DICTIONARY OF
CONCEPTS IN HISTORY

DICTIONARY OF CONCEPTS IN HISTORY

Harry Ritter

Reference Sources for the Social Sciences and Humanities, Number 3

Greenwood Press
New York • Westport, Connecticut • London

Library of Congress Cataloging-in-Publication Data

Ritter, Harry.
  Dictionary of concepts in history.

  (Reference sources for the social sciences and
humanities, ISSN 0730–3335 ; no. 3)
  Bibliography: p.
  Includes index.
  1. Historiography—Dictionaries. I. Title.
II. Series.
D13.R49 1986   907'.2'0321   85–27305
ISBN 0–313–22700–4 (lib. bdg. : alk. paper)

Library of Congress Catalog Card Number: 85–27305
ISBN: 0–313–22700–4
ISSN: 0730–3335

First published in 1986

Greenwood Press, Inc.
88 Post Road West, Westport, Connecticut 06881

Printed in the United States of America

The paper used in this book complies with the
Permanent Paper Standard issued by the National
Information Standards Organization (Z39.48–1984).

10 9 8 7 6 5 4 3 2

For Marian and Alan

Contents

List of Abbreviations

AHR	*The American Historical Review*
Berding	Helmut Berding, *Bibliographie zur Geschichtstheorie.* (Göttingen, 1977).
Birkos and Tambs	Alexander S. Birkos and Lewis A. Tambs, *Historiography, Method, History Teaching: A Bibliography of Books and Articles in English 1965–1973* (Hamden, Conn., 1975).
Bull. 54	Social Science Research Council, *Theory and Practice in Historical Study: A Report of the Committee on Historiography.* Bulletin 54 (New York, 1946).
Canary and Kozicki	Robert H. Canary and Henry Kozicki, eds., *The Writing of History: Literary Form and Historical Understanding* (Madison, Wis., 1978).
CSSH	*Comparative Studies in Society and History*
DHI	*Dictionary of the History of Ideas*, ed. Philip P. Wiener (New York, 1973). 5 vols.
Dray	William H. Dray, ed., *Philosophical Analysis and History* (New York, 1966).
EP	*The Encyclopedia of Philosophy*, ed. Paul Edwards (New York, 1967). 8 vols.
ESS	*Encyclopedia of the Social Sciences*, ed. Edwin R. A. Seligman (New York, 1930–34). 15 vols.
Gardiner	Patrick Gardiner, ed., *Theories of History* (New York, 1959).
GG	*Geschichtliche Grundbegriffe: Historisches Lexikon zur politisch-sozialen Sprache in Deutschland*, ed. Otto Brunner, Werner Conze, and Reinhart Koselleck (Stuttgart, 1972–). 5 vols. published.

Gilbert and Graubard　　　　　Felix Gilbert and Stephen R. Graubard, eds., *Historical Studies Today* (New York, 1972).

Higham　　　　　　　　　　　John Higham et al., *History* (Englewood Cliffs, N.J., 1965).

Hook　　　　　　　　　　　　Sidney Hook, ed., *Philosophy and History: A Symposium* (New York, 1963).

HT　　　　　　　　　　　　*History and Theory*

HT Beih.　　　　　　　　　　*Bibliography of Works in the Philosophy of History*, issued irregularly as Beihefte (supplements) to *History and Theory*; thus far bibliographies have appeared in Beihefte 1, 3, 7, 10, 13, 18, and 23.

HWP　　　　　　　　　　　*Historisches Wörterbuch der Philosophie*, ed. Joachim Ritter and Karlfried Gründer (Basel/Stuttgart, 1971–   ). 6 vols. published.

IESS　　　　　　　　　　　*International Encyclopedia of the Social Sciences*, ed. David L. Sills (New York, 1968). 17 vols.

Iggers and Parker　　　　　　Georg G. Iggers and Harold T. Parker, eds., *International Handbook of Historical Studies: Contemporary Research and Theory* (Westport, Conn., 1979).

JHI　　　　　　　　　　　*Journal of the History of Ideas*

JMH　　　　　　　　　　　*The Journal of Modern History*

JP　　　　　　　　　　　　*The Journal of Philosophy*

Kammen　　　　　　　　　　Michael G. Kammen, ed., *The Past Before Us: Contemporary Historical Writing in the United States* (Ithaca, N.Y., 1980).

Lane and Riemersma　　　　　Frederic C. Lane and Jelle C. Riemersma, eds., *Enterprise and Secular Change: Readings in Economic History* (Homewood, Ill., 1953).

MCWS　　　　　　　　　　*Marxism, Communism, and Western Society: A Comparative Encyclopedia*, ed. C. D. Kernig (New York, 1972). 8 vols.

Meyerhoff　　　　　　　　　Hans Meyerhoff, ed., *The Philosophy of History in Our Time: An Anthology* (Garden City, N.Y., 1959).

Nash　　　　　　　　　　　Ronald H. Nash, ed., *Ideas of History* 2 (New York, 1969).

OED　　　　　　　　　　　*The Oxford English Dictionary* (New York, 1971).

Stephens　　　　　　　　　　Lester D. Stephens, *Historiography: A Bibliography* (Metuchen, N.J., 1975).

Stern　　　　　　　　　　　Fritz Stern, ed., *The Varieties of History: From Voltaire to the Present* (1956; 2d ed., New York, 1972).

Strayer　　　　　　　　　　Joseph R. Strayer, ed., *The Interpretation of History* (1943; New York, 1950).

Bibliographical Note

The works listed above are the titles most frequently cited in this dictionary. Readers should also be aware of the following general bibliographical aids:

Frank Freidel, ed., *Harvard Guide to American History* (rev. ed., Cambridge Mass., 1974). 2 vols.

Hermann Heimpel and Herbert Geuss, eds. *Dahlmann-Waitz. Quellenkunde der deutschen Geschichte* (10th ed., Stuttgart, 1969), vol. 1.

George Frederick Howe et al., *The American Historical Association's Guide to Historical Literature* (New York, 1961).

In addition, there are important shorter bibliographies on historiography and philosophy of history in Bull. 54: 141–63 and in Louis Gottschalk, ed., *Generalization in the Writing of History: A Report of the Committee on Historical Analysis of the Social Science Research Council* (Chicago, 1963), pp. 213–47.

Series Foreword

In all disciplines, scholars seek to understand and explain the subject matter in their area of specialization. The object of their activity is to produce a body of knowledge about specific fields of inquiry. As they achieve an understanding of their subject, scholars publish the results of their interpretations (that is, their research findings) in the form of explanations.

Explanation, then, can be said to organize and communicate understanding. When reduced to agreed-upon theoretical principles, the explanations that emerge from this process of organizing understanding are called concepts.

Concepts serve many functions. They help us identify topics we think about, help classify these topics into related sets, relate them to specific times and places, and provide us with definitions. Without concepts, someone has said, "man could hardly be said to think."

Like knowledge itself, the meanings of concepts are fluid. From the moment an authority introduces a concept into a discipline's vocabulary, where it is given a specific meaning, that concept has the potential to acquire a variety of meanings. As new understandings develop in the discipline, inevitably the meanings of concepts are revised.

Although this pattern in the formation of the meaning of concepts is widely recognized, few dictionaries—certainly none in a consistent manner—trace the path a concept takes as it becomes embedded in a research topic's literature.

Dictionaries in this series uniformly present brief, substantive discussions of the etymological development and contemporary use of the significant concepts in a discipline or subdiscipline. Another feature that distinguishes these dictionaries from others in the field is their emphasis upon bibliographic information.

Volumes contain about 100 entries. Consistently, entries comprise four parts. In the first part, brief statements give the current meaning of a concept. Next, discursive paragraphs trace a concept's historical origins and connotative development. In part three, sources mentioned in part two are cited, and where appropriate, additional notes briefly highlight other aspects of individual references. Finally, in part four, sources of additional information (that is, extensive reviews, encyclopedia articles, and so forth) are indicated.

Thus with these volumes, whatever the level of their need, students can explore the range of meanings of a discipline's concepts.

For some, its is the most fundamental need. What is the current meaning of Concept X? Of Concept Y? For others with more intensive needs, entries are departure points for more detailed investigation.

These concept dictionaries, then, fill a long-standing need. They make more accessible the extensive, often scattered literature necessary to knowing a discipline. To have helped in their development and production is very rewarding.

Raymond G. McInnis

Preface

Professional historians—particularly those trained in English-speaking countries—sometimes say that history has no technical vocabulary; they take pride in the notion that their language is simply the plain language of good speech, believing that the avoidance of jargon protects their craft against the danger of becoming a remote, esoteric science—one inaccessible to the general public. This is no doubt one reason why there have been few serious efforts to compile English-language glossaries of historiographical concepts, and why those that have been undertaken (e.g., that of Sidney Hook in 1946[1]) have usually been half-hearted or disappointing. Indeed, in their widely used methods guide *The Modern Researcher*, Jacques Barzun and Henry F. Graff identify the very term *concept* as jargon and include it among their "Fifty Forbidden Words."[2]

It has frequently been remarked, as well, that historians are often reluctant to reflect on the general principles that underlie their own work; as a group, they traditionally prefer the modest satisfactions of painstaking research on specific events and situations to the delights of theory and preoccupation with "methodology."[3] A minor branch of the discipline, in fact, is dedicated to the Menckenesque debunking of social science and Marxist concepts (see, for instance, the entries CLASS, FASCISM, and FEUDALISM in this dictionary). G. R. Elton unquestionably expressed a widely shared professional opinion when he aired his suspicion that "a philosophic concern with such problems as the reality of historical knowledge or the nature of historical thought only hinders the practice of history," since (in his view) it does not "advance the writing of history."[4] Of course, history's association with the single-minded study of particular events has an ancient pedigree; it reaches back at least as far as chapter nine of Aristotle's *Poetics*, where history and poetry are distinguished on the grounds that the former, unlike poetry, deals more with particular rather than universal truths.

Still, statements regarding the language preferences and anti-theoretical biases of historians should not be accepted uncritically. Although historians are often inclined by training and temperament to avoid neologisms and cant, they nevertheless employ a professional vocabulary; and although this vocabulary is largely made up of common words, these terms are often used in uncommon ways (see, for example, entries on EVENT, FACT, HISTORY, and PAST). Furthermore, the work of historians inevitably rests on theoretical presuppositions. Although these controlling assumptions may not always be made explicit, they are there nonetheless, informing the research and writing that historians do. H. Stuart Hughes, commenting on the relationship of social science theory to historiography, made the point effectively when he observed that:

> In many cases, perhaps in a majority of cases, [the historian] does not really "apply" [social science concepts] at all. He lets them remain in the back of his mind, without bringing them explicitly into the foreground of his historical writing. He does not parade his knowledge of social science theory; he simply permits his thought to be informed by it. . . . A process of this kind subtly alters the character of a historian's work in ways that even the writer himself may be unaware of. To the unpracticed eye, his prose may remain just as untheoretical as in the past. But the new type of knowledge he has absorbed will actually have worked subterranean alterations in his whole mode of thought and expression; his choice of vocabulary and his explanatory line will be different, even though the cast of his prose remains irreproachably literary and discursive.[5]

Parenthetically, it should be noted that—contrary to widely held opinion[6]—historians are not always dependent on other disciplines for the theoretical concepts they employ; historians themselves have in fact played an important role in building many general concepts of modern social analysis, for example, HISTORISM, NATIONALISM, FASCISM, FEUDALISM, FRONTIER, and MODERNIZATION.

The concern with ordinary language and fear of generalization frequently encountered in the pronouncements of Anglo-American scholars is not necessarily characteristic of continental European historians. Nineteenth-century German historiography was strongly conditioned by philosophical idealism, and this provided the basis for a continuing German tradition of *Historik*—systematic reflection on history as a mode of inquiry—associated with the names Droysen, Meinecke, and others. In Germany the word *Begriff* is therefore not the cause for alarm that *concept* sometimes is among historians in Britain and the United States; there are, in fact, a number of sound disciplinary concept dictionaries in the German language.[7] Italy also has its own tradition of self-conscious theorizing, closely associated with idealism and the name of Benedetto Croce, and France is the birthplace of the positivist orientation in philosophy, a tradition that helps sustain the *Annales* historiography of Marc Bloch, Lucien Febvre, and their disciples.[8] Indeed, despite persistent clichés concerning the anti-theoretical nature of Anglo-American historiography, there is a substantial tradition of methodological reflection among historians of England and North America; more literature exists, certainly, than one person can hope to master easily. In

Britain the theorizing tradition is closely linked to idealism and the names of
R. G. Collingwood and Michael Oakeshott, and in the United States serious
interest in historical semantics and epistemological matters was spurred by the
controversy over "historical relativism" between World Wars I and II. There
is evidence that concern with such matters has increased since 1945, especially
in the founding and growth of the journal *History and Theory* after 1960. This
periodical is symptomatic of a new sensitivity to the importance of theory, an
awareness reflected in 1968, when C. Vann Woodward listed among historians'
"occupational shortcomings" the fact that "their premises are often unexamined,
their hypotheses ill-defined, their concepts vague, their interpretations confused."[9] Others evidently shared Woodward's concern, for, according to the
editor of a recent study, the 1970s witnessed a "revolution in methodological
awareness" reflected in a

> burst of books on how History ought to be done; in the proliferation of new journals
> that emphasize methodology; in books and essays that plead for greater self-
> consciousness on the part of historians about their assumptions and procedures;
> and in the appeal being made by some that historical methodology itself be rec-
> ognized as a discrete subdiscipline.[10]

Thus, even among the Anglo-Americans there is more evidence of serious interest
in historical semantics and epistemological matters than one might think, and
interest in theory seems to be growing. At the very least it should be clear that
these questions are crucial to the relatively underworked subfield of the history
of historical writing itself.[11]

In this book I survey some of the existing literature and attempt to identify
and discuss some of the key concepts of contemporary historical analysis. Each
entry is composed of four parts: (1) a concise definition of the idea in question;
(2) a discussion of the history of the idea, especially insofar as historiography
is concerned; (3) an annotated list of references cited in the entry; and (4)
suggestions for further reading. Various cross-references are also provided. The
entries in this dictionary summarize not only the thought of professional historians
but some work in the field of philosophy of history as well. I include philosophy
of history because, unlike an anonymous British reviewer, I emphatically do not
believe that modern philosophers have contributed nothing but "trivialities" to
our understanding of the activity of historians.[12] I am thinking especially of the
perceptive work of men such as W. H. Walsh, W. H. Dray, Louis O. Mink,
and Leon J. Goldstein.

In preparing this dictionary I have been inspired more than anything else by
J.G.A. Pocock's belief, expressed some twenty years ago, that historians must
assume "critical responsibility for their own professional vocabulary."

> The historian's employment of his professional vocabulary forms the main target
> of historical criticism [Pocock wrote], or should do so were that criticism specialized
> to a proper breadth of variety. . . . This [criticism] proceeds by enquiring where
> the historian found the terms of his conceptual vocabulary; how they were normally

used and how he used them; what logical, sociological, and other implications they carried; how their significance changed as, and has changed since, he used them; and how his construction of his statements was affected by the state of his language at the time when he made use of it. Such a mode of inquiry is less immediately concerned with logic and verifiability than with language as a social instrument and thought as social behavior.[13]

I would like to acknowledge the help of the following persons, who kindly read and commented on parts of this book. Among my friends on the faculty of Western Washington University, I wish to thank especially T.C.R. Horn and Ed Kaplan, who each read several draft entries. Other Western colleagues who assisted with their discussion and criticisms are Leonard Helfgott, Jim Hitchman, Merrill Lewis, Stephanie Mooers, George Mariz, Vladimir Miličić, and Louis Truschel. I also wish to acknowledge the comments of Georg Iggers of SUNY–Buffalo, Ron Loftus of Willamette University, David Paul of Seattle, Rod Sievers of Humboldt State University, and Rod Stackelberg of Gonzaga University. Ray McInnis, general editor of the series of concept dictionaries in which this volume appears, was unfailing in his help and encouragement. Student assistants Kevin Boers, Randy Guy, and Patrick St. Louis undertook bibliographical searches. Evelyn Darrow and Dorothy Sherwood in the interlibrary loan and periodicals departments of Wilson Library were always helpful. Departmental secretaries Sally Wirth and Phyllis Paterson assisted with occasional typing and related matters. Finally, the Bureau for Faculty Research of Western Washington University provided a much-appreciated summer research grant.

Above all, I am grateful to Oron J. Hale of the University of Virginia and Thomas W. Parker of the University of Arizona, former teachers (both now retired) who encouraged and deepened my interest in the study of history.

NOTES

1. Charles A. Beard and Sydney Hook, "Problems of Terminology in Historical Writing," in Social Science Research Council, *Theory and Practice in Historical Study: A Report of the Committee on Historiography* (New York, 1946), pp. 103–30.

2. Jacques Barzun and Henry F. Graff, *The Modern Researcher*, rev. ed. (New York, 1970), pp. 281, 286. See chapter twelve, "Plain Words: The War on Jargon and Clichés," and cf. Charles Tilly, "In Defense of Jargon," *Canadian Historical Association, Annual Report* (1966): 178–86.

3. E.g., Joseph R. Strayer, "Introduction," in Joseph R. Strayer, ed., *The Interpretation of History* (1943; reprint, New York, 1950), pp. 24–25. Cf. Jurgen Herbst, "Theoretical Work in History in American University Curricula," *History and Theory* 7 (1968): 336–54.

4. G. R. Elton, *The Practice of History* (New York, 1967), p. v. Ironically, Elton has since devoted a considerable part of his time to methodological matters. See also the remarks of Martin Malia in "On the Languages of the Humanistic Studies," *Daedalus* 98 (Fall 1969): 1019–20.

5. H. Stuart Hughes, "The Historian and the Social Scientist," *The American Historical Review* 66 (Oct. 1960): 33–34.

6. See Carl Schorske's remarks in the discussion on "New Trends in History," *Daedalus* 98 (Fall 1969): 955: "I do not think of historians as doing this [making theoretical contributions]. History has always seemed to me to be a parasitic discipline. History borrows concepts from other fields; it does not really develop them."

7. See Helmut Berding, *Bibliogaphie zur Geschichtstheorie* (Göttingen, 1977), pp. 41–47.

8. Though even among theoretically inclined continental scholars one may encounter hostility to epistemology. For instance, Fernand Braudel, *On History* (Chicago, 1980), p. 64, believes that a philosophical approach encourages a "tendency to see history as a discipline whose rules have been defined utterly and once and for all"; Pierre Chaunu, another member of the *Annales* group, has said that "Epistemology is a temptation one must resolutely cast aside. . . . At most it is opportune that a few leading minds dedicate themselves to it . . . in order to preserve the robust craftsman who is busy forging a knowledge still under construction" (cited in Paul Ricoeur, *The Contribution of French Historiography to the Theory of History* [Oxford, 1980], p. 33, n. 2). Ricoeur refers to the "deliberately anti-epistemological attitude of French historians" (p. 33).

9. "History and the Third Culture," *Journal of Contemporary History* 3 (1968): 24.

10. Michael G. Kammen, ed., *The Past Before Us: Contemporary Historical Writing in the United States* (Ithaca, N.Y., 1980), p. 31.

11. See the remarks of W. H. Walsh, "History as Science and History as More Than Science," *Virginia Quarterly Review* 44 (Spring 1973): 212.

12. *History* 45 (1960): 304.

13. Review of J. H. Hexter, *Reappraisals in History, History and Theory* 3 (1963–64): 121.

THE DICTIONARY

A

ALIENATION. A sense of separation from established institutions and values due to social change; social estrangement.

The 1960s and 1970s witnessed a surge of interest in human alienation and its relationship to the study of society. The idea's brief history reflects ways in which non-scholarly factors may become involved in the rise of an influential social concept and illustrates many of the difficulties historians typically associate with the explicit use of theory in their research. To a large degree, current interest in alienation is politically motivated by the desire of west European and North American leftists to rescue the doctrines of Karl Marx from the philosophically untenable "Marxist-Leninist" orthodoxy of Soviet Russia (see HISTORICAL MATERIALISM). Although modern usage has been largely inspired by Marx, Soviet scholars have displayed scant interest in the subject (Ludz, 1976: 14). Thus, although "alienation" has become an important idea in western social science, it has also been an ideological weapon in the philosophical conflict between East and West.

Current interest is very recent in origin. The 1930 edition of the *Encyclopedia of the Social Sciences*, for example, contained no entry on *alienation*, and the term did not even appear in the index. In contrast, specialized encyclopedias such as the *International Encyclopedia of the Social Sciences* (1968), the *Encyclopedia of Philosophy* (1967), and the *Dictionary of the History of Ideas* (1968) all contain weighty essays on alienation, and a recent bibliography (Geyer, 1972) lists more than 1,100 references on alienation and related subjects. In the past half-century the idea has emerged as "one of the most prominent subjects of conscious concern to twentieth century man, especially in the West" (Tucker, 1972: 238; cf. Nisbet, 1953: 15).

In consequence there has been a "proliferation of alienation concepts," and there is little scholarly agreement on the precise meaning of the term (Geyer and Schweitzer, 1976: xxiii; Ludz, 1976: 16–17). To complicate matters, *alienation* became a vogue word in the 1960s and was inflated in journalistic and popular usage as a label for virtually any unsatisfactory condition (McLellan, 1968: 40). Serious theoretical interest in the idea is strongest in disciplines such as sociology and social psychology (e.g., Nisbet, 1953: 15; Seeman, 1959). Historians, who sometimes view social theory as a needless distraction from empirical research (Elton, 1967: v), have not written extensively on the subject per se; the bibliography cited above, for instance, cites literature from fields such as political science, philosophy, criminology, and anthropology but does not include history. The concept is nonetheless implicit—and occasionally explicit—in much contemporary historical thinking about the impact of social change (Stern, 1961; Walzer, 1963–64), especially in the subfields of SOCIAL HISTORY, INTELLECTUAL HISTORY, and CULTURAL HISTORY.

The modern term derives from the ancient Latin *alienato*, which referred to three distinct kinds of "separation": legal (the transfer of property); social (separation from one's community); and medical (dementia, insania—separation from one's self). With the rise of Christianity the term was adapted to designate separation from God. According to the *OED*, the earliest English use of the term occurs in Wyclif's translation of the book of Job (1388): "Alienacioun of God is to men worchynge wickidnesse." In the Lutheran protestantism that developed after the sixteenth century the term also signified Christ's renunciation of his own divine nature to bring salvation to man (Tuveson, 1968: 34–35; Lichtheim, 1968: 264). Current social science usage ultimately derives from these ancient social, medical, and religious traditions (Ludz, 1976: 5).

The key event in the rise of the twentieth-century social concept, however, was the discovery in the 1920s of Karl Marx's previously unknown "Economic and Philosophical Manuscripts of 1844," which were partially published in Russian translation in 1927 and appeared in their original German entirety, as well as in English and French editions, in 1932. These fragments have been called—perhaps with some exaggeration—"the most talked about philosophical work in this century" (Mészáros, 1970: 11); there is wide agreement that their central idea is "alienation" (e.g., McLellan, 1968: 39).

Marx's concept of alienation was the product of three specifically German sources: (1) the eighteenth-century literary and philosophical tradition of *Bildung* (cultivation, education), which stressed the importance of cultivating a balanced, fully rounded personality as opposed to a fragmented, one-sided one (Bruford, 1962; 1975); (2) G.W.F. Hegel's speculative and highly abstract PHILOSOPHY OF HISTORY (in many ways a secularized version of Lutheran theology), which depicted history as the progress of human consciousness toward recognition of its own freedom (so long as consciousness [or "mind," "spirit"] did not realize its own freedom, it was "estranged" [e.g., Hegel, (1807) 1967: 72, 81, 96]); and (3) the critique of Hegel's philosophy by "young Hegelian" thinkers of the 1830s and 1840s, especially Ludwig Feuerbach (McLellan, 1968: 37). Feuerbach's *Essence of Christianity* (1841) is a classic statement of the "humanist" notion that the concept of God is a creation of man, and that man betrays (or "alienates") his own nature when he subordinates himself to an idea of his own making.

Marx took the idea that man creates his own gods, historicized it, and linked it to his analysis of economic life under nineteenth-century CAPITALISM (although he also allowed for alienation under pre-capitalist socioeconomic systems [Ollman, 1976: 252]); his theory of "alienated labor" (Marx, [1844] 1959: 64–78) arose from his analysis of the division of labor under capitalism. Man's essential human activity, Marx believed, is labor; under capitalism—a system of man's own creation—the great majority are unjustly denied the product of this activity. Thus,

> the worker is related to the *product of his labour* as to an *alien* object. . . . it is clear that the more the worker spends himself, the more powerful the alien objective world becomes which he creates over against himself, the poorer he himself—his inner world—becomes, the less belongs to him as his own. It is the same in religion. The more man puts into God, the less he retains in himself. The worker puts his life into the object; but now his life no longer belongs to him but to the object. . . . The *alienation* of the worker in his product means not only that his labor becomes an object, an external existence, but that it exists *outside him*, independently, as something alien to him, and that it becomes a power of its own confronting him; it means that the life which he has conferred on the object confronts him as something hostile and alien. (Marx, [1844] 1959: 66–67)

This is the core of Marx's analysis. Against this image of alienated man, enslaved by idols of his own making, he pits the ideal of the free, whole, balanced life of the "non-specialist and fully developed individual" (Ludz, 1976: 9). Elsewhere, in a famous passage from *The German Ideology* he and Engels speak of a life under communism

> where nobody has one exclusive sphere of activity but each can become accomplished in any branch he wishes, society regulates the general production and thus makes it possible for me to do one thing today and another tomorrow, to hunt in the morning, fish in the afternoon, rear cattle in the evening, criticise after dinner, just as I have a mind, without ever becoming hunter, fisherman, shepherd or critic. ([1845–46] 1972: 124)

Beyond this specific notion of "estranged labor," Marx extends the idea of alienation to three other broad categories: (1) alienation from physical nature (through industrialization and urbanization); (2) alienation from other men and women (through the growing depersonalization of life); and (3) alienation from one's "species being," or one's nature as a member of the human species (Marx, [1844] 1959: 70–73). These ideas have been exhaustively analyzed in the recent "avalanche of exegetic material on Marxism" (Ollman, 1976: xvii; cf. Mészáros, 1970; Lukes, 1967).

In "alienation" (psychological disorientation under the impact of social change) Marx identified an evident malady of modern western culture, one that social analysts have increasingly perceived as acute in the past hundred years. Although Marx's reflections remained unknown in his own lifetime, many late-nineteenth-century writers adopted similar views: the historian Jacob Burckhardt, the historian-sociologist Max Weber, and the sociologists Ferdinand Tönnies and Emile Durkheim are only a few names that might be mentioned (Durkheim's idea of "anomie"—the feeling of rootlessness that sometimes accompanies rapid social change—has been carefully distinguished from Marx's "alienation" by Lukes [1967]).

Contemporary historians employ the idea most frequently in connection with the impact of INDUSTRIALIZATION. As one would expect, Marxists have made explicit use of the notion (e.g., Aptheker, 1965), although (with some exceptions [e.g., Aronowitz, 1973: 6, 255–56]) the idea of "alienated labor" in Marx's special sense of self-enslaved labor does not seem to have significantly influenced historical writing. Historians—even Marxists (e.g., Thompson, 1967)—have not adopted the idea self-consciously from Marx so much as they have absorbed it from current sociology. Thus, they use the idea in the loose sense of general social estrangement and psychological disorientation. Until very recently, even this conception had not influenced English and American labor historians because they have traditionally approached their task—with some exceptions (e.g., Ware, [1924] 1964)—almost exclusively from the viewpoint of the political struggles of the organized trade union movement, rather than in terms of the emotions of working people. Only since the 1960s have labor historians begun to conceptualize their research systematically in social-psychological terms and to employ the concept of alienation—either tacitly (e.g., Thompson, 1967; Gutman, 1976) or explicitly (Stearns, 1972: 3, 155; 1975: 346–53)—to define and interpret worker disorientation under the impact of industrialization.

More significant, perhaps, is the usage of cultural and intellectual historians. Since the late 1930s (Brinton, 1963: 208) the term and concept of *alienation* have been used by these scholars to designate the estrangement of intellectuals (particularly in the nineteenth and twentieth centuries) from the mainstream of their own societies (e.g., Graña, 1964; Stern, 1961; Lasch, 1965; Johnston, 1972: 20; Schorske, 1980). This theme became popular among American writers in the 1950s, partly due to their own sense of social estrangement during the anti-intellectual "McCarthy era" (Brinton, 1963: 210). The idea is also commonly used to designate the disenchantment of any social or religious group, especially in revolutionary situations (Brinton, [1938] 1965; Walzer, 1963–64: 59, 81–84; Stone, 1966: 164, 166; Kramnick, 1972: 39; Toynbee, 1972). It is occasionally linked to the politics of counterrevolution, which are sometimes explained as manifestations of "anxiety, alienation, and fear" (Mayer, 1971: 120).

References

Aptheker, Herbert, ed. 1965. *Marxism and Alienation*. New York. See Aptheker's "Alienation and the American Social Order," pp. 15–25.

Aronowitz, Stanley. 1973. *False Promises: The Shaping of American Working Class Consciousness*. New York.

Brinton, Crane. 1963. "Reflections on the Alienation of the Intellectuals." In Alexander V. Riasanovsky and Barnes Riznik, eds., *Generalizations in Historical Writing*. Philadelphia. Brinton asserts that the expression "alienation of the intellectuals" was "almost certainly in common use twenty-five years ago" (p. 208). He suggests the possibility of a comparative history of intellectual alienation in different periods of western history to determine, among other things, if there is a "set of normal attitudes" that intellectuals display toward their own societies (p. 225).

———. [1938] 1965. *The Anatomy of Revolution*. New York. This is a pioneering work on the theory of revolution; it uses the expression "desertion of the intellectuals" rather than "alienation of the intellectuals," which Brinton (1963: 209) considers related to, but not precisely synonymous with, social alienation.

Bruford, W. H. 1962. *Culture and Society in Classical Weimar, 1775–1806*. Cambridge.

———. 1975. *The German Tradition of Self-Cultivation: "Bildung" from Humboldt to Thomas Mann*. Cambridge.

Elton, G. R. 1967. *The Practice of History*. New York. Elton thinks that "a philosophic concern with such problems as the reality of historical knowledge or the nature of historical thought only hinders the practice of history" because it does not "advance the writing of history" (p. v).

Geyer, R. Felix. 1972. *Bibliography Alienation*. Amsterdam.

Geyer, R. Felix, and Schweitzer, David R., eds. 1976. *Theories of Alienation*. Leiden. The introduction provides a good overview of the multiplicity of ways that sociologists and philosophers have found to use the term.

Graña, César. 1964. *Bohemian versus Bourgeois: French Society and the French Man of Letters in the Nineteenth Century*. New York. This book was later republished in paperback under the title *Modernity and Its Discontents*.

Gutman, Herbert G. 1976. *Work, Culture, and Society in Industrializing America: Essays in American Working-Class and Social History*. New York. See especially the first essay, "Work, Culture, and Society in Industrializing America, 1815–1919," which is largely organized around an implicit idea of social alienation. Many of the footnote citations are excellent sources of bibliographical information on American and British labor history (e.g., no. 6, no. 8).

Hegel, G.W.F. [1807] 1967. *The Phenomenology of Mind*. New York.

Johnston, William M. 1972. *The Austrian Mind: An Intellectual and Social History, 1848–1938*. Berkeley, Calif. Johnston employs Ferdinand Tönnies' distinction between cohesive, pre-industrial "community" (*Gemeinschaft*) and impersonal industrial "society" (*Gesellschaft*) to analyze the Austrian intelligentsia's disorientation in the face of social modernization (see p. 20).

Kramnick, Isaac. 1972. "Reflections on Revolution: Definition and Explanation in Recent Scholarship." *HT* 11: 26–63. Kramnick speaks of "the economic and psychological bases of revolutionary alienation" (p. 39).

Lasch, Christopher. 1965. *The New Radicalism in America, 1889–1963: The Intellectual as Social Type*. New York. See the essay "Woman as Alien," pp. 38–68.

Lichtheim, George. 1968. "Alienation." *IESS* 1: 264–68.

Ludz, Peter C. 1976. "Alienation as a Concept in the Social Sciences." In R. Felix Geyer and David R. Schweitzer, eds., *Theories of Alienation*. Leiden: 3–37. Ludz complains that scholars "probably have not even reached a minimal consensus about what they mean by 'alienation'."

Lukes, Steven. 1967. "Alienation and Anomie." In Peter Laslett and W. G. Runciman, eds., *Philosophy, Politics and Society*. Third Series. Oxford: 134–56.

McLellan, David. 1968. "Alienation in Hegel and Marx." *DHI* 1: 37–41.

Marx, Karl. [1844] 1959. *Economic and Philosophical Manuscripts of 1844*. Moscow.

Marx, Karl and Engels, Friedrich. [1845–46] 1972. *The German Ideology*. In Robert C. Tucker, ed., *The Marx-Engels Reader*. New York: 110–64.

Mayer, Arno J. 1971. *Dynamics of Counterrevolution in Europe, 1870–1956: An Analytic Framework*. New York.

Mészáros, István. 1970. *Marx's Theory of Alienation*. 2d ed. London.

Nisbet, Robert. 1953. *The Quest for Community*. New York.

Ollman, Bertell. 1976. *Alienation: Marx's Conception of Man in Capitalist Society*. 2d ed. Cambridge.

Schorske, Carl E. 1980. *Fin-de-Siècle Vienna: Politics and Culture*. New York. Although it seldom uses the term *alienation* explicitly (see pp. 360, 363), this book is organized around the theme of the social estrangement of the segments of the turn-of-the-century Viennese middle class.

Seeman, Melvin. 1959. "On the Meaning of Alienation," *The American Sociological Review* 24: 783–91.

Stearns, Peter N., ed. 1972. *The Impact of the Industrial Revolution: Protest and Alienation*. Englewood Cliffs, N.J.

———. 1975. *Lives of Labor: Work in a Maturing Industrial Society*. New York. See especially pp. 346–53.

Stern, Fritz. 1961. *The Politics of Cultural Despair*. Berkeley, Calif. Here "cultural despair" functions as a synonym for "alienation."

Stone, Lawrence. 1966. "Theories of Revolution." *World Politics* 18: 159–76.

Thompson, E. P. 1967. "Time, Work-Discipline, and Industrial Capitalism." *Past and Present* 38: 56–97. This article deals with problems of adjusting to heightened regimentation in the industrial system.

Toynbee, Arnold J. 1972. "The Century of Alienation." *International Affairs* 48: 267–70. Review of Alan Bullock's *The Twentieth Century: A Promethean Age*. Toynbee seeks to elevate alienation into a general concept for understanding the decline of entire civilizations, such as those of ancient Greece and Egypt (p. 269).

Tucker, Robert C. 1972. *Philosophy and Myth in Karl Marx*. 2d ed. Cambridge. This is an unsympathetic interpretation of Marx's theory of alienation on grounds that it is not an accurate description of capitalist society but a projection of Marx's own split personality. See especially pp. 136–49 and 218–32. Cf. Ollman (1976) and Mészáros (1970).

Tuveson, Ernest. 1968. "Alienation in Christian Theology." *DHI* 1: 34–37.

Walzer, Michael. 1963–64. "Puritanism as a Revolutionary Ideology." *HT* 3: 59–90. Walzer uses the concept of social alienation to analyze the psychology of English Puritanism.

Ware, Norman. [1924] 1964. *The Industrial Worker, 1840–1860: The Reaction of American Industrial Society to the Advance of the Industrial Revolution*. Chicago. Ware's interest in the psychological reactions of workers to industrialization reflects an idea of social alienation long before the term became fashionable. See pp. x-xi.

Sources of Additional Information

See especially Geyer (1972) and Geyer and Schweitzer (1976), as well as Lichtheim (1968). For lengthy bibliographies see the following entries in specialized encyclopedias: G. Petrović, "Alienation," *EP* 1: 76–81; Nicholas Lobkowicz, "Alienation," *MCWS* 1: 88–93, and E. Ritz, "Entfremdung," *HWP* 2: 510–26. Ritz's entry is especially good for linking Marx's ideas to the German literary and philosophical context. The sociologist Melvin Seeman (1959) has made a specialty out of review articles on the subject; see his "Alienation and Engagement," in Angus Campbell and Philip E. Converse, eds., *The Human Meaning of Social Change* (New York, 1972), and "Alienation Studies," *Annual Review of Sociology* 1 (1975): 91–123. For use in political science see Ada W. Finifter, "Dimensions of Political Alienation," *The American Political Science Review* 64 (June 1970): 389–410. Vicky Rippere, a literary critic, approaches the 1960s debate as less a matter of substance than intellectual fashion in her *Schiller and "Alienation"* (Berne, 1981). A widely cited work is Heinrich Popitz, *Der entfremdete Mensch: Zeitkritik und Geschichtsphilosophie des jungen Marx* (Basel, 1953). Consult also David McLellan, *Marx Before Marxism* (New York, 1970). For an anthology of Feuerbach's writings see *The Fiery Brook: Selected Writings of Ludwig Feuerbach* (Garden City, N.Y., 1972). A concise survey of the literature on American labor is Thomas A. Krueger, "American Labor Historiography, Old and New," *Journal of Social History* 4 (1971): 277–85.

ANACHRONISM. Awareness that the past differs in fundamental respects from the present.

The sense of anachronism, or "obsolescence," is a characteristic feature of modern historical thinking; together with critical regard for EVIDENCE and concern for social CAUSATION, it has been called one of the three basic aspects of the modern "sense of history" (Burke, 1969: 1). The underlying idea is regularly expressed in various ways: the "sense of a contrast between ourselves and the ancients," a "peculiar sense of the exotic" (Bloch, [1928] 1953: 497), the "sense of historical discontinuity" (Harbison, 1956: 93), and the "sense of historical perspective," "historical sensibility," "feeling for the past," or "sympathetic awareness of different values in ... different period[s]" (Burke, 1969: 1, 24, 49; cf. also Wedgwood, 1960: 32–33). In a classic dictum, the nineteenth-century German historian Leopold von Ranke ([1854] 1981: 159) declared that each epoch in history stands "immediate to God" and therefore must be understood in terms of its own unique, unrepeatable context. From the standpoint of professional historians today, the conscious or unconscious attribution of present attitudes, values, and modes of behavior upon the past is "presentism," an inexcusable violation of the past's integrity and the "historical sin of sins" (Manuel, 1972: 218).

The assumption that the past was characteristically different from the present has become so familiar to the contemporary western sense of time—reflected in the acute feeling for anachronism often displayed by modern film audiences—that it is sometimes difficult to imagine that people in general, much less historians, should ever have been insensitive to the representation of temporal or cultural incongruity. Barzun observes that in modern cinema the

> atttempt to be [historically] exact is painful and intense. The country is apparently full of persons who will detect trifling errors and write indignant letters to Hollywood. So we may be relatively sure that Henry VIII's table manners will be true to his period and that George Washington will wear the right wig. ([1943] 1950: 43)

It would nonetheless be wrong to exaggerate the extent to which the historical sensibility has presently become common psychological property. Despite a generalized concern for historical fidelity, modern cinema and historical fiction usually overlook the more subtle problems of depicting change in attitudes and styles of behavior as opposed to those in external physical appearance and costume. Moreover, modern audiences regularly display an inability to sympathize with the underlying values, motives, and even technical methods of films produced only a decade or two previously.

In fact, it seems that the sense of anachronism has only recently begun to establish itself firmly in western consciousness; hardly evident in antiquity, it was virtually non-existent in the Middle Ages and appears to have begun to develop seriously only from about the fourteenth century onwards.

With regard to antiquity, it is usually held that the Greeks and Romans lacked a sense of anachronism. Burke (1969: 138–39), however, believes that at least one Greek historian—Herodotus (c. 484–c. 425 B.C.), the "father of history"—exhibits the historical sense to some degree. Moreover, he argues that a number of Roman authors occasionally display an awareness of the qualitative difference between past and present—Varro (116–27 B.C.), Cicero (106–43 B.C.), Lucretius (94–55 B.C.), Vergil (70–19 B.C.), and Horace (65–8 B.C.). On the other hand, he denies (1969: 141) that historical perspective was a facet of ancient Hebrew culture.

There is general agreement that the awareness of historical anachronism was, for practical purposes, lost during the Middle Ages (Hay, 1977: 91; Haddock, 1980: 2).

> Medieval men lacked a sense of the past being different in quality from the present. They did not deny that in some ways the past was unlike the present; they knew, for example, that the ancients had not been Christians. But they did not take the difference very seriously. (Burke, 1969: 1)

In sculpture and illuminated manuscripts, for example, ancient personalities such as Moses and Alexander the Great were typically depicted in medieval dress.

Such disregard of temporal propriety is reminiscent of attitudes anthropologists attribute to primitive societies, where the lack of historical sensibility is a basic aspect of consciousness. Burke (1969: 18–19) cites several reasons for the lack of historical sense in a culture: a slow rate of change, which makes fundamental structural change difficult to detect; the lack of writing, which makes it easy for past outlooks to be revised in accordance with present standards; and the lack of sophisticated means for measuring the passage of time, such as mechanical clocks.

The origins of the modern historical sense of anachronism seem to lie in the early RENAISSANCE (Hay, 1977: vii). The work of the Italian poet and antiquarian Petrarch (1304–74) is often considered symptomatic of the beginnings of the transition. Petrarch's attitude toward Roman antiquity reflects a new "feeling for the past": "Unlike medieval writers, Petrarch did not take the ruins of Rome for granted. He was, one might say, the first modern antiquarian in the sense of someone who is interested in the reconstruction of the past from its physical remains" (Burke, 1969: 23; also Haddock, 1980: 2) (see ANTIQUARIANISM). Petrarch and subsequent authors of his period introduced the conception of history as comprising three distinct periods—ancient, medieval, and modern—each of which was understood to be qualitatively different in ambience. "With the creation of a new series of epochs came a sense of anachronism which was also new" (Hay, 1977: 91). In the fifteenth century, Lorenzo Valla (c. 1407–57) successfully used the concept of anachronism to challenge the authenticity of the forged "Donation of Constantine" (Harbison, 1956: 44–45), and the new sensibility began to influence the thinking of classicists, legal scholars, artists, and architects. Writers slowly became "more and more conscious that all sorts of things—buildings, clothes, words, laws—changed over time" (Burke, 1969: 39).

From Italy, awareness of anachronism slowly spread to scholars in northern Europe, such as Erasmus of Rotterdam (c. 1466–1536) (Harbison, 1956: 93). In the north the Protestant Reformation, too, was important in the development of a sense of the distinctiveness of past periods, insofar as it emphasized the necessity of returning to a "pure," original faith, which the reformers perceived as differing fundamentally from the practice of sixteenth-century Christianity (Burke, 1969: 40).

The beginnings of the early modern sense of anachronism are most graphically displayed in the figurative arts of Renaissance Italy. The painter Piero della Francesca (1420–92), for instance, exhibited a half-developed historical sense in his Arezzo frescoes of the life of Constantine, which portray soldiers in both ancient Roman and fifteenth-century costume participating in the same battle. In the same period, the architect Antonio Filarete admonished artists: "if you have to represent antiquity, do not dress [your figures] in modern dress" (quoted in Burke, 1969: 27). A major stimulus to this kind of thinking was the creation of the notion of a "gothic" style identified with the Middle Ages and the desire of Renaissance critics to distinguish clearly this "inferior" style from their own (allegedly superior) neo-classicism, derived from the study of monuments of antiquity (Panofsky, [1930] 1955: 187–88).

Although the growth of anachronist consciousness is clearly displayed in painting, sculpture, and philology from the fifteenth century onwards, the new sensibility was ironically slow to emerge in the writing of history itself. This was largely due to revered interpretive canons that stressed that history's importance lay in the *timeless* moral and political lessons the study of the past could provide, and because historians traditionally assumed that human behavior and circumstances remained essentially similar throughout time (see PHILOSOPHY OF HISTORY). These assumptions, ancient in origin, were reinforced by the "philosophical history" of the eighteenth-century ENLIGHTENMENT. In his essay on history, for example, David Hume (1711–76) maintained that:

> The chief use of history is to discover the constant and universal principles of human nature . . . records of wars, intrigues, factions and revolutions are so many collections of experiments by which the politician or moral philosopher fixes the principles of his science. (quoted in Burke, 1969: 143)

Only in the late eighteenth and early nineteenth centuries did the awareness of anachronism finally triumph in historiography, with the fusion of the traditions of ANTIQUARIANISM and NARRATIVE history (Hay, 1977: 169–85) and with the rise of certain ideas associated with ROMANTICISM (Wedgwood, 1960: 27) and the doctrine of HISTORISM. Reacting against ancient and Enlightenment assumptions that human nature remains basically the same, historians now affirmed that human attitudes and behavior change fundamentally over time; the very concept of a uniform and constant "human nature" was questioned. The new outlook was first systematically displayed in the thought of the Italian philosopher Giambattista Vico (1668–1744) (Haddock, 1980: 60–72) and, later, in the work of the much more influential social theorist Johann Gottfried von Herder (1744–1803). The work of these scholars implied that the historian's job was to "understand the 'otherness' of the past" (Burke, 1969: 143—see UNDERSTANDING), a position that became the basis for the present "conviction that history can only be studied by entering sympathetically into the thought and feeling of the past" (Wedgwood, 1960: 32–33).

In the nineteenth century the historical sense spread rapidly to the educated public through popular media such as the historical novel and historical drama. For professional historians, unswerving fidelity to the past and the sense of historical distance became a key ingredient of the notion of SCIENTIFIC HISTORY (e.g., Fustel de Coulanges, [1862] 1972: 184–85, 187).

References

Barzun, Jacques. [1943] 1950. "History, Popular and Unpopular." In Strayer: 27–57.
Bloch, Marc. [1928] 1953. "Toward a Comparative History of European Societies." In Lane and Riemersma: 494–521.
Burke, Peter. 1969. *The Renaissance Sense of the Past*. London. This is a key work for defining the *historical sense*.
Fustel de Coulanges, N. D. [1862] 1972. "An Inaugural Lecture." In Stern: 179–90. For a classic indictment of anachronistic thinking, see p. 187.
Haddock, B. A. 1980. *An Introduction to Historical Thought*. London.
Harbison, E. Harris. 1956. *The Christian Scholar in the Age of the Reformation*. New York.

Hay, Denys. 1977. *Annalists and Historians: Western Historiography from the Eighth to the Eighteenth Centuries*. London.

Manuel, Frank E. 1972. "The Use and Abuse of Psychology in History." In Gilbert and Graubard: 211–37.

Panofsky, Erwin. [1930] 1955. "The First Page of Giorgio Vasari's 'Libro': A Study on the Gothic Style in the Judgment of the Italian Renaissance with an Excursus on Two Facade Designs by Domenico Beccafumi." In Erwin Panofsky, *Meaning in the Visual Arts: Papers in and on Art History*. Garden City, N.Y.: 169–235. This essay by a famous art historian contains many excellent passages regarding the early history of consciousness of anachronism. Footnote references are valuable for further reading.

Ranke, Leopold von. [1854] 1981. "The Epochs of Modern History." In Leopold von Ranke, *The Secret of World History: Selected Writings on the Art and Science of History*. New York: 156–64.

Wedgwood, C. V. 1960. "The Sense of the Past." In C. V. Wedgwood, *Truth and Opinion: Historical Essays*. New York: 19–41. The author asserts that "In its perfect state . . . the sense of the past should carry with it a capacity for eliminating the consciousness of the future, so that we could examine and consider the quality of an epoch *for itself alone*, without any attention to what came after it" (p. 38). For related thoughts, see J. Huizinga, "The Idea of History" [1934], in Stern: 292.

Sources of Additional Information

Despite its central role in modern historical consciousness, the sense of anachronism has not been the object of extensive theoretical reflection. Art historians seem to have paid most penetrating attention to the question; see the references in Panofsky ([1930] 1955) and those cited in the entry on ANTIQUARIANISM. Isaiah Berlin, "The Concept of Scientific History," *HT* 1: 28–30, contains some pertinent observations; see also David E. Stannard, *Shrinking History: On Freud and the Failure of Psychohistory* (Oxford, 1980), pp. 151, 156, and especially David Hackett Fischer, *Historians' Fallacies: Toward a Logic of Historical Thought* (New York, 1970), pp. 132–40. R. W. Southern, "Aspects of the European Tradition of Historical Writing: 4. The Sense of the Past," *Transactions of the Royal Historical Society*, Fifth Series, 23 (1973): 243–63, cites Henry James as the first to use the expression "the sense of the past" and defines it as an ambivalent condition of "alienation and desire for union with the past" (p. 244–45); it is, Southern believes, the result of our "recurrent need to understand and stabilize the present by reviving the experience of the past" (p. 263). For a related view see T. S. Eliot, "Tradition and Individual Talent," in Walter Jackson Bate, ed., *Criticism: The Major Texts* (New York, 1970): 525–29, who defines *historical sense* in terms of "a perception, not only of the pastness of the past, but of its presence . . . a sense of the timeless as well as of the temporal and of the timeless and the temporal together" (pp. 525–26).

ANTIQUARIANISM. 1. Interest in the past based on the love of old things. 2. Learned curiosity about the past purely for its own sake, irrespective of present, future, or other broad interpretive concerns; in this sense, normally pejorative. 3. A branch of scholarship that flourished in Europe, particularly from the fifteenth to eighteenth centuries, devoted to the appreciation and classification of relics, monuments, and old texts.

Antiquarianism refers to an impulse, extant since ancient times, that flourished especially in early modern Europe. Although antiquarianism was in some ways crucial to the emergence of the modern concept of HISTORY, and although the antiquarian spirit is still in certain respects central to professional historical consciousness, the term itself—with certain exceptions (for example, Huizinga, [1929] 1959: 23)—usually has derogatory connotations in contemporary usage. Today, serious historical work is frequently understood in terms of its contrast to "mere" antiquarianism (for instance, Turner, [1891] 1972: 201; Winks, 1969: xx); antiquarianism conventionally designates a naive approach to the past, which "simply collects bits and pieces of data, more or less without regard to their importance or interrelationships" (Landes and Tilly, 1971: 8). It is "data collection for data collection's sake" (Stone, 1972: 132) arising out of "curiosity rather than deep personal concern" (Hughes, 1964: 96).

The word *antiquario* was used in Italian as early as the late fifteenth century (Momigliano, 1950: 290, n. 1); the earliest examples of English usage cited by the *OED* are 1586 (for *antiquary*, in the sense of a "student, or collector, of antiquities"), 1771 (*antiquarian*), and 1779 (*antiquarianism* itself). It derives from the classical Latin *antiquitates*, a term used, and perhaps introduced, by the Roman erudite Varro (116–c. 27 B.C.). Varro's *Antiquitates divinae et humanae* reflected the idea of a past "civilization recovered by systematic collection of all the relics of the past," and he has been called the "father of modern antiquarian studies" (Momigliano, 1950: 289, 288). There is, however, even earlier evidence of an implicit distinction between "history" and what would now be called "antiquarianism." Among the Greeks, *history* rather narrowly implied the very recent political past (as in Thucydides), whereas *archaeology* dealt more comprehensively with geneology and the remote origins of the city states; thus,

> already towards the end of the fifth century B.C. political history and learned research on the [more distant] past tended to be kept in two separate compartments. . . . History was chiefly [recent] political history. What remained outside was the province of learned curiosity. (Momigliano, 1950: 287–88)

Traditionally, as well, "history" was understood as a branch of rhetoric or literature, while "archaeology," or "antiquarianism" (a lesser pursuit), was compilation and classification. In accordance with this ancient tradition, history from the eighteenth century was "always distinguishable from 'mere' scholarship and antiquarianism, and the ground of the distinction was in large measure that the historian was a writer, whereas the scholar and the antiquarian were not" (Gossman, 1978: 4–5).

The classical traditions of archaeology and "antiquities" were largely lost during the Middle Ages but were revived in Italy in the fourteenth century, beginning with Petrarch (1304–74) (Weiss, 1964; Burke, 1969: 23). The chief model for the genre in Renaissance Italy was Flavio Biondo's *Rome Restored* (1440–46), a "topographical account of ancient Rome, describing baths, temples, gates, obelisks and so on, using literary sources as well as information obtained from [Biondo's] own visits to the sites" (Burke, 1969: 25). Most writers of the time, such as Francis Bacon, considered *antiquaries* to be "imperfect historians who helped to salvage relics of the past too fragmentary to be the subject of proper history"; they dealt in "static descriptions" of previous life, as oppposed to "historical expositions" (Momigliano, 1950: 292, 294).

Antiquarianism was widely cultivated in the seventeenth and eighteenth centuries, when antiquaries played a key role in combatting historical SKEPTICISM (doubt regarding the possibility of reliable knowledge about the past) by developing systematic procedures for the evaluation of historical EVIDENCE, including non-literary evidence (see CRITICISM). Antiquarianism came under increasing attack in the eighteenth century, however, with the rise of "philosophical history" exemplified by the work of figures such as Voltaire, Montesquieu, Hume, and Robertson (see PHILOSOPHY OF HISTORY). "Philosophical" historians criticized "mere" erudition inspired by interest in the past for its own sake, divorced from broader social concerns and trends; they insisted that the study of the past be made directly relevant to present interests and that it be related to general patterns of social development.

Although they attacked the antiquarians in name, philosophical historians began to adopt the exacting scholarly methods for evaluating and classifying evidence that antiquarians had helped to devise. In addition, they often assimilated the antiquaries' broad approach to the past as including more than simply political history. Moreover, an appreciation for ANACHRONISM—the necessity of viewing past situations in their own contexts—was strengthened, largely as the result of antiquarian labors. Thus arose the synthesis of antiquarian erudition and broader interpretive concerns, which is the mark of modern professional historical consciousness. Antiquarianism was not, in fact, repudiated by history, but rather subsumed by it. Semantically, however, the tendency to ascribe a pejorative meaning to the word and concept of *antiquarianism* (evident since antiquity) was strengthened: "The antiquary was a connoisseur and an enthusiast; his world was static, his ideal was the collection. . . . he lived to classify" (Momigliano, 1950: 311).

References

Burke, Peter. 1969. *The Renaissance Sense of the Past*. London. This is a good, brief introduction to the history of early modern attitudes toward the past, with substantial citations from original documents.

Gossman, Lionel. 1978. "History and Literature: Reproduction or Signification." In Canary and Kozicki: 3–39.

Hughes, H. Stuart. 1964. *History as Art and as Science: Twin Vistas on the Past*. New York.

Huizinga, Johan. [1929] 1959. "The Task of Cultural History." In Johan Huizinga, *Men and Ideas*. New York: 17–76. Huizinga counsels, within limits, a "rehabilitation of the antiquarian interest." "The direct, spontaneous, naive zeal for antiquated things of earlier days which animates the dilettante of local history and geneologist," writes Huizinga, "is not only a primary form of the urge to historical knowledge but also a full-bodied one" (p. 23).

Landes, David S., and Tilly, Charles, eds. 1971. *History as Social Science.* New York.

Momigliano, Arnaldo. 1950. "Ancient History and the Antiquarian." *Journal of the Warburg and Courtauld Institutes* 13: 285–315. Also reprinted in Momigliano's *Studies in Historiography* (London, 1966): 1–39. This is one of the best introductions to the subject in terms of both subject and bibliographical information.

Stone, Lawrence. 1972. "Prosopography." In Gilbert and Graubard: 107–40.

Turner, Frederick Jackson. [1891] 1972. "The Significance of History." In Stern: 198–208.

Weiss, Roberto. 1964. "Petrarch the Antiquarian." In Charles Henderson, Jr., ed., *Classical, Medieval and Renaissance Studies in Honor of Berthold Louis Ullman* 2. Rome: 199–209.

Winks, Robin W. 1969. *The Historian as Detective: Essays on Evidence.* New York.

Sources of Additional Information

Literature is relatively sparse. The footnote citations in Momigliano (1950) are an excellent source of general bibliography. On antiquarianism in Renaissance Italy see chapter fifteen of Erich Cochrane, *Historians and Historiography in the Italian Renaissance* (Chicago, 1981), which also contains rich bibliographical footnotes. Joan Evans, *A History of the Society of Antiquaries* (Oxford, 1956), traces the development of antiquarianism in England and includes a bibliography that deals mainly with England. The most comprehensive general survey of historical scholarship in the age of antiquarian erudition is still Eduard Fueter, *Geschichte der neueren Historiographie* (1911; reprint ed., New York, 1968), although it should be used cautiously. More concise surveys in English are Denys Hay, *Annalists and Historians: Western Historiography from the Eighth to the Eighteenth Centuries* (London, 1977), and B. A. Haddock, *An Introduction to Historical Thought* (London, 1980). Art historians have made significant contributions to the history of antiquarianism as it relates to the growth of historical sensibility in painting, costume design, and so on. See, for example, Roy Strong, *Recreating the Past: British History and the Victorian Painter* (London, 1978), an appreciation of the role of antiquarianism in the development of British historical painting in the eighteenth and nineteenth centuries; see also J. G. Mann, "Instances of Antiquarian Feeling in Medieval and Renaissance Art," *Archaeological Journal* 89 (1932): 254–74. Finally, see David Hackett Fischer's discussion of the "antiquarian fallacy"—the effort to deliberately cut oneself off from one's own time—in his *Historians' Fallacies: Toward a Logic of Historical Thought* (New York, 1970), pp. 140–42.

B

BIOGRAPHY. In history, the life story of an individual with special emphasis on his or her social role. Recent usage also allows the term to mean the collective life portrait of a group of individuals.

Biography—from the Greek *bios* (life), conventionally understood as an account of the life of a "single man or woman" (Nevins, 1938: 318)—has been closely but ambiguously linked to history since antiquity. From Hellenistic times to the present (Thayer, 1920: 14; Stauffer, 1941: 4), custom has loosely distinguished two genres: biography per se and historical biography. The concerns of the former are private and personal rather than social; in the latter, emphasis is on the public significance of the life or lives in question (James, 1968: 95; Momigliano, 1971: 1–2). This distinction is mirrored in the existence of two theoretical traditions, the one viewing biography as a branch of historical scholarship (Garraty, [1957] 1966: 56), the other as an "art" akin to "literature" (Stauffer, 1941: 4). The "biographical approach" is widely recognized as a legitimate method for history proper (Neale, 1951), and modern historical biography emerged and flourished alongside professional historiography in the late eighteenth and nineteenth centuries.

That the ultimate objects of historical research are the lives of past human individuals is a truism that historians and philosophers broadly acknowledge (e.g., Butterfield, 1955: 1, 4). W. H. Walsh (1969: 157) remarks the "commonplace" that individual people are the "irreducible substances in any historical account." History, Walsh believes,

> must be restricted to whatever touches the fortunes of human beings. . . . Natural happenings and conditions in remote corners of the universe will thus be irrelevant to history, except in a few cases, like the appearance of a comet, where they impinge on human consciousness and excite human hopes or fears. (p. 157)

According to Neale (1951: 203), "many [historical] questions in their nature presupppose biographies; the facts are unobtainable without at least skeleton biographies."

From the historian's viewpoint, *biography* is, simply defined, "the record of a life" and is "thus a branch of history, a small segment of a bigger pattern, just as the story of the development of a town, a state, or a nation may be thought of as an element in a larger whole" (Garraty, [1957] 1966: 56). All biographies are historically interesting since each one necessarily includes some information about its subject's time (p. 56). Not all biographies are "historical biographies," however. To qualify, a study must be informed by a systematic desire to add to our knowledge of a past society, that is, to relate its subject to his unique temporal context (Malone, [1943] 1950: 141). Emphasis may vary— the primary point may be to understand the *individual* against the backdrop of his "times" (a typical nineteenth-century approach) or to use the life as a document or "text" to understand the society (more common in the twentieth century). Whatever the case, social relations must be prominent, for

> history deals with societies as well as individuals, and any society is far more than the sum of its parts. Vast economic, social, and cultural forces, which obviously transcend the lives of individuals, are basic elements in history. (Garraty, [1957] 1966: 58; cf. Mandelbaum, 1967: 417; Dray, 1963: 105–6; Walsh, 1969: 160–61)

The western tradition of writing "life stories of famous mortals" apparently originated among the Greeks of Asia Minor between 500 and 480 B.C. (Momigliano, 1971: 28–33, 101; Breisach, 1983: 25–26). The notion of "lives that teach a lesson" is found in Herodotus (c. 485–c. 425 B.C.) and Thucydides (c. 460–c. 400 B.C.)—see, for example, Thucydides' sketches of Pericles and Cleon in his *Peloponnesian War*. Both men considered personality a decisive influence in human affairs, although they did not use life history as an organizing principle in their works. The *Cyropaedia* of Xenophon (c. 430–c. 355 B.C.), an account of Cyrus the Great's education as a leader, is perhaps the earliest biography by a historian (Breisach, 1983: 26), although Momigliano (1971: 8) refers to it as a "philosophic novel."

Classical authors valued both history and biography primarily as educational tools; the lives of eminent men, like the record of politics and war, provided vicarious experience that served to instruct future generations. This tradition persisted into the RENAISSANCE and well beyond. Down to the eighteenth century, biographers often followed the model of Plutarch's (c. A.D. 46–c. 120) *Parallel Lives*, which, in keeping with classical didacticism and the ancient belief that human nature is unchanging, stressed character over history (Garraty, 1954: 569; 1957: 46). For Plutarch biography, unlike history, dealt with the soul rather than public events:

> . . . it is not Histories that I am writing, but Lives; and in the most illustrious deeds there is not always a manifestation of virtue or vice, nay, a slight thing like a

phrase or a jest often makes a greater revelation of character than battles where thousands fall, or the greatest armaments, or seiges of cities. (1919: 225)

Biography, thought Plutarch, deals (like portraiture) with "signs of the soul in men, and by means of these [portrays] the life of each, leaving to others the description of their great contests." This model fostered a non-empirical understanding of biography as the representation of lives as standard "types." To be sure, another tradition, exemplified by Suetonius' (c. A.D. 69–c. 140) *Twelve Caesars*, encouraged a closer association between history and biography (Breisach, 1983: 71–72) and encouraged a somewhat more empirical approach (as in Einhard's ninth-century *Life of Charlemagne*). Only under the influence of the eighteenth-century cults of inductive reasoning, empathetic understanding, and sensibility, however (reflected in the refinement of characterization in fiction), did biography assume much psychological depth, reaching its epitome in Boswell's famous *Life of Samuel Johnson* (1791), "the most universally admired biography in any language" (Garraty, [1957] 1966: 69). In this climate eighteenth-century historians such as Voltaire and Robertson organized works around the lives of figures such as Louis XIV, Peter the Great, and Charles V (Vercauteren, 1966: 559–60).

In the early nineteenth century, with its romantic and patriotically motivated interest in heroic individuals, biography flourished (Vercauteren, 1966: 554–55). The striking character sketch became an important component of the historian's narrative technique, and historians recognized full-scale biography as an important pursuit. A Belgian scholar reflected widespread opinion when he asserted that "biography is history individualized" (cited in Vercauteren, 1966: 555). Hegel's notion of "world historical individuals"—inspired by Napoleon's career—suggested that extraordinary individuals embody the progressive forces of their age and drive history forward; the idea was popularized in the English-speaking world by Thomas Carlyle, who considered the "History of the World" synonymous with the "Biography of Great Men" ([1840] 1972: 103) and called history the "essence of innumerable Biographies" ([1830] 1972: 93; cf. Stover, 1967). Leopold von Ranke (1795–1886), the foremost role model for academic historiography, agreed that "universal tendencies alone do not decide the outcome of history, they always require the great personalities to bring them into play" (cited in Wines, 1981: 19).

Many nineteenth-century historical biographies were "ponderous" in the fashion of the "panegyric and the commemorative life" (Garraty, 1957: 98), but authors also sought intuitively to plumb the hidden motivations of their subjects, strengthening the notion—still encountered today—that good biography requires the "art" and "imagination" of the novelist (Tolles, [1954] 1966: 82, 72). Also important was the growing popularity of introspective autobiography, a further reflection of the age's psychologism. The realms of scholarship and fiction were often blurred, but standards of research were also refined: biographers "made increasing use of personal documents . . . diaries, journals, and other personal jottings" (Garraty, 1957: 82). In the most sophisticated instances this material was evaluated according to the exacting standards of historical CRITICISM, which led in turn to the use of evidence above and beyond the purely personal kind, that is, documentation regarding the *society* within which the subject lived. Thus emerged the familiar "life-and-times" biography of the late nineteenth century, in which historical context played a central role. Indeed, the genre "often lost sight of the 'life' while multiplying details of the times" (Kraus, 1954: 609). An important by-product of this interest was the appearance of national bio-graphical dictionaries such as the British *Dictionary of National Biography* and the German *Allgemeine Deutsche Biographie*. In the United States the *Dictionary of American Biography* was launched in 1928 and completed in 1937. It should be noted that these works departed from the "great-man" tradition, insofar as they included entries on relatively obscure individuals alongside those of political celebrities (Vercauteren, 1966: 565).

Toward the end of the nineteenth century, various forms of determinism—economic, biological, sociological—worked to undermine the conviction that the extraordinary individual is the key to human affairs. Historians, even when they rejected such doctrines, began to repudiate the "biographical zeal" of the immediate past, with its excessive individualism (Vercauteren, 1966: 554, 561–63). Biography, it was now believed, neglected the broad sweep of history at the expense of single individuals, sacrificing factual accuracy to the requirements of "character study" (Plumb, 1956: xxi; James, 1968: 95); institutions replaced individuals as the focal point for leading scholars such as Fustel de Coulanges in France, Waitz in Germany, and Stubbs in England (Vercauteren, 1966: 561–62). This position was reinforced by the emergence of modern social science, which warned against exaggerating the role of great men and the neglect of social and cultural circumstances. In the twentieth century the attraction of the "life-and-times" approach has declined, and individual biography is now "viewed with reserve by many historians" (James, 1968: 95). Although his-torical biography enjoyed a great publishing vogue in the early twentieth century (Nevins, 1938: 319), this was largely the work of non-academic authors—Emil Ludwig, Stefan Zweig, André Maurois, Lytton Strachey, and others—writers whose research standards were often impugned by academic historians (Neale, 1951: 194; Vercauteren, 1966: 563; Momigliano, 1971: 1). Yet professional interest in the individual life did not entirely disappear, especially in the United States (Plumb, 1956: xxi), where the high degree of political stability fostered continuing reverence for eminent men of the past (cf. Malone, [1943] 1950: 134; Higham, 1965: 220). The growth of the specialized subfield of INTELLEC-TUAL HISTORY also fostered continued interest in great individuals in the form of "intellectual biography" (cf. Rickman, 1979). Since the late 1950s, psy-choanalytic theory has been adapted to the study of exceptional individuals of the past—once again, especially in the United States (see PSYCHOLOGICAL HISTORY).

More important, however, is the rise of "group" or "collective" biography

in the twentieth century; it is in this form that biography survives most prominently in the thinking of the methodologically informed. The idea of collective
biography, (also called "multiple career-line analysis," or "prosopography"
[Stone, 1972: 107]) is a product of the broadened social awareness that profoundly
affected many academic disciplines at the turn of the twentieth century, when
the conviction arose that individuals cannot truly be understood apart from the
groups to which they belong—classes, professional groups, nationalities, and so
on (cf. Hughes, 1958). A pioneering work of composite biography was Charles
Beard's *Economic Interpretation of the Constitution of the United States* (1913),
which analyzed the lives and economic interests of authors of the American
constitution. Beard paid little attention, however, to kinship or social relationships in developing his group portrait (Stone, 1972: 111).

More influential in this regard was Sir Lewis Namier, whose *Structure of
Politics at the Accession of George III* (1929) popularized "Namierism" (a
synonym for prosopography) in Britain. Namier believed that social groups
cannot be understood apart from the people who compose them (Neale, 1951).
Using biographical studies and dictionaries that had accumulated since the eighteenth century, Namier "worked impressionistically through case studies and
personal vignettes, which [he] used to build up a picture of elitist personal
interests, mainly kinship groupings, business affiliations, and a complicated web
of favors given and received" (Stone, 1972: 112). Since the 1950s Namier's
approach has been attacked on various grounds, for example, for exaggerating
group interest at the expense of individual personality and for creating the image
of a "political world too radically sundered from the general intellectual background of the time" (Butterfield, 1959: 297). It remains influential, nonetheless.

The approach exemplified by Beard and Namier has been called the "elitist
school" (Stone, 1972: 109) because it deals with political and socioeconomic
leadership groups. It has helped inspire large projects that aim at compiling and
correlating masses of biographical information about social elites (in many cases
with the aid of teams of scholars and computer banks), as well as smaller-scale
collective biographies that focus on "representative" personalities—individuals
whose lives allegedly embody characteristic features of a larger social group (for
example, Rosenberg, 1958; Stern, 1961). The latter method, pioneered by the
German sociologist and social historian Max Weber (1864–1920) (see IDEAL
TYPE), is an adaptation of the sociological "case study," which has extended
beyond professional to POPULAR HISTORY (for example, Tuchman, 1979).

A "mass school" of collective biography has also emerged since the 1930s
(Stone, 1972: 109), based largely on the adaptation of the statistical methods of
quantitative demography to history. Practitioners of this approach tend to think
that human affairs are controlled more by mass opinion and popular "mentalities" than the actions of elites (pp. 108–9). Their focus is the composite study
of "ordinary people" about whom little can be known as individuals, and their
work reflects a recent concern—associated particularly with SOCIAL HISTORY—
to shift emphasis away from exceptional individuals (even in groups) toward the

study of the behavior of the inarticulate (Fogel, 1975: 345) (see also the discussion of the study of *mentalités* under INTELLECTUAL HISTORY). Among the subjects that have benefited from inquiry along these lines are the histories of social mobility, relationships between popular attitudes and cultural milieux, and "psephology," or the analysis of mass voting behavior (Stone, 1972: 108–9, 113). But such topics depart so far from inquiry into the concrete detail of individual lives—either singly or in groups—that it is debatable whether they can justly be called "biography" at all.

References

Breisach, Ernst. 1983. *Historiography: Ancient, Medieval, and Modern*. Chicago. This work fully integrates material on the history of biography and its relationship to history.

Butterfield, Herbert. 1955. "The Role of the Individual in History." *History*, N.S., 40: 1–17. "The genesis of historical events lies in human beings," writes Butterfield. "Minute researches, concentrated on the action of individuals day by day, are the solid rock on which historical scholarship is built" (pp. 1, 4).

———. 1959. *George III and the Historians*. New York.

Carlyle, Thomas. [1830] 1972, "On History." In Stern: 91–101.

———. [1840] 1972. *On Heroes, Hero-Worship, and the Heroic in History*. In Stern: 101–107.

Dray, William. 1963. "The Historical Explanation of Actions Reconsidered." In Hook: 105–35. Dray suggests, following Maurice Mandelbaum, that "individual actions as such are below the threshold of proper historical interest; they enter history only insofar as they have 'societal significance' " (pp. 105–6).

Fogel, Robert William. 1975. "The Limits of Quantitative Methods in History." *AHR* 80: 329–50.

Garraty, John A. 1954. "The Interrelations of Psychology and Biography." *Psychological Bulletin* 51: 569–82.

———. [1957] 1966. "The Nature of Biography." In A. S. Eisenstadt, ed., *The Craft of American History: Selected Essays* 2. New York: 56–70.

———. 1957. *The Nature of Biography*. New York.

Higham, John. 1965. *History*. Englewood Cliffs, N.J.

Hughes, H. Stuart. 1958. *Consciousness and Society: The Reorientation of European Social Thought, 1890–1930*. New York.

James, Robert Rhodes. 1968. "Britain: Soldiers and Biographies." *Journal of Contemporary History* 3: 89–101.

Kraus, Michael. 1954. "Biography since 1900." *The Mississippi Valley Historical Review* 40: 608–13.

Malone, Dumas. [1943] 1950. "Biography and History." In Strayer: 121–48.

Mandelbaum, Maurice. 1967. "A Note on History as Narrative." *HT* 6: 413–19.

Momigliano, Arnaldo. 1971. *The Development of Greek Biography: Four Lectures*. Cambridge, Mass. This work is of general interest since these lectures were designed as an introduction to the "difficult and important" problem of the separation of biography and history. The introduction contains many references to the opinions of historians and philosophers regarding biography. Momigliano detects a resurgence of interest in biography among historians and concludes with a very useful bibliography of general as well as specialized works.

Neale, J. E. 1951. "The Biographical Approach to History." *History*, N.S., 34: 193–302. Neale's essay is a good statement of Namier's approach by a convinced supporter.

Nevins, Allan. 1938. *The Gateway to History*. Boston. Chapter twelve is entitled "Biography and History."

Plumb, J. H. 1956. "The Interaction of History and Biography." *The Times Literary Supplement*, Jan. 6: xxi.

Plutarch's Lives. 1919. Ed. T. E. Page, E. Capps, W.H.D. Rouse. London.

Rickman, H. P. 1979. "Wilhelm Dilthey and Biography." *Biography* 2: 218–29.

Rosenberg, Hans. 1958. *Bureaucracy, Aristocracy, and Autocracy: The Prussian Experience, 1660–1815*. Cambridge, Mass.

Stauffer, Donald A. 1941. *The Art of Biography in Eighteenth Century England*. 2 vols. Princeton, N.J. Stauffer asserts that "emphasis should fall upon biography as an art rather than as a science. Individual pieces are to be judged, in other words, according to their success in conveying the sense of a life being lived, rather than according to the quantity or the accuracy of the facts they contain" (p. 4).

Stern, Fritz. 1961. *The Politics of Cultural Despair: A Study in the Rise of Germanic Ideology*. Berkeley, Calif.

Stone, Lawrence. 1972. "Prosopography." In Gilbert and Graubard: 107–40. This is a concise survey of the field and its literature. It defines *prosopography*, a term used by classical scholars since the eighteenth century, as "the investigation of the common background characteristics of a group of actors in history by means of the collective study of their lives" (p. 107).

Stover, Robert. 1967. "Great Man Theory of History." *EP* 3: 378–82. Stover's entry includes a useful bibliography.

Thayer, William Roscoe. 1920. *The Art of Biography*. New York. This work is a general history of biography from antiquity through the nineteenth century.

Tolles, Frederick B. [1954] 1966. "The Biographer's Craft." In A. S. Eisenstadt, ed., *The Craft of American History: Selected Essays* 2. New York: 72–83.

Tuchman, Barbara. 1979. "Biography as a Prism of History." In Marc Pachter, ed., *Telling Lives: The Biographer's Art*. Washington, D.C.: 132–47.

Vercauteren, Fernand. 1966. "La Biographie et l'Histoire." *Bulletin de l'academie Royale de Belgique, classe des lettres et de science morales et politiques* 52: 554–65. Vercauteren's article is a brief and valuable historical survey.

Walsh, W. H. 1969. "The Notion of an Historical Event II." *Aristotelian Society Supplementary Volume* 43: 153–64. While acknowledging the truism that history deals with individual human beings, Walsh rejects the notion that history is "essentially the story of the doings and sufferings of individual human beings. . . . these are the subject-matter of biography which, whether or not it is reckoned to belong to history, is at most only part of the latter study. . . . History is concerned with man in society, more specifically with man in his different social groupings. . . . social groups and not individuals are the units on which historians concentrate" (pp. 160–61, 164; see also pp. 162–63).

Wines, Roger. 1981. "Introduction." In Leopold von Ranke, *The Secret of World History: Selected Writings on the Art and Science of History*. New York: 1–31. See also the comments on pp. 165–66.

Sources of Additional Information

Momigliano (1971) includes an invaluable bibliography of general and specialized works; the same author has also written "History and Biography," in M. I. Finley, ed., *The Legacy of Greece* (Oxford, 1981): 155–84. The journal *Biography* regularly publishes theoretical articles and bibliographies on the subject. Garraty (1957) contains an extensive bibliography on all facets of biography. Charles F. Mullett, *Biography as History: Men and Movements in Europe since 1500* (Washington, D.C., 1963), also includes a long list of titles. There are relevant comments in Kurt von Fritz, *Aristotle's Contribution to the Practice and Theory of Historiography* (Berkeley, Calif., 1958), pp. 129–35. Daniel Aaron, ed., *Studies in Biography* (Cambridge, Mass., 1978), contains eleven essays, including one by the historian John Clive. Paul Murray Kendall, *The Art of Biography* (London, 1965), is a general survey along the lines of the earlier work by Thayer (1920). Of related interest is Sidney Hook, *The Hero in History: A Study in Limitation and Possibility* (New York, 1943). Daniel Bertaux, ed., *Biography and Society: The Life History Approach in the Social Sciences* (Beverly Hills, Calif., 1981), treats the subject from the standpoint of sociology. See also Grete Klingenstein et al., *Biographie und Geschichtswissenschaft* (Munich, 1980). Catherine Drinker Bowen, a prolific American biographer, has written *Biography: The Craft and the Calling* (Boston, 1968). There is much on Namier, for example, Herbert Butterfield, "George III and the Namier School," *Encounter* 8 (April 1957): 70–76, and two articles by John Brooke, "Namier and His Critics," *Encounter*, Feb. 1965: 47–49, and "Namier and Namierism," *HT* 3 (1963–64): 331–47. On the "mass school" see D. K. Rowney and J. Q. Graham, *Quantitative History* (Homewood, Ill., 1969). On the unreliability of some biographical dictionaries see Margaret C. Schindler, "Fictitious Biography," *AHR* 42 (July 1937): 680–90. Of further interest is K. D. Barkin, "Autobiography and History," *Societas* 6 (Spring 1976): 83–108.

C

CAPITALISM. 1. A system of economic organization and production—typical of many western societies since the sixteenth century and especially since the INDUSTRIAL REVOLUTION of the late eighteenth century—animated by a preference for acquisition over consumption and based on the calculated investment of savings for the production of new wealth. Sixteenth-, seventeenth-, and eighteenth-century pre-industrial capitalism is often referred to as "mercantile" capitalism, in contrast to the later "industrial" capitalism. 2. Less frequently, any economic view or practice, regardless of historical period or geographical location, based on the systematic investment of wealth to produce more wealth.

The term *capitalism*—derived from the Latin *caput* ("head," or "chief") and its adjective *capitalis* (Cannan, 1920–21: 469)—was introduced in French, English, and German in the mid-nineteenth century to denote the modern European system of economic production. The word's popularity, especially in continental journalism and social criticism, derived largely from the fact that it became a loose socialist slogan used to attack existing economic and social conditions. Its use in the social sciences, including history, became widespread only in the early twentieth century (Braudel, [1967] 1975: xiii). Today it is basic to much historical thinking on socio-economic development in the early modern and modern periods of western history (for example, Braudel, [1967] 1975; Morazé, 1968). Indeed, economic and social historians are primarily responsible for legitimizing academic use of the term (Hilger, 1982: 449). Still, the word is normally not well defined, retains its polemical associations, and, ironically, has long been resisted by economists (Passow, 1927: 4–5, 8–9). Hilger (1982: 448) notes that scholars often accept the word itself but display either an imprecise idea of the underlying concept or repudiate the concept outright.

The early history of the term is vague; presumably, it originated in the early-nineteenth-century French literature of social reform (Hilger, 1982: 443). One of the earliest uses of *capitalism*—possibly the first—appears in the ninth edition of Louis Blanc's *Organization of Labor* (1850), where the French socialist refers to *capitalisme* as the "appropriation of capital by some to the exclusion of others" (cited in Passow, 1927: 2). The earliest English use noted in the *OED* is Thackeray's novel *The Newcomes* (1854): "The sense of capitalism sobered and dignified Paul de Florac." Carl von Rodbertus was evidently first to use the word in German, as late as 1869 (Hilger, 1982: 443).

The term was a logical outgrowth of the older words *capitalist* and *capital*. In both English and French, *capital*, in the sense of "money which is to be invested or has been invested" (Cannan, 1920–21: 481), slowly evolved from the sixteenth century onward (Sée, 1928: 2, 187, n. 1; Richards, 1925–26); a "usurer's and accountant's word" (Bloch, 1953: 170), it was apparently borrowed in its commercial sense from Italian bookkeeping texts. By the seventeenth century, *capital* understood as "wealth . . . used to help in producing more wealth" was widely employed in English (*OED*) and, in a loose sense, was simply equated with "moneyed wealth"; Arthur Young, for example, referred to "capitalists" as "moneyed men" in his *Travels in France* (1792) (*OED*). In *The Wealth of Nations* (1776), Adam Smith introduced an important extension of the word: while continuing to employ *capital* in the sense of invested wealth, he also used it to refer to "things" in which money is invested, which are in turn used to produce more wealth (Cannan, 1920–21: 480). The term could now denote "capital goods," for example, a warehouse or factory, as well as a sum of invested wealth.

Early-nineteenth-century usage assumes the existence of a concept of capitalism (that is, a distinct economic system) before the term itself appeared. The German economist Julius von Soden used the expression "capitalist production" as early as 1815 (Hilger, 1982: 443). Williams (1976: 42) cites Thomas Hodgskin's *Labour Defended against the Claims of Capital* (1825): "betwixt him who produces food and him who produces clothing, betwixt him who makes instruments and him who uses them, in steps the capitalist, who neither makes nor uses them and appropriates to himself the produce of both."

All of this suggests that Werner Sombart's claim that Karl Marx "virtually discovered the phenomenon" of capitalism is an exaggeration (Sombart, 1930: 195; cf. Parsons, 1928: 661). Marx was certainly important in shaping Sombart's idea of capitalism—and that of twentieth-century German sociology in general (Parsons, 1929: 50)—but he never employed the word *Kapitalismus* (Passow, 1927: 3, n. 2; Braudel, [1967] 1975: xiii; Hilger, 1982: 442–43) and, in fact, merely formalized terminology and attitudes that were widespread in the early and mid-nineteenth century. The idea that Marx is responsible for creating the concept is largely the result of efforts by anti-Marxist writers, especially Germans (e.g., Passow, 1927), to discredit the idea by linking it to socialist polemics. Through his socialist disciples, Marx was undoubtedly important in disseminating the set of ideas we now call "capitalism" on the European continent, although this is probably less true for England. In one of the earliest English-language histories of capitalism, for example, J. A. Hobson (1894: 4–5)—who was thoroughly familiar with socialist ideas—mentioned Marx only a few times and justified his use of the term on grounds of its acceptance by businessmen rather than social theorists. As an instrument of academic analysis, it is nonetheless true that "capitalism" was largely the creation of Marx and two other German thinkers who followed his lead: Sombart himself (1863–1941) and Max Weber (1864–1920) (Dahrendorf, [1959] 1969: 37–38).

Marx viewed his own society as an interlocking system of economic production and social domination that was the logical outgrowth of the early industrial stage of historical development (see HISTORICAL MATERIALISM). If he did not specifically use the term *capitalism*, he nevertheless made liberal use of the adjective *capitalist*—for example, "capitalist production," "capitalist mode of production," "capitalist accumulation"—and this helped link the word—particularly in German—to the prevailing system of production in western Europe and North America (Hoover, 1968: 295). In scattered passages of his *Contribution to the Critique of Political Economy* (1859) and the first volume of *Capital* (1867), Marx characterized the basic features of this system: mechanized production, private ownership of the means of production, wage labor, and the creation of "surplus value" (i.e., the profit margin that, according to Marx's now largely discredited labor theory of value, is created by the worker but unfairly appropriated by the employer).

Socialist usage, following Marx, spread the concept on the European continent. In the socialist vocabulary, *capitalism* was a pejorative label for an economic order that had to be overthrown, as well as a concept of historical periodization, "a great epoch in social and economic development" (Parsons, 1928: 642).

The work of Sombart and Weber, although non-socialist, retains many of the pejorative overtones that socialist theory had attached to *capitalism*. Sombart's *Der moderne Kapitalismus* (1st ed., 1902)—perhaps the single most important work for establishing the idea of capitalism as an economic system in academic circles—was explicitly conceived as an extension of Marx's ideas (Parsons, 1928: 661). But Sombart's view of capitalism also owes much to romantic conservatism, which viewed industrialization as a negative force in the destruction of the supposed "organic" unity of agrarian society (Parsons, 1928: 651). Moreover, Sombart's analysis is "idealistic" rather than "materialistic": whereas Marx considered capitalism's profit mentality a surface reflection of underlying material conditions, Sombart reversed this, emphasizng the rationalist and acquisitive "spirit" as the essence of capitalism; at its core, capitalism for Sombart is a way of looking at the world that reduces everything—including human beings—to the status of means of production (Parsons, 1928: 648–50, 659–60). Thus, Sombart forged a melodramatic, pessimistic view of the capitalist world as a prison for everyone involved; such histrionic associations remain strong in popular and scholarly usage (cf. Hayek, 1954).

From the 1920s onward, Sombart's influence was inescapable, even for those historians who did not share his melancholy attitudes (e.g., Gras, [1942] 1953). His impact on historiography is typically reflected in the work of the French historian Henri Sée (1928: xiii, xv), who embraced Sombart's two-stage scheme of periodization and depicted capitalism as a "phenomenon" that was "international in scope."

Max Weber's theory of capitalism shares the melancholy spirit of Sombart's analysis. His famous *Protestant Ethic and the Spirit of Capitalism* ([1920] 1958) concludes by evoking the image of an "iron cage" created by the capitalist system—which Weber sees as the product of the mechanistic *rationalization* of economic life and fetishistic worship of material production (cf. Mitzman, 1970; Hughes, 1958: 318). Even more influential among English-speaking historians than Sombart's *Der moderne Kapitalismus*, Weber's *Protestant Ethic* did much to encourage use of the term and concept of *capitalism*. Aspects of Weber's interpretation were elaborated in a widely read work by R. H. Tawney (1926), and the German original was itself translated into English in 1930.

In his writings, Weber used the term *capitalism* in two ways, often without carefully distinguishing them: as a general concept, or IDEAL TYPE, which designated any economic system based on "(rationally conducted) exchange for profit," regardless of time or place; and as a historically specific designation for the modern European economic system. According to Weber, only in the latter case has the rationalist, acquisitive spirit of capitalistic enterprise completely dominated an entire society (Parsons, 1929: 34–36, 48–49).

Weber's concept made its greatest immediate impact on historians via his theory that the modern spirit of acquisition was religious in origin; the roots of European capitalism lay in the asceticism, regimentation, and routinization of life inculcated by sixteenth-century Calvinist protestantism. This was the celebrated and now partly discredited "Weber thesis," which became a storm center of scholarly debate in the 1930s and remained controversial for some time after World War II.

Interestingly, Sombart, Weber, and other early disseminators of the concept such as Joseph Schumpeter (1950) thought of capitalism "as being on the eve of replacement by quite a different economic system" (Hoover, 1968: 298), an assumption that obviously owed much to their own personalities and to the Marxist and socialist traditions, yet one that persists as an implicit assumption in much historical scholarship, both polemical and otherwise. The idea was strengthened by the world depression of the 1930s, which was popularly interpreted as a "crisis of capitalism" and led many historians to entertain socialist and socialist-inspired ideas for the first time (see CRISIS).

There have been numerous objections to use of the term by historians, in much the same vein as objections to the word FEUDALISM. The French scholar Marc Bloch (1953: 174) called *capitalism* a potentially "useful word" but complained of its ambiguity. In stronger terms, Alfred Cobban (1956: 11) maintaned that *capitalism* has become a "mere bogy, a term of abuse like fanaticism and with as little precise content." "What are significant historically," he added, "are not the remote similarities but the essential differences hidden by these omnibus terms."

On the other hand, Fernand Braudel ([1967] 1975: xiii), while admitting that the term "has been much used and perhaps abused," argues that "If we use it so much it is because there is a need for it, or for a word serving the same purpose; because it points to certain forms of economic life in past centuries that are already modern, as though oriented to the future."

References

Bloch, Marc. 1953. *The Historian's Craft*. New York.

Braudel, Fernand. [1967] 1975. *Capitalism and Material Life, 1400–1800*. New York. Braudel, a leading French scholar, is willing to embrace the idea of "capitalist civilization" (p. xiii).

Cannan, Edwin. 1920–21. "Early History of the Term Capital." *Quarterly Journal of Economics* 35: 469–81.

Cobban, Alfred. 1956. "The Vocabulary of Social History." *Political Science Quarterly* 71: 1–17.

Dahrendorf, Ralf. [1959] 1969. *Class and Class Conflict in Industrial Society*. Stanford, Calif. Dahrendorf, a sociologist concerned to surmount the polemical and time-bound associations of "capitalism," wishes to augment the idea of "capitalism" with the more comprehensive concept of "industrial society" (p. 37, 40).

Gras, N.S.B. [1942] 1953. "Capitalism—Concepts and History." In Lane and Riemersma: 66–79. Gras distinguishes five concepts of capitalism: "the technological concept" of classical economists such as Adam Smith and J. S. Mill; the "ethical concept" of the socialists; the identification of capitalism with "individual ownership, regardless of the ethical element"; the idea of capitalism as a "system of production in which capital predominates"; and (his own favorite) the notion of capitalism as a "capitalist-administrator system," that is, "an organization of production in which the owner of capital enters into partnership with the administrator to produce an income for all concerned" (pp. 66–67).

Hayek, F. A., ed. 1954. *Capitalism and the Historians*. Chicago. This is a collection of essays designed to defend capitalism against socialist and socialist-inspired attacks.

Hilger, Marie-Elisabeth. 1982. "Kapital, Kapitalist, Kapitalismus." *GG* 3: 399–454. Hilger's article has an excellent bibliography in the footnote citations. She notes that Marx and Engels displayed an embryonic concept of capitalism in *The German Ideology* (1845–46), which they labeled *Weltmarkt* (p. 443), and stresses the usage of the economist Schäffle in 1870; her piece includes a short contribution by Lucian Hölscher on Marx's concept of "capital."

Hobson, John A. 1894. *The Evolution of Modern Capitalism: A Study of Machine Production*. London. Hobson's book makes capitalism virtually synonymous with the mechanization of production.

Hoover, Calvin B. 1968. "Capitalism." *IESS* 2: 294–302. Hoover accepts the basic Marx-Sombart-Weber paradigm.

Hughes, H. Stuart. 1958. *Consciousness and Society: The Reorientation of European Social Thought, 1890–1930*. New York. This work contains a lengthy discussion of Weber.

Mitzman, Arthur. 1970. *The Iron Cage: An Historical Interpretation of Max Weber.* New York.

Morazé, Charles. 1968. *The Triumph of the Middle Classes.* Garden City, N.Y.

Parsons, Talcott. 1928. " 'Capitalism' in Recent German Literature: Sombart and Weber." *The Journal of Political Economy* 36: 641–61. This is the first section of a valuable two-part article (see the next citation). This segment deals with Sombart, the second with Weber.

————. 1929. " 'Capitalism' in Recent German Literature: Sombart and Weber." *The Journal of Political Economy* 37: 31–51. This segment stresses that in Weber "all the specific elements of capitalism which we think of as contrasting it with socialism . . . are of secondary importance as compared with the great central fact of bureaucracy" (pp. 38–39).

Passow, Richard. 1927. *"Kapitalismus:" Eine begrifflich-terminologische Studie.* 2d ed. Jena, E.Ger. According to Hilger (1982: 448), this is still the most basic study of the term and concept. It repudiates the word as a nebulous slogan of social polemic and notes that the late-nineteenth-century historian Theodor Mommsen frequently used the terms *Kapitalwirtschaft* and *Kapitalistenwirtschaft* in *History of Rome* (p. 3). On early use by other French and German historians such as Pirenne and Dopsch, see pp. 6–7.

Richards, R. D. 1925–26. "Early History of the Term Capital," *Quarterly Journal of Economics* 40: 329–38. Richards corrects some errors in Cannan (1920–21).

Schumpeter, Joseph A. 1950. *Capitalism, Socialism, and Democracy.* 3rd ed. New York.

Sée, Henri. 1928. *Modern Capitalism: Its Origin and Evolution.* New York. This work illustrates the stereotypes and clichés that gained wide acceptance in the 1920s. The citations are a good source for early literature.

Sombart, Werner. 1930. "Capitalism." *ESS* 3: 195–208. This piece is good for older bibliography.

Tawney, R. H. 1926. *Religion and the Rise of Capitalism: A Historical Study.* New York.

Weber, Max. [1920] 1958. *The Protestant Ethic and the Spirit of Capitalism.* New York. Weber's book first appeared in the form of articles published in 1904 and 1905.

Williams, Raymond. 1976. *Keywords: A Vocabulary of Culture and Society.* New York. Williams is evidently incorrect in the contention that the term *capitalism* was introduced in the early 1800s; the word seems to date only from the mid-nineteenth century (cf. Hilger, 1982: 443).

Sources of Additional Information

See "Capitalism" and related entries in James Russell, *Marx-Engels Dictionary* (Westport, Conn., 1980), and in Tom Bottomore, ed., *A Dictionary of Marxist Thought* (Cambridge, Mass., 1983). For a Soviet account see the *Great Soviet Encyclopedia*, 3rd ed. (1976), 11: 99–105. On Marx see also Zbigniew A. Jordan, ed., *Karl Marx: Economy, Class and Social Revolution* (London, 1971), pp. 39–54, and the clear explication in Roy Enfield, "Marx and Historical Laws," *HT* 15 (1976): 267–77, especially 270–71, 273. There is much bibliography in the entries "Capital" and "Capitalism" in volume one of *MCWS*: 375–98. William Ebenstein and Edwin Fogelman, *Todays Isms: Communism, Fascism, Capitalism, Socialism*, 8th ed. (Englewood Cliffs, N.J., 1980), includes a short bibliography. For the history of the word *capital* see Bernhard Laum, "Über Ursprung und Frühgeschichte des Begriffes 'Kapital'," *Finanzarchiv* 15 (1954–

55): 72–112. Richard Romano and Melvin Leiman, eds., *Views on Capitalism* (Beverly Hills, Calif., 1970), is an anthology of excerpts from the writings of economic theorists, from the classical economists to the present. On the immense influence of the concept in studies of IMPERIALISM see Wolfgang J. Mommsen, *Theories of Imperialism* (New York, 1980). Chapter one of Norman Ware, *The Industrial Worker, 1840–1860* (1924; reprint ed., Chicago, 1964), is "Modern Capitalism." For a sampling of more recent use by historians see Christopher R. Friedrichs, "Capitalism, Mobility and Class Formation in the Early Modern German City," *Past and Present* 69 (Nov. 1975): 24–49; John Day, "Fernand Braudel and the Rise of Capitalism," *Social Research* 47 (Autumn 1980): 507–48; Joyce Appleby, *Capitalism and a New Social Order in the 1790s* (New York, 1984); and David S. Landes, ed., *The Rise of Capitalism* (New York, 1966).

CAUSATION. The establishment of relations of cause and effect in historical explanation; the representation of historical events, conditions, and processes as consequences of prior conditions and/or human actions.

Since its beginnings history has been intimately concerned with causation (Oakeshott, [1933] 1966: 193). The idea of cause—from the Latin *causa*—has been called "the great central pillar" of historical thought (Tapp, 1952: 67; cf. Bayer, 1980: 272) and is often identified as the factor that distinguishes history from more rudimentary forms such as annals and chronicles (Mandelbaum, 1942: 40; Beard and Hook, 1946: 112). E. H. Carr ([1961] 1964: 87) states flatly that *history* is "a study of causes." The French scholar Marc Bloch ([1928] 1953: 504) called history an "exhilarating, never-ending search for causes"; Maurice Mandelbaum ([1938] 1967: 271–72) considers the discovery of causal connections between events "the goal of technical historical investigation," and the Italian philosopher Croce ([1919] 1960: 80) thought of *cause* as the "cement" that historians use to bind their accounts together.

The idea of causation surfaces most obviously whenever the word *because* is used in historical writing (Hughes, 1960: 27–28), but Michael Scriven (1966: 238)—who considers causation "the most important explanatory notion in history"—notes that the idea's significance cannot be "gauged by the frequency with which the actual word 'cause' occurs" since "the notion is very frequently embedded in other terms." Despite its importance, it is only in the past century that the concept of causation has been closely scrutinized, and the ideas of cause, DETERMINISM, LAW, EXPLANATION, and PROCESS have often overlapped. With certain exceptions (for instance, Dray, 1978) thought on the subject has unfortunately been highly generalized, divorced from close analysis of actual historical studies and controversies. In the early 1960s W. H. Walsh ([1962–63] 1969: 245; cf. Hughes, 1960: 24–25) could still refer to historians' "general confusion about what a cause is."

In classical philosophy and legal thought, *cause* evoked the image of an orderly universe governed by law (Cohen, 1942: 13); *inquiry*, according to Aristotle, was at bottom a quest for causes (Nash, 1969: 228–29). Herodotus (c. 484–c. 425 B.C.) inaugurated the tradition that historians should explain the events they describe; from his time forward *historical explanation* was understood as a search for social causes, particularly the roots of war and political unrest (Momigliano, [1958] 1966: 116). Thucydides (c. 460–c. 400 B.C.) discriminated between immediate and long-range causes, as well as genuine causes and mere pretexts (Momigliano, 1978: 4). Polybius (c. 203–c. 120 B.C.), who believed that "the indication of cause makes history fruitful" (cited in Oakeshott, [1933] 1966: 193), distinguished between "the motive force, the excuse or reason, and the beginning or origin" (Cohen, 1942: 13). Ancient historians (notably Thucydides) tended to depict *cause* in the narrow sense of deliberate human intentions. "Fortune," divine will, and geographical influences were also important, however (Walsh, [1962–63] 1969: 245–46; Momigliano, 1978: 4) (see DETERMINISM).

Interest in causation—aside from divine will—diminished in medieval historiography (Burke, 1969: 13), but in early modern historiography the role of causation was reaffirmed and has since been vastly extended beyond ancient practice (Walsh, [1962–63] 1969: 48). In the sixteenth century cause became closely associated with science, understood as the discovery of cause-effect relationships in nature. The notion that history should imitate science and uncover such relationships in human affairs ultimately became a hallmark of historiographical POSITIVISM. The British positivist H. T. Buckle (1821–62), for instance, sought to use statistics to demonstrate the "reign of iron laws of causality" in history (Cohen, 1942: 12). Nineteenth-century historiography treated the importance of causation as self-evident, although the explicit quest for cause was often subordinated to dramatic NARRATIVE, as in the work of Ranke and his school in Germany (Bayer, 1980: 272). According to the Hegelian idealist tradition of "internal relations"—from which Marxist historiography sprang—"it is *a priori* assumed that there *must* be a causal connection among all events" (Wiener, 1941: 321).

In the 1870s a shift occurred. German idealists such as Droysen, Dilthey, Windelband, and Rickert, together with the Italian Croce, joined in denying that history must conform to scientific models. *Science*, they argued, formulates generalized laws of cause and effect, whereas *history* studies unique, non-recurring events (see IDEALISM). This suggested that a general concept of causation might be inappropriate to history (Mandelbaum, 1942: 30–31). In Britain many historians simultaneously grew skeptical of efforts to isolate historical causes, based on their belief in the "unity" and "continuity" of history; "Such is the unity of all history," wrote two scholars of the day (Pollack and Maitland, [1898] 1968: 1), "that anyone who endeavors to tell a piece of it must feel that his first sentence tears a seamless web."

Croce became especially influential in England and the United States; he wished, in essence, to expunge the ideas of "cause" and "law" from historical discourse (Hughes, 1960: 24). In Britain the idealist philosopher Michael Oakeshott rallied to this position (Walsh, [1962–63] 1969: 238). Without rejecting the usefulness of causal concepts for science or ordinary life, Oakeshott ([1933]

1966: 198–99, 196) considered the effort to isolate historical causes irrelevant, since it "implies that a single historical event may be abstracted from the world of history, made free of all its relations and connexions, and then spoken of as the cause of all that followed it or of certain selected events which followed it." The idea of historical causation, Oakeshott believed, was a "monstrous incursion of science into the world of history."

In the United States the question of causation became part of the debate over historical RELATIVISM (the doctrine that written history is inevitably slanted by the subjective viewpoint of the historian). Relativists were especially troubled by wide disagreement over the causes of key events such as the American Civil War and World War I (Beale, 1946; Walsh, [1962–63] 1969: 235; Potter, 1963: 179). In a famous presidential address to the American Historical Association ([1934] 1959: 144–45; cf. Higham, 1965: 126), Charles Beard, for example, attacked the "falsity" of the "assumption of causation" as one of the "intellectual formulas borrowed from natural science, which have cramped and distorted the operations of history" (cf. Williams, 1956: 60–61, 73). Beard linked the idea of historical causation to DETERMINISM and the fallacious quest for general social laws similar to "laws such as are found in hydraulics." Later (1936: 79), he took up a theme of Croce and Oakeshott, maintaining that causal judgments violated the "seamless web" of the past.

Beard's address focused attention on historical causation for the next two decades. Writing in the early 1940s, Mandelbaum (1942: 30) identified "distrust with . . . the concept of causation" as one of the "most widely current prepossesions in the theory of historiography." Like Beard, many historians concluded that *cause* implied rigid necessity and the quest for historical laws. In response, defenders of the concept sought to refurbish the notion and fix its precise role in historical inquiry.

On the one hand, advocates of a neo-positivist position such as C. G. Hempel ([1942] 1959) reaffirmed on new grounds what Beard and the idealists denied: that historical EXPLANATION, like explanation in the natural sciences, proceeds by relating individual occurrences to general causal laws (see COVERING LAW). Their arguments, however, did not convince most historians.

In less scientistic fashion, philosophers such as Morris Cohen (1942), Maurice Mandelbaum (1942), and Sidney Hook (Beard and Hook, 1946) upheld the ideal of necessary cause-effect relationships in history, while underscoring the question's complexity. All stressed the importance of some notion of cause in ordinary thinking. According to Cohen (1942: 14), "we all believe that human, like other events, are in some way connected, and that there is always a reason or ground why anything happens." Cohen denied that historical causation may be understood in terms of statistical correlation (a view advanced by the American scholar Frederick J. Teggart [1942]), since *correlation*—mere recognition that two things have occurred in some regular relationship—may be the result of coincidence. *Cause*, in contrast, implies necessary connection; it "affirms that there is some reason or ground why, whenever the antecedent occurs, the consequent must follow'' (Cohen, 1942: 15–16) Cohen's understanding of historical explanation was still modeled on scientific method, that is, the demonstration of rigorous cause-effect relationships that identify ''the necessary and sufficient conditions for the occurrence of any event.'' He argued, however, that historians operate under special handicaps that prevent the perfect realization of this ideal: the fragmentary nature of evidence, the fact that human affairs (which involve ''mental'' and ''biologic'' factors) are more complex than mechanics, and the historian's primary obligation (according to Cohen) to narrate rather than analyze. As a consequence, historians normally display loose conceptions of causality. Cohen concluded that the historical search for cause is

> both a necessary ideal and yet inherently difficult of attainment. The best we can achieve by rigorous scientific procedure is some progress in the approximation to this ideal. . . . But we can say with a great deal of confidence that some things are altogether irrelevant and some conditions are more directly involved than others in bringing about certain events. (p. 29)

Mandelbaum (1942: 30, 39) maintained that historians unavoidably use some notion of causation, no matter what they say in theory; the mere suggestion that one event is ''relevant'' to another is an instance of the idea. Causal analysis in history, he conceded, cannot be as rigorous or predictive as in natural science since the historian does not enjoy laboratory control over his material and human events do not recur exactly; human events are nonetheless similar enough to be comparable (pp. 30–32). The idealists, he believed, erred in understanding cause only in its special natural scientific sense; there are other legitimate meanings, such as the sense of cause in ordinary life and the law, which are more appropriate for history (pp. 33–34; Mandelbaum, [1938] 1967: 272–73). Mandelbaum's stress on the resemblance between historical reasoning and ordinary thinking— where *cause* is understood to mean simply ''an event, action or omission but for which the whole subsequent course of events would have been significantly different'' (Walsh, [1962–63] 1969: 236; also Scriven, 1966)—became a hallmark of future reflection on the subject. Exploration of similarities between concepts of causation in history and the law have been especially fruitful (Hart and Honoré, [1959] 1966; Walsh, [1962–63] 1969: 244–45; Dray, 1978).

According to Hook (Beard and Hook, 1946: 110), *cause* is an ''ambiguous and difficult'' term best used with caution; it is nevertheless ''employed in every day affairs, in all branches of science, and in the writings of all historians.'' Like Cohen and Mandelbaum, Hook (pp. 110–11) maintained that *cause* implies necessity, but he also stressed that

> Since every historical occurrence involves the interaction of several elements, we cannot intelligibly speak of *the* cause of the occurrence if by that term we mean the sole or exclusive element. But usually ''the cause'' of an event, as used by historians, means not the only cause but ''the most important cause'' . . . among a complex of causal conditions, or the condition which was most decisive to what

occurred, or which made the difference between what occurred and what probably
would have occurred in its absence. (pp. 110–11)

Hook recognized that subjective factors condition the historian's thought, and
he acknowledged that causal reasoning in history is always a matter of probability;
on the other hand, "the attribution of causes is either true or false and *in principle*
ascertainable although in practice we may not at any moment know enough to
provide the answer" (p. 111). In a key passage, Hook argued that historians
typically show cause by a twofold technique of "comparison and hypothetical
construction." *Comparison* "involves constructing a class of instances and proceeding . . . to eliminate alternative hypotheses. . . . The validity of the historian's
findings will depend upon his ability to discover a method of roughly measuring
the relative strength of the various factors present" (p. 111). *Hypothetical construction* (see COUNTERFACTUAL ANALYSIS) involves

> envisaging the historical consequences that would have ensued if a given antecedent
> event had not occurred and in giving an answer, of varying degrees of probability,
> in terms of approximate regularities observable in other instances. The degree of
> probability marks the difference between wild speculation and well grounded lik-
> lihood. (p. 113; cf. Hughes, 1960: 29)

The use of adjectives such as *decisive* or *basic* in connection with cause reflects
a comparative evaluation:

> It is an elliptical way of saying that some necessary condition is *more* decisive (or
> basic, etc.) than some other conditions. . . . In general, a factor is more decisive
> than others in any situation if it enables us to predict the development of the
> situation, and of more aspects of the situation, *more reliably* than predictions based
> on other factors. In the study of historical situations this prediction is a retrospective
> prediction or post-diction. (p. 114)

Hook concluded that disagreements between historians over the causes of events
should not be unduly troubling, since such disagreements occur in natural science
as well (p. 115).

The debate over *causation* made many historians squeamish about employing
the term in the 1940s and 1950s—a sensitivity that persists (Zeldin, 1976: 243)—
and substitute terms such as *factor* began to replace *cause* in historical writing
(Hexter, 1961: 200). Eventually, the subject became tiresome to many scholars.
Controversy subsided in the 1950s, although debates flared as late as the 1960s.
A small minority of historians adopted variations of Hempel's positivist view;
a far greater number sought refuge in the conviction that human affairs are too
complex to be understood according to the methods of natural science (Higham,
1965: 138; cf. Benson and Strout, 1961). H. Stuart Hughes, who undertook a
balanced exploration of the problem in the late 1950s, underscored the "complexity" of questions of historical causation, arguing that

> an event like the outbreak of the First World War can be explained in several
> different and complementary ways. It is not necessary to argue endlessly over

whether immediate diplomatic events or more sustained imperial rivalries or the intensification of nationalism in popular psychology or the development of capitalism into its "highest stage" was the "basic" cause. From one point of view or another, any and all of these explanations can lay claim to historical "truth." (1960: 30)

In the same spirit, many authorities stress the appropriateness of the idea of "overdetermination" or "causal pluralism" to history, that is, "multiple causation where the causes are not mutually exclusive" (Scriven, 1966: 260; Walsh, [1962–63] 1969: 246–47; Gay, 1976: 7; cf. MacIntyre, 1976; Carlyle, [1830] 1972: 95).

References

Bayer, Erich, ed. 1980. *Wörterbuch zur Geschichte: Begriffe und Fachausdrücke*. 4th ed. Stuttgart.

Beale, Howard K. 1946. "What Historians Have Said about the Causes of the Civil War." In Bull. 54: 53–102. Beale's piece includes a bibliography of works related to this subject.

Beard, Charles A. 1936. *The Discussion of Human Affairs*. New York.

————. [1934] 1959. "Written History as an Act of Faith." In Meyerhoff: 140–51.

Beard, Charles A., and Hook, Sydney. 1946. "Problems of Terminology in Historical Writing: The Need for Greater Precision in the Use of Historical Terms; Illustrations." In Bull. 54: 103–30. "Cause" is dealt with on pp. 110–15. Hook, who actually wrote this discussion, later recalled disagreements between Beard and himself (see Sidney Hook, ed., *Philosophy and History: A Symposium* [New York, 1963]: 253–54). In contrast to Hook, Beard maintained (Bull. 54: 136, n.3) that "the terms 'cause' and 'causality' should never be used in written-history. . . . the word 'cause' . . . is unnecessary to the making of true statements concerning history-as-actuality, and owing to the ambiguity and connotations of its meanings, is more likely to be misleading than correctly informing the reader."

Benson, Lee, and Strout, Cushing. 1961. "Causation and the American Civil War: Two Appraisals." *HT* 1: 163–85.

Bloch, Marc. [1928] 1953. "Toward a Comparative History of European Societies." In Lane and Riemersma: 494–521.

Burke, Peter. 1969. *The Renaissance Sense of the Past*. London. Considers interest in causation—along with a sense of ANACHRONISM and an appreciation of EVIDENCE—crucial to the true "sense of history" (p. 1).

Carlyle, Thomas. [1830] 1972. "On History." In Stern: 91–101. See Carlyle's famous evocation of the idea of multiple causation, p. 95.

Carr, E. H. [1961] 1964. *What is History?* Harmondsworth, Eng. Chapter Four is entitled "Causation in History."

Cohen, Morris R. 1942. "Causation and Its Application to History." *JHI* 3: 12–29. Cohen's article reviews some major objections to the use of the concept of cause in history and seeks to refute them.

Croce, Benedetto. [1919] 1960. *History: Its Theory and Practice*. New York.

Dray, W. H. 1978. "Concepts of Causation in A.J.P. Taylor's Account of the Origins of the Second World War." *HT* 17: 149–74. This is a close analysis of the debate over Taylor's controversial reading of the causes of World War II that supports

Hart and Honoré ([1959] 1966). It identifies several models of causal thinking in the debate, while suggesting that the exchange was often logically muddled.

Gay, Peter. 1976. *Art and Act: On Causes in History—Manet, Gropius, Mondrian.* New York.

Hart, H.L.A., and Honoré, A.M. [1959] 1966. "Causal Judgment in History and in the Law." In Dray: 213–37. The authors argue that in history as in law *cause* is normally understood in terms of the categories of abnormality and human volition: "in distinguishing between causes and conditions two contrasts are of prime importance. These are the contrasts between what is abnormal and what is normal, . . . and between a free deliberate human action and all other conditions. In both fields, causal statements are 'singular' rather than 'general' as in the case in natural science" (pp. 214–16).

Hempel, Carl G. [1942] 1959. "The Function of General Laws in History." In Gardiner: 344–56.

Hexter, J. H. 1961. "Personal Retrospect and Postscript." In J. H. Hexter, *Reappraisals in History.* Evanston, Ill.: 185–214.

Higham, John. 1965. *History.* Englewood Cliffs, N.J.

Hughes, H. Stuart. 1960. "The Historian and the Social Scientist." *AHR* 66: 20–46. Hughes characterizes the typical historian's position as an unexamined "residual or truncated positivism" that retains the idea of cause but rejects the notion of law (pp. 24–25). He suggests that "exhaustive causal explanation" is "logically impossible" in history and argues that the concepts of cause and law are closely related, since "any coherent explanation in terms of cause suggests a lawful universe: in rather summary fashion, a causal explanation may be considered as simply an example of the operation of a more general law" (pp. 27–28). Hughes supports the idea of a close connection between counterfactuals and causal explanation (p. 29).

MacIntyre, Alistaire. 1976. "Causality and History." In Juha Manninen and Raimo Tuomela, eds., *Essays on Explanation and Understanding: Studies in the Foundations of Humanities and Social Sciences.* Dordrecht, Holland: 137–58. This essay is a rare criticism of the mainstream position of "causal pluralism." The anthology contains several other relevant essays.

Mandelbaum, Maurice. 1942. "Causal Analysis in History." *JHI* 3: 30–50. The author defines *historical causation* as "a relation of dependence, the cause of an event being the complete set of those events 'without which the event would not have occurred, or whose non-existence or non-occurrence would have made some difference to it.' " (p. 39).

———. [1938] 1967. *The Problem of Historical Knowledge: An Answer to Relativism.* New York. Mandelbaum discusses cause in framework of a doctrine of historical REALISM, which holds that "the concrete structure and continuity to be found in every historical work is not a product of valuational judgments, but is implicit in the facts themselves" (pp. 270).

Momigliano, Arnaldo. [1958] 1966. "Some Observations on Causes of War in Ancient Historiography." In Arnaldo Momigliano, *Studies in Historiography.* London: 112–26.

———. 1978. "Greek Historiography." *HT* 17: 1–28.

Nash, Ronald H., ed. 1969 *Ideas of History* 2. New York.

Oakeshott, Michael. [1933] 1966. "Historical Continuity and Causal Analysis." In Dray: 193–212. In Oakeshott's view, "the only explanation of change relevant or possible in history is simply a complete account of change. History accounts *for* change by means of a full account *of* change. The relation *between* events is always other events, and it is established in history by a full relation *of* the events. The conception of cause is thus replaced by the exhibition of a world of events intrinsically related to one another in which no *lacuna* is tolerated" (p. 209).

Pollack, Sir Frederick, and Maitland, Frederic William. [1898] 1968. *The History of English Law Before the Time of Edward I.* Cambridge.

Potter, David M. 1963. "Explicit Data and Implicit Assumptions in Historical Study." In Louis Gottschalk, ed., *Generalization in the Writing of History: A Report of the Committee on Historical Analysis of the Social Science Research Council.* Chicago: 178–94. This is a helpful discussion.

Scriven, Michael. 1966. "Causes, Connections, and Conditions in History." In Dray: 238–64. Scriven attacks the covering law position and attempts to subdivide the concept of cause into various types.

Tapp, E. J. 1952. "Some Aspects of Causation in History." *JP* 49: 67–79.

Teggart, Frederick J. 1942. "Causation in Historical Events." *JHI* 3: 3–11.

Walsh, W. H. [1962–63] 1969. "Historical Causation." In Nash: 234–52. This is an excellent summary that includes a critique of Oakeshott ([1933] 1966) and a brief survey of reasons why historians became concerned with the problem of cause in the 1930s.

Wiener, Philip P. 1941. "On Methodology in the Philosophy of History." *JP* 38: 309–24.

Williams, William Appleman. 1956. "A Note on Charles Austin Beard's Search for a General Theory of Causation." *AHR* 62: 59–80. Williams asserts that Beard's late work is muddled and that he misunderstood much of the work of the German idealists (p. 61).

Zeldin, Theodore. 1976. "Social History and Total History." *Journal of Social History* 10: 237–45. Zeldin avoids the term *cause* and favors "juxtaposition, so that the reader can make what links he thinks fit for himself. This has the advantage that I can show the whole complexity of each factor, without having to suppress all those that do not fit into a causal pattern. Causation has been almost as merciless a tyrant to history as chronology" (p. 243).

Sources of Additional Information

Almost every work on methodology contains some reference to the subject. For general subject and bibliographical information see Richard Taylor, "Causation," *EP* 2: 56–66. There is a short bibliography in Dray: 384. See also Berding: 158–64. Milic Capek, "Toward a Widening of the Notion of Causality," *Diogenes*, No. 28 (Winter 1959): 63–90, is a sweeping assessment of various theoretical trends. For a basic introduction to the problems of causation in history see two books by William H. Dray, *Laws and Explanation in History* (Oxford, 1957), chapter four, and *Philosophy of History* (Englewood Cliffs, N.J., 1964), also chapter four. See also chapters four and five of Morton White, *Foundations of Historical Knowledge* (New York, 1965), which review and analyze specific notions of causation in the work of various historians and contain a criticism of Hart and Honoré (pp. 150–51). Maurice Mandelbaum, *The Anatomy of Historical Knowledge* (Baltimore, 1977), is an important revision of the author's earlier position in *The Problem of Historical Knowledge* ([1938] 1967), cited above; see also the review of this book by Louis Mink, *HT* 17 (1978): 211–23, which claims that

Mandelbaum "has stopped just one step short of acknowledging that narrative explanation is not a kind of causal explanation at all, but an incompatible alternative to it" (p. 219). Paul K. Conkin, "Causation Revisited," *HT* 13 (1974): 1–20, is a helpful survey of some basic themes and problems. In his well-known *The Idea of History* (Oxford, 1946), R. G. Collingwood sought to distinguish historical causation from causation in natural science by linking it exclusively to human intention and action (see pp. 214–15; cf. Nash, 1969: 232). Note the curious remarks in Johan Huizinga, *Men and Ideas* (New York, 1959), pp. 38–39, 55, and the comments on Dray's *Laws and Explanation in History* in Perez Zagorin, "Historical Knowledge: A Review Article on the Philosophy of History," *JMH* 31 (1959): 243–55, especially 251–52. Kieran Egan, "Thucydides, Tragedian," in Canary and Kozicki: 63–92, is suggestive on the possible relationship between causality and "mythic paradigms" used by historians. Elazar Weinryb, "The Justification of a Causal Thesis: An Analysis of the Controversies over the Theses of Pirenne, Turner, and Weber," *HT* 14 (1975): 32–56, and Raymond Martin, "Causes, Conditions, and Causal Importance," *HT* 21 (1982): 53–74, are (like Dray [1978]) investigations of concepts of cause in specific historiographical controversies. Mary Forrester, "Practical Reasoning and Historical Inquiry," *HT* 15 (1976): 133–40, extends the "ordinary thinking" approach of Mandelbaum. In general, see also François Simiand, "Causal Interpretation and Historical Research" [1903, 1906], in Lane and Riemersma: 469–88; R. M. MacIver, "History and Social Causation," *Journal of Economic History Supplement* (1943): 135–45; David Hackett Fischer, *Historians Fallacies: Toward a Logic of Historical Thought* (New York, 1970), pp. 164–86; Murray G. Murphey, *Our Knowledge of the Historical Past* (Indianapolis, Ind., 1973); Peter D. McClelland, *Causal Explanation and Model Building in History, Economics, and the New Economic Theory* (Ithaca, N.Y., 1975); Samuel H. Beer, "Causal Explanation and Imaginative Re-enactment," *HT* 3 (1963–64): 6–29 (which argues that the positivist and idealist traditions are potentially compatible); Elazar Weinryb, "Von Wright on Historical Causation," *Inquiry* 17 (1974): 327–44; F. M. Barnard, "Herder's Treatment of Causation and Continuity in History," *JHI* 24 (1963): 197–212 (which includes a brief sketch of David Hume's views in their relation to historical causation); and, also by Barnard, "Accounting for Actions: Causality and Teleology," *HT* 20 (1981): 291–312. For an expression of the mainstream view that social processes are "overdetermined" or "multi-causal," see Wolfgang J. Mommsen, *Theories of Imperialism* (New York, 1980).

CIVILIZATION. 1. An advanced stage of social development, characterized by a complex social structure, a high level of technological and administrative sophistication, and a high degree of intellectual and aesthetic accomplishment. 2. The process by which a society attains a high level of social, technological, administrative, intellectual, and aesthetic development. 3. A synonym for the anthropological meaning of the term CULTURE, that is, the totality of a society's material and mental way of life.

Civilization (Fr., *civilisation*), a word coined in mid-eighteenth-century France, has been used in various senses during the past two hundred years. The term's history displays parallels with the history of the concept of CULTURE, with which the idea of "civilization" has traditionally been closely associated.

Etymologically, *civilization* is derived from the ancient Latin *civis* (citizen), *civitas* (city-state), and *civilitas* ("citizenship" or, alternatively, "politeness," particularly in the sense of deference). In medieval Latin, *civilitas* acquired broad social connotations. In his *De monarchia*, for example, Dante, spoke of *humana civilitas* in the sense of the "largest and most comprehensive social entity" (Kroeber and Kluckhohn, 1952: 15; Brinkmann, 1930: 525–26).

The emergence of the modern concept of civilization predates the word itself by at least two centuries. In both France and England, the expressions "to civilize" and "civilized" were commonly used in the sixteenth and seventeenth centuries (Febvre, [1930] 1973: 224); they were part of a field of expressions that dealt with levels of human behavior and comparative social development— from *savagry* and *barbarism* at the lower end of the scale to *politesse* (cultivated refinement) and *police* (refinement in law, administration, and government) at the top. As early as 1560 (Huppert, 1971: 765–69) French scholars, seeking an antonym to *savagery* and a more comprehensive concept than "police," used the term *civilité* in one of the modern senses of "civilization," that is, an evolutionary process that leads to sophistication in manners, laws, and government. The actual introduction of the word *civilization* in mid-eighteenth-century France served a specific historical purpose: the need for a term to "designate . . . the triumph and spread of reason not only in the constitutional, political and administrative field [*police*] but also in the moral and intellectual field" (Febvre, [1930] 1973: 228).

Febvre ([1930] 1973: 222), in his pioneering study, traced the word to M. Boulanger's *Antiquité dévoilée par ses usages* (1766), where it is used to designate the process by which a "savage" people may be elevated to a higher level of life. Moras (1930) and Benveniste (1953) pushed this date back to the Marquis de Mirabeau's *L'Ami des Hommes ou Traité de la population* (1757), where the word has two meanings: an activity or process, namely the refinement of social life; and the condition achieved as a result of this process (Rauhut, 1953: 84). From French, the word quickly passed into the English and German languages.

Initially, there was broad consensus on the term's meaning. It referred to the idea of a universal and irresistible human process of moral and social perfection in which the educated classes of western Europe were already well advanced and toward which the human race as a whole was steadily progressing. It was thus a key aspect of the ENLIGHTENMENT idea of PROGRESS (Gilbert, 1960: 41). This ethical ideal became the broad philosophical foundation for the ideas of CULTURAL HISTORY and UNIVERSAL HISTORY (or "world history") in the late eighteenth century and a general conceptual framework for western historiography in the nineteenth and early twentieth centuries (Masur, 1962).

Civilization was typically understood ethnocentrically, strictly according to European norms (Liebel, 1967–68: 457). The German philosopher Hegel displayed the unshakable confidence of the European intelligentsia in the power of European traditions: "The Europeans have sailed around the world and for them it is a sphere," he wrote. "Whatever has not yet fallen under their sway is either not worth the trouble or is destined to fall under it" (cited in Masur, 1962: 607). In his lectures on *La civilisation en Europe* (1828), the historian François Guizot expressed the view that underpinned most European historiography before World War I:

> For my part I am convinced that there is such a thing as the general destiny of humanity, and the transmission of humanity's assets and, consequently, one universal history of civilization which needs to be recorded and written about. . . . The idea of progress and development seems to me to be the fundamental idea contained in the word civilization. (cited in Febvre, [1930] 1973: 241)

Soon after the turn of the nineteenth century the term began to be used in a second, "ethnographic" sense, as a designation for particular social and intellectual traditions, for example, "French civilization," "Chinese civilization." This foreshadowed the late-nineteenth-century rise of the modern archaeological and anthropological concept of "culture." The *OED*, for example, cites an 1814 reference in the British House of Commons to "Hindoo . . . civilization"; in the same year the German explorer Alexander von Humboldt referred to "more than five centuries of civilization" among the Malays of Sumatra, and the French philosopher Pierre-Simon Ballanche alluded to "ancient civilizations" and "the legacy of all previous civilizations" in his *Le Vieillard et le jeune homme* (1819) (Febvre, [1930] 1973: 235–36). Such usage implied that any human group, no matter how complex its level of material and intellectual development, could have its own brand of civilization (Febvre, [1930] 1973: 247). In addition, there arose a tendency to combine the "moral" and "ethnographic" concepts and to associate the term with a particular *country's* political, cultural, and moral contribution to human history—the legacy, heritage, or hard-earned "assets" that it passed on from generation to generation. As Febvre noted, the view that "asserts the existence of each individual people and each individual civilization does not prevent the old concept of a general human civilization remaining alive in people's minds" (fp. 248). The two could (and still often do) exist side by side as part of the assumption that national "civilizations" feed the growth of human civilization, just as tributaries feed a great river (Brinkmann, 1930: 528). In this sense, *civilization* was treated as a "positive accomplishment, something that only a few societies had managed to attain" (Bierstedt, 1966: 485). This nationalistic use of the term still persists in textbook surveys of "American civilization," "French civilization," "English civilization," and so on, although it is now often branded narrowly ethnocentric (Schneider, 1968: 188).

In German-speaking Europe, *civilization* was initially used in Mirabeau's original sense; but in a third important development, it became entangled in a complex relationship with the word CULTURE (*Cultur, Kultur*) (Gilbert, 1960: 40–41). During the nineteenth century, many German writers adopted the practice of sharply distinguishing between the concepts of civilization and culture. Accordingly, *civilization* designated the material, mechanical, man-made aspects of social life, those refinements developed through the exercise of conscious reason such as writing, business methods, and agricultural techniques. *Culture* designated the "more subjective aspects of human existence which are not socially cumulative and cannot be borrowed or learned by outsiders," such as "ideas and ideals, arts and literature, morals and ethics, philosophy and religion" (Schneider, 1968: 187). This distinction was also adopted by some English-speaking writers, although it never became popular in France. Since 1945 many authorities have maintained that *culture* and *civilization* have become virtually synonymous in scholarly discourse (Gilbert, 1960: 41, 52). This is true especially in archaeology, anthropology, and sociology. In history, however, the two terms are rarely considered completely synonymous; usually, *civilization* designates a particular phase of culture, that is, a higher stage of social evolution (for example, Polišenský, 1980: 62).

The rise of the disciplines of archaeology, sociology, and anthropology in the late nineteenth century coincided with efforts to define *civilization* as an object of scientific study; the result was an array of often amorphous and overlapping definitions (see Armillas, 1968; Bierstedt, 1966; Childe, 1951). This effort, spurred by scholarly preoccupation with evolution in the wake of Charles Darwin's *Origin of Species* (1859), is exemplified in the work of Herbert Spencer (1820–1903), the British pioneer of theoretical sociology, and the writings of the early American anthropologist Lewis Henry Morgan (1818–81). Spencer, Morgan, and like-minded theorists believed that the social traditions of the world could be classified in terms of levels of advancement along a standard scale of development, from the lower rungs of "savagery" and "barbarism" to the highest rungs of "civilization." This became a way of discriminating between groups of "advanced" ("civilized") and "backward" peoples. A wide range of indices of "civilization" were suggested—literacy, organized agriculture, money, the existence of large cities, and so on. Morgan's *Ancient Society* (1877) emphasized the transition from social structures founded on descent to those based on social function (Armillas, 1968: 219). The association of "civilization" with the rise of large cities and urban modes of behavior was especially influential in the early twentieth century, exemplified in the idea of an "urban revolution" advanced by the British archaeologist V. Gordon Childe (1936; 1942). (Interestingly, the 1968 *International Encyclopedia of the Social Sciences* treats "civilization" as a subcategory of "urban revolution.") Thus arose the widespread convention of identifying the concept of civilization with "values, institutions and customs . . . appropriate to urban life" (Schneider, 1968: 186). This provided a convenient way for some scholars to differentiate between "civilization" and "culture": any society, no matter what its level of material and intellectual development, possessed a culture; "civilization," however, required a high level of urbanization, with the associated social complexity and advanced level of technical development.

In history, art history, and sociology, the idea of civilization—often loosely defined or not defined at all—was widely used in the first half of the twentieth century as the theoretical basis for the speculative world histories of figures such as Spengler ([1918–22] 1932) and Toynbee (1934–61) and a host of popularizers (e.g., Durant, 1935–75; Clark, 1970) who understood the notion in the sense of the "most comprehensive identifiable unit working in history" (Gilbert, 1960: 54) (see PHILOSOPHY OF HISTORY; METAHISTORY). Much early twentieth-century interest in the rise and fall of "civilizations" was directly related to a perceived "crisis" in "Western civilization," variously understood as the Greco-Roman/ Christian heritage or the "quest for the good life" (Marcell, 1969: 74). In American colleges, classes in "western civilization" were introduced in the early twentieth century as a means of assimilating immigrants from areas outside western and northern Europe. With growing appreciation of non-European historical traditions in the second half of the twentieth century, *civilization*, with its value-charged burden of teleological and ethnocentric associations (Masur, 1962: 607–8), has to some extent given way to newer terms and concepts (e.g., MODERNIZATION) to designate the attainment of social complexity and sophistication.

References

Armillas, Pedro. 1968. "The Concept of Civilization." *IESS* 16: 218–21.

Benveniste, E. 1953. "Civilisation: Contribution à l'histoire du mot." In *Hommage à Lucien Febvre*. Paris: 47–54.

Bierstedt, Robert. 1966. "Indices of Civilization." *The American Journal of Sociology* 71: 483–90. This is a concise summary of several major theories of civilization since the late nineteenth century; it criticizes the carelessness with which the term is conventionally used.

Brinkmann, Carl. 1930. "Civilization." *ESS* 3: 525–29. Brinkmann's entry is confusing and inaccurate in some places.

Childe, V. Gordon. 1936. *Man Makes Himself*. London.

———. 1942. *What Happened in History*. Harmondsworth, Eng.

———. 1951. *Social Evolution*. New York.

Clark, Kenneth. 1970. *Civilization*. New York.

Durant, Will. 1935–74. *The Story of Civilization*. New York.

Febvre, Lucien. [1930] 1973. "*Civilisation*: Evolution of a Word and a Group of Ideas." In Peter Burke, ed., *A New Kind of History: From the Writings of Febvre*. New York: 219–57. This is a pioneering work in the history of the concept and in historical semantics generally.

Gilbert, Felix. 1960. "Cultural History and Its Problems." *Comité International des Sciences Historiques, Rapports* 1: 40–58.

Huppert, George. 1971. "The Idea of Civilization in the Sixteenth Century." In Anthony Molho and John A. Tedeschi, eds., *Renaissance Studies in Honor of Hans Baron*. Dekalb, Ill.: 757–69.

Kroeber, A. L., and Kluckhohn, Clyde. 1952. *Culture: A Critical Review of Concepts and Definitions*. New York.

Liebel, Helen P. 1967–68. "The Historian and the Idea of World Civilization." *The Dalhousie Review* 47: 455–66. The piece is not as helpful as the title suggests but is still worth consulting.

Marcell, David W. 1969. "Charles Beard: Civilization and the Revolt Against Empiricism." *American Quarterly* 21: 65–86.

Masur, Gerhard. 1962. "Distinctive Traits of Western Civilization: Through the Eyes of Western Historians." *AHR* 67: 591–608. Masur presents a survey of the importance of the idea for western historiography during the past two hundred years; he highlights European ethnocentrism (p. 593).

Moras, Joachim. 1930. *Ursprung und Entwicklung des Begriffs der Zivilisation in Frankreich, 1756–1830.* Hamburg.

Polišenský, Josef. 1980. *Aristocrats and the Crowd in the Revolutionary Year 1848: A Contribution to the History of Revolution and Counter-Revolution in Austria.* Albany, N.Y.

Rauhut, Franz. 1953. "Die Herkunft der Worte und Begriffe 'Kultur,' 'Civilisation,' und 'Bildung'." *Germanisch-Romanischer Monatsschrift*, N.S., 3: 81–91.

Schneider, Carl J. 1968. "Civilization." In Joseph Dunner, ed., *Handbook of World History.* London: 186–89.

Spengler, Oswald. [1918–22] 1932. *The Decline of the West.* London.

Toynbee, Arnold J. 1934–61. *A Study of History.* Oxford.

Sources of Additional Information

See also CULTURE; PROGRESS; UNIVERSAL HISTORY. Raymond Williams, "Culture and Civilization," *EP* 2: 273–76, and Frederick M. Barnard, "Culture and Civilization in Modern Times," *DHI* 1: 613–21, provide substantive and bibliographical information, although both are primarily concerned with the concept of culture. Andrew D. White's "On Studies in General History and the History of Civilization," *Papers of the American Historical Association*, 1 (1885): 49–72, reflects widely held late-nineteenth-century attitudes and assumptions. *Civilization* (Berkeley, Calif., 1959) is an anthology of philosophical papers originally presented in 1941; included are the essays "The Idea of Civilization," "Conceptions of Civilization," and "Civilizations in Historical Perspective." G. M. Pflaum has written a doctoral dissertation entitled *Geschichte des Wortes "Zivilisation"* (University of Munich, 1961). For a critical analysis of Toynbee's usage see Pitirim A. Sorokin, "Arnold J. Toynbee's Philosophy of History," *JMH* 12 (Sept. 1940): 374–87. Alan Donagan, "Determinism in History," *DHI* 2: 22–23, also discusses Toynbee. Eric R. Wolf, "Understanding Civilizations: A Review Article," *CSSH* 9 (1966–67): 446–65, is an evaluation of five studies of "civilization" published in the early 1960s. Roger W. Wescott's "Enumeration of Civilizations," *HT* 9 (1970): 59–75, is an interesting catalogue of the various ways authors have classified and enumerated civilizations; Wescott concludes that "civilization is a conceptual elephant in which our scholarly blindness may be forgiven for perceiving many very different, if only partial, truths" (p. 75).

CLASS. A category of social standing defined in terms of economic function.

The French medievalist Marc Bloch (1931) called *class* one of the most equivocal words in the historical vocabulary. Despite its ambiguity, the idea of social class has undoubtedly been a touchstone for historical scholarship in the twentieth century. During the 1950s and 1960s the role of the concept of class in historiography became a focus of controversy that led to important refinements in the understanding and use of the idea.

The modern term *class* comes from the Latin *classis*, a word the Romans used to designate groups for property taxation. The chief general sense of the word today is "a number of individuals (persons or things) possessing common attributes, and grouped together under a general or 'class' name; a kind, sort, division" (*OED*). Use of the term to designate "social class"—that is, social division or social status—is quite recent and closely linked to the INDUSTRIAL REVOLUTION of the late eighteenth and early nineteenth centuries. In this regard, the origins of the idea must be seen in the context of efforts to deal with the problem of social and economic inequality.

Before the nineteenth century the words *rank*, *order*, *estate*, or *degree*— categories that might be defined in terms of heredity, occupation, prestige, and so on—were most commonly used in English to convey the idea of social status; in French and German similar terms were used, for example, *état* (estate), *Stand* (station, order). In English the word *class* was primarily an educational category (Coser, 1973: 441; Williams, 1976: 51). By the early 1820s, however, *class* was solidly established as a social term (Briggs, 1960: 43).

This development was closely related to several late-eighteenth-century trends: growing interest in economic matters (see ECONOMIC HISTORY), heightened consciousness of the social importance of the division of labor and economic function, awareness of rapid economic and technological change, sharpened perception of disparities in wealth created by industrialization, and preoccupation with political revolution and social conflict. A new vocabulary was needed to reflect rapidly changing circumstances and perceptions, and in the new lexicon the word *class* evoked primarily economic rather than genealogical or political associations; a *class* was a group of people bound together by common economic function and interest (Coser, 1973: 441). The shift is reflected in Charles Hall's *Effects of Civilization on the People in European States* (1805), which argued that

> The people in a civilized state may be divided into different orders; but for the purpose of investigating the manner in which they enjoy or are deprived of the requisites to support the health of their bodies and minds, they need only be divided into two classes, viz. the rich and the poor. (cited in Briggs, 1960: 48)

According to Coser,

> class is a less definite and more fluid term than "rank" or "order," and the use of this less specific term subtly indicates the erosion since the Industrial Revolution of the earlier clear-cut hierarchical rank order which used to govern the . . . social structure and a shifting of focus from [ascribed] social status to economic criteria. (1973: 441)

Williams (1976: 52) notes that use of the word *class* was related to "the increasing consciousness that social position is made rather than merely inherited."

The title of John Wade's *History of the Middle and Working Classes* (1833) reflects the establishment of the chief modern subcategories of the idea. On the European continent, the ideas of "middle" and "working" classes were commonly conveyed by the words *bourgeoisie* (townspeople) and *proletariat*, popularized first in France. The idea of a "middle class" appears to have crystallized before the idea of "working class." In English, *middle class* was used in a positive sense from the 1790s onward by authors who wished to set themselves apart from the "non-productive" nobility. The term *working class* was evidently first used by the English philanthropist Robert Owen in his *Essays on the Formation of Character* (1813), later retitled *A New View of Society* (Briggs, 1960: 52). *Proletariat* was derived from the Latin *proletarii*, members of the ancient Roman tax group whose sole form of property was their children (*proles*) (Dahrendorf, [1959] 1969: 3). *Prolétaire* appears in French as early as the fourteenth century, but only with reference to Roman history. The same is true of the English *proletary* and *proletarian*, which were in use by the seventeenth century. The word was applied to modern society in the eighteenth century, for example, by Jean Jacques Rousseau in 1761. As a label for industrial wage laborers, *proletariat* was popularized in the mid–1830s by disciples of the French socialist Charles Fourier. From France, its use quickly spread to Germany and Eastern Europe. Albert Brisbane, an American Fourierist, first used *proletaries* in English to refer to the "wages-classes" in 1845 (Bestor, 1948: 272, 275).

The notion of history as an arena for conflict between economic classes became a focus of liberal and socialist historiography in the early nineteenth century (see LIBERALISM; SOCIALISM). The rise and triumph of the middle class was a theme commonly used to explain historical PROGRESS, as in the classic liberal accounts of English and French history by Augustin Thierry and François Guizot and in lesser works such as W. A. Mackinnon's *History of Civilization* (1846) (Briggs, 1960: 57). Socialist theory and historiography mirrored liberal practice, with the working class supplanting the middle class as the engine of progress. This is most dramatically illustrated in the HISTORICAL MATERIALISM of Karl Marx and Friedrich Engels, whose *Communist Manifesto* (1848) declared that the "history of all hitherto existing society is the history of class struggles." For the authorized English translation of this famous polemic (1888), Engels supplied special Marxist definitions of *bourgeoisie* and *proletariat*: "By bourgoisie is meant the class of modern Capitalists, owners of the means of social production and employers of wage-labor. By proletariat the class of modern wage-laborers who, having no means of production of their own, are reduced to selling their labor-power in order to live."

Directly or indirectly, Marxist theory has been the chief vehicle for transmitting the early-nineteenth-century concept of class to twentieth-century scholarship. Engels is especially important in this regard; his exposure to the British terminology of *class* during his stay in England in the early 1840s led to his publication in German of *The Condition of the Working Class in England in 1844* (1845), a key early contribution to the theory of social class. Marx himself planned a section on "class" for his *Capital* but never completed it; nevertheless, his and

Engels' work displays a general understanding of class as the fundamental social reality, a type of group identity determined essentially by one's functional relation to the prevailing system of production in a given society but also by one's subjective consciousness of that relation (Russell, 1980: 16; Coser, 1973: 447). In practice, however, the two men used the term in a range of simple and complex ways (O'Boyle, 1952: 392). For example, they sometimes present a simple picture of two classes—bourgeoisie and proletariat—locked in combat; elsewhere they make finer distinctions, as between the "financial" and "industrial" middle class or between the true proletariat and the *Lumpenproletariat* ("ragged" or "vagabond" proletariat, rendered "social scum" in the English translation approved by Engels). Still, the "major emphasis is on the separation between those who own the means of production and those who, owning no means of production, must sell their labor power" (Coser, 1973: 447). What made Marx's and Engels' approach especially appealing to historians—despite its polemical underpinnings—was the fact that the two men did not understand class as an unchanging aspect of an eternal "natural" social order but presented it as a *historical* phenomenon, that is, something that changes over time as production methods change.

Nevertheless, the idea of class was suspect in professional historical circles in the late nineteenth century, chiefly due to its close association with partisan causes. As a framing device for historical conceptualization it was largely replaced by the idea of NATIONALITY. In the United States, academic and amateur historians strongly resisted the notion of class because it was associated with European radicalism (Benson, 1960: 101), and because it was considered inappropriate to the allegedly egalitarian social scene in America; indeed, American-trained historians have yet to accept the term *working class* completely (Berthoff, 1962: 119).

Around 1900 the concept of socioeconomic class began to regain scholarly respectability in consequence of its influence on pioneers of sociology such as Max Weber and by virtue of its use by a few important historians (e.g., Beard, 1913). At the same time, the language of *rank*, *order*, and so on that survived in English usage and coexisted with the new idea of class throughout the nineteenth century finally began to die (Briggs, 1960: 73). Whether or not historians agreed with Marxist doctrine, they increasingly "borrowed their vocabulary, and therefore the presuppositions of their history, from the Marxian analysis" (Cobban, 1956: 3). By the mid-twentieth century, "practically all historians of the modern period" had come to treat social class as "the most important grouping in nineteenth- and twentieth-century societies" (O'Boyle, 1952: 392). At the same time, important differences developed regarding ways the idea could be legitimately used by historians.

In the 1950s various writers charged that historians habitually used the idea of class simplistically, anachronistically, and imprecisely (e.g., O'Boyle, 1952; Cobban, 1956). Historians were alleged to have fallen into use of Marxist terminology "even when their own researches call for something different"; *middle class* and *working class* were declared "omnibus terms" that hid "essential differences" among social groups and acted as "a mental blockage to prevent further enquiry" (Cobban, 1956: 3, 11). The nineteenth-century idea of the "rise of the middle class" was denounced as a "myth" used anachronistically as "the ultimate solution of all the problems of explanations in European history from the eleventh century on" (Hexter, 1961: 112). The underlying concern was that the Marxian understanding of socioeconomic class was not sufficiently supple to deal with the multi-faceted, fluid status system created by industrialization. Historians had "focussed so narrowly on [economic] class" that they "failed to sense the possible importance of other social groupings" (O'Boyle, 1952: 397). The "simple pattern of social classes which has served generations of historians well," concluded Alfred Cobban (1956: 6), "has lost its usefulness."

Such criticisms became a springboard for efforts to refine the idea of class. They were inspired largely by sociological theory and especially by the work of Max Weber (for instance, O'Boyle, 1966; Leff, 1971). In Weber's thought, class was only one aspect of the larger question of social stratification. Weber believed that Marx and Engels placed too much emphasis on economic factors as the basis of group cohesion. Weber's concept of class was less narrow than that of Marx, and he sought to refurbish the older idea of *Stand* (usually translated in English as "status" [Dahrendorf, (1959) 1969: 7, n. 5]) for purposes of modern social analysis. For Weber,

> class refers to men sharing a common economic situation, without however attempting to relate it to the mode of production. . . . [He] confines men's class position to their economic role—which is in turn conceived not as a fixed state but as a compound of their actual situation, their opportunties and their expectations. (Leff, 1971: 170)

Beyond "class" understood in this way, Weber stressed the importance of two non-economic social categories: "status" and "power." *Status* refers to the "honor or prestige and hence the amount of deference accorded to individuals or positions"; *power* designates "the ability of a man or a group to impose its will on others even, if necessary, against their opposition" (Coser, 1973: 445). Marx and Engels explained power in terms of control over the means of economic production, whereas Weber argued that "in the modern world commanding positions in a variety of administrative and bureaucratic hierarchies may confer social power on men whose purely economic power is minimal and who have but little social honor" (p. 445).

The concept of class used by most historians today is a compound of Marx's and Weber's views. As the result of theoretical refinements undertaken in the 1960s and 1970s, historians have generally become more discriminating in their use of the idea and have added new expressions to their vocabulary such as *social role* and *status group* for use in analyzing the non-economic foundations of social differentiation, cohesion, and action.

References

Beard, Charles A. 1913. *An Economic Interpretation of the Constitution.* New York.

Benson, Lee. 1960. *Turner and Beard: American Historical Writing Reconsidered.* Glencoe, Ill.

Berthoff, Rowland. 1962. "The Working Class." In John Higham, ed., *The Reconstruction of American History.* London: 119–36.

Bestor, Arthur E., Jr. 1948. "The Evolution of the Socialist Vocabulary." *JHI* 9: 259–302. This is very useful for the early history of many social terms.

Bloch, Marc. 1931. *Les caracteres originaux de l'histoire rurale française.* Paris.

Briggs, Asa. 1960. "The Language of 'Class' in Early Nineteenth-Century England." In Asa Briggs and John Saville, eds., *Essays in Labour History.* London: 43–73. Briggs' essay is a key source for English usage.

Cobban, Alfred. 1956. "The Vocabulary of Social History." *Political Science Quarterly* 71: 1–17. This article is an important criticism of the Marxian theory of class.

Coser, Lewis A. 1973. "Class." *DHI* 1: 441–49. Coser's entry is an excellent survey by a sociologist; it is particularly good for its discussion of Weber's ideas and includes a useful bibliography oriented toward works in sociology.

Dahrendorf, Ralf. [1959] 1969. *Class and Class Conflict in Industrial Society.* Stanford, Calif. This is an influential study by a West German sociologist.

Hexter, J. H. 1961. "The Myth of the Middle Class in Tudor England." In J. H. Hexter, *Reappraisals in History.* Evanston, Ill.

Leff, Gordon. 1971. *History and Social Theory.* Garden City, N.Y. Chapter nine, "Class," illustrates the extent to which Weber's views have influenced the thinking of some historians.

O'Boyle, Lenore. 1952. "The Class Concept in History." *JMH* 24: 391–97. Brief but important, this essay concentrates on problems arisng out of Hannah Arendt's use of *class* in her *Origins of Totalitarianism* (1951). It is one of the first calls by a historian for refinements in the idea of class along Weberian lines.

———. 1966. "The Middle Class in Western Europe, 1815–1848." *AHR* 71: 826–45. This article is a rejoinder to Alfred Cobban's position that the idea of the "middle class" has become useless to historians.

Russell, James. 1980. *Marx-Engels Dictionary.* Westport, Conn. This work contains entries on "class" and a number of related ideas such as "class consciousness," "middle class," and "working class."

Williams, Raymond. 1976. *Keywords: A Vocabulary of Culture and Society.* New York. Williams' book contains a useful entry on "class."

Sources of Additional Information

Literature is extensive. There is a lengthy bibliography in Peter Calvert's comprehensive *Concept of Class: An Historical Introduction* (New York, 1982). Many older titles are listed in Paul Mombert, "Class," *ESS* 3: 531–36. For recent sociological theory see (in addition to Coser [1973]) Stanislaw Ossowski, *Class Structure in the Social Consciousness* (New York, 1963), and the bibliographies on "Stratification, Social" in *IESS* 15: 288–377. For both Marxist and non-Marxist theory see the pertinent articles in *MCWS*—"Class, Class Struggle" (2: 1–19); "Bourgeoisie" (1: 280–90); "Proletariat" (7: 50–67); and "Working Class" (8: 357–62). All contain extensive bibliographies. Rudolf Hermstadt, *Die Entdeckung der Klassen: Die Geschichte des Begriffs Klasse von den*

Anfängen bis zum Vorabend der Pariser Julirevolution 1830 (Berlin, 1965), written from
a Marxist standpoint, is a thorough investigation of the early history of the concept. On
the relationships of Marx's and Weber's notions of class see Richard Ashcraft, "Marx
and Weber on Liberalism as Bourgeois Ideology," *CSSH* 14 (1972): 130–68, especially
145–47, 149. In *GG* see the entries "Hierarchie" (3: 103–30), "Proletariat" (5: 27–68),
"Mittelstand" (4: 49–92), "Adel" (1: 1–48), "Arbeiter" (1: 216–42), "Bauer" (1: 407–
39), and "Beruf" (1: 490–507). Roland Mousnier, "Le concept de classe social et
l'historie," *Revue d'historie économique et sociale* 48 (1970): 449–59, shares with most
non-Marxist work an emphasis on the fluid nature of social stratification; in this regard
see also Edward N. Saveth, "Class," in Edward N. Saveth, ed., *American History and
the Social Sciences* (London, 1964): 202–14, and Thomas C. Cochran, "The Historian's
Use of Social Role," in Louis Gottschalk, ed., *Generalization in the Writing of History*
(Chicago, 1963): 103–10. E. P. Thompson's *Making of the English Working Class* (New
York, 1963) contains important observations on the idea of class from the viewpoint of
a leading English Marxist historian; see especially pp. 9–11. For a discussion of concerns
arising directly from a specific historical problem see the exchange of views in "Class
in the French Revolution," *AHR* 72 (Jan. 1967): 497–522; the footnotes there are a good
source of bibliographical information.

CLIMATE OF OPINION. See ZEITGEIST.

COLLIGATION. A method of historical interpretation in which a past event
is considered to have been understood when it has been related to the particular
context of events and circumstances in which it occurred.

The word *colligation* was introduced to the vocabulary of critical PHILOSOPHY
OF HISTORY in 1942 by the British philosopher W. H. Walsh (1942: 133–34)
and later popularized in Walsh's widely read *Philosophy of History: An Introduction* (1960: 23, 57–64) as part of the author's effort to augment the COVERING
LAW theory of historical EXPLANATION. In response to criticism (Levich, 1964–
65: 338–41), Walsh subsequently revised his position slightly and came to associate colligation primarily with historical INTERPRETATION rather than explanation (Walsh, 1967: 75).

Walsh borrowed the word from the nineteenth-century philosopher William
Whewell (Walsh, 1942: 133; 1960: 23; 1967: 72), who first introduced *colligation*
as a technical philosophical term. In Book XI of his *Philosophy of the Inductive
Sciences Founded upon Their History* (1840), Whewell used the word to refer
to a process common to all sciences, involving "the binding together or connection of a number of isolated facts by a suitable general conception or hypothesis" (*OED*; also Cebik, 1969: 41; McCullagh, 1978: 269). Cebik (1969:
41–42) links the pre-history of the idea as a historiographical concept to the neo-
idealist thought of Heinrich Rickert, L. Reis, P. Kristeller, Wilhelm Dilthey,
Michael Oakeshott, and R. G. Collingwood (see IDEALISM). In introducing the
concept, Walsh—although not a professed idealist (1942: 134)—acknowledged

the influence of the idealist tradition (Walsh, 1960: 59, 62; Thompson, 1967: 87–88).

According to covering law theory, knowledge is uniform in its logical structure, and therefore historical explanations follow the same logical form as explanations in natural science (i.e., deduction from universal laws). Walsh (1960: 62) did not deny that some historical explanations may take this form, but he held that covering law theory does not account for all instances of historical explanation. There are, he maintained, certain "peculiarities" about the way historians typically account for events, and there is thus a need for a "special concept of explanation" that reflects "the steps historians actually take when they set out to elucidate an historical event or set of events" (Walsh, 1969: 22–23).

Walsh's key point was that historians, although they use generalizations in explanation, do not normally use them in the same way as natural scientists. Instead of representing events as instances of general laws, historians often "colligate" them, that is, trace connections between them and other events or circumstances with which they stand "in inner relationship" (Walsh, 1960: 23). The historian "wishes to show that his facts form a unified whole, or a series of such wholes, in much the same way in which a work of pictorial art or a piece of music is unitary" (Walsh, 1942: 130).

> What every historian seeks for [Walsh maintained] is not a bare recital of unconnected facts, but a smooth narrative in which every event falls as it were into its natural place and belongs to an intelligible whole. In this respect the ideal of the historian is in principle identical with that of the novelist or the dramatist. Just as a good novel or a good play appears to consist not in a series of isolated episodes, but in the orderly development of the complex situation from which it starts, so a good history possesses a certain unity of plot or theme. And where we fail to find such a unity we experience a feeling of dissatisfaction: we believe we have not understood the facts we set out to investigate so well as we should. (1960: 23)

From this standpoint, events are considered to have been "explained" when they have been shown to be part of a *particular context, or web of circumstances*.

> The underlying assumption . . . [Walsh explained] is that different historical events can be regarded as going together to constitute a single process, a whole of which they are all parts and in which they belong together in a specially intimate way. And the first aim of the historian, when he is asked to explain some event or other, is to see it as part of such a process, *to locate it in its context* [emphasis added] by mentioning other events with which it is bound up. (1960: 23; cf. McCullagh, 1978: 267)

Colligation, then, is "the procedure of explaining an event by tracing its intrinsic relations to other events and locating it in its historical context" (Walsh, 1960: 59).

In this procedure events are explained by being grouped under "appropriate" general concepts (Walsh, 1960: 62). The historian wants to "make a coherent whole out of the events he studies," and his method of achieving this goal is

> to look for certain dominant concepts or leading ideas by which to illuminate his facts, to trace connections between those ideas themselves, and then to show how the detailed facts become intelligible in the light of them by constructing a "significant" narrative of the events of the period in question. (p. 62)

Specific examples of such "colligatory" concepts are RENAISSANCE, ENLIGHTENMENT, ROMANTICISM, MODERNIZATION, FASCISM, and REVOLUTION. Such generalizations express the sense of a unique complex of inwardly related events and circumstances, a whole that is more than the sum of its parts. When an event is represented as having been part, for instance, of the "Renaissance," it is regarded as having been in some sense understood or explained. The examples cited above are cases of unplanned sets of ideas and values; however, *colligation* may also refer to the explanation of *deliberate* sets of related actions; for example, Hitler's invasion of Poland in 1939 might be explained by representing it as part of a larger whole, such as his expansionist foreign policy (McCullagh, 1978: 267).

But to have a notion of a "context" one needs to have a notion of "how things turned out," and this is where the element of "hindsight" or "perspective" comes in. The historian is able to develop a clear conception of "wholes" into which individual events can be fit because he knows the outcome of past events. Thus "historical thinking, because of the nature of the historian's subject matter, often proceeds in teleological terms" (Walsh, 1960: 60; 1967: 67; Thompson, 1967: 91, 100).

Although professional historians seldom use the word *colligation*, Walsh's theory appears to correspond closely to their own conception of one form historical reasoning. Wallace Ferguson (1948: 392), for example, once described the "credo" of the working historian as "the belief that all elements of a civilization are related to one another as parts of a total configuration, just as, by the dynamic nature of history, they are related in causal sequence to the past and the future."

Since the 1940s, the idea of colligation has been an important reference point for scholars who seek to carry the discussion of historical explanation beyond the covering law theory. W. H. Dray, for example—a leading critic of the covering law thesis—uses Walsh's idea to elucidate the process of "synthesis" in historical writing. *Synthesis*, according to Dray, involves explaining how individual events in the past should be regarded, and this requires classification:

> explaining what a thing is, where this means explaining it as a so-and-so, might be characterized in a preliminary way as explanation by means of a general concept rather than a general law. For the explanation is given by finding a satisfactory *classification* of what seems to require explanation. . . . explaining what a thing is, i.e., how it should be regarded, is just not the same enterprise at all as explaining why it (whatever it may have been) happened, or why it ran the course it did, or

how it came about, or how it could have happened in light of so-and-so. (1959: 404–5)

Dray argues that this type of "explanation by concept" (1959: 405) is "summative," rather than deductive; that is, the explanation is complete when the various particulars are shown to add up to a greater whole. Instead of taking the form "whenever x then y," they argue "x, y, and z amount to a Q." Thus, colligatory concepts enable historians "to bring a wide range of facts into a system or pattern" (p. 407). Dray further argues that colligatory explanations do not in any way require amplification by covering law theory: "colligatory explanations . . . , insofar as they provide satisfactory unifying concepts, *can* be perfectly complete explanations *of their type*—i.e., as answers to 'what' rather than 'why' questions" (p. 408).

Louis Mink ([1965] 1966), in turn, amplifies Walsh's asides on similarities between historiography and literary representation to illuminate the relationship between explanation and NARRATIVE in historical writing. "In *some* sense," Mink argues "we may understand a particular event by locating it correctly in a narrative sequence" (p. 172). He asserts that there are things such as "*sequential* explanations," arguments in which intelligibility "depends on [an event's] position in a sequence of acitons," as for instance in the performance of mime (p. 172). Here again, the key is the idea of "context"; the "actual meanings are provided by the total context" (pp. 178, 181). When the historian shows that a series of events or circumstances add up to a greater whole, or context, he performs, in Mink's terms (p. 182), an act of "synoptic judgment"; this is based on the historian's effort to "discover the *grammar* of events," in contrast to covering law theory, which represents the historian's task as the discovery of the "logic of events alone."

The intellectual historian Hayden White (1973: 17–21) has synthesized the ideas of Walsh, Dray, and Mink and presented them under the label "contextualism" as one of four possible modes of historical explanation. According to White (p. 18), *contextualism* is a " 'functional' conception of the meaning or signficance of events discerned in the historical field. The informing presupposition of Contextualism is that events can be explained by being set within the 'context' of their occurrence" (p. 18). This, in White's view, is the orthodox method of explanation among professional historians (p. 19).

Finally, McCullagh (1978: 284) has revised Walsh's arguments in certain important ways. For instance, whereas Walsh depicted colligatory concepts as being all of one kind, McCullagh distinguishes between different types of colligation. Although all colligatory terms identify sets of events as parts of greater wholes, some do so in a "formal" sense—point to the "formal structure of an historical process"—and some perform this task in a "dispositional" way—designate a "disposition, a set of ideas or values which a group of events can all be said to manifest." Moreover, whereas Walsh claimed that colligatory terms always referred to *unique* sets of circumstances, McCullagh (p. 284) maintains that there can be both singular and *general* concepts of colligation, for "some of the historical wholes they refer to have common features." *Renaissance*, for example, may refer exclusively to a unique set of values and circumstances that existed in certain parts of Europe between the fourteenth and sixteenth centuries, but *revolution* may designate a general class of circumstances that occurs at different times and places in history. Morever, some "complex" concepts combine formal and dispositional features, such as the idea of "democratic revolution" (p. 277).

Finally, in what has become a specialized subdebate on the issue, some authors claim (following Dray) that colligation is a special kind of classification (Cebik, 1969); McCullagh (1978: 284), however, maintains that some colligatory concepts may involve classification—those which are general—but singular colligatory statements do not.

References

Cebik, L. B. 1969. "Colligation and the Writing of History." *Monist* 53: 40–57.
Dray, William. 1959. " 'Explaining What' in History." In Gardiner: 403–8.
Ferguson, Wallace K. 1948. *The Renaissance in Historical Thought*. Cambridge, Mass.
Levich, Marvin. 1964–65. Review of Sidney Hook, ed., *Philosophy and History: A Symposium* in *HT* 4: 328–49.
McCullagh, C. Behan. 1978. "Colligation and Classification in History." *HT* 17: 267–84. An excellent introduction, this essay provides a good description of Walsh's theory, highlights differences between the ideas of Walsh and Dray, and makes sensible suggestions for the refinement of the idea of colligation.
Mink, Louis O. [1965] 1966. "The Autonomy of Historical Understanding." In Dray: 160–92. This is a key contribution to literature on the role of narrative in historiography.
Thompson, D. 1967. "Colligation and History Teaching." In W. H. Burston and D. Thompson, eds., *Studies in the Nature and Teaching of History*, London: 85–106.
Walsh, W. H. 1942. "The Intelligibility of History." *Philosophy* 17: 128–43.
———. 1960. *Philosophy of History: An Introudction*. New York. Originally published in 1951 and revised in 1958. This is the most important source for understanding the idea. Walsh believes that "though historical thinking does . . . possess certain peculiarities of its own, it is not *toto coelo* different from scientific thinking. In particular, it is hard to deny that the historian, like the scientist, does make appeal to general propositions in the course of his study, though he does not make these explicit in the same way as the scientist does. History differs from the natural sciences in that it is not the aim of the historian to formulate a system of general laws; but this does not mean that no such laws are presupposed in historical thinking" (p. 24).
———. 1967. "Colligatory Concepts in History." In W. H. Burston and D. Thompson, eds., *Studies in the Nature and Teaching of History*. London: 65–84.
White, Hayden. 1973. *Metahistory: The Historical Imagination in Nineteenth-Century Europe*. Baltimore.

Sources of Additional Information

Literature is not extensive. Cebik (1969: 40) asserts that "Rarely has a theory of comparable scope and potential importance received so little critical treatment. The criticism which has appeared is altogether bland and dismissive, while those who have seen some merit in the notion adapt it freely to their own purposes." The remarks of J.W.N. Watkins, "Ideal Types and Historical Explanation," [1952] in Herbert Feigl and May Brodbeck, eds., *Readings in the Philosophy of Science* (New York, 1953): 723–43, exemplify the truth of this statement, although the situation has improved with the appearance of the essay by McCullagh (1978). The best bibliographies, perhaps, are footnote citations in the articles by Cebik and McCullagh. L. Pompa and W. H. Dray, eds., *Substance and Form in History: A Collection of Essays in Philosophy of History* (Edinburgh, 1981), contains a bibliography of the writings of W. H. Walsh, pp. 187–93, as well as an essay by Dray, "Colligation Under Appropriate Conceptions," pp. 156–70. For the relationship of colligation to economic history see J.R.T. Hughes, "Fact and Theory in Economic History," in Ralph L. Andreano, ed., *The New Economic History: Recent Papers on Methodology* (New York, 1970): 43–66, especially 51–52.

COMPARATIVE HISTORY. 1. An orientation toward the study of the past, based on the use of analogies between two or more societies or periods. 2. A subdiscipline of historiography characterized by the systematic comparison of carefully defined ideas or institutions in different societies. 3. A specific method of historical explanation in which developments in one social situation are explained by comparing them to developments in other social situations.

As a loosely defined approach to the study of the past, comparative history is as old as the idea of history itself. Both explicit and tacit comparisons between the Greeks and non-Greek "barbarians" appear in the earliest examples of western historiography written by Herodotus (c. 484–c. 425 B.C.) and Thucydides (c. 460–c. 400 B.C.). An eye for comparing different epochs and cultures is likewise evident in the eighteenth-century historical work of writers such as Voltaire and the Baron de Montesquieu (Pflug, [1954] 1971: 12–14). Indeed, "All history that aims at explanation or interpretation involves some type of explicit or implicit comparison" (Fredrickson, 1980: 457).

Only in the mid-nineteenth century, however, did such considerations give rise to the self-conscious use of comparative methods in history, and only in the twentieth century—particularly since 1945—have historians attempted to define precisely the idea of comparative history and render its use systematic. Since the nineteenth century there have been two distinct stages in the development of the idea. The first, before 1900, was based on the comparison of whole cultures remote from one another in space and time and stressed comparison as a means of uncovering broad social regularities and patterns of historical development. The second phase, predominant since 1945, stresses a more cautious approach based on the careful definition of particular aspects of societies to be compared and understands comparative history primarily as a way of illuminating social differences rather than similarities.

Late-nineteenth-century comparative history was inspired by a variety of influences: the methods of philology, evolutionist biology, and comparative anatomy, and—to some degree—the philosophy of POSITIVISM (Semmel, 1976: 372, 377). Just as philologists used comparison to study the origins and relationship of words, and naturalists sought to uncover relationships between species on the basis of anatomical resemblance, so historians such as H. T. Buckle in England and Herbert Baxter Adams in the United States attempted to plot broad institutional evolution by comparing the histories of various societies. Comparison was understood as a means of discovering common social origins, as in the *Comparative Politics* (1873) of the English historian Edward Augustus Freeman. One of the most popular hypotheses of the day—the so-called germ theory, which located the origins of modern Anglo-Saxon institutions in the forests of ancient Germany—was based on a loosely conceived comparison of ancient and modern Germany, England, and the United States (Saveth, 1964: 10–11). Scholars such as the British historian Lord Acton believed that a comparative approach modeled on natural science could scientifically uncover regularities of social development (Thrupp, 1958–59: 1). Marxian theory, as well, with its belief in the existence of general stages of socioeconomic development, encouraged comparative analysis (see HISTORICAL MATERIALISM).

Even before 1900, however, widespread confidence in historical comparison began to elicit a counter-reaction, and skepticism regarding the historical validity of comparative methods strengthened following World War I. Many scholars, zealous in their quest for LAW and rhythm in history, had ignored crucial differences between societies (Thrupp, 1058–1959: 1). In contrast, the influential doctrine of HISTORISM emphasized the uniqueness of past events and situations and discouraged the comparative search for uniformities and regularities. The vogue of historical RELATIVISM—which stressed subjectivity in historical interpretation—strengthened interwar doubts regarding the reliability of comparative approaches. Finally, sweeping studies of comparative social decay (such as Spengler's *Decline of the West* [1918–22] and Toynbee's *A Study of History* [1934–61]), while finding favor with the lay public and some sociologists, helped to discredit the idea of comparative history among academic historians because the units they compared ("cultures" and "civilizations") were vaguely defined, and because these vast surveys were not rigorously based on monographic research.

But despite the climate of skepticism, a few interwar historians made noteworthy contributions to the theory and practice of comparative history, for example, the American Crane Brinton ([1938] 1965) and especially the French medievalist Marc Bloch ([1928] 1953). Brinton's technique was broadly conceived and, in some respects (e.g., his search for uniformities in societies widely separated in space and time—seventeenth-century England, eighteenth-century France and America, and twentieth-century Russia), was reminiscent of late-nineteenth-century tradition. Instead of comparing whole cultures, however,

Brinton believed that a carefully defined social phenomenon such as REVOLUTION should be the unit of comparison. In the period since 1945, a number of comparative studies organized around similarly broad themes or concepts have appeared, for example, MODERNIZATION (Black, 1966) and RACISM (Fredrickson, 1981).

Even more influential for long-term theoretical development was Bloch, whose essay "Toward a Comparative History of European Societies" ([1928] 1953) has been a springboard for most post–1945 reflection on comparative studies. Bloch, a champion of INTERDISCIPLINARY HISTORY who was influenced by work in comparative linguistics (Walker, 1980), defined two distinct ways historians might use comparison: the first, "comparative method in the grand manner," was the sort familiar to the late nineteenth century in which "the units of comparison are societies far removed from one another in time or space." In the second—more restrained, more cautious, and (he believed) more promising— "the units of comparison are societies that are geographical neighbors and historical contemporaries, constantly influenced by one another" (Bloch, [1928] 1953: 497–98; Sewell, 1967: 214). Here differences were as important as similarities; in fact, "Correctly understood, the primary interest of the comparative method is . . . the observation of differences" (Bloch, [1928] 1953: 507). Bloch predicted that the emergence of a truly rigorous comparative history would be slow, since all comparisons had to be based on painstaking monographic research: "The old maxim remains true that a day of synthesis requires years of analysis" (pp. 518–19, 521).

Since the 1950s, there has been renewed interest in comparative history, inspired in large part by Bloch's ideas. The revival has been encouraged by various factors: the more extreme varieties of historical relativism and historism have fallen out of fashion, and the rationale for narrowly ethnocentric histories has been undermined by the two world wars—catastrophes widely blamed on the ideology of NATIONALISM (Thrupp, 1958–59: 1). A compelling argument holds that the "comparative perspective reduces our biases by presenting us with alternative systems of values and world views, and by imparting to us a sense of the richness and variety of human experience" (Sewell, 1967: 218). From the point of view of many historians, the matter is a practical one: "Historical comparisons are notoriously dangerous and misleading, and historians as a rule are reluctant to make them. But since comparisons are inevitable, it would seem best that they be handled by expert historians" (Woodward, 1968: x; also Grew, 1980: 769).

Post-war interest is reflected in numerous ways; new journals emphasize the comparative orientation (e.g., *Comparative Studies in Society and History*, 1958—, *The Journal of Interdisciplinary History*, 1970—), and widely praised exercises in the approach have appeared (for example, Palmer, 1959–64; Black, 1966). "Comparative history" provided the theme for the 1978 convention of the American Historical Association. To date, however, comparative studies represent only a small percentage of the total production of historical works.

In recent decades there have been renewed efforts to define more precisely and justify comparative history. In this literature—following Bloch's example—stress is no longer on the search for uniform morphology or general patterns. Comparative history is seen primarily as a way to explain the *differences* rather than similarities between situations and societies separated in space and time (Degler, 1968: 426; Grew, 1980: 769–70). With a few exceptions (e.g., Coulborn, 1969), the tendency has been to move away from the comparison of large, ill-defined units such as "civilizations" or "cultures" and toward more "well-defined categories of analysis" (Grew, 1980: 770; Black, 1966: 40). A recurring theme (following Brinton) has been the call to work with "middle-range comparisons"—comparisons of institutions and ideas on a more limited level than that of "culture" or the "nation" (such as "slavery" and "revolution") (Black, 1966: 42).

As yet, however, "there is no firm agreement on what comparative history is or how it should be done" (Fredrickson, 1980: 457); the status of the idea is still tenuous and uncertain. Often, *comparative history* is loosely understood to include any history that uses analogies—no matter how eclectic, brief, or casual—to illuminate situations separated in space or time (e.g., Woodward, 1968). It may well be objected that the "limited use of a generalized 'comparative perspective' or exotic analogy as a way of shedding additional light on some phenomenon in a single nation or society is not comparative history in the full sense" (Fredrickson, 1980: 457).

Some theorists define comparative history more rigorously as a distinct "method" or "logic" of research, a "set of rules which can be methodically and systematically applied in gathering and using evidence to test explanatory hypotheses" (Sewell, 1967: 217). According to one view, the "comparative method" is

> a tool for dealing with problems of explanation . . . a single logic . . . underlies these various uses. This is the logic of hypothesis testing. If an historian attributes the appearance of phenomenon A in one society to the existence of condition B, he can check this hypothesis by trying to find other societies where A occurs without B or vice versa. (Sewell, 1967: 208–9; cf. Beard and Hook, 1946: 113)

Other scholars, however, deny that a single "comparative method" exists, arguing that there are many logically different ways to compare historical phenomena. Raymond Grew (1980: 776–77), himself a dedicated supporter of historical comparison, even suggests that the expression *comparative history* is best avoided.

Some authors prefer to think of comparative history as a historiographical genre rather than a method. Fredrickson (1980: 458) reserves the term for a "relatively small but significant body of scholarship that has *as its main objective* the systematic comparison of some process or institution in two or more societies that are not usually conjoined within one of the traditional geographical areas of historical specialization." He denies, however, that comparative history in this sense exists as a distinct field—or even trend—of historical inquiry, since the idea "does not possess a self-conscious community of inquirers who are aware of each other's work and build on it or react critically to it" (p. 459). The overwhelming majority of predoctoral students, he notes, continue to be narrowly trained in the history of a single nation or region; and the profession tends to reward those scholars who, in traditional fashion, pursue narrowly defined regional research throughout their lifetimes (pp. 472–73).

Despite the post–1945 revival, much of the profession continues to be wary of the notion of comparative history (Grew, 1980: 763). In an age of increasing specialization, many scholars doubt that any historian can genuinely master the literature of more than one field, narrowly delimited by region and period; under these circumstances, broad comparisons over space and time are considered highly risky (Thrupp, 1958–59: 1–2). Generally, historians are not inclined to support pronouncements by political scientists and sociologists to the effect that comparisons can skip painstaking monographic research and be made on the basis of theoretical models that may "violate the texture and detail of the concrete historical occasion" (Apter, 1971: 265–66). The "conventional tendency of historians to look for particularity, complexity, and ambiguity" (Fredrickson, 1980: 461) feeds this skepticism, for "the very act of comparison requires [general] categories that are comparable and some presuppositions about what is constant and predictable in human motivation or behavior." Against the skeptics, however, it has been persuasively argued that claims for historical uniqueness can be confirmed only by undertaking the risk of comparison (Degler, 1968: 425; Fredrickson, 1980: 462).

References

Apter, David E. 1971. "Radicalization and Embourgeoisement: Some Hypotheses for a Comparative Study of History." *The Journal of Interdisciplinary History* 1: 265–303. Apter is sociologist who argues that it may be "necessary to treat history explicitly as a testing ground for analytically derived propositions and, even in a rough-and-ready fashion, to plunder events in order to do hindsight analysis." Historians are not apt to be consoled by the author's view that "since history is subject to continuous revision, such violations can only be regarded as minor transgressions" (p. 266).

Beard, Charles A., and Hook, Sydney. 1946. "Problems of Terminology in Historical Writing." In Bull. 54: 103–30. The authors maintain that "In place of the controlled experiment, [the historian] uses the method of historical comparison and hypothetical construction" (p. 113).

Black, C. E. 1966. *The Dynamics of Modernization: A Study in Comparative History.* New York.

Bloch, Marc. [1928] 1953. "Toward a Comparative History of European Societies." In Lane and Riemersma: 494–521. This is a key source that appears in another translation in Marc Bloch, *Land and Work in Medieval Europe: Selected Papers by Marc Bloch* (New York, 1969): 44–81.

Brinton, Crane. [1938] 1965. *The Anatomy of Revolution.* New York.

Coulborn, Rushton. 1969. "A Paradigm for Comparative History." *Current Anthropology*. April-June: 175–77.

Degler, Carl N. 1968. "Comparative History: An Essay Review." *The Journal of Southern History* 34: 425–30. Degler's article is a critical evaluation of Woodward (1968).

Fredrickson, George M. 1980. "Comparative History." In Kammen: 457–73.

————. 1981. *White Supremacy: A Comparative Study of American and South African History*. New York.

Grew, Raymond. 1980. "The Case for Comparing Histories." *AHR* 85: 763–78.

Palmer, R. R. 1959–64. *The Age of Democratic Revolution*. 2 vols. Princeton, N.J.

Pflug, Günther. [1954] 1971. "The Development of Historical Method in the Eighteenth Century." *HT Beih.* 11: 1–23.

Saveth, Edward N. 1964. "The Conceptualization of American History." In Edward N. Saveth, *American History and the Social Sciences*. London: 3–22.

Semmel, Bernard. 1976. "H. T. Buckle: The Liberal Faith and the Science of History." *British Journal of Sociology* 27: 370–86.

Sewell, William H., Jr. 1967. "Marc Bloch and the Logic of Comparative History." *HT* 6: 208–18.

Thrupp, Sylvia L. 1958–59. "Editorial." *CSSH* 1: 1–4. Thrupp's comments are a good introduction to the spirit behind the post–1945 revival of the idea of comparative history.

Walker, Lawrence D. 1980. "A Note on Historical Linguistics and Marc Bloch's Comparative Method." *HT* 19: 154–64. Walker discusses the influence of the linguistic scholar Antoine Meillet on Bloch. His article complements the essay by Sewell (1967) and asserts that the comparative method in history has proven much less successful than Bloch hoped.

Woodward, C. Vann. 1968. "Preface." In C. Vann Woodward, *The Comparative Approach to American History*. New York. This is a book widely criticized for the ill-defined nature of its conception of comparative history, which nevertheless drew attention to the subject. See reviews by Degler (1968) and Paul F. Bourke in *HT* 9 (1970): 110–16. For further reflections by Woodward on comparative history, see his *Burden of Southern History* (Baton Rouge, La., 1960), p. 177.

Sources of Additional Information

See especially the footnote citations in Grew (1980) and Fredrickson (1980). Shmuel N. Eisenstadt, "Social Institutions: Comparative," *IESS* 14: 421–29, contains a helpful bibliography. The October and December 1980 numbers of the *AHR* are dedicated to comparative history; for a discussion of the origins and nature of Marc Bloch's idea of comparative history see, in the October issue, Alette Olin Hill and Boyd H. Hill, "Marc Bloch and Comparative History" (pp. 828–46), followed by the comments of William H. Sewell, Jr., and Sylvia L. Thrupp. The "AHR Forum" in *AHR* 87 (Feb. 1982): 123–43, is devoted to an exchange of views on comparative history. Paul Bourke cites a number of recent comparative studies in the footnotes to his review of Woodward (1968) in *HT* 9 (1970): 110–16; note especially references to the work of Louis Hartz. For a brief discussion of the relationship of comparative history to COUNTERFACTUAL ANALYSIS see George Green, "Comment," in Ralph L. Andreano, ed., *The New Economic History: Recent Papers on Methodology* (New York, 1970): 101–7, especially 105–6. On some problems of comparative political history see William O. Aydelotte, *Quantification in History* (Reading, Mass., 1971), p. 11.

CONSTRUCTIONISM, CONSTITUTION. The doctrine that historians construct, or "constitute," the past to which their accounts refer.

Constructionism—together with the related expression *historical constitution*—designates a special class of theories of historical knowledge in the broader tradition of IDEALISM (Mandelbaum, 1966: 894; Nowell-Smith, 1977a: 2; Goldstein, 1977). These labels have lately acquired limited currency among philosophers of history, primarily as the result of books by Jack Meiland (1965) and Leon J. Goldstein (1976)—although it is not clear if all of those who have been called "constructionists" fully accept the term (e.g., Goldstein, 1977: 30). The names of several twentieth-century philosophers and historians—Benedetto Croce, Michael Oakeshott, R. G. Collingwood, and Carl Becker (Meiland, 1965: v; Nowell-Smith, 1971: 5; Goldstein, 1972a, 1972b; cf. Dray, 1974)—have also been associated with the doctrine, even though they may not personally have identified themselves as constructionists. Defenders of constructionism are thus far a distinct minority among philosophers, and their arguments often conflict radically with key assumptions of working historians.

Constructionism is based on the truism that past events are inaccessible to present observation; in other words, historians "purport to tell us what happened in the past, and yet have no direct access to it" (Walsh, 1977: 53). Thus, history is not perceptual or sensory. Unlike eyewitnesses, who testify to what they have seen, historians report what they have "*reason to believe* at the conclusion of an inquiry which is intellectual only and in no way perceptual" (Goldstein, 1976: xiii).

> what we come to believe about the human past can never be confirmed by observation—can never be known by acquaintance—and so can never be put to the test of observation, the method of confirmation which is virtually the only one explicitly recognized by science and philosophy. (p. xii)

From this, constructionists draw two basic conclusions (Meiland, 1965: 192). First, historians should not be regarded as discovering factual information about an independently existing past—either because such a realm may not exist or, more likely, because it cannot be demonstrated that the historian can have direct acquaintance with such a past, even if it does exist; the historian must therefore be regarded as the *creator*, rather than the *discoverer* of the past to which his accounts refer. Second, history is nonetheless a socially significant and cognitively valid activity, because it tries to account for the present existence of phenomena, which scholars traditionally call "Historical Evidence" (written documents, artifacts, social traditions, and so on) according to the widely recognized disciplinary conventions of source CRITICISM and INTERPRETATION (Goldstein, 1976: 56–58). Properly understood, therefore, *history* is an activity that "accounts for the existence and nature" of historical evidence, and the historian is important because he "helps, along with those working in other fields, to give a coherent account of the *present* world as a whole" (Meiland, 1965: 192).

fields, to give a coherent account of the *present* world as a whole" (Meiland, 1965: 192).

Constructionists pit their thesis against the "discovery" or "reconstructionist" view of historiography, a position held (explicitly or, more often, implicitly) by the majority of philosophers and historians. This, in turn, is based on the assumptions of historical REALISM, the doctrine that historians discover the factual nature of real phenomena (events, personalities, institutions, and so on) that exist or existed in a "real" PAST that "actually happened" (Meiland, 1965: 4). Constructionism denies this and asserts—although most (possibly all) historians presume the contrary—that historical accounts are only "ostensibly" about past events (Meiland, 1965: 4). Constructionists insist that the "real" past—whether or not it exists—has nothing at all to do with history. They do not deny that historians think that they are recovering or reconstructing a real past; they maintain, however, that history is actually—in the words of Oakeshott and Collingwood ([1946] 1956: 180)—only "what the evidence obliges us to believe." Realists might agree but would contend that "what the evidence compels us to believe" *corresponds* to an independently existing actual past (Nowell-Smith, 1977a: 4–5). Constructionists, in contrast, maintain that this compelling belief does not correspond to a real past; rather, the historian's past—a "historical" (i.e., disciplinary, not real) past—is a construct of his own thought.

Constructionism may or may not lead to some form of historical SKEPTICISM, or doubt about the reliability of history as knowledge. Goldstein (1972b; 1976: xvi, xix-xx), perhaps the most important advocate of the doctrine, argues that constructionism is in fact the only way to *avoid* skepticism about history, since a real past can never be directly known, and since the only philosophically reliable knowledge we have of anything is, in any case, disciplinary. He stresses the fact that professional historians have been able to reach an extraordinary level of agreement concerning the historical past, using time-honored methods of inquiry (Goldstein, 1976: xii). Thus, the process of historical constitution is not a matter of isolated subjective judgments by individual scholars but rather the informed consensus of a community of scholars. Supporters of constructionism deny that, in holding that the historian "creates" his past, they destroy the distinction between "history" and historical fiction: "the basic difference is that written history is largely if not entirely based on documents, whereas much of historical fiction has no basis at all in the documents" (Meiland, 1965: 197).

Constructionists concede that the notion that the "real past" is "irrelevant to the practice of history" (Goldstein, 1977: 32) appears paradoxical. This is true not only from the viewpoint of common sense, but from the standpoint of the nineteenth-century's confident realism (based on the idea that the historian *re*constructs the past "as it actually happened" [Ranke, (1824) 1972: 57]), as well as that of today's guarded realism (according to which historians "are concerned and committed to tell about the past the best and most likely story that can be sustained by the relevant extrinsic evidence" [Hexter, 1967: 5]). They assert, nonetheless, that their theory correctly describes what historians *actually do*.

The constructionist position is extremely controversial. On the positive side, Goldstein's version has been applauded for its emphasis on the largely overlooked fact that professional historical inquiry is a corporate rather than isolated individual activity and that, therefore, the "consensus or near consensus of historians is important both when it comes to saying what is to be explained and when we ask what explains it" (Walsh, 1977: 55). But most commentary has thus far been hostile. The entire view that written history is not about a real past is widely considered "remarkable" and unacceptable (Nowell-Smith, 1977b: 315–16). More specifically, Meiland has been soundly criticized on the grounds that his arguments are all of a general epistemological kind and are not based on a thorough analysis of historical practice (Mandelbaum, 1966: 894). Some critics (e.g., Gorman, 1977: 72–73) reject the view that a high degree of agreement or consensus among historians makes history "epistemically licit." Many practicing historians would probably agree with Maurice Mandelbaum in saying that the "basic flaw" in Goldstein's thought is his

> failure . . . to be explicit regarding his view of what, for a historian, constitutes evidence relevant to the task of constructing the historical past. . . . Goldstein stresses the historian's need for "evidence," yet if all forms of historical realism are to be rejected as playing no part in historical inquiry, it is hard to see what the historian would mean when he held that a particular statement, artifact, or document is *evidence* for anything at all. (1977: 293–94)

Nowell-Smith (1977a: 6–7) argues for a moderate realist position, which he considers compatible with a constructionist theory of *historical practice* but not with a constructionist theory of reality. He defends the idea of a real past to which historical accounts, with greater or lesser accuracy, correspond and argues that no constructionist has adequately demonstrated that "in the case of past events alone what the historian constructs is not an account of an event but the event itself" (Nowell-Smith, 1977a: 16). In Goldstein's case, Walsh suggests that much of the difficulty ultimately arises from an effort to "combine an idealist theory of history with a realist theory of perception" (1977: 67).

References

Collingwood, R. G. [1946] 1956. *The Idea of History*. New York. Collingwood's name has been associated with constructionism, partly due to his emphasis on the fact that the past "has vanished and our ideas about it can never be verified as we verify our scientific hypotheses" (p. 5) and partly on the grounds of his theory of the historical IMAGINATION, which stresses the historian's "web of imaginative construction" and "constructive imagination." The claim that he was a constructionist has been challenged on the grounds that his conception of history as the process of "rethinking" thoughts of past individuals (see UNDERSTANDING) assumes that a "real" past is the true object of the historian's inquiry (Meiland, 1965: 64, 81–82).

Dray, William. 1974. Review of Michael Krausz, ed., *Critical Essays on the Philosophy of R. G. Collingwood*. HT 13: 291–305.

Goldstein, Leon J. 1972a. "Collingwood on the Constitution of the Historical Past." In
    Michael Krausz, ed., *Critical Essays on the Philosophy of R. G. Collingwood*.
    London.
————. 1972b. "Historical Realism: The Ground of Carl Becker's Scepticism." *Phi-
    losophy of the Social Sciences* 2: 121–31.
————. 1976. *Historical Knowing*. Austin, Tex. This is the most important defense of
    constructionism, which Goldstein prefers to call "historical constitution," or the
    "primacy of knowing" theory. Goldstein's position differs from that of Meiland
    (1965) in that it is not based on historical skepticism and insofar as it involves a
    close analysis of several actual cases of historical reasoning.
————. 1977. "History and the Primacy of Knowing." *HT Beih.* 16: 29–52. This is a
    concise statement of the idea that "in history there is no reference except as it is
    constituted or constructed by means of the techniques of historical investigation"
    (p. 51).
Gorman, J. L. 1977. Review of Leon J. Goldstein, *Historical Knowing*. *HT* 16: 66–80.
    Gorman complains that Goldstein's conclusions are not argued through and that
    his position displays "very little philosophical refinement" (p. 80).
Hexter, J. H. 1967. "The Rhetoric of History." *HT* 6: 3–13.
Mandelbaum, Maurice. 1966. Review of Jack W. Meiland, *Scepticism and Historical
    Knowledge*. *AHR* 71: 894.
————. 1977. Review of Leon J. Goldstein, *Historical Knowing*. *JMH* 49: 292–94.
Meiland, Jack W. 1965. *Scepticism and Historical Knowledge*. New York. This inter-
    esting analysis of constructionism has exercised slight influence on philosophers
    and historians, largely because its arguments are highly generalized and not related
    to actual examples of historical writing.
Nowell-Smith, P. H. 1971. *What Actually Happened*. Lawrence, Kans. This book is a
    concise summary and criticism of the constructionist position.
————. 1977a. "The Constructionist Theory of History." *HT Beih.* 16: 1–28. In this
    important criticism of Goldstein by a moderate realist and leading advocate of the
    label "constructionism" the author argues that Goldstein's "correct account of
    historical methodology" is "intertwined with a *philosophical* thesis that is . . .
    totally unacceptable" (p. 2). Pages 3–5 contain a concise description of
    constructionism.
————. 1977b. Review of Leon J. Goldstein, *Historical Knowing*. *Philosophy of the
    Social Sciences* 7: 315–16.
Ranke, Leopold von. [1824] 1972. Preface to *Histories of the Latin and Germanic Nations
    from 1494–1514*. In Stern: 55–58.
Walsh, W. H. 1977. "Truth and Fact in History Reconsidered." *HT Beih.* 16: 53–71.
    This is a generally favorable assessment of Goldstein's constructionism.

Sources of Additional Information

See also IDEALISM; PAST; REALISM. Constructionism is relatively new as an articulated
doctrine, and literature on the subject is sparse. The essays by Nowell-Smith (1977a),
Goldstein (1977), and Walsh (1977) conveniently appear together in Beiheft 16 of *HT*.
This volume, together with Goldstein (1976), constitutes the best introduction to the
question. Also relevant is Goldstein's essay "Evidence and Events in History," *Philosophy of Science* 29 (1962): 175–94. For an important essay on Oakeshott see David
Boucher, "The Creation of the Past: British Idealism and Michael Oakeshott's Philosophy

of History,'' *HT* 23 (1984): 193–214. Margit Hurup Nielson, ''Re-enactment and Re-construction in Collingwood's Philosophy of History,'' *HT* 20 (1981): 1–31, argues that Collingwood was a ''constructivist.'' There is a critique of the position in B. C. Hurst, ''The Myth of Historical Evidence,'' *HT* 20 (1981): 278–90. Beyond this, the reader should consult reviews of Meiland (1965) and Goldstein (1976). Among the more important reviews not cited above are Basil Mitchell, *Mind*, 77 (1968): 298–99 (on Meiland), Richard Peterson, *Philosophy and Phenomenological Research*, 38 (1977–78): 273–75, and Ronald E. Roblin, *Philosophy of the Social Sciences*, 7 (Sept. 1977): 317–19 (on Goldstein).

CONTEMPORARY HISTORY. 1. The history of one's own lifetime. 2. The history of the twentieth century, or some segment thereof. 3. A historical method that uses present concerns as criteria for selecting problems for study in the past.

The expression *contemporary history* has become popular since 1945, primarily as a label for works that deal with the ''recent past''—roughly understood as the twentieth century—or, more broadly, for studies of any period whose time frame is the historian's own life span. A few scholars also understand contemporary history as a method of selection, according to which one chooses the historical subjects one studies on the basis of present issues and concerns.

The practice of writing histories of the recent—as opposed to the remote—past is ancient. *The Peloponnesian War* of Thucydides (c. 460–c. 400 b.c.), an interpretation of events that occurred in the author's own lifetime and in some of which he was himself directly involved, is usually cited as the first great example (e.g., Woodward, 1966: 1). Indeed, until the nineteenth century most histories necessarily focused on the recent past since, before the refinement of source CRITICISM in the sixteenth and seventeenth centuries, historians lacked the research techniques required to deal scientifically with the remote past. Moreover, before the invention of printing and the simultaneous rise of modern states with their record-keeping bureaucracies, written evidence about the distant past was frequently non-existent or at best fragmentary, disorganized, and difficult to obtain. Thus, the pre-modern historian normally had little upon which to base his accounts aside from personal observations and interviews. The fact that researchers were restricted in the foregoing ways was a perennial source of SKEPTICISM about history as a branch of knowledge. Historians themselves widely viewed the distant past—regrettably but inevitably—as the sphere of received tradition and myth, beyond the scope of critical historiography; Thucydides (1954: 35), for example, said that he ''found it impossible, because of its remoteness in time, to acquire a really precise knowledge of the distant past or even of the history preceding our own period.''

Nevertheless the PAST, in popular consciousness, gradually became identified with the remote past. This was because historians such as Thucydides had written accounts of their own recent pasts, and these pasts, as they faded into time, became identified as ''the past,'' or ''history.'' ''The tendency to regard what was more remote as by definition more 'historical' increased . . . and this tendency was finally institutionalized with the professionalization of history in the nineteenth century'' (Schlesinger, 1967: 69).

In the nineteenth century, academic historians began to frown on efforts to write historical accounts of the recent past, even though some historians—including the profession's chief disciplinary role model, Leopold von Ranke—often wrote on contemporary subjects (Ritter, 1961–62: 268), and certain scholars (e.g. the French historian Alexis de Tocqueville) openly defended the historical study of recent events (Schlesinger, 1967: 74). Despite these cases, it became common practice for late-nineteenth-century professionals to speak ''as historians'' only about the more distant past; when one wrote of the recent past, one did so not as a historian but as a journalist or ''publicist.'' Accounts of the immediate past were disqualified as true history because written documentation was usually sparse and, more importantly, because these events were considered too close in time to allow the proper distance and dispassionate ''perspective'' necessary to scholarly OBJECTIVITY. Most historians believed that the passing of at least a generation was required before a period qualified for historical scrutiny (Schlesinger, 1967: 69); this attitude became strongly ingrained and persists to some extent in late twentieth century (Hughes, 1964: 89–90).

In the early twentieth century, however, thinking slowly began to shift. Systematic philosophical efforts to compare the methods of history and natural science led to new awareness of the subjective factor in *all* historical writing, whether it concerned the remote or the recent past. Doubt spread about the possibility of perfect OBJECTIVITY in historiography as the result of philosophical neo-IDEALISM, which fed the rise of historical RELATIVISM. Among the first to use the term *contemporary history* in a positive sense was the Italian neo-idealist Benedetto Croce (1866–1952), who used the term to designate historical writing that was ''living,'' or emotionally charged with the personal values and imagination of the historian himself. Croce articulated the now famous dictum ''every true history is contemporary history'' (Croce, [1919] 1960: 12), a statement conventionally interpreted to mean that ''the writing of history necessarily changes with the standpoint of the historian, that *all* history is contemporary in the sense that its presentation reflects the circumstances and attitudes of those who write it'' (Hughes, 1964: 94). In the United States, the concurrent rise of the NEW HISTORY reflected a desire for history to be more pragmatic, in the sense of contributing in some direct way to the understanding and control of present circumstances. These traditions gradually prepared the way for the positive reception of the concept of ''contemporary history'' after 1945.

Beyond philosophical considerations, the occurrence of certain events—especially the First and Second World Wars—aroused an urgent desire for historical explanations of current trends (Thomson, 1967: 30). For some historians, World War II represented a radical break with the past and ushered in a new epoch (Barraclough, 1964: 2). These dramatic developments—which also included the accelerated rate of social change caused by INDUSTRIALIZATION (Schlesinger,

1967: 69–70) and (later, in the United States in 1963) the assassination of President Kennedy (Commager, 1966)—convinced some historians that they would be shirking their duty as citizens and scholars if they refused to study them.

Such perceptions were initially strongest in West Germany, where the changes were most dramatic; there, traditional, socially disengaged "scholarly history" was widely believed to have "failed as a guide to life" (Ritter, 1961–62: 262) and *Zeitgeschichte*, or "contemporary history," quickly became an accepted genre (Besson, 1961). An *Institut für Zeitgeschichte* was founded with its own periodical (*Vierteljahrshefte für Zeitgeschichte*), which published articles primarily on German history since World War I and especially on the subject of National Socialism (Rothfels, 1953: 8). Similar institutes and journals were founded in other European countries. In England, with its imperial tradition, particular stress was placed on the global scope of contemporary studies (Barraclough, 1964: 2; also Rothfels, 1953: 6–8). In the United States, a general session on contemporary history at the 1951 conference of the American Historical Association met with mixed response (Lamar, 1952: 802), but the propriety of inquiry into the immediate past was soon fully accepted. According to some authorities (e.g., Woodward, 1966: 3), U.S. historians are now in danger of "going to the other extreme and concentrating too much on contemporary history and neglecting the development of western civilization for a superficial study of the past of Africa and Asia."

Apologists for contemporary history countered their opponents by arguing that lack of official documentation on current subjects is not a serious problem, since rapid communications in the contemporary world have rendered written documents less important forms of evidence than previously was the case. Many important decisions are now made by telephone, and modern technology makes possible personal consultations between leaders and their advisors that may never be recorded. On the other hand, the "information explosion" has resulted in such a mass of documentation on some matters that no single historian could thoroughly analyze it along the classic lines of nineteenth century textual criticism (Hughes, 1964: 90–93).

With regard to the alleged threat to detached "perspective," the defenders drew inspiration from Croce. Thus,

> perspective is merely the standpoint from which the viewer and his own generation regard the past. One has only to read the historiography of any period to realize how quickly this standpoint changes. . . . Events in the past do not sort themselves out in the course of time by some automatic process; the present observer does the sorting, and contemporary reasons determine his order of arrangement. (Woodward, 1966: 4; also Hughes, 1964: 95)

In certain respects, indeed, the historian of his own times enjoys a decided advantage; for example, the establishment of a relationship of empathy with the past (see UNDERSTANDING) is in some respects rendered easier (Rothfels, 1953:

6). Finally, champions of contemporary history note that *someone* will inevitably interpret the recent past and argue that by and large it is best for those systematically trained as historians to do it (Hughes, 1964: 107).

Although the general notion of historical inquiry into the recent past has thus triumphed, attempts to delineate precisely a clear idea of "contemporary history" have proven difficult. French historians, for example, customarily use the term to refer to the period since the French Revolution of 1789, but English-speaking historians regard this as much too broad (Woodward, 1966: 1, n.1). The best attempts at definition have produced only a loose, working formula—for example, the scholarly treatment of the "history of our own time" (Rothfels, 1953; 2; Woodward, 1966: 1, n.1)—rather than a rigorous, logically consistent concept. Most definitions start with an effort to discriminate between "contemporary history" on the one hand, and "journalism," or "current affairs" on the other. Louis Halle (1967: 566), for example, draws a distinction between *contemporary history*—"the history of our own times"—and *current events*. *Current events* refers to the "immediate present" while *contemporary history* "pertains to the quite recent past, and the rest of history belongs to the more distant past." He admits that there are "gray zones" in which the "categories merge imperceptibly" but maintains that "we need not quibble about precisely where, for working purposes, to draw the line" (p. 567).

Beyond this purely chronological distinction, it is often argued that current affairs deals with day-to-day change on the superficial level, and contemporary history identifies and explains "deeper historical trends" (Barraclough, 1964: 8) or long-range "secular trends" associated with things such as "the progress of science and technology," "demographic changes," and the "attrition of natural resources" (Halle, 1967: 576–77). The contemporary historian is primarily interested in the long-term consequences of events, whereas journalism is mainly interested in momentary, "dramatic importance." Unlike journalism, contemporary history is not vitally interested in the "intergovernmental exchanges of notes and the formal institutional arrangements that belong to the superficial level" (Halle, 1967: 572–73, 575–76). The purpose of contemporary history is rather to "clarify the basic structural changes which have shaped the modern world" (Barraclough, 1964: 9).

In these respects, it is conceded, the method of contemporary history is no different from that of history in general. According to Barraclough (1964: 9–10, 12), however, there is a methodological distinction to be made. The "causal or genetic" approach used in much traditional historiography, he believes, is "unsuitable" for contemporary history; instead of working—in the conventional manner—toward the future from a starting point in the past, contemporary history self-consciously takes the present as its starting point and searches the past for the origins of current issues and trends. The contemporary historian need look no farther into the past than that point at which "the problems which are actual in the world today first take visible shape." This position has been attacked, however, as an instance of the "presentist" fallacy, a form of ANACHRONISM in which

> the antecedent in a narrative series is falsified by being defined or interpreted in terms of the consequent . . . it is the mistaken idea that the proper way to do history is to prune away the dead branches of the past, and to preserve the green buds and twigs which have grown into the dark forest of our contemporary world. (Fischer, 1970: 138, 135)

In contrast to Barraclough, many historians would agree that research should remain "quite unaffected by whether our subject is one we have ourselves been well situated to observe or one remote from us in time. The process of the historian's thought is the same when he writes a history of naval actions in the Second World War or in the war of the Greeks against Persia" (Zagorin, 1956: 9).

Because the expression *contemporary history* has been so closely associated with a specific historical situation—the dramatic changes that have followed World War II—it is probably to some degree a vogue term that will be used less frequently in the future than it has in the immediate past. Likewise, use of the term to designate a special method (Barraclough, 1964) seems somewhat idiosyncratic and logically flawed. On the other hand, the expression has become common enough to suggest that it will endure in the historical lexicon. Moreover, recent arguments in defense of historian's right to analyze the events of his own time make it seem unlikely that the *idea* of the historical study of the very recent past will soon fall out of favor.

References

Barraclough, Geoffrey. 1964. *An Introduction to Contemporary History*. New York. This is an important but occasionally confusing work. At one point the author states that the contemporary era should be dated from 1890; at another, from 1960; at another, from no particular point at all, but from the points "when the problems which are actual in the world today first take visible shape (p. 12).
Besson, Waldemar, ed. 1961. *Geschichte: Das Fischer Lexikon*. Frankfurt am Main.
Commager, Henry Steele. 1966. "Should Historians Write Contemporary History?" *Saturday Review*, Feb. 12: 18–20, 47.
Croce, Benedetto [1919] 1960. *History: Its Theory and Practice*. New York.
Fischer, David Hackett. 1970. *Historians' Fallacies: Toward a Logic of Historical Thought*. New York.
Halle, Louis J. 1967. "What is Contemporary History?" *The Virginia Quarterly Review* 43: 566–79.
Hughes, H. Stuart. *History as Art and as Science: Twin Vistas on the Past*. New York. Chapter Five originally appeared as "Is Contemporary History Real History?" in *The American Scholar*, 32 (Autumn 1963): 516–25.
Lamar, Howard R. 1952. "The New York Meeting, 1951." *AHR* 57: 795–822.
Ritter, Gerhard. 1961–62. "Scientific History, Contemporary History, and Political Science." *HT* 1: 261–79. Consult this work for references to literature in German.

Rothfels, Hans. 1953. "Zeitgeschichte als Aufgabe." *Vierteljahrshefte für Zeitgeschichte*
    1: 1–8.
Schlesinger, Arthur, Jr. 1967. "On the Writing of Contemporary History." *The Atlantic
    Monthly*. March: 69–74. Schlesinger believes that the "ultimate explanation for
    the rise of contemporary history undoubtedly lies in the acceleration of the rate
    of change. The world has altered more in the last century than it had in the
    thousand years preceding" (pp. 69–70).
Thomson, David. 1967. "The Writing of Contemporary History." *Journal of Contem-
    porary History* 2: 25–34.
Thucydides. 1954. *The Peloponnesian War*. Trans. Rex Warner. Harmondsworth, Eng.
Woodward, Llewellyn. 1966. "The Study of Contemporary History." *Journal of Con-
    temporary History* 1: 1–13. Woodward's article is one of the best brief introduc-
    tions to this subject.
Zagorin, Perez. 1956. "Carl Becker on History. Professor Becker's Two Histories: A
    Skeptical Fallacy." *AHR* 62: 1–11.

Sources of Additional Information

In general see Dietrich Gerhard, "Periodization in History," *DHI* 3 (1973): 476–81.
The *Journal of Contemporary History* 2 (Jan. 1967) is devoted to a survey of work in
contemporary history in various countries. Some of these essays are reprinted in Donald
C. Watt, ed., *Contemporary History in Europe: Problems and Perspectives* (New York,
1969). See also "Contemporary History: Problems and Perspectives," *Journal of the
Society of Archivists* 3 (Oct. 1969): 511–25; Llewellyn Woodward, "The Study of Contemporary History," *Journal of Contemporary History* 1 (1966): 1–13; W. H. Burston, "The Nature and Teaching of Contemporary History," in W. H. Burston and D.
Thompson, eds., *Studies in the Nature and Teaching of History* (London, 1967): 107–
36; and Yehuda Bauer, "Contemporary History—Some Methodological Problems,"
History, N.S., 61 (Oct. 1976): 333–43, which seeks to illuminate "the extent to which
contemporary history in our own century reveals aspects and poses problems that are
unique" (p. 335) but nevertheless reaffirms the conventional position that contemporary history "should not be considered a separate branch of knowledge, but simply a
branch of the historical discipline with specific problems" (p. 333). E. H. Carr, *What
Is History?* (1961; reprint ed., Harmondsworth, Eng., 1964), makes some relevant
points on pp. 96–98.

COUNTERFACTUAL ANALYSIS. Inquiry that utilizes counterfactual prop-
    ositions, i.e., premises (explicit or tacit) that are at least in part contrary to
    fact. In historiography, counterfactual assertions are often explicitly used in
    ECONOMETRIC HISTORY; implicit counterfactual premises are also generally
    found in discussions of historical CAUSATION and wherever historical expla-
    nation involves an assessment of the relative significance of any person, event,
    process, situation, and so forth.

The use of counterfactual propositions—also called "subjunctive conditionals," "counterfactual conditionals," and "contrary-to-fact conditionals"—has
recently aroused interest in analytical philosophy (Goodman, 1965: 3–27) and
historiography, especially among students of quantitative economic history (or

ECONOMETRIC HISTORY). Although history is rightly understood as a factual enterprise, historians often use contrary-to-fact reasoning in at least two distinct ways (McClelland, 1975: 149): (1) in the analysis of social CAUSATION and (2) in speculation about the possible consequences of events that did not actually occur. In the first case, counterfactual assertions or assumptions are employed to highlight the special causal significance of certain factors. According to H. Stuart Hughes (1960: 29), the "most satisfactory type of causal explanation in history simply tries to locate the factor which, when removed, would make the decisive difference in a given sequence of events—that is, the factor which, if thought away, would render the events in question inconceivable." An illustration is the assertion: "The Civil War would not have been fought had it not been for slavery." Here "the historian begins with the causal facts of the case, mentally removes one of those operative causal factors [that is, the institution of Negro slavery], and speculates about the residual in order to assess the importance of the factor mentally removed" (McClelland, 1975: 149).

The second type of counterfactual thinking involves the addition rather than subtraction of one or more factors; the possible result of the added factor(s) then becomes a basis for the analysis of actual events. It is not unusual, for instance, for historians of twentieth-century international relations to suggest that strong Anglo-French resistance to German remilitarization of the Rhineland in 1936— something that did not occur—might have nipped Nazi expansionism in the bud (Barraclough, 1979: 76). A recent example of this type is the work of Neuburger and Stokes (1979: 187), which examines pre–1914 Britain's fear of being commercially overtaken by Germany and attempts to show how this rivalry would have developed had World War I not occurred; the added factors here are the failure of World War I to occur and a set of hypothetical developments projected by statistical inference. The authors' point is to "suggest a sequence of events that never occurred but may nonetheless be used as a guide in evaluating the views and expectations of contemporaries" (p. 187). Although this second kind of counterfactual reasoning is not uncommon in historical analysis, officially it is usually frowned upon since it does not center upon the analysis of established fact (cf. Carr, [1961] 1964: 97). More generally, the distinctions between various kinds of counterfactual reasoning are sometimes blurred or go unrecognized (Fales, 1951: 85; Fischer, 1970: 15–21).

As employed in econometric history (that is, quantitative economic history), counterfactuals conform primarily to the first type (McClelland, 1975: 150); they are deliberate falsifications used to assess the economic impact of technological innovation, social change, and so on:

> The net effect of such things on development [writes Robert Fogel] involves a comparison between what actually happened and what would have happened in the absence of the specified circumstance. However, since the counterfactual condition never occurred, it could not have been observed, and hence is not recorded in historical documents. In order to determine what would have happened in the absence of a given circumstance the economic historian needs a set of general

> statements (that is, a set of theories or a model) that will enable him to deduce a
> counterfactual situation from institutions and relationships that actually existed.
> (1966: 653; cf. Davis, 1971: 110)

In econometric history, these counterfactual models are generated by the use of
statistical inference from existing data. Systematic use of this method was initially
inspired by the COVERING LAW theory of historical EXPLANATION, which holds
that historical reasoning is a species of scientific explanation and that all scientific
explanation proceeds from "hypothetico-deductive" laws or generalizations;
according to Fogel (1966: 655), a champion of econometric history, "counterfactual propositions [in quantitative economic history] are merely inferences from
hypothetico-deductive models" (cf. Davis, 1971: 107, 112).

> In order to determine what would have happened in the absence of a given institution
> [Fogel writes], the economic historian needs a set of general statements that will
> allow him to deduce a counterfactual situation from institutions and relationships
> that actually existed (1967: 285).

In economic history, explicit interest in counterfactuals dates from the late
1950s, when Alfred H. Conrad and John R. Meyer ([1957] 1964) advocated the
use of statistically designed counterfactual hypotheses to test the validity of
traditional interpretations in economic history. The idea was enthusiastically
adopted by advocates of quantitative, or "new," economic history (Davis, 1966:
657; 1971: 112–13). A well-known application of counterfactual analysis is
Fogel's study *Railroads and American Economic Growth* (1964), which seeks
to measure the importance of the railroad industry for U.S. economic development in the nineteenth century. More specifically, Fogel tested the widely
held theory that railroad expansion was crucial to nineteenth-century American
economic growth by designing a counterfactual model of an American trans-
portation system based on waterways rather than railroads; he concluded that
railroads were not actually an "indispensable" factor in America's nineteenth-
century development. In explaining his procedure, Fogel stated:

> Estimation of the net benefit of railroads involves a comparison between the actual
> level of national income and the level that would have obtained in the absence of
> railroads. The amount of national income in the absence of railroads cannot be
> computed directly. It is necessary to construct a hypothetico-deductive model on
> the basis of which one can infer, from those conditions that were actually observed,
> a set of conditions that never occurred. (1966: 650)

Use of counterfactual analysis has aroused strong criticism in some quarters.
Among the most outspoken critics is the economic historian Fritz Redlich (1965;
[1968] 1970). Redlich ([1968] 1970: 91) draws a sharp distinction between social
science and history (see SOCIAL SCIENTIFIC HISTORY) and argues that figments—
"research on what would have happened if something had happened that did
not happen"—might (if carefully designed) be useful in some branches of the
former but are inappropriate to history where "the question of what would have
happened 'if,' is non-permissable."

historical research deals with the past that was and not with the past that might have been [Redlich maintains]. . . . I cannot see how one can know in exact quantitative terms . . . something that actually never happened. The result of such investigations is for me "as if" history, quasi-history, fictitious history—that is, not really history at all. ([1968] 1970: 91)

Yet despite the severity of his remarks, Redlich is ambiguous on the possible usefulness of quantitative counterfactuals for historians: "I do not take a stand against this kind of research per se, nor do I consider it worthless; I only want to have it recognized as part and parcel of the social sciences and to stress its tool character as far as history is concerned" ([1968] 1970: 92).

Despite such objections, it has long been recognized that counterfactual speculation in history is not novel at all but (as suggested above) is an important—although frequently unacknowledged—part of historical explanation (Cohen, 1942: 20; Beard and Hook, 1946: 113; Nowell-Smith, 1971: 11; Climo and Howells, 1974: 461). For example, "Every historical statement regarding the effect of a change must be implicitly measured against an assumed counterfactual continuity" (Cochran, 1969: 1568; cf. Fogel, 1966: 655; Green, [1968] 1970: 103–4). Recent theoretical interest in the question marks a distinct advance, since informed discussion about counterfactuals can only occur once they have been made explicit. At least one writer (Davis, 1966: 658) argues that

any argument carries with it some assumptions about a counterfactual world—a world no one has ever seen, but a world of what might have been. . . . It is only through a comparison of what was with what might have been that we are able to make statements about the nature of events.

This seems to be an exaggeration, however, and even the idea that all causal statements are based on counterfactuals—which many econometric historians appear to hold—is at best dubious (McClelland, 1975: 146–47; Gerschenkron, 1967: 456).

References

Barraclough, Geoffrey. 1979. *Main Trends in History*. New York. 1979. See ns. 319 and 320 for further bibliography.

Beard, Charles A., and Hook, Sydney. 1946. "Problems of Terminology in Historical Writing." In Bull. 54: 103–30.

Carr, E. H. [1961] 1964. *What Is History?* Harmondsworth, Eng. Carr's disdain for the practice of playing "parlour games" with the "might-have-beens of history" (p. 97) typifies the attitude of many historians.

Climo, T. A., and Howells, P.G.A. 1974. "Cause and Counterfactuals." *The Economic History Review*, 2d Series, 27: 461–68. A critique of J. D. Gould's "Hypothetical History," *The Economic History Review*, 2d Series, 22 (1969): 195–207, this article recognizes counterfactuals as "a fundamental part of the traditional conception of causation" (p. 461) but stresses the limitations of their use in causal analysis.

Cochran, Thomas C. 1969. "Economic History, Old and New." *AHR* 74: 1561–72.

Cohen, Morris R. 1942. "Causation and Its Application to History." *JHI* 3: 12–29.
" . . . all practical activity involves weighing the consequences of alternatives only
one of which is realized," writes Cohen. "Indeed, we cannot grasp the full
significance of what happened unless we have some idea of what the situation
would have been otherwise. Nor is there much logical force in the argument that
all our evidence bears on what did happen and not at all on what might have
happened" (p. 20).
Conrad, Alfred H., and Meyer, John R. [1957] 1964. "Economic Theory, Statistical
Inference, and Economic History." In Alfred H. Conrad and John R. Meyer, *The
Economics of Slavery and Other Studies in Econometric History*. Chicago: 3–30.
Davis, Lance. 1966. "Professor Fogel and the New Economic History." *The Economic
History Review*, 2d Series, 19: 657–63.
———. 1971. "Specification, Quantification, and Analysis in Economic History." In
George Rogers Taylor and Lucius F. Ellsworth, eds., *Approaches to American
Economic History*. Charlottesville, Va.: 106–20.
Fales, Walter. 1951. "Historical Facts." *JP* 48: 85–94. See n. 1 for a bibliography.
Fischer, David Hackett. 1970. *Historians' Fallacies: Toward a Logic of Historical
Thought*. New York.
Fogel, R. W. 1964. *Railroads and American Economic Growth: Essays in Econometric
History*. Baltimore.
———. 1966. "The New Economic History." *The Economic History Review*, 2d Series,
19: 642–56. Fogel's article cites various ways in which counterfactual analysis is
used in traditional economic history (p. 655). He argues that counterfactual propositions "can be verified in at least two ways. The first involves the determination
of whether the proposition asserted follows logically from its premises. The second
requires a determination of whether the assumptions of the model are empirically
valid. . . . A third level of verification, the test of the predictive power of a model,
may often be possible" (pp. 655–56; also n. 1, p. 656).
———. 1967. "The Specification Problem in Economic History." *The Journal of Economic History* 27: 283–308. This article repeats many of the arguments of Fogel
(1966).
Gerschenkron, Alexander. 1967. "The Discipline and I." *The Journal of Economic
History* 27: 443–59.
Goodman, Nelson. 1965. *Fact, Fiction and Forecast*. 2d ed. Indianapolis, Ind. Goodman's book contains references to the philosophical literature.
Green, George. [1968] 1970. "Comment." In Ralph L. Andreano, ed., *The New Economic History: Recent Papers on Methodology*. New York: 101–7.
Hughes, H. Stuart. 1960. "The Historian and the Social Scientist." *AHR* 66: 20–46.
McClelland, Peter, D. 1975. *Causal Explanation and Model Building in History, Economics, and the New Economic History*. Ithaca, N.Y. This is a thorough examination, which argues that counterfactual thinking is unavoidable in determining
the relative importance of factors in causing a given event but denies that counterfactuals are implicit in all causal reasoning (p. 152). McClelland identifies some
logical difficulties associated with the use of counterfactuals, such as the problem
of determining if the results of counter-to-fact reasoning are persuasive (pp. 146–
68). He concludes that the counterfactuals employed by econometric historians
"are . . . destined frequently to strain (although not necessarily rupture) the bonds
of credibility" (p. 168).

Murphy, George G. S. 1969. "On Counterfactual Propositions." *HT* Beih. 9: 14–38.

Neuburger, Hugh, and Stokes, Houston H. 1979. "The Anglo-German Trade Rivalry, 1887–1913: A Counterfactual Outcome and Its Implications." *Social Science History* 3: 187–201. The authors apply Markov probability analysis.

Nowell-Smith, P. H. 1971. *What Actually Happened*. Lawrence, Kans.

Redlich, Fritz. 1965. " 'New' and Traditional Approaches to Economic History and Their Interdependence." *Journal of Economic History* 25: 480–95.

———. [1968] 1970. "Potentialities and Pitfalls in Economic History." In Ralph L. Andreano, ed., *The New Economic History: Recent Papers on Methodology*. New York: 85–99.

Sources of Additional Information

For philosophical literature see R. S. Walters, "Contrary-to-Fact Conditional," *EP* 2 (1967): 212–16; also Nelson Goodman, "The Problem of Counterfactual Conditionals," *JP* 44 (Feb. 27, 1947): 113–28. On the benefits and pitfalls of counterfactual reasoning in history see Sidney Hook, *The Hero in History: A Study in Limitation and Possibility* (New York, 1943), especially chapter seven entitled " 'If' in History." Various passages in Murray G. Murphey, *Our Knowledge of the Historical Past* (Indianapolis, Ind., 1973), touch on the role of counterfactuals in historical explanation. For the special application of counterfactuals in economic history see the brief annotated bibliography in George Rogers Taylor and Lucius F. Ellsworth, *Approaches to Economic History* (Charlottesville, Va., 1971), pp. 130–32; also the footnote citations and bibliography in McClelland (1975) and Lance E. Davis, " 'And It Will Never Be Literature.' The New Economic History: A Critique" [1968], in Ralph L. Andreano, ed., *The New Economic History: Recent Papers on Methodology* (New York, 1970): 67–83. Stefano Fenoalter, "The Discipline and They: Notes on the Counterfactual Methodology and the 'New Economic History'," *The Journal of European Economic History*, 2 (1973): 729–46, argues that some of the counterfactual conclusions of econometric history are "untenable"—including some of Fogel's work on railroads. David F. Laschky, "Are Counterfactuals Necessary to 'The Discipline' and They?" *The Journal of European Economic History* 4 (1975): 481–85, stresses the "extreme difficulty in constructing sound, internally consistent counterfactual tests" (p. 485).

COVERING LAWS. Empirically verifiable generalizations from which, according to one theory of historical knowledge, historians derive explanations concerning the past.

The term *covering law* was first used by W. H. Dray (1957: 1) to designate the concept that underlies a controversial theory of historical EXPLANATION advanced by Carl G. Hempel ([1942] 1959), Karl Popper (1950: 445–49), and Morton White (1943). The "covering law model" of explanation is also variously known as the "deductive-nomological" theory, the "hypothetico-deductive model," the "regularity theory," the "Hempelian model," and the "positivist theory" (see POSITIVISM). "Covering law model" or "covering law theory" are, however, the most widely used labels. Hempel's position was originally conceived in opposition to the widely held idea that history is an "idiographic" discipline that—unlike natural science—does not appeal to or seek to discover general LAWS. The theory is based on the following premises: (1) all scientific explanation is identical in logical form; (2) scientific explanation is deductive and syllogistic; (3) history is (or should be) a branch of science; therefore (4) historical explanations must conform to the deductive pattern of scientific explanation. Since the 1940s various forms of the covering law theory have been advanced and its validity has been vigorously debated by philosophers. Most historians have either been uninterested in the controversy or have strongly opposed the idea that they explain the past by appealing to covering laws.

Popper and, especially, Hempel are the most important advocates of the theory. Despite certain differences (Donagan, 1964–65: 3–7; Perry, 1967: 27–29), both agree that historical explanations, in order to qualify as genuine and complete, must differ in no fundamental way from explanations in the natural sciences. The form of a complete historical explanation must be deductive; the major premise from which the conclusion is deduced must incorporate a universal law (Olafson, 1979: 2). (Strictly speaking, it was only the second part of this position that Dray originally referred to as the "covering law model." Nevertheless, the two ideas are customarily grouped together as the "covering law" theory.) A *general law* is defined as "a statement of universal conditional form which is capable of being confirmed or disconfirmed by suitable empirical findings" (Hempel, [1942] 1959: 345). Hempel declares himself "entirely neutral with respect to the problem of '*specifically historical laws*' " and does not attempt to indicate a "particular way of distinguishing historical from sociological and other laws"; the laws he alleges that historians use are normally physical, psychological, or sociological laws discovered by other (natural or social) scientists and borrowed by historians (p. 355). Usually, the historian is "not a producer of general laws, but a consumer of them. His position vis-a-vis the sciences is essentially parasitic" (Joynt and Rescher, 1961–62: 154). The general law "covers" the particular case "in the sense that the case is itself an instance of what has been stated by the law" (Mandelbaum, 1961–62: 235; Dray, 1957: 1); in Hempel's own words:

> In history as anywhere else in empirical science, the explanation of a phenomenon consists in subsuming it under general empirical laws; and the criterion of its soundness is . . . exclusively whether it rests on empirically well confirmed assumptions concerning initial conditions and general laws. ([1942] 1959: 353)

Hempel concedes that actual explanations produced by historians seldom explicitly satisfy this prescription; nevertheless, he maintains that any complete explanation must conform to it, at least implicitly. Neither he nor Popper are essentially concerned with actual historical practice but rather wish to outline a properly rigorous mode of explanation for history. According to this view most historians do not in fact construct bona fide scientific explanations but produce proto-scientific approximations of explanations, or "explanation sketches," that consist of "a more or less vague indication of the laws and initial conditions considered as relevant'' and that require '' 'filling out' in order to turn into a full-fledged explanation'' (Hempel, [1942] 1959: 351).

The theory has exercised a strong influence on many contemporary philosophers of science, although it has been vigorously attacked and various revisions have been suggested. The questions it raises have been largely responsible for the lively interest that has developed in "critical" PHILOSOPHY OF HISTORY since 1945. Even opponents of the theory often acknowledge their debt to its formulators (e.g., Donagan, 1964–65: 25; Perry, 1967: 46). The leading critics have been Dray (1957) and Donagan (1964–65). Most opponents agree that it is wrong to assume that explanation in the natural sciences must be the model for explanation in other fields. They stress that scholarship as it is in fact practiced by professional historians does not usually conform to the covering law paradigm, and they often defend existing historical practice as an autonomous and legitimate form of knowing (Mink, [1965] 1966; Goldstein, 1976). It is frequently argued that proper historical explanations do not depend at all on the appeal to general laws but proceed by COLLIGATION, that is, by locating whatever is to be explained in the context of its unique spatial and temporal setting (Walsh, [1951] 1960: 59–64). It is also suggested that illustrations of covering laws cited by supporters of the theory do not amount to genuine laws at all but are "nothing more than the immediate generalization of the particular historical explanation [they] purport to justify" (Goldstein, 1976: 96). Others object that the theory does not take the allegedly intrinsic "narrative character" of historical explanation into account (Porter, 1975: 299–301; see also NARRATIVE). On the other hand, some significant studies of the character of historical narrative attempt to incorporate the covering law theory (for example, Danto, 1964; M. White, 1965).

In response to criticisms, Hempel modified his position somewhat by dividing explanations into two general categories: "deductive-nomological" and "inductive probabilistic." Explanations in the former class are scientifically complete and correspond to his initial statement of the covering law theory. In the second category—into which most historical explanations fall—the generalization appealed to is not a universal law but a statement of statistical probability (Donagan, 1964–65: 6). This revision, however, fails to satisfy most critics (e.g., Fischer, 1970: 128–29, n. 38).

Historians with an active interest in the controversy—and they have been a small minority—generally display a profound skepticism toward the covering law model. By training, professional historians are usually eclectic "pluralists" in matters of theory and often resent the efforts of philosophical "outsiders" to reduce their mode of reasoning to one logical form (Krieger, 1963: 137). They frequently maintain that the appeal to general laws is not a significant part of historical explanation at all (Zagorin, 1959: 251). Many object that covering law theorists, unfamiliar with history as a discipline, unfairly seek to impose a logic on history that is simply inappropriate and does not accord with actual practice (Krieger, 1963; Leff, [1969] 1971: 66–90; Hexter, 1971: 14–18, 21–42). D. H. Fischer (1970: xii, 130) describes the model as a "Procrustean bed" in which covering law theorists would make historians lie "even if their heads must be removed to make them fit"; he declares that philosophers have "squandered" their time in an "absurd" effort to relate the theory to historical practice. Such sarcasm is fairly typical of professional historical opinion.

There are noteworthy exceptions, however. Some advocates of SOCIAL SCI-ENTIFIC HISTORY, for example, support the theory as part of their effort to make history conform more closely to the methods of the natural sciences (for instance, Fogel, 1966: 656). Hayden White (1972: 14), an intellectual historian, has accepted the theory as one *possible* way historians explain, although he adds that it is "not the only one, and it may not even be the most important one." Murray G. Murphey (1973) has attempted to adapt the theory to his idea of "limited" historical LAWS.

References

Danto, Arthur C. 1964. *Analytical Philosophy of History*. Cambridge.

Donagan, Alan. 1964–65. "Historical Explanation: The Popper-Hempel Theory Reconsidered." *HT* 4: 3–26. In this key source Donagan describes the covering law theory as an "infatuation" that "mutilate[s] research into human affairs by remodelling the social sciences into deformed likenesses of physics" (p. 25).

Dray, William. 1957. *Laws and Explanation in History*. Oxford. This is the most important early critique of the covering law theory.

Fischer, David Hackett. 1970. *Historians' Fallacies: Toward a Logic of Historical Thought*. New York.

Fogel, R. W. 1966. "The New Economic History." *The Economic History Review*, 2d Series, 19: 642–56.

Goldstein, Leon J. 1976. *Historical Knowing*. Austin, Tex.

Hempel, Carl G. [1942] 1959. "The Function of General Laws in History." In Gardiner: 344–56. In terms of its impact, this is perhaps the most important single publication in current critical philosophy of history.

Hexter, J. H. 1971. *The History Primer*. New York.

Joynt, Carey B., and Rescher, Nicholas. 1961–62. "The Problem of Uniqueness in History." *HT* 1: 150–62.

Krieger, Leonard. 1963. "Comments on Historical Explanation." In Hook: 136–42.

Leff, Gordon. [1969] 1971. *History and Social Theory*. Garden City, N.Y.

Mandelbaum, Maurice. 1961–62. "Historical Explanation: The Problem of 'Covering Laws'." *HT* 1: 229–42. Mandelbaum places the controversy in the context of the past century of philosophical discussion.

Mink, Louis O. [1965] 1966. "The Autonomy of Historical Understanding." In Dray: 16–92.

Murphey, Murray G. 1973. *Our Knowledge of the Historical Past*. Indianapolis, Ind.

Olafson, Frederick A. 1979. *The Dialectic of Action: A Philosophical Interpretation of History and the Humanities*. Chicago. Chapter one contains a concise introduction to the controversy.

Perry, L. R. 1967. "The Covering Law Theory of Historical Explanation." In W. H. Burston and D. Thompson, eds., *Studies in the Nature and Teaching of History*. London: 27–48.

Popper, Karl. 1950. *The Open Society and Its Enemies*. Princeton, N.J. This book cites sources on the nineteenth-century prehistory of the covering law controversy, pp. 722–23, n. 3. Popper maintains that he was the first to advance the covering law theory in his *Logik der Forschung* (Vienna, 1935); regardless, Hempel ([1942] 1959) has had the greatest impact.

Porter, Dale H. 1975. "History as Process." *HT* 14: 297–313. This article contains a concise summary of the covering law debate, pp. 298–301.

Walsh, W. H. [1951] 1960. *Philosophy of History: An Introduction.* New York.

White, Hayden. 1972. "The Structure of Historical Narrative." *Clio* 1: 5–20.

White, Morton. 1943. "Historical Explanation." *Mind*, N.S., 52: 212–29.

Zagorin, Perez. 1959. "Historical Knowledge: A Review Article on the Philosophy of History." *JMH* 31: 243–55. Zagorin summarizes a point made by many critics: "the historian need not, and usually does not, make use of laws at all. Naturally, he takes for granted the truth of all laws, physical, psychological, and others, that have been established. He assumes, for example, that the bullet at Sarajevo followed a path accountable for by the laws of mechanics. But these laws do not enter into his explanations in the sense of determining their logical structure or giving them their force" (p. 251).

Sources of Additional Information

See also LAWS. *HT Beih.*, Birkos and Tambs, and Stephens are indispensable bibliographies. A number of anthologies of writings in the philosophy of history include selections and helpful editorial comments on the controversy: Hook, Gardiner, Dray, and Nash. The latter three, especially Nash (pp. 157–58), contain additional bibliographical information. The citations in chapter one of Olafson (1979) are also an important source of bibliography. There is a useful introduction to the subject in William H. Dray, *Philosophy of History* (Englewood Cliffs, N.J., 1964), pp. 5–18. The early literature is reviewed in Rudolph H. Weingartner, "The Quarrel about Historical Explanation," *JP* 58 (1961): 29–45 (reprinted in Nash), and some of the refinements of the Hempel thesis are summarized in William Dray, "The Historical Explanation of Actions Reconsidered," in Hook: 105–35.

CRISIS. A short period of decisive challenge, a turning point that determines the survival of a person, institution, or condition, or its disappearance.

Crisis is one of the most loosely used words in the vocabulary of social analysis. Occasionally, it is effectively used in the succinct sense of "moments of vital decision [which] quickly pass" (Trevor-Roper, 1981: 360). However, indiscriminate use has inflated and trivialized the word to such a degree that its value as an analytical term is seriously threatened; as a journalistic catch-word it actually impedes understanding. This danger is sometimes acknowledged (e.g., Le Roy Ladurie, 1981: 270); yet "crisis" remains one of the most frequently and thoughtlessly employed notions in historiography.

Some idea of the volume of scholarship employing the notion may be gained by consulting the subject index of any annual compilation of the *Social Sciences Citation Index.* The fashionable term is used to designate situations that range from the urgently "revolutionary" to the merely "problematic" or virtually any sort of tension or disagreement in politics or international affairs. *Crisis* is even more nebulous than some other ambiguous terms such as REVOLUTION and PROGRESS since, unlike them, it is not "heavily burdened with specifically historical identifications" (Starn, 1971: 17); in this regard, it closely resembles *tragedy*, another protean term often abused by historians.

Specialized dictionaries and encyclopedias are not often helpful in obtaining a grasp of the term's possible legitimate meanings, since they tend to offer extremely broad or conflicting definitions, definitions that are too narrow, or definitions that contradict actual usage (for instance, Reading, 1977: 53; Zadrozny, 1959: 74; Masur, 1973: 593). The 1931 edition of the *Encyclopedia of Social Sciences* defined the term exclusively from the specialized perspective of economics, characterizing *crisis* as a "grave and sudden disturbance of economic equilibrium" (Lescure, 1931: 595). In contrast, the editors of the 1968 *International Encyclopedia of the Social Sciences* assigned the term to a specialist in "decision making," whose entry was written from the special point of view of that novel field of endeavor (Robinson, 1968). The idea of radical change within a "short span of time," or "revolutionary" change (Brinton, 1939: 145), is often considered important; yet in practice scholars frequently use the term to refer to changes occurring over periods of a century (Aston, 1965) or even several centuries (Crocker, 1959; 1964: 433; Le Roy Ladurie, 1981: 272). After exhorting his readers to exercise caution in using the word, one authority refers melodramatically to the "permanent crisis in which we are forced to live [today]" and invokes the hackneyed notion of the "crisis which has engulfed our century" (Masur, 1973: 594–95).

Does the history of historiographical usage suggest any genuinely disciplined and useful ways in which the term can be employed? Actually, the fact that the term is used so indiscriminately is ironic, since its ancient Greek root meant "to separate or to divide" (Masur, 1973: 589; *OED*; Starn, 1971: 3), that is, to "discriminate" or "decide." *Critical* is a related term. Early historiographical use was adapted from the law; Thucydides (c. 460–c. 400 B.C.) used the term six times in his *Peloponnesian War* in the sense of judicial decision and in the wider sense of decision in general—for example, his assertion that war "rendered the crisis" (verdict) between the Persians and the Greeks (Starn, 1971: 4).

Among the Greeks the word also carried a medical meaning—the turning point that "occurs in diseases whenever the diseases increase in intensity or go away or change into another disease or end altogether" (quoted in Starn, 1971: 4). Thucydides also used the term in this sense in his account of the plague in Athens. Starn, in fact, argues that Thucydides

> may have adopted [the medical concept] as a general model of historical expla-
> nation, as a rationale for establishing the facts of a case and ordering them into
> patterns of development. . . . Like the physician, the historian had to get his facts
> straight and place them in relation to decisive turning points, their antecedents and
> consequences, observed and plotted as on a fever chart. (1971: 4)

Historians' use of the idea after Thucydides has not been carefully studied; "a precise history of the word does not exist" (Masur, 1973: 590). Starn (1971: 5) believes that the idea "did not appear significantly in Roman, medieval or Renaissance historians," although it did survive in medical usage. In this form it entered English, as early as the mid-sixteenth century (*OED*). The term also acquired a related astrological meaning: "a conjunction of the planets which determines the issue of a disease or critical point in the [general] course of events" (*OED*). The association with astrology may be responsible for the word's reemergence as a social term, beginning in the seventeenth century (Starn, 1971: 5), since some other modern terms relating to change (such as REVOLUTION) share an astrological pedigree. At any rate, the broad modern sense of *historical crisis* had been established by the early seventeenth century: "a vitally important or decisive stage in the progress of anything; a turning point; also, a state of affairs in which a decisive change for better or worse is imminent" (*OED*). By the eighteenth century, use of the term in relation to religious, political, and economic matters had become relatively common, as reflected in Thomas Paine's *American Crisis* (1776) and in the text of Edward Gibbon's *Decline and Fall of the Roman Empire* ([1776–88] 1952: 518).

In the nineteenth century, the idea of "crisis" was inflated to

> cover virtually any time of trouble or tension. . . . Many of the great national histories of the nineteenth century—those of Ranke, Sybel, Michelet, Thiers and Taine, for example—were "crisis histories" in the sense that they focused on critical moments [decisive turning points] when national character and institutions were thought to have been decisively shaped and tested. (Starn, 1971: 6, 9)

The concept's popularity may have been related to the vogue of organic metaphors as modes of conceptualization, which encouraged the belief that society is like a living organism that experiences growth, health, sickness, recovery, or possibly death.

This is evident, for example, in the work of social theorists such as Marx and Engels and historians such as the Swiss scholar Jacob Burckhardt. In the early nineteenth century, *crisis* had won popularity in the vocabulary of political economy as a label for the periodic outbreaks of disorder that characterized the economic system of CAPITALISM. Using this meaning as a starting point, Marx and Engels and their followers broadened the notion of crisis into a comprehensive social theory in which every stage of economic development (except communism) had its inevitable turning point, leading to its decline and destruction.

The work of Jacob Burckhardt (1818–97) is even more symptomatic of the diffuse associations and melodramatic connotations of urgency that the word acquired. Burckhardt employed *crisis* to explain the general pattern of historical change, and his use forshadows in some ways certain twentieth-century theories of REVOLUTION, notably that of Crane Brinton (1938 [1965]). He developed his ideas in lectures delivered at Basel in 1868, couched in the romantic imagery of storm, stress, spiritualism, and the sublime. Burckhardt's vivid although rambling thoughts are based on reflections on Greek and Roman history, the Reformation, and especially the French Revolution; they amount to a general view of "the accelerated movements of the whole process of history . . . of crises and revolutions" (Burckhardt, 1943: 79). Everything is portrayed in the imagery of violent climatic change and pathology and subsumed under what Burckhardt calls the "theory of storms"—"the occasional abrupt absorption of all other movements, the general ferment of all the rest of life, the ruptures and reactions" (p. 79). *Crises* are "accelerations of the historical process"; he cites as examples sweeping collective experiences such as the *Völkerwanderung* of late antiquity and (more generally) war, which he regards as "a crisis in the relations of the peoples and a necessary factor of higher development" (pp. 257, 259). Burckhardt's metaphors are organic, based on the idea of "accelerations" in "growth" and "development." In a crisis, the "historical process is suddenly accelerated in terrifying fashion. Developments which otherwise take centuries seem to flit by like phantoms in months or weeks" (p. 267). Moreover he revives the ancient medical analogy, comparing crisis to "an epidemic" and "a fever"; when the "hour and the real cause has come, the infection flashes like an electric spark over hundreds of miles. . . . The message goes through the air. . . . *Things must change*" (pp. 276, 289, 269). Throughout, crises are viewed as storms that clear the air, terrifying but necessary cathartic trials that humanity must periodically endure in order to grow: "The crisis is to be regarded as a new nexus of growth. Crises clear the ground, firstly of a host of institutions from which life has long since departed, and which, given their historical privilege, could not have been swept away in any other fashion" (p. 289). In the end, however, the "permanent result . . . remains astonishingly meagre in comparison with the great efforts and passions which rise to the surface during the crisis" (p. 281).

Burckhardt distinguishes between "real" crises and "counterfeit" crises — "so called crises" and "mere tempestuous episodes" (pp. 265, 273); he does not, however, provide any real criteria for doing so. He does assert that "genuine crises are rare." By *genuine crisis* he seems to mean what might loosely be termed "revolution," since he states that they are situations that lead to "vital transformations" in which the "political and social foundations of the State" are "shaken" (p. 266). As Starn (1971: 9) notes, "In the end Burckhardt's theory of crisis is not a theory at all but an affirmation of the mysterious vitality, variety, and challenging discontinuities of history."

The experience of World War I—called the "world crisis" by Winston Churchill (1923–29) and others—pushed the notion of crisis into the forefront of western consciousness, both popular and scholarly. The fashionable use of the word by economists in an apparently technical sense (e.g., Lescure, 1931) in the 1920s and 1930s "carried the cachet of a scientific-seeming organicism with an invitation to a sense of historical drama" (Starn, 1971: 10). The term gained further scholarly popularity in connection with research on the economic origins of the French Revolution, and the American historian Crane Brinton ([1938] 1965) appealed to the idea in both a metaphorical and "social scientific" sense in the first chapter of his widely read *Anatomy of Revolution*. Social scientific usage was further broadened by popular and scholarly perceptions of the rise of FASCISM, diagnosed as a symptom of the "crisis of liberalism," and which gave rise to a whole genre of "crisis literature" (Starn, 1971: 11–12) (see LIBERALISM).

The problems of usage associated with *crisis* will not be solved by efforts to refine more precise definitions. The notion should be recognized as a metaphor and loose synonym for "turning point" and used with discretion. Thucydides worked effectively with the judicial and medical associations of the term centuries ago. One European historian has recently advised historians to avoid mere chronology and concentrate on *crises*—understood as

> definite point[s] of rupture between two methods of production, between two systems of social relationships, between two dominant ideologies. The crisis should be the moment of change which sheds light on all the elements of social formation, and all the levels of reality" (Benoit Verhaegen, quoted in Dhondt, 1971: 57)

However, the word itself has been recently so overworked that considerations of clarity and taste suggest that it be avoided in the great majority of cases.

References

Aston, Trevor, ed. 1965. *Crisis in Europe, 1560–1660*. London.
Brinton, Crane. 1939. "The 'New History' and 'Past Everything'." *The American Scholar* 8: 144–57.
————. [1938] 1965. *The Anatomy of Revolution*. New York.
Burckhardt, Jacob. 1943. *Force and Freedom: Reflections on History*. New York.
Churchill, Winston. 1923–29. *The World Crisis*. New York.
Crocker, Lester G. 1959. *An Age of Crisis: Man and World in Eighteenth-Century French Thought*. Baltimore. Crocker interprets the period from the late seventeenth to the late twentieth century as an age of "crisis."
————. 1964. "Recent Interpretations of the French Enlightenment." *Cahiers d'histoire mondiale* 8: 426–56.
Dhondt, Jan. 1971. "Recurrent History." *Diogenes* 75: 24–57.
Gibbon, Edward. [1776–88] 1952. *The Portable Gibbon: The Decline and Fall of the Roman Empire*. New York.
Le Roy Ladurie, Emmanuel. 1981. "The Crisis and the Historian." In Emmanuel Le Roy Ladurie, *The Mind and Method of the Historian*. Chicago: 270–89.
Lescure, Jean. 1931. "Crises." *ESS* 4: 595–99. The usage in this entry was dictated by the economic depression of the early 1930s; Lescure states that "it would seem that for the term crisis one may henceforth substitute that of depression."
Masur, Gerhard. 1973. "Crisis in History." *DHI* 1: 589–96. This entry includes a helpful bibliography. Masur defines *crisis* as "a precipitous change over a short span of time affecting the very vitals of institutions, mores, modes of thought and feeling, power structures, and economic organizations."
Reading, Hugo F. 1977. *A Dictionary of the Social Sciences*. London. Reading defines *crisis* as "a turning point faced by a society."

Robinson, James A. 1968. "Crises." *IESS* 3: 510–14.

Starn, Randolph. 1971. "Historians and 'Crisis'." *Past and Present* 52: 3–22. This is the most important analysis of the subject. Starn suggests that Thomas S. Kuhn has developed a workable theory of historical crises in his *The Structure of Scientific Revolutions* (Chicago, 1960).

Trevor-Roper, Hugh. 1981. "History and Imagination." In Hugh Lloyd-Jones, Valerie Pearl and Blair Worden, eds., *History and Imagination: Essays in Honor of H. R. Trevor-Roper.* London: 356–69.

Zadrozny, John T. 1959. *Dictionary of Social Science.* Washington, D.C. This dictionary defines *crisis* as "any event which disrupts an established way of behaving on the part of a person, or a group of people, and which points up a conflict which the person or the group, is not prepared to meet."

Sources of Additional Information

The footnote citations in Starn (1971) and the short bibliography in Masur (1973) are the best introductions to the literature, which is not extensive. Some relevant titles are cited in Berding: 250–62. For additional comments about overuse of the term see Elizabeth L. Eisenstein, "Clio and Chronos: An Essay on the Making and Breaking of History-Book Time," *HT Beih.* 6: 38. Since the 1950s, historians of early modern Britain have been preoccupied with a "crisis" in the seventeenth century; on this see various issues of the British journal *Past and Present* since 1954—for example, E. J. Hobsbawm, "The General Crisis of the European Economy in the Seventeenth Century," *Past and Present*, No. 5 (1954): 33–53, and No. 6 (1954): 44–65; also Aston (1965). For a recent interpretation of crisis in the thought of Karl Marx see Melvin Rader, *Marx's Interpretation of History* (New York, 1979), especially pp. 186–99. Among the many historical studies that use the notion of crisis as a broad conceptual framework see, for example, Paul Hazard, *La crise de la conscience européenne, 1680–1715* (Paris, 1935) (published in English as *The European Mind, 1680–1715* [London, 1953]), and Hans Baron, *The Crisis of the Early Italian Renaissance* (Princeton, N.J., 1955).

CRITICISM. 1. The appraisal of historical EVIDENCE for the purpose of determining its origin, authenticity, and credibility—that is, "source criticism." 2. Less frequently, analysis and evaluation of the written work of historians.

Kritikós—from the ancient Greek *krités*, "a judge," and *krineín*, "to judge"—was used to designate "a judge of literature" as early as the late fourth century B.C.; it passed into Latin as *criticus*. The word fell out of use in the Middle Ages but was revived by classical scholars of the RENAISSANCE to mean the editing of old texts. In Jan Wower's *Tractatio de Polymathia* (1602), for example, the neo-Latin *critica* refers to *iudicium* (establishment of textual authenticity) and *emendation* (correct interpretation) (Wellek, 1963: 22, 24).

The term entered the vernacular languages in the seventeenth century—for example, Richard Simon's *Histoire critique du Vieux Testament* (1678). Francis Bacon's *Advancement of Learning* (1605) discriminates between "critical" and "pedantical" approaches to knowledge and defines five characteristics of critical knowledge: the correction of texts, the explanation of meaning, historical analysis (placing the work in temporal context), the evaluation of texts, and analysis of syntax. By the eighteenth century the term's field of meaning, originally narrowly restricted to classical philology, had broadened to include general problems of judgment and epistemology (Wellek, 1963: 25–26)—as, for example, in Immanuel Kant's *Kritik der reinen Vernunft* (1781).

In modern scholarship the term may refer narrowly to the philological analysis of texts or, more broadly, to the interpretation and judgment of either fiction or scholarly writing. Since the late seventeenth century (e.g., Dryden's "Grounds of Criticism in Tragedy" [1679]; Alexander Pope's *Essay on Criticism* [1711]), *criticism* has been widely used in English to designate literary theory, poetics, and, indeed, "all study of literature" (Wellek, 1963: 3, 21; Frye, 1957).

In historiography, both the narrow and broad meanings of *criticism* were established in early nineteenth-century German scholarship—for example, Leopold von Ranke's *Zur Kritik neuerer Geschichtsschreiber* (1824), which was simultaneously a treatise on research methodology and a verdict on the work of fellow historians. For most historians, however, *criticism* traditionally refers to the narrower meaning, "source criticism"—the application of standard techniques for determining the origin, authenticity, and meaning of EVIDENCE about the past (e.g., Bourne, 1901: vii–viii; Bury, [1902] 1972: 211–12; Hockett, 1955: 9; Müller, 1967: 303). (Discussions of criticism in this sense often concentrate on the analysis of *written* evidence; this is a flaw in the literature. It must be stressed that historical evidence is not limited to written documentation and that the general principles of source criticism apply equally to written and non-written sources.) These procedures were codified by philologists, monastic scholars, and antiquarians between the sixteenth and eighteenth centuries (Haddock, 1980: 32–59—see ANTIQUARIANISM) and established in academic historiography at the turn of the nineteenth century, particularly through the example of the German scholars Barthold Georg Niebuhr (1776–1831) and Ranke (1795–1886) (Gooch [1913] 1959: 14–23, 72–97; Guilland, 1915: 41–119). The techniques are also often referred to collectively as "the historical METHOD."

Following the convention established by Ernst Bernheim ([1914] 1970: 326), source criticism is traditionally subdivided into two categories: "external (or lower) criticism" and "internal (or higher) criticism" (e.g., Langlois and Seignobos, [1898] 1926: 66–67; Johnson, 1926: 51, 75; Garraghan, 1946: 168; Renier, 1950: 108; Hockett, 1955: 14). *External criticism* ascertains the *origin* and *authenticity* of the written source (date and location of origin, authorship, historical antecedents), eliminates possible textual corruptions (falsifications, interpolations, and so on), and restores written documentation to its original form (i.e., "textual criticism"). *Internal criticism*, which follows the preliminary operations of external criticism, determines the *meaning* and *credibility* of information contained in the source; it renders a verdict, in other words, on the source's significance as historical evidence.

It should be noted that external and internal *criticism* differs from questions of external and internal *evidence*. The two sets of terms are sometimes interchanged, with resulting confusion. For example, *internal evidence* (evidence based on material found within a written document, such as style, content, and script, as opposed to *external evidence*, or evidence extraneous to the document) may be employed in solving a question of *external criticism*, such as the author's identity. "What many, if not most writers have in mind when they speak of internal criticism," Garraghan notes (1946: 169), "is not discussion of a problem of credibility (Bernheim), but the application of internal criteria of evidence to any problem whatsoever of criticism, whether external or internal."

Aside from the narrow meaning of "source criticism," historians occasionally use the term *criticism* in the broader sense of inquiry into the nature and judgment of their own scholarship. This usage (also sometimes referred to as METHODOLOGY) corresponds to the idea that criticism is the "science of judging" (White, 1974: 760), and "a critic is a person able and willing to go over somebody else's thoughts for himself to see if they have been well done" (Collingwood, [1946] 1956: 252).

There is considerable variation in the ways this broad notion of criticism may be understood. For example, book reviews, review articles, critical bibliographies, and monographs that "critically appraise" historical publications logically fall into this category (Caughey, 1954). More specifically, "historical criticism" may be understood as the analysis of history as a general way of knowing (Beard and Vagts (1937: 465)—what since 1945 has come to be known among philosophers as "analytical" or "critical" PHILOSOPHY OF HISTORY. Or it may be understood as a branch of semantics concerned with "language as a social instrument and thought as social behavior"; J. G. A. Pocock, for example, believes that:

> The historian's employment of his professional vocabulary forms the main target of historical criticism, or should do so were that criticism specialized to a proper breadth of variety. . . . [It] proceeds by enquiring where the historian found the terms of his conceptual vocabulary; how they were normally used and how he used them; what logical sociological, and other implications they carried; how their significance changed as, and has changed since, he used them; and how his construction of his statements was affected by the state of his language at the time when he made use of it. (1963–64: 120)

Criticism may also be understood as "literary criticism of history," that is, an approach to the study of historical writing that combines "literary and intellectual history with literary criticism" (Levin, 1959: viii, x; 1967: 22; Lewis, 1976: 403). This form of analysis

> concentrates on individual works of history and how they are conceived and written. . . . [The critic's] ultimate concern will be the value of the entire work rather than merely the validity of its paraphraseable content, its argument. He will devote himself to the relationship between that argument and the form and language in which it is presented. (Levin, 1967: 22)

References

Beard, Charles A. and Vagts, Alfred. 1937. "Currents of Thought in Historiography." *AHR* 42: 460–83.

Bernheim, Ernst. [1914] 1970. *Lehrbuch der historischen Methode und der Geschichtsphilosophie*. New York. First edition published in 1889. This is the classic manual of historical methodology.

Bourne, Edward Gaylord. 1901. *Essays in Historical Criticism*. New York. This is a good example of the traditional understanding of "historical criticism" as source criticism. Interestingly, Bourne apologizes for including some essays that today might be included in the category of criticism (understood as the evaluation of the writing of historians) but that did not fit his narrow conception of the idea (p. viii).

Bury, J. B. [1902] 1972. "The Science of History." In Stern: 210–23. For Bury, *criticism* means the "microscopic criticism" that "gave historians the idea of a systematic and minute method of analysing their sources" (p. 212).

Caughey, John W. 1954. "Trends in Historical Criticism." *The Mississippi Valley Historical Review* 40: 619–28. This is an interesting plea for more *historical criticism*, understood as the "critical appraisal" of published historical studies (p. 620).

Collingwood, R. G. [1946] 1956. *The Idea of History*. New York.

Frye, Northrop. 1957. *Anatomy of Criticism: Four Essays*. Princeton, N.J. This is an influential recent theoretical study by a famous literary scholar.

Garraghan, Gilbert J. 1946. *A Guide to Historical Method*. New York. This book is sometimes confusing, particularly in use of the terms *higher* and *lower* criticism.

Gooch, G. P. [1913] 1959. *History and Historians in the Nineteenth Century*. Boston.

Guilland, Antoine. 1915. *Modern Germany and Her Historians*. New York.

Haddock, B. A. 1980. *An Introduction to Historical Thought*. London.

Hockett, Homer Carey. 1955. *The Critical Method in Historical Research and Writing*. New York. Hockett believes that the principles of source criticism are "in reality little more than common-sense rules carefully formulated" (p. 9).

Johnson, Allen. 1926. *The Historian and Historical Evidence*. New York.

Langlois, Ch. V., and Seignobos, Ch. [1898] 1926. *Introduction to the Study of History*. New York. This book was very influential in the early twentieth century.

Levin, David. 1959. *History as Romantic Art*. Stanford, Calif.

———. 1967. *In Defense of Historical Literature*. New York. Levin presents a well-argued plea on behalf of "literary criticism of history." See especially chapter one.

Lewis, Merrill. 1976. "Language, Literature, Rhetoric, and the Shaping of the Historical Imagination of Frederick Jackson Turner." *Pacific Historical Review* 45: 399–424. Lewis looks forward to the establishment of a "formal 'historical criticism' which will do for history what literary criticism has done for its imaginative counterparts—the novel, the poem, and the drama" (p. 403).

Müller, Gert. 1967. "History as a Rigorous Discipline." *HT* 6: 299–312.

Pocock, J. G. A. 1963–64. Review of J. H. Hexter, *Reappraisals in History*. *HT* 3: 121–35. Pocock uses Hexter's book as a model for the semantic approach to historical criticism since it highlights "the use of concepts and language by historians" and argues that historians must assume "critical responsibility for their own professional vocabulary" (p. 122).

Renier, G. J. 1950. *History: Its Purpose and Method*. Boston.
Wellek, René. 1963. *Concepts of Criticism*. New Haven, Conn. See especially the second
      essay, "The Term and Concept of Literary Criticism."
White, Hayden. 1974. "Structuralism and Popular Culture." *Journal of Popular Culture*
      7: 759–75.

Sources of Additional Information

According to Wellek (1963: 21), "there seems to be practically no literature on the
history of the term 'criticism' or even 'critic'." Of related general interest is Wellek's
own entry, "Literary Criticism," in *DHI* 1 (1973): 596–607, which includes a short but
well-chosen list of titles. See also the article "Textual Criticism" in the *Encyclopedia
Britannica* 24, 11th ed. (1911): 708–15; chapter three of Marc Bloch's *Historian's Craft*
(New York, 1953), "Historical Criticism"; and chapter three of Peter Burke's *Renaissance Sense of the Past* (London, 1969). Hockett (1955: 265–66) contains a brief bibliography of manuals of historical method; more extensive are the citations in Robert
Marichal, "La critique des textes," in Charles Samaran, ed., *L'historie et ses méthodes*
(Paris, 1961): 1360–66, and Berding: 25–28. See also the short entry *Ouellen* (sources)
in Erich Bayer, ed., *Wörterbuch zur Geschichte: Begriffe und Fachausdrücke* (Stuttgart,
1974). For a concise history of historical source criticism, see chapter seven of Herbert
Butterfield, *The Origins of History* (New York, 1981). *Clio*, an American journal founded
in 1971, is largely devoted to the literary criticism of historiography. Among the individual
scholars who have attempted to implement David Levin's call for a criticism in this sense
are Gene Wise, "Implicit Irony in Perry Miller's *New England Mind*," *JHI* 29 (1968):
579–600, and Richard Reinitz, "The Use of Irony by Historians and Vice-Versa: Toward
a Methodology of Liberation," *Clio* 6 (Spring 1977): 275–88.

CULTURAL HISTORY. A subfield of history that attempts to achieve an
      integrated treatment of human activity—literary, aesthetic, intellectual, and
      so on, as well as political, social, and economic—through the study of social
      forms, symbols, metaphors, styles, modes of thought.

Cultural history, one of the oldest subfields of modern historiography, is
presently beset by many doubts and difficulties (Gilbert, 1960: 40, 56). Some
scholars argue that the idea of cultural history is too broad and imprecise to be
the basis for a distinct specialization with its own method and its own goals
(Ritter, 1951: 294, 300–301). The recent publication of widely praised examples
of the genre, however (e.g., Le Roy Ladurie, 1978; Schorske, 1980), indicates
that the concept remains very much alive.

The expression *culture history* (*Culturgeschichte*) was first employed in German at least as early as the 1780s; the earliest known uses of the term appeared
in Johann Christoph Adelung's *Versuch einer Geschichte der Cultur des Men-
schlichen Geschlechts* (1782) and D. H. Hergewisch's *Allgemeine Uebersicht
der teutschen Culturgeschichte* (1788). Between 1843 and 1852 Gustav E.
Klemm published a ten-volume *Allgemeine Culturgeschichte der Menschheit*.
By the 1890s, the term *cultural history* (*Culturgeschichte* or *Kulturgeschichte*)
was sufficiently established in general German usage to be included in M.

Heyne's *Deutsches Wörterbuch* (1890–95) (Kroeber and Kluckhohn, 1952: 31, 14).

Among the early practitioners of the genre were Voltaire (1694–1778) and the German philosopher Johann Gottfried Herder (1744–1803). Perhaps the first great expression of the idea was Voltaire's *Age of Louis XIV* (1751)—a study designed to provide a comprehensive account not only of politics but of "philosophy, oratory, poetry and criticism; to show the progress of painting, sculpture and music; of jewelry, tapestry making, glassblowing, gold-cloth weaving, and watchmaking" (Voltaire, [1738] 1972: 40). Aside from the comprehensive attitude and "synthetic" impulse (which have ever since typified the cultural history approach) Voltaire exhibited a second attitude that has, until very recently, been characteristic of the genre: he proposed to focus on only the highest achievements of human endeavor, to "depict only the geniuses that have excelled in these undertakings" (p. 40). Despite occasional nods in the direction of folklore and "popular culture," most scholarly cultural history has been written by professional aesthetes for narrow, highly educated audiences—although this fact has sometimes been obscured by the professed intent of many authors to reach a "general" readership, as opposed to an audience of specialists. Traditionally, the object of cultural history has been culture understood as "high culture"— art, literature, and the life-style of the well-to-do—as opposed to culture in the modern anthropological sense, that is, the total complex of a way of life, material and social as well as intellectual and spiritual (see CULTURE).

The two undisputed classics of the genre are Jacob Burckhardt's *Civilization of the Renaissance in Italy* (1860) and Johan Huizinga's *Waning of the Middle Ages* (1919). These two books, the one by a Swiss, the other by a Dutch historian, represent cultural history in the grand manner; they are panoramas of whole civilizations at particular points in time. Efforts to define the concept of cultural history usually involve an analysis of these two works.

Huizinga himself made a major contribution to the theory of cultural history in his essay "The Task of Cultural History" ([1929] 1959; also, Colie, 1964).

> The object of cultural history is culture [wrote Huizinga], and this concept . . . will always be exceedingly difficult to define. . . . Cultural history is distinct from political and economic history in that it is worthy of the name only to the extent that it concentrates on deeper, general themes. The state and commerce exist as configurations, but also in their details. Culture exists only as a configuration. The details of cultural history belong to the realm of morals, customs, folklore, antiquities, and easily degenerate into curios. ([1929] 1959: 27–28)

Huizinga defined the key problems of cultural history as

> problems of the form, structure, and function of social phenomena. . . . The cultural historian . . . not only sketches the contours of the forms he designs, but colors them by means of intuition and illuminates them with visionary suggestion . . . the great cultural historians have always been historical morphologists: seekers after the forms of life, thought, custom, knowledge, art. (p. 59)

Furthermore:

> Only when the scholar turns to determining the patterns of life, art, and thought
> *taken all together* [emphasis added] can there actually be a question of cultural
> history. The nature of those patterns is not set. They obtain their form only beneath
> our hands. And for this reason—that cultural history is to such a great extent the
> product of the free spirit of scholars and thinkers—greater caution is required in
> formulating the questions. (p. 28)

This characteristic emphasis on intangible "configurations" as the object of
inquiry in cultural history—"forms" or "patterns" of social life impressionistically given shape "beneath our hands"—has aroused considerable skepticism
regarding the field's scholarly legitimacy (cf. Heaton, [1943] 1950: 104–5; also
Barzun, [1956] 1972: 388).

Even leading practitioners of the approach—for example, Gombrich (1969)—
call attention to the questionable *a priori* assumptions of the tradition. Like
INTELLECTUAL HISTORY (to which some scholars would subordinate it [e.g.,
Darnton, 1980]), cultural history owes much to nineteenth-century philosophical
and historiographical IDEALISM. Nineteenth-century idealists made major contributions to the methodological underpinnings of cultural history; especially
significant were ideas of the philosopher G. W. F. Hegel (1770–1831), although
Hegel is not remembered as a cultural historian. Gombrich (1969: 6) persuasively
argues that both cultural history (*Kulturgeschichte*) and the overlapping concept
of *Geistesgeschichte* (history of the human spirit)—as they developed under the
late-nineteenth-century inspiration of Burckhardt, Wilhelm Dilthey, Karl Lamprecht, Aby Warburg, and Huizinga—were based on dubious Hegelian assumptions. Both were based on the idea that it was possible to analyze literature, the
arts, society, and ideas as a unit. This is reflected primarily in the "exegetic
method" that they used, based on the assumption of the existence of the "structural unity of culture" (Gombrich, 1969: 27), that is, the inner connectedness
of all aspects of life in a given society. Gombrich maintains that most of this
"study of structures and patterns . . . is rarely free of Hegelian holism" (p. 46).
In his lectures on the philosophy of history, Hegel had maintained that all social
phenomena represent expressions of a hidden "spirit" that manifests itself in
different places and times in various unique ways and is the common reference
point for all social life. All historical phenomena—religion, law, customs, politics, ethics, science, technology, art, and so on—are integrally interrelated as
a result of the fact that they are outward expressions of this "spirit." Spirit,
then, provided the cohesion for later works of cultural history; it was a hidden
essence—a "common centre" (p. 10).

> Postulating [*a priori*] the unity of all manifestations of a civilization, the [exegetic]
> method consists in taking various elements of culture, say Greek architecture and
> Greek philosophy, and asking how they can be shown to be expressions of the
> same spirit. The end of such an interpretation must always be a triumphant Eu-

clidean Q.E.D., since Hegel has bequeathed to the historian that very task: to find
in every factual detail the general principle that underlies it. (pp. 24–25)

One begins by begging the question, assuming that all social phenomena are
related; the achievement of the synthesis thus becomes a self-fulfilling prophecy.
Gombrich conceded (p. 30) that "obviously there is something in the Hegelian
intuition that nothing in life is ever isolated, that any event and any creation of
a period is connected by a thousand threads with the culture in which it is
embedded." But he adds, it is "one thing to see the interconnectedness of things,
another to postulate that all aspects of a culture can be traced back to one key
cause of which they are the manifestations" (p. 30).

With Burckhardt, Dilthey, and Lamprecht, there was a shift away from Hegel's
original concept of "national spirit" toward collective psychology; the underlying essence was assumed to be a mentality, style, or "spirit" of the age (see
ZEITGEIST). This assumption of an underlying "spirit" or essence imparts a
unifying quality to all aspects of social life and provides the basis for the traditional view in cultural history that a synthetic pattern can be uncovered.

Today, the line between "cultural" and "intellectual" history remains hazy,
a situation that promises to persist as long as historians—under the influence of
the anthropological concept of culture and the impact of the idea of SOCIAL
HISTORY—treat ideas increasingly as social products rather than living entities
to be studied in themselves. It has been noted that there is an "increasing tendency
of historians to substitute the word 'cultural' in places where they might earlier
have employed the word 'intellectual' " (Bouwsma, 1981: 284). Traditionally,
however, there has been a rough distinction between the two genres insofar as
cultural history has cast its net wider than intellectual history, to include the
analysis of non-rational as well as rational patterns in the arts, ceremony, ritual,
and so on, whereas intellectual history has emphasized until very recently
"ideas" in the articulated sense (see INTELLECTUAL HISTORY).

Lately, also under the influence of anthropology, there is a significant effort
to broaden cultural history to include "popular culture" as well as "high culture." *Popular culture* is defined by one scholar as "unofficial culture, the
culture of the non-elite, [of] the 'subordinate classes' " (Burke, 1978: Prologue).
Although this idea is by no means entirely new (Darnton, 1980: 345), it is
especially evident since the mid–1960s, developing in more or less conscious
reaction to what some historians regard as the implicit snobbery of traditional
cultural history's emphasis on "high culture" (White, 1974). The traditional
approach, even on the relatively rare occasions when it directed attention to
"popular" culture, tended to view it condescendingly from above and as the
product of the vulgarization of the ideas of the elite (e.g., Barzun, [1956] 1972:
396–97). The new trend draws strong inspiration from Lucien Febvre's idea of
reconstructing the popular *mentalité* (or group consciousness) of a society and
derives many of its techniques and modes of conceptualization from folklore
and cultural anthropology (Walters, 1980). The central stress on synthesis and

the holistic approach of traditional cultural history are still present in newer work, although a possible way of circumventing the metaphysics of the older school has been suggested: to treat each culture as a "code" or "communications system," tied together by a set of "grammatical" rules in a fashion similar to a spoken language. Thus the various manifestations of a culture can be viewed as interrelated; the thing considered to link them is not a hidden "essence" but a culturally inherited set of shared "grammatical" rules of deportment and expression (White, 1974: 774; Burke, 1978: Prologue).

References

Barzun, Jacques. [1956] 1972. "Cultural History as a Synthesis." In Stern: 387–402. Barzun notes that as late as the 1920s the idea of cultural history "carried a taint of fraud" in the United States (p. 388). As a graduate student in history at Columbia at the time, Barzun was warned to relegate his interest in "culture" to the status of an avocation.
Bouwsma, William J. 1981. "From History of Ideas to History of Meaning." *Journal of Interdisciplinary History* 12: 279–91.
Burke, Peter. 1978. *Popular Culture in Early Modern Europe*. New York. This book contains the best comprehensive bibliography on the history of popular culture.
Colie, R. L. 1964. "Johan Huizinga and the Task of Cultural History." *AHR* 69: 607–30.
Darnton, Robert. 1980. "Intellectual and Cultural History." In Kammen: 327–54. This essay includes a good bibliography in the footnote citations.
Gilbert, Felix. 1960. "Cultural History and Its Problems." *Comité International des Sciences Historiques, Rapports* 1: 40–58. Gilbert presents an excellent discussion of the history of the words *culture* and *civilization*, the importance of Burckhardt's work, and the logical problems underlying the "concept of the unity of a cultural epoch" (p. 50).
Gombrich, E. H. 1969. *In Search of Cultural History*. Oxford. This is a good analysis of the German tradition. Gombrich believes that cultural history can avoid the pitfalls of its "belief in the existence of an independent supra-individual collective spirit . . . [only] if it . . . fixes its attention on the individual human being" (p. 37). By doing so, the historian "will not deny that the success of certain styles may be symptomatic of changing attitudes, but he will resist the temptation to use changing styles and changing fashions as indicators of profound psychological changes" (p. 37).
Heaton, Herbert. [1943] 1950. "The Economic Impact on History." In Strayer: 85–117.
Huizinga, Johan. [1929] 1959. "The Task of Cultural History." In Johan Huizinga, *Men and Ideas*. New York: 17–76.
Kroeber, A. L., and Kluckhohn, Clyde. 1952. *Culture: A Critical Review of Concepts and Definitions*. New York.
Le Roy Ladurie, Emmanuel. 1978. *Montaillou: The Promised Land of Error*. New York. This book represents an effort to reconstruct the popular culture of a medieval village.
Ritter, Gerhard, 1951. "Zum Begriff der 'Kulturgeschichte': Ein Diskussionsbeitrag." *Historische Zeitschrift* 171: 293–302. Ritter raises many of the fundamental issues.
Schorske, Carl E. 1980. *Fin-de-Siècle Vienna: Politics and Culture*. New York.

Voltaire. [1738] 1972. "Letter to Abbé Jean Baptiste Dubos: On *The Age of Louis XIV*."
    In Stern: 38–40.
Walters, Ronald G. 1980. "Signs of the Times: Clifford Geertz and Historians." *Social
    Research* 47: 536–56. Walters discusses the impact of the anthropologist's ideas
    on American historians; see especially pp. 550–51.
White, Hayden. 1974. "Structuralism and Popular Culture." *Journal of Popular Culture*
    7: 759–75.

Sources of Additional Information

See also CULTURE. Consult the bibliographies in E. H. Gombrich's article "Style" in
IESS 15 (1968): 352–61, and Frederick M. Barnard's entry "Culture and Civilization in
Modern Times," *DHI* 1 (1973): 613–621. An early history of the concept is Friedrich
Jodl, *Die Culturgeschichtsschreibung, ihre Entwicklung und ihr Problem* (Halle, 1878).
Gombrich (1969) may be supplemented by Leonard B. Meyer's review in *HT* 9 (1970):
397–99. Caroline F. Ware's *Cultural Approach to History* (New York, 1940) is an
anthology of papers presented at the 1939 conference of the American Historical Asso-
ciation. Wallace K. Ferguson's *Renaissance in Historical Thought* (Cambridge, Mass.,
1948) contains noteworthy passages on the concept. Chapter four of Ernst Troeltsch's
famous *Der Historismus und seine Probleme* (Tübingen, 1922) is entitled "Über den
Aufbau der europäischen Kulturgeschichte." On Voltaire, see Paul Sakmann, "The
Problems of Historical Method and of Philosophy of History in Voltaire" [1906], *HT*
Beih. 11 (1971): 24–59. For additional literature on Lamprecht see the entry INTERDIS-
CIPLINARY HISTORY; for work on Burckhardt see RENAISSANCE. Werner Kaegi's biography
of Burckhardt (Basel, 1947–67) and his *Vom Begriff der Kulturgeschichte, zum hundersten
Geburtstag Johan Huizingas* (Leiden, 1973) are important. For the more recent work see
Patrick H. Hutton, "The History of Mentalities: The New Map of Cultural History,"
HT 20 (1981): 237–59. For an American historian's point of view see John William
Ward, *Red, White and Blue: Men, Books, and Ideas in American Culture* (New York,
1969), especially p. 13.

CULTURE. 1. The total complex of intellectual and material life of a particular
society. 2. A condition of moral and intellectual refinement attained by individual persons. 3. A level of development attained by an entire society. 4.
The arts in general—music, the visual arts, literature, and so on.

The term *culture* is "one of the two or three most complicated words in the
English language" (Williams, 1976: 76). Since the eighteenth century—when
it initially gained popularity—it has been closely associated with the vocabulary
of the history of philosophy and the history of history itself. Modern theories
of culture are to a large degree the product of dislocations associated with the
social processes of rationalization and industrialization, sometimes referred to
collectively as MODERNIZATION (Meyer, 1952: 405; Ward, 1969: 16).

Two families of meaning may be distinguished: "humanistic" and "anthropological" (Barnard, 1973: 614). Both are often found combined in the thought
of influential social theorists and historians, such as Johann Gottfried Herder
and Jacob Burckhardt (see below). Humanistic concepts of culture are normative

and selective; they imply that certain human activities—labeled "cultural"—
are superior to other kinds of activity and include definitions 2 through 4 above.
In contrast, the "anthropological" concept—definition 1—is descriptive, neutral, and inclusive.

The word itself is derived from the Latin verb *colere*, which had several
meanings in antiquity: "inhabit, cultivate, protect, honor with worship" (Williams, 1976: 77). *Cultura*, derived from *colere*, acquired the meaning of cultivation of the land. The associations of the word remained primarily agricultural,
although Cicero, in his *Tusculanae disputationes*, set an isolated precedent for
later social meanings when he compared "culture of the soul" to cultivated
fields that bear fruit. With the revival of interest in Roman learning during the
RENAISSANCE, Cicero's usage was resurrected, and from the sixteenth century
onward, the term became closely associated with the idea of human development.
This social meaning is evident, for example, in the work of the German scholar
Samuel von Pufendorf (1632–94), who used *cultura* to refer to the intellectual
and emotional development of both the individual and society as a whole. For
Pufendorf, *cultura* included all that was not given by nature but rather was
created by man (Rauhut, 1953: 81–83).

In the mid-eighteenth century the equally complex term CIVILIZATION came
into wide use in France, and this word became involved in a complex relationship
with "culture," especially in Germany. At first, eighteenth-century German
authors used the term *Cultur* as a synonym for the French *civilisation*, to designate
either "a general process of becoming 'civilized' or 'cultivated' " or "the secular
process of human development," that is, improvement (Williams, 1976: 78).
Herder, for example, used *Cultur* to mean "a progressive cultivation or development of faculties" (Kroeber and Kluckhohn, 1952: 32, 39). But Herder also
introduced an important new shade of meaning when he spoke of human "cultures" in the plural. In so doing he made *culture* into a noun referring to a given
society's total way of life, and he argued that every nation had its own unique
and intrinsically valuable form of culture. This would develop into the anthropological meaning of the word, although it was relatively rare in German until
the mid-nineteenth century and in English until the late nineteenth century (Williams, 1976: 78–79).

Another important development occurred in the nineteenth century, particularly in Germany. Although the eighteenth-century practice of equating "culture"
and "civilization" persisted, perhaps in the majority of cases (Kroeber and
Kluckhohn, 1952: 30), some writers began to draw polar distinctions between
the two words. One term (either *culture* or *civilization*, depending on the author)
would be associated with material and technological (or "artificial") values and
development, the other with social and "spiritual" (and, by implication,
"higher") values and development. The historian Leopold von Ranke (1795–
1886), for example, differentiated " 'civilization' (the social realm of techniques)
and the extensive nature of the progress of 'culture' (the social realm of the
spirit)" (Krieger, 1951: 490, n.15). By the turn of the twentieth century, German

usage had established *culture* as the appropriate designation for the higher "spiritual" forms of social life; *civilization* became a pejorative to refer to base "mechanical" or "artificial" aspects of moral and social development (Gilbert, 1960: 40). During World War I, these words became instruments of propaganda for German writers, who used *culture* to refer to the "healthy" form of social life represented by Germany and *civilization* to refer to the "superficial" and "materialistic" west European social tradition. This usage spawned an enormous volume of polemical literature (see Bruford, 1962), and it is something of an exaggeration to dismiss it as "mainly an episode in German thought" (Kroeber and Kluckhohn, 1952: 29); important nineteenth-century English writers such as Samuel Taylor Coleridge and Matthew Arnold made the distinction as well. C. P. Snow's widely read book *The Two Cultures* (1960) reflects the fact that the distinction was still being made in the mid-twentieth-century English-speaking world (Barnard, 1973: 617). In English-speaking countries today, however, the two terms are most often used as virtual synonyms (Gilbert, 1960: 41, 52).

Another meaning level has had a more enduring influence, in both general and historiographical usage: *culture* acquired (either positive or pejorative) connotations of social class and became associated with the personal and aesthetic "refinement" of the individual. Here, *culture* was understood as a "value, which had to be maintained and defended" (Gilbert, 1960: 45). This conception was already well established in Germany in the mid-eighteenth century, where the term *Bildung* was widely used to designate the cultivation of the individual personality; this meaning crystallized in the work of Christoph Wieland (1733–1813), who used *Bildung* to designate Cicero's *cultura animi* ("culture of the spirit") (Rauhut, 1953: 89). The equation of "culture" with "high culture," or the "finer things of the mind" (Weintraub, 1966: 9; Kroeber and Kluckhohn, 1952: 56, 60–61)—very prominent in the older forms of CULTURAL HISTORY (as in the work of the Swiss historian Jacob Burckhardt)—was established in English during the controversy surrounding the publication of Matthew Arnold's *Culture and Anarchy* in 1869. Arnold defined *culture* as an activity of the individual, "a pursuit of total perfection by means of getting to know, on all the matters which most concern us, the best which has been thought and said in the world" (cited in Kroeber and Kluckhohn, 1952: 54).

From the standpoint of present historiography, however, the most important nineteenth-century development was the scholarly world's gradual adoption of Herder's "anthropological," or "ethnographic," concept of culture. This descriptive, non-evaluative concept designates "material and technological as well as intellectual and artistic aspects of human activity" (Gilbert, 1960: 40) and is today widespread in German, Scandinavian, Slavic, and English-speaking scholarship, although not so common in French or Italian usage (Williams, 1976: 81). In history, this meaning was already apparent in Gustav E. Klemm's ten-volume *Allgemeine Culturgeschichte der Menschheit* (1843–52). Although Klemm's text still betrayed the familiar eighteenth-century associations of "advancement" or "improvement," he also used *culture* as a neutral term to designate the general pattern of life of a particular human group. This understanding was then widely disseminated by Jacob Burckhardt in his famous *Die Cultur der Renaissance in Italien* (1860), which represented the life of late medieval and early modern Italy in terms of an interlocking pattern. Burckhardt's usage was soon adopted by other cultural historians, for example, Karl Lamprecht (1856–1915), who understood culture as "the totality of life to which a people gives expression" (Weintraub, 1966: 170). In the first edition of his influential methodological work *Lehrbuch der historischen Methode* (1889), Ernst Bernheim defined *culture* as the "totality 'of the forms and processes of social life, of the means and results of work, spiritual as well as material'." This sense of the word was introduced to English by the pioneer British anthropologist E. B. Tylor in his *Primitive Culture* (1871) (Kroeber and Kluckhohn, 1952: 31, 11).

An important subsequent refinement was the recognition, in the 1930s, that that within a particular society there might be "different levels or strata of culture," for example:

> The agrarian sector of the population or subject classes may remain untouched or only slowly accept the cultural life of the cities or of the ruling group . . . particularly in modern times, the existence of different classes claiming equal status requires a pluralistic picture, because each class has its own culture. (Gilbert, 1960: 50)

The anthropological notion of culture has had a great impact on the writing and conceptualization of history in the twentieth century, despite the fact that it is rejected in a few quarters (e.g., Barzun [1956] 1972: 392–93). As early as 1939 the American Historical Association dedicated its annual conference to the theme of cultural history (Ware, 1940). After 1945, the anthropological idea provided strong impetus for "area studies" programs, such as the "American Studies" movement in the United States, in which "professors of American literature, art, music, as well as history realized that all their narrow specialties really were engaged in the same basic endeavor encompassed in the new meaning of culture" (Berkhofer [1972] 1973: 81; also Sykes, 1963). In the 1950s, two important works explicitly recommended use of the anthropological concept: Social Science Research Council Bulletin 64 (1954) and David Potter's *People of Plenty* (1954). In the early 1960s, H. Stuart Hughes (1960; 1964) argued that anthropology, with its particular concept of culture, was the scholarly discipline most closely related to history.

Despite the suggestion of Berkhofer ([1972] 1973: 98) that historians "more and more feel the need to move beyond the cultural analysis of history," appeals to the anthropological concept continue to grow (for instance, Ward, 1969; Kinser, 1971: 708, n.3; Sheehan, 1981: 7, n.14; Burke, 1978: xi), stressing the idea that *culture* implies social "sharing," "meaning," and "symbol." This is the result of a further refinement in the anthropological concept, dating from the 1920s and 1930s (although already implicit in the work of Burckhardt and Huizinga)—that is, the idea that the analysis of culture should involve the exploration of the "ideational components" behind patterns of social life (Berkhofer, [1972] 1973: 80). The 1970s witnessed growing interest in the historical adaptation of the latest refinements in anthropological theory (see Walters, 1980; Higham and Conkin, 1979). Especially influential were the ideas of the American anthropologist Clifford Geertz, who approaches culture as "the informal logic of actual life" (Walters, 1980: 542).

It should be noted that there is a common tendency to mix senses in which the word is used. Weintraub (1966: 11), for example, employs the word primarily in the anthropological sense but also believes that "culture is man's jurisdiction, the creative effort by which he saves himself from chaos, boredom, vice, and barbarism"—an opinion that evokes the usage of eighteenth-century moralists.

References

Barnard, Frederick M. 1973. "Culture and Civilization in Modern Times." *DHI*: 613–21. Barnard's entry stresses the importance of Herder and the Italian Giambattista Vico in the evolution of the modern concept.

Barzun, Jacques. [1956] 1972. "Cultural History as a Synthesis." In Stern: 387–402.

Berkhofer, Robert F., Jr. [1972] 1973. "Clio and the Culture Concept: Some Impressions of a changing Relationship in American Historiography." In Louis Schneider and Charles M. Bonjean, eds., *The Idea of Culture in the Social Sciences*. Cambridge: 77–100. This is a valuable analysis of specific historiographical uses of the anthropological concept.

Bruford, W. H. 1962. *Culture and Society in Classical Weimar, 1775–1806*. Cambridge.

Burke, Peter. 1978. *Popular Culture in Early Modern Europe*. New York. Burke defines *culture* as "a system of shared meanings, attitudes and values, and the symbolic forms (performances, artifacts) in which they are expressed or embodied" (p. xi).

Gilbert, Felix. 1960. "Cultural history and Its Problems." *Comité International des Sciences Historiques, Rapports* 1: 40–52.

Higham, John, and Conkin, Paul K., eds. 1979. *New Directions in American Intellectual History*. Baltimore. See especially the "Introduction" by Higham, pp. xi-xix.

Hughes, H. Stuart. 1960. "The Historian and the Social Scientist." *AHR* 66: 20–46.

———. 1964. *History as Art and as Science: Twin Vistas on the Past*. New York.

Kinser, Samuel, 1971. "Ideas of Temporal Change and Cultural Process in France, 1470–1535." In Anthony Molho and John A. Tedeschi, eds., *Renaissance Studies in Honor of Hans Baron*. Dekalb, Ill. Kinser uses the word *culture* to mean "the ensemble of symbol-making and symbol-using activities of man."

Krieger, Leonard. 1951. "The Idea of Progress." *The Review of Metaphysics* 4: 483–94.

Kroeber, A. L., and Kluckhohn, Clyde. 1952. *Culture: A Critical Review of Concepts and Definitions*. New York. This is a key source, which synthesizes a vast amount of etymological work.

Meyer, Alfred G. 1952. "Historical Notes on Ideological Aspects of the Concept of Culture in Germany and Russia." In A. L. Kroeber and Clyde Kluckhohn, *Culture: A Critical Review of Concepts and Definitions*. New York: 403–13.

Rauhut, Franz. 1953. "Die Herkunft der Worte und Begriffe, 'Kultur', 'Civilisation', und 'Bildung'." *Germanisch-Romanische Monatsschrift*, N.S., 3: 81–91.

Sheehan, James J. 1981. "What Is German History? Reflections on the Role of the *Nation* in German History and Historiography." *JMH* 53: 1–23. Sheehan characterizes culture as "a set of shared symbols and values" and stresses that "culture is a process, not just a body of ideas and artifacts; it is *shared* symbols, not just symbols. One must always be aware, therefore, of the institutional network through which the sharing takes place" (p. 7, n. 14).

Sykes, Richard E. 1963. "American Studies and the Concept of Culture: A Theory and Method." *American Quarterly* 15: 253–70.

Walters, Ronald G. 1980. "Signs of the Times: Clifford Geertz and Historians." *Social Research* 47: 537–56. Walters evaluates the impact of Geertz on the study of cultural and intellectual history; he suggests potential dangers in Geertz's use of semiotics and the concept of "thick description" (p. 556).

Ward, John William. 1969. *Red, White, and Blue: Men, Books, and Ideas in American Culture*. New York. Ward defines *culture* as "the organization of social experience in the consciousness of men made manifest in symbolic action" (p. 6).

Ware, Caroline, ed. 1940. *The Cultural Approach to History*. New York.

Weintraub, Karl. *Visions of Culture* (Chicago, 1966). This is an important introduction to use of the concept in historical writing during the past two centuries.

Williams, Raymond. 1976. *Keywords: A Vocabulary of Culture and Society*. New York.

Sources of Additional Information

Compare Sidney Hook's discussion "Civilization and Culture" in Bull. 54: 118–19. G. Weiss, "Scientific Concept of Culture," *American Anthropologist* 75 (October 1973), attempts to define the anthropological concept more precisely than previous authors and cites much of the basic literature. Two articles in *DHI* contain brief, helpful bibliographies: Barnard (see above) and Clarence J. Glacken, "Environment and Culture" 2: 127–34. Milton Singer, "Culture: The Concept of Culture," *IESS* 3: 527–43, contains an extensive bibliography of recent work in anthropology. For the older anthropological literature see the entry "Culture" in *ESS* 4: 621–46 by Bronislaw Malinowski—a major contributor to the consolidation of the modern concept. See also chapter three of V. Gordon Childe's *Social Evolution* (London, 1951), "Culture in Archaeology and Anthropology." For a useful anthology see Louis Schneider and Charles M. Bonjean, eds., *The Idea of Culture in the Social Sciences* (Cambridge, 1973). Raymond Williams, *Culture and Society, 1780–1950* (London, 1958), is a widely cited work of major significance. Robert Berkhofer's *Behavioral Approach to Historical Analysis* (New York, 1969), pp. 98–168, also deals with the subject. For a French view see E. de Dampierre, "Note sur 'Culture' et 'Civilization'," *CSSH* 3 (1960–61): 328–40. W. H. Bruford's *German Tradition of Self-Cultivation: 'Bildung' from Humboldt to Thomas Mann* (Cambridge, 1975) is, together with his *Culture and Society in Classical Weimar* (cited above), the best introduction in English to the German tradition of culture as personal refinement. John H. Moore, "Cultural Concept as Ideology," *American Ethnologist* 1 (August 1974): 537–49, criticizes mainstream anthropological views. Stephen Porter Dunn, "Culture," *MCWS* 2: 282–87, discusses Soviet opinion.

D
_____

DECLINE, DECADENCE. Related terms associated with special aspects of social change. *Decline* refers to the loss of cohesion in a society, leading to potential public disorder, diminishment of political power, loss of economic wealth, and social disintegration. *Decadence* may be synonymous with *decline* or may more specifically refer to a distinct late-nineteenth-century cultural style that emphasized pessimism and often celebrated that which is conventionally regarded as morally or socially corrupt.

Since ancient times, the idea of the decay and dissolution of human cultures has been a central theme of historical analysis. In his *History of Florence* (1532), Niccolo Machiavelli expressed a time-honored belief when he wrote: "since nature has not allowed worldly things to remain still, when they arrive at their final perfection, they have no further to climb and so they have to descend" (cited in Burke, 1976: 144). Before the eighteenth-century ENLIGHTENMENT—which strongly emphasized PROGRESS in human development—mainstream speculation about social change was vitally concerned with the possibility of social deterioration; traditionally, decline was widely presumed to be "natural, more natural in fact than stability" (Burke, 1976: 144).

There are two ways of approaching the semantic complex of decline/decadence: (1) as a process of social degeneration and, perhaps, dissolution (the "social" concept); and (2) as a specific movement in high culture that arose in the nineteenth century (the "aesthetic" concept, or "decadentism"). Although twentieth-century historians are often wary of using the value-laden terms, they retain a vigorous interest in the *idea* of social decay—especially in the subfields of CULTURAL HISTORY and INTELLECTUAL HISTORY (Drake, 1982). Moreover, the metaphorical convention of conceptualizing social change in terms of the human life cycle, or the cycle of nature generally, promotes a persistent popular belief in the inevitability of social decay; this often conditions the thinking of professional scholars. Both popular and scholarly notions of decline are usually associated in some way with images of the "fall" of ancient Rome, "the dominant historical catastrophe in the imagination of the West" (Winegarten, 1974: 68).

Images of decline and decadence predate recorded history. The notion of a "golden age" followed by decay is a "basic expression of mythical thinking attested in all cultures" (Spitzlberger and Kernig, 1972: 279). This may originate, as the German poet Schiller suggested in his essay *On Naive and Sentimental Poetry* (1795), in a basic human tendency to regard childhood as a lost age of innocence; nostalgia and the sense of decline are often closely associated modes of sensibility.

Mythological images of decadence were translated into the earliest written speculations about time, for example, the *Works and Days* (c. 650 B.C.) of the Greek poet Hesiod, who depicted history as a succession of descending epochs— golden, silver, bronze, and iron. F. C. White (1977: 352) suggests that the major concern in Plato's *Republic* is "not with metaphysics or epistemology, but with the decline and decay of societies." Many Roman writers bemoaned decay or corruption in their society, often basing their views on an idea of historical RECURRENCE in which the idea of decline was prominent.

Although *decline* (*declinatio*, "bend," or "slope") and *decadence* (*decadentia*, "falling down") are of ancient Latin origin, explicit use of the terms in a historical sense is first encountered only in medieval Latin. The chronicler Otto of Freising (d. 1158) was among the earliest to employ *decline* to refer to government: "if it is at its height, soon it will need decline." Similar use of *decadentia* appeared in the early thirteenth century (Starn, 1975: 4). The popularity of decline as a literary theme was aided especially by the Italian poet Petrarch (1304–74), whose work legitimized the idea of a "middle age" of cultural regression following the end of Roman hegemony over the European and Mediterranean world. Other representatives of the Italian RENAISSANCE created an "explicit [Latin] vocabulary of decline" (Starn, 1975: 5) and a "large repertoire of metaphors or schemata . . . to characterize . . . change for the worse" (Burke, 1976: 138). From Latin, this verbal arsenal passed to French and the other vernacular languages. "From the sixteenth and seventeenth centuries . . . usage of 'decline' (and increasingly of 'decadence') with reference to history was widely accepted" (Starn, 1975: 7).

Burke (1976: 138–41) classifies the early-modern language of decline under six main headings: (1) "cosmic decline," that is, the idea that the universe itself ages, in a literal sense; (2) "moral decline," associated with original sin, or the debasement of manners; (3) religious decline; (4) "political decline," the loss of power by governments; (5) "cultural decline," the debasement of language, learning, or the arts; and (6) "economic decline," the loss of wealth or commercial vigor.

These categories were, in turn, explained according to three basic "theories of decline" (Burke, 1976: 142–44): divine, natural, and human. Divine causes included providence, divine punishment, and "fortune." Among the natural causes were the world's "old age" and the influence of the stars. Human explanations included the influx of alien peoples into established communities, a "loss of virtue" (that is, sense of civic duty), or the corrupting influence of luxury or power. Especially popular was the idea that there are three basic forms of government—monarchy, aristocracy, and democracy—all naturally subject to decay; this could be avoided only through some form of mixed government, which would preserve social equilibrium.

Human theories of decline began to prevail over divine and astrological explanations in the seventeenth century. Despite the fact that the eighteenth century witnessed the birth of the modern idea of PROGRESS, there was also great interest in social decline. Decline was part of the theory of historical recurrence devised by the Italian philosopher Giambattista Vico (1668–1744); the Baron de Montesquieu (1689–1755) and Edward Gibbon (1737–94) wrote classic studies of the decline and fall of the Roman empire (cf. Trevor-Roper, 1967: 420); and the French moralist Jean Jacques Rousseau repopularized the ancient idea that "progress, insofar as it involved luxury, necessarily brought decadence in its train" (Buckley, 1966: 70).

In the nineteenth century, "decline" became increasingly associated with the notion of social PROCESS, and the "social concept" of decline, following the tradition of Montesquieu and Gibbon, was firmly established. The idea that most authors who use the concept are "*socially and politically conservative*" (Winthrop, 1971: 511) is incorrect; during the past two hundred years the theme of social disintegration has been as important to the liberal and radical orientations in historical scholarship, for the ideas of decline and decadence do not *necessarily* imply irreversible deterioration. One may envision social change in terms of a " 'mixed' time pattern" in which decline may be "considered part of larger wholes which move in circles, spirals, or undulating lines" (Starn, 1975: 17; Burke, 1976: 144); indeed, "many of those who think that our own society is decadent draw attention to this supposed fact partly because they desire to see the tendency reversed" (White, 1977: 359).

A rough semantic division occurred in the nineteenth century, in which *decadence* assumed more explicitly value-laden connotations than *decline* and took on a second meaning; it came to refer to a sensibility symptomatic of the avantegarde intelligentsia's estrangement from mainstream society (see ALIENATION), a self-conscious fascination with corruption and decay. Thus emerged the "aesthetic concept" of decadence, or (after the usage of the Italian critic Walter Binni) "decadentism" (Drake, 1982: 72). A contributing factor to interest in social "decay," aside from specific political calamities and economic disruptions (Buckley, 1966: 78–79), was the hostility of part of the leisure class and literary intelligentsia to the rapid urbanization, industrialization, and material affluence that characterized the late nineteenth century (Weber, 1982: 3) (see MODERNIZATION). Hallmarks of the "decadent" sensibility (as in Mallarmé and Verlaine in France, Oscar Wilde in England) were cultural pessimism, subjectivism, hostility to mainstream morality, and obsessive interest in the perverse and bizarre (Buckley, 1966: 92–93). In many ways these attitudes continue to influence the temper of the western intelligentsia.

These developments affected social science theory in general and historiographical practice in particular. In the usage of a wide range of political camps— from conservatives to Marxists—*decadence* became a "polemical term of moral opprobrium" (Drake, 1982: 71). To the Italian philosopher and historian Benedetto Croce (1866–1952), for example, *decadence* was "a perverse rejection of the moral and intellectual standards that had made Western civilization the conscience and guide of the world" (Drake, 1982: 81). In this period, especially, many historians understood *decline* not as a mere figure of speech but as a palpable reality. "The corruption and decline of Rome is one of the most important and suggestive things in human annals," wrote Andrew D. White (1885: 64), first president of the American Historical Association. "This corruption and decline is as real as the existence of Rome itself" (p. 64). In White's view, the "most precious" historical works were those that demonstrated "what cycles of birth, growth, and decay various nations have passed" (p. 51).

Among the causes of political and moral degeneration cited at the time were "the failure of idealism, the substitution of self-interest for civic virtue, the decay of manners, the surrender of reason to sensuality" (Buckley, 1966: 74)— classic indices of social pathology that Gibbon had already identified as reasons for Rome's collapse. Some historians—such as Henry and Brooks Adams in the United States (Conley, 1972)—found "scientific" justification for their social anxiety in the second law of thermodynamics, which taught that the universe's energy would gradually dissipate through the diffusion of heat. As a rule, however, nineteenth-century authors did not understand social decomposition fatalistically, as the inevitable consequence of a cosmic order of things; rather, it was understood as the consequence of some flaw or failure of human action (Buckley, 1966: 75).

Until recently the idea of decadence was taken seriously as a useful analytical concept by many social scientists (e.g., Todd, 1931), and today the idea still plays an important, even explicit, role in the work of some leading historians (e.g., Kohn, 1969; Lasch, 1978). At present, however, most historians are wary of the strong emotive and normative overtones of the terms. Sweeping accounts of the "rise" and "fall" of civilizations in the tradition of Gibbon's classic panorama of *The Decline and Fall of the Roman Empire* (1776–88) have not been well received by the historical profession in the twentieth century (see METAHISTORY). The theories of decline presented in such studies are considered unempirical, and more generally, the analogy of the natural life cycle as a guide for scholarship is widely mistrusted. Appeals to "decadence" are apt to be considered evidence of "modish intellectual pessimism" (Winegarten, 1974: 67), and the historian who explicitly uses the terms today may well be called to task for evoking the "portentously ominous" (e.g., Cecil, 1976: 1276–77). Current historiographical criticism often treats the ideas of decline and decadence ironically, representing them not as objective processes but as patterns subjectively imposed on the past by the historical IMAGINATION (Stern, 1961). The British philosopher R. G. Collingwood offered a classic caveat:

> in history as it actually happens there are no mere phenomena of decay: every decline is also a rise, and it is only the historian's personal failures of knowledge or sympathy—partly due to mere ignorance, partly to the preoccupations of his own practical life—that prevent him from seeing this double character, at once creative and destructive, of any historical process whatever. (1946: 164–65)

References

Buckley, Jerome Hamilton. 1966. *The Triumph of Time: A Study of the Victorian Concepts of Time, History, Progress, and Decadence.* Cambridge, Mass. See especially chapter five, "The Idea of Decadence."

Burke, Peter. 1976. "Tradition and Experience: The Idea of Decline from Bruni to Gibbon." *Daedalus* 105: 137–52.

Cecil, Lamar. 1976. Review of Ekkehard-Teja P. W. Wilke, *Political Decadence in Imperial Germany: Personal-Political Aspects of the German Government Crisis, 1894–97. AHR* 82: 1276–77.

Collingwood, R. G. [1946] 1956. *The Idea of History.* Oxford.

Conley, Patrick T. 1972. "Brooks Adams' Law of Civilization and Decay." *Essex Institute Historical Collections* 108: 89–98.

Drake, Richard. 1982. "Decadence, Decadentism and Decadent Romanticism in Italy: Toward a Theory of *Décadence.*" *Journal of Contemporary History* 17: 69–92. This is a survey of late-nineteenth-century Italian theories of decadence, especially the ideas of Walter Binni, Benedetto Croce, and Antonio Gramsci. It includes a critique of Gilman (1979), as well as an extensive bibliography in footnote citations.

Gilman, Richard. 1979. *Decadence: The Strange Life of an Epithet.* New York. Gilman explores the term's literary and social associations; his book is designed to debunk popular use of the term in contemporary English. He argues that decadence "is not a fact but a value judgment, a category of belief or opinion" (p. 129).

Kohn, Hans. 1969. "A Turning Point." *JHI* 30: 283–90.

Lasch, Cristopher. 1978. *The Culture of Narcissism: American Life in an Age of Diminishing Expectations.* New York.

Spitzlberger, Georg, and Kernig, Claus D. 1972. "Periodization." *MCWS* 6: 278–91.

Starn, Randolph. 1975. "Meaning-Levels in the Theme of Historical Decline." *HT* 14: 1–31. This is an essential source that addresses the problem of "when—in what circumstances—are historical individuals likely to use word and idea structures entailed in speaking and thinking of historical decline?" (p. 22) The author pinpoints some of the attractions of the concepts of decline and decadence for the historian—their possible associations with paradox, irony, and so on.

Stern, Fritz. 1961. *The Politics of Cultural Despair: A Study in the Rise of the Germanic Ideology.* Berkeley, Calif. This work is among the first and best-known studies in what has become a popular genre—the history of "cultural pessimism."

Todd, Elizabeth. 1931. "Decadence." *ESS* 5: 39–43. Although dated, this entry is good for an older bibliography.

Trevor-Roper, H. R. 1967. "The Idea of the Decline and Fall of the Roman Empire."

In *The Age of Enlightenment: Studies Presented to Theodore Bestermann*. Edinburgh and London.

Weber, Eugen. 1982. "Introduction: Decadence on a Private Income." *Journal of Contemporary History* 17: 1–20. Weber analyzes the sources and implications of the idea in nineteenth-century Europe, primarily among *rentier* income groups in France. He ascribes the literary intelligentsia's fascination with "decadence" primarily to the "ancient and familiar prejudice against material goods most prevalent among those who enjoy them" (p. 5). There is an excellent bibliography in the footnote citations.

White, Andrew D. 1885. "On Studies in General History and the History of Civilization." *Papers of the American Historical Association* 1: 47–72.

White, F. C. 1977. "On Properties and Decadence in Society." *Ethics* 87: 352–62. White takes the concept seriously as a moral and social category.

Winegarten, Renee. 1974. "The Idea of Decadence." *Commentary* 58 (Sept.): 65–69. This piece is similar in tone to Gilman (1979).

Winthrop, Henry. 1971. "Variety of Meaning in the Concept of Decadence." *Philosophy and Phenomenonological Research* 31: 510–26. Winthrop treats the concept seriously.

Sources of Additional Information

Historians have written much less about the concept of decline than about its opposite, the idea of PROGRESS. For a bibliography see the footnote citations in both Starn (1975) and Burke (1976). A widely cited work is Walter Rehm, *Der Untergang Roms im abendländischen Denken. Ein Beitrag zur Geschichtsschreibung und zum Dekadenzproblem*, 2d ed. (Darmstadt, 1966), originally published in 1930. Also relevant are many parts of Robert A. Nisbet, *Social Change and History: Aspects of the Western Theory of Development* (New York, 1969). The summer, 1976 issue of *Daedalus* is devoted to "Edward Gibbon and the Decline and Fall of the Roman Empire." Also, the January 1982 number of the *Journal of Contemporary History* deals with decadence as a theme of intellectual and cultural history. Of related interest are Frederic Cople Jaher's *Doubters and Dissenters: Cataclysmic Thought in America, 1885–1918* (New York, 1964) and Susan Sontag's perceptive *Illness as Metaphor* (New York, 1978). On the aesthetic concept of decadence see especially A. E. Carter, *The Idea of Decadence in French Literature, 1830–1900* (Toronto, 1958); Koenraad W. Swart, *The Sense of Decadence in Nineteenth Century France* (The Hague, 1964); and Cesar Graña, *Bohemian versus Bourgeois: French Society and the French Man of Letters in the Nineteenth Century* (New York, 1964). For further reading see *The Princeton Encyclopedia of Poetry and Poetics* (Princeton, N.J., 1974).

DETERMINISM. 1. Most often, the belief that historical events are controlled by factors other than the motives and free volition of human beings—for example, supernatural agencies such as providence, fate, and destiny or natural circumstances such as geography, climate, heredity, and social tradition. 2. Less commonly, the view that events are the unavoidable results of definite causes.

The idea of determinism in history, a species of the more general category of historical CAUSATION, has interested historians and philosophers on various occasions—most recently during the 1940s and 1950s, when it was fashionable for western moralists to contrast the allegedly "non-determinist" underpinnings of LIBERALISM with the reputedly "deterministic" and pernicious doctrines of Nazi and Soviet collectivism (for example, Popper, 1950; [1957] 1964; Berlin, 1954; cf. Carr, [1961] 1964: 91–93). Historians, as well as some philosophers, typically associate *determinism* with a range of other terms that imply necessity or inevitability—for example, fatalism, predestinarianism, fortune—although this may not always be logically defensible (Donagan, 1973: 19–21). Some writers identify the term with the distractions of airy speculation and advise an attitude of "indifference" toward the metaphysical aspects of determinist controversies (Fischer, 1970: 13). Especially confusing is the fact that writers who use the word in the sense of definition 1 do not usually acknowledge that it may be employed in sense number 2. Understood in sense number 1, as is most common (e.g., Gustavson, 1976: 158; Hook, 1943: 65–66; Berlin, 1954: 7; Geyl, 1958: 264; Leff, 1971: 43–59; Nash, 1969: 300–301; cf. White, 1965: 181), discussions of determinism normally focus on the role of the individual in history and the degree of freedom that he enjoys. More specifically, they concern the extent to which human beings are able to shape events through free acts of their own volition and the degree to which events are controlled by factors extraneous to the human will—for example, divine will or other metaphysical influences, genetic factors, geographical circumstances, social tradition, economic conditions, and so on. Approached in this way the term became a favored epithet in cold war polemics, a fact deplored by theorists who maintain that *determinism* understood in sense number 2 is not only logically plausible but essential to the practice of history as an empirical discipline (e.g., Carr, [1961] 1964: 93–98; Nagel, [1960]: 1969: 343, 349–50).

In its broadest and most neutral sense, *determinism* is the position that "for everything that ever happens there are conditions such that, given them, nothing else could happen" (Taylor, 1967: 359). Three types of *historical* determinism may be identified (Dray, 1967: 373–76), always allowing for the possibility of overlap: (1) *Fatalistic and providential varieties*, which posit a supernatural power (such as God or destiny) that manipulates events inexorably in a way "outside the mechanism of ordinary causal connection." This form is typically used selectively and normally implies only that "certain things will necessarily come to pass, not that everything happens necessarily." (2) *Doctrines of "historical inevitability*,*"* which regard history as a teleological PROCESS displaying a definite pattern controlled by some internal dynamic, or LAW. (Again, such theories seldom hold that *all* events happen necessarily; "the claim is usually limited to the main trend or the more significant events.") (3) *"Scientific" determinisms*, which hold that events occur in accord with empirically demonstrable relationships of cause and effect. These latter types may be further subdivided into two classes: (a) "single-factor theories," which claim that scientific research can isolate one cause—for example, geography, heredity, economic conditions—as the controlling factor in all historical change; and (b) more modest versions that claim only that "for every event there is a sufficient condition, no matter how disparate the causal elements that may sometimes be required to constitute it" (cf. Carr, [1961] 1964: 93; Nagel, [1960] 1969: 322–25; White, 1965: 271–91).

The view that humankind has a preordained "destiny" of some kind is common to the myths and religions of many cultures, early and modern (Plumb, 1969: 62–63). Most speculative PHILOSOPHY OF HISTORY also involves some form of determinism, understood in sense number 1 (Nash, 1969: 30). Ancient Greek and Roman historians—despite noteworthy efforts to move beyond mythological categories toward explanations in terms of human motives (cf. Breisach, 1983: 14–15)—typically attributed a large role to non-human factors beyond human control such as "fortune," "fate," "destiny," and "divine will." The notion of "fate," for example, which designated the inexorable aspects of causality (Cioffari, 1973: 226), is central to the Greek concept of tragedy, which arguably underpins Thucydides' famous history of the Peloponnesian War (Egan, 1978). "Fortune" is a distinct but sometimes related idea; as employed from antiquity to the RENAISSANCE, it might refer to pure accident but more often implied a mysterious power beyond normal causation (Cioffari, 1973: 226–27). In the latter sense it was used by Polybius to explain the rise of Roman power (Breisach, 1983: 48) and was later used in the histories of Froissart and Machiavelli (Breisach, 1983: 150, 158; Cioffari, 1973: 235–36). Ancient historians regularly appealed to fate and fortune not only because their outlook was still partly informed by myth but because—lacking standardized methods for collecting and evaluating EVIDENCE—they doubted the accuracy with which the past could be known (see SKEPTICISM). According to Michael Grant (1970: xvii), appeals to destiny in ancient historiography are often no more than conventions reflecting a "humble agnosticism about matters on which the writers regarded it as a mistake to feel too certain" (p. xvii).

Christian historians of medieval Europe were even more inclined to supernatural explanations of events, since Christianity viewed human affairs as an extension of divine providence. As a systematic thesis, this "theology of history" had its roots in the work of St. Augustine (Cioffari, 1973: 230) and was later reinforced in the theology and historiography of the Protestant Reformation.

The growth of rationalism in the seventeenth and eighteenth centuries slowly shifted the focus of social thought away from providence, fate, and fortune toward secular explanations (see ENLIGHTENMENT). This ultimately influenced historiography, which, ever since its professionalization at the turn of the nineteenth century (coincidentally, the classical age of liberal individualism), has usually been linked to belief in the sanctity of the individual and his ability freely to shape the present and future.

Thus the suggestion that extra-human factors might dictate or otherwise control human affairs contradicts widely accepted values; one often encounters voluntarism even in historians who are usually not identified as liberals (e.g., Ranke, [n.d.] 1972: 60–61). Charles Kingsley's 1860 reference to "man's mysterious power of breaking the laws of his own being" (cited in Carr, [1961] 1964: 93) is representative. The rule generally holds, despite nineteenth-century revivals of the providential thesis as the notion that nations may have "manifest destinies" in world history (Plumb, 1969: 84–94). This helps to explain professional historians' reluctance to embrace metaphysical philosophies of history such as those of Hegel, Herbert Spencer, Oswald Spengler, and A. J. Toynbee, as well as Marx's HISTORICAL MATERIALISM (Hook, 1943: 75) (see also PHILOSOPHY OF HISTORY; METAHISTORY). (Ingrained aversion to alleged determinism in Marxism leads some American-trained scholars to equate any special emphasis on economic causes with "determinism," so that the term may be employed to mean mere sensitivity to the causal significance of material conditions; by this loose standard, the work of liberal scholars such as Frederick Jackson Turner, Charles Beard, or David Potter may even be considered "deterministic" [e.g., Higham, 1965: 224].)

The cardinal sin of all of these approaches—aside from their perceived violation of the requirements of rigorous empiricism (Plumb, 1969: 99)—is that (rightly or wrongly [cf. Dray, 1964: 74 and Donagan, 1973: 20, 24–25]) they are understood as "fatalistic" and "impersonal" systems (Higham, 1965: 198, 209) that dehumanize history by robbing past individuals of an open future— that is, the ability to choose freely the alternative courses of action and thereby decisively influence the shape of human affairs. "To any practising historian," writes Gordon Leff,

> it must be the first principle from which he begins that events happen which need not happen and which could frequently have happened differently. Their contingency varies from sheer chance and accident . . . to a precarious equilibrium between forces—nations, armies, parties—which could have been tipped the other way by the merest addition. (1971: 42)

Exceptions can be cited, particularly among theorists who believe that history can become a science in the same methodological sense as the natural sciences (see POSITIVISM). The British scholar H. T. Buckle ([1856] 1972: 127), for example, believed that "the actions of men, being guided by their antecedents, are in reality never inconsistent, but, however capricious they may appear, only form part of one vast scheme of universal order, of which we in the present state of knowledge can barely see the outline." In similar fashion the American E. P. Cheyney (1927: 7) maintained that long-term social changes are the result of "great cyclical forces" that occur "with a certain inevitableness"; in these transformations, Cheyney believed,

> there seems to have been an independent trend of events, some inexorable necessity controlling the progress of human affairs. . . . Events come of themselves, so to speak; that is, they come so consistently and unavoidably as to rule out as causes not only physical phenomena but voluntary human action" (p. 7).

Today such views are apt to be considered quaint relics of Victorian scientism. Current scholars are more likely to sympathize with Buckle's German critic, J. G. Droysen ([1868] 1972: 142), who believed that history deals most significantly with "anomaly, the individual, free-will, responsibility, genius . . . [and] the movements and effects of human freedom and of personal peculiarities." Determinism is thus a "temptation" that is best avoided (Gustavson, 1976: 158). Although it is still common for academic historians to allude to "underlying tides and currents" or "great social forces" (Dray, 1967: 374), such expressions are normally purely rhetorical; theories perceived to make individuals pawns "helplessly caught in the grip" of external forces are typically repudiated (for example, Geyl, 1958: 264).

It is nonetheless true that most historians acknowledge the conditioning nature of the social traditions and physical contexts within which individuals operate. This is simply to recognize that although "human beings . . . may have a considerable range of free choice in their actions, their actual choices and actions will fall within certain limits"; in other words, "not everything which is logically possible is also historically possible during a given period and for a given society of men" (Nagel, [1960] 1969: 331). The nineteenth-century German historian Ranke, while maintaining that history's "greatest attraction" lay in its concern with "scenes of . . . freedom," also argued that

> freedom . . . is accompanied by force, by primal force. . . . [In history] there prevails a deep, pervasive connection as well, of which no one is entirely independent and which penetrates everywhere. Freedom and necessity exist side by side. Necessity inheres in all that has already been formed and that cannot be undone, which is the basis of all new, emerging activity. ([n.d.] 1972: 60–61; cf. Holborn, [1955] 1972: 190)

In the twentieth century the point is made most strongly by French historians associated with the periodical *Annales*, for example, Fernand Braudel:

> Can it not be said [asks Braudel] that there is a limit, a ceiling which restricts all human life, containing it within a frontier of varying outline, one which is hard to reach and harder still to cross? This is the border which in every age, even our own, separates the possible from the impossible, what can be done with a little effort from what cannot be done at all. (1981: 27)

For *Annales* historians, the term *structure* functions as a code word to evoke the sum of the social, biological, and psychological limitations that exist for every age (Braudel, 1981: 29; [1958] 1980: 31; cf. Stoianovich, 1976).

Closely related to the issue of the limiting role of circumstances on human thought and action is the question of the role of "accident," coincidence, or "chance" in history—something many historians, fearful of doctrines of inevitability, have been concerned to emphasize (see, for instance, Trevelyan, [1903] 1972: 233; Leff, 1971: 42). A key source here is still J. B. Bury's famous 1916 essay "Cleopatra's Nose," inspired by Pascal's statement: "Had Cleopatra's nose been shorter, the whole face of the world would have been different" (cited in Gustavson, 1976: 162–63). Bury, a champion of SCIENTIFIC HISTORY, wished to vindicate the "law of causation" in historical analysis; by this he meant the principle that "every phenomenon is the consequent of antecedent causes, and that no phenomenon contains any element which is not determined by a sequence of causes and effects" (Bury, [1916] 1964: 60). Without this idea, he insisted, there could be no question of scientific research. This law of causation, Bury argued, was compatible with the hypothesis that human affairs might sometimes turn on such apparent coincidences as the shape of a woman's nose. He did so by defining *chance* as "the valuable collision of two or more independent chains of causes—'valuable' meaning that it is attended with more or less important consequences" (p. 61). The shape of Cleopatra's nose, for example, was in the strictest sense no accident (in the sense of something "*inherently* unforeseeable" [Nagel, (1960) 1969: 342]) but the result of definite hereditary causes. The power of the Roman state and Antony's position in it were likewise the result of specific causes, although they were primarily social rather than biological and therefore of a different order than the first set. The collision of these two independent causal chains in Antony's infatuation with the Egyptian queen was the contingency that significantly influenced events; but this "chance" could not be comprehended apart from the idea of cause and effect. Bury illustrated this rule with reference to a number of other examples, concluding with characteristic optimism that the role of contingency diminishes as man gains greater control over his environment through scientific PROGRESS (Bury, [1916] 1964: 68–69). Although later scholars may question his optimism, Bury's argument is still valued for the way it allows historians to retain the idea of chance without sacrificing strict adherence to the doctrine of secular causation (cf. Carr, [1961] 1964: 98–108; Gustavson, 1976: 163–65).

References

Berlin, Isaiah. 1954. *Historical Inevitability*. London. This is a celebrated study that influenced many historians (cf. Geyl, 1958: 264–71; Carr, [1961] 1964: 92–93). Berlin defines *determinism* as the "proposition that everything that we do and suffer is part of a fixed pattern" (p. 30) and *historical inevitability* as "the assumption that belief in the importance of the motives is delusive; that the behaviour of men is in fact made what it is by factors largely beyond the control of individuals" (p. 7). Berlin is interested in human responsibility and considers determinism pernicious because "all forms of genuine determinism" involve the "elimination of the notion of individual responsibility" (p. 25). He fears that *determinism* understood in his sense will prompt historians to evade their duty to render moral judgments in their work. For a criticism of the idea that determinism and the ability to render moral judgments are incompatible, see White (1965: 273–77), who subscribes to definition 2 and argues that even voluntary actions are caused by something: "all events, including choices, are determined" (p. 277; on this point, cf. also Carr, [1961] 1964: 95–96).
Braudel, Fernand. [1958] 1980. "History and the Social Sciences: The *Longue Durée*." In Fernand Braudel, *On History*. Chicago: 25–54.

————. 1981. *The Structures of Everyday Life: The Limits of the Possible*. New York.

Breisach, Ernst. 1983. *Historiography: Ancient, Medieval, and Modern*. Chicago.

Buckle, H. T. [1856] 1972. *History of Civilization in England*. In Stern: 121–137.

Bury, J. B. [1916] 1964. "Cleopatra's Nose." In Harold Temperley, ed., *Selected Essays of J. B. Bury*. Amsterdam: 60–69.

Carr, E. H. [1961] 1964. *What Is History?* Harmondsworth, Eng. This is a key source. Carr defines *determinism* as the view that "everything that happens has a cause or causes, and could not have happened differently unless something in the cause or causes had also been different" (p. 93). The work contains a spirited attack on Berlin and Popper and generally complements the work of Bury ([1916] 1964), Nagel ([1960] 1969), and White (1965).

Cheyney, Edward P. 1927. "Law in History." In Edward P. Cheyney, *Law in History and Other Essays*. New York: 1–29.

Cioffari, Vincenzo. 1973. "Fortune, Fate, and Chance." *DHI* 2: 225–36. This entry includes a short bibliography. It covers the period from antiquity to the Renaissance.

Donagan, Alan. 1973. "Determinism in History." *DHI* 2: 18–25. Donagan maintains that the ideas of determinism and historical inevitability must be carefully distinguished, since historical inevitability "may be asserted on either determinist or nondeterminist grounds" (p. 20–21).

Dray, W. H. 1964. *Philosophy of History*. Englewood Cliffs, N.J. See especially the discussion of the "non-deterministic" nature of Hegel's idea of necessity, pp. 74–75, which underscores the importance of the notion of contingency—"the fortunate timely availability of both men and conditions."

————. 1967. "Determinism in History." *EP* 2: 373–78. Dray notes that it is "generally agreed that the conflict between historical determinists and indeterminists cannot be resolved by the offering of proofs and disproofs" but that "few contemporary philosophers regard indeterminism as an acceptable assumption to carry into historical or social investigation" (p. 378).

Droysen, J. G. [1868] 1972. "Art and Method." In Stern: 137–44.

Egan, Kieran. 1978. "Thucydides, Tragedian." In Canary and Kozicki: 63–92.

Fischer, David Hackett. 1970. *Historians' Fallacies: Toward a Logic of Historical Thought*. New York.

Geyl, Pieter. 1958. *Debates with Historians*. Cleveland, Ohio. The author supports Berlin (1954) in arguing that the crucial point is "not that *determinism* is a fallacy, but that *to apply determinism to history* is an impossible and necessarily misleading method" (p. 267).

Grant, Michael. 1970. *The Ancient Historians*. New York.

Gustavson, Carl G. 1976. *The Mansion of History*. New York. Gustavson characterizes *determinism* as the belief that "powerful causal forces beyond human control" determine the course of history (p. 158).

Higham, John. 1965. *History*. Englewood Cliffs, N.J.

Holborn, Hajo. [1955] 1972. "Misfortune and Moral Decisions in German History." In Hajo Holborn, *History and the Humanities*. Garden City, N.Y.: 187–95. Holborn illuminates appeals to necessity in German historiography, especially in the work of Ranke and Friedrich Meinecke.

Hook, Sidney. 1943. *The Hero in History: A Study in Limitation and Possibility*. New York. Chapters four and five deal with "social determinism." Hook argues, like

Berlin (1954), that determinism is reprehensible because it involves the elimination of individual responsibility. See especially the discussion of the shared assumptions of various forms of social determinism, pp. 65–66. Hook considers Marxism the "most impressive system of social determinism in our times" (p. 75).

Leff, Gordon. 1971. *History and Social Theory*. Garden City, N.Y. This work is representative of mainstream professional views. Chapter three deals with "contingency" and is a strong defense of the "indeterminacy" of human affairs (see p. 44).

Nagel, Ernest. [1960] 1969. "Determinism in History." In Nash: 319–50. This is a key article, also reprinted in Dray: 347–82. Note the helpful discussion of "chance" in historiographical usage, pp. 340–43.

Nash, Ronald H., ed. 1969. *Ideas of History* 2. New York. This book contains a section on "historical determinism," pp. 300–350.

Plumb, J. H. 1969. *The Death of the Past*. Boston. Chapter two is entitled "The Past as Destiny."

Popper, Karl R. 1950. *The Open Society and Its Enemies*. Princeton, N.J.

———. [1957] 1964. *The Poverty of Historicism*. New York. This was first published as a series of articles in 1944–45. Popper argues that social determinisms confuse the fallacious notion of historical laws with the legitimate idea of historical trends.

Ranke, Leopold von. [n.d.] 1972. "A Fragment from the 1860's." In Stern: 60–62. Compare this translation with that of Holborn (1972: 190).

Stoianovich, Traian. 1976. *French Historical Method: The Annales Paradigm*. Ithaca, N.Y. See especially pp. 139–41.

Taylor, Richard. 1967. "Determinism." *EP* 2: 359–73.

Trevelyan, George Macaulay. [1903] 1972. "Clio, A Muse." In Stern: 227–45.

White, Morton. 1965. *Foundations of Historical Knowledge*. New York. A valuable contribution, especially on the question of the alleged incompatibility of determinism and value judgment; see p. 283. The author thinks that Berlin's argument (1954) is based on logically dubious "moral judgment" that "*No one should judge an action as right or as wrong unless he thinks it is voluntary*" (p. 289).

Sources of Additional Information

See LAW; HISTORICAL MATERIALISM; VALUE JUDGMENT. Taylor (1967) is a good introduction to the varieties of philosophical determinism, with a substantial bibliography. See also Robert M. Kingdon, "Determinism in Theology: Predestination," *DHI* 2: 25–31, and Bernard Berofsky, "Free Will and Determinism," *DHI* 2: 236–42. In *The Anatomy of Historical Knowledge* (Baltimore, 1977), Maurice Mandelbaum uses *determinism* to refer narrowly to "any process that takes place under boundary conditions that exclude the influence of outside factors, and in which what occurs can be said to represent the self-transformation of a system according to some set of laws" (p. 105). Good starting points for information on *historical* determinisms are the short bibliographies in Dray (1967), Nash (1969), and Donagan (1973). See especially Sidney Hook's discussion of the terms *cause; chance, accident*, and *contingency*; and *destiny, fate*, and *predestination* in Bull. 54, pp. 110–16, 119–20. See also Pieter Geyl, "The American Civil War and the Problem of Inevitability," in Pieter Geyl, *Debates with Historians* (Cleveland, 1958): 244–63. R. G. Collingwood comments on Bury's position in *The Idea of History* (1946; reprint ed., New York, 1956), pp. 148–51. There is an excellent discussion of some aspects of the problem in W. H. Walsh, "Colligatory Concepts in History," in W. H. Burston and D. Thompson, eds., *Studies in the Nature and Teaching of History* (London, 1967): 65–84, especially 68–72. Gardiner contains several relevant selections, including Georgi Plekhanov's famous "Role of the Individual in History." Ellsworth Huntington, *Mainsprings of Civilization* (New York, 1945), by a geographer, is often cited as a recent effort to argue for geographical determinism. Melvin Rader, *Marx's Interpretation of History* (New York, 1979), defends Marx against the charge of determinism, for example, pp. 14–18. For more on the concept of "structure" see the footnote citations in Stoianovich (1976) and—in connection with Marxism—Alfred Schmidt, *History and Structure: An Essay on Hegelian—Marxist and Structuralist Theories of History* (Cambridge, Mass., 1981). Consult also the titles on "Funktionalismus, Strukturalismus, und Systemtheorie" in Berding: 128–37. On "manifest destiny" in American history see Frederick and Lois B. Merk, *Manifest Destiny and Mission in American History: A Reinterpretation* (New York, 1963); also the titles listed in volume two of the *Harvard Guide to American History*, rev. ed. (Cambridge, Mass., 1974): 813–21. John Passmore has written an essay on "History, Freedom, and Inevitability," *Philosophical Review* 68 (1959): 93–102. Meyerhoff contains many relevant selections, including excerpts from the work of Berlin and Popper.

DEVELOPMENT. See PROCESS.

DIALECTIC. 1. In speculative PHILOSOPHY OF HISTORY, a principle of social development according to which events move progressively forward through a process of conflict and transcendence of opposing forces. 2. More generally, a style of thought or broad approach to historical explanation that represents social change in terms of tensions, conflicts, and contradictions.

Dialectic is an old and extremely complex term of ancient Greek origin; one of its earliest meanings in Greek was "art of conversation" (Hall, 1967: 385). Since the eighteenth century the word has "passed into fairly common if often difficult usage" (Williams, 1976: 92). The term is regularly encountered in modern historical writing, where its meaning is, however, almost never precisely defined. Most historians who use the term proceed as though its meaning were generally understood, and context is seldom very helpful in understanding a given writer's exact understanding of the word.

In characterizing the term, special care must be taken to speak of loosely related traditions of usage rather than exact or generally agreed upon meanings. Sidney Hook ([1940] 1966: 250) states that "Few philosophers have ever employed the term in the same sense as any of their predecessors. Indeed, rarely is it the case that any philosopher has consistently adhered to any one meaning in his writings." Roland Hall (1967: 385) cites eight meanings that have been "among the more important" in the history of philosophy; additional senses of the word have developed outside the realm of systematic thought. A major source of mystification is the widespread practice of referring indiscriminately to *dialectic, dialectical theory*, the *dialectic, dialectics*, and so on. Some of these words suggest an imminent force that propels the course of history; others imply an intellectual method. In many cases (especially in the Hegelian and Marxian traditions) there is the suggestion of interlacing meanings. The use of *method* in connection with *dialectic* is—outside the Platonic tradition (see below)—a source of frequent difficulty; in the cases of Hegel and Marx, for example, the "dialectical method" can be described as such only in the most casual sense (comparable, e.g., to the loose way METHOD is sometimes used in the expression *historical method*); *method* here does not refer to a precise technique with clearly established rules and procedures but to a broad approach or orientation.

For these reasons—and because of its associations with the philosophically untenable doctrine of Soviet "dialectical materialism" (see HISTORICAL MATE-RIALISM)—the word has recently fallen out of favor among Anglo-American philosophers (e.g., Popper, 1940); even those who seek to refurbish the term admit its difficulty and often find it easier to specify what *dialectic* does *not* mean than to say what it is (for instance, Mink, 1969: 22–23; 1972: 168). Perhaps because of its very obscurity, combined with its ancient pedigree, the word enjoys a certain mystique that attracts many historians. They often use it as a high-sounding substitute for more mundane terms such as *alteration, interaction*, or *struggle* (for example, Stromberg, 1975: 568; Stoianovich, 1976: 77, 140). On the other hand, it would be wrong to dismiss *dialectic* as nothing but a glib catch-word; too many important philosophers have taken the term seriously. Moreover, there are understandable reasons for its appeal to historians (see below).

Philosophical usage dates from the fifth century B.C. The best-known ancient meaning of the term is the one employed by Plato to describe Socrates' style of debate—a "prolonged cross-examination [in the form of a conversation or dialogue] which refutes the opponent's original thesis by getting him to draw from it, by means of a series of questions and answers, a consequence that contradicts it" (Hall, 1967: 386). In teaching theory this is sometimes called the "Socratic method," that is, the technique whereby an instructor, through question and answer, attempts to "bring out of the pupil's mind that which lies hidden in it" (Boas, 1973: 543). Here we see a hint of certain associations prominent in nonpedagogical uses of the term—for example, the notion that truth emerges through argument, opposition, and resolution.

Of special importance was the usage of the Greek stoic philosophers, who employed *dialectic* as a broad synonym for *logic*. This extremely generalized usage, transmitted by the Romans, was common in the Middle Ages and the early-modern period and was the way the word was originally understood in English (Hall, 1967: 387; Williams, 1976: 91).

Modern use received its main impulse from late-eighteenth and early-nineteenth-century German philosophy. Immanuel Kant (1724–1804) first popularized the word by calling his critique of abstract rationalism "transcendental dialectic"; to Kant, *dialectic* implied the exposure of illusion by setting out the contradictions in a philosophical position, and he used the terms *thesis* and *antithesis* to refer to such contradictions (Hall, 1967: 387). In his *Grundlage der gesamten Wissenschaftslehre* (1794), J. G. Fichte, another German thinker, introduced the triad "thesis-antithesis-synthesis" as a formula for the explanation of change, and this idea influenced other idealist philosophers, notably Schelling and G. W. F. Hegel (1770–1831).

Hegel is the most important modern employer of the term, and despite the abstract nature of his thought, his dialectical theory of human events (the unfolding of history's meaning through the conflict and transcendence of particular expressions of the human "spirit" [*Geist*]) put a "peculiar metaphysical leaven into historical thinking," a "fermenting power [that] is not yet spent" (Kuhn, 1949: 16). According to Kuhn (p. 16), "the wide-spread willingness to see history as a field in which antagonist 'forces' operate, testifies to the spectral but effective afterlife" of Hegelian theory.

More than anyone else, Hegel ([1807] 1967: 93) endowed the word *dialectic* with a mystique—referring, for example, to "the portentous power of the negative," "this mighty power," and the "magic power." His ideas are set out in compressed form in the preface to his *Phenomenology of Mind* (1807). Hegel did not invoke Fichte's "thesis-antithesis-synthesis" triad and in fact expressly repudiated the formula (Mueller, 1958: 411; Lichtheim, 1965: 7). The idea that he did use the triad is nevertheless perpetuated in textbooks and classroom lectures, and many authorities appear unwilling to discuss his ideas without referring to it (e.g., Popper, 1940: 404; Körner, 1973: 359). In fact, although Hegel rejected the Fichtean schema, it is at least arguable that his dialectic can be described in Fichtean terms (Lichtheim, 1967: xxiv).

For Hegel (as for his follower Marx), *dialectic* is both a world process and a mode of thought, because he believes that human inquiry mirrors the natural pattern of social evolution. The driving idea that underlies Hegel's spiritualist conception of history (see IDEALISM) is the notion that the whole of reality interacts with its individual components:

> The dialectical method is meant to conform to the actual structure of reality, conceived as a process in which the logical subject unfolds itself into its own predicates . . . the content and the method are seen to coincide . . . for Hegel there is in the last analysis no distinction between mind and its object. . . . Spirit is both subjective and objective, and its "internal contradictions" are resolved in the dialectical process, whereby the potentialities of all things unfold in a pattern of self-transcendence to a higher unity. (Lichtheim, 1965: 8)

The notion of preservation in transformation, captured in the German verb *aufheben*, is crucial to Hegel's understanding.

Hegel's position is based on the idea that history is a process comprehensible to human reason. He believed that each "World Historical People . . . makes its contribution to spiritual advance through the development and cultural assertion of its own distinctive idea or principle" and that

> these principles are related in such a way that they represent a "logical" progression . . . they have the kind of [logical] order which he believes can be found in the

stages of any constructive piece of rational reflection which proceeds from an inadequate, one-sided understanding of its object to an ever more sophisticated, many-sided grasp of it. . . . Hegel regards such a pattern of tension and resolution as the very "mechanism" of reason; and this is what he claims to discover, although in a much less definite form, in the rational progress of history. . . . The principles of Greece and Rome, for example, are seen as antithetical ways of trying to express the idea of freedom in society, the latter being a reaction against the one-sidedness of the former. (Dray, 1964: 73–74)

As far as most historians' working understanding of this abstruse theory is concerned, Herbert Heaton's rough characterization is probably fairly representative—that is, a

method of rebutting one argument with another, of seeing one line of development reach a certain point, then be challenged and pushed aside by an opposite one, which in turn was elbowed out of the way by a third; and so-on, zig-zag, toward a less imperfect, yet never fully perfect world. ([1943] 1950: 88)

Marx's and Engels' position is an outgrowth of Hegel's thought; like Hegel's theory, it is based on the idea of an interlocking relationship between human thought and historical development. For Marx, history is the unfolding of human freedom, a process driven forward by contradiction, conflict, and transcendence manifested in recurring struggles between economic CLASSes. That he understood dialectic as an intellectual method as well as a social process is clear—he explicitly referred to "my dialectic method" (Marx, [1873] 1972: 197)—although precisely what he understood the nature of this method and its operation to be is the subject of highly technical debate (see, for example, Rosdolsky, 1974; Rabinbach, 1974; Moore, 1971). Some appreciation of the difficulties involved may be gained by reading Marx's afterword to the second German edition of *Capital* ([1873] 1972: 195), where he complains that his "method . . . has been little understood." It would be possible to interpret Marx's remarks in this passage in various ways; what seems important is that it reflects a loose sense of dialectic as an outlook, or intellectual stance, rather than as a disciplined technique of inquiry. Indeed, some scholars are wary of referring to dialectic as a "method" in Marx, preferring to speak of it in terms of an "approach" or style of "presentation" (Shaw, 1978: 107–8). One author (Rader, 1979: xv, xvii-xix) has sought to domesticate the idea by suggesting that dialectic in Marx is best understood metaphorically as a broad analogy or "heuristic model," that is, "an imaginary construction intended to guide somebody in the pursuit of knowledge." This seems useful, although it must be remembered that the theory of intellectual "models" is an expression of twentieth-century sociology, not a product of Marx's own day (see IDEAL TYPE; MODEL).

The term *dialectic* and *dialectics* took on new meaning in the work of Marx's friend Engels, who sought to popularize Marx's ideas. Hook ([1940] 1966: 184–95) identifies seven distinct meanings, some incompatible, in the work of Engels alone. In the so-called "Anti-Dühring" (*Herr Eugen Dühring's Revolution in*

Science [1878]), as well as in manuscripts published posthumously under the title *Dialectics of Nature*, Engels represented *dialectic* as a general law of change analogous to the laws of natural science. His usage inspired the doctrine of "dialectical materialism," the official philosophy of Soviet Russia since the Bolshevik Revolution of 1917. Whether or to what extent this doctrine corresponds to Marx's own views is a subject of controversy (see HISTORICAL MATERIALISM). Generally, in current Marxist scholarship the word *dialectic* is used to elicit the sense of relatedness in opposition and unity in diversity; but this often evaporates into what one critic, in a slightly different context, calls a "scholasticism of resolving antimonies" (Skinner, 1969: 22) where references to Marx's notion can be absolutely mystifying (e.g., Levine, 1975: 11, and *passim*).

On the positive side, some implications of the term have received unusually clear exposition in Louis O. Mink's short essay on dialectic in the thought of the twentieth-century British philosopher R. G. Collingwood (1972). Mink's theme is the dialectical mode of conceptualization, which, he alleges, informs Collingwood's outlook on history. According to Mink, Collingwood viewed human experience in terms of series, or sequences, of becoming. These series he understood in terms reminiscent of Hegel: "each form of experience undergoes its own typical development in the course of which it generates tensions which it cannot resolve within its own form. At the same time it has developed in an implicit and rudimentary way the elements of the next form of experience" (Mink, 1972: 169). Collingwood considered human thought and social processes interrelated on various levels, "so that one includes but transforms the other" (Mink, 1972: 168). History from his standpoint is a complex of changing relations in which the past is both preserved and transformed. In the most general sense, *dialectic* refers only to a type of relationship that may exist within a series; a

> dialectical series is *cumulative* in the sense that earlier or "lower" members are not merely replaced by later or "higher" members but are preserved although modified in the later ones; elements of the earlier may even survive unmodified. Thus in the transition of one architectural style to another the former is not (usually) entirely abandoned. (Mink, 1972: 173)

It is not difficult to see why such a general notion might appeal to historians, since it enables them to grasp not only the interconnectedness of historical phenomena but simultaneously to account as well for both novelty and the persistence of tradition in social change—a complex kind of awareness that virtually every historian comes to appreciate in the course of his work.

Unfortunately, in most historiographical usage the meanings attributed to the term are simply not made clear. If *dialectic* is understood as an "axiom" that "posits change and contradiction as fundamental features of social reality" (Henretta, 1979: 1301) or a pattern by which one generation "may not wholly assimilate, but may partly challenge," traditions inherited from another (Barnard, 1963: 205), then this is simply banal and requires no assistance from a word with such esoteric overtones. Occasionally, the term appears to serve a useful purpose when, for example, it is employed to designate a situation in which some institution, event, and so on seems to create a challenge to itself—for example: "The crown had thus, by a kind of dialectic, raised up forces which it could not control" (Pocock, [1957] 1967: 118). The term has also been suggestively employed in connection with strategies of historical EXPLANATION and NARRATIVE. Cushing Strout ([1961] 1966: 60–61), for instance, uses it to refer to the poetic "logic" of dramatic tension that he believes is necessary to historical exposition, adding that his usage "does not entail any Hegelian scheme." Even in this regard, however, it has been noted that the concept of "dialectical tension" can function as a protean "catch-all device for dealing with a multitude of problems" (Pomper, 1980: 33). Recent efforts to use the idea as a broad conceptual framework for interpreting long-range trends (e.g., Gay, 1966: xi) have aroused suspicions of glib "window dressing" (Darton, 1971: 116). Indeed, much usage seems inspired by little more than rhetorical fashion—for example, the stark, unamplified assertion that twentieth-century FASCISM was "one of the products of the dialectical movement of European civilization" (Sauer, [1967] 1975: 112). In historiography, *dialectic* is in most cases probably best understood not as a precise concept but as a kind of "imagination" (Jay, 1973: 63), sensibility, or cast of mind that organizes and depicts social reality in terms of organic PROCESS, conflict, and flux.

References

Barnard, F. M. 1963. "Herder's Treatment of Causation and Continuity in History." *JHI* 24: 197–212.

Boas, George. 1973. "Idea." *DHI* 2: 542–48.

Darnton, Robert. 1971. "In Search of the Enlightenment: Recent Attempts to Create a Social History of Ideas." *JMH* 43: 113–32. This is a critical review of Peter Gay's *Enlightenment* (see below), which regards Gay's use of the idea of dialectic as theoretical scaffolding imposed on the evidence.

Dray, William H. 1964. *Philosophy of History*. Englewood Cliffs, N.J. Chapter six includes a concise sketch of Hegel's theory.

Gay, Peter. 1966. *The Enlightenment: An Interpretation* 1. New York.

Hall, Roland. 1967. "Dialectic." *EP* 2: 385–89. This piece includes a concise bibliography that slights the literature on Marx.

Heaton, Herbert. [1943] 1950. "The Economic Impact on History." In Strayer: 87–117.

Hegel, G. W. F. [1807] 1967. *The Phenomenology of Mind*. New York. The preface contains Hegel's most compressed discussion of the idea of dialectic. This edition includes a bibliography of Hegel's writings as well as critical studies of Hegel.

Henretta, James A. 1979. "Social History as Lived and Written." *AHR* 84: 1293–1322.

Hook, Sidney. [1940] 1966. *Reason, Social Myths, and Democracy*. New York. Hook argues that "it would be best in the interests of clarity to let the term [*dialectic*] sink into the desuetude of archaisms" (p. 250).

Jay, Martin. 1973. *The Dialectical Imagination: A History of the Frankfurt School and the Institute of Social Research, 1923–1950*. Boston. Jay presents a sympathetic though critical study of the twentieth-century "Frankfurt School" of Marxism.

He notes that for this group "Dialectics was superb at attacking other systems' pretensions to truth, but when it came to articulating the ground of its own assumptions and values, it fared less well" (p. 63).

Körner, Stephan. 1973. "Necessity." *DHI* 3: 351–62.

Kuhn, Helmut. 1949. "Dialectic in History." *JHI* 10: 14–29. Kuhn argues that "the thesis of the intrinsically dialectical character of the historical process" is erroneous, and that "the prevalence of the dialectic schema in historical thinking tends to dehumanize history" (pp. 16, 26).

Levine, Norman. 1975. *The Tragic Deception: Marx Contra Engels*. Santa Barbara, Calif. This book exemplifies fetishistic and careless usage.

Lichtheim, George. 1965. *Marxism: An Historical and Critical Study*. New York.

———. 1967. "Introduction." In G. W. F. Hegel, *The Phenomenology of Mind*. New York: xv–xxxii. This work is recommended, along with the preceding title, because of Lichtheim's skill in translating the concepts of German idealism for the benefit of English-speaking readers.

Marx, Karl. [1873] 1972. "Afterword" to the Second German edition of *Capital*. In Robert C. Tucker, ed., *The Marx-Engels Reader*. New York: 195–98.

Mink, Louis O. 1969. *Mind, History, and Dialectic: The Philosophy of R. G. Collingwood*. Bloomington, Ind.

———. 1972. "Collingwood's Historicism: A Dialectic of Process." In Michael Krausz, ed., *Critical Essays on the Philosophy of R. G. Collingwood*. Oxford: 154–78. This piece is highly recommended.

Moore, Stanley. 1971. "Marx and the Origin of Dialectical Materialism." *Inquiry* 14: 420–29.

Mueller, Gustav E. 1958. "The Hegel Legend of 'Thesis-Antithesis-Synthesis'." *JHI* 19: 411–14. Mueller asserts that the identification of Hegel with the Fichtean triad was begun by the philosopher Heinrich Mortiz Chalybäus in the 1830s and spread by left-wing Hegelians, especially Marx. Lichtheim (1965: 7, n.2) maintains that Mueller "exaggerates Marx's part in furthering the misconception."

Pocock, J. G. A. [1957] 1967. *The Ancient Constitution and the Feudal Law: A study of English Historical Thought in the Seventeenth Century*. New York.

Pomper, Philip. 1980. "Typologies and Cycles in Intellectual History." *HT Beih.* 19: 30–38.

Popper, Karl R. 1940. "What Is Dialectic?" *Mind*, N.S., 49: 403–26. Popper calls *dialectic* "an empirical descriptive theory" that often has a loose sort of validity but is "rather vague" (pp. 411–12). He considers Hegel's theory "absurd" (p. 415) and Marx's position "even worse than dialectic idealism" (p. 422). Cf. the comments of Mink (1972: 176, n. 1).

Rabinbach, Anson G. 1974. "Roman Rosdolsky, 1897–1967: An Introduction." *New German Critique* 1: 56–61. The author refers to the *dialectic* as "an historical logic in Marx."

Rader, Melvin. 1979. *Marx's Interpretation of History*. New York. This book contains interesting reflections on the relevance of the notion of "Socratic dialogue" for Marx's idea of dialectic.

Rosdolsky, Roman. 1974. "Comments on the Method of Marx's Capital and Its Importance for Contemporary Marxist Scholarship." *New German Critique* 1: 62–72.

Sauer, Wolfgang. [1967] 1975. "National Socialism: Totalitarianism or Fascism?" In Henry A. Turner, Jr., ed., *Reappraisals of Fascism*. New York: 93–116.

Shaw, William H. 1978. *Marx's Theory of History*. Stanford, Calif.

Skinner, Quentin. 1969. "Meaning and Understanding in the History of Ideas." *HT* 8: 3–53.

Stoianovich, Traian. 1976. *French Historical Method: The Annales Paradigm*. Ithaca, N.Y.

Stromberg, R. N. 1975. "Some Models Used by Intellectual Historians." *AHR* 80: 563–73.

Strout, Cushing. [1961] 1966. "Causation and the American Civil War: Two Appraisals." In A. S. Eisenstadt, ed., *The Craft of American History: Selected Essays* 1: 34–62. Strout suggests that "in telling a story the historian is committed to the 'logic' of drama. In explaining [for example] the Civil War he necessarily seeks to recreate the strife of opposing forces out of which the war came. The connective tissue of his account then has a dialectical form: a person or group takes a position and performs an action because of and in relation to the position or action of another position or group. The historian's story becomes a narrative of this reciprocal response" (p. 60).

Williams, Raymond, 1976. *Keywords: A Vocabulary of Culture and Society*. New York.

Sources of Additional Information

For general bibliography see, in addition to Hall (1967), the comprehensive entry "Dialektik" in *HWP* 2: 164–226 and the article "Dialectics" in *MCWS* 2: 405–20. There is a brief characterization of "dialectic" by Sidney Hook in Bull. 54: 120–22; see also chapter five of Hook's *Hero in History: A Study in Limitation and Possibility* (New York, 1943). James Russell defines *dialectics* as the "logical system underlying Marxian science" in his *Marx-Engels Dictionary* (Westport, Conn., 1980), p. 28. There are relevant passages in Philip P. Wiener, "On Methodology in the Philosophy of History," *JP* 38 (June 5, 1941): 309–24, and Otto Hintze, "Troeltsch and the Problems of Historism," in Felix Gilbert, ed., *The Historical Essays of Otto Hintze* (New York, 1975): 368–421. Ronald H. McKinney, "The Origins of Modern Dialectics," *JHI* 44 (1983): 179–90, contains a discussion of the idea's range of meanings in ancient and medieval philosophy. On Hegel see Herbert Marcuse, *Reason and Revolution: Hegel and the Rise of Social Theory* (1941; reprint ed., Boston, 1960), which contains a preface entitled "A Note on Dialectic"; also Walter Kaufmann, *Hegel: A Reinterpretation* (Garden City, N.Y., 1965), and Carl J. Friedrich's "Introduction" to his anthology *The Philosophy of Hegel* (New York, 1953). One of the most influential Marxist discussions is contained in Georg Lukács, *History and Class Consciousness: Studies in Marxist Dialectics* (1922; reprint ed., London, 1971); see, for example, pp. 140–49. Also relevant are many parts of M. M. Bober, *Karl Marx's Interpretation of History* (Cambridge, Mass., 1948), and Z. A. Jordan, *The Evolution of Dialectical Materialism* (London, 1967).

DIALECTICAL MATERIALISM. See HISTORICAL MATERIALISM.

E

ECONOMETRIC HISTORY, NEW ECONOMIC HISTORY, CLIOMET-

RICS. *Econometric history*, the most specific of the three terms, refers to the kind of ECONOMIC HISTORY that systematically employs the statistical models of "econometrics" (that is, quantitative economics). *New economic history* and *cliometrics*—the latter a hybrid of the name Clio (the ancient muse of history) and the idea of measurement—are often used interchangeably with *econometric history*. However, *cliometrics* logically implies any kind of (economic or otherwise) history that makes use of mathematical and statistical theory.

Econometric history, new economic history, and *cliometrics* are American labels coined in the 1960s to designate an approach to ECONOMIC HISTORY characterized by an emphasis on the use of mathematical and statistical techniques. The expression *new economic history* was introduced in 1961 (Davis, Hughes, and McDougall, 1961: vii; Davis, 1971: 106). *Econometric history* was popularized by the titles of two books that appeared three years later (Conrad and Meyer, [1957] 1964; Fogel, 1964). *Cliometrics* has been broadly equated with SCIENTIFIC HISTORY generally (Fogel and Elton, 1983: 23–24), although it is most often used with reference to quantitative economic history. There is no firm consensus on whether these words are synonyms or precisely when and how they should be used, but there is general agreement that all three refer to the systematic use of contemporary, neo-classical economic theory in economic history; since that theory is highly mathematical, this means the use of mathematics and statistical inference.

The three terms were initially employed as synonyms to mean the use of any kind of quantification in the study of economic history, and they are still often used interchangeably (as in Marczewski, 1968: 179–80; Fogel and Engerman,

1974: 6–7; Fogel, 1975: 331). Critics of the approach (e.g., Redlich, 1965: 480, 483), however, pointed out that the adjective *new* was somewhat misleading in that quantitative methods—although never predominant in the field—had been used by economic historians since the nineteenth century. In response there has been some effort to define more precisely *new economic history* as the sort of quantitative economic history that makes use of the "econometric" theoretical models of contemporary neo-classical economics—as opposed to the more traditional use of statistics merely to illustrate conventional narrative. (*Econometrics* refers to the branch of economics that uses mathematical models to solve economic problems [Bannock, Baxter and Rees, 1972: 129]). Lance Davis, for instance, states that

> the "new" history does (or attempts to do) four things. First to state precisely the questions subject to examination and to define operationally the relevant variables. Second, to build explicit models that are relevant to the questions at hand. Third, to produce evidence (frequently quantitative, but at times qualitative) of the world as it actually existed. And finally, to test the model (a logical statement of assumptions and conclusions) against the evidence (the world that did exist) and the counterfactual deduction (the world that did not exist). (1966: 657)

G. N. von Tunzelman ([1968] 1970: 151; cf. Conrad, [1968] 1970: 110) goes further, distinguishing between *new economic history* ("that branch of economic history involving the use of theoretically ordered quantitative data to reject or provisionally accept its given hypothesis") and *econometric history* (a subcategory of new economic history limited to analysis "in which the theoretical ordering of the data follows the precepts of current econometric theory . . . specifically, regression and correlation analysis"). (*Correlation* is a method of statistical inference used to determine the extent to which variations in the values of one factor, or "variable"—for example, investment—are associated with variations in values of another—for example, interest; *regression analysis* is a related technique used to quantify the relationship between two or more variables, often used for economic forecasting).

There is general agreement that the "cliometric" approach dates from the late 1950s and the publication of two articles by Alfred H. Conrad and John R. Meyer ([1957] 1964; [1958] 1964). Before the 1950s, historical use of econometric methods was not practical because theoretical economists were primarily interested in market *equilibrium*, whereas historians were interested in understanding *change*; since the 1940s, however, theoretical economics has attempted to measure and forecast change in the form of economic growth (Redlich, 1965: 482–83; Habakkuk, 1972: 30). This shift in focus opened the door to communication between the two fields, although the underlying emphasis on equilibrium in neo-classical econometric theory is still considered a problem (North, 1977; see ECONOMIC HISTORY).

Conrad's and Meyer's first essay, a plea for the use of statistical and quantitative methods in economic history, argued that statistical inference could be applied to economic history in accordance with the COVERING LAW theory of historical EXPLANATION (Conrad and Meyer, [1957] 1964: 24, 3). Some later practitioners also linked the approach to covering law theory (e.g., Fogel, 1964: 247–49; 1966: 656). Conrad's and Meyer's second essay ([1958] 1964: 44–45) was an analysis of American Negro slavery that used a statistical model based on capital theory to support the controversial conclusion that slavery was a profitable institution in the antebellum South.

Interest in quantitative economic history grew rapidly following the appearance of these two articles. Perhaps the best known examples are Fogel (1964), which used an econometrically designed counterfactual model (see COUNTERFACTUAL ANALYSIS) to contest the widespread view that railroads were indispensable to industrial growth in nineteenth-century America; and Fogel and Engerman (1974), which summarized quantitative research on the slavery question. In addition, since about 1960 articles using the econometric approach have been well represented in scholarly periodicals that specialize in economic history. By the mid–1970s, according to one authority, "econometric" economic history had

> become the predominant form of research in this field, at least in the United States. The majority of the articles published in the main economic history journals of the United States are now quite mathematical, and cliometricians predominate in the leadership of the Economic History Association. (Fogel, 1975: 331–32)

Despite Conrad's and Meyer's ([1957] 1964: 3) desire to "avoid *methoden-streit*," the idea of quantitative economic history aroused heated debate. ECONOMIC HISTORY, since its crystallization as a historiographical subfield in the late nineteenth century, had been primarily based on prose narrative rather than mathematics (Habakkuk, 1972: 30); the discipline was traditionally more descriptive than theoretical and analytical. The focus of most intense controversy was the use of counterfactual (i.e., "contrary to fact") models (Fogel, 1967: 283), a practice that was attacked as "quasi-history" (Redlich, 1965: 484, 486–91; [1968] 1970: 90–96; Chandler, [1968] 1970); the very notion of creating a detailed picture of the past as it might have occurred—even for purposes of comparison with the "actual" past—was bound to arouse debate in a discipline such as history, traditionally devoted to the reconstruction of the past "as it actually happened" (see REALISM; SCIENTIFIC HISTORY).

Equally controversial was the fabrication of missing data by the use of statistical inference from existing evidence. This practice utilizes

> indirect rather than direct measurement, that is, when the information sought cannot be obtained directly by counting in the most appropriate source, but must instead be inferred from the measurement of some other attribute. Such inference requires that there be a mathematical relationship between what is wanted and what one measures, and this means bringing "equations into a literary discipline." (Beringer, 1978: 308)

By "postcasting" such "statistical reconstructions," econometric historians sought to bridge lacunae in documentary evidence, gaps that were abundant for periods before the twentieth century when governments did not keep extensive statistical records (Conrad, [1968] 1970: 120; Tunzelmann, [1968] 1970: 154; Habakkuk, 1972: 31). Again, the notion of fabricating evidence ran strongly against the grain of disciplinary tradition. According to Habbakuk,

> Propositions derived from economic reasoning of these kinds, when used in the construction of quantitative data, are particularly liable to give rise to false conclusions, because they are based on assumptions which do not correspond to reality. Econometric history raises the same difficulties as econometrics itself. (1972: 35)

Despite such criticisms, econometric history continues to attract and inspire practitioners—although champions of the approach are now somewhat chastened in their expectations of what it can accomplish (see, for example, Fogel, 1975; North, 1977). In summing up, a judicious observer concludes that "So far the methods have had a high degree of success and have advanced thought and knowledge of a surprisingly wide range of problems" (Habakkuk, 1972: 41).

References

Bannock, G., Baxter, R. E., and Rees, R. 1972. "Econometrics." *The Penguin Dictionary of Economics*. Harmondsworth, Eng.: 129.

Beringer, Richard E. 1978. *Historical Analysis: Contemporary Approaches to Clio's Craft*. New York. This book includes excerpts from quantitative studies that illustrate the use of statistical techniques such as regression analysis; there is a valuable bibliography.

Chandler, Alfred D., Jr. [1968] 1970. "Comment." In Ralph L. Andreano, ed., *The New Economic History: Recent Papers on Methodology*. New York: 143–50. Chandler suggests that the attempt to combine econometrics and economic history was generally ill-advised, since econometrics is designed largely as a tool for the formulation of economic policy and forecasting.

Conrad, Alfred H. [1968] 1970. "Econometrics and Southern History." In Ralph L. Andreano, ed., *The New Economic History: Recent Papers on Methodology*. New York: 109–27. The author stresses the crucial role of mathematical model-building in econometric history (see pp. 110–11).

Conrad, Alfred H., and Meyer, John R. [1957] 1964. "Economic Theory, Statistical Inference, and Economic History." In Alfred H. Conrad and John R. Meyer, *The Economics of Slavery and Other Studies in Econometric History*. Chicago: 3–30. This is the pioneering manifesto of econometric history, in which the authors nevertheless acknowledge hazards in the approach (p. 24).

————. [1958] 1964. "The Economics of Slavery in the Antebellum South." In Alfred H. Conrad and John R. Meyer, *The Economics of Slavery and Other Studies in Econometric History*. Chicago: 43–114.

Davis, Lance E. 1966. "Professor Fogel and the New Economic History." *The Economic History Review*, 2d Series, 19: 657–63.

————. 1971. "Specification, Quantification, and Analysis in Economic History." In George Rogers Taylor and Lucius F. Ellsworth, eds., *Approaches to American*

Economic History. Charlottesville, Va.: 106–20. This piece contains a brief annotated bibliography.

Davis, Lance E., Hughes, Jonathan R. T., and McDougall, Duncan M. 1961. *American Economic History: The Development of a National Economy*. Homewood, Ill.

Fogel, Robert William. 1964. *Railroads and American Economic Growth: Essays in Econometric History*. Baltimore.

———. 1966. "The New Economic History." *The Economic History Review*, 2d Series, 19: 642–56. This is an early survey of methods and points of controversy. It links the new economic history to covering law theory, arguing that "the fundamental methodological feature of the new economic history is its attempt to cast all explanations of past economic development in the form of valid hypothetico-deductive mdoels" (p. 656).

———. 1967. "The Specification Problem in Economic History." *The Journal of Economic History* 27: 283–308.

———. 1975. "The Limits of Quantitative Methods in History." *AHR* 80: 329–50. The author, the most celebrated champion of econometric history in the 1960s, expresses some second thoughts about the approach.

Fogel, Robert William, and Elton, G. R. 1983. *Which Road to the Past? Two Views of History*. New Haven, Conn. According to Fogel, the "common characteristic of cliometricians is that they apply the quantitative methods and behavioral models of the social sciences to the study of history" (p. 24). In this exchange Elton, once an opponent of quantitative methods, tempers his views.

Fogel, Robert William; and Engerman, Stanley L. 1974. *Time on the Cross: The Economics of American Negro Slavery*. Boston.

Habakkuk, John. 1972. "Economic History and Economic Theory." In Gilbert and Graubard: 27–44. This is a balanced assessment.

Marczewski, Jean. 1968. "Quantitative History." *Journal of Contemporary History* 3: 179–91.

North, Douglass C. 1977. "The New Economic History after Twenty Years." *American Behavioral Scientist* 21: 187–200.

Redlich, Fritz. 1965. " 'New' and Traditional Approaches to Economic History and Their Interdependence." *The Journal of Economic History* 25: 480–95. This is an important essay by the chief early critic of new economic history.

———. [1968] 1970. "Potentialities and Pitfalls in Economic History." In Ralph L. Andreano, ed., *The New Economic History: Recent Papers on Methodology*. New York: 85–99.

Tunzelman, G. N. von. [1968] 1970. "The New Economic History: An Econometric Appraisal." In Ralph L. Andreano, ed., *The New Economic History: Recent Papers on Methodology*. New York: 151–75.

Sources of Additional Information

See also the references cited in the entries ECONOMIC HISTORY, QUANTIFICATION, and COUNTERFACTUAL ANALYSIS. Good sources of bibliography are Harry N. Schreiber, "On the New Economic History—And Its Limitations: A Review Essay," *Agricultural History* 41 (1967): 383–95, and Thomas C. Cochran, "Economic History, Old and New," *AHR* 74 (1969): 1561–72. See also Paul Janssens, "Historie économique ou économie retrospective?" *HT* 13 (1974): 21–38 (with an English abstract in *HT* 16 [1977]: 95), as well as the heated exchange between David Landes, R. M. Hartwell, and Robert Higgs in

AHR 76 (1971): 467–74, 1633–37, and 77 (1972): 237–39, provoked by Landes' failure to use explicit economic theory in his *Unbound Prometheus* (1969). Peter D. McClelland, *Causal Explanation and Model Building in History, Economics, and the New Economic History* (Ithaca, N.Y. 1975), is a comprehensive study. Jacques Barzun, *Clio and the Doctors: Psycho-History, Quanto-History, and History* (Chicago, 1974), contains an angry attack on quantification in history. Ralph L. Andreano, ed., *The New Economic History: Recent Papers on Methodology* (New York, 1970), is an invaluable anthology. Other useful anthologies that contain illustrations of the method include Peter Temin, ed., *New Economic History* (Harmondsworth, Eng., 1973), and Robert W. Fogel and Stanley L. Engerman, eds., *The Reinterpretation of American Economic History* (New York, 1971). Most of the basic issues were raised in the storm of controversy that followed the publication of Fogel and Engerman's *Time on the Cross* (1974); consult the *Book Review Index* for critical response. There are several general guides to quantitative methods, including Roderick Floud, *An Introduction to Quantitative Methods for Historians* (Princeton, N.J., 1973); Edward Shorter, *The Historian and the Computer: A Practical Guide* (Englewood Cliffs, N.J., 1971); Charles M. Dollar and Richard J. Jensen, *Historian's Guide to Statistics: Quantitative Analysis and Historical Research* (New York, 1971); and V. O. Key, Jr., *A Primer of Statistics for Political Scientists* (New York, 1966).

ECONOMIC HISTORY. The subfield of history devoted to the study of past economic events; *economic events* may mean (1) economic life in its broad relationship to institutional, social, and cultural life or (2) more narrowly, problems of supply, demand, economic growth, and income distribution. The use of quantitative data and mathematical analysis is often closely associated with the field.

Research on the early history of economic history is still sparse, but it is clear that specialized historical interest in economic subjects arose quite recently; insofar as professional historiography is concerned, the field is mainly a product of the late nineteenth and early twentieth centuries (Jacunsky, 1964: 576, 584). Frederic Seebohm's *English Village Community: An Essay in Economic History* (1883) was the first important study in English to use the term, and the first chair of economic history in either Britain or America was established at Harvard in 1892 (Clapham, 1931b: 318; Gras, 1931: 326).

Historians had displayed occasional interest in economic matters from the earliest times, and scattered passages relating to economic life may be found in the work of various ancient, medieval, and early modern authors. The *Florentine Chronicles* of Giovanni Villani (c. 1272–1348), for example, contain substantial information on economic matters (Jacunsky, 1964: 576). Economic subjects were long considered unworthy of consideration (Clapham, 1931b: 315), however, and pre-modern historiography was overwhelmingly political or religious in emphasis, never systematically economic. Indeed, specialized interest in economic history did not originate among historians themselves but among the merchants and public officials of seventeenth-century Europe. Among the earliest examples of the genre are Peter De la

Court's *Interest van Holland* (1662), by a Dutch woolen mill owner (which includes a history of European trade from the tenth century onward), and several studies of economic life in antiquity (e.g., Wilhelm Gues's agrarian history of Rome, *Rei agrariae auctores legesque varii* [1674]. The rise of the field was related to the rapid commercial expansion of seventeenth-century western Europe and the resulting growth of interest in the collection of economic data and regulation of mercantile life as an aspect of state power (Clapham, 1931b: 315).

In the eighteenth century, many studies of public finance appeared, such as François de Forbonnais' *Recherches et considérations sur les finances de la France* (1758) and James Postlethwayt's *History of the Public Revenue from 1688 to 1758* (1759). William Petty, an Englishman, dreamed of creating a "political arithmetic" that would enable states to establish policy quantitatively (Clapham, 1931b: 315); systematic collection of statistics by governments began in the late eighteenth century, paving the way for efforts to measure past economic performance. (The immediate impact of statistical compilation should not be overstressed, however; as Clapham [1931b: 317] notes, "until 1850 and in some fields until much later the gaps were immense.")

Especially significant was work on the history of international trade from the second half of the eighteenth century, particularly in Britain—for example, Adam Anderson's *Historical and Chronological Deduction of the Origin of Commerce from the Earliest Accounts* (1763) (a South Seas Company official's effort to write a UNIVERSAL HISTORY from an economic point of view). At this time the expression *history of trade* (or *commerce*) was an umbrella label for the historical study of economic life. Not all early studies were general in scope, however; many histories of specialized topics appeared, for example, John Smith's *Chronicon rusticum-commerciale*; or, *Memoirs of Wool* (1747), and Bishop Fleetwood's *Chronicon preciosum* (1707), a history of prices. The latter work was used and revised by Adam Smith, whose "incidental use" of economic history was typical of the early political economists (Gay, [1941] 1953: 407).

The early-nineteenth-century rise of NATIONALISM and the advent of INDUSTRIALIZATION were crucial in stimulating a more systematic interest in economic history. In Germany, particularly, the growth of national consciousness and the desire for economic policies that would benefit the nation drew attention to the significance of the economic past; for example, Friedrich List's *Das nationale System der politischen Okonomie* (1841) encouraged economists to "study problems of wealth not at a point in time and all on one plane but to think of live changing nations on different and shifting planes and of the growth of their productive powers" (Clapham, 1931b: 317; also Gay, [1941] 1953: 407–8). This orientation triumphed in the new "historical school" of economics inspired by Wilhelm Roscher's *Staatswirthschaft nach geschichtlicher Methode* (1843) and was carried to its peak in the mid- and late-nineteenth century by Karl Knies (1821–1898) and, particularly, Gustav Schmoller (1838–1917) (Lane and Riemersma: 432–36). The historical school repudiated the abstract theorizing of classical economics and, especially in Schmoller, displayed a bias against mathematics (Gay, [1941] 1953: 411). The work of this school established models for historians in Germany, where economic history in its "comprehensive and independent" form first appeared, exemplified by Karl von Inama-Sternegg's *Deutsche Wirthschaftsgeschichte*" (1879–99) (Clapham, 1931b: 318). The Schmoller school sought to establish stage theories of economic development based on empirical research into the economic past, and its influence on historiography culminated in Werner Sombart's controversial *Der moderne Kapitalismus* (1902–27) (Pirenne, 1931: 322) (see CAPITALISM). Early twentieth-century economists rejected the historical approach on the grounds that the "central problems of economic theory, although they may be stated in terms of some particular historic phase, are in essence independent of history" (Clapham, 1931a: 329; Heckscher, [1928] 1953: 421). Still, the historical school dominated economic thought in late-nineteenth-century Germany and had a powerful impact on historians as well as economists in Britain, France, and the United States.

In the earliest work by professional historians, economic history was typically approached as an adjunct of legal and institutional history (Clapham, 1931b: 319); this is illustrated in many scholarly works, for example, in Fustel de Coulanges' famous study *La cité antique* (1864) and in Bishop Stubbs' *Select Charters of Constitutional History* (1870). Most of the important early work was done on the classical, medieval, and early-modern periods, since previous work in source collection and criticism was most highly developed for these periods (Clapham, 1931b: 319). Among medievalists, a controversy raged throughout the nineteenth century over the "Roman" or "Teutonic" origin of the institutions of the Middle Ages. The debate really concerned legal and political issues, but it also stimulated research on economic themes. This tradition culminated in the landmark studies of the Austrian medievalist Alfons Dopsch, which—along with the work of the Belgian scholar Henri Pirenne, the Russian Mikhail Rostovtzeff, and the American James Westfall Thompson—helped to solidify the concept of economic historiography at the turn of the twentieth century.

By this time, especially in Germany, economic history had largely broken its links with political history and was tied to the history of society under the rubric "social and economic history." The first scholarly periodical devoted to economic history was the *Vierteljahrschrift für Sozial- und Wirtschaftsgeschichte*, established in 1893. By now the economic component was not overshadowed but was "overwhelmingly preponderant"—an extremely important development for historiography in general since it "revealed the desire for an approach to history systematically different from the classical Rankean one" (Hobsbawn, 1972: 2–3), that is, one primarily oriented to the study of politics and diplomacy. J. H. Clapham (1931a: 329), the greatest of the early-twentieth-century British economic historians, expressed the feeling of most specialists of his generation when he said that "as the main concerns of society are and always have been economic, by far the greater part of social history . . . is simply economic history" (see SOCIAL HISTORY). Despite some continuing resistance (Gras, 1931: 327), economic history had gained recognition as one of the major categories of historical study.

The new appreciation of economic factors undoubtedly owed something to the influence of Marxism, which stressed the primacy of economic conditions in historical change (see HISTORICAL MATERIALISM). It is likely, however, that the sheer impact of industrialization on late-nineteenth-century consciousness was more important than any specific doctrine in drawing historians' attention to the importance of economic forces. Still, Marx had published the first volume of *Capital* in 1867, and beginning in the 1870s the "Marxian conception of capitalism slowly acquired a prominent place in historical thought" (Clapham, 1931b: 319). Arnold Toynbee's lectures on the Industrial Revolution delivered at Oxford in 1881–82 reflected a knowledge of Marx's work in French translation; yet in 1887 Thorold Rogers (author of a *History of Agriculture and Prices* [1866–87]) gave "no sign of having heard of Marx" in his course "The Economic Interpretation of History" at the same university; the usual view is that Marxism did not exert a strong influence on academic work until at least the 1890s (Heaton, [1943] 1950: 93–94).

Scholarly interest in economic history in France lagged behind that in Germany and England, but there were significant pioneers such as Henri Sée; the *Revue d'histoire des doctrines économiques et sociales* was founded in 1908 (Pirenne, 1931: 323). Since the 1920s, France has played a leading role in development of the field, especially since the founding of the journal *Annales d'histoire économique et sociale* by Marc Bloch and Lucien Febvre in 1929.

In America serious interest dates from the 1890s, largely under inspiration from Europe. A course in economic history was introduced at Harvard in 1883 and a chair of economic history was established there in 1892 (Gras, 1931: 326). Frederick Jackson Turner's essay "The Significance of History" ([1891] 1972: 199–200) noted the appearance of a school that wished to "rewrite history from the economic point of view" and asserted: "Today the questions that are uppermost, and that will become increasingly important, are not so much political as economic questions." Turner's own FRONTIER thesis concerning the uniqueness of American development aroused much interest in economic topics such as agriculture and the fur trade (Gras, 1931: 326). Charles Beard's controversial *Economic Interpretation of the Constitution of the United States* (1913) and *Economic Origins of Jeffersonian Democracy* (1915), although not, strictly, economic histories (Cochran, 1947: 5), drew much attention to the economic orientation. Agricultural, business, and labor history emerged as important branches of the field in the 1920s. Edwin F. Gay of Harvard, trained under Schmoller in Germany, played a leading role in promoting the study of economic history in early-twentieth-century America (Cochran, 1947: 8).

Before 1950 most work was descriptive rather than analytical. This was partly a legacy of the German historical school's bias against abstract theory and mathematical analysis, partly the result of history's traditional emphasis on the narrative description of unique events. To some degree economic history had always been "quantitative," since much of its evidence was numerical in form—for example, prices, trade volume, and so on. Quantitative data was usually scarce, however, and the methods of statistical inference were either primitive or not specially adapted for use in historical study. Thus Clapham (1931a: 327), while affirming that the "methodological distinctiveness" of economic history rested on its "marked quantitative interests," complained that "for all but the most modern period the absence of statistical material may make only very rough and uncertain quantitative treatment possible." Despite occasional calls for the greater use of economic theory (e.g., Heckscher, [1928] 1953), and despite conventional recognition of the importance of the "statistical sense" in economic history (Clapham, 1931a: 328; cf. Cochran, 1947: 21), most studies were in fact based primarily on literary rather than quantitative evidence. Where statistics were used, they were normally employed in an auxiliary sense—illustrative tables, graphs, and so on—not in the sense of rigorous quantitative analysis (see QUANTIFICATION).

During the 1950s, however, a "substantial departure" occurred in the study of economic history, especially in the United States and France (Habakkuk, 1972: 30; North, 1968: 468; Barraclough, 1978: 74, 84). This is not to say that important work in the older, descriptive fashion did not continue to appear (for example, Landes, 1969); the degree of reorientation should not be overemphasized, nor should one exaggerate its long-term impact (Engerman, 1977: 75). Clearly, however, the focus of attention by the 1960s and 1970s was on the rise of ECONOMETRIC HISTORY (also called the "new economic history" and "cliometrics"), a novel and self-consciously "revolutionary" approach based on the systematic use of statistical inference and (especially in the United States) on the theoretical MODELS of neo-classical economics. "What is new in the new economic history," wrote Habakkuk (1972: 32), "is that the move from the known to the unknown is based explicitly upon a chain of economic reasoning which is derived from the working of a theoretical model." Although the approach involved certain dangers, many authorities agreed that it represented an advance since "Theory of some sort is implicit in even the most rudimentary attempts to explain events. The great merit of making the model explicit is that the assumptions can be argued about and, in some degree, tested by the collection of additional data" (Habakkuk, 1972: 36). At the same time, the focus of the field became more narrowly defined in terms of the study of market forces, in the spirit of Heckscher's objection ([1928] 1953: 425–26) that "a very great . . . part of what is commonly called Economic History is something else, such as social, legal, political or otherwise institutional, or, on the other hand, technological history"; the "legal or social character of institutions," he had insisted, "is distinct from their economic character."

In France, on the other hand, the approach was considerably more eclectic. There models were drawn not only from neo-classical theory but from classical economics, Marxism, and other schools as well (North, 1977: 191), and quantitative historians remained much more concerned with relating closely defined economic themes such as the history of prices to broader social and institutional questions.

In America the quantitative movement coincided with the reawakening of historical interests among theoretical economists in the 1950s, and many of the first American econometric historians were trained primarily in economics departments (Engerman, 1977: 72). The chief advantage of the new approach was its ability to expand the usefulness of available data through the application of sophisticated techniques of statistical sampling and projection, often computer-assisted (North, 1968: 472; 1977: 192; Engerman, 1977: 77). In some cases this allowed scholars to "deduce evidence . . . when direct evidence is lacking" (Habakkuk, 1972: 31). Unlike most of the older economic history, the "new economic history" was not primarily concerned with the description and explanation of particular events; rather, it sought to explain recurring patterns and generalized group behavior (North, 1977: 188). This, along with the apparent mathematical rigor of its methods, led some practitioners to lay special stress on the "scientific" nature of the approach (see SCIENTIFIC HISTORY; SOCIAL SCIENCE HISTORY).

Despite its advantages, even champions of the econometric orientation had begun to underscore its limitations by the late 1970s (e.g., North, 1977: 192–94). By this time the approach had proven valuable for testing older interpretations but had not led to the construction of new syntheses. Its limitations were to a large degree related to the fact that most work in the field—at least in the United States—had been narrowly tied to neo-classical economic theory, which came under attack from economists themselves in the 1970s (Engerman, 1977: 81). From the historical point of view, perhaps the chief disadvantage is that neo-classical theory assumes economic equilibrium, whereas historians are most often interested in problems of uneven change over time, such as economic growth or decline. Moreover, neo-classical theory addresses problems of supply, demand, and distribution exclusively from the point of view of free markets, whereas non-market forces, such as governments and households, have played the dominant role in the actual allocation of resources in the past (North, 1977: 194). Thus, neo-classical theory appears to be unsuited for the analysis of all but a few historical problems.

References

Barraclough, Geoffrey. 1978. *Main Trends in History*. New York.

Clapham, John H. 1931a. "Economic History: Economic History as a Discipline." *ESS* 5: 327–30. Clapham defines *economic history* as "a branch of general institutional history, a study of the economic aspects of the social institutions of the past. Its methodological distinctiveness hinges primarily upon its marked quantitative interests."

———. 1931b. "Economic History: Survey of Development to the Twentieth Century." *ESS* 5: 315–20. This is still enormously valuable; North (1968) calls it "definitive of earlier views."

Cochran, Thomas C. 1947. "Research in American Economic History: A Thirty Year View." *Mid-America*, N.S., 18: 3–23. This article is indispensable for the early history of the field in the United States. There are bibliographical references in text and footnotes. The author states that the "most distinctive methodological feature of economic history is emphasis on quantitative analysis . . . the economic historian feels lost unless he can use measurements" (p. 21).

Engerman, Stanley L. 1977. "Recent Developments in American Economic History." *Social Science History* 2: 72–89.

Gay, Edwin F. [1941] 1953. "The Tasks of Economic History." In Lane and Riemersma: 407–14. This piece was written by a pioneer of economic historiography in the United States.

Gras, N.S.B. 1931. "Economic History: Economic History in the United States." *ESS* 5: 325–27. The author was a founder of "business history" as a subcategory of economic history in the United States.

Habakkuk, John. 1972. "Economic History and Economic Theory." In Gilbert and Graubard: 27–44. This is a good introduction to the new econometric history.

Heaton, Herbert. [1943] 1950. "The Economic Impact on History." In Strayer: 85–117. The author assesses the impact of Marxist doctrine.

Heckscher, Eli F. [1928] 1953. "A Plea for Theory in Economic History." In Lane and Riemersma: 421–30. This is a famous paper that argues that generalized theory is indispensable in the identification, selection, and explanation of facts; theory determines the kinds of questions that scholars put to their data (pp. 425, 429).

Hobsbawn, E. J. 1972. "From Social History to the History of Society." In Gilbert and Graubard: 1–26.

Landes, David S. 1969. *The Unbound Prometheus: Technological Change and Industrial Development in Western Europe from 1750 to the Present.* London.

Jacunsky, V. K. 1964. "The Rise of Economic Historiography." *Cahiers d'histoire mondiale* 8: 576–584. This is a survey of developments in the seventeenth and eighteenth centuries by a Soviet historian.

Lane, Frederic C., and Riemersma, Jelle C. 1953. "Introduction to Arthur Spiethoff." In Lane and Riemersma: 431–43. This piece contains a concise discussion of the German "historical school" of economics.

North, Douglass C. 1968. "History: Economic History." *IESS* 6: 468–74. The entry includes a bibliography. It is of limited historical use since the author, a leading practitioner of econometric history, "essentially offers a methodological prescription for the present and the future instead of surveying the past literature of the field."

———. 1977. "The New Economic History after Twenty Years." *American Behavioral Scientist* 21: 187–200. North is critical of the French *Annales* school, which "builds on bits and pieces of theory—geographic determinism, Marxism, Malthusianism: at its best . . . it is more an art form than a scientific approach to history" (p. 191).

Pirenne, Henri. 1931. "Economic History: Study and Research in the Twentieth Century, Continental Europe." *ESS* 5: 322–25. This piece was written by a great Belgian medievalist and early practitioner of "social and economic" history.

Sources of Additional Information

See ECONOMETRIC HISTORY; HISTORICAL MATERIALISM; INDUSTRIAL REVOLUTION; QUANTIFICATION. There is a very useful bibliography in Peter D. McClelland, *Causal Explanation and Model Building in History, Economics, and the New Economic History* (Ithaca, N.Y., 1975). The section "Wirtschafts- und Sozialgeschichte" in Berding: 196–207 is useful for literature in both German and English; Berding also includes the related sections

"Quantifizierung" (pp. 183–90), "Geschichte und Okonomie" (pp. 229–30), and "Wirtschaftliche Entwicklung: Kapitalismus und Industrialisierung" (pp. 287–302). Lane and Riemersma is still an important anthology. Jerzy Topolski, "The Role of Theory and Measurement in Economic History," in Iggers and Parker: 43–54, is a helpful review of recent literature, European as well as American. In the same volume, Richart T. Vann, "The New Demographic History," pp. 29–42, reviews literature in a field traditionally associated with economic studies. For recent work in labor history see David Brody, "Labor History in the 1970s: Toward a History of the American Worker," in Kammen: 252–69; in the same volume see also J. Morgan Kousser, "Quantitative Social-Scientific History," pp. 433–56. Aside from Jacunsky (1964), there is some information on earlier periods in N.S.B. Gras, "The Rise and Development of Economic History," *Economic History Review* 1 (1927–28): 12–34, and Amintore Fanfani, *Introduzione allo studio della storia economica* (Milan, 1941). The text and footnote citations in Cochran (1947) are an excellent source of older titles published in the United States; on this subject see also Arthur H. Cole, "Economic History in the United States: Formative Years of a Discipline," *Journal of Economic History* 28 (Dec. 1968): 556–89, and the same author's *Birth of a New Social Science Discipline: Achievements of the First Generation of American Economic and Business Historians, 1893–1974* (New York, 1974).

ENLIGHTENMENT. 1. An intellectual movement in eighteenth-century Europe and North America, centered primarily but not exclusively in France and characterized by an emphasis on secularization; cosmopolitanism; a critical attitude toward tradition and authority; a pragmatic, instrumentalist attitude toward knowledge; the appeal to reason as an ultimate authority; an idea of nature as orderly and predictable; and the notion of historical PROGRESS. 2) The period in which this movement occurred—the eighteenth century (the "Age of Enlightenment"). 3. Less commonly, any period or movement that resembles the eighteenth-century Enlightenment.

As a historical concept, the idea of the Enlightenment (Ger. *Aufklärung*) originated in late-eighteenth- and early-nineteenth-century Germany. It was then embraced by non-German scholars and to a limited extent has since acquired the generic meaning of any movement reminiscent of eighteenth-century progressivism (e.g., Holmes, 1969). The word initially carried both positive and pejorative connotations but has enjoyed an essentially positive meaning in historiography since the late nineteenth century. In isolated cases it may still carry negative connotations, and as late as 1960 a British scholar (Cobban, 1960: 7) claimed that the "term 'Enlightenment' is hardly naturalized in English." This, however, is a serious exaggeration. The *OED*—which associates the historical meaning of *enlightenment* with "shallow and pretentious intellectualism, unreasonable contempt for tradition and authority"—is correct for mid- and late-nineteenth century English but totally inaccurate for contemporary historiographical usage.

The word's German origins have been meticulously examined by Horst Stuke (1972), who begins by citing a 1691 dictionary definition of *Aufklärung* as the equivalent of the Latin *senenitas* (clear, bright, fair weather). Concurrently, the philosophical works of Leibnitz helped to popularize the metaphor of *clarity* by their use of the French terms *éclairer*, *éclarcir*, and *éclairissement*; the image of light was common to both Cartesian philosophy and German pietist theology in the seventeenth century. Also important were translations of early-eighteenth-century English weeklies, which often used the phrase "to enlighten" (Stuke, 1972: 247–49; Schalk, 1968: 250–51).

By the 1780s *Aufklärung* had become a "vogue word" in Germany (Stuke, 1972: 246), but it was used in a variety of (sometimes contradictory) senses. Confusion over the term's meaning led Johann Friedrich Zöllner to pose a celebrated question in 1783: "What is enlightenment? Surely this question, which is nearly as important as 'what is truth?', should be answered before we begin our efforts to enlighten!" (Stuke, 1972: 244–45). Zöllner's query elicited definitions from Moses Mendelssohn ("Uber die Frage: Was heisst aufklären?" [1784]) and a host of lesser known authors in the 1780s and 1790s; these definitions ranged from emotional warmth and religious awakening—senses dramatically opposed to the presently accepted conception of the European Enlightenment as a process of secularization and "demystification"—to "popular moral instruction." The most famous of these efforts was Immanuel Kant's "Reply to the Question 'What is Enlightenment?' " (1784).

Kant defined *enlightenment* in highly positive terms as a process of maturation leading to intellectual courage and moral self-reliance:

> Enlightenment is man's emergence from his self-imposed nonage. Nonage is the inability to use one's own understanding without another's guidance. This nonage is self-imposed if its cause lies not in lack of understanding but in indecision and lack of courage to use one's own mind without another's guidance. *Dare to know!* (*Sapere aude*.) "Have the courage to use your own understanding" is therefore the motto of the enlightenment. ([1784] 1973: 384)

Kant also connected the idea of Enlightenment to the notion of historical periods: "When we ask, Are we now living in an enlightened age? the answer is, No, but we live in an age of enlightenment" (p. 388).

Kant's fame as a philosopher has sometimes led scholars to consider his definition representative of his time and to use it as a starting point for a consideration of the modern historical concept (for instance, Cassirer, [1932] 1955: xi; Ford, 1968: 17; Gay, 1966: 3). According to Stuke (1972: 246, 267), however, Kant did not use the term consistently, and his definition came to be considered important only at the end of the nineteenth century, during the "neo-Kantian" revival. Much more important for the rise of the modern period concept were early nineteenth-century romantic authors (such as the poet Novalis) and idealist philosophers (especially Hegel); as sometimes happens, the opponents of a movement are those mainly responsible for establishing its name. In his essay "Christianity or Europe" (1799), for instance, Novalis used the expression *Aufklärung* as a pejorative to designate the ideas, methods, and institutions through which "modernization" (*Modernisierung*) establishes itself (Stuke, 1972: 305).

Hegel seems to have been the most important figure in this process. In the 1820s he identified *Aufklärung* with the period from the accession of Frederick II of Prussia (1740) to the French Revolution (1789) and with abstract rationalism, radical materialism, and atheism in both France and Germany (Stuke, 1972: 315–16). Although he recognized a positive side to the contributions of the period, in the last analysis he considered its characteristic mode of thought flawed and outdated and in need of replacement by his own system of idealism (pp. 315–16). Thus, while helping to endow the idea with historical specificity, he added to the pejorative identity the term had acquired as a result of the romantic critique. This was true especially when he spoke of the "German Enlightenment," which he associated with banality, shallowness, barrenness, and often (though not always) depicted as a feeble reflection of French philosophy. Hegel's position was to prove especially influential in shaping future conceptions of eighteenth-century German intellectual life, both in Germany and elsewhere. It is still evident, for example, in the widespread but mistaken idea that the Enlightenment had "only a superficial and transient influence on the German mind" (e.g., Cobban, 1960: 7).

It took several decades for Hegel's conception to establish itself fully in general usage. Not until the late nineteenth century was this accomplished, largely as the result of the work of historians of philosophy such as Wilhelm Windelband (1878), who popularized "the Enlightenment" as a general label for the period in European philosophy stretching from the time of John Locke to that of Herder. Following this example, general historians and historians of literature and culture began to employ the term on a wide scale (Stuke, 1972: 340–41). The idea's development culminated in Ernst Troeltsch's 1897 essay "Die Aufklärung," which defined the Enlightenment as a period of cultural transformation that affected all spheres of life (Cassirer, [1932] 1955: ix).

The twentieth-century historiography of the subject has been vigorous, especially since the end of World War II. Crocker (1964) and Niklaus (1967) usefully summarize a broad sampling of the literature from the 1920s to the early 1960s, although both appeared too early to include an assessment of the most ambitious recent study by Peter Gay (1966–69).

Generally, the historiography of the Enlightenment has been liberal in spirit (Anchor, 1967: 152) and therefore essentially sympathetic toward the movement, which is normally depicted as the fount of modern secularism and LIBERALISM (e.g., Martin, 1929). Late-nineteenth-century scholarship had established the idea that the Enlightenment was the most important source of many characteristic features of modern western civilization—secularization, empiricism, individualism, anti-traditionalism, political and social democracy, the idea of PROGRESS, and so on. During the past fifty years the term has gradually—though not entirely—lost the associations of "shallowness" and superficiality that it often had in the nineteenth century (see, for instance, Cassirer, [1932] 1955: ix; Crocker,

1959, 1963; Gay, 1966: ix). In the eyes of the majority of historians, the Enlightenment has superseded the RENAISSANCE as the "prototype of the modern world." In fact, "many, if not most, historians view the last two and a half centuries as forming a single historical unit" and consider the Enlightenment "the last and most vigorous phase in the transition from the medieval to the modern world" (Anchor, 1967: 3, 143; Dorn, 1958: 68), the "take-off point of modern Western civilization" (Brinton, 1967: 521).

There are some major exceptions to this pattern, however, notably Becker (1932)—a now classic work that stresses the Enlightenment's similarities to the medieval Christian world view—and Talmon (1952), a widely discussed study that locates the origins of twentieth-century TOTALITARIANISM in the Enlightenment. But Becker's interpretation is now generally considered unacceptable for many reasons (see Rockwood, 1958), and Talmon's book is widely believed to seriously distort and exaggerate certain ideas of the Enlightenment at the expense of the context of the movement as a whole.

References

Anchor, Robert. 1967. *The Enlightenment Tradition*. New York. This is an excellent
    brief introduction.
Becker, Carl L. 1932. *The Heavenly City of the Eighteenth-Century Philosophers*. New
    Haven, Conn.
Brinton, Crane. 1967. "Enlightenment." *EP* 2: 519–25.
Cassirer, Ernst. [1932] 1955. *The Philosophy of the Enlightenment*. Boston. This is an
    interwar study that is still highly regarded, although virtually all English-speaking
    writers reject Cassirer's idea that Kant's idealism was the epitome of the
    Enlightenment.
Cobban, Alfred. 1960. *In Search of Humanity: The Role of the Enlightenment in Modern
    History*. New York.
Crocker, Lester G. 1959. *An Age of Crisis: Man and World in Eighteenth Century French
    Thought*. Baltimore. Crocker and Gay (1966–69), represent opposing poles of
    contemporary interpretation, Gay sympathizing with the Enlightenment's con-
    structive work, Crocker arguing that the Enlightenment culminates in a moral
    "crisis" that continues to haunt modern society.
————. 1963. *Nature and Culture: Ethical Thought in the French Enlightenment*.
    Baltimore.
————. 1964. "Recent Interpretations of the French Enlightenment." *Cahiers d'histoire
    mondiale* 8: 426–56. This article relates post–1945 interest in the Enlightenment
    to the sobering experiences of World War II.
Dorn, Walter L. 1958. "*The Heavenly City* and Historical Writing on the Enlightenment."
    In Raymond O. Rockwood, ed., *Carl Becker's Heavenly City Revisited*. Ithaca,
    N.Y.: 52–69.
Ford, Franklin L. 1968. "The Enlightenment: Towards a Useful Redefinition." In R. F.
    Brissenden, ed., *Studies in the Eighteenth Century: Papers Presented at the David
    Nichol Smith Memorial Seminar, Canberra, 1966*. Toronto: 17–29. Ford defines
    the *Enlightenment* as a "cultural movement" (i.e., "a cluster of ideas and [the]
    people who espouse some or all of them") based on four "attitudes": (1) secular

humanism, (2) an analytical way of reasoning, (3) the idea that human affairs were changeable and "amenable to direction," and (4) a "sense of dedication to the cause of liberty" (pp. 18, 25–27).

Gay, Peter. 1966–69. *The Enlightenment: An Interpretation*. 2 vols. New York. This is the most important recent synthesis, although Gay underestimates the importance of traditional Christian concerns at the expense of his theme of the Enlightenment as the "rise of modern paganism." Cf. Ford (1968: 21).

Holmes, George. 1969. *The Florentine Enlightenment, 1400–50*. New York.

Kant, Immanuel. [1784] 1973. "What Is Enlightenment?" In Peter Gay, ed., *The Enlightenment: A Comprehensive Anthology*. New York: 383–90.

Martin, Kingsley: 1929. *French Liberal Thought in the Eighteenth Century: A Study of Political Ideas from Bayle to Condorcet*. London.

Niklaus, Robert. 1967. "The Age of the Enlightenment." In W. H. Barber, ed., *The Age of Enlightenment: Studies Presented to Theodore Besterman*. Edinburgh and London: 395–412. This is a useful historiographical essay.

Rockwood, Raymond O., ed. 1958. *Carl Becker's Heavenly City Revisited*. Ithaca, N.Y. See especially the essays by Peter Gay ("Carl Becker's Heavenly City," pp. 27–51) and Walter L. Dorn (cited above).

Schalk, Fritz. 1968. "Zur Semantik von 'Aufklärung' in Frankreich." In Kurt Baldinger, ed., *Festschrift Walther von Wartburg zum 80. Geburtstag*. Tübingen: 251–66.

Stuke, Horst. 1972. "Aufklärung." *GG* 1: 243–342.

Talmon, J. L. 1952. *The Rise of Totalitarian Democracy*. Boston.

Windelband, Wilhelm. 1878. *Die Geschichte der neueren Philosophie in ihrem Zusammenhange mit der allgemeinen Cultur und den besonderen Wissenschaften*. Leipzig.

Sources of Additional Information

Bibliographical resources are extensive. In addition to Crocker (1964) and Niklaus (1967) see both volumes of Gay (1966–69), which contain exhaustive bibliographical essays. For a sober, thoughtful review of Gay see James A. Leith, "Peter Gay's Enlightenment." *Eighteenth-Century Studies* 5 (Fall 1971): 157–71. Gay has reviewed the first volume of Crocker (1959) in "An Age of Crisis: A Critical View," *JMH* 33 (June 1961): 174–77. Gay's *Enlightenment: A Comprehensive Anthology* (New York, 1973), more than 800 pages, is the best of many available anthologies; it also contains much valuable bibliographical information. See also Hellmut O. Pappe, "Enlightenment," and Isaiah Berlin, "Counter-Enlightenment," *DHI* 2: 89–112; and Hans Kohn, "The Multidimensional Enlightenment," *JHI* 31 (July–Sept. 1970): 465–74. For Marxist views see Iring Fetscher and Eberhard Müller, "Enlightenment," *MCWS* 3: 170–82; also chapter eight of Martin Jay, *The Dialectical Imagination* (Boston, 1973). Interesting review articles include Robert Darnton, "In Search of the Enlightenment: Recent Attempts to Create a Social History of Ideas," *JMH* 42 (1971): 113–32; and Carolyn C. Lougee, "The Enlightenment and the French Revolution: Some Recent Perspectives," *Eighteenth-Century Studies* 11 (1977–1978): 84–102. On the Enlightenment in the New World see Henry F. May, "The Problem of the American Enlightenment," *New Literary History* 1 (Winter 1970): 201–14, and May's *Enlightenment in America* (New York, 1976), as well as Arthur P. Whitaker, "Changing and Unchanging Interpretations of the Enlightenment in Spanish America," *Proceedings of the American Philosophical Society*, 114

(Aug. 20, 1970): 256–71. The entire Summer 1973 issue of the *American Quarterly* is devoted to the "American Enlightenment."

EVENT. Any segment of past human action or experience defined in the course of historical inquiry.

History is often understood in terms of its relationship to *events*. *Webster's Third New International Dictionary* (1981), for instance, defines *history* as a "narrative of events," a "systematic written account . . . of events," or a "branch of knowledge that records and explains past events." The same source defines *event* as "something that happens" and "a noteworthy occurrence or happening." Since antiquity history has been closely identified with the description of *res gestae* (things done, deeds, exploits), what French scholars sometimes call *l'histoire événementielle*—the narration of great political events. The historian is still conventionally viewed as one who seeks to describe or understand past events; Maurice Mandelbaum ([1938] 1967: 26), for example, asserts that "the historian's task lies in understanding the concrete nature of some event with reference to a series of events which determined its character." This statement is undoubtedly true, although it fails to appreciate the key role played by the analysis of *situations* as well as events in historical inquiry (Walsh, 1969: 153–54, 160).

Yet despite the basic and perhaps indispensable function of the notion of "event" for history (Gruner, 1969: 152; Walsh, 1969: 153–54, 160), "hardly any concept is less clear" (Mink, 1978: 145). Behind the word *event* lies an ambiguous, "rough and ready" idea (Smart, 1949: 486) that historians—like others in everyday language—regularly employ in the loose but pragmatic sense of "any past happening" (e.g., Fischer, 1970: xv, n. 1). The term is used to designate things as broad as "the Reformation," "the French Revolution," or "the Cold War" and as circumscribed as the momentary actions or decisions of individuals. Indeed, in speculative PHILOSOPHY OF HISTORY the entire course of human development may be seen as one great event—as, for example, in the idea of human history as the product of God's will. Surprisingly little has been written on the implications of this ambiguous usage for the study of history, and the issues surrounding the concept of historical events have never become a focus of theoretical debate. "No historian," observes Rolf Gruner (1969: 141), "spends sleepless nights over the question 'What is an historical event?' " If the matter occurs to historians at all they incline to regard it as a technical problem for philosophers that does not impinge on their own work. But Gruner's assertion evidently applies to philosophers as well, considering the scarcity of philosophical literature on the subject. There are nevertheless logical problems linked to the use of the idea, some of them reminiscent of difficulties associated with the notion of historical FACT; the categories of "fact" and "event" are, indeed, often conflated in historiography (Gruner, 1969: 141).

There are two broad ways of understanding the logical place of the event

concept in historiography, the one "realistic," the other "constructionist." RE-
ALISM, the mainstream view, assumes that *events* are discrete occurrences that
possess their own intrinsic, unalterable structure and constitute the raw data of
inquiry. On this view, events "happened in the way that they happened, and
not in any other way" (Fischer, 1970: 66, n. 4). It is the business of the historian
to "apprehend" the determinate structure of these occurrences (Mandelbaum,
[1938] 1967: 239).

In realism, historical "facts" may be equated with events or may be considered
items of knowledge that correspond to them, more or less perfectly. The work
of Carl Becker supplies a good illustration. In his celebrated essay "What Are
Historical Facts?" ([1955] 1959) Becker uses the term *event* frequently. At one
point he seems to equate *fact* and *event* ([1955] 1959: 131), although this is
clearly not his overall intention. What he wants to argue, instead, is that a *fact*
is a "symbolic" statement that an event occurred (p. 124; cf. Gruner, 1969:
141–42). Becker employs *event* to designate loosely "anything that has to do
with the life of man in the past—any act or . . . emotion which men have expressed, any idea, true or false, which they have entertained" (p. 124). The
event is something "ephemeral . . . which disappears" (pp. 124, 126) but is
nonetheless "actual." Events have their own structure, but historical facts—
human affirmations about past events—can never perfectly reproduce this reality.

A more recent illustration of the realist position is David Fischer's *Historians'
Fallacies* (1970: 66, n. 4). Although critical of Becker on various points, Fischer
agrees that "events happened in the way that they happened, and not in any
other way" and defines *facts* as "true statements about past events." As already
noted, he defines an *event* simply as "any past happening" (p. xv, n. 1). The
overwhelming majority of historians unreflectively employ some version of this
view in commonsense fashion. A historian's work, for instance, is conventionally
judged by his peers in terms of its faithfulness to the presumed integrity of past
events.

CONSTRUCTIONISM, in contrast, rejects realism and holds that *events* are intellectual constructs that lack an independent existence or structure of their own.
The constructionist position is best represented by the philosopher Leon Goldstein
(1962; 1976), who refines and extends objections already raised against realism
by nineteenth-century proponents of historical IDEALISM. For example, the German idealist Wilhelm von Humboldt maintained that although a "simple presentation" of events is the goal of every historian, these events are

> only partially visible in the world of the senses; the rest has to be added by intuition,
> inference, and guesswork. The manifestations of an event are scattered, disjointed,
> isolated; what it is that gives unity to this patchwork, puts the isolated fragment
> into its proper perspective, and gives shape to the whole, remains removed from
> direct observation. ([1821] 1967: 57–58)

In this tradition Gruner, who defines an *event* as something that occasions *change*
in a state of affairs (1969: 142–44), speaks of an "inherent relativity in the use

of the word 'event,' in the sense that a question such as 'Is a battle an event?' demands a counter-question 'An event relative to what?' In other words . . . whether it is conceived as an event or as something else is dependent on context'' and "the position adopted" by the historian (pp. 148, 150). The event is thus a function of the historian's purposes, and the "event-character of an item" lies "in the eyes of the beholder" (p. 151)—although Gruner adds that he does not "deny reality in any meaningful sense of this word to any individual historical phenomenon. . . . There still was or occurred a French Revolution, whether the item which goes under this name is conceived as an event" or as something else. This coincides with the opinion of William Riker (1957: 60): "The motion and action in an event are objectively existent; but the boundaries are subjectively imposed."

Going beyond Humboldt and Gruner, Goldstein entirely rejects the notion that historical events exist in any sense apart from the operations of historians:

> The historical event [Goldstein argues]—the only historical event that figures in the work of historians—is an hypothetical construct. The historian does not look for evidence in order to explain the event, as if the event is clearly before him and he is required to make sense of it, but, rather, he calls it forth for the purpose of explaining his evidence. (1962: 177)

The event, in other words, is something created by the historian "for the purpose of making our evidence intelligible" (p. 179); "the historian does not describe an event which is there to be described; rather, following the techniques of his craft he constitutes the event" (Goldstein, 1976: 57–58). From a methodological point of view, the issues attending the "constitution" of a historical event in this sense are akin to those associated with the processes of COLLIGATION and historical PERIODIZATION:

> There emerges in the course of research a constellation of kinds of historical evidence [writes Goldstein]. To account for the particular constellation becomes a question of some interest, and it is at this point that the historical event enters into consideration. It is the function of the event to explain the evidence, that is, it must make intelligible the grouping together of some particular constellation of historical evidence which is believed to belong together. (Goldstein, 1962: 182)

In a related argument, the philosopher Louis Mink links the concept of historical event to NARRATIVE. Common sense, writes Mink, assumes that there is some standard account or "untold story" of the past that includes the true form of any event. The historian's presumed task is to uncover this untold story. But this is fallacious, for there "can in fact be no untold stories at all, just as there can be no unknown knowledge. There can be only past facts not yet described in a context of narrative form" (Mink, 1978: 145–47). Events, then, are defined by their function in some particular story about the past that a historian wishes to tell:

> it is clear that we cannot refer to events as such, but only to events *under a discription*. . . . "Events" (or more precisely, descriptions of events) are not the

raw material out of which narratives are constructed; rather an event is an abstraction from a narrative. An event may take five seconds or five months, but in either case whether it is one event or many depends not on a definition of "event" but on a particular narrative construction which generates the event's appropriate description. This conception of "event" [Mink continues] is not remote from our ordinary responses to stories: in certain stories we can accept even something like the French Revolution as a simple event, because that is the way it is related to characters and plot, while in other stories it may be too complex to describe as a single whole. But if we accept that the description of events is a *function of particular narrative structures* [emphasis added], we cannot at the same time suppose that the actuality of the past is an untold story. (p. 145–47)

The positions of both Goldstein and Mink recall Riker's point (1957: 57) that a "general term like 'event,' which is the product of abstraction, cannot be defined ostensively and must, therefore, be defined in context and genetically." Riker believes that "we ourselves . . . are the masters of the boundaries of events," (p. 70).

Some historians display a similar understanding. H. Stuart Hughes (1964: 6), for instance, asserts "what we conventionally call an 'event' in history is simply a segment of the endless web of experience that we have torn out of context for purposes of clearer understanding." Even more explicit is Peter Munz, who states that

The thoughtful professional will know that every event, no matter how small, is a construction and that for every time and every place many events can be constructed . . . any event, no matter how small, is divisible and . . . we can therefore think of any event only as a construction or a putting together of other events. In this sense the concept of "narration" is really implicit in the concept "event". (1977: 32, 304, n. 6)

References

Becker, Carl L. [1955] 1959. "What Are Historical Facts?" In Meyerhoff: 120–37. Originally read as a paper in 1926, this essay was not published until 1955.
Fischer, David Hackett. 1970. *Historians' Fallacies: Toward a Logic of Historical Thought*. New York.
Goldstein, Leon J. 1962. "Evidence and Events in History." *Philosophy of Science* 29: 175–94. This is a concise account of Goldstein's views.
———. 1976. *Historical Knowing*. Austin, Tex.
Gruner, Rolf. 1969. "The Notion of An Historical Event, I." *Aristotelian Society Supplementary Volume* 43: 141–52. Gruner asserts that events are things that "*happen, occur* or *take place*"; "if something is said to *be* or to *exist* it is not conceived as an event" (p. 142). He believes that an event must occasion a change (or have the potential to occasion a change) in a "state of affairs" (p. 144). Gruner's analysis seems helpful in defining the semantic boundaries of *event*, but as Walsh suggests (1969: 154), it seems to apply more to change in general than to change as it is specifically represented in the work of historians.
Hughes, H. Stuart. 1964. *History as Art and as Science*. New York.

Humboldt, Wilhelm von. [1821] 1967. "On the Historian's Task." *HT* 6: 57–71.

Mandelbaum, Maurice. [1938] 1967. *The Problem of Historical Knowledge: An Answer to Relativism*. New York. This is a classic of critical philosophy of history by the chief defender of historical realism. For Mandelbaum *events* are the "strands of history"; an *event* is "an enduring entity, pervaded by a specific unity, and at the same time comprised of multiple subevents" connected by a "relation of existential dependence" (p. 225); he believes that "historical events in themselves possess a structure which the historian apprehends and does not invent" (p. 259).

Mink, Louis O. 1978. "Narrative Form as a Cognitive Instrument." In Canary and Kozicki: 129–49.

Munz, Peter. 1977. *The Shapes of Time: A New Look at the Philosophy of History.* Middletown, Conn.

Riker, William H. 1957. "Events and Situations." *JP* 54: 57–70. Riker defines *event* as "any subjectively differentiated portion of motion or action" (p. 58), "some sort of perceived motion or action, sometime, someplace" (p. 57). "Faced with the complexity of continuous reality," Riker states, "humans understand it by breaking it up into pieces. Although a continuous reality cannot, by definition, consist of discrete motions and actions, we imagine stops and starts. What lies between the starts and stops we call events" (p. 59).

Smart, J.J.C. 1949. "The River of Time." *Mind*, N.S., 58: 483–94.

Walsh, W. H. 1969. "The Notion of An Historical Event, II." *Aristotelian Society Supplementary Volume* 43: 153–64. Walsh generally accepts Gruner's (1969) "relativist" characterization of the notion of event and in some respects pushes it farther, arguing that in certain contexts even a person might be considered an event (pp. 155–56). He qualifies Gruner's argument by maintaining (following R. G. Collingwood) that *historical events* are "constituted by the actions *and reactions* of human beings." This excludes "happenings in the physical world," which "are important not for what they are in themselves, but for the reactions they produce in men's minds. They have to be mediated by human thought if they are to be effective" (p. 158; also p. 163). The most interesting feature of the essay is Walsh's argument that although "history without events is logically inconceivable," it is nonetheless not "exclusively concerned with events" (pp. 153–54). It also deals with social structures and situations (see pp. 154, 160).

Sources of Additional Information

See also FACT; PROCESS. For criticisms of history understood as the "history of events" along the same lines as those advanced by Walsh (1969), see Traian Stoianovich, *French Historical Method: The Annales Paradigm* (Ithaca, N.Y.), as well as Frederick J. Teggart, *Theory and Processes of History* (1925; Berkeley, Calif., 1960), p. 77. For some observations by a literary critic see Richard Gilman, *Decadence: The Strange Life of an Epithet* (New York, 1979), pp. 53, 68. See also chapter seven of Margaret Macdonald, ed., *Philosophy and Analysis* (Oxford, 1954), which contains several related essays; the remarks of Louis O. Mink in his review of Maurice Mandelbaum's *Anatomy of Historical Knowledge*, *HT* 17 (1978): 220 and 222; Bruce Waters, "The Past and the Historical Past," *JP* 52 (May 12, 1955): 256; as well as Dale H. Porter, "History as Process," *HT* 14 (1975): especially 302–4.

EVIDENCE. Anything within the range of the historian's experience—document, opinion, monument, artifact, tradition, and so on—that can be used as a basis for statements about the past; often called "sources."

For many authorities, evidence is the central concept of history. With some exceptions (cf. Hurst, 1981), it is generally agreed that, in the absence of evidence, there can be no history (e.g., Johnson, 1926: 153). Some philosophers define *history* as the "science of historical evidence" and argue that the chief distinction between *fiction* and *history* is the latter's "peculiar relation to something called evidence" (Goldstein, 1970: 36; Collingwood, [1946] 1956: 246, 251–52).

It is widely agreed that everything has the potential to be historical evidence; pragmatically, however, a thing can only become evidence if some historian can find a way to bring it to bear on a particular question in which he is interested. In order for anything to count as evidence, it has to be viewed as the inferential basis *for* something about the human past. "The whole perceptible world . . . is potentially and in principle evidence to the historian," wrote Collingwood ([1946] 1956: 246). "It becomes actual evidence in so far as he can use it." Nothing, in other words, is automatically historical evidence; to become evidence it must be related to some problem by a historian—"Otherwise it is merely perceived fact, historically dumb" (p. 246).

> At the outset [the historian] has only raw data, scraps of parchment, inscriptions, letters, codices, pamphlets, or what-not, and he himself must *constitute* these as evidence and decide what they are evidence for [emphasis added]. Then he interrogates and criticizes the evidence he has thus established. (Zagorin, 1956: 9; cf. Johnson, 1926: 76–77; Walsh, [1951] 1960: 18–19, 83; Meiland, 1965: 21; Cebik, 1970: 76)

Johnson (1926: 4) divides historical evidence into two broad categories: "records" and "remains." *Records* are "documents designed to transmit information, in order either to perpetuate popular traditions and the memory of events, or to serve immediate practical purposes." *Remains* are "mere inanimate vestiges of human life." Actually, he adds (pp. 76–77), remains is an "all-inclusive term. Every form of historical record is—quite apart from its contents—an example of human activity. From this point of view manuscripts may be regarded as remains quite as much as fragments of pottery." Johnson (p. 61) also conveniently defines the conventional distinction between *original* (or *primary*) and *secondary evidence* (or *sources*): strictly speaking, *original evidence* means only eyewitness testimony. Any evidence not derived from eyewitness testimony is *secondary evidence*. In practice, however, historians widely regard any material contemporary to the problem they are studying as "primary"—"Contemporaneousness becomes the real test." This distinction between original and derivative evidence was firmly established by antiquarian scholars of the late seventeenth century (Momigliano, 1950: 286—see ANTIQUARIANISM); since the early nineteenth century, tradition requires that, whenever possible, historians must base their conclusions mainly on original evidence.

Disagreement exists over the precise relationship between historical evidence and the PAST to which historical accounts refer. It is widely held that *evidence* should be regarded as "traces" of the past. In a formal sense, this idea goes back at least to the mid-eighteenth century (Johnson, 1926: 122, 133–34); for example, J. M. Chladenius' *Allgemeine Geschichtswissenschaft* (1751) refers to *historical evidence* as *Spuren* (traces) and *Uberbleibsel* (remains). The idea was reaffirmed in the mid-nineteenth century by Johann Gustav Droysen in his influential *Grundriss der Historik* (1858) and was a fundamental assumption of many subsequent manuals (e.g., Langlois and Seignobos, [1898] 1926: 63–65; Johnson, 1926: 22; Renier, 1950: 119–22). It is explicitly stated in some historical studies (e.g., Brinton, [1930] 1961: 4), and we may assume that it is a working premise of most, if not all, professional historians (Walsh, [1951] 1960: 18). The view presumes that historical evidence represents presently existing vestiges of past situations once present but now forever gone, "real" pasts independent of the thought of historians that are "recovered" or "reconstructed" by inference from their "traces" (see REALISM). These traces presumably provide the historian with a means of indirect contact with the past. According to Langlois and Seignobos, for example,

> The facts of the past are only known to us by the traces of them which have been preserved. These traces . . . are directly observed by the historian, but, after that, he has nothing more to observe; what remains is the work of reasoning, in which he endeavors to infer, with the greatest possible exactness, the facts from the traces. ([1898] 1926: 63–64)

Or, according to Johnson (1926: 22), "we can know the past only as it has left its traces in records and remains. . . . The present which we would hold has slipped into the limbo of the past and can only be reclaimed, as all human experience is recovered, through the traces which it has left." The position is endorsed by recent philosophers of history as well, for example, Walsh ([1951] 1960: 18): "Although the past is not accessible to direct inspection it has left ample traces of itself in the present, in the shape of documents, buildings, coins, institutions, procedures and so forth."

But the work of some philosophers—notably those espousing some form of CONSTRUCTIONISM—challenges the conception of evidence as "traces." For example, Michael Oakeshott maintains that the evidence used by historians really refers to the present—in the sense of the present concerns of historians—rather than to a once existing "past" (Oakeshott, 1933; Walsh, [1951] 1960: 82). From this standpoint there is no way of demonstrating a connection between "evidence"—data presently available to historians—and the "past," of which we have, after all, no immediate perceptual experience; we cannot speak meaningfully of a connection between the two (Meiland, 1965: 49). Since we cannot demonstrate that there is such a connection, *evidence*, by implication, cannot be regarded as "traces." More recently, Goldstein (1962: 176) has adopted a similar position, explicitly denying that *evidence* can properly be regarded as "traces" that "provide some more or less direct contact between the present and the past."

> The historical event [he writes]—the only historical event that figures in the work of historians—is an hypothetical construct. The historian does not look for evidence in order to explain the event, as if the event is clearly before him and he is required to make sense of it, but, rather, he calls it forth for the purpose of explaining his evidence. (1962: 177)

For Goldstein, the past to which historical accounts refer is a "historical past" *constructed* or *constituted* by historians, not a "real past" that somehow exists independently of the disciplinary activities of the historical profession; consequently, it is not possible to view historical evidence in terms of the notion of "traces" of what "really happened."

References

Brinton, Clarence Crane. [1930] 1961. *The Jacobins: An Essay in the New History*. New York.
Cebik, L. B. 1970. "Collingwood: Action, Re-enactment, and Evidence." *The Philosophical Forum*, N.S., 2: 68–90. This is a valuable essay that generally endorses Collingwood's views on evidence while rejecting some of his other ideas.
Collingwood, R. G. [1946] 1956. *The Idea of History*. New York. This book includes a celebrated discussion of the nature of historical evidence in which the author discriminates between mere "testimony" and "evidence," which involves the interpretation of testimony.
Goldstein, Leon J. 1962. "Evidence and Events in History." *Philosophy of Science* 29: 175–94.
———. 1970. "Collingwood's Theory of Historical Knowing." *HT* 9: 3–36. This is a controversial interpretation of Collingwood's ideas.
Hurst, B. C. 1981. "The Myth of Historical Evidence." *HT* 20: 278–90. Hurst rejects the term *evidence* in favor of *data* on the grounds that any material used as a basis for explanation by the historian is actually inseparable from his narrative and therefore cannot be regarded as having an independent status.
Johnson, Allen. 1926. *The Historian and Historical Evidence*. New York. This is a thorough analysis by a professional historian, still in many ways the most reliable introduction to the subject.
Langlois, Ch. V., and Ch. Seignobos. [1898] 1926. *Introduction to the Study of History*. New York. This classic manual reflects a remarkably narrow view of historical evidence; it limits the idea almost entirely to written documentation.
Meiland, Jack W. 1965. *Scepticism and Historical Knowledge*. New York.
Momigliano, Arnaldo. 1950. "Ancient History and the Antiquarian." *Journal of the Warburg and Courtauld Institutes* 13: 285–315.
Oakeshott, Michael. 1933. *Experience and Its Modes*. Cambridge. Relevant passages are found in chapter three, "Historical Experience."
Renier, G. J. 1950. *History: Its Purpose and Method*. Boston.
Walsh, W. H. [1951] 1960. *Philosophy of History: An Introduction*. New York. This book contains a criticism of Oakeshott's views (p. 89).

Zagorin, Perez. 1956. "Carl Becker on History. Professor Becker's Two Histories: A Skeptical Fallacy." *AHR* 62: 1–11.

Sources of Additional Information

Cebik (1970: 81) notes that the "notion of evidence has drawn sparse attention in philosophic writing" and affirms that the subject has not received as much interest among historians as one might expect. H. B. George, *Historical Evidence* (Oxford, 1909), is an older but in some respects still useful study; it has, however, been strongly criticized (see Johnson, [1926: 139]). Robin W. Winks, ed., *The Historian as Detective: Essays on Evidence* (New York, 1968), is an anthology designed to introduce general readers to some of the ways historians understand and use evidence. It includes brief biblio-graphical references, although few of the items cited deal specifically with evidence as a concept. Similar in spirit (though not an anthology) is James West Davidson and Mark Hamilton Lytle, *After the Fact: The Art of Historical Detection* (New York, 1982). Leon J. Goldstein's controversial views on the nature of historical evidence have been incor-porated in his general study *Historical Knowing* (Austin, Tex., 1976), especially pp. 124–31, where Goldstein denies that the relationship between evidence and historical judgment is one of inference. Among the many essays that illustrate how the same data may be constituted as evidence in different ways and for different things, see especially Jay Mechling, "Advice to Historians on Advice to Mothers," *Journal of Social History* 9 (Fall 1975): 44–63, and W. H. Dray, "Concepts of Causation in A.J.P. Taylor's Account of the Origins of the Second World War," *HT* 17 (1978): 149–74. Similarities and differences between the use of evidence in history and in the law have attracted some attention; see, for example, George (1909: 18–20) and especially Nicholas Rescher and Carey B. Joynt, "Evidence in History and in the Law," *JP* 56 (June 18, 1959): 561–78. See also G. R. Elton's attack on historiographical appeals to the legal model of evidence in Robert William Fogel and G. R. Elton, *Which Road to the Past? Two Views of History* (New Haven, Conn., 1983), pp. 90–93.

EVOLUTION. See PROCESS.

EXPLANATION. The mode of reasoning used by historians to make the past intelligible; the way historians account for the occurrence of EVENTS.

Explanation has been generally characterized as "the process at the end of which we are rewarded with the understanding of a fact" (Gruner, 1967: 153). The nature of historical explanation has been a key issue in PHILOSOPHY OF HISTORY since the late nineteenth century; in Anglo-American critical philosophy of history, explanation has been the single most important focus of debate since the publication of Carl G. Hempel's essay "The Function of General Laws in History" in 1942 (Mandelbaum, [1960] 1969: 124). For many English and American philosophers, in fact, philosophy of history is synonymous with the discussion of historical explanation (Leff, 1971: 60). Note that issues associated with historical UNDERSTANDING are sometimes discussed under the heading "ex-planation," although distinct traditions of usage suggest that the two terms should be treated separately.

Before the late nineteenth century there was no precisely defined theory of historical reasoning. Indeed, an old tradition often traced to Aristotle (1940: 25) regards history as narrowly descriptive, denying it any significant explanatory function whatsoever (cf. M. White, 1945: 316; Fritz, 1958: 132–33). To be sure, an equally ancient tradition teaches that history is a treasury of moral and political lessons (Nadel, 1964), which suggests explanation in the sense of demonstration by example. Moreover, eighteenth- and nineteenth-century philosophy of history and "philosophical history" (see PHILOSOPHY OF HISTORY) implied a notion of explanation, insofar as they assumed that historical inquiry yields consciousness of patterns that constitute the "meaning" of human destiny. Such orientations, however, differ fundamentally in spirit from the epistemological thrust of analytical philosophy in the past century.

Contemporary interest in historical explanation springs from the nineteenth-century philosophical conflict between POSITIVISM and IDEALISM. Nineteenth-century positivists, following Auguste Comte (1798–1857), considered history a natural process that develops in accordance with general scientific LAWS. Historical understanding means that the historian "discovers" and elucidates these laws, in the same sense that natural scientists discover and explain the laws of physical nature. In contrast, idealists such as Wilhelm Dilthey (1833–1911), Wilhelm Windelband (1848–1915), and Heinrich Rickert (1863–1936)—while differing among themselves in various ways—denied that the methods of historical inquiry and explication are analogous to those of the natural sciences. They maintained—to use Windelband's terminology ([1894] 1980: 175)—that *history* is an "idiographic" form of knowledge, based on the capacity of empathy with the uniqueness of past situations, not on the "nomothetic" discovery of general laws (Mandelbaum, [1960] 1969: 127) (see HISTORISM; UNDERSTANDING). Idealists generally enjoyed the upper hand in history and philosophy of history in the early twentieth century, as reflected in the work of theorists such as Benedetto Croce, Michael Oakeshott, and R. G. Collingwood, as well as the thought of leading historians such as Friedrich Meinecke, Carl Becker, and Charles Beard (see IDEALISM, RELATIVISM).

In his 1942 essay Hempel, reacting against idealism, asserted the neo-positivist position that historians account for past events by appealing to laws or law-like generalizations; according to Hempel ([1942] 1959: 345), history is a branch of science and historians explain their subjects by proceeding deductively from "universal hypotheses" that are identical with the laws of physical science. Hempel conceded that historians normally perform this operation unconsciously and admitted that historical accounts are not usually characterized by the full rigor of explanations in the natural sciences; typically, he believed, *histories* are "explanation sketches" of a proto-scientific kind (p. 351). He insisted, however, that his theory accurately portrayed the logic of historical reasoning, which he considered identical with the logic of all explanation in general. In the words of one of his followers, May Brodbeck, "There is no such thing as 'historical explanation,' only the explanation of historical events" (cited in Mink [1965]

1966: 163). This position has become known as the COVERING LAW model of explanation, after the usage of one of Hempel's critics, William H. Dray (1957: 1). Since the 1940s the covering law position has been refined by Hempel himself, as well as others who accept the model in whole or in part (for example, M. White, 1943; Popper, 1950: 720–23; Mandelbaum, [1960] 1969: 138).

With few exceptions (e.g., Fogel, 1966: 656; Munz, 1967: 111), historians have displayed a "visceral reaction" to Hempel's claims (Krieger, 1963: 136–37). By training and temperament, academic historians are traditionally "confirmed pluralists" (p. 137) and instinctively reject the idea that their mode of reasoning can be reduced to one logical form; different problems, they believe, call for different explanation procedures. Some historians are wary of the term *explanation* because they think it implies "conclusive proof," and this, they believe, the historian can never provide (see Bullock, 1977: 20). Others complain that covering law theory is not based on a thorough knowledge of the actual assumptions and procedures of professional historiography (Krieger, 1963: 136–37). In itself, this is insufficient reason for rejecting the covering law model, for historians might not themselves be knowledgeable regarding the underlying principles of their work, and their working assumptions might not truly reflect the nature of their enterprise. In any event, when they hold explicit views on the matter at all, historians have usually sympathized with the idealist contention that the logic of historical inquiry differs substantially from that of natural science—that history is a unique endeavor based on the relation of particular events to the contexts in which they occurred (see COLLIGATION), not on deduction from general laws (cf. Carr, [1961] 1964: 21). In Leonard Krieger's words (1963: 137), "When an historian seeks to explain a particular action what he wants explained is precisely the particularity of the action: why it was produced by this man at this place at this time."

These views are supported by a number of theorists who either reject covering law theory outright or maintain that it describes only one possible form of historical explanation (e.g., Dray, 1957; Gallie, 1955; Danto, 1956; Donagan, 1964; Mink, [1965] 1966; H. White, 1972). Zagorin (1959) and Weingartner ([1961] 1969) summarize and classify some of these positions. According to Zagorin (1959: 250), the laws that covering law theorists suggest as a basis for historical explanation "are often so loose as not to be laws at all; or if they are laws, their connection with the explanation in which they are alleged to be implicit is so tenuous as to deprive them of any explanatory value." It is trivial to suggest, for instance, that the statement "Louis XIV died unpopular because he pursued policies detrimental to French interests" is the result of a deduction from the general rule that "Rulers who pursue policies detrimental to their countries' interests become unpopular"; moreover, the generalization itself is not universally true (p. 250). " . . . the historian need not, and usually does not, make use of laws at all," Zagorin (1959: 251) continues.

> Naturally, he takes for granted the truth of all laws, physical, psychological, and others, that have been established. He assumes, for example, that the bullet at

Sarajevo followed a path accountable for by the laws of mechanics. But these laws do not enter into his explanations in the sense of determining their logical structure or giving them their force. (p. 251)

W. H. Walsh ([1951] 1960) offers what is perhaps the most widely accepted alternative to the covering law model in his notion of explanation by COLLIGA-TION. According to this view, historians typically explain the occurrence of an event not by appealing to general laws but "by tracing its intrinsic relations to other events and locating it in its historical context" (p. 59). Walsh's position is in some respects a refinement of Michael Oakeshott's "continuous series model of explanation" (1933), according to which historians explain the past by simply providing a detailed description of changes that have transpired (cf. Nash, 1969: 78).

A theme frequently encountered in attacks on covering law theory is the idea that NARRATIVE is a key to historical explanation. Proponents of this view argue that historical explanations are constituted by the order in which data are positioned in accounts of the past; the "event to be explained *is* explained in virtue of the fact that it 'falls into place' as the terminal phase of a sequence . . . coherent narrative is taken to be the model of explanation" (Weingartner, [1961] 1969: 145). The most elaborate variation on this theme is offered by Hayden White (1973). Although not rejecting covering law theory entirely, White argues that historical explanation proceeds on numerous levels and is often a function of various kinds of narrative form and figurative representation. Building on traditional and contemporary poetic and linguistic theory, White maintains, for example, that explanation in history may be achieved by "emplotment"—the working up of data into the four generally recognizable plot forms of romance, comedy, tragedy, or satire. Here the historian accomplishes explanation as "a sequence of events fashioned into a story is gradually revealed to be a story of a particular kind" (1973: 7; also 1972: 9). Other possible levels exist as well, such as explanation by "motific organization" or "thematic configuration" (1972: 15). A related account of the problem is the "paradigm" theory of historical explanation advanced by Gene Wise (1973).

References

Aristotle. 1940. *The Art of Poetry*. Ed. W. Hamilton Fyfe. Oxford. In chapter nine Aristotle declares that *poetry* "is something more philosophic and of graver import than history, since its statements are of the nature rather of universals, whereas those of history are singulars" (p. 25). This has been called the "traditional view of history," which "never allows it to transcend facts or particulars—by definition"; it persists in some circles in the twentieth century (M. White, 1945: 316). See the remarks below under Fritz (1958).

Beard, Charles A., and Hook, Sydney. 1946. "Problems of Terminology in Historical Writing." In Bull. 54: 103–30.

Bullock, Alan. 1977. *Is History Becoming a Social Science? The Case of Contemporary History*. Cambridge.

Carr, E. H. [1961] 1964. *What Is History?* Harmondsworth, Eng. This work refers to the idealist Collingwood as "the only British thinker in the present century who has made a serious contribution to the philosophy of history" (p. 21).

Danto, Arthur C. 1956. "On Explanations in History." *Philosophy of Science* 23: 15–30. The author argues that history cannot and ought not be a science.

Donagan, Alan. 1964. "Historical Explanation: The Popper-Hempel Theory Reconsidered." *HT* 4: 3–26.

Dray, William H. 1957. *Laws and Explanation in History*. Oxford. This is one of the best-known criticisms of the covering law model of historical explanation.

————. 1970. "Theories of Historical Understanding." *Transactions of the Royal Society of Canada*, Series 4, 8: 267–85. This is a good basic survey with specific examples drawn from the work of historians.

Fogel, R. 1966. "The New Economic History." *The Economic History Review*, 2d Series, 19: 642–56.

Fritz, Kurt von. 1958. *Aristotle's Contribution to the Practice and Theory of Historiography*. Berkeley, Calif. The author argues that Aristotle did not deny history's connection with universal truth—although his remarks in chapter nine of *The Art of Poetry* have often been so construed: "Aristotle's statement means that both (dramatic) poetry and history make something universal visible through the medium of the specific and the particular, but that poetry is nearer to the universal, while in history there is more of the fortuitous and particular" (p. 133).

Gallie, W. B. 1955. "Explanations in History and the Genetic Sciences." *Mind* 64: 160–80.

Gruner, Rolf. 1967. "Understanding in the Social Sciences and History." *Inquiry* 10: 151–63.

Hempel, Carl G. [1942] 1959. "The Function of General Laws in History." In Gardiner: 344–56.

Krieger, Leonard. 1963. "Comments on Historical Explanation." In Hook: 136–42.

Leff, Gordon. 1971. *History and Social Theory*. Garden City, N.Y. Chapter four deals with "explanation."

Mandelbaum, Maurice. [1960] 1969. "Historical Explanation: The Problem of 'Covering Laws'." In Nash: 124–40. Mandelbaum believes that the logic used by scientists and historians is identical and that "at least an implicit appeal to a knowledge of general laws is needed in history" (p. 138).

Mink, Louis O. [1965] 1966. "The Autonomy of Historical Understanding." In Dray: 160–92.

Munz, Peter. 1967. "The Skeleton and the Mollusc: Reflections on the Nature of Historical Narratives." *New Zealand Journal of History* 1: 107–23.

Nadel, George. 1964. "Philosophy of History Before Historicism." *HT* 3: 291–315.

Nash, Ronald H., ed. 1969. *Ideas of History* 2. New York.

Oakeshott, Michael. 1933. *Experience and Its Modes*. Cambridge.

Popper, Karl. 1950. *The Open Society and Its Enemies*. Princeton, N.J. Popper maintains that it was he, and not Hempel, who first advanced the covering law position in his *Logik der Forschung* (1935).

Walsh, W. H. [1951] 1960. *Philosophy of History: An Introduction*. New York.

Weingartner, Rudolph H. [1961] 1969. "The Quarrel about Historical Explanation." In Nash: 140–58.

White, Hayden. 1972. "The Structure of Historical Narrative." *Clio* 1: 5–20.

————. 1973. *Metahistory: The Historical Imagination in Nineteenth-Century Europe*. Baltimore.

White, Morton G. 1943. "Historical Explanation." *Mind*, N.S., 52: 212–29.

————. 1945. "The Attack on the Historical Method." *JP* 42: 314–31.

Windelband, Wilhelm. [1894] 1980. "History and Natural Science." *HT* 19: 169–85.

Wise, Gene. 1973. *American Historical Explanations: A Strategy for Grounded Inquiry*. Homewood, Ill.

Zagorin, Perez. 1959. "Historical Knowledge: A Review Article on the Philosophy of History." *JMH* 31: 243–55. This article is good for additional bibliography.

Sources of Additional Information

See also COVERING LAW; UNDERSTANDING; *HT Beih.*; Birkos and Tambs; Stephens. In general see Berding, especially the section *"Erklären und Verstehen,"* pp. 158–64; also Rudolph H. Weingartner, "Historical Explanation," *EP* 4: 7–12, which includes a good bibliography. The footnotes in Mandelbaum ([1960] 1969) are also rich in bibliographical information. Two anthologies provide excellent introductions to the subject, as well as bibliographical information: Nash (1969) and Gardiner (1959). Also valuable are Hook (1963), Dray (1966), and Juha Manninen and Raimo Tuomela, eds., *Essays on Explanation and Understanding: Studies in the Foundations of the Humanities and Social Sciences* (Dordrecht, Holland, 1976). Some of the refinements of covering law theory are conveniently summarized in William Dray, "The Historical Explanation of Actions Reconsidered," in Hook: 105–35. See also the discussions in: Patrick Gardiner, *The Nature of Historical Explanation* (Oxford, 1961), especially p. 99; Quentin Skinner, "The Limits of Historical Explanations," *Philosophy* 41 (1966): 199–215; Louis O. Mink, "Philosophical Analysis and Historical Understanding," *The Review of Metaphysics* 21 (June 1968): 667–98; Murray G. Murphey, *Our Knowledge of the Historical Past* (Indianapolis, Ind., 1973), especially chapter three (as well as William Dray's review of this book in *JP* 72 [Dec. 18, 1975]: 805–9); J. O. Wisdom, "Current Explanation in History," *HT* 15 (1976): 257–66; Maurice Mandelbaum, *The Anatomy of Historical Knowledge* (Baltimore, 1977); Rex Martin, *Historical Explanation: Re-Enactment and Practical Inference* (Ithaca, N.Y., 1977); Dale H. Porter, *The Emergence of the Past: A Theory of Historical Explanation* (Chicago, 1981); and Peter Burke, *The Renaissance Sense of the Past* (London, 1969), chapter four and pp. 134–36. Hayden White's position is the subject of several papers published in Beih. 19 (1980) of *HT*.

F

FACT. A claim to knowledge established by the methods of historical inquiry.

History is commonly distinguished from fiction on the grounds that it rests on fact. It is this factual basis, above all, that is generally believed to set history apart from fable, legend, and myth (Lévy-Bruhl, 1935–36: 264). The historian E. H. Carr ([1961] 1964: 30) characterizes history as "a continuous process of interaction between the historian and his facts." "The historian without his facts is rootless and futile," Carr asserts; "the facts without their historian are dead and meaningless." Yet despite a substantial literature on the subject—some of it authored by historians—use of the term *fact* in history is remarkable for its lack of rigor. In many cases *fact* is a thought-arresting word, an impenetrable category beyond which analysis fails to proceed. Even scholars who try to address the subject head on often circumvent the problem of precise definition. Much of the difficulty stems from failure to distinguish carefully the categories of fact and EVENT.

Since the late Middle Ages the noun *fact*—derived from the Latin *factum*—has implied "something definitely done" (Gilliam, 1976: 233). The word entered English from Latin indirectly, via the French *fait* (deed) (Lukacs, 1968: 100). It first became a key term in historical discourse in the nineteenth century, when historians sought to free their discipline from the domain of "literature"—where it had been loosely classified since antiquity. The young Leopold von Ranke (1795–1886), his thirst for REALISM unsatisfied by Walter Scott's historical novels, concluded that "historical evidence was more beautiful and, at any rate, more interesting than all romantic fiction. I turned away from it and resolved to avoid all invention and fabrication in my works and stick to the facts" (cited in Cassirer, [1944] 1970: 192). For Ranke the "supreme law" of history became the "strict presentation of the facts, contingent and unattractive though they may be" (Ranke, [1824] 1972: 57). In like spirit, Thomas Carlyle announced: "How impressive the smallest historical *fact* may become as contrasted with the grandest *fictitious* event" (cited in Lukacs, 1968: 100).

The notion of fact was not usually viewed as a problem in historical writing until the end of the nineteenth century. True, a few writers acknowledged the tenuousness of an idea that, in previous times, "had not borne the importance of a major category of reality" (Gilliam, 1976: 233; Lukacs, 1968: 100). Goethe's famous opinion that "Das Höchste wäre: zu begreifen, dass alles Faktische schon Theorie ist" (cited in Cassirer, [1944] 1970: 192, n. 5) was shared, for example, by Wilhelm von Humboldt ([1821] 1967: 58), who asserted that every fact has an "invisible part" that the historian cannot perceive directly but has to add. Said Humboldt, "the facts of history are in their several connecting circumstances little more than the results of tradition and scholarship which one has agreed to accept as true, because they—being most highly probable in themselves—also fit best into the context of the whole" (p. 58). In accordance with the realist presuppositions of most nineteenth-century scholarship, however, facts were generally treated as fixed entities, somewhat like the atoms of physical science. They were things to be ascertained and "collected" (Taine, [1863–67] 1970: 503)—the building blocks of historical NARRATIVE. According to this "cult of facts" (Carr, [1961] 1964: 9), the historian "need make no interpretation of them; he need only say what they are. . . . a fact, like a sense-impression, impinges on the observer from outside and is then given immediately in perception" (Gilliam, 1976: 234). This was the basis for the widespread belief that the assembled facts would "speak for themselves," a notion reflected in Fustel de Coulanges' (1830–89) assertion that it was not he who spoke in his histories but "history which speaks through me" (cited in Stern, 1972: 25).

Variations of this position persist (e.g., Fales, 1951: 85, 91), but it is now widely agreed that *fact* is an ambiguous word.

> In most historical contexts [writes Gilliam] it is unclear whether *fact* refers to the deed itself or to a statement implying a judgment that the deed was done. . . . [This ambiguity focuses] attention on the historian's primary predicament—his need to resolve the discrepancy between fact and interpretation, the objective and the subjective. (1976: 233–34)

Historians today regularly disavow the "nineteenth-century fetishism of facts," to cite an expression of Carr ([1961] 1964: 16), who disclaims as a "preposterous fallacy" the "belief in a hard core of historical facts existing objectively and independently of the interpretation of the historian" (p. 12).

Present thinking owes much to the neo-idealist Italian philosopher Benedetto Croce (1866–1952). Croce rejected as an "illusion of naturalism" the notion of "brute" facts, that is, the idea that historians begin with facts "which do not already involve interpretation" (Meiland, 1965: 21; Croce, [1919] 1960: 73, 76). Facts, he argued, are not simply *there*, ready-made for discovery, but are "posited" by the historian for purposes of his own. The true starting point for the historian is thus "the mind that thinks and constructs the fact" (Croce, [1919] 1960: 75). Facts are not external to the historian's mind but precisely the reverse; they are human constructs, the "end product[s] of the historian's work, not its starting point" (Meiland, 1965: 20). This challenged the stock assumption that "fact and interpretation are different and that interpretations are built on facts" (p. 21).

One might suppose that Croce erred in denying the existence of certain kinds of "brute" facts—for example, the fact that a particular manuscript is found in a certain place or that it is handwritten. Such cases do not seem to require interpretation. One might ask, however, if these sorts of facts are *historical* facts, that is, facts known by virtue of the methods of history. If not, Croce was probably right to deny the existence of "brute *historical* facts" (even though he did not himself clearly distinguish categories of historical and non-historical fact [Meiland, 1965: 22]).

After World War I important examinations were undertaken by the French scholar Henri Lévy-Bruhl (1926; 1935–36) and the American historian Carl Becker ([1955] 1959). Lévy-Bruhl's conclusions were ambiguous. In his first paper (1926) he concluded that historians are essentially concerned with what society has *believed* to be true rather than with actual, or "brute," fact (pp. 55, 58–59, n. 1). Thus, the *historical* fact about a spurious document such as the Donation of Constantine is not that it was a forgery but that medieval society considered it genuine (p. 56; also Goldstein, 1976: 65). Again, a statesman who is admired during his lifetime may be exposed as incompetent by evidence discovered after his death; what interests the historian is the appearance of greatness that prevailed while he lived. Lévy-Bruhl did not explain how historians *establish* "social facts" of this nature; he was concerned with classifying the kinds of facts that are objects of historical inquiry, not the epistemic basis such facts.

In his second paper (1935–36: 268–69) Lévy-Bruhl moved to the epistemological plane, asserting that his first essay had been too narrow. After surveying a range of possible meanings he concluded that the expression *historical fact* was a "confused notion" not susceptible of precise definition. It was, he believed, a semantic atavism—a vestige of the annalist stage of historiography when *fact* simply meant a remarkable event and *history* was understood as the straightforward description of such occurrences. The term was therefore inadequate to the contemporary needs of "explanatory" historical science (p. 274; cf. Goldstein, 1976: 63–64).

Carl Becker's "What Are Historical Facts," written in 1926 but not published until 1955, is perhaps the best-known treatment of the subject by an English-language historian. In this essay—and in a later presidential address to the American Historical Association (1932)—Becker extended ideas that he had advanced, partly under Croce's influence, as early as 1910 (Destler, 1970: 340). Becker noted that the use of expressions such as *hard facts* and *solid foundation of fact* lends a "sense of stability" to historical narratives. "By virtue of talking in this way," he wrote ([1955] 1959: 120), "the facts of history come in the end to seem something solid, something substantial like physical matter, . . . something possessing definite shape, and clear persistent outline—like bricks or scantlings." But in reality "the facts . . . do not say anything, do not impose any meaning. It is the historian who speaks, who imposes a meaning" (p. 131).

For Becker a "fact" could be delimited in a variety of ways depending on the goals and interests of the individual historian; there were no "simple" facts. The fact that Caesar crossed the Rubicon in 49 B.C., for instance, may be subdivided into an almost infinite number of lesser facts. A *fact* is actually a generalization, based on a selection made by the individual historian. Moreover, a fact cannot be understood *historically* unless it is seen in the context of a broader set of circumstances. A *historical fact*, he concluded, is

> not a hard, cold something with a clear outline, and measurable pressure, like a brick. It is so far as we can know it, only a *symbol*, a simple statement which is a generalization of a thousand and one simpler facts which we do not for the moment care to use, and this generalization itself we cannot use apart from the wider facts and generalizations which it symbolizes. (p. 123; cf. Cassirer, [1944] 1970: 189–228, especially pp. 192–93)

As symbols, *facts* are "illusive and intangible" *statements* made by individual historians, subject to all of the psychological and cultural pressures that affect human beings. It is even doubtful if they can be said to be true or false. "The safest thing to say about a symbol," Becker asserted ([1955] 1959: 125), "is that it is more or less appropriate."

> There is thus a distinction of capital importance to be made [he concluded]: the distinction between the ephemeral event which disappears, and the affirmation about the event which persists. For all practical purposes it is this affirmation about the event that constitutes for us the historical fact. If so the historical fact is not the past event, but a symbol which enables us to recreate it imaginatively. (p 124)

Whatever else it did, Becker's statement of the problem made scholars sensitive to the use of the term *fact* and obliged traditionalists to articulate their assumptions. Thus the philosopher Maurice Mandelbaum, an opponent of Becker's RELATIVISM, deliberately argued that "the facts of the past are fixed, as dead flies on fly paper" (1952: 360). But it is doubtful if many historians or philosophers would subscribe to Mandelbaum's position today. D. H. Fischer (1970: 66, n. 4), for example, maintains that although past events "happened in the way that they happened, and not in any other way . . . facts, or true statements about past events, can and will change, as other events occur." Fischer amplifies this by suggesting that "the significance of events is always, in part dependent upon later events; and therefore . . . the significance of past events is partly dependent upon future events" (p. 66, n. 4).

Certainly, few scholars would now openly endorse the once-respectable notion that facts "speak for themselves" (although it may be true that the "old error still survives, deep in the dark recesses of every historian's heart'' [Fischer, 1970: 7]). Although most would emphatically reject Becker's idea that truth and falsehood are not relevant to historical fact, many would agree that facts are best understood as statements or affirmations by historians rather than as independent entities. Fischer (1970: xv, n.; 66, n. 4), for instance, defines a *historical fact* as a "true descriptive statement about past events.'' On the other hand, E. H. Carr's analogy ([1961] 1964: 23) comparing facts to "fish swimming in a huge and sometimes inaccessible ocean'' that the historian tries to "catch'' reflects a persistent belief that facts exist apart from the scholar's operations. The facts, Carr thinks (p. 30), "belong to the past,'' whereas the historian is "part of the present.'' In his view, "basic facts'' (p. 11) are found and collected by historians, but they become *historical* facts only when they are judged historically significant by selection and interpretation. The same would apply to Rolf Gruner's idea (1968: 128) that the facts of history are like pieces in a jigsaw puzzle, which the historian fits together in ways that may vary. This conventional orientation undoubtedly prevails among many—perhaps most—historians, who often pride themselves on employing the terms and assumptions of common sense and ordinary language. On the other hand, some scholars take a middle position, suggesting that some facts are "given'' and others are "created'' (Berr and Febvre, 1932: 363). It is worth noting that the ideas of "fact'' and EVENT are traditionally used interchangeably (for instance Fales, 1951: 85), a conflation that blurs matters by erasing the useful distinction between historical facts and past occurrences.

A key question is whether a fact is a statement that *corresponds* to a past event. Most historians believe that this is the case. Becker ([1955] 1959: 124), for instance, thought that the object of history is a true realm of past events— what Croce might have called "brute facts''—but that these events, because they are past, cannot be directly known; historical facts are the historians' imperfect or "symbolic'' affirmations about these events. Fischer appears to agree, despite his opinion that Becker's relativism was a "great blight upon historical scholarship'':

> there is an infinity of particulars in the past [he asserts, preferring to use the term *particular* where *fact* might once have appeared]. Their truth value is an objective entity that exists independently of an inquirer. But their particularity is separately defined by each inquiry. (1970: 5, x)

The mainstream position thus seems to be that historians do not exercise interpretation in the creation of facts but only in their selection and classification; the very notion that facts can be created would be considered highly unorthodox. Ultimately, *facts* are statements that refer or correspond to phenomena that once existed in the real world, events or processes that "actually happened.''

A recent, opposing view is that of Leon Goldstein (1976: 67), who rejects the realist premises of most existing thought on the subject and favors a "methodological'' approach. While admitting that the term *fact* has "no generally

agreed to and unambiguous use," Goldstein maintains that the word "is somewhat useful as a diagnostic tool" (p. 63); "historical facts are not to be located
in the real past," he writes (p. 81) but are "products of research." Like Becker,
he considers a *fact* an affirmation,

> something established in the course of some kind of intellectual activity, in the
> course of some inquiry initiated for the purpose of establishing claims to knowledge.
> . . . a historical fact would be a claim to knowledge arrived at by means of historical
> investigation—what is known in the historical way is a historical fact. (p. 81)

Historical facts, then, are statements about the past "established through historical research" (p. 66).

Crucial to Goldstein's view is the idea that we do not know the facts of the
past in the same way that we know the facts of the present. The facts of the
present can be confirmed by immediate experience, but the facts of the past, no
matter how much agreement upon them may exist, are only established in a
disciplinary way, by the methods of historical scholarship (p. 69). Moreover,
since we have no way of directly experiencing the "real" past, we cannot say
that facts are statements that correspond, more or less, to past events; for it
makes no sense to say that something corresponds to something else that tran-
scends our experience. There would be no basis for asserting such a correspondence. More accurately, *facts* are statements that historians "constitute" (pp. 71,
84) on the basis of EVIDENCE; they are constructions of the community of scholars
that earn their status as facts by virtue of professional consensus and their logical
relationship to evidence. Goldstein attributes variations or anticipations of this
approach to Becker ([1955] 1959), Langlois and Seignobos ([1898] 1926), H.-
I. Marrou (1966), and G. Kitson Clark (1967).

References

Becker, Carl L. 1932. "Everyman His Own Historian." *AHR* 37: 221–236. Reprinted
        in Carl L. Becker, *Everyman His Own Historian: Essays on History and Politics*
        (New York, 1935): 233–55. Becker's 1931 presidential address to the American
        Historical Association which repeated—in the same terminology—some of the
        arguments advanced in his unpublished paper "What Are Historical Facts?" (see
        below). See especially pp. 249–51.
————. [1955] 1959. "What Are Historical Facts." In Meyerhoff: 120–37. This was
        first read as a paper at Cornell and at the American Historical Association in 1926;
        it was first published, however, in *The Western Political Quarterly* 8 (Sept. 1955):
        327–40. It is reprinted in Phil L. Snyder, ed., *Detachment and the Writing of
        History: Essays and Letters of Carl L. Becker* (Ithaca, N.Y., 1958): 41–63.
Berr, Henri, and Febvre, Lucien. 1932. "History." *ESS* 7: 357–68.
Carr, E. H. [1961] 1964. *What Is History?* Harmondsworth, Eng.
Cassirer, Ernst. [1944] 1970. *An Essay on Man*. New York. The author views the historical
        fact as symbol (see the chapter "History," pp. 189–228, and especially pp. 192–
        93).
Clark, G. Kitson. 1967. *The Critical Historian*. New York.
Croce, Benedetto. [1919] 1960. *History: Its Theory and Practice*. New York.

Destler, Chester McArthur. 1970. "The Crocean Origin of Becker's Historical Relativism." *HT* 9: 335–42. Destler stresses the importance of Becker's 1910 essay
"Detachment and the Writing of History" (*The Atlantic Monthly* 106 [1910]:
524–36).

Fales, Walter. 1951. "Historical Facts." *JP* 48 (Feb. 15, 1951): 85–94. Fales defines a
historical fact as "an event which influences the minds of people so as to bring
about unique, irreversible changes in their pattern of thinking, initiating an indefinite series of noticeable effects upon their style of living" (p. 85).

Fischer, David Hackett. 1970. *Historians' Fallacies: Toward a Logic of Historical
Thought*. New York.

Gilliam, Harriet. 1976. "The Dialectics of Realism and Idealism in Modern Historiographic Theory." *HT* 15: 231–56. This work contains a discussion of fact from
both realist and idealist points of view (pp. 233–36).

Goldstein, Leon J. 1976. *Historical Knowing*. Austin, Tex. Chapter three, "Historical
Facts," discusses several ways historical facts have been understood.

Gruner, Rolf. 1968. "Historical Facts and the Testing of Hypotheses." *American Philosophical Quarterly* 5: 124–29. The author believes it is necessary to distinguish
"between a fact and the assertion of a fact" (p. 125); a fact is something that
"was the case in the past" (p. 125), and "sometimes historians even stumble on
a fact by pure chance" (p. 127).

Humboldt, Wilhelm von. [1821] 1967. "On the Historian's Task." *HT* 6: 57–71.

Langlois, Ch. V., and Seignobos, Ch. [1898] 1926. *Introduction to the Study of History*.
New York.

Lévy-Bruhl, Henri. 1926. "Qu'est-ce que le fait historique?" *Revue de Synthèse Historique* 42: 53–59.

————. 1935–1936. "Une notion confuse: Le fait historique." *Recherches Philoso-
phiques* 5: 264–274.

Lukacs, John. 1968. *Historical Consciousness or the Remembered Past*. New York. This
book contains an interesting discussion in chapter three, "Facts and Fictions."
Lukacs belives that "facts ought to mean something that was accomplished in the
past" (p. 103).

Mandelbaum, Maurice. 1952. "Comments." *JP* 49: 359–62.

Marrou, Henri-Irénée. 1966. *The Meaning of History*. Baltimore.

Meiland, Jack W. 1965. *Scepticism and Historical Knowledge*. New York.

Ranke, Leopold von. [1824] 1972. *Histories of the Latin and Germanic Nations from
1494–1514*. In Stern: 55–58.

Stern, Fritz. 1972. "Introduction." In Stern: 11–32.

Taine, Hippolyte. [1863–67] 1970. *The History of English Literature*. In Walter Jackson
Bate, ed., *Criticism: The Major Texts*. New York: 501–7.

Sources of Additional Information

See the bibliography cited in Peter Munz, *The Shapes of Time* (Middletown, Conn.),
p. 305. For discussions of fact in formal philosophy consult the index to *EP* and especially
the entry by A. N. Prior, "Correspondence Theory of Truth," 2: 223–32; also Edward
W. Strong, "Fact and Understanding in History," *JP* 44 (Nov. 6, 1947): 617–25.
Fischer's position (1970) is based partly on Arthur Danto's *Analytical Philosophy of
History* (Cambridge, 1965). In his essay "The Burden of History," *Tropics of Discourse*
(Baltimore, 1978), p. 47, Hayden White suggests that "*what constitutes the facts them-*

selves'' is a product of the "choice of the metaphor by which [the historian] orders his
world, past, present, and future." On the idea of fact in late-nineteenth-century SCIENTIFIC
HISTORY see W. Stull Holt, "The Idea of Scientific History in America," *JHI* 1 (June
1940): 352–62. See also Harold N. Lee, "The Hypothetical Nature of Historical Knowledge," *JP* 51 (1954): 213–20; and Maurice Mandelbaum, "Societal Facts" [1955], in
Gardiner: 476–88. Sidney Hook discusses "Fact" in Bull. 54: 123–25. G. R. Elton
devotes a part of his *Practice of History* (New York, 1967), pp. 58–66, to a consideration
of "Facts and Method." See also W. H. Walsh, *Philosophy of History: An Introduction*
(1951; New York, 1960), pp. 72–93, on "truth and fact in history." On the idea of fact
in the British idealist tradition, see David Boucher, "The Creation of the Past: British
Idealism and Michael Oakeshott's Philosophy of History," *HT* 23 (1984): 193–214,
especially 195 and 197. For a rambling treatment from the standpoint of HISTORICAL
MATERIALISM see Adam Schaff, "Historical Facts and Their Selection," *Diogenes*, no.
69 (Spring 1970): 99–125. Volume 38 (Sept. 1951): 265–66 of the *Mississippi Valley
Historical Review* summarizes a discussion, "The Use of Evidence to Establish Facts,"
that occurred at a meeting of the Mississippi Valley Historical Association.

FASCISM. 1. A political doctrine created by Benito Mussolini and his followers
in Italy following World War I—militantly nationalist, radical in style, authoritarian, anti-liberal, anti-socialist, and anti-conservative; became fashionable in many parts of Europe between 1919 and 1945. 2. A concept of
comparative political and social analysis employed by many scholars, particularly since the early 1960s, to explain various non-socialist forms of authoritarianism in the twentieth century, especially Italian Fascism and German
National Socialism.

Fascism has been called the "vaguest of contemporary political terms"
(Payne, 1980: 4). Some historians (for instance, Allardyce, 1979) argue that it
is meaningless to speak of fascism as a general phenomenon and recommend
that the term be used only to refer to the self-designated Fascist party of Mussolini
in Italy. Most scholars embrace the concept, but there is wide disagreement over
the origins, nature, and significance of fascism.

The idea of fascism as a general political phenomenon arose in the 1920s and
1930s as the consequence of efforts to account for the rise of Mussolini and
Hitler. The word *fascio*, derived from the Latin *fasces* (a bundle of rods surrounding an axe, which symbolized authority in ancient Rome; also, an organized
group or union), had come into use in late-nineteenth-century Italy as a term for
workers' organizations. The term *fascism* (*fascismo*) itself appeared at the turn
of the century, although it seems to have been rarely used before the 1920s.
Variations of the term were used by socialist and nationalist organizations alike;
it had not yet gained a firm ideological definition. On March 23, 1919, Mussolini,
a former Marxist who had renounced socialism for nationalism during the war,
founded an organization called the Fasci di combattimento (Nolte, 1975: 329–
36). This became the nucleus of the Fascist party, which Mussolini led to power
in late 1922; in 1926 it was declared the only legal party in Italy.

Italian and German Marxists pioneered in formulating a general theory of fascism, based on the idea that it was the creation of beleaguered CAPITALISM. In the early and mid–1920s, Marxist theorists generalized from the Italian case, linking their interpretation of the Italian case to the Marxist theory of historical development, HISTORICAL MATERIALISM. According to this view, fascism was the political and socioeconomic form appropriate to late monopoly capitalism, a last-ditch means by which the forces of big capital sought to defend their privileged status. The official position adopted by the Communist International stated that fascism was "the openly terroristic dictatorship of the most reactionary, most chauvinistic and most imperialistic elements of finance-capital" (Rabinbach, 1974: 136; Nolte, 1975: 332). This was an "agent" theory that held that Mussolini's Fascist party and similar movements such as Hitler's National Socialism were tools of financial and industrial interests working behind the scenes. The majority of West European and American historians have always rejected this agent theory as simplistic and crude; in doing so, they have sometimes presented it as the *only* Marxist concept of fascism. There have in fact been various shadings of Marxist theory, all tied to the idea that fascism is the product of a CRISIS of "late capitalism"; many are less simplistic than the Comintern formulation (Rabinbach, 1974).

Aside from the Marxists, Mussolini himself helped to create the idea that fascism was a general phenomenon that extended beyond the frontiers of Italy. In a well-known article of 1932, "The Doctrine of Fascism," written for the *Encyclopedia Italiana*, Mussolini ([1932] 1977: 329, 340) represented fascism as a general "political conception" that could provide the "solutions of certain universal problems." It was a "whole way of conceiving life, a spiritualized way," in which self-sacrifice and duty to the state were paramount. Fascism was anti-liberal and anti-Marxist, avowedly elitist, authoritarian, and collectivist. In contrast to Marxist theory, Mussolini denied that fascism was "reactionary"; fascism did not want to "make the world return to what it was before 1789 [i.e., before the French Revolution]. . . . It is not reactionary, but revolutionary" (p. 340).

During the 1930s *fascism* was still widely used to refer to Mussolini's regime in Italy, a fact reflected in the entry that appeared in volume six of the *Encyclopedia of Social Sciences* (1931). However, Hitler's rise to power in 1933 at the head of National Socialism, so apparently similar in style and values to Mussolini's movement, helped to popularize the idea that fascism was indeed an international phenomenon. In the late 1930s journalists and other writers depicted the Spanish civil war as a struggle between the forces of democracy and "international fascism." At this time the term was firmly established in the general vocabulary of politics.

After World War II the concept of fascism fell temporarily out of favor among scholars, at least among non-Marxists. Some preferred to explain the events of the recent past in terms of unique national traditions rather than general concepts (e.g., Taylor, 1946). In the "cold war" climate of the late 1940s and 1950s, the concept of TOTALITARIANISM tended to replace fascism among non-Marxists as a theory to explain the rise of twentieth-century authoritarian regimes. The Nazi and Fascist regimes of Germany and Italy were depicted as bureaucratic despotisms that were, at bottom, essentially similar to Stalin's Soviet regime, and "fascism" was denigrated as a product of Marxist ideology.

In the early 1960s, however, the theory of totalitarianism was widely (although by no means completely) discredited as a by-product of cold war LIBERALISM, and interest in the theory of fascism revived, especially among historians (Sauer, 1967). Since this time the concept of fascism has been widely used as an IDEAL TYPE, or hypothetical model, for purposes of comparative historical analysis. Simultaneously, the word *fascism* experienced a renaissance as a political catch-word, and in journalistic and polemical usage it was generalized in the extreme, a practice that occasionally crept into historical texts. A widely used textbook, for example, suggests that the term may properly refer to "any noncommunistic authoritarian movement or government in the contemporary Western world" (Beatty and Johnson, 1977: 320). Some historians have adopted this broad usage and have attempted to extend the concept beyond the historical confines of interwar Europe to other settings, such as Japan, Latin America, and contemporary Africa (e.g. Laqueur, 1976). Inflated to this degree, the concept ceases to carry much genuine analytical power.

The key work in the concept's revival among historians was Ernst Nolte's *Three Faces of Fascism*, published in West Germany in 1963 and translated into English in 1966. Nolte accepts the idea that fascism was a general phenomenon but argues that use of the concept should be strictly limited to the anti-socialist authoritarian movements and regimes of Europe between the First and Second World Wars. He traces the intellectual roots of fascism to the late-eighteenth-century formulators of the idea of counterrevolution and defines *fascism* very abstractly as a reactionary or anti-progressive "resistance to transcendence," by which he seems to mean opposition to democratization and liberalization by social groups threatened in various ways by the progressive ideas of the eighteenth-century ENLIGHTENMENT. Despite its high level of abstraction, Nolte's theory has been widely adopted by working historians as a framework for conceptualization (e.g., Edmondson, 1978).

Following Nolte's work, there have been a variety of approaches to the study of fascism. Three broad currents may be identified: (1) a continuing commitment among Marxists to the idea of fascism as the political expression of "decadent" capitalism, along with many efforts, especially in West Germany, to refine this theory; (2) the outright rejection of the idea of fascism as a generic concept; (3) the development of a new theory of fascism, inspired partly by Nolte's work, as the response of certain early-twentieth-century European societies to the process of MODERNIZATION (which may be roughly characterized in terms of democratization, urbanization, industrialization, and secularization), either as an effort to accelerate the process (the Italian case [Cassels, (1969) 1975]) or to resist it (the German case [Turner, (1972) 1975]). Although "modernization" theories of fascism are usually presented as alternatives to Marxist theory, they often draw on Marxist arguments, with the notion of modernization functioning in some respects as a substitute for the Marxist concept of capitalism. For example, the Marxist idea that fascism drew its decisive mass support from the lower middle class has long been widely endorsed in non-Marxist circles (but cf. Hamilton, 1982). Marxist and "modernization" theories differ, however, in that non-Marxist historians usually contend that fascist movements were in some sense "revolutionary" (Carsten, 1976: 428; De Felice, 1977) and stress the differences as well as the family similarities between the national varieties of fascism; Marxists contend that fascist movements were "counterrevolutionary" and emphasize their essential similarity.

The modernization theory was especially popular among academic historians in Western Europe and America in the 1970s. Thus, despite occasional calls for abandonment of the concept of fascism, most historians assume that fascism existed as an international phenomenon, at least in Europe between the two world wars. The view of Payne (1979: 389) is representative: "Historical understanding requires us to identify certain common features or qualities of new forces within a given period, if only to recognize and clarify their differences and uniqueness."

References

Allardyce, Gilbert. 1979. "What Fascism Is Not: Thoughts on the Deflation of a Concept." *AHR* 84: 367–88. This brief history of the development of the idea debunks Fascism as a generic concept, as a political ideology, and as a personality type. The article is followed by rejoinders by Stanley G. Payne and Ernst Nolte that defend use of the concept.

Beatty, John Louis, and Johnson, Oliver A., eds. 1977. *Heritage of Western Civilization* 2. 4th ed. Englewood Cliffs, N.J.

Carsten, Francis L. 1976. "Interpretations of Fascism." In Walter Laqueur, ed., *Fascism: A Reader's Guide. Analyses, Interpretations, Bibliography*. Berkeley, Calif.

Cassels, Alan. [1969] 1975. "Janus: The Two Faces of Fascism." In Henry A. Turner, Jr., ed., *Reappraisals of Fascism*. New York: 69–92.

De Felice, Renzo. 1977. *Interpretations of Fascism*. Cambridge, Mass. This is a survey of interpretations by one of the leading Italian students of the problem. It includes an introduction by Charles F. Delzell discussing De Felice's own controversial position on Italian fascism, which stresses its "progressive" nature.

Edmundson, C. Earl. 1978. *The Heimwehr and Austrian Politics, 1918–1934*. Athens, Ga.

Hamilton, Richard F. 1982. *Who Voted for Hitler?* Princeton, N.J. Hamilton argues that lower middle-class support was not decisive to Hitler.

Laqueur, Walter. 1976. "Fascism—The Second Coming." *Commentary* 61 (Feb. 1976): 57–62.

Mussolini, Benito. [1932] 1977. "The Doctrine of Fascism." In John Louis Beatty and Oliver A. Johnson, eds., *Heritage of Western Civilization* 2. 4th ed. Englewood Cliffs, N.J.: 329–41.

Nolte, Ernst. 1975. "Fascismus." *GG* 2: 329–36. This very important discussion is by one of the most widely cited authorities.

Payne, Stanley G. 1979. "Comments." *AHR* 84: 389–91. This piece is by a specialist
    in modern Spanish history and one of the leading American defenders of the idea
    of fascism as a generic concept.
————. 1980. *Fascism: Comparison and Definition.* Madison, Wis. This is an excellent
    introduction; it presents a "typological description" of fascism based on its "ne-
    gations," "ideology and goals," and "style and organization."
Rabinbach, Anson G. 1974. "Toward a Marxist Theory of Fascism and National So-
    cialism: A Report on Developments in West Germany." *New German Critique*
    1: 127–53. The author presents a good survey of some recent refinements in
    Marxist theory.
Sauer, Wolfgang. 1967. "National Socialism: Totalitarianism or Fascism?" *AHR* 73:
    404–22. This article is reprinted in Henry A. Turner, Jr., ed., *Reappraisals of
    Fascism* (New York, 1975) but without the footnotes of the original essay, which
    are rich in bibliographical information.
Taylor, A.J.P. 1946. *The Course of German History: A Survey of the Development of
    Germany since 1815.* New York.
Turner, Henry A., Jr. [1972] 1975. "Fascism and Modernization." In Henry A. Turner,
    Jr., ed., *Reappraisals of Fascism.* New York. This is the best introduction to the
    theory of German National Socialism as a movement opposed to "modernization."

Sources of Additional Information

See also TOTALITARIANISM. An excellent guide is Philip Rees, ed., *Fascism and Pre-
Fascism in Europe, 1890–1945: A Bibliography of the Extreme Right* (Sussex, Eng.,
1984), which is comprehensive. Consult also Berding: 317–28. There are a number of
articles on fascism in specialized encyclopedias that include helpful bibliographies, for
example, *ESS, IESS,* and, particularly, *MCWS.* Topical interest in fascism during the
1960s and 1970s spawned a great many anthologies and reviews of research. The most
useful anthology is Henry A. Turner, Jr., ed., *Reappraisals of Fascism* (New York,
1975). Others include Walter Laqueur and George L. Mosse, eds., *International Fascism,
1920–1945* (New York, 1966); S. J. Woolf, ed., *European Fascism* (London, 1968);
and Walter Laqueur, ed., *Fascism: A Reader's Guide. Analyses, Interpretations, Bibliography* (Berkeley, Calif., 1976). An important survey of research on the Nazi movement
is Pierre Ayçoberry, *The Nazi Question: An Essay on the Interpretations of National
Socialism (1922–1975)* (New York, 1981). The best survey of Italian research is De
Felice (1977). Chapter five of Martin Jay, *The Dialectical Imagination* (Boston, 1973),
contains an analysis of interwar Marxist interpretations of Nazism as fascism. For a
critique of recent German Marxist literature, with a wealth of citations, see Heinrich
August Winkler, "Die 'neue Linke' und der Fascismus: Zur Kritik neomarxistischer
Theorien über den Nationalsozialismus," in Heinrich August Winkler, *Revolution, Staat,
Fascismus: Zur Revision des Historischen Materialismus* (Göttingen, 1978): 65–117.

FEUDALISM (Fr. *féodalité*). 1. A medieval military and political relationship
in which a vassal pledged homage and fealty (or loyalty) to a lord and was
given in return a fief (i.e., sustenance)—usually in the form of land—with
which to support himself as a warrior; typical of many parts of Western Europe
(but especially northern France) from the ninth to the thirteenth century. 2.
In Marxist doctrine, a stage of economic development or "mode of produc-

tion'' based on large estate agriculture controlled by an aristocracy and worked by a servile peasantry. This usage is normally rejected by non-Marxist scholars, who see feudalism and its economic counterpart, manorialism, as separate systems.

The difficulties of defining *feudalism* were clearly recognized by the French historian Marc Bloch, who once remarked that ''Nearly every historian understands the word as he pleases'' (1953: 176). Among medievalists, the idea of feudalism and the associated notion of ''feudal system'' have long been notorious for their ambiguity and polemical overtones; nonetheless, both continue to be widely employed. Indeed, for more than a century

> the concepts of feudalism and the feudal system have dominated the study of the medieval past. The appeal of these words, which provide a short, easy means of referring to the European social and political situation over an enormous stretch of time, has proved virtually impossible to resist. (Brown, 1979: 1065)

The idea of feudalism has been so compelling that, in the twentieth century, it has become a popular basis for comparing highly differentiated Western and non-Western societies and has been adapted for a wide range of other purposes as well—for example, the analysis of administrative relationships in Nazi Germany (Koehl, 1960; Mommsen, 1981: 159).

The idea of feudalism is a product of sixteenth- and seventeenth-century legal and political thought, although the relationships it designates are medieval and had largely disappeared by the time the notion was invented. The term itself is derived from *feudum*, tenth-century Latin for *fief*. *Fief* is a medieval French word apparently derived from the Frankish *fehu*, which meant cattle or, by extension, money or property in general. *Feudum* appeared first in France around the year 1000 and gradually displaced earlier Latin terms for property, such as *beneficium* and *honor*. Its meaning was at first narrowly technical and assumed the relationship of vassalage, ''for a fief could not exist apart from a vassal to hold it'' (Stephenson, 1941: 797; Brunner, 1975: 337). *Vassalage* may be defined as a relationship in which ''a man gives himself to a lord while remaining free, performing military service in return for a usufruct in a piece of land'' (Pocock, [1957] 1967: 73). Vassalage itself seems to have been a common arrangement as early as the eighth century.

Sixteenth- and seventeenth-century jurists laid the groundwork for the formal concept of feudalism on the basis of their studies of a single code: the *Libri Feudorum*, a twelfth-century compilation of the laws of Lombardy. For various scholarly and political reasons, these scholars—for example, Jacques de Cujas (1522–90) and François Hotman (1524–90) of France, the Scotsman Sir Thomas Craig (1538–?), and the Englishman Sir Henry Spelman (?–1641)—were interested in divorcing the history of law in their own lands from the Roman legal tradition.

The Lombard code was the only comprehensive written version of feudal law that became part of the general legal tradition of early-modern Europe and was considered to possess "the status of universal law" (Pocock, [1957] 1967: 70–71). Earlier commentators tried to explain it as an extension of ancient Roman law. Toward the end of the sixteenth century, however, largely due to philological considerations (the medieval latin terms of the Lombard books could not be found in ancient texts), Hotman and others began to construct a new, "Germanic" interpretation (Pocock, [1957] 1967: 72). According to this reading, the incursions of German tribes into the Roman empire—especially the Lombards—brought new legal forms that became the basis for an entirely new system of personal and economic relationships. Thus, the idea of "feudalism" as a *legal relationship* became widely accepted.

The French term *féodalité*, from which the English *feudalism* is derived, has been found to exist as early as 1515 (Mackrell, 1973: 5), but regular use dates only from the seventeenth century (Bloch, [1939–40] 1961: xvii). In English, the expressions *feudal* (*feudall*, *feodal*, *fewdal*) and *feudal law* were established in the seventeenth century, although the *OED* does not cite instances of *feudal system* or *feudalism* itself before the late eighteenth and early nineteenth century.

For a long time *féodalité* was a specialized legal term that referred narrowly to the fief and obligations arising from feudal tenure. In 1630, for example, a French lexicographer described *feodum*, *féodal*, and *féodalité* as "lawyers jargon" (Bloch, [1939–40] 1961: xvii). But as early as the sixteenth century isolated suggestions forshadowed the later notion that the idea could become the conceptual basis for cross-cultural comparisons. Craig, for example, suggested that medieval European relationships might be compared to the *timar* system of Ottoman Turkey (Pocock, [1957] 1967: 81–82). (Later, in the eighteenth century, Voltaire asserted that "Feudalism . . . is a very old form which, with differences in its workings, subsists in three quarters of our hemisphere" [cited in Bloch, (1939–40) 1961: 441]).

The idea was vastly broadened in early-eighteenth-century France (Mackrell, 1973). Then the terms *Gouvernement féodal* and *féodalité* came to be used to "designate a state of society"—first in the *Histoire de l'ancien Gouvernement de France* (1727) of the Comte de Boulainvilliers (1658–1722) and then, most significantly, in the *Spirit of the Laws* (1748) by the Baron de Montesquieu (Bloch, [1939–40] 1961: xvii). Both men were defenders of the French nobility and sought to refurbish the ancient "feudal law" to enhance the legal position of the aristocracy against the absolutist Bourbon kings.

> Montesquieu's famous chapters "Des lois féodales" . . . established the basis for all future discussion of feudal origins [writes Stephenson]. According to Montesquieu the essence of feudalism lay in the custom of vassalage, which can be traced to the *comitatus* [or warrior band] described by Tacitus. (1941: 789)

Although Montesquieu did not actually use the term *féodalité*, "it was unquestionably he who convinced the educated public of his time that the *lois féodales* were the distinguishing marks of a particular period of history" (Bloch, [1939–40] 1961: xviii).

Montesquieu's usage was rapidly disseminated in France and abroad, and the work of popularizing the idea of an entire "feudal regime" was finally completed during the French Revolution. By the late eighteenth century the expression *feudal regime* "embraced the manifold phenomena of political and social life which had made up the ancien régime" (Neubauer, 1972: 328). During the eighteenth century in France, the original legal term had become inflated and imprecise, so it encompassed not only the idea of "land tenure in return for military service" (Mackrell, 1973: 1) but the *economic system* of manorialism, a type of plantation system based on serfdom:

> it became customary, in spite of etymology, to describe as "feudal rights" the burdens to which peasant holdings were subject. Thus when the men of the [French] Revolution announced their intention to destroy feudalism, it was above all the manorial system that they meant to attack. [Actually] the manor was in itself an older institution, and was destined to last much longer. (Bloch, [1939–40] 1961: 442)

This broad sense of *feudalism* as a cultural system—in which the lord-vassal relationship was combined with and virtually superseded by manorialism—was popularized in the nineteenth century by many authors, such as the French Saint-Simonians and the German philosopher Hegel (Brunner, 1975: 345). The pejorative associations of social oppression forged during the French Revolution remained strong, so in some cases *feudalism* implied virtually any oppressive economic system, agrarian or otherwise. "How many polemicists since then have held up to public obloquy the 'feudalism' of bankers or industrialists!" writes Bloch ([1939–40] 1961: 442). Patriotic French historians—for example, François Guizot and Benjamin Guérard—portrayed feudalism as an anarchic and predatory system imposed on Gaul by German invaders, "destroyers of civilization, who substituted for the orderly government of Rome the chaotic relationships of vassals and lords" (Stephenson, 1941: 788).

Against this background, Marx and Engels introduced their idea of feudalism as a "system of industry" ([1848] 1977: 198), a stage of production relations through which all societies generally pass in their development toward CAPITALISM and eventually SOCIALISM. It should be remarked, however, that Marx and Engels themselves "neither systematically discussed nor gave a coherent account of feudalism," which interested them only as a preliminary stage to capitalism (Neubauer, 1972: 330). Although the idea of feudalism as a "mode of production" (that is, an *economic category* characteristic of a certain level of historical development) is still presumed by Marxist scholars, it is generally repudiated or simply ignored by non-Marxists (for example, Brown, 1979) on the grounds that it confuses *feudalism* with *manorialism* and other pre-industrial economic forms (e.g., Bloch, [1939–40] 1961: 442; Ganshof, [1947] 1952: xvi–xvii; Lyon, 1965: 13; Mackrell, 1973: 1).

In the late nineteenth century there were lively debates on the origins of feudalism, involving the question of whether it began in ancient Rome or among the ancient Germans or was an eighth-century fusion of German and Roman traditions (Stephenson, 1941; Lyon, 1965: 22–23). At the same time, some medievalists became skeptical of the concept; as early as 1887–88 the English constitutional historian Frederic William Maitland wondered if the idea of an English "feudal system" was not really the seventeenth-century invention of Sir Henry Spelman (Brown, 1979: 1064). As knowledge of the Middle Ages deepened and appreciation of the diverse nature of medieval life, law, and custom grew, historians increasingly doubted that the notion of such a uniform, widespread social order actually corresponded to European conditions between the eleventh and thirteenth centuries. In the early twentieth century a major effort was mounted to divest the term of its polemical accretions and to use it more precisely. Marc Bloch, keenly aware of the importance of historical semantics, pioneered in writing the concept's history and in pointing up the need to draw a clear distinction between *feudalism* and *manorialism* (Bloch, [1939–40] 1961: 442). In the United States Carl Stephenson (1941: 809–11; 1942: 14) championed the same cause. By the early 1940s, at the latest, academic orthodoxy held that "Although men in the Middle Ages were quite familiar with vassals and fiefs and with vassalage and feudal tenure, they apparently did not think in terms of a broad feudal theory—a set of feudal principles by which to construct a social and political framework" (Stephenson, 1941: 797). From this standpoint the practice of lumping medieval institutions under the heading "feudalism" or "the feudal system" was an instance of anachronism—the "most unpardonable of sins in a time-science" (Bloch, 1953: 173).

Yet the term remained in wide use. In some respects (e.g., as an IDEAL TYPE or conceptual reference point for comparing historically diverse societies such as medieval France and early-modern Japan [see Duus, 1976]) its popularity actually grew, as evidenced in the 1950s by a leading academic press's publication of a collaborative volume dealing with the concept per se (Coulborn, 1956). Paradoxically, it was the work of Bloch that, more than anything else, appeared to legitimize expansive use of the concept. For despite pleas for greater discrimination, Bloch's own book on *Feudal Society* ([1939–40] 1961) defined its subject broadly as a "system of human relations" characteristic of a particular era in western history (Postan, 1961: xii), advocated the use of *feudalism* as a heuristic concept for cross-cultural comparison (Bloch, [1939–40] 1961: 446–47), and included the following list of "fundamental features of European feudalism" (p. 446):

> A subject peasantry; widespread use of the service tenement (i.e., the fief) instead of a salary, which was out of the question; the supremacy of a class of specialized warriors; ties of obedience and protection which bind man to man and, within the warrior class, assume the distinctive form called vassalage; fragmentation of authority—leading inevitably to disorder; and, in the midst of all this, the survival of other forms of association, family and State.

Today, despite occasional admonitions to jettison the concept (Brown, 1979: 1080–84), *feudalism* is still widely used, generally with caution by medievalists and comparative historians (for instance, Duus, 1976: 3), although often with less care by other historians (for example, Taylor, [1948] 1976: 14; Okey, 1982: 18, 21).

Bloch, Marc. 1953. *The Historian's Craft*. New York.

————. [1939–40] 1961. *Feudal Society*. London. This classic study warns that "In the interests of sound terminology it is important that [the words *feudalism* and *manorialism*] should be kept clearly separate" (p. 442).

Brown, Elizabeth A. R. 1979. "The Tyranny of a Construct: Feudalism and Historians of Medieval Europe." *AHR* 79: 1063–88. This is a good introduction that recommends discarding the concept: "The tyrant feudalism must be declared once and for all deposed and its influence over students of the Middle Ages finally ended" (p. 1088). It defines *feudalism* as "a construct devised in the seventeenth century and then subsequently used by lawyers, scholars, teachers, and polemicists to refer to phenomena, generally associated more or less closely with the Middle Ages, but always and inevitably phenomena selected by the person employing the term and reflecting that particular viewer's biases, values, and orientations" (p. 1086). It does not consider Marxist usage.

Brunner, Otto. 1975. "Feudalismus, feudal." *GG* 2: 337–50.

Coulborn, Rushton. 1956. *Feudalism in History*. Princeton, N.J.

Duus, Peter. 1976. *Feudalism in Japan*. New York. Duus considers the concept "indispensable" (p. 3).

Ganshof, F. L. [1947] 1952. *Feudalism*. London. This is a much-cited study.

Koehl, Robert. 1960. "Feudal Aspects of National Socialism." *The American Political Science Review* 54: 921–33.

Lyon, Bruce. 1965. *The Middle Ages in Recent Historical Thought: Selected Topics*. Washington, D.C. This book contains useful sections on "The Meaning of Manorialism" and "The Significance of Feudalism." With regard to the Marxist interpretation, the author asserts: "Feudalism, in spite of being termed an economic system of exploitation by Marx, was the political and military system which came into prominence some four centuries after manorialism and was superimposed upon it" (p. 13).

Mackrell, J.Q.C. 1973. *The Attack on "Feudalism" in Eighteenth-Century France*. London. Mackrell focuses on the early development of polemical usage; his work has an extensive bibliography.

Marx, Karl, and Engels, Friedrich. [1848] 1977. *Manifesto of the Communist Party*. In John Louis Beatty and Oliver A. Johnson, eds., *Heritage of Western Civilization* 2. 4th ed. Englewood Cliffs, N.J.: 197–213.

Mommsen, Hans. 1981. "The Concept of Totalitarian Dictatorship vs. the Comparative Theory of Fascism: The Case of National Socialism." In Ernest A. Menze, ed., *Totalitarianism Reconsidered*. Port Washington, N.Y.: 146–66.

Neubauer, Helmut. 1972. "Feudalism." *MCWS* 3: 328–34. This entry includes a helpful bibliography, especially with regard to Soviet scholarship.

Okey, Robin. 1982. *Eastern Europe, 1740–1980*. Minneapolis, Minn. Okey refers to *feudalism* broadly as "a regime of underdevelopment" (p. 21).

Pocock, J.G.A. [1957] 1967. *The Ancient Constitution and the Feudal Law: A Study of English Historical Thought in the Seventeenth Century*. New York.

Postan, M. M. 1961. "Foreword." In Marc Bloch, *Feudal Society*. London: xi–xv.

Stephenson, Carl. 1941. "The Origin and Significance of Feudalism." *AHR* 46: 788–812. Stephenson surveys the nineteenth- and early-twentieth-century historiography of *feudalism*.

————. 1942. *Medieval Feudalism*. Ithaca, N.Y. "By 'feudalism'," asserts the author, " . . . we properly refer to the peculiar association of vassalage with fief-holding that was developed in the Carolingian Empire and thence spread to other parts of Europe" (p. 14).

Taylor, A.J.P. [1948] 1976. *The Habsburg Monarchy, 1809–1918*. Chicago. The author's allusion to eighteenth-century Hungary's "feudal" diet (p. 14) reflects a widespread practice of using the term *feudal* as a virtual synonym for *aristocratic*.

Sources of Additional Information

For year-by-year coverage of the literature, consult the semi-annual *International Medieval Bibliography* (Leeds, Eng., 1967–). See also Joseph R. Strayer, "Feudalism," *Dictionary of the Middle Ages* 5 (1975): 52–57. Articles on "feudalism" in *ESS* 6: 203–20 (by Marc Bloch and others) and *IESS* 5: 393–403 reflect the idea's rise as a comparative social concept; both entries include useful bibliographies. In the same vein, see the bibliography in Coulborn (1956). Bloch's *Feudal Society* received a thoughtful review by Lawrence Walker in *HT* 3 (1963–64): 247–55. The footnote citations in Stephenson (1941) are a good source of information on nineteenth- and early-twentieth-century literature—especially n. 34. See also Donald R. Kelley, "De Origine Feudorum: The Beginnings of an Historical Problem," *Speculum* 39 (1964): 207–28; Kelley also touches on the subject in "The Rise of Legal History in the Renaissance," *HT* 9 (1970): 174–94, especially 187–90. A classic study is F. Pollock and F. W. Maitland, *The History of English Law Before the Time of Edward I*, 2 vols. (2d ed., Cambridge, 1898). The following studies refine the definition of *feudalism* and its role in medieval society by illustrating its connection to *vassalage*: Jacques Le Goff, "The Symbolic Ritual of Vassalage," in Jacques Le Goff, *Time, Work, and Culture in the Middle Ages* (Chicago, 1980): 237–87, and Georges Duby, *The Three Orders: Feudal Society Imagined* (Chicago, 1980). On Japan see John W. Hall and Marius B. Jansen, eds., *Studies in the Institutional History of Early Modern Japan* (Princeton, N.J., 1968), especially chapters one and two. For Marxist usage see the debate on the transition from "feudalism" to "capitalism," which appeared in the periodical *Science and Society* between 1950 and 1953. On abuse of the term see Alfred Cobban, "The Vocabulary of Social History," *Political Science Quarterly* 71 (1956): 11.

FRONTIER. 1. In U.S. history, the edge of settlement of Europeans and their descendents that moved gradually westward in the seventeenth, eighteenth, and nineteenth centuries. According to Frederick Jackson Turner's celebrated "frontier hypothesis," first advanced in 1893, this moving demographic boundary produced a unique American social ethic based on democracy and individualism. 2. In European usage, the boundary between two states.

In the first half of the twentieth century the "frontier hypothesis" of Frederick Jackson Turner (1861–1932) was the most widely used and debated interpretive concept in United States historiography (Billington, 1958: 1). Few historical theories can claim to have had such a broad impact, extending far beyond the sphere of serious scholarship; for several decades the frontier thesis "embodied the predominant American view of the American past" (Hofstadter, 1949: 433).

Turner advanced his frontier hypothesis in a paper entitled "The Significance of the Frontier in American History," presented to the American Historical Association in 1893; the theory was intended to assist in explaining the uniqueness of America's social evolution. In a celebrated passage ([1893] 1938: 186), Turner claimed that "The existence of an area of free land, its continuous recession, and the advance of American settlement westward explain American development." In Turner's view, the characteristic features of the American psychology and social tradition—especially belief in democracy—originated in a common "pioneering experience in which the leveling influence of poverty and the uniqueness of local problems encouraged majority self-rule" (Billington, 1966b: 138).

An emphasis on the significance of the frontier in the growth of American values was certainly not original with Turner. Early statesmen such as Franklin and Jefferson, as well as widely read scholars such as Francis Parkman and Alexis de Tocqueville, had previously commented on the importance of frontier conditions (Billington, 1966a: 4). These writers had attributed various meanings to the word *frontier* but used it primarily in the traditional European sense, dating from the seventeenth century—that is, the boundary between two states (Febvre, [1928] 1973: 212; Mood, 1948). Early use of the term *frontier* in North America simply extended this meaning to the shifting lines of settlement between the white and Indian populations (Juricek, 1966: 31).

In the mid-nineteenth century the term *frontier* began to take on new connotations that foreshadowed Turner's usage; British conservatives, for example, developed the idea that the American frontier was unique, a notion used to buttress the argument that democracy was unsuitable for England (Tuttle, 1967). Moreover, the usage of U.S. government demographers working in the 1870s, 1880s, and 1890s directly inspired Turner's notion of the American frontier as the westward-moving line of settlement (Mood, 1945). Turner's essay was, however, the first systematic statement of the idea by a historical scholar. That it created such a sensation within the historical profession was largely due to the fact that it directly challenged an established theory of the origins of American democracy: the "germ theory," which held that the democratic institutions of the United States were European rather than uniquely American in origin and had evolved from the "germ" of ancient German custom via England.

Other circumstances ensured that Turner would capture an audience beyond the historical guild. During the 1880s many public figures had expressed concern over the social implications of the disappearance of free or inexpensive land in the western wilderness. Did this mark the end of the release valve of westward migration that had allegedly prevented festering social tension, and possibly revolution, in the eastern cities? Turner himself was bothered by this question, and from a non-professional standpoint the secret of his essay's success lies less in its originality than its timeliness: it articulated widely existing assumptions and fears in a particularly dramatic way. Thus, an "altered intellectual atmosphere [in the 1880s and 1890s] created a climate of opinion suited to receive and nurture the frontier theory" (Billington, 1966a: 5, 13–14; Riegel, 1956: 359, 362).

A remarkable fact was the vagueness with which Turner employed the word *frontier*; his understanding of the word was much looser than previous usage (Juricek, 1966: 29). While stressing that his frontier should not be understood in the European sense—"a fortified boundary line running through dense populations"—Turner openly avowed that "The term is an elastic one, and for our purpose does not need sharp definition" ([1893] 1938: 187). He excused this lack of precision on the grounds that his aim was not "to treat the subject exhaustively" but "simply to call attention to the frontier as a fertile field for investigation, and to suggest some of the problems which arise in connection with it" (p. 188). Thus, he referred to the frontier variously as "an area of free land" (which could be taken to mean either land that was simply unsettled or that was inexpensive or free for the taking [Hofstadter, 1949: 440]); as "the outer edge of the wave [of expansion]—the meeting point between savagery and civilization"; as "the margin of that settlement which has a density of two or more to the square mile"; as a "belt" that encompassed "the Indian country and the outer margin of the 'settled area' of the census reports"; and as "the line of most rapid and effective Americanization" (Turner, [1893] 1938: 186–88). Moreover, he sometimes referred to the frontier and the "west" even more vaguely as though these were not geographical categories but a "social process" (Hofstadter, 1949: 437). Although he underscored the idea that the "most significant" aspect of the frontier was that "it lies at the hither edge of free land" (Turner, [1893] 1938: 187), this was itself an indirect characterization referring only to one of the features of the frontier. The vagueness of Turner's usage has given rise to a large literature that tries either to pin down his precise meaning or to expose him as a muddled thinker, but it has been wisely suggested that Turner had two basic things in mind: the notion of a geographical frontier and the idea of a "frontier process" (Billington, 1958: 9):

> The "frontier" can be defined as "the geographic area adjacent to the unsettled portions of the continents in which a low man-land ratio and abundant natural resources provide an unusual opportunity for the individual to better himself economically and socially without external aid." The "frontier process" may be described as "that process by which individuals and their institutions were altered through contact with an environment which provided unique opportunity to the individual by making available to him previously untapped natural resources."

Turner's suggestion of a frontier process had a deep resonance in the United States; it conformed to the idea of a cutting edge of civilization as it pushed back the wilderness. . . . a "frontier" meant to most Americans the forward surge of white occupation. . . . Even today many Americans continue to think more easily of a frontier in terms of cultural and economic expansion, as a frontier of learning, than as a boundary between nations. (Riegel, 1956: 357)

One of the chief preoccupations of American historical scholars in the 1920s was the effort to flesh out the spare outlines of Turner's thesis and render his vague images more precise. The theory does not at this time appear to have been widely known or appreciated in Europe, however. Lucien Febvre, for example, one of France's more theoretically ecumenical historians, analyzed the term *frontière* in 1928 but (aside from a passing allusion to American usage) only from the perspective of the evolution of the idea of state boundaries (Febvre, [1928] 1973: 212; cf. Clark, 1947).

In the 1930s and 1940s Turner's thesis came under attack on a number of grounds. Disillusionment produced by the Great Depression led to a reassessment of orthodox theories of American development, Turner's included. Marxism, which became popular in many circles, fostered an interest in social classes as opposed to geography and regionalism. INTELLECTUAL HISTORY won converts in the historical guild and shifted attention from the west to the intellectual centers of the east—Philadelphia, Boston, and New York. The frontier thesis was increasingly assailed as at best one-sided, at worst a major obstacle to historical inquiry. Turner's terminology, it was said, was hopelessly vague, and his influence had led to a simplistic, monocausal understanding of American history. The frontier thesis was denounced as a form of geographical determinism that overemphasized the uniqueness of American development. Richard Hofstadter (1949: 437–38) charged that the "obsession with uniqueness, the subtly demagogic stress on 'the truly American part of our history,' diverted the attention of historical scholarship from the possibilities of comparative social history." Particularly offensive was the so-called safety-valve thesis associated with Turner's concept—the idea that "the availability of free land as a refuge for the oppressed and discontented has alleviated American social conflicts, minimized industrial strife, and contributed to the backwardness of the American labor movement" (p. 449). Many monographic studies demonstrated the inaccuracy of this notion. It was found, for example, that the mainstream of American migration in the late nineteenth century was not from east to west but from rural to urban areas; Turner's emphasis on "free land" in the west had thus led to a "major distortion" of America's history (p. 442).

Turner's apologists maintain that critics fail to appreciate that he never intended to advance anything more than a hypothesis to stimulate inquiry (Billington, 1958: 4). Still, criticisms took a heavy toll, and the frontier theory is no longer the focus of attention that it once was. On the other hand, the idea of "frontier" has by no means vanished as a working part of American historians' theoretical equipment. "The Turner generalizations have been questioned, modified, and sometimes discarded," writes Riegel (1956: 380), "but the apparent implication of some critics that the frontier had no influence of importance seems unreasonable on its face.'' Despite criticisms of the imprecision with which Turner used the term *frontier*, ''there has been a more or less passive acceptance of Turner's main definition . . . [as] 'the edge of settlement, rather than, as in Europe, the political boundary' '' (Juricek, 1966: 10).

The concept of the frontier was debated with such intensity for so many years that it developed its own mystique, and the term continues to exercise its spell over North American historical conceptualization (McNeill, 1983). Since World War II American-trained historians, following the advice of an American Historical Association president (Hayes, 1946), have been especially active in using the idea as a comparative concept to analyze frontiers and their significance for societies as disparate as medieval Europe, modern Russia, Canada, Australia, South America, and Africa (Wyman and Kroeber, 1957; Hess, 1978; Lamar and Thompson, 1981). Turner himself—despite his stress on American uniqueness— implied that his idea might be used as a benchmark for historical comparison when he claimed that ''the most important effect of the frontier has been in the promotion of democracy here and in Europe'' and asserted that

> What the Mediterranean Sea was to the Greeks, breaking the bond of custom, offering new experiences, calling out new institutions and activities, that, and more, the ever retreating frontier has been to the United States directly, and to the nations of Europe more remotely. (Turner, [1893] 1938: 219, 229; cf. Riegel, 1956: 369)

So far as comparative studies are concerned, most of the completed work thus far suggests that ''frontier conditions throughout the world were far from uniform, and that the encouragement of ways of life such as democracy and individualism was anything but universal, as varied cultures moved into various 'open spaces' '' (Riegel, 1956: 370).

References

Billington, Ray Allen. 1958. *The American Frontier*. Washington, D.C. This is a basic historiographical survey intended for use by high school teachers of American history.

————. 1966a. *America's Frontier Heritage*. New York. This book is by Turner's most prolific and sympathetic commentator.

————. 1966b. ''How the Frontier Shaped the American Character: Turner's Frontier Hypothesis.'' In A. S. Eisenstadt, ed., *The Craft of American History: Selected Essays*. New York: 135–48.

Clark, George. 1947. *The Seventeenth Century*. Oxford. Originally published in 1929; this book contains a chapter on ''Frontiers,'' which like Febvre ([1928] 1973) illustrates European usage uninformed by Turner's theory.

Febvre, Lucien. [1928] 1973. ''*Frontière*: The Word and the Concept.'' In Peter Burke, ed., *A New Kind of History: From the Writings of Febvre*. New York: 208–18. Febvre does not refer to Turner's concept explicitly but notes that in English *frontier* ''is used above all in a metaphorical, abstract or philosophical sense'' (p. 217).

Hayes, Carlton J. H. 1946. "The American Frontier—Frontier of What?" *AHR* 51: 199–216. This presidential address to the American Historical Association encourages the broadening of Turner's concept to mean the world-wide frontier of European civilization.

Hess, Andrew C. 1978. *The Forgotten Frontier: A History of the Sixteenth-Century Ibero-African Frontier*. Chicago.

Hofstadter, Richard. 1949. "Turner and the Frontier Myth." *The American Scholar* 18: 433–43. This is a handy summary of objections to the frontier thesis.

Juricek, John T. 1966. "American Usage of the Word 'Frontier' from Colonial Times to Frederick Jackson Turner." *Proceedings of the American Philosophical Society* 110: 10–34. Juricek argues that "Turner became the United States' first important nationalist historian, for earlier scholars . . . had not succeeded in discovering such an all-encompassing yet uniquely American theme" (p. 33).

Lamar, Howard, and Thompson, Leonard, eds. 1981. *The Frontier in History: North America and Southern Africa Compared*. New Haven, Conn. The introductory essay "Comparative Frontier History" is rich in bibliographic citations. On Turner see especially n. 2, p. 4.

McNeill, William H. 1983. *The Great Frontier: Freedom and Hierarchy in Modern Times*. Princeton, N.J. This is a global version of the frontier thesis.

Mood, Fulmer. 1945. "The Concept of the Frontier, 1871–1898." *Agricultural History* 19: 24–30. Mood, an extreme case of professional fascination with the Turner thesis, advises historians to "leave off the compounding of textbooks and the cultivation of 'new' approaches" in order to "concentrate on the main professional obligation of the times, namely the resolving of the frontier issue" (p. 30).

———. 1948. "Notes on the History of the Word *Frontier*." *Agricultural History* 22: 78–83. This is a useful history of the word and concept since ancient times.

Riegel, Robert E. 1956. "American Frontier Theory." *Cahiers d'histoire mondiale* 3: 356–80. This concise, balanced summary of all aspects of the question is a good starting point for further inquiry.

Turner, Frederick Jackson. [1893] 1938. "The Significance of the Frontier in American History." In Frederick Jackson Turner, *The Early Writings of Frederick Jackson Turner*. Madison, Wis.: 185–229. This anthology contains a useful bibliography of Turner's work.

Tuttle, William M., Jr. 1967. "Forerunners of Frederick Jackson Turner: Nineteenth-Century British Conservatives and the Frontier Thesis." *Agricultural History* 41: 219–27.

Wyman, Walker D., and Kroeber, Clifton B., eds. 1957. *The Frontier in Perspective*. Madison, Wis. This anthology of essays relates Turner's thesis to various historical periods and areas of the world.

Sources of Additional Information

Discussion and criticism of the role of the "frontier" in American history have produced a flood of secondary literature that few can hope to master. See the list of titles in the *Harvard Guide to American History* (Cambridge, Mass., 1974), 1: 261–62 and 324–44, especially 342–44. For a bibliography of Turner's own work see Turner [1893] (1938). The footnote citations in Riegel (1956) provide a comprehensive bibliography until the mid–1950s. A judicious selection of general titles is contained in footnote citations to the introductory essay in Lamar and Thompson (1981). See also two additional works by Ray Allan Billington: "Frontiers," in C. Vann Woodward, ed., *The Comparative Approach to American History* (New York, 1968): 75–90, and *The Genesis of the Frontier Thesis: A Study in Historical Creativity* (San Marino, Calif., 1971). The latter book—an exhaustive analysis of the personal factors that led Turner to his thesis—illustrates the intensiveness with which the theme has been mined. The following are also useful: Lee Benson, *Turner and Beard: American Historical Writing Reconsidered* (Glencoe, Ill., 1960); David M. Ellis et al., *The Frontier in American Development* (Ithaca, N.Y., 1969); Richard Hofstadter, *The Progressive Historians* (New York, 1969); Richard Hofstadter and Seymour Martin Lipset, eds., *Turner and the Sociology of the Frontier* (New York, 1968); and George M. Frederickson, "Comparative History," in Kammen: 457–73, especially 462–65. The University of Oklahoma has sponsored a series of symposia on "Comparative Frontier Studies," the results of which appear in *The Frontier: Comparative Studies*, volumes I (1977, edited by David Harry Miller and Jerome O. Steffan) and II (1979, edited by William W. Savage, Jr. and Stephen I. Thompson). Walter P. Webb, *The Great Frontier* (Boston, 1952), attempts to explain the whole of western history since the Renaissance in terms of the frontier thesis.

H

HISTORICAL MATERIALISM. 1. Generally, the belief that material or physical conditions fundamentally influence historical events. 2. In Marxist theory, the doctrine that every society is based on a characteristic system of economic relationships (*Produktionsweise*, or "mode of production") and that this system of production decisively conditions all aspects of social life.

The notion that human history is influenced in some basic sense by material conditions is very old. W. H. Walsh (1942: 136–37) finds the idea already loosely expressed in the last section of Herodotus' *Histories* (5th century B.C.), where human courage is attributed to the physical conditions in which men live. Over the centuries many writers have emphasized the social and historical importance of environmental factors such as climate and geography, notably the Baron de Montesquieu in his *Spirit of the Laws* (1748) and Henry Thomas Buckle in his *History of Civilization in England* (1857–61). Nineteenth-century historical materialism was an outgrowth of the social beliefs of the eighteenth-century EN-LIGHTENMENT, for example, the view of the French reformer Saint-Simon that "the first need for man is to secure his subsistence" (Jordan, 1971: 31). By the late nineteenth century scholars were increasingly drawn to explanations in materialistic terms. In 1888 Thorold Rogers wrote an *Economic Interpretation of History*, which, without suggesting that economics are necessarily decisive, nevertheless emphasized the importance of economic conditions for social change. In the United States the influential essays of Frederick Jackson Turner on the FRONTIER in American history presumed that environmental conditions are decisive in social life. "Today," wrote Turner ([1891] 1972: 200), "the questions that are uppermost, and that will become increasingly important, are not so much political as economic questions."

The most elaborate nineteenth-century theory of historical materialism was jointly created by Karl Marx and Friedrich Engels in the 1840s. Today one thinks first of their names when the expression *historical materialism* is used—or any of the terms employed (in some cases erroneously) as synonyms for it: *materialist conception of history*, *economic interpretation of history*, *economic determinism*, or *dialectical materialism*. Marx himself did not use any of these labels (certainly not *dialectical materialism*, which was coined in the late nineteenth century by the Russian socialist Georgi Plekhanov [1857–1918]), although he did refer to his "materialistic and thus scientific method" (Lichtheim, 1973: 452–53). Both Marx and Engels referred to "the writing of history [on] a materialistic basis" in their jointly written *German Ideology* (1845–46). It was evidently Engels who introduced the expressions *materialist conception of history* (in 1859, with reference to Marx's *Critique of Political Economy* of the same year) and *historical materialism* (in a letter of 1890 and again in the 1892 introduction to the English translation of his *Socialism: Utopian and Scientific*) (Weiss, 1972: 139). Actually, *historical materialism* is in some respects misleading as a designation for Marx's and Engels' views, since (as the German social theorist Georg Simmel [(1905) 1977: 185] observed) "the theory has nothing to do with any sort of metaphysical materialism" (i.e., the doctrine that only matter exists). In this regard, the interpretations of Montesquieu and Buckle are more accurately called materialistic than those of Marx and Engels, since

> these theories are reductive and materialistic in the original sense of this term; they reduce all social change to the ultimate action of the physical world. . . . The historical materialism of Marx is not a materialistic theory in this sense. . . . For its basic premise is not the proposition "only matter exists" but the assumption that a scientific study of society and history can be based on observation of the world in which men live. (Jordan, 1971: 38–39)

What is now usually called Marxian historical materialism is a species of historical REALISM that Marx and Engels formulated in conscious opposition to the historical IDEALISM of G.W.F. Hegel. Their aversion to the word *ideal* helps explain their self-conscious emphasis on terms like *real* and *material*. It has been correctly said that the "core of [Marx's] materialism lay in the primacy it allotted to man's economic activities in society" (Leff, [1961] 1969: 26). Current authorities (following Engels) often regard the preface to Marx's *Contribution to the Critique of Political Economy* (1859) as the "*locus classicus* of historical materialism" (Tucker, 1972: 3). There Marx succinctly outlines a general theory of history based on the belief that

> legal relations as well as forms of state are to be grasped neither from themselves nor from the so-called general development of the human mind, but rather have their roots in the material conditions of life. . . . the anatomy of civil society is to be sought in political economy. . . . In the social production of their life, men enter into definite relations that are indispensable and independent of their will, relations of production which correspond to a definite stage of development of their material productive forces. The sum total of these relations of production constitutes the

economic structure of society, the real foundation, on which rises a legal and political superstructure and to which correspond definite forms of social consciousness. The mode of production of material life conditions the social, political and intellectual life process in general. It is not the consciousness of men that determines their being, but, on the contrary, their social being that determines their consciousness. (Marx, [1859] 1972: 4)

Implicit in this passage is a general view of social change that has come to be called "dialectical" (see DIALECTIC), although Marx did not so designate it himself—that is, the idea that the transition from one form of society to its successor is the result of conflict between existing legal and mental conventions and the emergence of new productive methods. More specifically, Marx (p. 5) identified four distinct "modes of production" that he claimed had characterized the "economic formation of society" until the nineteenth century—"Asiatic, ancient, feudal, and modern bourgeois." He predicted the emergence of a fifth, socialistic mode from the "womb of bourgeois society." It is unclear, however, if Marx intended this pattern of stages to apply universally and necessarily to all human history or whether he merely believed that it described the peculiar evolution of west European society. In the preface of 1859 this schema is presented in general terms, and many of Marx's readers believed that he meant it to be understood as universally valid; but later, in a letter of 1877 regarding the future of Russia, Marx objected to "generalizing his sketch of the origin of capitalism in Western Europe into 'a historico-philosophical theory of the general path imposed by fate on all peoples regardless of their historical circumstances' " (cited in Bober, 1948: 41). In light of the discovery of many of Marx's unpublished notes and manuscripts—especially those published under the title *Grundrisse der Kritik der politischen Okonomie* (*Outlines of a Critique of Political Economy*) in 1953—some scholars now believe that Marx never considered the "list of historical epochs as necessarily following each other in the indicated order" (Jordan, 1971: 311, n. 54).

An important problem in defining *historical materialism* is the question of its relationship to the twentieth-century communist doctrine of "dialectical materialism" created by Russian and Soviet Marxists such as Plekhanov and Joseph Stalin. *Dialectical materialism* is a metaphysical doctrine based on the belief that all change—whether in society or in nature—is deterministically controlled by dialectical LAWS; *dialectic*, in other words, is understood as a universal mechanism of change. Orthodox Soviet scholarship considers "historical materialism" a subclass of the broader category of "dialectical materialism" and regards Marx as the originator of both. Many non-Soviet scholars once shared this view (e.g., Bober, 1948: 30, n. 5; 44–45), and it became the basis for polemical attacks on Marxism as a metaphysical doctrine during the 1940s and 1950s. Today, leading non-Soviet authorities agree that dialectical materialism is untenable but sharply distinguish it from the more philosophically respectable doctrine of historical materialism (for instance, Lichtheim, 1973; Jordan, 1967; 1971).

Whether Marx was in any sense an author of dialectical materialism is a separate and controversial question; unfortunately, certain aspects of his thought are obscure. Many scholars stress Engels' role in the transformation of historical materialism into dialectical materialism. Engels sought to popularize historical materialism in a number of late-nineteenth-century works, especially the so-called "Anti-Dühring" (*Herr Eugen Dühring's Revolution in Science* [1878]), which became the basic textbook of Marxist doctrine. In argument and imagery Engels stressed the methodological identity of Marx's "science of society" (i.e., historical materialism) with natural science and introduced the notion of "dialectics" as a general principle of change that applies universally to physical nature and human affairs. In recent years dialectical materialism has become an embarrassment to western Marxists and Marxist sympathizers, who have sometimes tried to tie the albatross of dialectical materialism around Engels' neck and so vindicate Marx (for example, Levine, 1975). But there is opposition to this trend, based on the older idea that Marx and Engels were basically of one mind and that the roots of the two doctrines of dialectical materialism and historical materialism are to be found in the thought of Marx as well as that of Engels (e.g., Moore, 1971; Gouldner, 1980: 250–86).

Since the 1890s, Marxian historical materialism—usually divested of its polemical elements—has exercised a powerful though often indirect influence on historical writing. Its appeal stems largely from the fact that it requires the historian to look beneath the surface of events for underlying social relationships, something that nineteenth-century historiography, with its prevailing conception of history as past politics, tended to overlook. The doctrine was discussed at a meeting of the American Historical Association as early as 1899, where one scholar asserted "for the last two or three years everybody who has ventured to write about economic history at all has been liable to be called upon to 'stand up and deliver' his opinion as to the materialistic conception of history at a moment's notice" (cited in Heaton, [1943] 1950: 94). In the United States the expression *economic interpretation of history* has always been favored over *historical materialism* because it seems less closely tied to Marx's radical political views (e.g., Seligman, 1907; Beard, 1913; Knight, [1929] 1968: 9). Rightly or wrongly, most American-trained historians and many philosophers consider *historical materialism* an *a priori*, speculative PHILOSOPHY OF HISTORY designed to "fully explain the course of history" (e.g., Walsh, 1942: 140; Bober, 1948; Sée, [1929] 1968). On the other hand, most concede that Marx and Engels were correct in

> calling attention to the very important part which is played in history by economic factors, and in pointing out that all historical actions take place against a certain material background. The nature of the latter in all cases conditions, and in some actually determines, what men do. (Walsh, 1942: 140)

By the 1940s historical materialism, domesticated by doses of non-Marxist sociological theory (especially that of Max Weber), had become part of historiographical orthodoxy, as suggested by the following representative passage from the work of Wallace Ferguson:

> . . . economic conditions, the way men make a living, form the necessary basis of civilization. They determine in large part the character and interests of the social classes and set a limit to the variety of cultural forms possible at a given time. . . . And when there is a fundamental change in this necessary basis of civilization, it is only reasonable to expect roughly corresponding changes in the political, social and cultural superstructure, though the latter may be delayed and modified by the force of tradition and custom. (1940: 7)

Today the influence of historical materialism is pervasive in historical studies, as reflected in the wide (though often tacit) use of concepts closely associated with Marxist social theory such as CLASS, IDEOLOGY, and ALIENATION. It is hardly an exaggeration to say that there are "Marxists who don't know that they are Marxists . . . and no American historian will write a book on any particular period of the past without first introducing his readers to its economic foundations" (Pachter, 1967: 104). Even critics of historical materialism are forced to attack the idea in terms strongly conditioned by the concept itself (e.g., Leff, [1961] 1969).

References

Beard, Charles A. 1913. *An Economic Interpretation of the Constitution*. New York. This celebrated study advanced the thesis that framers of the American constitution were motivated by economic interests.

Bober, M. M. 1948. *Karl Marx's Interpretation of History*. 2d ed. Cambridge, Mass. This is a revised version of a study originally published in 1927; it contains detailed discussions of all aspects of Marx's theory and its subordinate concepts, such as "mode of production," "dialectic," "ideology," and "crisis."

Ferguson, Wallace K. 1940. *The Renaissance*. New York.

Gouldner, Alvin W. 1980. *The Two Marxisms: Contradictions and Anomalies in the Theory*. New York. This work is good on the intellectual relationship between Marx and Engels.

Heaton, Herbert. [1943] 1950. "The Economic Impact on History." In Strayer: 87–117. This is a convenient survey of the influence of historical materialism on historical studies before the 1940s.

Jordan, Z. A. 1967. *The Evolution of Dialectical Materialism: A Philosophical and Sociological Analysis*. London. This is an important analysis of dialectical materialism and its relationship to historical materialism.

————. 1971. *Karl Marx: Economy, Class and Social Revolution*. London. This anthology brings together scattered passages from the work of Marx and Engels on many subjects, including historical materialism. The "Introductory Essay" is a concise statement of Jordan's belief that Marxism shares important similarities with Comtean sociology and that Marx's doctrine should be called a form of "naturalism" rather than "materialism."

Knight, Melvin M. [1929] 1968. "Introduction." In Henri Sée, *The Economic Interpretation of History*. New York: 9–42. This is an interesting survey of early-twentieth-century opinion.

Leff, Gordon. [1961] 1969. *The Tyranny of Concepts: A Critique of Marxism*. London.

Levine, Norman. 1975. *The Tragic Deception: Marx Contra Engels*. Santa Barbara, Calif. This is an extreme statement of the idea that Engels, not Marx, was the author of dialectical materialism.

Lichtheim, George. 1973. "Historical and Dialectical Materialism." *DHI* 2: 450–56. This is an opinionated article by a widely read authority on Marx. Many problematic points are presented as straightforward fact. It has a valuable annotated bibliography.

Marx, Karl. [1859] 1972. Preface to *A Contribution to the Critique of Political Economy*. In Robert C. Tucker, ed., *The Marx-Engels Reader*. New York: 3–6.

Moore, Stanley. 1971. "Marx and the Origin of Dialectical Materialism." *Inquiry* 14: 420–29. Moore argues that Marx and Engels both contributed to the rise of dialectical materialism but that they did so in distinct ways.

Pachter, Henry M. 1967. "Marxism and America's New Left." *Survey*, no. 62: 104–13.

Sée, Henri. [1929] 1968. *The Economic Interpretation of History*. New York. More superficial than Bober (1948), this book reflects the mainstream position that historical materialism "contains solid materials and a notable element of truth," and that its "outstanding merit has been to free us from the idea that great men make history, and to draw the attention of historians to the less dramatic phenomena which reveal economic life" (p. 123).

Seligman, Edwin R. A. 1907. *The Economic Interpretation of History*. 2d ed. New York. This was one of the first American efforts to separate carefully the methodological facets of Marxian theory from its polemical aspects.

Simmel, Georg. [1905] 1977. *The Problems of the Philosophy of History: An Epistemological Essay*. New York.

Tucker, Robert C., ed. 1972. *The Marx-Engels Reader*. New York.

Turner, Frederick Jackson. [1891] 1972. "The Significance of History." In Stern: 198–208.

Walsh, W. H. 1942. "The Intelligibility of History." *Philosophy* 17: 128–43.

Weiss, Andreas von. 1972. "Historical Materialism." *MCWS* 4: 138–51.

Sources of Additional Information

For general bibliography, in addition to Weiss (1972) and Lichtheim (1973), see Berding: 106–20. The entries in *MCWS* provide exhaustive bibliographies on all aspects of Marxist theory. The *Marx-Engels Cyclopedia*, now being issued by Schocken Publishers, promises to include a bibliography of all writings by Marx and Engels. The collected writings of Marx and Engels in their original German are available in Karl Marx and Friedrich Engels, *Werke*, 39 vols. ([East] Berlin, 1963–70); International Publishers is issuing a similar set in English translation. Useful dictionaries include James Russell, *Marx-Engels Dictionary* (Westport, Conn., 1980); Tom Bottomore, ed., *A Dictionary of Marxist Thought* (Cambridge, Mass., 1983); and Josef Wilczynski, *An Encyclopedic Dictionary of Marxism, Socialism, and Communism* (Berlin and New York, 1981). Beih. 20 of *HT* (1981) is dedicated to four "Studies in Marxist Historical Theory." George Lichtheim's *Marxism: An Historical and Critical Study* (London, 1964) is an influential study of the history of Marx's and Engels' views on society and history. On dialectical materialism see, in addition to Jordan (1967), Gustav A. Wetter, *Dialectical Materialism* (London, 1958). On Marx's and Engels' intellectual relationship see two excellent studies:

Terrell Carver, *Marx and Engels: The Intellectual Relationship* (Bloomington, Ind., 1983), and Gareth Stedman Jones, "Engels and the History of Marxism," in Eric J. Hobsbawm, ed., *The History of Marxism* 1 (Bloomington, Ind., 1982): 290–326. Two important studies are William H. Shaw, *Marx's Theory of History* (Stanford, Calif., 1978), and Melvin Rader, *Marx's Interpretation of History* (Oxford, 1979). For Marx's broad impact on turn-of-the-century social theory see H. Stuart Hughes, *Consciousness and Society: The Reorientation of European Social Thought, 1890–1930* (New York, 1958), especially chapters three and eight. On Charles Beard's materialism and its influence see especially Richard Hofstadter, "Beard and the Constitution: The History of an Idea" [1950], in A. S. Eisenstadt, ed., *The Craft of American History: Selected Essays* (New York, 1966), 1: 149–68.

HISTORICISM, HISTORISM. (From Ger. *Historismus* and It. *storicismo.*) Both terms refer to the belief that human affairs can be adequately understood "historically," that is, by tracing them to their origins and describing their relationship to a process of development through time. In addition, this basic meaning may be amplified in directly opposing ways to refer to: (a) a doctrine, developed particularly in nineteenth- and early-twentieth-century Germany, based on the assumption that past events and situations are unique and non-repeatable and therefore cannot be understood in universal terms but only in terms of their own particular contexts; (b) the view that the study of history can lead to the discovery of general laws of social development that may be used to predict future events.

Historicism is often used in any or all of these senses. *Historism* usually refers to meaning (a). Both terms, but especially *historicism*, may have pejorative connotations.

The terms *historicism* and *historism* (the former more frequent in English) are notorious for having been used during the past two centuries in confusing, sometimes diametrically opposed, ways. They may be employed in a neutral, analytical sense (Reill, 1975: 213); used as terms of highest praise (Meinecke, [1936] 1972: liv); or understood as terms of opprobrium that designate something "profoundly hateful" (Fischer, 1970: 156, n. 53). The same author may use them in widely varying senses (e.g., Beard, 1935; Beard and Vagts, 1937). There is still remarkable disagreement over their use, despite an extensive literature on the subject; indeed, this literature, although designed to clarify the situation, has often added to the problem. According to one authority (Iggers, 1968: 287), *historicism* "defies definition." Some of the confusion could perhaps be avoided, however, if *historicism* were restricted to meaning (b), and *historism* were reserved for meaning (a). The need for clearer distinctions, as well as certain traditions of usage, would seem to recommend this as a general rule.

The German word *Historism* appeared as early as 1797, when the poet and essayist Friedrich Schlegel used it to refer to a " 'kind of philosophy' which places the main stress on history" (Iggers, 1973: 456; Rothacker, 1960: 4). By the mid-nineteenth century the term was in relatively wide use among philosophers and scholars in central Europe. About the same time, the word *Histori-zismus* appeared (Rothacker, 1960: 5); it was used interchangeably with *Historism* (Liebel, 1971–72: 595), although the latter term appears to have been favored. There was no firm consensus on the meaning of these terms. They were used variously to designate an appreciation of the importance of history, a superficial approach to past events that neglects underlying connection or meaning, or an outlook that comprehends things in terms of the web of particular circumstances in which they occur.

In the 1880s an important precedent for pejorative uses of the term was established by the Austrian economist Carl Menger. Menger's *Die Irrtümer des Historismus in der deutschen Nationalökonomie* (*The Errors of Historism in German Political Economy*, 1884) defended an *a prioristic*, deductive method of economic analysis and attacked the descriptive *historism* of the then dominant "historical school" of economics led by Gustav Schmoller. Menger's polemic became a basis for later depreciatory uses of the term.

In the early twentieth century the work of three men—the Italian philosopher Benedetto Croce, the Protestant theologian Ernst Troeltsch, and the historian Friedrich Meinecke—gave the term wider currency in both Europe and North America. Croce coined the terms *istorismo* and *storicismo*—variations on the German *Historismus*—to designate his neo-idealist philosophy of history (see IDEALISM). Even more important was Troeltsch, whose *Der Historismus und seine Probleme* (*Historism and Its Problems*, 1922) popularized the idea of "historism" as a uniquely modern outlook in which all aspects of life—including human ethics—are understood relativistically, in terms of change. The rise of the "historist" world view was, in Troeltsch's opinion, one of the great achievements of European civilization. As a theologian, however, he feared the relativist implications of this conclusion, for if the tenets of "historism"—in his sense— were valid, all values and norms were historically contingent and there could be no eternal standards of conduct. Troeltsch's usage, then, signified a historical RELATIVISM that complemented the rise of cultural and ethical relativism in anthropology and some branches of philosophy in the early twentieth century; his work helped popularize the idea of a "crisis of historism" in the 1920s and 1930s (e.g., Heussi, 1932).

In the same period, Friedrich Meinecke ([1936] 1972) introduced an important elaboration of Troeltsch's usage. For Meinecke, *historism* designated a specific conception of the past developed in late-eighteenth- and early-nineteenth-century Germany, and which he associated with figures such as the philosopher Johann Gottfried von Herder, the poet Goethe, and the historian Leopold von Ranke. This approach was based on the notion of historical "individuality," that is, the idea that historical phenomena—whether individual people or cultural institutions such as states, religions, and so on—develop according to their own unique principles and therefore cannot be understood in terms of universal laws. (The term *historicity*, in fairly wide use among historians and philosophers, carries this same implication of "historical particularity" [Kuzminski, 1976: 139]—

that is, the condition of being time and place specific). Meinecke also believed that historians, by acts of aesthetic intuition or empathy, could relive and recreate the uniqueness of past human experience (Iggers, 1968: 216–17). It is in this special sense that the term is often understood by professional historians today, especially in Germany but also in England and America (Besson, 1961: 102–116; Bayer, 1974: 226–27; Butterfield, 1955: 17–18; Meyerhoff, 1959: 9–18; Gustavson, 1976: 263–64; Kelley, 1967: 807–8).

Historism and *historicism* were introduced to English after World War I as translations of the German and Italian terms. *Historism*—technically a more appropriate rendering of the German *Historismus*—was initially popular but has been largely replaced by *historicism*, which apparently originated as a translation of Croce's *storicismo* (Iggers, 1973). There is some evidence of a revival of *historism*, however, most notably in the 1972 English version of Meinecke's *Die Entstehung des Historismus*, where *Historismus* is translated as *historism* rather than *historicism*.

There has never been a clear tradition of conceptual usage in English. Charles Beard (1935), for example, used *historicism* idiosyncratically to refer to the widely held but (in his opinion) unattainable "noble dream" that the historian can know the past impartially and objectively, "as it actually happened." This usage was not generally adopted, even by Beard himself; a few years later he employed the word in a sense very close to that of Meinecke (Beard and Vagts, 1937: 461–62, 466, 476–77). One of the broadest meanings of the term is simply "a serious commitment to historical understanding" (Struever, 1970: 37). Lee and Beck (1954: 577) suggest two "intentionally general" definitions: (1) "the belief that the truth, meaning, and value of anything, i.e., the basis of any evaluation, is to be found in its history"; and (2) "more narrowly," the "antipositivistic and antinaturalistic view that historical knowledge is a basic, or the only, requirement for understanding and evaluating man's present political, social, and intellectual position or problems." Hayden White (1959: xvii) proposes a more specific definition, based on Troeltsch: "the tendency to interpret the whole of reality, including what up to the romantic period had been conceived as absolute and unchanging human values, in historical, that is to say, relative terms."

White's definition, like those of Lee and Beck, is neutral; however, in English the term is frequently used as a pejorative. Most important in this regard is the usage of the Austrian-British philosopher Karl Popper (1957), who employs *historicism* to designate the belief—in his opinion, utterly false—that the study of the past leads to the discovery of historical "laws" that permit one to predict the future. Occasionally, Popper draws a distinction between two types of historicism: the one just cited, the other close to Meinecke's idea (e.g., Popper, 1940: 423–24). It was Popper's idiosyncratic linking of historicism with the idea of the quest for pattern and prediction, however, and his negative use of the word—inspired, perhaps, by the example of his fellow Austrian Menger—that made the most powerful impact on English usage. Popper's work has been widely read and discussed and has undoubtedly strengthened use of the word as a term of disparagement (e.g., Zagorin, 1959: 245).

Georg Iggers (1968; 1973), a leading authority on the history of this semantic tangle, has done much to document the careers of these terms and ideas (cf. Liebel, 1971–72: 602–3). For Iggers (1968), *historicism* is a congeries of attitudes based on the assumption that the best way to understand a thing is to explain it historically and the recognition that everything human is subject to change; it is the time and place-bound product of nineteenth-century west European scholarship, which, since the collapse of Europe's world hegemony in World War II, is being replaced by a neo-positivistic "analytic, structural approach" to historical understanding (Iggers, 1973: 462).

Maurice Mandelbaum (1971: 42), a noted philosopher of history, defined *historicism* as the "belief that an adequate understanding of the nature of any phenomenon and an adequate assessment of its value are to be gained through considering it in terms of the place which it occupied and the role which it played within a process of development." "The thesis of historicism," he writes,

> demands that we reject the view that historical events have an individual character which can be grasped apart from viewing them as embedded within a pattern of development. What is, then, essential to historicism is the contention that a meaningful interpretation or adequate evaluation of any historical event involves seeing it as part of a stream of history. (p. 43)

But this idea of a transcendent "stream of history," according to Mandelbaum, is neither empirically nor logically demonstrable; historicism is therefore a nineteenth-century "belief"—exemplified in the work of figures such as Herder, Hegel, Comte, Marx, and Spencer—that has been (or at least should be) left behind.

Despite important differences of usage, Popper, Iggers, and Mandelbaum agree that *historicism* perverts the proper historical impulse because it seeks to make historical evidence conform to some preconceived, metahistorical framework. Hayden White (1975) challenged this distinction between the genuine "historical" approach and specious "historicism," arguing that all historical explanation is really "historicist" since every historian inevitably shapes his account of the past according to some preconceived framework, even if that framework consists of nothing more than the structure of language itself.

References

Bayer, Erich, ed. 1974. "Historismus." *Wörterbuch zur Geschichte: Begriffe und Fachausdrücke*. Stuttgart: 226–27.

Beard, Charles A. 1935. "That Noble Dream." *AHR* 41: 74–87.

Beard, Charles A., and Vagts, Alfred. 1937. "Currents of Thought in Historiography." *AHR* 42: 460–83.

Besson, Waldemar. 1961. "Historismus." In Waldemar Besson, ed., *Das Fischer Lexikon: Geschichte*. Frankfurt: 102–16.

Butterfield, Herbert. 1955. *Man on His Past: The Study of the History of Historical Scholarship*. Cambridge. Butterfield's work is strongly influenced by Meinecke.

Fischer, David Hackett. 1970. *Historians' Fallacies: Toward a Logic of Historical Thought*. New York. This work exemplifies the confusing usage that is so widespread.

Gustavson, Carl G. 1976. *The Mansion of History*. New York.

Heussi, Karl. 1932. *Die Krisis des Historismus*. Tübingen. This is among the most influential works of the interwar period.

Iggers, Georg G. 1968. *The German Conception of History: The National Tradition of Historical Thought from Herder to the Present*. Middletown, Conn. This book is indispensable for placing *historism* in the context of modern German intellectual history. Footnote 1, pp. 287–90, contains an important discussion of the term and its history. The book includes a valuable annotated bibliography.

———. 1973. "Historicism." *DHI* 2: 456–64. This is a concise introduction with a useful bibliography.

Kelley, Donald R. 1967. "Guillaume Budé and the First Historical School of Law." *AHR* 72: 807–34. Kelley displays informed usage.

Kuzminski, Adrian. 1976. "A New Science?" *CSSH* 18: 129–43.

Lee, Dwight E., and Robert N. Beck. 1954. "The Meaning of Historicism." *AHR* 59: 568–77. The authors outline five ways the term was used in the early twentieth century.

Liebel, Helen P. 1971–72. "Reply to Georg Iggers." *Eighteenth-Century Studies* 5: 594–603.

Mandelbaum, Maurice. 1971. *History, Man, and Reason: A Study in Nineteenth-Century Thought*. Baltimore. This is a broad, thoroughly supported investigation.

Meinecke, Friedrich. [1936] 1972. *Historism: The Rise of a New Historical Outlook*. London, 1972. Translation of *Die Entstehung des Historismus*. The classic of the field, this work is strongly stamped by Meinecke's scholarly and political outlook, which was typical of the German profession in the late nineteenth and early twentieth centuries. Meinecke's interpretation of the origins of modern historical consciousness is increasingly questioned as more research accumulates on the early-modern history of historiography.

Meyerhoff, Hans. 1959. "History and Philosophy: An Introduction." In Meyerhoff: 1–25. This essay, together with Geoffrey Barraclough's "Historian in a Changing World," reprinted in the same anthology, influenced many American-born historians in the 1960s and 1970s.

Popper, Karl. 1940. "What Is Dialectic?" *Mind*, N.S., 49: 403–26.

———. 1957. *The Poverty of Historicism*. Boston.

Reill, Peter Hanns. 1975. *The German Enlightenment and the Rise of Historicism*. Berkeley, Calif.

Rothacker, Erich. 1960. "Das Wort Historismus." *Zeitschrift für deutsche Sprache*, N.S., 1: 3–6.

Struever, Nancy. 1970. *The Language of History in the Renaissance*. Princeton, N.J.

White, Hayden. 1975. "Historicism, History, and the Figurative Imagination." *HT Beih.* 14: 48–67. This particular supplement to *History and Theory* contains three additional articles on the idea of historicism.

White, Hayden. 1959. "Translator's Introduction: On History and Historicisms." In Carlo Antoni, *From History to Sociology: The Transition in German Historical Thinking*. Detroit: xv–xxviii.

Zagorin, Perez. 1959. "Historical Knowledge: A Review Article on the Philosophy of History." *JMH* 31: 243–55.

Sources of Additional Information

The importance of the annotated bibliography in Iggers (1968) must be underscored. In general see *HT Beih.*, as well as Berding: 7–79, which includes a lengthy list of titles on *"Historismus und Historismuskritik."* Maurice Mandelbaum, "Historicism," *EP* 4: 22–25, includes a short bibliography. G. Scholtz, "Historismus, Historizismus," *HWP* 3: 1141–46, includes an extensive bibliography of German titles and is particularly valuable for its discussion of nineteenth-century uses. Karl-Georg Faber, "Ausprägungen des Historismus," *Historische Zeitschrift* 228 (Feb. 1979): 1–22, is a recent review of the literature. Arnaldo Momigliano, "Historicism in Contemporary Thought," [1961], reprinted in the Momigliano's *Studies in Historiography* (London, 1966): 221–38, discusses the concept with reference to various national historiographical traditions; see also Momigliano's "Historicism Revisited" [1974] in his *Essays in Ancient and Modern Historiography* (Middletown, Conn., 1977), which contains important bibliographical references on p. 373, n. 1. Friedrich Engel-Janosi, *The Growth of German Historicism* (Baltimore, 1944), was especially influential in shaping the usage of American scholars in the 1940s and 1950s. There is an interesting discussion of usage in Alan Donagan, "Determinism in History," *DHI* 2: 20–21. Note also the remarks of Hans Meyerhoff, ed., *The Philosophy of History in Our Time* (Garden City, N.Y., 1959), pp. 9–11 and (on Popper's usage) 299–300. For Italian usage see Carlo Antoni, "Storicismo e anti-storicismo" [1931], in Carlo Antoni, *Storicismo e antistoricismo* (Naples, 1964); also Antoni's *Lo storicismo* (Turin, 1957), which is available in French translation, and his *From History to Sociology: The Transition in German Historical Thought* (1940; reprint ed., Detroit, 1959). Many of the writings of Iggers, aside from those already cited, touch on the subject; for example, his "German Historical Thought and the Idea of Natural Law," *Cahiers d'Histoire Mondiale* 8 (1964): 564–75, contains an analysis of Meinecke's views. Iggers and Helen P. Liebel engaged in heated but sometimes illuminating exchanges over the definition and significance of *historicism* in *Eighteenth-Century Studies* 4 (Summer 1971): 359–85 and 5: 587–503 and in *Clio* 3 (1974). H. Stuart Hughes' *Consciousness and Society* (New York, 1958) contains a good account of the so-called crisis of historicism in interwar Europe; see also Colin T. Baader, "German Historicism and Its Crisis," *JMH* 48 (On Demand Supplement): 85–119. Note the usage of Dorothy Ross, "Historical Consciousness in Nineteenth-Century America," *AHR* 89 (1984): 910. Historicism stimulates discussion in disciplines other than history, such as literary criticism and political science; see, for example, Roy Harvey Pearce, *Historicism Once More: Problems and Occasions for the American Scholar* (Princeton, N.J., 1969), and Eugene F. Miller, "Positivism, Historicism, and Political Inquiry," *The American Political Science Review* 66 (Sept. 1972): 796–817, followed by "Comments" and a "Rejoinder" by Miller. On the idea of "historicity" see L. von Renthe-Fink, "Geschichtlichkeit," *HWP* 3: 404–8.

HISTORIOGRAPHY. 1. Written history; the writing of history. 2. The study of the development of historical scholarship; the history of history as a general branch of learning, or the history of historical interpretation of particular periods and problems.

Historiography is used in two senses by English-speaking historians: broadly, to refer to written history in general or to the act of writing history (*historiographer* is a synonym for *historian*, now rare); and, more narrowly, as a technical term to designate the study of the history of historical writing, methods, interpretation, and controversy (Hexter, 1967: 3). The first meaning is much the older of the two; in English, use of *historiography* in the traditional sense of "written history" dates at least from the sixteenth century. The *OED*, in fact, gives only this definition, citing 1569 as the earliest known date of usage. Historians continue to use the word in this sense with fair regularity, although it has to a large degree been supplanted by the shorter, though ambiguous, HISTORY (which can refer either to the course of human events or to written accounts of the course of events). The second, technical meaning has grown in popularity since the early twentieth century, as appreciation for the history of historical scholarship has increased (e.g., Flint, 1874; Robinson, 1912) and professionalization has led to conflicting interpretations creating, in turn, the need for a specialized term to designate the study of historical controversy.

Although technical use of the word is very recent, the idea of studying historical scholarship historically is by no means new. Polybius (c. 203–c. 120 B.C.), for example, surveyed and criticized previous work on Roman history (Barnes, [1937] 1962: 399), and RENAISSANCE humanists studied the classical Greek and Roman historians from a historical point of view. In 1599 the French scholar Lancelot Voisin de la Popelinière even published a "history of histories" (*Histoire des Histoires, avec l'idée de l'histoire accomplie*) (Butterfield, 1955: 2). Before the late eighteenth century, however, such efforts amounted to little more than chronological lists of titles and authors. It was primarily among late-eighteenth- and early-nineteenth-century German historians at Göttingen University— J. G. Gatterer, August Ludwig Schlözer, Friedrich Ruhs, Friedrich Creuzer, and Ludwig Wachler—that the idea of an analytical and critical history of historical scholarship crystallized. This culminated in the publication of Wachler's *Geschichte der historischen Forschung und Kunst seit der Wiederherstellung der literärischen Cultur in Europa* (1812–20) and, much later, F. X. von Wegele's *Geschichte der deutschen Historiographie seit dem Auftreten des Humanismus* (1885) (Butterfield, 1955: 4–22).

Specialized English and American use of the word seems to have begun about 1900 as an indirect by-product of German usage. The term *Historiographie* was frequently employed by late-nineteenth-century German-language historians of history (for instance Wegele, 1885; Wyss, 1895). In 1911 the Swiss Eduard Fueter published the influential *Geschichte der neueren Historiographie*, which he described as a "history of European historical writing" ([1911] 1968: v). Fueter and other German-speaking scholars continued to use the word *historiography* in the traditional sense (i.e., as a synonym for *historical writing*, or *Geschichtsschreibung*), but their example established a close link between "historiography" and the *analysis* of historical writing and methods. (To this day, *Historiographie* primarily seems to have retained its traditional meaning in German, even among historians; in his dictionary of technical expressions, Bayer [1974], for example, discusses *Historiographie* under the entry *Darstellung* [representation], which he defines as "often synonymous with *Geschichtsschreibung*, *Historiographie*"). German usage made a strong impression on British historians such as G. P. Gooch who, at least in part following German precedent, used the expression "the development of modern historiography" in the 1913 preface to his *History and Historians in the Nineteenth Century* ([1913] 1959: vi). The specialized English term is probably a simple abbreviation of the expression "history of historiography," which occurred during or immediately after the First World War; it was then established in the vocabulary of English, and particularly American, historians during the 1920s and 1930s.

The Cornell historian Carl Becker was especially important in defining and popularizing the technical term in North America. In a paper of 1926 Becker ([1955] 1959: 132) defined *historiography* as "the history of history: the history, that is, of what successive generations have imagined the past to be like." In the late 1930s, he devoted an entire essay to *historiography* understood as the "study of the history of historical study," which he described disparagingly as

> little more than the notation of historical works since the time of the Greeks, with some indication of the purposes and points of view of the authors, the sources used by them, and the accuracy and readability of the works themselves. The chief object of such enterprises . . . is to assess, in terms of modern standards, the value of historical works for us. At this level historiography gives us manuals or information about histories and historians, provides us, so to speak, with a neat balance sheet of the "contributions" which each historian has made to the sum total of verified historical knowledge now on hand. (1938: 20).

But Becker believed that historiography should be something more; it should be

> in some sense a phase of intellectual history, that phase of it which records what men have at different times known and believed about the past, the use they have made in the service of their interests and aspirations, of their knowledge and beliefs, and the underlying presuppositions which have made their knowledge seem to them relevant and their beliefs seem to them true. (1938: 22)

Other Americans who helped establish the term's technical meaning were Harry Elmer Barnes, James Westfall Thompson, and Charles Beard. Barnes explicitly cast his *History of Historical Writing* ([1937] 1962) in Fueter's mold. Although he did not define *historiography* as a specialized term, he did argue that

> like other forms of culture, [historical writing] is truly a historical product and must be considered against the background of the civilization out of which it grew. So, a history of historical writing must necessarily be, to a large degree, a phase of the intellectual history of mankind. (p. ix)

Thompson (1942: viii) explicitly wrote his own *History of Historical Writing* to encourage the creation of courses in historiography at American colleges. Beard

(Beard and Vagts, 1937: 464) had already complained that few schools offered classes in the "history of historiography" and used his influence to popularize the founding of such courses. He used the term *historiography* often in both the traditional and technical senses (e.g., Beard, [1935] 1972: 327, 328; Beard and Vagts, 1937: 467, 477), and his example was undoubtedly important.

The popularity of historiography as a genre has grown rapidly since 1945. According to John Higham, American historians, although

> still uncomfortable in the rarefied regions of philosophy of history . . . have become addicted to the more tangible sort of commentary we call historiography . . . The historiographer has stepped in as a middleman in scholarly discourse, taking over where the book reviewer leaves off. He conserves the scholarship of the past that seems currently relevant. He directs attention to convergent aspects of current scholarship, helping individual historians discover the relation of their own interests to larger currents of thought. (1965: 89)

Highham adds that historiography can also become a "critical weapon" because, insofar as it "blends historical explanation with critical appraisal," it supplies a "vehicle of emancipation from ideas and interpretations one wishes to supersede" (p. 89).

On the negative side, some historians display a certain aversion to the idea of writing about the history of their own occupation, as if this were an activity less than worthy of the primary attention of first class scholars, people who should be concerned with "History, not historians" (Bloch, [1939–40] 1961: xxi). From this perspective, *historiography* in the technical sense is often treated with mild derision; a "branch—or perhaps a twig—of the sociology of knowledge" (Hexter, 1967: 3) or a "form of disciplinary narcissism" (Berkhofer, [1972] 1973: 77).

References

Barnes, Harry Elmer. [1937] 1962. *A History of Historical Writing*. New York. This is a pioneering survey in English that is still widely used; along with Thompson (1942), however, it has been criticized by Denis Hay (*Annalists and Historians* [London, 1977]: v) as "mainly scissors-and-paste; wherever one can check them, the facts are often wrong and the interpretation banal."

Bayer, Erich, ed. 1974. *Wörterbuch zur Geschichte: Begriffe und Fachausdrücke*. 4th ed. Stuttgart.

Beard, Charles A. [1935] 1972. "That Noble Dream." In Stern: 315–28.

Beard, Charles A., and Vagts, Alfred. 1937. "Currents of Thought in Historiography." *AHR* 42: 460–83.

Becker, Carl L. 1938. "What Is Historiography." *AHR* 44: 20–28. In this review of Barnes (1937) Becker reaffirms Barnes' opinion that *historiography* is a "phase of intellectual history," although Becker refers to the word *historiography* itself as "unlovely" (p. 20). He goes beyond Barnes in arguing that historians of historical scholarship should "forget entirely about the contributions of historians to present knowledge and . . . concentrate wholly upon their role in the cultural

pattern of their time"; historical writing would thus be viewed as "one of the literary forms in which current ideas about the past find expression" (pp. 25–26).
————. [1955] 1959. "What Are Historical Facts." In Meyerhoff: 120–37. This was originally presented as a paper in 1926.

Berkhofer, Robert F., Jr. [1972] 1973. "Clio and the Culture Concept: Some Impressions of a Changing Relationship in American Historiography." In Louis Schneider and Charles M. Bonjean, eds., *The Idea of Culture in the Social Sciences*. Cambridge.

Bloch, Marc. [1939–40] 1961. *Feudal Society*. London.

Butterfield, Herbert. 1955. *Man on His Past: The Study of the History of Historical Scholarship*. Cambridge. This is a key study by a strong British defender of the technical concept.

Flint, Robert. 1874. *The Philosophy of History in Europe: France and Germany*. Edinburgh. Flint deals with historical writing as well as with speculative philosophy of history.

Fueter, Eduard. [1911] 1968. *Geschichte der neueren Historiographie*. New York.

Gooch, G. P. [1913] 1959. *History and Historians in the Nineteenth Century*. Boston.

Hexter, J. H. 1967. "The Rhetoric of History." *HT* 6: 3–13.

Higham, John, et al. 1965. *History*. Englewood Cliffs, N.J. This is a basic history of historical scholarship in the United States; it includes chapters on Europe by Felix Gilbert and Leonard Krieger as well.

Robinson, James Harvey. 1912. "The History of History." In James Harvey Robinson, *The New History: Essays Illustrating the Modern Historical Outlook*. New York: 26ff.

Thompson, James Westfall. 1942. *A History of Historical Writing*. 2 vols. New York. See the annotation on Barnes ([1937] 1962).

Wegele, Franz Xaver von. 1885. *Geschichte der deutschen Historiographie seit dem Auftreten des Humanismus*. Munich.

Wyss, Georg von. 1895. *Geschichte der Historiographie in der Schweiz*. Zurich.

Sources of Additional Information

In general see Berding, especially 66–70; *HT Beih.*; Stephens; Birkos and Tambs. There is an interesting discussion of the term *historiography* in Sterling P. Lamprecht, "Historiography of Philosophy," *JP* 36 (Aug. 17, 1939): 449. Ernst Breisach's *Historiography: Ancient, Medieval, and Modern* (Chicago, 1983) is a comprehensive survey that includes a lengthy bibliography. For the early modern and modern periods see B. A. Haddock, *An Introduction to Historical Thought* (London, 1980). Butterfield (1955) is in many ways the best introduction to the subject. For substantive and bibliographical information see also Butterfield's essay "Historiography" in *DHI* 2: 464–98. See also the articles by several scholars collected under the heading "Historiography" in *IESS* 6: 368–480. Barnes ([1937] 1962: 399–404) includes "Note on the History of History," which contains many bibliographic references. M. A. Fitzsimmons et al., *The Development of Historiography* (Harrisburg, Pa., 1954), is a general survey that complements Barnes ([1937] 1962) and Thompson (1942). Since 1982 *Storia della Storiografia*, a journal devoted to the history of historiography, has been published in Milan; its articles appear in the major European languages. For the history of ancient historiography see James T. Shotwell, *An Introduction to the History of History* (New York, 1922), and two more recent studies: Herbert Butterfield, *The Origins of History (New York, 1981)*, and Charles William Fornara, *The Nature of History in Ancient Greece and Rome*

(Berkeley, Calif., 1983). The most convenient general analysis of medieval and early-modern historiography is Denis Hay, *Annalists and Historians: Western Historiography from the Eighth to the Eighteenth Century* (London, 1977). On medieval historiography see also Gray Cowan Boyce, ed., *Literature of Medieval History, 1930–1975* 4 (New York, 1981), pp. 2188–2204. For the early-modern period Fueter ([1911] 1968), although outdated in some respects, is still valuable. The same is true of Gooch ([1913] 1959) for the nineteenth century. Higham et al. (1965) is the most convenient survey of American scholarship. For the twentieth century see especially Georg G. Iggers, *New Directions in European Historiography* (Middletown, Conn., 1975)—revised in 1984—and Geoffrey Barraclough, *Main Trends in History* (New York, 1979). The major anthologies of primary readings are Fritz Stern, ed., *The Varieties of History* (New York, 1972), and Peter Gay et al., *Historians at Work*, 4 vols. (New York, 1972–75).

HISTORY. 1. In ordinary usage, the human past. 2. In professional usage, either the human past or (more significantly) inquiry into the nature of the human past, with the aim of preparing an authentic account of one or more of its facets. The term may also refer in both popular and professional usage to a written account of past events. From the *historical* viewpoint—that is, from the standpoint of the history of historical thinking itself—*history* may be generally defined as a tradition of learning and writing, dating from ancient times, based on rational inquiry into the factual nature of the human past.

The word *history* has an ambiguous meaning in the languages of modern Europe: it may refer either to the EVENTS of the PAST themselves (*res gestae*, or "things done" in Latin); to the *activity* of studying and writing about the past (Barzun, [1943] 1950: 31; Rothfels, 1961: 7); or to a finished *written account* of the past—as in the expression "Gibbon's history of the decline of Rome." (In German, *Geschichte* [from *geschehen*, to happen] shares the ambiguities of *history*. It appeared as a synonym for *Historie* in the seventeenth century and had replaced the latter word by the nineteenth century as the favored German label for study of the past [Berr and Febvre, 1932: 357].) These three meanings already existed in classical Greek and Latin, although the original Greek *historia* meant simply "inquiry" of any kind. In the technical usage of modern professional historiography, *history* still retains that archaic message—it is the act of inquiry by which one studies and communicates about the past (e.g., Berr and Febvre, 1932: 358; Strayer [1943] 1950: 6). A *historian* is one who "pursues this inquiry, and the best historian is he who pursues it best" (Zagorin, 1956: 9).

The Greek *historia* came from the root "to see," and *histor* first meant "eyewitness"; from this evolved the meaning: "one who examines witnesses and obtains truth through inquiry" (Arendt, 1961: 284–85, n. 1; Press, 1977: 284). Herodotus (c. 484–c. 425 B.C.), who established *historia* as the standard word for the study of the past, used the term in the dual sense of testimony and inquiry (Arendt, 1961: 285). Testimony implied statements of factual truth regarding actual events, and this distinguished his sort of inquiry from myth and mythically inspired epic and drama—which, despite the creation of factual history by Herodotus and his successor Thucydides (c. 460–c. 400 B.C.), always remained the favored Greek ways of interpreting the past. As Finley (1964–65: 299) writes, "Acceptance and belief were what counted, and [in myth] the Greeks had all the knowledge of the past they needed without the help of historians."

In Hellenistic and Roman times, *history* came to designate the *narrative* of the inquirer; a semantic shift occurred in which the ideas of investigation and testimony were subordinated to the art of presentation. From this developed the custom of using *history* in the sense of "story," that is, to refer to fictional as well as factual narratives (Press, 1977: 285, 288)—as, for example, in Fielding's eighteenth-century *History of Tom Jones*. This rhetorical tradition—which led to history's classification as a branch of literature, important as a means of edification and entertainment as well as a source of factual knowledge—remained paramount until the eighteenth century, the eve of the rise of "scientific" history (Johnson, 1926: 21–22; Stromberg, 1951: 297–98).

During medieval times *history* gradually took on the meaning of the entire course of human events, a sense that probably did not exist at all in antiquity (Press, 1977: 283) but that came to play a key role in Christian theology, in speculative PHILOSOPHY OF HISTORY, and in the ordinary discourse of modern times. (Many older accounts of ancient historical consciousness [e.g., Holborn, 1949: 6–7] sharply contrast the classical and Judeo-Christian traditions, assuming that the Greeks and Romans understood *history* as a cyclical process while the Hebrews viewed it as a progressive, teleological process of development. This view is now disputed, either on grounds that a notion of *history* as a developmental PROCESS was simply non-existent in antiquity [Press, 1977: 281–82], or that ancient Greco-Roman and Judeo-Christian thought both display concepts of PROGRESS and RECURRENCE [Trompf, 1979].)

The idea of history as a developmental process (which may have roots in the work of St. Augustine [Press, 1977: 294–95]) implies that history is a kind of "untold story" (Mink, 1978: 134), a "series of happenings in time and space, [which exists] apart from the records"; it suggests that the past "has a sort of objective reality with which, in some unexplained way, the historical scholar may compare and verify the written records" (Johnson, 1926: 22). Critics of this tradition warn that "we can know the past only as it has left its traces in records and remains. The past does not exist except in human consciousness" (Johnson, 1926: 22).

How and to what end historical inquiry should be conducted has always been contested. As Berr and Febvre (1932: 357) note, "there is no branch of knowledge which in the course of intellectual evolution has exhibited more varied modalities and answered to more contradictory conceptions than has history. There is none which has had and continues to have more difficulty in discovering its definitive status." Frederick Jackson Turner's ([1891] 1972: 198) statement that "conceptions of history have been almost as numerous as the men who have written history" is surely an exaggeration, but Johan Huizinga ([1936] 1963: 8–

9) rightly suggests that every period and society produces a conception of history "adequate" to it, that is, one that answers its intellectual needs. For Herodotus—called the "father of history" by Cicero—history was a matter of erecting monuments to noble deeds; Thucydides understood it as the analysis of recent events that (he believed) would yield general truths about human behavior (Holborn, 1949: 3, 5). Following chapter nine of Aristotle's *Poetics*, however, most ancient thinkers considered history unimportant. In contrast to Thucydides, they believed that history dealt merely with the merely literal, the mundane, and the particular, not with the higher realm of timeless, universal truth (Holborn, 1949: 6; Press, 1977: 287–87; but cf. Fritz, 1958). What the Greeks wanted were not facts but truths. Indeed, even for Thucydides, "The past can yield nothing more than paradigmatic support for the conclusions one has drawn from the present; the past, in other words, may still be treated in the timeless fashion of myth" (Finley, 1964–65: 301).

In contrast to the ancient historians, medieval Christian scholars understood history not as human inquiry but as the allegorical contemplation of divine will (White, 1942; Holborn, 1949: 7–8). The most renowned early modern historians, however—for example, Machiavelli (1469–1527) and Guicciardini (1483–1540)—revived the secular models of antiquity (Weisinger, 1945: 417; Holborn, 1949: 8). Beginning in the fourteenth and fifteenth centuries a new attitude toward the past slowly crystallized, a "sense of temporal perspective, . . . born at about the same time that Italian painters began to represent figures in spatial perspective" (Harbison, 1956: 36). This was the sense of the past as alien, as fundamentally different from the present (see ANACHRONISM), an orientation pioneered in the work of the poet Petrarch and the philologist Lorenzo Valla. Simultaneously, an erudite interest in facts of the past for their own sake took shape, associated especially with philology, legal scholarship, and the editing of old manuscripts (see ANTIQUARIANISM). Whether or not these developments constituted a historiographical "revolution," as some have claimed, is disputed (cf. Preston 1977: 357). What is certain is that antiquarian scholarship—typically encyclopedic in form—was not initially considered history at all, since history (according to classical rhetorical canons) had to display a narrative structure (Hay, 1977: 133, 184).

During the eighteenth century the ancient tradition of history as narrative was wedded to the antiquarian concern for facts, and around 1800 the modern concept of SCIENTIFIC HISTORY took shape. Then *history* was inquiry into the nature of the past for its own sake, pursued with the aim of establishing a narrative record of events as they "actually happened" (Ranke, [1824] 1972: 57).

All professional historians currently agree that *history* means scholarly inquiry into the factual nature of the human past. Since the late eighteenth century three characteristics have been generally regarded as indispensable to this task: (1) a critical sense of EVIDENCE; (2) a sense of ANACHRONISM; and (3) a sense of secular CAUSATION (cf. Burke, 1969: 1). Beyond this basis consensus, however, the past two centuries have abounded in conflicting efforts to prescribe what the

activity of history should and should not be. For example, the French historian
Fustel de Coulanges ([1862] 1972: 179)—like many other scholars before and
since (e.g., Strayer, [1943] 1950: 17)—believed that history necessarily deals
with human *change* in the past. In the late nineteenth century it became fashionable to think that the search for social regularities had no legitimate place in
historiography—that history must deal exclusively with the "occurrence of particular event-complexes" (Trompf, 1977: 137); this notion, which implies a
radical difference between the methods of history and those of natural science,
still persists in many circles (see IDEALISM).

Some theorists stress history's similarities to literature. The Italian philosopher
Benedetto Croce (1866–1952), for example, insisted on a distinction between
"history" proper and "chronicle" on the grounds that *history* implies sustained
narrative built on cause-effect relationships, and *chronicle* merely suggests a
series of disconnected fragments (cf. Barzun, 1945: 81; Meiland, 1965: 17);
Croce's usage is not always helpful, however, since some medieval chronicles
were in fact coherent narratives based on cause and effect connections (see
Breisach, 1983: 126–30).

Disputes over the "nature" of history have intensified in the twentieth century;
most have involved efforts to define *history* as either an "art" or a "science"
in its methods and aims (e.g., Hughes, 1964). At the turn of the century the
British historian G. M. Trevelyan ([1903] 1972: 234) led the attack against the
scientific model, arguing that "history is, in its unchangeable essence, 'a
tale',"—by which he meant that "the art of history remains always the art of
narrative"; Trevelyan's conception of history as a "liberal art" or "part of
humane letters" has remained popular (Strayer, [1943] 1950: 3; Barzun, 1945:
81). On the other hand, some historians are adamant in their insistence that
history is a social science (see SOCIAL SCIENTIFIC HISTORY). A popular way of
avoiding commitments in this debate is to hold that *history* is a unique combination of art and science and to argue that it occupies an autonomous status
among the branches of human learning. But much more important than this
controversy is the fact that inquiry has been vastly broadened in scope and method
in the twentieth century and is no longer narrowly identified with the reconstruction of past politics or church affairs on the basis of written texts (see INTER-
DISCIPLINARY HISTORY).

The foregoing summary hardly begins to suggest the variety of ways *history*
has been characterized; a detailed overview may be gained from standard texts
such as Stern (1972) or Briesach (1983). The laudable impulse to prescribe
carefully the boundaries of any intellectual activity is easily understood, particularly from the standpoint professionals who wish to vindicate the cognitive
legitimacy of their field and defend standards of responsible scholarship. From
a historical standpoint, however, the notion that history should have a "definitive" status or an "unchangeable essence" seems curious. Circumstances have
changed radically over time and views about the past have also changed (cf.
Huizinga, [1936] 1963: 3). The word *history* implies an ensemble of traditions

of thinking and writing about the past; to some, it may also suggest the possibility of a relatively open-ended future with regard to the discipline's further development. The point may seem obvious. That it needs to be said points up an interesting paradox; in their efforts to define their discipline, historians regularly betray the fact that they have collectively paid surprisingly little attention to the overall history of history itself (Walsh, 1973: 211–12). Of course, every competent historian is thoroughly familiar with the history of scholarship in his own specialized subfield; but such historiographical sophistication rarely extends to the discipline as a whole. Thus, attempts to characterize the discipline in general are often undermined by a prescriptive impulse that is uninformed by a true appreciation of the overall evolution of historical consciousness itself. Such efforts are "unhistorical" reflections of the definer's own particular view of what history *should* be, rather than what history presently is, or has been, or may become.

References

Arendt, Hannah. 1961. "The Concept of History: Ancient and Modern." In Hannah Arendt, *Between Past and Future: Eight Exercises in Political Thought*. New York: 41–90.

Barzun, Jacques. 1945. "History as a Liberal Art." *JHI* 6: 81–88. This is a classic characterization of history as an enriching source of "perspective, of judgment, of wisdom—in short of humanity." History is said to achieve these "liberal" effects in two ways: "it sets the mind free from the obsession of immediate place and it sets the mind free from the obsession of immediate time" (p. 84).

———. [1943] 1950. "History, Popular and Unpopular." In Strayer: 27–57.

———. 1974. *Clio and the Doctors: Psycho-History, Quanto-History, and History*. Chicago. One reviewer has said of this book by a well-known humanist: "Seldom has a less satisfactory answer been given to the ancient query, 'What is history?' " (*HT* 15: 98).

Berr, Henri, and Febvre, Lucien. 1932. "History and Historiography: History." *ESS* 7: 357–68. The authors define *history* as "the study of human facts of the past" (p. 358). This is an opinionated essay in which the authors seek to propagate their notion of history as "synthesis."

Breisach, Ernst. 1983. *Historiography: Ancient, Medieval, and Modern*. Chicago.

Burke, Peter. 1969. *The Renaissance Sense of the Past*. London.

Croce, Benedetto. [1919] 1960. *History: Its Theory and Practice*. New York.

Finley, M. I. 1964–65. "Myth, Memory, and History." *HT* 4: 281–302.

Fritz, Kurt von. 1958. *Aristotle's Contribution to the Practice and Theory of Historiography*. Berkeley, Calif. Fritz argues that the generally accepted view that Aristotle was indifferent toward history is "totally wrong" (p. 132).

Fustel de Coulanges, N. D. [1862] 1972. "An Inaugural Lecture." In Stern: 179–88.

Harbison, E. Harris. 1956. *The Christian Scholar in the Age of the Reformation*. New York.

Hay, Denys. 1977. *Annalists and Historians: Western Historiography from the Eighth to the Eighteenth Century*. London.

Holborn, Hajo. 1949. "Greek and Modern Concepts of History." *JHI* 10: 3–13.

Hughes, H. Stuart. 1964. *History as Art and as Science: Twin Vistas on the Past.* New York.

Huizinga, Johan. [1936] 1963. "A Definition of the Concept of History." In Raymond Klibansky and H. J. Paton, eds., *Philosophy and History: Essays Presented to Ernst Cassirer.* New York: 1–10. Huizinga's general definition of *history* as "the intellectual form in which a civilization renders account to itself of its past" (p. 9) is obviously too broad, since it would include myth, poetry, drama, and so on. The Dutch scholar is correct, however, in seeking an ecumenical definition that "comprises every form of historical record; that of the annalist, the writer of memoirs, the historical philosopher, and the scholarly researcher [and which] comprehends the smallest antiquarian monograph in the same sense as the vastest conception of world history" (p. 10).

Johnson, Allen. 1926. *The Historian and Historical Evidence.* New York.

Meiland, Jack W. 1965. *Scepticism and Historical Knowledge.* New York.

Mink, Louis O. 1978. "Narrative Form as a Cognitive Instrument." In Canary and Kozicki: 129–49.

Press, Gerald A. 1977. "History and the Development of the Idea of History in Antiquity." *HT* 16: 280–96. This is an important study based on a close examination of the meaning of the word in antiquity.

Preston, Joseph H. 1977. "Was There an Historical Revolution?" *JHI* 38: 353–64. This valuable review essay correctly chides historians for their tendency to write histories of historiography from a naively presentist point of view, that is, from the standpoint that the only noteworthy aspects of history's past are those that foreshadow twentieth-century practice (p. 363); cf. Stromberg (1951).

Ranke, Leopold von. [1824] 1972. Preface to *Histories of the Latin and Germanic Nations from 1494–1514.* In Stern: 55–58.

Rothfels, Hans. 1961. "Einleitung." In Waldemar Besson, ed., *Geschichte: Das Fischer Lexikon.* Frankfurt.

Stern, Fritz. 1972. *The Varieties of History.* New York. This justly admired anthology reflects, however, the modernist bias in the history of historical thinking; it includes only one group of selections (all from the work of Voltaire) that antedates the nineteenth century.

Strayer, Joseph R. [1943] 1950. "Introduction." In Strayer: 3–26. The author defines *history* as "the study of all past human activities" (p. 6).

Stromberg, R. N. 1951. "History in the Eighteenth Century." *JHI* 12: 295–304. Overgeneralized and somewhat dated, this article neglects developments in Germany. The author's conclusion (p. 304) exemplifies the historiographically naive presentmindedness criticized by Preston (1977: 363).

Trevelyan, George Macaulay. [1903] 1972. "Clio, A Muse." In Stern: 227–45.

Trompf, G. W. 1977. "Social Science in Historical Perspective." *Philosophy of the Social Sciences* 7: 113–38.

———. 1979. *The Idea of Historical Recurrence in Western Thought: From Antiquity to the Reformation.* Berkeley, Calif.

Turner, Frederick Jackson. [1891] 1972. "The Significance of History." In Stern: 198–208.

Walsh, W. H. 1973. "History as Science and History as More Than Science." *Virginia Quarterly Review* 49: 196–212.

Weisinger, Herbert. 1945. "Ideas of History During the Renaissance." *JHI* 6: 415–35. This work identifies six basic ideas of history that were important during the Renaissance, especially after the middle of the sixteenth century: the idea of progress, the theory of the plenitude of nature, the climate theory, the cyclical theory of history, the doctrine of uniformitarianism, and the idea of decline (p. 416). It stresses parallels between developments in natural science and in history.

White, Lynn. 1942. "Christian Myth and Christian History." *JHI* 3: 145–58.

Zagorin, Perez. 1956. "Carl Becker on History. Professor Becker's Two Histories: A Skeptical Fallacy." *AHR* 62: 1–11.

Sources of Additional Information

See also HISTORIOGRAPHY. Consult *HT Beih.*; Berding; Stephens; Birkos and Tambs. For general bibliography see, in addition to the older survey by Berr and Febvre (1932), the extensive treatment of "History and Historiography" in *IESS* 6: 368–480 and the long article by Herbert Butterfield, "Historiography," in *DHI* 2: 464–98. Consult, as well, H. W. Bartsch, "Geschichte/*Historie*," in *HWP* 3: 398–99; also, in the same volume, M. Hahn, "Historia," pp. 401–2. R. G. Collingwood's famous *Idea of History* (1946; reprint ed., New York, 1956) is strongly opinionated but nonetheless indispensable. An important text, which supplements Breisach (1983), Hay (1977) and Stern (1972), is B. A. Haddock, *An Introduction to Historical Thought* (London, 1980); it includes an annotated bibliography. See also Herbert Butterfield, *The Origins of History* (New York, 1981). There are a host of attempts by historians to characterize the nature of history, among the more famous of which are Marc Bloch's *Historian's Craft* (New York, 1953) and E. H. Carr's *What Is History?* (1961; reprint ed., Harmondsworth, Eng., 1964). On antiquity see Kurt von Fritz, "The Influence of Ideas on Ancient Greek Historiography," *DHI* 2: 499–511; Arnaldo Momigliano, "Greek Historiography," *HT* 17 (1978): 1–28; and Charles William Fornara, *The Nature of History in Ancient Greece and Rome* (Berkeley, Calif., 1983). For a more complete development of Press's views on the ancient conception of history see his *Development of the Idea of History in Antiquity* (Kingston and Montreal, 1982). The book contains a wealth of bibliographical information in footnote citations, especially in the concluding chapter. For the medieval period see Gray Cowan Boyce, ed., *Literature of Medieval History, 1930–1975* 4 (New York, 1981): 2188–2204, and Beryl Smalley, *Historians of the Middle Ages* (London, 1975). On the Renaissance and early-modern periods see, in addition to Burke (1969) and the review essay by Preston (1977), Felix Gilbert, *Machiavelli and Guicciardini: Politics and History in Sixteenth-Century Florence* (Princeton, N.J., 1965); Eric W. Cochrane, *Historians and Historiography in the Italian Renaissance* (Chicago, 1981); and Donald R. Kelley, *Foundations of Modern Historical Scholarship* (New York, 1970). Kelly's "Faces in Clio's Mirror: Mistress, Muse, Missionary," *JMH* 47: 679–90, is a review of literature on the early-modern period, also of more general interest. Also relevant is Arnaldo Momigliano, "Ancient History and the Antiquarian," in Arnaldo Momigliano, *Studies in Historiography* (London, 1966). On the eighteenth century consult, besides Stromberg (1951), Hugh Trevor-Roper, "The Historical Philosophy of the Enlightenment," in T. Bestermann, ed., *Studies on Voltaire and the Eighteenth Century* 27 (1963): 1667–87, and especially Peter Hanns Reill, *The German Enlightenment and the Rise of Historicism* (Berkeley, Calif., 1975). For the modern conception of history see the articles "Historische Methode'' (pp. 78–91) and ''Historisches Denken der Gegenwart'' (pp. 92–102) in Waldemar Besson, ed., *Geschichte* (Frankfurt, 1961). Leon J. Goldstein's provocative *Historical Knowing* (Austin, Tex., 1976) is inspired by the ancient idea that history is best understood as inquiry.

I
_____

IDEAL TYPE, MODEL. Synonyms denoting simplified, schematic character-
izations of social phenomena (institutions, movements, processes, human
groups, and so on) that serve as aids to reflection and research.

Current social science (for instance, Bendix, 1960: 281; Roth, 1971b: 119;
Brown, 1974: 1063; Iggers, 1975: 100; Burger, 1976: 164, 212, n. 8) employs
the terms *model* and *ideal type* as loose synonyms to designate "heuristic" (i.e.,
inquiry-aiding) mental constructs that, though simplifications, purport to capture
in some way general features of reality and so stimulate thought, discussion,
and social comparison (see COMPARATIVE HISTORY). Since the 1960s—following
the usage by Thomas S. Kuhn (Hollinger, 1973)—the word *paradigm* has also
been employed in this sense (for example, Wise, 1968: 579, 585; Menze, 1981:
3). A working definition of *model* to which many historians subscribe is "simplified description" (e.g., Burke, 1978: 23; Habakkuk, 1972: 34; cf. Gustavson,
1976: 321, 324). Examples might include many of the ideas discussed in this
dictionary, such as "feudalism," "totalitarianism," "revolution," "fascism,"
"imperialism," and so on, insofar as each of these ideas suggests an "ideal
picture" (Weber, [1904] 1949: 90) of some social phenomenon; such labels do
not *precisely* describe any particular case but nevertheless purport to give us a
selective approximation of some facet of actuality and help us begin to grasp
the "infinite variety of facts" that constitute social reality (Parsons, 1929: 31).

The methodological concept of "ideal types" (Ger. *Idealtypus*) was popularized by Max Weber (1864–1920). Weber, conventionally identified as a sociologist, was also a historian interested in comparing ideas and institutions in
different social settings; his work has had an "extraordinary" impact on historical
method in the twentieth century (Mommsen, 1972: 65). Under the influence of
Weber's successors such as Joseph Schumpeter, the term *model* has gradually

replaced "ideal type" (e.g., Roth, 1976: 309, 311) and has become "an enormously popular stock-in-trade among social scientists" (Hughes, 1958: 314); today, scholarly discussion of models is often conducted without reference to Weber's ideal types at all (Cohen, 1966: 75). Of the two terms, *model* is the more ambiguous and in many instances has become semantically "overburdened" (Cohen, 1966: 70; McClelland, 1975: 28–29; Burger, 1976: 212–13, n. 8). *Paradigm* is, if anything, even more elusive. One sociological dictionary gives five meanings for the word *model*, asserting that social scientists sometimes use it as a synonym for *theory*, as well as any kind of proposition whatever! (Gellner, 1964: 435)

Weber first employed the expression *ideal type* in his essay of 1904: " 'Objectivity' in Social Science and Social Policy" ([1904] 1949: 90). The term was actually coined by the legal scholar Georg Jellinek (Hughes, 1958: 313; Roth, 1971a: 260), but it was Weber who gave it its modern social science meaning (Roth, 1971a: 260–61). English-language audiences were introduced to Weber's ideas through the glosses and translations of R. H. Tawney and Talcott Parsons in the 1920s and 1930s—especially Parson's English version of Weber's *Protestant Ethic and the Spirit of Capitalism* (1930).

Weber devised the concept during his commentary on a famous dispute between rival German economists: Carl Menger (1840–1921), who understood *economics* as a science of general laws, and Gustav Schmoller (1838–1917), who approached *economics* as a matter of individual historical facts (Antoni, [1940] 1959: 169—see also ECONOMIC HISTORY). Weber was concerned to show that Menger's "laws"—for example, the "acquisitive impulse," the "free market"—were not transcendent principles but actually constructs of his own making, invented to explain economic behavior.

Weber understood *ideal types* as "bench mark concepts . . . which deliberately simplify and exaggerate the evidence" (Bendix, 1968: 499). They are one-sided distillations of those features of social phenomena that the researcher considers "essential and logically consistent" (Zadrozny, 1959: 157). The fabrication of these intellectual "tools," he believed, is unavoidable because human affairs are so complex (MacRae, 1974).

Such imaginary standards may be tested against reality by empirical research; thus, "the adequacy of our imagination, oriented and disciplined by reality, is *judged*" (Weber, [1904] 1949: 93). For instance, CAPITALISM—an idealized general image of prevailing economic conditions in nineteenth-century Western Europe—may be compared against actual conditions in specific regions of Europe, as well as economic systems in various other periods and areas, such as ancient China. In his most famous illustration of the technique, Weber (1930) constructed an ideal value system—the "Protestant ethic," based largely on his reading of Benjamin Franklin's *Autobiography*—and used it as a standard for interpreting the rise of capitalism in Western Europe between the sixteenth and eighteenth centuries. Although Weber was the first to make deliberate use of this device, he regarded such "concept-construction . . . to a certain extent, indispensable, to [all] the cultural sciences" (Weber, [1904] 1949: 89), among which he included history.

Weber stressed that the *Idealtypus*, though a construct of IMAGINATION, is not a haphazard product of fantasy; it must always be "objectively probable, i.e., conform to our nomological knowledge of social behavior and of its motivation" (Rogers, 1969: 42). He also emphasized that his use of the term *ideal* was ethically neutral: it "has no connection at all with *value-judgments*, and it has nothing to do with any type of perfection other than a purely *logical* one. There are ideal types of brothels as well as of religions" (Weber, [1904] 1949: 98–99).

Anticipating objections to the use of "utopias" in social science, Weber argued ([1904] 1949: 92) that the usefulness of ideal types could not be determined *a priori*;

> there is only one criterion, namely, that of success in revealing concrete cultural phenomena in their interdependence, their causal conditions and their *significance*. The construction of abstract ideal-types recommends itself not as an end but as a *means*. (p. 92)

He conceded that the device was "unhistorical" because it did not represent reality in all its concrete detail but considered it a matter of "simplification" rather than "falsification," since it was not arbitrary (Bendix, 1960: 280). In any case, Weber maintained that historians, whether or not they like it, unavoidably use such constructs in all studies that seek to go beyond mere description (Weber, [1904] 1949: 92; cf. MacRae, 1974: 71; Bendix, 1960: 281), and he cited abstractions such as individualism, imperialism, feudalism, and mercantilism as ideal types that historians use regularly.

The logical status of the ideal-type concept has been widely discussed. Most scholars follow the German sociologist Alexander von Schelting (1934: 329–35, 354–61) in arguing that Weber actually developed two distinct classes of ideal types and failed to distinguish clearly between them (e.g., Parsons, 1929: 33, 49; Watkins, 1952; Hughes, 1958: 313; Bendix, 1960: 280–81, n. 27). Those who argue that Weber is not inconsistent or imprecise include Burger (1976) and McIntosh (1977). According to the mainstream view, Weber spoke ambiguously in terms of "generalized" ideal types and "individualized" ideal types (Rogers, 1969: 88–89). *Generalized ideal types* are idealizations of *recurrent* social phenomena, for example, the three basic types of social authority identified by Weber: legal, charismatic, and traditional. *Individualized ideal types* are idealizations of *specific* historical structures, events, or ideas and comprise two distinct subcategories: (1) idealizations of "concrete historical individuals," *unique* phenomena such as the institutions of modern capitalism; and (2) "relative-historical concepts," or idealizations of tendencies in thought, for example, the value system of European Protestantism and the Brahmanic tradition of karma. Bendix (1960: 280–81, n. 27) agrees that Weber confuses types drawn from concrete instances, such as groups like the Chinese literati, with types constructed as the result of the historical comparison of a variety of instances, such as charisma. These latter types are "different from models such as the economists' 'free competitive market'."

Whatever the epistemological status of Weber's idea, it is now widely acknowledged that historians commonly use the range of mental constructs that he grouped under the label "ideal types"—although the term *model* is generally preferred (e.g., Hobsbawm, 1972: 19; Walker, 1980: 156, 161; Menze, 1981: 3–4). (Weber himself [(1904) 1949: 97] employed both terms but did not use them synonymously; *model type* to him implied a value judgment, an exemplar to be followed, and *ideal type* was value neutral.) Although recognizing model building as part of their method, historians often express strong reservations and warnings about the practice. Disciplinary tradition holds that the construction of abstract concepts (often identified with models and ideal types) is not appropriate to historiography, which must deal only in specific detail. D. H. Fischer (1970: 7) refers to a guild "antipathy to questions and hypotheses and models, which is apt to run below the surface of a historian's thought." Some historians wish to sharply distinguish history from social science (see SOCIAL SCIENTIFIC HISTORY) and understand models as the typical device of the social scientist, one "resorted to" and often abused. A recurring objection concerns the danger— warned against by Weber himself—that

> these constructs . . . may be allowed to escape the gravitation of the data supposedly being represented and to be themselves mistaken for reality. The whole, ideal type, or model may be made to dominate the data, determine the observer's selectivity, and become a Procrustean bed into which data are crammed, whether suited or not. (Gustavson, 1976: 324; Redlich, 1965: 490; Skinner, 1969: 10)

Indeed, an important subgenre of historiographical criticism is devoted to debunking methodological constructs on these very grounds (for example, Brown, 1974; Allardyce, 1979).

References

Allardyce, Gilbert. 1979. "What Fascism Is Not: Thoughts on the Deflation of a Concept." *AHR* 84: 367–88.

Antoni, Carlo. [1940] 1959. *From History to Sociology: The Transition in German Historical Thinking*. Detroit. This is an early attempt to fit Weber's ideas into the German intellectual context. Note 61, p. 242, contains bibliographical references to the history of the concept of types.

Bendix, Reinhard. 1960. *Max Weber: An Intellectual Portrait*. Garden City, N.Y. This basic survey is by one of the best-known interpreters of Weber's thought.

———. 1968. "Max Weber." *IESS* 16: 493–502.

Brown, Elizabeth A. R. 1974. "The Tyranny of a Construct: Feudalism and Historians of Medieval Europe." *AHR* 79: 1063–88. Brown maintains that medievalists have overlooked important data due to their use of FEUDALISM as "model or Ideal Type" (p. 1063).

Burger, Thomas. 1976. *Max Weber's Theory of Concept Formation: History, Laws, and Ideal Types*. Durham, N.C. This book contains a concise discussion of the relevance of the dispute between Menger and Schmoller (pp. 140–53). Burger denies the existence of logical ambiguities in Weber's theory and proclaims existing literature on the subject to be seriously incorrect: "Were it not for two or three notable essays, it would hardly be an exaggeration to say that in 60 years practically nothing has been achieved as far as the clarification of the methodological status of the ideal type is concerned" (p. 156). There is a comprehensive bibliography.

Burke, Peter. 1978. *Popular Culture in Early Modern Europe*. New York.

Cohen, Percy S. 1966. "Models." *The British Journal of Sociology* 17: 70–78. Cohen asserts that *model* is used "almost indiscriminately by sociologists and anthropologists to dignify any form of analysis or explanation. . . . the term becomes overburdened and its use unnecessary." He recognizes two sound usages—"a set of assumptions which attributes to some relatively unknown or unobservable process a form which is similar to that which is known to operate elsewhere" (p. 70) and "a set of assumptions which is deliberately used to simplify or limit the number of relationships or related processes which are to be studied in any area of reality" (p. 71).

Fischer, David Hackett. 1970. *Historians' Fallacies: Toward a Logic of Historical Thought*. New York.

Gellner, E. A. 1964. "Model." In Julius Gould and William L. Kolb, eds., *A Dictionary of the Social Sciences*. Glencoe, Ill.: 435.

Gustavson, Carl G. 1976. *The Mansion of History*. New York. The author defines *model* as a "simplified version of reality" (p. 324).

Habakkuk, John. 1972. "Economic History and Economic Theory." In Gilbert and Graubard: 27–44. Habakkuk states that "By definition a model contains assumptions which depart from reality. This is precisely what models are for; they are attempts to understand reality by simplifying it."

Hobsbawm, E. J. 1972. "From Social History to the History of Society." In Gilbert and Graubard: 1–26. As examples of "models," Hobsbawm mentions E. P. Thompson's concept of the "moral economy" of pre-industrial England, as well as his own "social banditry."

Hollinger, David A. 1973. "T. S. Kuhn's Theory of Science and Its Implications for History." *AHR* 78: 370–93.

Hughes, H. Stuart. 1958. *Consciousness and Society: The Reorientation of European Social Thought, 1890–1930*. New York. This is a positive evaluation of Weber, "the original model-builder—the man who first made explicit the procedure of abstract theoretical construction that alone renders possible the rational understanding of the human world" (p. 314).

Iggers, Georg G. 1975. *New Directions in European Historiography*. Middletown, Conn.

McClelland, Peter D. 1975. *Causal Explanation and Model Building in History, Economics, and the New Economic History*. Ithaca, N.Y. See the discussion of the terms *model* and *theory*, which are often used synonymously, pp. 28–29.

McIntosh, Donald. 1977. "The Objective Bases of Max Weber's Ideal Types." *HT* 16: 265–79. McIntosh argues that Weber's use of ideal types in empirical studies suffers from fewer inconsistencies than his theoretical exposition of the idea.

MacRae, Donald G. 1974. *Max Weber*. New York.

Menze, Ernest A. 1981. "Introduction. Totalitarianism: An Outmoded Paradigm?" In Ernest A. Menze, ed., *Totalitarianism Reconsidered*. Port Washington, N.Y.: 3–8.

Mommsen, Wolfgang J. 1972. "Max Weber." In H.-U. Wehler, ed., *Deutsche Historiker* 3. Göttingen: 65–90. This concise introduction argues that Weber should be considered not only a social and cultural historian but a writer of UNIVERSAL HISTORY. It is good for its German-language bibliography.

Parsons, Talcott. 1929. " 'Capitalism' in Recent German Literature: Sombart and Weber, II." *Journal of Political Economy* 37: 31–51.

Redlich, Fritz. 1965. " 'New' and Traditional Approaches to Economic History and Their Interdependence." *The Journal of Economic History* 25: 480–95. Redlich presents the view that "a model is never a piece of history" (p. 490).

Rogers, Rolf E. 1969. *Max Weber's Ideal Type Theory*. New York. Unusually conceived but nonetheless useful, this book includes selected translations from Weber's writings as well as excerpts from the work of others dealing with ideal types.

Roth, Guenther. 1971a. "The Genesis of the Typological Approach." In Reinhard Bendix and Guenther Roth, eds., *Scholarship and Partisanship: Essays on Max Weber*. Berkeley, Calif.: 253–65.

———. 1971b. "Sociological Typology and Historical Explanation." In Reinhard Bendix and Guenther Roth, eds., *Scholarship and Partisanship: Essays on Max Weber*. Berkeley, Calif.: 109–28.

———. 1976. "History and Sociology in the Work of Max Weber." *British Journal of Sociology* 27: 306–18.

Schelting, Alexander von. 1934. *Max Webers Wissenschaftslehre*. Tübingen. Extracts from this work are translated in Rogers (1969: 45–55).

Skinner, Quentin. 1969. "Meaning and Understanding in the History of Ideas." *HT* 8: 3–53.

Walker, Lawrence D. 1980. "A Note on Historical Linguistics and Marc Bloch's Comparative Method." *HT* 19: 154–64. Walker asserts that Bloch's concept of "feudalism" is an *ideal type*, or *model*, although Bloch did not use these terms.

Watkins, J.W.N. 1952. "Ideal Types and Historical Explanation." *The British Journal for the Philosophy of Science* 3: 22–43. Watkins links the use of ideal types to the COVERING LAW theory of historical explanation.

Weber, Max. 1930. *The Protestant Ethic and the Spirit of Capitalism*. London.

———. [1904] 1949. " 'Objectivity' in Social Science and Social Policy." In Max Weber, *The Methodology of the Social Sciences*. Glencoe, Ill.: 50–112.

Wise, Gene. 1968. "Implicit Irony in Perry Miller's *New England Mind*." *JHI* 29: 579–600.

Zadrozny, John T. 1959. *Dictionary of Social Sciences*. Washington, D.C.

Sources of Additional Information

There is a comprehensive bibliography in Burger (1976). See also the sections "Max Weber und verstehende Soziologie" (pp. 121–27) and "Vergleichende Methoden und Typologie" (pp. 165–71) in Berding. For substantive as well as bibliographical information see Mary Hesse, "Models and Analogy in Science," *EP* 5: 354–59, and, in volume 8 of the same work, Peter Winch, "Max Weber," pp. 282–83. Some of the literature is reviewed in John Torrance, "Max Weber: Methods and the Man," *Archives of European Sociology* 15 (1974): 127–65. For further evidence of the prevailing confusion see Roy Harrod, "What Is a Model," in J. N. Wolfe, ed., *Value, Capital, and Growth* (Chicago, 1968): 173–91. See also Jerzy Topolski, "The Model Method in Economic History," *Journal of European Economic History* 1 (Winter 1972): 713–26. Chapter one of Jürgen Kocka, *Sozialgeschichte: Begriff-Entwicklung-Probleme* (Göttingen, 1977), deals with Weber.

IDEALISM. 1. Broadly, any approach to history that attributes a crucial role to ideas, either in the course of human events or the methods of historical inquiry. 2. A metaphysical orientation, prevalent especially in nineteenth-century Germany, that holds that history's goal is the discovery of "leading ideas" that are presumed to lie hidden beneath the outward appearance of human affairs. 3. In critical philosophy of history, the position that historical inquiry fundamentally differs from the natural sciences insofar as it deals with human ideas, values, non-repeatable events; in contrast, natural science seeks to discover the regularities of physical nature.

Idealism and REALISM have been the two philosophical poles of historical theory and inquiry since the early nineteenth century (Gilliam, 1976: 231). The term itself was used by Leibnitz as early as 1702 to refer to the doctrines of Plato (Acton, 1967: 111). A word with "a multitude of shifty meanings" (Kelly, 1969: 2), *idealism* is linked to modern historiography in two distinct but inter-related senses—one metaphysical, the other epistemological. These two may be referred to as the "old" and "new" idealist traditions (Hughes, 1964: 7–13).

Idealism's central place in modern historiography stems largely from the fact that the modern approach to history first crystallized in late-eighteenth- and early-nineteenth-century Germany, where the "old," or metaphysical, idealism was the dominant philosophical current. German idealism was an extension of the ancient tradition of western idealism, which stems from Plato. This tradition, based on the familiar dichotomy between "appearance" and "reality," teaches that ultimate truth resides in a realm of hidden "ideas" that transcend the finite material world and the powers of human perception. The perceived (or phenom-enological) world is an incomplete reflection of these universal ideals, which can be experienced, however imperfectly, only by the spirit or intellect—not by the physical senses (Mandelbaum, 1971: 7; Gilbert, 1972: 149).

Key figures in the transfer of metaphysical idealism to historiography were the philosopher Wilhelm von Humboldt (1767–1835) and the historian Leopold von Ranke (1795–1886)(Liebel, 1963–64: 316). Humboldt's position ([1821] 1967: 5–6; 23) rests on the classic idealist assumption that historical events have an "inner truth" that is "only partially visible in the world of the senses"; the historian's goal, he believed, is the "presentation of the struggle of an idea to realize itself in actuality." His essay "On the Historian's Task" ([1821] 1967) concisely expresses the three basic presuppositions of German idealist histo-riography (Iggers and Moltke, 1973: 3–4): (1) the doctrine of ideas (*Ideenlehre*), according to which "historical phenomena are merely the external manifestation of underlying eternal ideas"; (2) the concept of "individuality," that is, the belief that these ideas cannot be grasped in the abstract but must be studied as they "express themselves in concrete historical individualities" (such as partic-

ular personalities, social institutions, nations, situations)(see HISTORISM); and
(3) the notion of "sympathetic understanding" (*Verstehen*) (see UNDERSTAND-
ING), that is, the idea that the historian must penetrate the outward appearance
of events to grasp the inner essence of historical individualities in their unique
particularity. This is achieved through a combination of painstaking source CRIT-
ICISM—during which the detached scholar steeps himself in remains of the past—
and intuitive contemplation (*ahnen*), which permits him to fathom the "inner
structure of the historical individuality under study."

The histories of Ranke, although products of a meticulously empirical mind,
represent the practical reflection of Humboldt's theory; in Ranke's work, careful
source criticism and idealist metaphysics are combined. Underlying his scholarship is the assumption that human affairs embody a definite logic, and this
meaning is presumed to derive from an invisible world of "leading ideas." For
Ranke, the ultimate end of historical inquiry was an "empathetic understanding"
of this secret meaning (Iggers, 1962–63: 32)(see also UNIVERSAL HISTORY).
Although cautious regarding the historian's ability to define the logic of this
process (he repudiated the *a priori* presumption of Hegel's speculative philosophy
of history) Ranke was "convinced that each period of history was [the] reflection
of an individual idea and that this idea molded its various aspects" (Gilbert,
1972: 147; Liebel, 1963–64: 316–17)(see ZEITGEIST). The point of history was
to "understand the inner form" or "peculiar truth" of a period by grasping the
invisible idea operative within it (Liebel, 1963–64: 316). Ranke's interests—
like those of most nineteenth-century historical scholars—were mainly political
and religious, and in practical terms he understood the "leading ideas" of history
to be "the general principles according to which religions are founded and states
are built" (Momigliano, [1954] 1966: 105, 110; Fueter, [1911] 1936: 474). In
the final analysis, God stands behind the ideas, and history for Ranke is a " 'holy
hieroglyph,' a divine puzzle worthy of a life-time of decipherment" (Wines,
1981: 6)(it should be noted that Lutheran theology strongly conditioned the
thought of north German idealists; in some ways their thought is best understood
as a partly secularized version of Lutheran doctrine). Thus, history was really
a religious exercise, a reverent "search for the 'hand of God' through a method
of 'intuitive approximation' " (Hughes, 1964: 8). That this religious mind-set
was also strongly political was due to state domination of ecclesiastical institutions in post-Reformation north Germany. The *Ideenlehre* thus became closely
entwined with the concepts of the state, NATION, and NATIONAL CHARACTER,
and each nation-state was presumed to embody a particular idea, or "spirit";
Germans in general were bearers of the idea of "freedom," Prussians carried
forward the idea of the "state," and so on (Momigliano, [1954] 1966: 106).

Although his exacting research techniques became the standard for the nineteenth-century historical profession, Ranke was not a systematic theorist, and it
was relatively easy to one-sidedly divorce his erudition from its metaphysical
framework (Iggers, 1962–63: 31; cf. Liebel, 1973: 146); beyond Germany—
and especially in the United States—the vital role of the *Ideenlehre* in his schol-

arship was generally ignored or unappreciated (Iggers, 1962–63: 31, 19–27). The result was a serious misunderstanding not only of Ranke's own work but of the importance of idealism in German historiography generally. Outside Germany "the notion of history as a process reflecting ideas and controlled by them was abandoned" (Gilbert, 1972: 149), and the concept of ideas as "principles of historical development" gave way to the approach that still prevails, that is, that ideas are simply "themes of historical research" (Momigliano, [1954] 1966: 110).

In Germany itself the idealist framework was rarely challenged, although it was revised in various ways (Iggers, 1962–63: 27–38). Articles in the leading German review, the *Historische Zeitschrift*, were strongly idealist through World War I and beyond, and leading historians (e.g., Otto Hintze) held fast to the belief that, in the last analysis, "science left one on the doorstep of a great unknown. The unknown possessed a real existence and to affirm this fact . . . by no means made one a mystic. What could not be perceived by science could be understood through artistic perception" (Liebel, 1963–64: 326). It should be noted, however, that even outside Germany metaphysical idealism left an important legacy, namely, its stress on the tenuousness of historical knowledge and the necessity of subjective INTERPRETATION; this was carried over in the "new," or epistemological, idealism (neo-idealism) that arose in the final decades of the nineteenth century.

Neo-idealism is closely associated with "Neo-Kantianism," the revival of interest in Kant that flourished in central Europe about 1870–1920 (Beck, 1967). It was part of a reaction against Hegel and speculative philosophy in general that set in about 1850 and the subsequent rise of the idea that philosophy's proper task was not metaphysical but epistemological: the analysis of human knowledge. This was seen in terms of Kant's distinction between knowledge of things "in themselves" and things as they are perceived. In history neo-idealism arose from the controversy over the relationship of the methods of natural science vis-à-vis other branches of learning. Pioneers of the new approach—for example, Wilhelm Dilthey, Wilhelm Windelband ([1894] 1980), Heinrich Rickert—argued that the "cultural sciences" or "sciences of the mind" (*Geisteswissenschaften*) differed radically from the "natural sciences" (*Naturwissenschaften*). According to this distinction precise and impersonal observation is possible in the natural sciences, but cultural sciences (including history) depend strongly on intuition and empathy; the point of (nomothetic) natural science is the discovery of timeless laws of nature, whereas the (idiographic) cultural sciences seek to comprehend human affairs in their unique temporal contexts (Windelband, [1894] 1980: 175). In contrast to the old idealism, neo-idealism viewed history as a discipline, or system of ideas with its own logic of investigation, not an esoteric spiritual process (Goldstein, 1962: 175). Yet—especially in Germany—the new idealism was still decidedly "spiritual" in tone. Dilthey, for instance, held that the subject matter of history was "Objective Mind." By this he meant that the "human spirit" is

objectified in certain visible phenomena such as language, literature, laws, architecture, religion, music, tools, art, towns, etc. . . . The historian can study these
objective expressions of man's mind in the past and through them he can enter
into and "relive" the human experiences of the past. (Nash,1969: 6)

In England neo-idealism was inaugurated by F. H. Bradley's essay on "The
Presuppositions of Critical History" (1874) (Boucher, 1984: 202), which applied
Kantian and Hegelian premises to problems of historical methodology. Not until
after World War I would Michael Oakeshott and R. G. Collingwood elaborate
on Bradley's foundations. More important in the immediate sense was Benedetto
Croce in Italy, who extended the work of the German neo-idealists, emphasizing
that historical understanding is unavoidably subjective, inseparably linked to the
life and times of the individual historian. In simplest terms, Croce taught that
history is an intellectual enterprise, and each historian inevitably writes about
the past from his own present viewpoint—the meaning of his famous dictum
"every true history is contemporary history" (Croce, [1919] 1960: 12).

The new idealism, with its stress on the logic of historical reasoning, had a
profound influence on the rise of historical RELATIVISM in the United States in
the 1920s and 1930s and on the related "crisis of HISTORICISM" in German-
speaking Europe during the same period—controversies that had an enduring
impact on the assumptions of working historians. Most historians today follow
the idealists in distinguishing their enterprise from the "realm of necessity"
associated with natural science (Hughes, 1960–61: 29), and few present scholars
would "deny the neoidealists' central contention that historical understanding is
a subjective process—a mighty effort to recall to life what is irrevocably over
and done with" (Hughes, 1964: 10). Moreover, the idealist "emphasis on the
[sympathetic understanding of] the individual and on the unique has remained
characteristic of nearly all historians" (Hughes, 1960–61: 24).

In Britain, Michael Oakeshott (1933; 1962) and R. G. Collingwood ([1946]
1956) extended the idealist legacy and perpetuated idealism as a living tradition
in the English-speaking world. Oakeshott helped lay the foundations of CON-
STRUCTIONISM, the doctrine that the PAST which historians study is not a "real"
past—as common sense suggests and historians usually assume—but an intellectual construct, a "world of ideas" created by the community of professional
historical scholars (Oakeshott, 1933: 95–96; also Meiland, 1965: 39–82;
Boucher, 1984: 206 and *passim*). Collingwood ([1946] 1956) stressed that history
is at bottom the study of thought and argued that the historian's method consists
in "rethinking" the ideas and intentions of people in the past (Dray, 1958). His
theory has received much attention as part of the controversy over historical
EXPLANATION since the 1940s. In this debate, *idealism* refers to the view that
"human actions are sharply to be distinguished from events in nature, that they
arise out of human thinking, willing and desiring, that the mind is capable of
reenacting human thought, and that it is the job of history to study these concrete
acts of thought, will and desire in their individuality"; this position is pitted
against POSITIVISM, which "holds that there is one and only one scientific method

(best exemplified in physics), and *genuine* historical or any other kind of knowledge has to be founded upon this method and its search for universal laws or statements of statistical probability" (Golob, 1980: 55). To date, Collingwood probably enjoys more admiration among practicing historians than any other philosopher of history; E. H. Carr ([1961] 1964: 21), for instance, calls Collingwood "the only British thinker in the present century who has made a serious contribution to the philosophy of history." On the other hand, Collingwood's doctrine of historical inquiry as "rethinking" has occasionally been ridiculed as "antihistorical, antiempirical, and absurd" (Fischer, 1970: 197).

References

Acton, H. B. 1967. "Idealism." *EP* 4: 110–18.

Beck, Lewis White. 1967. "Neo-Kantianism." *EP* 5: 468–73.

Boucher, David. 1984. "The Creation of the Past: British Idealism and Michael Oakeshott's Philosophy of History." *HT* 23: 193–214. Boucher grounds Oakeshott's thought in the context of the British idealist tradition. For a bibliography see especially p. 193, n. 2.

Carr, E. H. [1961] 1964. *What Is History?* Harmondsworth, Eng. This book calls attention to some pitfalls of Collingwood's approach, pp. 26ff.

Collingwood, R. G. [1946] 1956. *The Idea of History*. New York.

Croce, Benedetto. [1919] 1960. *History: Its Theory and Practice*. New York.

Dray, W. H. 1958. "Historical Understanding as Re-thinking." *University of Toronto Quarterly* 27: 200–215.

Fischer, David Hackett. 1970. *Historian's Fallacies: Toward a Logic of Historical Thought*. New York.

Fueter, Eduard. [1911] 1968. *Geschichte der neueren Historiographie*. New York.

Gilbert, Felix. 1972. "Intellectual History: Its Aims and Methods." In Gilbert and Graubard: 141–58.

Gilliam, Harriet. 1976. "The Dialectics of Realism and Idealism in Modern Historiographic Theory." *HT* 15: 231–56. Gilliam suggests that the tension between these two tendencies is the source of much of the richness of modern historiography.

Goldstein, Leon J. 1962. "Evidence and Events in History." *Philosophy of Science* 29: 175–94.

Golob, Eugene O. 1980. "The Irony of Nihilism." *HT Beih.* 19: 55–65.

Hughes, H. Stuart. 1960–61. "The Historian and the Social Scientist." *AHR* 66: 20–46.

———. 1964. *History as Art and as Science: Twin Vistas on the Past*. New York.

Humboldt, Wilhelm von. [1821] 1967. "On the Historian's Task." *HT* 6: 57–71.

Iggers, Georg G. 1962–63. "The Image of Ranke in American and German Historical Thought." *HT* 2: 17–40.

Iggers, George G., and Moltke, Konrad von. 1973. *Leopold von Ranke: The Theory and Practice of History*. Indianapolis, Ind.

Kelly, George Armstrong. 1969. *Idealism, Politics, and History: Sources of Hegelian Thought*. Cambridge.

Liebel, Helen P. 1963–64. "Philosophical Idealism in the *Historische Zeitschrift*, 1859–1914." *HT* 3: 316–30.

———. 1973. "Ranke's Fragments on Universal History." *Clio* 2: 145–59. This piece is informative on Ranke's idealism and his knowledge of Kant. Liebel argues that Ranke's work "does rest on well thought out theoretical foundations" (p. 146).

Mandelbaum, Maurice. 1971. *History, Man, and Reason: A Study in Nineteenth-Century Thought*. Baltimore. This book is conventional but somewhat misleading in its stark juxtaposition of German idealism and the Enlightenment (p. 7).

Meiland, Jack W. 1965. *Scepticism and Historical Knowledge*. New York. Meiland's work contains chapters on Oakeshott and Collingwood.

Momigliano, Arnaldo. [1954] 1966. "A Hundred Years After Ranke." In Arnaldo Momigliano, *Studies in Historiography*. London.

Nash, Ronald H., ed. 1969. *Ideas of History* 2. New York.

Oakeshott, Michael. 1933. *Experience and Its Modes*. Cambridge. Chapter three is entitled "Historical Experience."

————. 1962. *Rationalism in Politics, and Other Essays*. London. See especially the essay "The Activity of Being an Historian," pp. 137–67.

Windelband, Wilhelm. [1894] 1980. "History and Natural Science." *HT* 19: 165–85. This piece includes a useful introduction by the translator, Guy Oakes.

Wines, Roger. 1981. "Introduction." In Leopold von Ranke, *The Secret of World History: Selected Writings on the Art and Science of History*. New York: 1–31. This is a very good introduction to Ranke's work and its place in the context of German idealism.

Sources of Additional Information

For general bibliography see Acton (1967) and *HT Beih*. For literature on neo-idealism in contemporary philosophy of history see Nash (1969): 71–74, 157–58. On Humboldt, see Paul Sweet, *Wilhelm von Humboldt: A Biography*, 2 vols. (Columbus, Ohio, 1980). On Ranke see the annotated bibliography in Wines (1981) and Leonard Krieger, *Ranke: The Meaning of History* (Chicago, 1977). The early sections of Georg G. Iggers, "The Decline of the Classical National Tradition of German Historiography," *HT* 6 (1967): 382–412, deal with the idealist paradigm. See also Helen P. Liebel, "The Enlightenment and the Rise of Historicism in German Thought," *Eighteenth-Century Studies* 4 (1971): 359–85, and Georg Iggers' comments in the same periodical, 5 (1972): 587–603. On the close association between metaphysical idealism and the spiritualization of state power in nineteenth-century German historiography, see Peter Paret's introduction to Friedrich Meinecke, *The Age of German Liberation, 1795–1815* (Berkeley, Calif., 1977). See, as well, Georg G. Iggers, *The German Conception of History: The National Tradition of Historical Thought from Herder to the Present* (Middletown, Conn., 1968). On the impact of German idealism in the United States see Jürgen Herbst, *The German Historical School in American Scholarship* (Ithaca, N.Y., 1965). For a Soviet critique of the western idealist tradition see I. S. Kon, *Die Geschichtsphilosophie des 20. Jahrhunderts. Kritischer Abriss* (Berlin, 1964); see also the generally sympathetic review by Geoffrey Barraclough in *HT* 6 (1967): 230–36. On Collingwood see the bibliography in Michael Krausz, ed., *Critical Essays on the Philosophy of R. G. Collingwood* (Oxford, 1972), pp. 327–48, and Fischer (1970): 196, n. 25. On Oakeshott see David Boucher, "The Creation of the Past: British Idealism and Michael Oakeshott's Philosophy of History," *HT* 23 (1984): 193–214.

IDEOLOGY. 1. Thought—or, more broadly, consciousness—that reflects social and economic interests. 2. In Marxist usage, political and social beliefs that reflect narrow class interests and constitute a distorted, one-sided view of reality; "false consciousness," as opposed to truth. 3. An ideal vision of the social and political order; a political creed, belief system, or world view.

The meaning of the word *ideology* has changed significantly since its introduction at the end of the eighteenth century, and the term is still used in various related and overlapping ways. Some scholars (notably Marxists) reserve it for only particular kinds of belief systems; others use it to refer to "all political doctrines" (Seliger, 1977: 1). In most contexts the word has pejorative connotations, although they may range from the subtle to the overt.

The history of the term is well documented. It began as a label for a specific program of social reform; became, in the mid-nineteenth-century writings of Marx and Engels, a polemical weapon and general concept of revolutionary social thought; and, in the twentieth century, was transformed into an analytical social science concept. On the popular level it also became a loose synonym for "political creed."

The neologism *idéologie* was coined in 1796 by the French social philosopher Antoine Louis Claude Destutt de Tracy (1754–1836) to designate his idea of a "science of ideas" (Kennedy, 1979: 353). Tracy and a group of associates who shared his views subsequently became known as *idéologues*, or "ideologists." According to the ideologues, the science of ideology would usher in an age of reason in accordance with the principles of the ENLIGHTENMENT and especially with the thought of the materialist philosopher Condillac (1715–1780). In his *Elemens d'idéologie* (1801–15), Tracy outlined his views and sought, as well, to vindicate the *laissez-faire* economic theory of the eighteenth-century French physiocrats—the economic doctrine that he considered most compatible with his viewpoint.

At the end of the 1790s Tracy and his associates supported Napoleon as the leader who would help them realize their goals; after coming to power, however, Bonaparte turned against the ideologues when they criticized his authoritarian methods. It was Napoleon who popularized the use of *ideology* as a pejorative, denouncing Tracy's *idéologie* as "idealistic trash" (Stein, 1956: 168). Tracy subsequently shifted his hopes for the future to the United States, beginning a correspondence with Thomas Jefferson; Jefferson translated some of Tracy's writings and, in so doing, helped to spread the word *ideology* in English (Stein, 1956: 170); the word had made its first English appearance in British reviews of Tracy's work as early as 1796 (*OED*).

Tracy's work was widely translated in the early nineteenth century, and the term *ideology* began to appear in the titles of numerous books. As its popularity grew, the word gradually lost its associations with the specific doctrines of the ideologues and began to be used broadly in connection with any political cause. Following the revolutions of 1848–49, use of the word and its variations became especially widespread among moderates and traditionalists, who identified it with abstract and impractical LIBERALISM. The German philosopher Wilhelm Dilthey, for example, contrasted "inspired ideologues" with "experienced politicians" in 1860 (Kennedy, 1979: 363–64).

Of key significance for twentieth-century usage—scholarly as well as popular—was the pejorative understanding displayed by the German social theorists Karl Marx and Friedrich Engels in the mid-nineteenth century; their work is conventionally viewed as a "watershed" (Rejai, 1973: 554) in the term's evolution. Pejorative usage had been widespread in German Europe following Napoleon's reference to the ideologues as "dangerous dreamers" in his Erfurt address of 1808. Goethe, the oracle of German letters, identified *ideology* with fantasy and so helped establish the term's range of denotation in central Europe (Kennedy, 1979: 364). Marx was apparently familiar only with the fourth volume of Tracy's *Elemens d'idéologie*, which was a "classic statement of liberal economic theory" (Kennedy, 1979: 366); it is therefore possible that he specifically identified the word with the economic theory that he considered a mere rationalization for capitalist exploitation.

The decisive work for the Marxist tradition of usage is Marx's and Engels' *German Ideology* (1845–46), an attack on the illusions of German idealism. There Marx and Engels display their understanding of *ideology*—an adjunct of their doctrine of HISTORICAL MATERIALISM—as "false" or "illusory" consciousness as opposed to truth. *Ideology* is associated with idealist "speculation" and "empty talk about consciousness" and is juxtaposed to "real, positive science" and "real knowledge" (Marx and Engels, [1845–46] 1972: 150). The basic distinction is between objective knowledge and subjective, self-serving ideology (Lichtheim, 1964–65: 176; Halpern, 1960: 131). *Consciousness* is understood as a social product, and *ideology* means "the whole system of religion, morality, and law, whereby a ruling class 'justifies' and upholds the social system dictated by its interests" (Halpern, 1960: 148; cf. Marx and Engels, [1845–46] 1972: 148–49). Much later, in a letter of 1893, Engels introduced the expression *false consciousness* as a synonym for *ideology* (Lichtheim, 1964–65: 173). But Marx and Engels did not regard the implications of their own thought as "ideological"—that is, time-bound to the particular social circumstances in which it was produced—an inconsistency that has often been remarked (for example, Roucek, 1944: 483; Seliger, 1977).

At the end of the nineteenth century Marxism began to influence the social science disciplines, especially sociology and political science, and the term *ideology* was firmly established in the vocabulary of social theory (Roucek, 1944: 483–88). In the 1940s, via thinkers such as Max Weber, Gaetano Mosca, Vilfredo Pareto, Georges Sorel (some of whom did not actually employ the term *ideology*), and especially Karl Mannheim (1936)—popularizer of the idea of "sociology of knowledge" (i.e., the study of the "relationship between knowledge and [material] existence" [Mannheim, 1936: 264])—the concept passed into the conceptual arsenal of non-Marxist historians (for instance, Roucek, 1944; Burks, 1949). Today the idea of ideology is widely regarded as "central to historical—as to all social—understanding" (Leff, 1971: 142). The appeal of the concept to historians, especially in forms derived from Mannheim's "sociology of knowledge," is not difficult to appreciate. Mannheim held that "All knowledge is relational; and hence knowledge is itself to be understood in terms of the relation of the possessor of knowledge to the particular historical and social context in which he is thinking" (Roucek, 1944: 487). This attitude nicely complements the concepts of ANACHRONISM and HISTORISM, which are basic to the outlook of modern historiography.

Following sociological usage—particularly that of Mannheim—historians in the late 1940s and 1950s adopted the word as a broad synonym for "belief system" or "philosophy of life," that is, "any pattern of symbols and ideas which 'serve the purpose of stabilizing the existing social reality' " (Burks, 1949: 183, 185). More importantly, since 1945 the concept of ideology has become a fundamental analytical tool in INTELLECTUAL HISTORY and SOCIAL HISTORY, especially in connection with efforts to transform traditional history of ideas into a "social history of ideas" (Gay, 1964: x), where the dominant trend has been based on the "notion that ideas are determined by social environment" (Kelly, 1969: 6)—although the idea that ideas are always rigid, direct reflections of specific class interests is regarded as "highly oversimplified" (Burks, 1949: 189). In particular, the historical study of modern political doctrines, such as LIBERALISM (e.g., Sheehan, 1978), is fundamentally conditioned by the assumption that political creeds are expressions of specific social circumstances and group economic interests.

References

Burks, Richard V. 1949. "A Conception of Ideology for Historians." *JHI* 10: 183–98. Burks understands *ideology* as any broad belief system; his essay is an amalgam of ideas drawn from sociology of knowledge and attitudes typical of the cold war.

Gay, Peter. 1964. *The Party of Humanity: Essays in the French Enlightenment*. New York.

Halpern, Ben. 1960. " 'Myth' and 'Ideology' in Modern Usage." *HT* 1: 129–49. The emphasis in this work is on the thought of Sorel and Mannheim.

Kelly, George Armstrong. 1969. *Idealism, Politics, and History: Sources of Hegelian Thought*. Cambridge.

Kennedy, Emmet. 1979. " 'Ideology' from Destutt de Tracy to Marx." *JHI* 40: 353–68. This is a good survey of the early history of the word and concept.

Leff, Gordon. 1971. *History and Social Theory*. Garden City, N.Y. Part two is an attack on the Marxian concept.

Lichtheim, George. 1964–65. "The Concept of Ideology." *HT* 4: 164–95. This important analysis by a well-known authority on Marxism was reprinted in Lichtheim's *Concept of Ideology and Other Essays* (New York, 1967).

Mannheim, Karl. 1936. *Ideology and Utopia: An Introduction to the Sociology of Knowledge*. New York. This classic study was originally published in German in 1929.

Marx, Karl, and Engels, Friedrich. [1845–46] 1972. "From *The German Ideology*." In Stern: 147–58.

Rejai, Mostafa. 1973. "Ideology." *DHI* 2: 552–59. This entry includes a bibliography.

Roucek, Joseph S. 1944. "A History of the Concept of Ideology." *JHI* 5: 479–88. This is a convenient summary of the contributions of early twentieth-century social scientists, especially those of Pareto and Mannheim.

Seliger, Martin. 1977. *The Marxist Conception of Ideology: A Critical Essay*. Cambridge. This comprehensive study of the history of the concept, written from a non-Marxist point of view, is especially valuable as a source of bibliography.

Sheehan, James. 1978. *German Liberalism in the Nineteenth Century*. Chicago.

Stein, Jay W. 1956. "Beginnings of 'Ideology'." *South Atlantic Quarterly* 53: 163–70. Stein's work complements Kennedy's (1979).

Sources of Additional Information

For general bibliography see, in addition to Seliger (1977) and Rejai (1973), Edward Shils and Harry M. Johnson, "Ideology," *IESS* 7: 66–85; Hans-Joachim Lieber and Hellmuth G. Bütow, "Ideology," *MCWS* 4: 199–211; David Braybrooke, "Ideology," *EP* 4: 124–27; and U. Dierse, "Ideologie," *HWP* 4: 158–86. Norman Birnbaum's "Sociological Study of Ideology (1940–60)," *Current Sociology* 9 (1960): 91–117, is an important review article, and Robin Blackburn, ed., *Ideology in Social Science: Readings in Critical Social Theory* (New York, 1972), is a handy anthology. Hans Barth's *Wahrheit und Ideologie*, 2d ed. (Zurich, 1961), originally published in 1945, is a widely cited general study. Colwyn Williamson, "Ideology and the Problem of Knowledge," *Inquiry* 10 (Summer 1967): 121–38, contains fresh ideas and concise definitions. On Marx, see Bhikhu Parekh, *Marx's Theory of Ideology* (Baltimore, 1982). The anthropologist Clifford Geertz has influenced some historians through his "Ideology as a Cultural System" in Clifford Geertz, *The Interpretation of Cultures: Selected Essays* (New York, 1973): 193–233. For historical perspectives on Karl Mannheim and the idea of "sociology of knowledge" see H. Stuart Hughes, *Consciousness and Society: The Reorientation of European Social Thought, 1890–1930* (New York, 1958), especially pp. 418–27, and William M. Johnston, *The Austrian Mind: An Intellectual and Social History, 1848–1938* (Berkeley, Calif., 1973), pp. 375–79. Among the many important historical works published since 1945 that broadly employ the notion of ideology as a conceptual framework, see C. Vann Woodward, *The Strange Career of Jim Crow* (New York, 1955), and Fritz Stern, *The Politics of Cultural Despair: A Study in the Rise of the Germanic Ideology* (Berkeley, Calif., 1961).

IMAGINATION. 1. The mental faculty that enables historians to establish relationships between items of historical EVIDENCE, so as to construct a meaningful picture of the PAST. 2. The capacity to attain a sympathetic understanding of past events and situations, apart from the values and assumptions of one's own time. 3. The ability to use language to create a vivid picture of the past. 4. The capacity to approach evidence about the past in fresh, original ways.

The word *imagination* is currently used in a variety of senses by literary theorists, art critics, philosophers, and historians. In history the term's possible meanings closely parallel those of the word STYLE. Aesthetic criticism presently invokes the term so regularly and unreflectively that it often degenerates to the level of cliché. It is less common in historiography, where conventional usage is nevertheless equally loose, confusing, or banal. Those who deny that history can be an exact science, for example, tend to employ the term to evoke the "commonplace" that "*all* historical accounts are 'artistic' in some way" (White, [1975] 1978: 107). Moreover, historians frequently mix meanings of the term or link it vaguely to an intuitive "sixth sense" or "gift" by virtue of which facts are "given life" (Curtis, 1970: 274; Trevor-Roper, 1958: 357; Hughes, 1960: 46). Such usage unnecessarily opposes the idea of imagination to traditions of rigorous scholarship and method.

Despite the word's broad range of meanings, it is possible to identify a "family likeness" that makes use of the concept of "imagination" valid and useful (Manser, 1967: 138). Before the nineteenth century history was normally considered a branch of literature, and its "fictive" nature was widely acknowledged (White, [1976] 1978: 123). (Here *fiction* implies not fantasy but the "action of fashioning or imitating," where *imagination* is understood as "that faculty of the mind by which are formed images or concepts of external objects not present to the senses, and their relations" [*OED*].) Most early-modern theorists acknowledged the "inevitability of a recourse to fictive techniques in the *representation* of real events" (White, [1976] 1978: 123), and this was often a source of SKEPTICISM regarding the cognitive worth of historical writing.

Around 1800 Immanuel Kant's reflections on the faculty of imagination began to influence German idealists, notably Wilhelm von Humboldt (1767–1835) who understood *imagination* as an aspect of cognition—a constructive mental activity that amounts to more than mere fancy. In his essay "On the Historian's Task" Humboldt observed that the

> truth of any event is predicated on the addition . . . of [the] invisible part of every fact, and it is this part, therefore, which the historian has to add. Regarded in this way, he does become active, even creative—not by bringing forth what does not have existence, but in giving shape by his own powers to that which by mere intuition he could not have perceived as it really was. Differently from the poet, but in a way similar to him, he must work the collected fragments into a whole. . . . if the historian . . . can only reveal the truth of an event by presentation, by filling in and connecting the disjointed fragments of direct observation, he can do so, like the poet, only through his imagination. The crucial difference [between poet and historian] . . . lies in the fact that the historian subordinates his imagination to experience and the investigation of reality. In this subordination, the imagination does not act as pure fantasy and is, therefore, more properly called the intuitive faculty or connective ability. ([1821] 1967: 58–59)

In the early and mid-nineteenth century, however, it became customary for historians to distinguish sharply fact from fiction and to regard imagination as an obstacle to the representation of past reality. Symptomatic was the attitude of Leopold von Ranke (1795–1886), who juxtaposed historical fiction and history proper:

> The writing of history cannot be expected to possess the same free development of its subject which, in theory at least, is expected in a work of literature. . . . The

strict presentation of the facts, contingent and unattractive though they may be, is
undoubtedly the supreme law. ([1824] 1972: 57)

After comparing history and the historical novel, Ranke found that "truth was
more interesting and beautiful than . . . romance. I turned away from it and
resolved to avoid all invention and imagination in my works and to stick to
facts" (quoted in Gooch, [1913] 1959: 74; also Weinstein, 1976: 264). On the
assumptions of nineteenth-century historical REALISM, the historian's task was
not "creative"; instead the scholar was expected to discover the "untold story"
of the past (Mink, 1978: 134–35), to uncover the already-existing links that
presumably existed between the facts. Speculation about a possible historical—
or "veracious"—imagination was left to aesthetes and writers of fiction, such
as George Eliot (Deegan, 1972: 25).

To be sure, Humboldt's idea of imagination as "connective ability" never
disappeared entirely. For example, Albert Bushnell Hart (1910: 246), an early
president of the American Historical Association, acknowledged the "impotence
of facts taken by themselves" and pointed to the "essential" role of imagination
in history, which he understood as the "power to assemble the dry bones [of
facts] and make them live." But Hart's ideas were presented as a kind of sermon,
couched in such romantic and imprecise terms that it may have alienated more
historians than it converted. Moreover, Hart conflated meaning levels when he
linked the practical matter of connecting facts with the mysterious "power" to
make facts "live."

Generally, late-nineteenth- and early-twentieth-century historians used *imagination* in two (sometimes overlapping) senses, the one positive, the other sometimes positive but often pejorative. The first usage related to the ability to
understand or *comprehend* the nature of the past, the second to the historian's
ability to *represent* or *communicate* that understanding to his readers. In the first,
or positive, sense the word was linked to the feeling for ANACHRONISM that had
come to be considered essential in the historian's attitude toward the past. Here,
imagination designated the sympathy by which the scholar, steeped in records
of a past period, attained an intimate feeling for that era in terms of its own
unique values and assumptions, apart from the values of his own time. This first
use is illustrated in Hart's statement (1910: 239) that a "little imagination helps
one to sympathize with the great men of the past; to understand the limitations
of their surroundings." It is in this sense that the idea is perhaps still most widely
understood by historians and by some philosophers as well (e.g., Hughes, 1964:
97; Wedgwood, 1960: 68; Curtis, 1970: 274; Walsh, [1951] 1960: 105–6).

The second usage—also current today—involved the historian's "art" as a
literary craftsman, that is, his ability to conjure through words a sense of im-
mediacy with the past, to *represent* the past verbally and make it "live." This
is the notion invoked by the nineteenth-century writer Macaulay ([1828] 1972:
72), who believed that the "perfect historian must possess an imagination sufficiently powerful to make his narrative affecting and picturesque." Here *imag-*

ination is essentially non-cognitive and is allied with one meaning of the notion of STYLE—that is, the ability to use language (diction, metaphor, and so on) to evoke a vivid feeling for the period and events in question, to craft consciously a picture, or "image," of the past for a reading audience (e.g., Wedgwood, 1960: 88). Yet *imagination* used in this way can have a pejorative as well as a positive connotation. Even Macaulay, an important advocate of "history as literature," distrusted *imagination* in this sense, warning that the historian "must control it so absolutely as to content himself with the materials which he finds, and to refrain from supplying deficiencies by additions of his own" ([1828] 1972: 72–73).

In the later nineteenth century the idea of imagination in the sense of "good writing" had increasingly come to mean mere "coloring" or "ornamentation" and was widely considered a hindrance to genuine "scientific" historical understanding. At best, it was something to be held under close rein. Underlying this caution was the "positivistic" assumption that "historical knowledge precedes rhetorical art" (Henderson, 1974: xvii), that is, that "art" is something added to history after the "facts" have been established.

A third level of meaning also became attached to the word in the early twentieth century and is now encountered with fair frequency: the ability to approach and interpret evidence about the past in innovative, original ways (e.g., Stannard, 1980: 155).

Recently, the notion of imagination in the Humboldtian sense of "connective ability" has enjoyed a revival, especially among representatives of the tradition of historical IDEALISM. This revival is to some degree also related to the rise of "sociology of knowledge" (see IDEOLOGY), which encourages the idea that "the only available reality [to anyone, not merely the historian or the novelist] is an imaginative construct" (Weinstein, 1976: 270). Current interest derives primarily from the work of the British philosopher R. G. Collingwood ([1946] 1956), who fashioned an explicit concept of the "historical imagination" in the 1930s and 1940s.

Collingwood believed that "the idea of history itself" was "the idea of an imaginary picture of the past. That is, in Cartesian language, innate; in Kantian language, *a priori*. It is not a chance product of psychological causes; it is an idea which every man possesses as part of the furniture of his mind." He introduced the notion of "historical construction," which he defined in terms of interpolation: "The historian's authorities tell him of this or that phase in a process whose intermediate phases they leave undescribed; he then interpolates [i.e., inserts] these phases for himself . . . relying on his own powers and constituting himself his own authority" (Collingwood, 1946: 237, 248). This is what Collingwood called "*a priori* imagination"; it is an activity that, "bridging the gaps between what our authorities tell us, gives the historical narrative or description its continuity" (pp. 240–41). Macaulay, according to Collingwood,

> underestimate[d] the part played by the historical imagination, which is properly not ornamental but structural. Without it the historian would have no narrative to

> adorn. . . . it is this [imagination] which, operating not capriciously as fancy but in its *a priori* form, does the entire work of historical construction. (p. 241)

The "constructive imagination" creates a "web of imaginative construction" that "so far from relying for its validity upon the support of given facts . . . actually serves as the touchstone by which we decide whether alleged facts are genuine"; it is not fanciful and insubstantial but something "solid and powerful" (pp. 242, 244).

Collingwood noted similarities and differences between this type of imagination and the kind of imagination employed by the novelist:

> As works of imagination, the historian's work and the novelist's do not differ. Where they do differ is that the historian's picture is meant to be true. The novelist has a single task only: to construct a coherent picture, one that makes sense. The historian has a double task: he has both to do this, and to construct a picture of things as they really were and of events as they really happened. (p. 246)

In the most important sense, this means that the

> historian's picture stands in a peculiar relation to something called evidence. The only way in which the historian or anyone else can judge, even tentatively, of its truth is by considering this relation; and, in practice, what we mean by asking whether an historical statement is true is whether it can be justified by an appeal to the evidence. (p. 246)

Collingwood's commentators have complained that his description of the historical imagination was too subjective (Weinstein, 1976: 265), was "rambling and frequently vague" (D. White, 1972: 17), was logically flawed (Donagan, 1962: 211), or that he substantially revised his position in later years (Mink, 1969: 183–86). Nevertheless, his idea of the "constructive imagination" in history continues to exert influence. This is reflected, at least in part, in the work of philosophers who uphold the theory of historical knowledge known as CON-STRUCTIONISM, although these theorists have largely abandoned use of the term *imagination*. Collingwood's influence is apparent, as well, in the work of historians who link *imagination* to the formulation of explanatory hypotheses in history and explanation in general (Sewell, 1967: 217; Hughes, 1960: 46; Lewis, 1976) or to the notion that the historian's reconstruction of the past involves "sympathetic" or "imaginative re-enactment" (Beer, 1963–64: 22–23; Walzer, 1963–64: 76–79). A contemporary British historian, H. R. Trevor-Roper (1981: 356, 360–61), recently used the term in a related way to refer to the historian's capacity to appreciate the possibility of unrealized alternative outcomes in past events. Collingwood's influence is also evident in the elaborate theory of the nineteenth-century European historical imagination suggested by Hayden White (1972; 1973; [1976] 1978; [1975] 1978). Together with Collingwood's study, White's *Metahistory* (1973) is to date the most important sustained effort to deal with the concept of the historical imagination. White, however, does not understand the power of "figuration" in metaphysical, Kantian terms as part of the innate "furniture of the mind"; rather, he maintains that the "constructive" historical imagination is a more or less subliminal reflection of the conventions of figurative language and sociocultural conditioning. His view, inspired also by work in the fields of linguistics and poetics, involves the "comprehension of the ways that traditionally provided modes of story telling function to inform us of the ways that our own culture can provide a host of different meanings for the same set of events" (D. White, 1972: 19). Here, *imagination* is conceived as an aspect of the "linguistic determinism to which the conventional narrative historian remains enslaved" (H. White, [1975] 1978: 117). For a more complete discussion of White's ideas, see INTERPRETATION.

References

Beer, Samuel H. 1963–64. "Causal Explanation and Imaginative Re-Enactment." *HT* 3: 6–29.

Collingwood, R. G. [1946] 1956. *The Idea of History*. Oxford.

Curtis, L. P., Jr. 1970. "Of Images and Imagination in History." In L. P. Curtis, Jr., *The Historian's Workshop*. New York: 245–76.

Deegan, Thomas. 1972. "George Eliot's Novels of the Historical Imagination." *Clio* 1: 21–33. Deegan maintains that Eliot defined "a veracious imagination in historical picturing" by which she meant "the working out in detail of the various steps by which a political or social change was reached, using all extant evidence and supplying deficiencies by careful analogical creation" (p. 25).

Donagan, Alan. 1962. *The Later Philosophy of R. G. Collingwood*. Oxford. Donagan calls Collingwood's notion of an *a priori* historical imagination "incredible" (p. 211).

Gooch, G. P. [1913] 1959. *History and Historians in the Nineteenth Century*. Boston.

Hart, Albert Bushnell. 1910. "Imagination in History." *AHR* 15: 227–51. Hart refers to *imagination* as a "high quality of the mind," a "noble . . . quality," and a "mysterious quality of mind" (pp. 237–238).

Henderson, Harry B. III. 1974. *Versions of the Past: The Historical Imagination in American Fiction*. New York. Henderson assumes that "history is itself a form of consciousness, an 'imaginative ordering' " (p. ix). He defines two broad types of *historical imagination* in nineteenth-century American historiography, the "progressive" and the "holist."

Hughes, H. Stuart. 1960. "The Historian and the Social Scientist." *AHR* 66: 20–46.

———. 1964. *History as Art and as Science: Twin Vistas on the Past*. New York. Hughes defines *historical imagination* as the "art . . . of making [the past] fully intelligible to us by enabling us to enter . . . into the minds and passions of people who . . . seem very different from us" (p. 97).

Humboldt, Wilhelm von. [1821] 1967. "On the Historian's Task." *HT* 6: 57–71.

Lewis, Merrill. 1976. "Language, Literature, Rhetoric, and the Shaping of the Historical Imagination of Frederick Jackson Turner." *Pacific Historical Review* 45: 399–424.

Macaulay, Thomas Babington. [1828] 1972. "History." In Stern: 72–89.

Manser, A. R. 1967. "Imagination." *EP* 4: 136–39. This entry includes a brief bibliography.

Mink, Louis O. 1969. *Mind, History, and Dialectic: The Philosophy of R. G. Colling-wood*. Bloomington, Ind.

————. 1978. "Narrative Form as a Cognitive Instrument." In Canary and Kozicki: 129–49.

Ranke, Leopold von. [1824] 1972. Preface to *Histories of the Latin and Germanic Nations from 1494–1514*. In Stern: 55–58.

Sewell, William H., Jr. 1967. "Marc Bloch and the Logic of Comparative History." *HT* 6: 208–18.

Stannard, David E. 1980. *Shrinking History: On Freud and the Failure of Psychohistory*. New York.

Trevor-Roper, Hugh. 1958. "Historical Imagination." *The Listener* 59 (Feb. 27, 1958): 357–58.

————. 1981. "History and Imagination." In Hugh Lloyd-Jones, Valerie Pearl, and Blair Worden, eds., *History and Imagination: Essays in Honour of H. R. Trevor-Roper*. London: 356–69. For Trevor-Roper, *imagination* seems related to COUNTERFACTUAL ANALYSIS: the capacity to visualize unrealized potentialities (p. 363).

Walsh, W. H. [1951] 1960. *Philosophy of History: An Introduction*. New York.

Walzer, Michael. 1963–64. "Puritanism as a Revolutionary Ideology." *HT* 3: 59–90.

Wedgwood, C. V. 1960. *Truth and Opinion: Historical Essays*. New York.

Weinstein, Mark A. 1976. "The Creative Imagination in Fiction and History." *Genre* 9: 263–77. This valuable survey argues that "we can reasonably maintain no more than that there are uncertain differences of degree between the two disciplines [i.e., fiction and history]: the historian is more limited by whatever evidence is available, while the historical novelist is more free to speculate over dark areas." (p. 267). It contains important bibliographical information in footnotes.

White, David A. 1972. "Imagination and Description: Collingwood and the Historical Consciousness." *Clio* 1, no. 2: 14–28.

White, Hayden. 1972. "The Structure of Historical Narrative." *Clio* 1, no. 3: 5–20.

————. 1973. *Metahistory: The Historical Imagination in Nineteenth-Century Europe*. Baltimore.

————. [1975] 1978. "Historicism, History, and the Figurative Imagination." In Hayden White, *Tropics of Discourse: Essays in Cultural Criticism*. Baltimore: 101–20.

————. [1976] 1978. "The Fictions of Factual Representation." In Hayden White, *Tropics of Discourse: Essays in Cultural Criticism*. Baltimore: 121–34.

Sources of Additional Information

See also STYLE; UNDERSTANDING. Manser (1967) provides a general introduction with a brief bibliography of works in philosophy. Even more helpful as a starting point is A.S.P. Woodhouse's "Imagination" in the *Princeton Encyclopedia of Poetry and Poetics* (Princeton, N.J., 1974), pp. 370–76. There are useful references in Canary and Kozicki: 151–58 and James R. Bennett et al., "History as Art: An Annotated Checklist of Criticism," *Style* 13 (Winter 1979): 5–36. The literature on Collingwood appears in Michael Krausz, ed., *Critical Essays on the Philosophy of R. G. Collingwood* (Oxford, 1972), pp. 327–48. Gordon Leff's *History and Social Theory* (Garden City, N.Y., 1971), pp. 102–6, includes a short discussion of "historical imagination." For a stimulating discussion of the rise of a theoretical distinction between *fantasy* and *imagination* at the turn of the nineteenth century, see M. H. Abrams, *The Mirror and the Lamp: Romantic Theory and the Critical Tradition* (Oxford, 1953). Also noteworthy are Harold Toliver,

Animate Illusions: Explorations in Narrative Structure (Lincoln, Neb., 1974), and Cushing Strout, *The Veracious Imagination: Essays on American History, Literature, and Biography* (Middletown, Conn., 1981). The periodicals *Clio* and *History and Theory* often publish relevant essays.

IMPERIALISM. The expansion of a state beyond its own frontiers with the aim of dominating other states or societies.

The word *imperialism*—coined in early-nineteenth-century France as a label for the policies of Napoleon I—has acquired various popular and technical meanings and has spawned a broad range of scholarly theories in the twentieth century (Mommsen, 1980; Baumgart, 1982). Its meaning in English has changed at least twelve times (Koebner and Schmidt, 1964: xiii). The term's enormous popularity as a political slogan complicates matters and impinges upon scholarly use. A survey conducted in 1960 concluded that the expression was employed, worldwide, in "at least one in every ten political broadcasts" (pp. xiii; xviii).

Although derived from the ancient Latin *imperator* (military commander) and *imperium* (empire), the term dates only from the 1840s. Thus, its use to describe the policies of pre-modern governments (e.g., Gruen, 1970; Lichtheim, 1971: 7; Brunt, 1964–65) is, strictly speaking, anachronistic. The concept of *imperium* is nevertheless an old and persistent idea in western history, one that survived the collapse of Rome to occur in various guises in the medieval and modern periods (Folz, [1953] 1969). To insist that *imperialism* may legitimately be used only to refer to the nineteenth century and subsequent periods would therefore be needlessly pedantic (Baumgart, 1982: 1–2).

The word arose to serve specific political needs; as early as 1832 the German poet Heine used the word *imperialists* to refer to Napoleon's admirers (Ladendorf, [1906] 1968: 133). Initially, there was no direct association with ancient Rome (Koebner and Schmidt, 1964: xix). The French *imperialisme*, coined in the 1840s, referred to the regime of Napoleon I and to the ambitions of Napoleon's nephew Louis Bonaparte (pp. 1–26). Following Louis Bonaparte's assumption of the title "Napoleon III" in 1852, the term was popularized by English journalists as a synonym for French *despotism*; the term first denoted Napoleon III's domestic policy, which was represented as alien to British liberty. The association with Napoleonic France dominated English usage until the fall of the Second French Empire in 1870. An important secondary development, however, was Whig use of the term to condemn Conservative leader Benjamin Disraeli's policies as "alien and undemocratic" (p. 164).

In the late 1850s the term began to acquire a different range of meanings, as a positive designation for the relationship between Britain and her colonies and policies designed to strengthen those ties (p. xxiv). This usage would gradually give rise to the broad meaning most commonly associated with the word today—a relationship of dominance of one government over another government or people.

The word entered the vocabulary of international relations in the 1880s and 1890s, when various European governments struggled to secure colonies and spheres of influence around the world, especially in Asia and Africa (Langer, [1931] 1950; [1935] 1950); *imperialism* was the term chosen by writers and politicians to refer to this competitive expansionism. At the turn of the century European theorists constructed a series of classic explanations of this burst of activity; these theories—all now considered more or less ethnocentric, simplistic, and outdated in specific detail—established the broad framework of discourse until the present.

Three basic approaches stand out as significant; in their original form, all sought to isolate a single (or at least "decisive") cause underlying European expansion. First, the predominantly *political* explanations accounted for expansion in terms of the natural desire of powerful governments to increase their dominion at the expense of weaker nations. This theory was widely used before the end of World War I, when imperialism was often considered positive evidence of a nation's vigor (e.g., Friedjung, 1919–22). The political approach could be cast in various ways, for example, in combination with "Social Darwinian" assumptions that viewed the world in terms of "natural" struggle between nations or in league with theories of NATIONALISM created in the 1920s and 1930s. Predominantly political theories declined in popularity at the expense of "economic" theories during the mid-twentieth century (see below) but have recently enjoyed new favor when combined with socioeconomic explanations (Mommsen, 1980: 143). It is in fact arguable that, over the years, political explanations have remained the most popular theoretical type among non-Marxist scholars (for instance, Hayes, 1941; Langer, 1935; Robinson and Gallagher, 1961; Fieldhouse, 1973; Baumgart, 1982).

A second major family of interpretations is *economic*. The key work here is unquestionably John Atkinson Hobson's enormously influential *Imperialism* (1902). Hobson, a British reform liberal whose interpretation grew from experience as a correspondent in the South African Boer War, maintained that British "imperialism" was directly linked to overseas investments. Using statistics, he sought to prove that the hidden impulse behind expansion was the quest of private interests for new markets overseas, after investment opportunities at home had allegedly been exhausted. Hobson did not, however, tie imperialism directly to the economic system of capitalism, as the Marxists would later do. Rather, he attributed it to Britain's traditional social and political system, which permitted the aristocracies of birth and wealth to use government as an instrument of their own selfish economic interests (Mommsen, 1980: 16).

Hobson's ideas were generalized beyond the British case by Marxist theorists. Marx himself did not construct an explicit theory, having died (in 1883) before theoretical interest in "imperialism" became fashionable. There are only hints in this direction in the work of Marx's partner Engels. Both revolutionists, however, generally supported European expansion and overseas domination in a tactical sense on grounds that it promoted world-wide economic modernization and so prepared the way for socialism.

The pioneer in Marxist theory was the Austrian Rudolf Hilferding (1910) who—like subsequent Marxists—handled the problem by tailoring Hobson's ideas to the doctrine of HISTORICAL MATERIALISM and depicting imperialism as a necessary stage in the development of world CAPITALISM. Hilferding maintained that European expansionism was an extension of monopoly capitalism, which was, in turn, a logical phase in the development of capitalism. The hidden force behind the process was "finance capital," that is, the big European banks.

From a polemical standpoint, Lenin's *Imperialism, the Highest Stage of Capitalism* (1916) is much more famous than Hilferding's book; it became the sacred work of the Marxist-Leninist position on imperialism. From a scientific point of view, however, Lenin's work is essentially derivative, based mainly on the ideas of Hilferding, Hobson, and Rosa Luxemburg (Mommsen, 1980: 47). Lenin's most original contribution was the notion that World War I, the end product of imperialist rivalries, would lead to the collapse of capitalism and the advent of world socialism. Supplemented by the work of Stalin and theorists of the Third International, who emphasized the use of nationalist movements in colonial areas to overthrow capitalism, Lenin's tract is still the basis of Soviet interpretation. Most non-communist scholars contest the economic arguments of Hobson, Hilferding, and Lenin alike on grounds that they are simplistic, reductionist, distorted, or inaccurate (for example, Langer, 1935; Mommsen, 1980: 18, 148; Baumgart, 1982).

A third important interpretive orientation is *sociological*. The classic study here—once again considered outdated in its specific arguments—is by the Austrian Joseph Schumpeter ([1919] 1951). Schumpeter, an economist, did not entirely discount the importance of economic motives (indeed, economic circumstances were seldom completely overlooked in any of the original theories). In Schumpeter's view, however, the decisive factor was the "atavistic" behavior of the European ruling classes who, he maintained, were socially conditioned toward aggressive behavior and war.

Although Schumpeter's nebulous use of the notion of social atavism is now generally rejected as far-fetched and unempirical, his analysis is considered important insofar as it underscored the significance of social-psychological factors; "in this respect he prepared the way for a modern sociological theory which would concentrate on showing how particular groups and classes within capitalist or non-capitalist systems were interested in imperialist expansion" (Mommsen, 1980: 27–28). The belief that imperialism was a tool used by traditional ruling castes to maintain their dominance in European societies is a "functional" interpretation that has recently gained wide acceptance—notably among some West German scholars (e.g., Wehler, 1970; 1972).

The present tendency among historians is to avoid monocausal or "one-dimensional" explanations in favor of an eclectic approach emphasizing combinations of political, economic, and social arguments. Among the more important recent developments is the introduction of the idea of "informal imperialism"— that is, the idea that the nineteenth-century European states (especially Britain) were, even during the early-nineteenth-century heyday of "free trade," involved in the indirect extension of their power, which, in some cases, even made the need for direct domination unnecessary (Robinson and Gallagher, 1953). Although criticized by some scholars as ill-defined (e.g., Baumgart, 1982: 5–7), Mommsen calls the idea of informal imperialism

> the most significant innovation in the development of Western theories of imperialism. . . . Generally speaking, most non-Marxist theoreticians admit nowadays that dependency of an imperialist sort may well result from the most varied kinds of informal influence, especially of an economic nature. (1980: 86)

A second recent tendency is to develop "peripheral" explanations, that is, theories that explain expansionism in terms of actions in the colonial areas themselves rather than in the European capitals, where the classical theories had focused their attention (p. 100). Key studies here are Robinson and Gallagher (1962) and Fieldhouse (1973).

References

Baumgart, Winfried. 1982. *Imperialism: The Idea and Reality of British and French Colonial Expansion, 1880–1914.* Oxford. Baumgart focuses on Britain and France, but the work is important for German imperialism as well; it includes a survey and critique of major theories and a lengthy bibliography. It was originally published in German in 1975.

Brunt, P. A. 1964–65. "Reflections on British and Roman Imperialism." *CSSH* 7: 267–88.

Fieldhouse, David K. 1973. *Economics and Empire, 1830–1914.* London.

Folz, Robert. [1953] 1969. *The Concept of Empire in Western Europe from the Fifth to the Fourteenth Century.* London.

Friedjung, Heinrich. 1919–22. *Das Zeitalter des Imperialismus 1884–1914.* 3 vols. Berlin. This work helped popularize the concept in non-Marxist circles in central Europe.

Gruen, Erich S., ed. 1970. *Imperialism in the Roman Republic.* New York. This is an anthology of writings on Roman expansionism, with annotated bibliography.

Hayes, Carlton J. H. 1941. *A Generation of Materialism.* New York.

Hilferding, Rudolf. 1910. *Das Finanzkapital.* Vienna.

Hobson, J. A. 1902. *Imperialism, A Study.* London. This most influential book ever written on the subject is "now out of date in almost all its details" (Mommsen, 1980: 11).

Koebner, Richard, and Helmut Dan Schmidt. 1964. *Imperialism: The Story and Significance of a Political Word, 1840–1960.* Cambridge. This painstaking study concentrates on the term's history as a political slogan and only secondarily as a scholarly concept.

Ladendorf, Otto. [1906] 1968. *Historisches Schlagwörterbuch.* Hildesheim.

Langer, William L. 1935. "A Critique of Imperialism." *Foreign Affairs* 14 (Oct.): 102–119. This is a famous critique of the economic orientation.

————. [1931] 1950. *European Alliances and Alignments, 1871–1890*. New York. To-
    gether with the following title, this is the standard diplomatic history of the "age
    of imperialism."
————. [1935] 1950. *The Diplomacy of Imperialism*. New York. See especially the
    "Bibliographical Note" in chapter three, pp. 96–100A.
Lichtheim, George. 1971. *Imperialism*. New York. Lichtheim's assertion that "The very
    term 'imperialism' nowadays carries unflattering connotations, but it did not do
    so for the ruling classes of the Roman empire" (p. 7) is a striking instance of
    semantic anachronism.
Mommsen, Wolfgang J. 1980. *Theories of Imperialism*. New York. This invaluable
    survey was originally published in German in 1977.
Robinson, Ronald, and Gallagher, John. 1953. "The Imperialism of Free Trade." *Eco-
    nomic History Review*, 2d series, 6: 1–25.
————. 1962. "The Partition of Africa." In the *New Cambridge Modern History* 11
    (1962): 593–640.
Robinson, Ronald, and Gallagher, John, with Alice Denny. 1961. *Africa and the Vic-
    torians: The Official Mind of Imperialism*. London.
Schumpeter, Joseph. [1919] 1951. *Imperialism*. New York.
Wehler, Hans-Ulrich. 1970. *Bismarck und der Imperialismus*. Cologne.
————. 1972. *Der Imperialismus*. Cologne.

Sources of Additional Information

The literature is overwhelming; "one gains the impression that there are more people
who have written on imperialism than people who have acted on it or fought for it"
(Baumgart, 1982: 8). A basic guide is Hans-Ulrich Wehler, *Bibliographie zum Imperialismus* (Göttingen, 1977). Berding: 308–16 also contains a substantial selection of titles.
Helmut Dan Schmidt and Wolfgang J. Mommsen, "Imperialism," *MCWS* 4: 211–29,
includes another useful list of sources. The importance of Mommsen (1980) and Baumgart
(1982) as review essays must be strongly underscored. See, as well, Charles Reynolds,
Modes of Imperialism (New York, 1981), and Norman Etherington, "Reconsidering
Theories of Imperialism," *HT* 21 (1982): 1–36. A useful anthology is Wm. Roger Louis,
ed., *Imperialism: The Robinson and Gallagher Controversy* (New York, 1976). Of key
importance are the annotated "Bibliographical Notes" that conclude volumes of the
University of Minnesota Press's ten-volume series, "Europe and the World in the Age
of Expansion"—for example, Raymond F. Betts, *The False Dawn: European Imperialism
in the Nineteenth Century* (Minneapolis, 1975). Several anthologies in Heath's "Problems
in World Civilization" and "Problems in Asian Civilization" series are relevant—for
example, Harrison M. Wright, ed., *The "New Imperialism"* (Boston, 1961); all contain
annotated bibliographies. Hannah Arendt's discussion of imperialism in *The Origins of
Totalitarianism* (New York, 1951) is widely cited. Of related interest is Richard Koebner's
Empire (Cambridge, 1961). For Marx's views see Shlomo Avineri, ed., *Karl Marx on
Colonialism and Modernization: His Dispatches and Other Writings on China, India,
Mexico, the Middle East and North Africa* (Garden City, N.Y., 1968). On the relationship
between modern technology and imperialism see Daniel R. Headrick, *The Tools of Empire:
Technology and European Imperialism in the Nineteenth Century* (New York, 1981). In
developing the concept of "social imperialism," Hans-Ulrich Wehler has been influenced
by the American historians William Appleman Williams (*The Contours of American*

History [New York, 1961]; *The Tragedy of American Diplomacy* [New York, 1962]) and Walter La Feber (*The New Empire, 1865–1898* [Ithaca, N.Y., 1963]).

INDUSTRIALIZATION. See INDUSTRIAL REVOLUTION.

INDUSTRIAL REVOLUTION, INDUSTRIALIZATION. In the narrow sense, the sudden and profound transformation of methods of commodity production that occurred in Britain between about 1760 and 1850. This change—the result of technological innovation (especially the harnessing of steam power) and increased capital investment—made an unprecedented level of material affluence possible. The pattern has subsequently been repeated in more or less similar fashion in many other parts of the world, and these developments are also typically considered "industrial revolutions" or, more broadly, as facets of a single ongoing "industrial revolution" set in motion by the original changes in Britain. *Industrialization*, a synonym for the broad meaning of Industrial Revolution, refers to the global process of refinement in methods of production and management—apparently self-sustaining.

Industrial Revolution has become a fixture in the vocabulary of contemporary historiography, as well as general modern usage. The term appeared in both French and German before it was adopted in English, but it has since become most widely used in English (Clark, 1953: 14). After a century of research on rapid economic change, scholarly interest in industrialization continues to grow, although many aspects of the subject remain unexplored (Hartwell, 1965: 164).

Arnold Toynbee's *Lectures on the Industrial Revolution* (delivered at Oxford in 1881–82 and published posthumously in 1884) first popularized the term *industrial revolution* in English and rendered it academically acceptable as well. For many years Toynbee (an uncle of the famous twentieth-century British historian of the same name) was credited with coining the expression (Hölscher, 1982: 295). However, a close association between the words *revolution* and *industry* had arisen much earlier in France, where the word REVOLUTION—which traditionally meant "recurrence" or "restoration"—first acquired its modern meaning of "sudden, radical change." The expression *révolution industrielle* was coined sometime in the very early nineteenth century to denote economic changes in France and Britain analogous to the radical political changes of the French Revolution (1789–99); by the 1820s it was in wide use in France and neighboring countries (Bezanson, 1921–22: 345; cf. Hölscher, 1982: 294). In 1837 the French economist Jérôme Adolphe Blanqui (not to be confused with the political activist Auguste Blanqui) was apparently the first to use the term as a concept of historical periodization to refer to the modern European era (Clark, 1953: 10, Hölscher, 1982: 294).

From France the expression spread to Germany where *industrielle Revolution* received its most significant early use in Friedrich Engels' *Condition of the*

Working Class in England in 1844 (1845). According to Engels ([1845] 1958: 9), it was "well known" that technological innovations such as steam power and spinning machines "gave the impetus to the genesis of an industrial revolution" that "had a social as well as an economic aspect since it changed the entire structure of middle-class society." In Engels' view, recent economic changes were "momentous" and "profound" and had given rise to a global PROCESS, the general features of which could best be understood by studying the situation in England, where it had all begun. The most important social result of these developments, Engels believed, was the creation of a new working CLASS, the "industrial proletariat." Thus, Engels laid the foundations for the Marxian concept of industrial revolution, which underpins the doctrine of HISTORICAL MATERIALISM and appears prominently in the first volume of *Capital*, Karl Marx's study of the modern system of production and distribution published in 1867 (Heaton, 1932: 3; Böhme, 1972: 275, 277–78).

Marx stressed the long-term emergence of modern CAPITALISM as a stage of historical development and emphasized technical innovation and the human impact of change rather than the suddenness of economic change itself. This concentration on the revolutionary *social* impact of industrial change has remained a prominent feature of Marxist thinking on the subject (Böhme, 1972: 277–79) and has been the focus of much non-Marxist scholarship as well. Since the late nineteenth century it has been common to designate this broad process—that is, "the industrial revolution, in the specifically technological and social sense, plus its economic consequences"—as "industrialization" (Landes, 1969: 5).

In England the term *industrial revolution* appeared relatively late; the adjective *industrial* itself was a nineteenth-century adaptation of the French *industriel* (*OED*). *Industrialism* was used in the early 1830s by Thomas Carlyle in *Sartor Resartus* to refer to the modern factory system, but *Industrial Revolution* seems not to have appeared until the late 1840s—as, for example, in John Stuart Mill's *Principles of Political Economy* (1848)(Mantoux, [1906] 1961: 25, n. 1). Toynbee's usage in the early 1880s was possibly influenced by Marx's *Capital* (Clark, 1953: 16).

The tradition established by Toynbee's lectures is so powerful that even those who question aspects of his theory of economic change concede that "the phrase 'Industrial Revolution' . . . has become so firmly embedded in common speech that it would be pedantic to offer a substitute" (Ashton, [1948] 1969: 4). Toynbee himself ([1884] 1920: 64) believed that a dramatic transformation of the British economy had occurred around 1760 and that this change—which led by about 1850 to the modern industrial system—was in "essence" the result of a shift from mercantilism (close government regulation of economic life) to *laissez-faire*. Many authorities still cite London's Crystal Palace Exposition of 1851 as the symbolic culmination of the "revolution." For Toynbee, the revolution was a matter of radical contrast between England before 1760, when production was based on hand work or rudimentary mechanization, and the highly mechanized "industrial England of to-day" (Toynbee, [1884] 1920: 7). The old system, he maintained, was suddenly destroyed by the introduction of technological innovations such as the steam engine and the power loom. During the next half-century writers shifted Toynbee's emphasis in various ways but retained his central idea that economic change had been sudden and radical, that is, "revolutionary." This was, for example, true of the most comprehensive early treatment of the subject by the French historian Paul Mantoux. Mantoux ([1906] 1961: 477, 35–36) depicted the *industrial revolution* as "the expansion of industrial forces, the sudden growth and blossoming of seeds which had for many years lain hidden or asleep"; its essence, he believed, was the transition from production by "manufacture" to "the modern factory system" based on machinery.

Some authors, however, began to strain the concept and extend it from the specific British experience to any sharp economic break with the past: for example, the "industrial revolution of the thirteenth century" or the "second industrial revolution" of the late nineteenth century (Landes, 1961: 1).

In the early 1920s there was a strong reaction against such elastic usage, and the very legitimacy of the notion of a sudden "industrial revolution" was called into question (Heaton, 1932: 4). This was not surprising considering the extremely oversimplified thinking the idea had often inspired. According to *Palgraves's Dictionary of Political Economy* (1923: 399), for example, before the late eighteenth century "the general character of industry in England presented broadly the same features as those which it had exhibited during the greater part of the middle ages." In response, a number of leading economic historians—for example, Henri Sée, J. H. Clapham, and John U. Nef—adopted the position that economic change is never sudden and "revolutionary" but is the result of long-term trends that are gradual and "evolutionary." Clapham's three-volume *Economic History of Modern Britain* (1926–38) was written without a single use of the term *industrial revolution* (Böhme, 1972: 279).

Since World War II there has been a decided swing back to the spirit of Engels', Marx's, and Toynbee's notion that economic changes that began in late-eighteenth-century Britain constituted a radical watershed in history. The idea of a rapid, structural transformation of material life was especially revitalized by the controversial work of the American economist and economic historian Walt W. Rostow ([1960] 1971), who introduced the aeronautical image of "take-off" to refer to the sudden surge of "economic growth" that had traditionally been called the "industrial revolution." *Take-off*, writes Rostow (p. 57), "is defined as an industrial revolution, tied directly to radical changes in methods of production, having their decisive consequence over a relatively short period of time." Although his views and metaphors often differ from those of Rostow, Alexander Gerschenkron (1962) also refurbished the traditional approach with his notion that modern economic change has often been characterized by "great spurts" of growth. Both Rostow and Gerschenkron seek to fuse the idea of a sudden economic surge with the opposing notion that economic change is gradual by arguing that economic acceleration in nineteenth-century Europe was preceded by the evolution of long-range "preconditions" dating from the sixteenth and seventeenth centuries.

Thus, there is now wide agreement that a series of events called the "Industrial Revolution" (often capitalized) "marked a major turning point in man's history" in the sense that it "initiated a cumulative, self-sustaining advance in technology whose repercussions [were] felt in all aspects of economic life" (Landes, 1969: 3). David Landes (p. 5) dramatically states that the "enormous increase in the output and variety of goods and services . . . alone has changed man's way of life more than anything since the discovery of fire." Another scholar (Hartwell, 1965: 165) claims that "On any historical accounting, the industrial revolution is one of the great discontinuities of history; it would not be implausible indeed, to claim that it has been the greatest." Although some post-war scholars may have had occasional qualms about using the expression (e.g. Ashton, [1948] 1969: 4) or may seek fresh ways to communicate the notion of rapid, qualitative economic discontinuity, the term itself is firmly entrenched. For historiographical surveys of the various positions and controversies see Böhme (1972: 279–81), Doty (1969: 1–10), Hartwell, (1965; 1970: 167–79), and Rudé (1972: 43–87).

References

Ashton, T. S. [1948] 1969. *The Industrial Revolution, 1760–1830*. New York.
Bezanson, Anna. 1921–22. "The Early Use of the Term Industrial Revolution." *Quarterly Journal of Economics* 35: 343–49.
Böhme, Helmut. 1972. "Industrial Revolution." *MCWS* 4: 275–83. This basic introduction to Marxist and non-Marxist views has an extensive bibliography.
Clark, George Norman. 1953. *The Idea of the Industrial Revolution*. Glasgow. Essential reading, this book is very good for setting Toynbee's usage in its historical context.
Doty, C. Stewart, ed. 1969. *The Industrial Revolution*. New York.
Engels, Friedrich. [1845] 1958. *The Condition of the Working Class in England*. Stanford, Calif.
Gerschenkron, Alexander. 1962. *Economic Backwardness in Historical Perspective*. Cambridge, Mass.
Hartwell, R. M. 1965. "The Causes of the Industrial Revolution: An Essay in Methodology." *The Economic History Review*, 2d Series, 18: 164–82. This is an excellent review essay. According to Hartwell, "historians have no agreed definition of the industrial revolution" in terms of rate of growth of output, or changing economic structure, or technical change, and so on, pp. 171–72.
———. 1970. "The Standard of Living Controversy: A Summary." In R. M. Hartwell, *The Industrial Revolution*. Oxford: 167–79.
Heaton, Herbert. 1932. "Industrial Revolution." *ESS* 8: 3–13. This piece has a good bibliography of the older literature.
Hölscher, Lucian. 1982. "Industrie, Gewerbe." *GG* 3: 237–304. The author states that the expression *révolution industrielle* first appeared in the *Moniteur Universal* of August 17, 1827.
"The Industrial Revolution." 1923. *Palgraves's Dictionary of Political Economy*. London: 399–401.

Landes, David S. 1969. *The Unbound Prometheus: Technological Change and Industrial Development in Western Europe from 1750 to the Present*. Cambridge. Landes includes a survey of the various meanings of *industrial revolution* (p. 1).

Mantoux, Paul. [1906] 1961. *The Industrial Revolution in the Eighteenth Century: An Outline of the Beginnings of the Modern Factory System in England*. New York. T. S. Ashton called this classic work "by far the best introduction to the subject in any language" (p. 22).

Rostow, W. W. [1960] 1971. *The Stages of Economic Growth: A Non-Communist Manifesto*. Cambridge.

George Rudé. 1972. *Debate on Europe, 1815–1850*. New York. Chapter two, "Industrial Revolution," is a good introduction to the historiographical field.

Toynbee, Arnold. [1884] 1920. *Lectures on the Industrial Revolution of the Eighteenth Century in England*. London. "The essence of the Industrial Revolution," according to Toynbee, "is the substitution of competition for the medieval regulations which had previously controlled the production and distribution of wealth" (p. 64).

Sources of Additional Information

For older literature see Eileen Power, *The Industrial Revolution, 1750–1850: A Select Bibliography* (London, 1927); also Heaton (1932). A comprehensive recent list of titles may be found in Böme (1972). See also Berding: 287–302. Doty (1969) is a useful anthology that includes a historiographical introduction and annotated bibliography. R. M. Hartwell has made a specialty out of historiographical essays on the subject; in addition to those works cited above, see his introduction in *The Causes of the Industrial Revolution in England* (London, 1967) and his *Industrial Revolution and Economic Growth* (London, 1971), especially pp. 42–59. Of related general interest is F. Eulen, "Industrie," *HWP* 4: 338–43. An interesting older work is Charles Beard, *The Industrial Revolution* (1902; reprint ed., Westport, Conn., 1969)(see Clark, 1953: 25–26). "The Origins of the Industrial Revolution," *Past and Present*, No. 17 (April 1960): 71–81, pinpoints some major research concerns. For a summary of recent scholarship by many scholars see Carlo M. Cipolla, ed., *The Fontana Economic History of Europe*, vols. 3 and 4 (London, 1973).

INTELLECTUAL HISTORY, HISTORY OF IDEAS. Both expressions refer to the branch of historiography devoted to the study of mental life. *Intellectual history*, the broader of the two, refers to the historical study of ideas in a comprehensive sense, including not only the history of articulate thought but consciousness in general, for example, inarticulate assumptions, unstated beliefs and presuppositions, implicit opinions, feelings, states of mind, collective mental processes. *History of ideas* refers more narrowly to the study of formal concepts in philosophy, political thought, imaginative literature, and so on.

The concept of a special field of history devoted exclusively to ideas and thought processes is relatively new, dating only from the latter years of the nineteenth and the early decades of the twentieth century. Since the mid-eighteenth century, however, historians have generally attached great importance to the role of ideas in social change, and the twentieth-century idea of intellectual history has a long and complex prehistory.

In his *Essai sur les moeurs* (1756), for example, Voltaire proclaimed the development of the mind to be the central object of historical scrutiny; the scholar's ultimate task, he believed, was to trace the advance of the human intellect through time, as manifested in the progress of science, art, and philosophy (Holborn, [1968] 1972: 198–99). This became the dominant historical view of the European ENLIGHTENMENT. French writers such as Voltaire and the Baron de Montesquieu also believed it possible to characterize an era in terms of its prevailing "spirit," or intellectual climate (*esprit du siècle*), and this idea was adopted and elaborated by late-eighteenth-century German authors as the notion of "spirit of the times," or ZEITGEIST (Schoeps, 1959: 13).

These traditions culminated in the historical IDEALISM of the German philosopher Hegel (1770–1831), who declared history's meaning to lie in the logical unfolding of "universal mind" in a sequence of stages (a view that may be interpreted as a secularized version of Christian "providence," or will of God). This transcendental process, according to Hegel, reveals itself in man's growing control over nature and through the work of "world historical" individuals who are "agents of the world mind" (Holborn, [1968] 1972: 199–200). Thus, Hegelian *panlogism* ("belief that, above . . . reality, eternal regulating principles exist" [pp. 200, 202]) made ideas the ultimate determinants of history; but since Hegel considered the *state* the primary vehicle for the objectification of universal mind, his doctrine also reinforced the ancient tradition that history's main concern was politics rather than ideas per se.

During the early nineteenth century, belief in the importance of ideas was implicit in the mainstream approach to history; ideas were presumed to be embedded or immanent in other things or processes, and the role of ideas in politics was a popular theme (Gilbert, 1972: 145). The work of the first generation of nineteenth-century historians—disciplinary "role models" such as Ranke (1795–1886), Michelet (1798–1874), and Bancroft (1800–1891)—was conditioned by the Enlightenment and Hegelian traditions, even though these men were empirical scholars who often explicitly rejected Hegel's *a priori* flights of abstraction. Christian theology was also an important influence on their work and, although their primary focus was political, they viewed politics as the outward expression of underlying "spiritual" forces (Gilbert, 1972: 147)—assuming the categories of "spirit" and "mind" to be complementary.

The key figure in the emergence of a special "intellectual" approach to history was the late-nineteenth-century German philosopher Wilhelm Dilthey (1833–1911), who attempted to demystify Hegel's idealism and refine the idea that institutions are concrete expressions of ideas. "More than any other scholar," Dilthey was "the father of the modern history of ideas" (Holborn, [1968] 1972: 202)—what in German became known as *Geistesgeschichte* (Schoeps, 1959: 9), best translated as "history of the human mind." Most of the conceptual and methodological issues in modern intellectual history become apparent through an analysis of Dilthey's approach.

For Dilthey, the world of the "spirit" (*Geist*, also translatable as "mind") did not lay—as Hegel had thought—beyond human experience but was rather the product of man himself and was objectified in human action and creativity. Man's knowledge of the world, Dilthey believed, is imaginatively formalized in *Weltbilder* ("world pictures," images of reality) and *Weltanschauungen* ("world views," conscious images of what the world should be like) (Holborn, [1968] 1972: 203); the dominant *Weltbilder* and *Weltanschauungen* constitute the *Zeitgeist* for any given period. *Geistesgeschichte*, then, is the historical study of these mental constructs, which express themselves outwardly in institutions, political systems, art, poetry, and all other manifestations of human culture. Thus, Dilthey's concept of intellectual history was theoretically broad, embracing not only formal philosophical systems but the general history of consciousness, feeling, and human endeavor as well. In practice, however, Dilthey and his followers (e.g., Friedrich Meinecke [1862–1954], whose *Ideengeschichte* revolved around the relationship of ideas to political power [Schoeps, 1959: 11]) focused somewhat narrowly on the study of "high culture" (see CULTURAL HISTORY); because they assumed ideas to be the ultimate determinants of history, they tended to isolate the study of ideas from other spheres of life, especially social structure and economic life (Holborn, [1968] 1972: 205–6). Although in principle they acknowledged the importance of social relations to the life of the mind, their treatment of the connection between ideas, economic interest, and social conditions "remained more of a painted backdrop of the stage instead of being used to explain the drama itself"; this is considered a major liability today, when many historians, under the influence of economic and sociological theory, regard ideas as responses to "practical human needs and not only as abstract syntheses" (pp. 207–8). A major concern in the twentieth century—especially since 1945—has been the problem of fleshing out traditional history of ideas by adding a "social dimension" (see below).

These theoretical problems were not paramount in the early twentieth century, however, when the idea of intellectual history first became fashionable. The main thrust behind the new interest was a desire to counterbalance history's narrow, traditional emphasis on politics (Gilbert, 1972: 149–50, 154). In the United States, James Harvey Robinson of Columbia University was a pioneer; in 1904 he introduced a course on "The Intellectual History of Western Europe" (Gilbert, 1972: 141) and called for the adoption of the new approach in his famous collection of essays, *The New History* (1912; see NEW HISTORY). In contrast to Dilthey, however, Robinson narrowly equated intellectual history with the progress of formal scholarship (Gilbert, 1972: 141, 156, n. 1). One of the earliest examples of the genre in Britain was J. B. Bury's *Idea of Progress* (1920), which traced the history of the concept of progress from antiquity to the present. In America, Carl Becker's *Declaration of Independence* (1921) was an early contribution to the field (Higham, 1951: 459). However, Perry Miller's *New England Mind* (1939) was apparently the first work to style itself explicitly as an exercise in "intellectual history" (Gilbert, 1972: 141).

Miller and Arthur O. Lovejoy (see below) established the broad framework within which most American intellectual historians worked in the mid-twentieth century (Darnton, 1980: 327), the heyday of the genre's fashionability. The compelling nature of Miller's model is reflected in the titles of numerous books that contain the word *mind* (e.g., Commager, 1950). Miller's goal was to analyze the complete thought system of an intellectual elite—the intelligentsia of Puritan New England. He reconstituted the group's logic, view of human nature, and vision of the universe—what Dilthey had designated by the terms *Weltbild* and *Weltanschauung*. All aspects of the Puritan "mind" were treated as an inter-related unit, or homogenous mental style (Gilbert, 1972: 143). By implication, it was assumed that the mental life of the intellectual elite typified the thought system of the society as a whole.

About the same time, Arthur O. Lovejoy ([1936] 1960) formulated his own concept of the "history of ideas." In contrast to Miller, who tried to reconstruct the thought system of a given society, Lovejoy sought to trace chronologically the "biography" of "unit-ideas" (i.e., ideas he regarded fundamental to the history of western culture, such as "the great chain of being" and "primitivism") from antiquity to the present. Lovejoy compared his method to the procedure by which chemists analyze compounds; *unit-ideas* in the history of philosophical doctrines were the metaphorical equivalents of chemical elements: "In dealing with the history of philosophical doctrines," wrote Lovejoy ([1936] 1960: 3; 1940: 4) " . . . [the method] cuts into the hard and fast individual systems and, for its own purposes, breaks them up into their component elements, into what may be called their unit-ideas." Lovejoy's approach was narrower and more closely tied to the history of articulate thought than Miller's, and it is now regularly criticized for its disregard of social and economic factors. The method was very influential in the United States, however, producing monuments such as the *Journal of the History of Ideas* (founded in 1940) and a valuable four-volume reference work entitled the *Dictionary of the History of Ideas* (1973).

Developments in France and Germany between the two world wars were very important. In its concept of the history of *mentalités* ("mentalities"), the French *Annales school* of Marc Bloch and Lucien Febvre refined and elaborated Dilthey's notion that intellectual history should deal comprehensively with the history of consciousness—popular sensibility, inarticulate assumptions, hopes, and expectations, unspoken opinions, amorphous beliefs, and so on—rather than merely with the history of formal ideas (e.g., Febvre, [1941] 1973—see SOCIAL HISTORY; INTERDISCIPLINARY HISTORY). In Germany the influence of Marxian HISTORICAL MATERIALISM produced Karl Mannheim's idea of the "sociology of knowledge" (*Wissenssoziologie*), the study of ideas as IDEOLOGY, that is, expressions and rationalizations of socioeconomic interests and social status (Mannheim, [1929] 1936: 236–80). Both of these schools involved "the expansion of inquiry from the intellectual elite to all intellectual producers" (Krieger, 1973: 511).

Since the 1960s, the methods and even the question of the usefulness of a special field of "intellectual history" have become the focus of much debate (Gilbert, 1972: 155; Krieger, 1973: 499, 515; Bouwsma, 1981: 279–80). Lovejoy's "unit-idea" approach, especially, has fallen out of favor (Mandelbaum, 1965). The "history-of-ideas" method, it is argued, narrowly stresses formal thought, written texts, and intellectual elites at the expense of popular consciousness and tends to endow "ideas" with a life of their own, as if they were living entities; moreover, the approach is "unhistorical" insofar as it divorces mental life from the social context in which it occurs (Skinner, 1969: 10; Gilbert, 1972: 150). Miller's assumption that the outlook of social elites reflects the thought processes of society as a whole has also been questioned (Gilbert, 1972: 149).

Nevertheless, the oft-expressed fear that intellectual history in the tradition of Dilthey, Miller, and Lovejoy will disappear seems unjustified; old fashioned intellectual history is still widely practiced, judging by the many university course offerings, dissertations, and journal articles that continue to appear in the field (Darnton, 1980: 335). Moreover, there have been important efforts to adjust intellectual history in response to legitimate complaints that ideas must be related to social and economic conditions and include the mental life of non-elite social groups. Thus, Peter Gay (1964: x; 1967) called for a synthesis of social and intellectual history, or "social history of ideas," and "l'histoire social des idées" is cultivated particularly by French historians of the *Annales* school, who seek to adapt QUANTIFICATION to the study of ideas (Darnton, 1971). Partly under the influence of cultural anthropology (Walters, 1980), another trend is to fashion a broadly conceived cultural, linguistic, and poetic search for social "idiom" (Darnton, 1980: 343), an interdisciplinary fusion of the techniques and aims of history, poetics, aesthetics, quantitative sociology, and anthropology (Bouwsma, 1981: 299–314). Despite the fact that these new approaches are typically pitted against the conceptions of Lovejoy and Miller, they nonetheless retain important features of the older approaches, notably Lovejoy's emphasis (1940: 4) on the need to study ideas from an interdisciplinary perspective and Miller's idea that ideas must be understood as part of a "system" in which all elements are logically interconnected.

References

Bouwsma, William J. 1981. "Intellectual History in the 1980s." *Journal of Interdisciplinary History* 12: 279–91. This concise survey of the entire problem samples recent literature; the author maintains that "intellectual history is now disappearing as one of the conventional specialities into which historians segregate themselves" (p. 280).
Commager, Henry Steele. 1950. *The American Mind*. New Haven, Conn. Typical of

sweeping, mid-century histories which reified the notion of "mind" and helped discredit intellectual history in the eyes of many scholars; cf. Darnton (1980: 340), as well as David Hackett Fischer, *Historians' Fallacies: Toward a Logic of Historical Thought* (New York, 1970), pp. 190–91.

Darnton, Robert. 1971. "In Search of the Enlightenment: Recent Attempts to Create a Social History of Ideas." *JMH* 43: 113–32.

———. 1980. "Intellectual and Cultural History." In Kammen: 327–54. Darnton is one of the most knowledgeable authorities; the footnote citations provide an excellent source of additional bibliography.

Febvre, Lucien. [1941] 1973. "Sensibility and History: How to Reconstitute the Emotional Life of the Past." In Peter Burke, ed., *A New Kind of History: From the Writings of Febvre*. New York: 12–26.

Gay, Peter. 1964. *The Party of Humanity: Essays in the French Enlightenment*. New York.

———. 1967. "The Social History of Ideas: Ernst Cassirer and After." In Kurt H. Wolff and Barrington Moore, Jr., eds., *The Critical Spirit: Essays in Honor of Herbert Marcuse*. Boston.

Gilbert, Felix. 1972. "Intellectual History: Its Aims and Methods." In Gilbert and Graubard: 141–58. This key assessment voices the now conventional opinion that the "investigation of subjects of intellectual history leads beyond the purely intellectual world and intellectual history per se does not exist" (p. 155).

Higham, John. 1951. "The Rise of American Intellectual History." *AHR* 56: 453–71. In this basic survey of names and titles the author asserts that Moses Coit Tyler (1835–1900) "inaugurated the critical study of American intellectual history" (p. 456).

Holborn, Hajo. [1968] 1972. "The History of Ideas." In Hajo Holborn, *History and the Humanities*. Garden City, N.Y.: 196–212. This is a clear statement of the idea that "social history is the necessary complement to the history of ideas" (p. 208). Holborn regards Dilthey as not only the father of the history of ideas but its greatest practitioner (p. 203). See also the closely related essay "Wilhelm Dilthey and the Critique of Historical Reason," pp. 125–52, originally published in *JHI* 11: 93–118.

Krieger, Leonard. 1973. "The Autonomy of Intellectual History." *JHI* 34: 499–516. Krieger concludes that intellectual history "is not now an integral or autonomous field of history" (p. 515). My general distinction between *intellectual history* and the *history of ideas* is taken from this essay, pp. 500–501.

Lovejoy, Arthur. 1940. "Reflections on the History of Ideas." *JHI* 1: 3–23. This is an important programmatic statement.

———. [1936] 1960. *The Great Chain of Being: A Study of the History of an Idea*. New York. Chapter one contains an outline of Lovejoy's concept of the "history of ideas."

Mandelbaum, Maurice. 1965. "The History of Ideas, Intellectual History, and the History of Philosophy." *HT Beih.* 5: 33–66. This work contains an extended consideration and critique of the Lovejoy approach—much bibliography.

Mannheim, Karl. [1929] 1936. *Ideology and Utopia*. New York.

Schoeps, Hans-Joachim. 1959. *Was ist und was Will die Geistesgeschichte? Über Theorie und Praxis der Zeitgeistforschung*. Göttingen.

Skinner, Quentin. 1969. "Meaning and Understanding in the History of Ideas." *HT* 8:

3–53. This influential essay argues that the history of ideas should concern itself primarily with the range of possible meanings and intentions open to past statements in political theory, philosophy, and so on.

Walters, Ronald G. 1980. "Signs of the Times: Clifford Geertz and Historians." *Social Research* 47: 537–56. The author analyzes the influence of Geertz, a cultural anthropologist, whose idea of "ideation" has recently had an impact on historians.

Sources of Additional Information

The literature is plentiful. The footnote citations in Darnton (1980) are a good place to begin. See also the section "Bewusstseins- und Ideengeschichte" in Berding: 222–28. Jeremy L. Tobey has published the two-volume *History of Ideas: A Bibliographical Introduction* (Santa Barbara, Calif., 1975–77): *Classical Antiquity* and *Medieval and Modern Europe*. Two recent, complementary anthologies are John Higham and Paul K. Conkin, eds., *New Directions in American Intellectual History* (Baltimore, 1979), and Dominick La Capra and Steven L. Kaplan, eds., *Modern European Intellectual History* (Ithaca, N.Y., 1982). La Capra has also published *Rethinking Intellectual History: Texts, Contexts, Language* (Ithaca, N.Y., 1983). Robert F. Berkhofer, Jr., "Clio and the Culture Concept: Some Impressions of a Changing Relationship in American Historiography," in Louis Schneider and Charles M. Bonjean, eds., *The Idea of Culture in the Social Sciences* (Cambridge, 1973): 77–100, contains good additional information in the text and in footnote citations, especially pp. 84–85. See also Robert Skotheim, *American Intellectual Histories and Historians* (Princeton, N.J., 1966), and Arthur A. Ekirch, Jr., *American Intellectual History: The Development of the Discipline* (Washington, D.C., 1973). Franklin L. Baumer, "Intellectual History and Its Problems," *JMH* 21 (1949): 191–203, is widely cited, as is John C. Greene, "Objectives and Methods in Intellectual History," *Mississippi Valley Historical Review* 44 (1957): 58–74. A related article is R. N. Stromberg's rambling "Some Models Used by Intellectual Historians," *AHR* 80 (1975): 563–73. Preston King, ed., *The History of Ideas: An Introduction to Method* (Totowa, N.J., 1983), includes a lengthy bibliography. The introductory chapter in H. Stuart Hughes, *Consciousness and Society: The Reorientation of European Social Thought, 1890–1930* (New York, 1958), is an important methodological essay. George Boas, *The History of Ideas: An Introduction* (New York, 1969), is by one of the founders of Lovejoy's "History of Ideas Club" at Johns Hopkins in 1923. Werner Stark has written "Sociology of Knowledge" in *EP* 7: 475–78. For more on Dilthey see Gerhard Masur, "Wilhelm Dilthey and the History of Ideas," *JHI* 13 (1952): 94–107; also see two articles in *HWP* by L. Geldsetzer: "Geistesgeschichte," 3: 207–10, and "Ideengeschichte," 4: 135–38, both with bibliography.

INTERDISCIPLINARY HISTORY. Historical scholarship that makes use of the methods or concepts of one or more disciplines other than history.

Discipline—in the sense of "a branch of instruction or education; a department of learning or knowledge"—is an old term in English. The earliest occurrence cited by the *OED* is the prologue to Chaucer's "Yeoman's Tale" (1386). The term derives from the word *disciple* and the idea of "instruction imparted to disciples or scholars." In the vocabulary of twentieth-century academic life the word normally refers to the specialized fields into which instruction and research have been divided in modern university curricula. The term *interdisciplinary* is of more recent vintage. The *OED* defines it as "Of or pertaining to two or more disciplines of learning; contributing to or benefitting from two or more disciplines," and cites a sociological article published in 1937 as the earliest instance of its use. American-trained historians have used the term since at least the late 1940s (e.g., Cochran, 1947: 22; Potter, 1954: xxvi). The expression *interdisciplinary history* became fashionable in the 1960s and was endowed with a degree of academic legitimacy with the founding of the scholarly *Journal of Interdisciplinary History* in 1970.

The underlying concept of interdisciplinary history considerably antedates introduction of the word itself. The idea arose in the late nineteenth century, when many of the modern social science disciplines were being institutionalized—for example, sociology, anthropology, psychology—and there was increasing concern over the growing specialization and fragmentation of knowledge. Key early manifestations of the idea were the work of Karl Lamprecht in Germany, the crusade of James Harvey Robinson and others for a NEW HISTORY in the United States, and the movement for "historical synthesis" led by Henri Berr in France. Each of these turn-of-the century currents in historiography arose in reaction against the prevailing late-nineteenth-century assumption that history is an autonomous discipline with its own unique methods, as well as the narrow idea that history is primarily the story of "past politics." In each case it was claimed that history must borrow ideas from science, especially from the new family of empirical social sciences—sociology, psychology, anthropology—as well as from the older science of economics. In general, historians continue to look primarily to the social sciences for interdisciplinary allies, although there are also many notable examples of interdisciplinary historical work that make use of the methods and concepts of "humanistic" disciplines such as art history, literary criticism, and poetics (e.g., Schorske, 1980).

Lamprecht (1856–1915) used the term *cultural history* (*Kulturgeschichte*; see CULTURAL HISTORY) as an umbrella label for his sweeping approach to the past, founded on a melange of the findings and concepts of traditional historiography, economics, art history, and psychology—especially the psychological theories of Wilhelm Wundt and Theodor Lipps (Popper, [1942] 1966: 228, 236, n. 43; Weintraub, 1966; Steinberg, 1971). The discipline of psychology was particularly important for Lamprecht, who described his orientation as "the comparative history of the factors of socio-psychic development" (cited in Popper, [1942] 1966: 223). He believed, however, that psychology could be useful for historians only if it were transformed from its traditional individualistic and introspective basis into a broadly based "social psychology," one that focused on groups and situations rather than single personalities. In 1905 he formulated his basic principle: "Modern historical science is above all a social-psychological science" (cited in Steinberg, 1971: 64). His grandiose, twenty-one volume *Deutsche*

Geschichte (1891–1915) was designed to trace the development of the collective German psyche through a progression of stages from antiquity to the twentieth century.

These unorthodox ideas became a storm-center of controversy among German scholars before World War I, and the approach of the isolated Lamprecht was eventually totally discredited as "eclectic trifling" (Steinberg, 1971: 58). It is only since the 1960s that a new generation of West German historians—themselves in conscious revolt against tradition—has taken an interest in his ideas; even now his endeavors are viewed primarily as a matter of antiquarian curiosity.

Lamprecht left little if any enduring legacy in Germany, but his ideas had an important impact in the United States, where they helped to inspire the movement known as the NEW HISTORY. This school, which flourished from about 1912 (i.e., the publication of James Harvey Robinson's *New History*) to the 1930s, called for an "enthusiastic alliance with the social sciences" (Higham et al., 1965: 113). According to Robinson (1912: 73), the New History's foremost advocate: "Each so-called science or discipline is ever and always dependent on other sciences and disciplines. It draws its life from them, and to them it owes, consciously or unconsciously, a great part of its chances of progress." The notion of a partnership between history and the social sciences grew in popularity in the 1920s and 1930s and became a matter of orthodoxy in the 1950s and 1960s (e.g., Hughes, 1960). Since 1945 interdisciplinary work in America has most often taken the form of (often cautious) borrowing from sociology and the "behavioral sciences" (Potter, 1954: xiii-xxvii; Cochran, [1954] 1972; Hofstadter, 1972; Berkhofer, 1969); the use of statistics, data processing, and other quantitative techniques has become increasingly widespread, especially in ECONOMIC HISTORY (see also ECONOMETRIC HISTORY; QUANTIFICATION). In the late 1960s and 1970s *interdisciplinary history* became a vogue term in the atmosphere of curricular innovation that then prevailed in American universities; in 1970 the editors of the new *Journal of Interdisciplinary History* declared that "the most rewarding stimulus to historical scholarship since World War II has been supplied by advances in other disciplines" (Rabb and Rotberg, 1970: 3). Although this sentiment was widely shared, disciplinary conservatives (e.g., Barzun, 1974) sought to defend the "autonomy" of history from other disciplines and strongly opposed the use of the methods and ideas of certain fields, especially statistics and psychoanalysis (see PSYCHOLOGICAL HISTORY).

A third—and, in some respects, the most important—manifestation of turn-of-the-century interdisciplinary theory arose in France under the leadership of the philosopher Henri Berr. Berr, founder of the *Revue de synthèse historique* in 1900, described his program as "basically an appeal for greater cooperation between social scientists and historians" (Siegel, 1970: 332, Berr, [1900] 1972). His *Revue de synthèse* became an international forum for the discussion of new ideas in a variety of fields—psychology, sociology, anthropology, and philosophy, as well as history. He was convinced that the organization and coordination of research was a crucial task and, like Lamprecht, he was especially interested in a union between history and social psychology.

The interdisciplinary momentum generated by Berr's journal helped lay the foundations for the rise of the "*Annales* school" of historiography in France in the late 1920s. This movement, led by Lucien Febvre and Marc Bloch (co-founders of the journal *Annales d'histoire économique et sociale* in 1929), sprang from the conviction that history should be "wide open to the findings and methods of other disciplines—geography, economics, sociology, psychology—and at the same time must resist the temptation, so marked in the 1920s and 1930s, to divide itself into a number of 'specialisms' (economic history, the history of ideas, etc.) each going its own independent way" (Barraclough, 1978: 264). Febvre, originally a member of Berr's circle, emphasized the need for "alert, inventive and ingenious brains looking for alliances; men who, when they come across any intellectual work, ask themselves the researcher's question, 'What use can this be to me? What use can be made of this though it was not made for me?' " (Febvre, [1938] 1973: 10–11). Since the 1930s the *Annales* school (the historiographical avante garde in Europe) has "promoted a view of history resting on the close collaboration of all the human and social sciences, to which the special contribution of the historian is *le sens du temps*" (Thomson, 1967: 33). In 1947 Febvre was named president of the newly created "Sixth Section" of the French *École des Hautes Études*, designed to "promote research and teaching of the most advanced kind in the area of economics and the social sciences" (Le Roy Ladurie, 1979: 17) and to encourage the kind of interdisciplinary teamwork that Berr had championed as a private intellectual impresario. Under Febvre's direction and that of his successors, the "Sixth Section" became the world's single most important center for the development of interdisciplinary theory, methodological innovation (notably in the areas of quantitative—or "serial"—analysis, historical demography, and the historical study of collective psychology [*mentalités*]), research, and publication. By the 1960s the record of the *Annales* school had become the major source of inspiration to advocates of interdisciplinary history in West Germany, Eastern Europe, Britain, and the United States.

References

Barraclough, Geoffrey. 1978. "History." In Jacques Havet, ed., *Main Trends in Research in the Social and Human Sciences* 2. Paris: 227–487. This major survey of innovative currents in twentieth-century historiography emphasizes the importance of interdisciplinary work, especially for the period since 1945. It was reprinted in 1979 by Holmes and Meier under the title *Main Trends in History*.

Barzun, Jacques. 1974. *Clio and the Doctors: Psycho-History, Quanto-History, and History*. Chicago. This is an angry attack on the "cult of the new" in historiography, including some varieties of interdisciplinary history.

Berkhofer, Robert F. 1969. *A Behavioral Approach to Historical Analysis*. New York.

Berr, Henri. [1900] 1972. "About Our Program." In Stern: 250–55.

Cochran, Thomas C. 1947. "Research in American Economic History: A Thirty Year View." *Mid-America* 29: 3–23.

―――. [1954] 1972. "The Social Sciences and the Problem of Historical Synthesis." In Stern: 348–59. This piece is by a leading mid-century advocate of cooperation between history and the social sciences.

Febvre, Lucien. [1938] 1973. "History and Psychology." In Peter Burke, ed., *A New Kind of History: From the Writings of Febvre*. New York: 1–11.

Higham, John, et al. 1965. *History*. Englewood Cliffs, N.J.

Hofstadter, Richard. 1972. "History and the Social Sciences." In Stern: 359–70. This is a good illustration of an attitude typical of American-trained historians toward cooperation between history and the social sciences: sympathetic but circumspect, committed to the idea of the autonomy of history as a "humanistic" discipline.

Hughes, H. Stuart. 1960. "The Historian and the Social Scientist." *AHR* 66: 20–46. The author calls for interdisciplinary cooperation but is wary of the use of quantitative methods.

Le Roy Ladurie, Emmanuel. 1979. *The Territory of the Historian*. Chicago. This is a collection of essays by a leading representative of the *Annales* school.

Popper, Annie M. [1942] 1966. "Karl Gotthard Lamprecht (1856–1915)." In Bernadotte E. Schmitt, ed., *Some Historians of Modern Europe: Essays in Historiography*. Port Washington, N.Y.: 217–39. There is a valuable bibliography in the footnote citations.

Potter, David M. 1954. *People of Plenty: Economic Abundance and the American Character*. Chicago. The introduction is a theoretical essay, "History, the Behavioral Studies, and the Science of Man."

Rabb, Theodore K., and Rotberg, Robert I. 1970. "Interdisciplinary History." *The Journal of Interdisciplinary History* 1: 3–5. This is an editorial credo.

Robinson, James Harvey. 1912. *The New History: Essays Illustrating the Modern Historical Outlook*. New York. Especially relevant is the essay "The New Allies of History," pp. 70–100.

Schorske, Carl E. 1980. *Fin-de-Siècle Vienna: Politics and Culture*. New York.

Siegel, Martin. 1970. "Henri Berr's *Revue de Synthèse Historique*." *HT* 9: 322–34.

Steinberg, Hans-Josef. 1971. "Karl Lamprecht." In Hans-Ulrich Wehler, ed., *Deutsche Historiker* 1. Göttingen: 58–68. This piece is conveniently concise, with excellent bibliographical notes.

Thomson, David. 1967. "The Writing of Contemporary History." *The Journal of Contemporary History* 2: 25–34.

Weintraub, Karl J. 1966. *Visions of Culture*. Chicago. Chapter four deals with Lamprecht.

Sources of Additional Information

See also NEW HISTORY; SOCIAL SCIENTIFIC HISTORY. Consult *HT Beih.*; Stephens; Birkos and Tambs; Berding. Barraclough (1978) is especially rich in bibliographical information; see also C. Vann Woodward, "History and the Third Culture," and Charles Morazé, "The Application of the Social Sciences to History," both in *The Journal of Contemporary History* 3 (April 1968). There is an abundance of literature on the *Annales* school; key sources are two essays by Jean Glénisson, "L'historiographie française contemporaine; tendances et réalisations," in Comité Français des Sciences Historiques, *La recherche historique en France de 1940 à 1965* (Paris, 1965): ix–lxiv; and "France," in Iggers and Parker: 175–92. See also Traian Stoianovich, *French Historical Method: The Annales*

Paradigm (Ithaca, N.Y., 1976); chapter two of Georg G. Iggers, *New Directions in European Historiography* (rev. ed., Middletown, Conn., 1984); and Paul Ricoeur, *The Contribution of French Historiography to the Theory of History* (Oxford, 1980). *JMH* 44 (1972) is a special issue devoted to the *Annales* school; also, the essays in Fernand Braudel, *On History* (Chicago, 1980), involve the concept of interdisciplinary cooperation. On Lamprecht see, in addition to titles already cited, the historian's own *What Is History?* (New York, 1905).

INTERPRETATION. The ensemble of procedures by which the historian—according to personal perspective, temperament, social conditioning, and conscious choice—imposes a pattern of meaning or significance on his subject; the process of selection, arrangement, accentuation, and synthesis of historical facts that establishes the personal stamp of an individual historian on an account of the past.

Interpretation has been a widely used though somewhat ill-defined word in the theory of historiography since the turn of the twentieth century. In the United States emphasis on interpretation dates from the pre–1914 rise of the NEW HISTORY with its present-oriented, functional conception of historical knowledge; especially important was the influence of Frederick Jackson Turner, whose FRONTIER thesis regarding American social development illustrated the potential fruitfulness of a self-consciously "interpretive" approach to the past (Randall and Haines, 1946: 44–45).

It is now broadly agreed that interpretation is an "inexpungeable" part of the historical enterprise (White, [1972–73] 1978: 51), perhaps even its "life-blood" (Carr, [1961] 1964: 28). The German scholar Gerhard Ritter (1961–62: 266–67) reflects mainstream opinion when he states that that history is "inevitably a *Deutungsversuch* [search for meaning], an effort by the thinking mind to bring a chaos of disconnected phenomena into a meaningful coherence by means of interpretation." The past, he explains,

> is indeed dead; it speaks to us only through evidence preserved in fragments, and consists of an altogether irreducible profusion of separate phenomena whose inner connections seem extraordinarily ambiguous. Writing history is not photography . . . but rather is comparable to the creative activity of a painter, who creates a picture by joining together separate strokes into a whole. . . . Historical pictures are not copies of past reality but a creative fashioning of an extremely diffuse substance which at first appears formless. (pp. 266–67)

It is now commonly held that history differs from "mere chronicle" on the grounds that *chronicle* is a simple, sequential ordering of facts, whereas genuine *history* requires the "structuring of facts into a cohesive narrative and an interpretation of those facts with respect to the causes and significance of past events" (Meiland, 1965: 17). Even *chronicle*, however, may be said to involve interpretation because the chronicler must choose to omit some things. Indeed, according to present orthodoxy the very notion that historians might dispense with interpretation is "in itself an interpretation" (Beale, 1946: 55, 87).

Despite the idea's popularity, neither historians nor philosophers normally supply explicit definitions of *interpretation*, prompting one theorist to label the idea a "neglected category" still in need of "detailed unpacking" (Levich, 1964–65: 338, 341; cf. Gruner, 1967: 151–53; White, [1972–73] 1978: 51). The notion is often used in loose association with the words IMAGINATION (e.g., Strayer, [1943] 1950: 16; Beard, 1946: 10) and especially EXPLANATION (for instance, Beale, 1946: 56), although English-language writers seldom clarify the relationship between *interpretation* and *explanation*. Levich (1964–65: 338–41), following continental European precedent (see below), maintains that a logical distinction should be drawn between *interpretation* and *explanation*; the latter word, he suggests, should designate arguments that answer *causal* questions of "why" and "how" events occurred, whereas *interpretation* should refer to the establishment of "meaning and import." Advocates of this distinction have traditionally defended a dualistic epistemology, arguing that the humanities employ an approach to knowledge distinct from that of the natural sciences. Those who would include the logic of all forms of inquiry under the heading of science, on the other hand, employ *explanation* as an umbrella term and neglect the category of *interpretation*.

In practice, both historians and philosophers often use *interpretation* to refer to speculative philosophies of history (for example, those of Hegel, Marx, or Toynbee) that purport to reveal the overall "meaning" of the totality of human history (Levich, 1964–65: 339; White, [1972–73] 1978: 52). Since most current English-speaking historians and philosophers doubt that the meaning of the entirety of human history can be known (see METAHISTORY, PHILOSOPHY OF HISTORY), this usage has pejorative overtones. Certain philosophers also use the term in a narrower, purely descriptive sense to designate the procedure whereby historians "understand" events by situating them within the framework of circumstances in which they occur (Levich, 1964–65: 339)(see COLLIGATION).

Comparison of a variety of uses in context, however, suggests that *professional historians* normally use the word to mean the *personal* (or "subjective") role of the individual historian in *selecting*, *evaluating*, *arranging*, and *synthesizing* his facts and in deciding the degree of *emphasis* he will accord to particular aspects of his subject (e.g., Beard, [1935] 1972: 319, 325; Strayer, [1943] 1950: 7–8; Beale, 1946: 56; Randall and Haines, 1946: 22; Carr, [1961] 1964: 11; White, [1972–73] 1978: 51). Charles Beard ([1935] 1972: 325), who did as much as anyone to formalize the English vocabulary surrounding the concept of historical interpretation, spoke of a "selection and organization of facts, hence an interpretation." The words that occur most frequently in allusions to the subject are *selection* and *organization* or *arrangement*. For Strayer ([1943] 1950: 7–8, 13) this amounts to finding a "pattern" in a "multitude of individual facts," culminating in the establishment of "meaning" or "significance." Ernst Breisach summarizes the position when he states that the "whole act of recreating the past" involves

> the historian's creative imagination in the combining of separate insights into a coherent whole according to a governing conceptual scheme—simply put, interpretation. . . . To acknowledge interpretation as an integral part of historiography is to recognize the link between a historical account and the person of the historian. (1983: 409)

Interpretation is thus the expression of a scholar's temperament and social conditioning; historians, themselves social products, view the past from within their own unique "frames of reference" (Beard and Hook, 1946: 125–26). Their conclusions will therefore be tentative and subject to modification in light of new circumstances; "the social sciences will always find themselves embroiled in a conflict of interpretations. . . . if they did not, they would thereby be conformist, complacent, and sterile" (Hoy, 1980: 661). Powerful or timely interpretations may establish theoretical traditions, for example, the "economic," "psychological," or "cultural" schools of interpretation.

This entire orientation stands in contrast to the prevailing late-nineteenth-century view that the historian's proper task was purely and simply the establishment of FACT; once established, the facts (it was widely presumed) would "speak for themselves" (Becker, [1932] 1935: 248; [1955] 1959: 129–30; Carr, [1961] 1964: 11). In this context *interpretation* was identified with tendentiousness and idle speculation (Randall and Haines, 1946: 32)—arbitrary "opinion" that could, and normally should, be avoided. To this day, some Anglo-American theorists think of *interpretation* as something that is "not knowledge but only opinion" (White, [1972–73] 1978: 54). But the notion of interpretation as a dispensable "pulp" surrounding the "hard core of facts" has been discarded by the majority of historians, who have come to believe that even the establishment of historical FACT necessarily involves some degree of personal selection and emphasis on the part of the individual scholar (Carr, [1961] 1964: 9–15).

Actually, present estimates of the importance of interpretation build on ancient traditions—temporarily suppressed in the late nineteenth century—that link historiography to rhetoric and the arts. Ritter's painting analogy (see above) echoes a theme common to writers of the eighteenth and early nineteenth centuries: Voltaire ([n.d.] 1972: 38), for instance, assumed that historians resemble an artist "who tries, with a weak but truthful brush, to show men as they were"; likewise, T. B. Macaulay ([1828] 1972: 74–75) compared great historians to painters who can "condense into one point of time, and exhibit at a single glance the whole history of turbid and eventful lives."

Nineteenth-century German idealist historiography also accorded a major role to interpretation (see IDEALISM)—hardly surprising considering that the analytical techniques and general approach of pioneers of professional historical scholarship such as Barthold Georg Niebuhr (1776–1831) and Leopold von Ranke (1795–

1886) were largely derived from "hermeneutic" methods of biblical and philological interpretation, originally developed in the seventeenth and eighteenth
centuries to extract meaning from the scriptures and other esoteric ancient texts
(Palmer, 1969; Liebel, 1971: 381; Blanke, Fleischer, and Rüsen, 1984: 338–
39, 342–43)(see CRITICISM). German *hermeneutics*—a "branch of philosophy
concerned principally with methodological questions about how to acquire correct
understanding and interpretation of texts" (Hoy, 1980: 649; cf. Reill, 1973: 25,
n. 2)—has, in turn, strongly influenced modern continental European theories
of historical UNDERSTANDING, especially through the work of Johann Gustav
Droysen (1804–84)(Maclean, 1982; Burger, 1977) and Wilhelm Dilthey (1833–
1911).

According to the hermeneutic tradition—first elaborated in detail by the Protestant theologian Friedrich Schleiermacher (1768–1834) (Palmer, 1969: 84–
97)—historical *understanding* (*Verstehen*) differs fundamentally from natural
scientific *explanation* (*erklären*) in that its objects are human beings and their
life expressions—written texts, monuments, institutions, and so on—understood
in temporal and spatial context. In this approach, the terms *interpretation* and
understanding are typically used interchangeably (for instance, Maclean, 1982:
356; Hoy, 1980: 658). *Interpretation* therefore presupposes a "divinatory" (Palmer, 1969: 90), "interpersonal" (Maclean, 1982: 356) capacity for "reliving"
the inner mental life of previous individuals and reexperiencing the situations
of earlier generations, based on intuitive sympathy and imagination that purely
empirical and rational explanations of the physical world and its "static categories" (Palmer, 1969: 101) do not require.

The sciences explain nature; the human studies understand expressions of
human life. Understanding grasps the individual entity, and science always views
the individual as a manifestation of a general type. A crucial facet of this view
(which later fed the doctrine of historical RELATIVISM) is the idea that *meaning*
is never "fixed and firm" but is "historical: it has changed with time; it is a
matter of relationship, always related to a perspective from which events are
seen. . . . Interpretation always stands in the situation in which the interpreter
himself stands; meaning hinges on this" (Palmer, 1969: 119–20). This stress on
"perspective" found expression in Dilthey's idea of *Weltanschauungen* ("world
views," mental orientations that characterize entire societies [see Ermarth, 1978])
and, later, in Beard's notion ([1935] 1972: 319; [1934] 1959: 151) that the
historian inevitably views the past from his own "angle of vision" or "frame
of reference." Although *perspective* was often viewed as a debilitating limitation
on OBJECTIVITY in the early twentieth century, by mid-century most historians
had come to regard it as a "positive opportunity to observe things that are
obscure" from various points of view (Hollinger, 1973: 388; Higham, 1965:
136).

Empirically oriented twentieth-century Anglo-American philosophy, while accepting the idea of perspective, has been generally skeptical of this continental
European tradition, based as it is on the idea that an essential part of historical

understanding involves a "mysterious process of mental transfer" (Palmer, 1969: 104); yet, especially through the influence of the Italian philosopher Benedetto Croce, the hermeneutic tradition has nevertheless made some significant inroads in English-language historiographical theory as manifested, for example, in the doctrine of historical RELATIVISM popular in the 1920s and 1930s, in the historical idealism of Michael Oakeshott and R. G. Collingwood ([1946] 1956), and in what is perhaps the most elaborate theory of historical interpretation proposed by a twentieth-century historian, that of Hayden White.

Inspired by the example of nineteenth-century theorists such as Hegel, Droysen, Nietzsche, and Croce and drawing heavily on the work of twentieth-century literary critics such as Northrop Frye and Kenneth Burke, White ([1972–73] 1978) develops a complex, multi-layered model of the mechanics of historical interpretation—a theory designed to suggest how, precisely, the historian may select his facts and make connections in order to create an overarching pattern of meaning. *Interpretation*, he argues, should be understood in terms of various possible combinations of (consciously or unconsciously held) poetic, logical, and rhetorical strategies that operate on four levels.

1. *The "aesthetic" level* (White, [1972–73] 1978: 70), in which the historian shapes his facts not only into a "story" but a "story of a particular kind" (e.g., comedy, tragedy, romance, epic, satire). White notes (p. 59) that this operation of "emplotment" does "not operate capriciously . . . [but] according to well-known . . . literary conventions, conventions which the historian, like the poet, begins to assimilate from the first moment he is told a story as a child" (p. 59). These plot forms constitute a "fund of *mythoi*" to which he may appeal in order to evoke the "odor of meaning or significance" for his readers (p. 60); as in drama or the novel, meaning is grasped when the audience recognizes the kind of story that is being told.

2. *The "epistemological" level* (p. 70), which is the level of "formal argument" or "explanation" (p. 63) (here explanation is thus made a subcategory of the broader concept of interpretation). On this plane the historian may use a variety of approaches, or explanatory "paradigms": a simple delineation of particular facts (the "ideographic" method), an organic synthesis, colligation (i.e., situating the particulars in context), or the "mechanistic reduction of the field in terms of universal causal laws" (p. 65).

3. *The "moral or ideological" level*—the level of value judgment, political or otherwise. Following Marx and others (see IDEOLOGY), White maintains that "every historical account of any scope or profundity presupposes a specific set of ideological commitments" (p. 68); he sees four basic types of ethical engagement: liberal, conservative, radical, and anarchist.

4. *The level of metaphor, or "tropology."* This, for White, is the deepest, most "essential" stratum of interpretation (p. 75), a level where "meaning . . . will be construed in terms of the possible modalities of natural language itself, and specifically in terms of the dominant tropological strategies by which unknown or unfamiliar phenomena are provided with meanings by different kinds

of metaphorical appropriations." Following Kenneth Burke, he identifies four "master tropes:" metaphor, metonymy, synechdoche, and irony" (p. 72). In White's theoretical scheme, these "tropes" function as "figures of thought" that condition and, in some way, ultimately direct or control the kinds of choices and combinations of aesthetic, explanatory, and ethical strategies that the particular historian may choose to make.

References

Beale, Howard K. 1946. "What Historians Have Said About the Causes of the Civil War." In Bull. 54: 53–92.
Beard, Charles A. 1946. "Grounds for a Reconsideration of Historiography." In Bull. 54: 3–14.
———. [1934] 1959. "Written History as an Act of Faith." In Meyerhoff: 140–51.
———. [1935] 1972. "That Noble Dream." In Stern: 315–28. Beard asserts that "Any overarching hypothesis or conception employed to give coherence and structure to past events in written history is an interpretation of some kind, something transcendent" (p. 324).
Beard, Charles A., and Hook, Sydney. 1946. "Problems of Terminology in Historical Writing: The Need for Greater Precision in the use of Historical Terms. Illustrations." In Bull. 54: 103–30. Beard defines *frame of reference* in four senses as (1) a "theory," or "hypothesis as to what constitutes the determining factor or factors in the problem or situation to be explained"; (2) "the historian's personal bias or prepossession"; (3) "the scope of the historian's interest"; and (4) "the philosophy of life or value by which the historian expresses his judgment of what is of most worth" (pp. 125–26).
Becker, Carl L. [1932] 1935. "Everyman His Own Historian." In Carl L. Becker, *Everyman His Own Historian: Essays on History and Politics.* New York: 233–55. This was Becker's 1931 presidential address to the American Historical Association.
———. [1955] 1959. "What Are Historical Facts." In Meyerhoff: 120–37.
Blanke, Horst Walter; Fleischer, Dirk; and Rüsen, Jörn. 1984. "Theory of History in Historical Lectures: The German Tradition of *Historik*, 1750–1900." *HT* 23: 331–56.
Briesach, Ernst. 1983. *Historiography: Ancient, Medieval, and Modern.* Chicago.
Burger, Thomas. 1977. "Droysen's Defense of Historiography: A Note." *HT* 16: 168–73.
Carr, E. H. [1961] 1964. *What Is History.* Harmondsworth, Eng. Carr labels as a "preposterous fallacy" the idea of "a hard core of historical facts existing objectively and independently of the interpretation of the historian." He discriminates between "facts" and "historical facts": *historical facts* are facts judged significant by interpretation (pp. 14–16). See also Carr's comments on pp. 90, 103, and 107.
Collingwood, R. G. [1946] 1956. *The Idea of History.* New York.
Ermarth, Michael. 1978. *Wilhelm Dilthey: The Critique of Historical Reason.* Chicago.
Gruner, Rolf. 1967. "Understanding in the Social Sciences and History." *Inquiry*: 151–63. Gruner states that the "process by which we ascertain the meaning or meanings of a symbol or group of symbols is usually called *interpretation*. Interpretation is the intellectual process at the end of which we are rewarded with the understanding

of a meaning." He distinguishes between *interpretation* and *explanation* on the grounds that the former leads to the understanding of meaning, whereas the latter leads to the understanding of fact (p. 153).

Higham, John. 1965. *History*. Englewood Cliffs, N.J.

Hirsch, E. D., Jr. 1967. *Validity in Interpretation*. New Haven, Conn.

Hollinger, David A. 1973. "T. S. Kuhn's Theory of Science and Its Implications for History." *AHR* 78: 370–93.

Hoy, David Couzens. 1980. "Hermeneutics." *Social Research* 47: 649–71. This survey of recent trends in philosophy refers broadly to *hermeneutics* as the "theory of understanding" (p. 658).

Levich, Marvin. 1964–65. Review of Sidney Hook, ed., *Philosophy and History: A Symposium*. *HT* 4: 328–49. Levich criticizes recent Anglo-American philosophers for subordinating the idea of interpretation to that of explanation. He argues that *explanations* answer questions of "why" and "how," whereas *interpretations* answer questions more difficult to characterize simply, such as "What did Marvell think of Cromwell when he wrote 'The Horatian Ode'? How do the writings of Dr. Johnson illustrate the interplay of commerce and political theory in the eighteenth century? To what extent was fifth-century Athens a democracy?" (pp. 340–41). "An historian *interprets* a stone inscription; he *explains* how it got there. . . . We *interpret* the nature of changes in eighteenth-century England; we explain, given their nature, how they came about" (pp. 340–41).

Liebel, Helen P. 1971. "The Enlightenment and the Rise of Historicism in German Thought." *Eighteenth-Century Studies* 4: 359–85. This work situates Ranke in the hermeneutical tradition (pp. 379–81).

Macaulay, Thomas Babington. [1828] 1972. "On History." In Stern: 72–89.

Maclean, Michael J. 1982. "Johann Gustav Droysen and the Development of Historical Hermeneutics." *HT* 21: 347–65. Maclean argues that Droysen made the "first attempt at a scholarly legitimation and employment of historical hermeneutics," initiated the *Verstehen* tradition, and made the original distinction between *erklären* (explanation) and *verstehen* (understanding) (pp. 347–348). Droysen's hermeneutic—inspired, in Maclean's view, by Hegel—was directed not only at the west European POSITIVISM of Comte and Buckle but against the political "quietism" of his own German colleagues (p. 362).

Meiland, Jack W. 1965. *Scepticism and Historical Knowledge*. New York.

Palmer, Richard E. 1969. *Hermeneutics: Interpretation Theory in Schleiermacher, Dithey, Heidegger, and Gadamer*. Evanston, Ill. This is a good introduction to the German hermeneutic tradition. The author is primarily concerned with the use of hermeneutics for literary interpretation but assumes that the hermeneutic tradition may become the foundation for a general science of interpretation appropriate to any discipline based on the analysis of written texts. There is an excellent bibliography. Palmer discusses six distinct meanings of the word *hermeneutics* (p. 33).

Randall, John Herman, Jr., and Haines, George, IV. 1946. "Controlling Assumptions in the Practice of American Historians." In Bull. 54: 15–52.

Reill, Peter Hanns. 1973. "History and Hermeneutics in the *Aufklärung*: The Thought of Johann Christoph Gatterer." *JMH* 45: 24–51. Reill defines *hermeneutics* as the "study of the grounds, reasons, and methods that allow us to understand . . . the productions of the human spirit (written documents, myth, art, architecture, law—anything that can be broadly defined as something that communicates meaning) and to incorporate this understanding into our own consciousness" (p. 25, n.2).

Ritter, Gerhard. 1961–62. "Scientific History, Contemporary History, and Political Science." *HT* 1: 261–79.

Strayer, Joseph R. [1934] 1950. "Introduction." In Strayer: 3–26. Strayer's loose remarks typify the casual usage characteristic of most historians. He links *interpretation* closely to the establishment of cause-effect relations.

Voltaire. [n.d.] 1972. "On History: Advice to a Journalist." In Stern: 36–38.

White, Hayden. [1972–73] 1978. "Interpretation in History." In Hayden White, *Tropics of Discourse*. Baltimore: 51–80. There is a rich bibliography in the footnotes.

Sources of Additional Information

See EXPLANATION, IMAGINATION, and UNDERSTANDING. Consult as well the extensive list of titles under "Hermeneutik" in Berding: 150–57. Although controversial at the time of its publication, Bull. 54 is a good sample of typical ways the term is presently used by historians trained in the United States. The entire pamphlet is a manifesto in support of interpretation; the very first of its "basic premises" describes the historian as an "interpreter of the development of mankind." "Every written history," its authors state (p. 135), "is a selection of facts made by some person or persons and is ordered or organized under the influence of some scheme of reference, interest, or emphasis— avowed or unavowed—in the thought of the author or authors."

Of related interest, though oriented more toward philosophy and literary criticism than historiography, are Arthur Child, *Interpretation: A General Theory* (Berkeley, Calif., 1965); and P. D. Juhl, *Interpretation: An Essay in the Philosophy of Literary Criticism* (Princeton, N.J., 1980). See also Heinrich Gomperz's older but important studies of the same type: *Interpretation: Logical Analysis of a Method of Historical Research* (The Hague, 1939) and "Interpretation," *Erkenntnis* VII (1938): 225–32. For more on history and the hermeneutic tradition see Joseph J. Kockelmans, "Hermeneutic Phenomenology and the Science of History," in Ernst W. Orth, ed., *Die Phänomenologie und die Wissenschaften* (Munich, 1976): 130–79. Hans-Georg Gadamer authored the article "Hermeneutik," in *HWP* 3: 1061–73; there is an entry by H. Anton, "Interpretation," in volume 4: 514–18 of the same reference work. Also relevant is Wilhelm von Humboldt, "On the Historian's Task," [1821], *HT* 6 (1967): 57–71. On Droysen see Jörn Rüsen, *Begriffene Geschichte: Genesis und Begründung der Geschichtstheorie J. G. Droysens* (Paderborn, 1969). For a complete explication of Hayden White's theory of interpretation, see his *Metahistory: The Historical Imagination in Nineteenth-Century Europe* (Baltimore, 1973). *Beih.* 19 of *HT* (1980) provides a sampling of reaction to White's ideas. Marvin Levich amplifies his ideas in "Interpretation in History: Or What Historians Do and Philosophers Say," *HT* 24 (1985): 44–61. Also relevant are the remarks of Georg G. Iggers on "meaning" in history in "The Idea of Progress: A Critical Reassessment," *AHR* 71 (1965), especially pp. 8–10.

IRONY. A complex rhetorical concept with a range of overlapping connotations, all based on the idea of disparity between literal meaning and underlying truth. The term may refer to a simple figure of speech, a dramatic or narrative strategy, or a broad orientation toward the world in general. In historical writing, *irony* is often understood as a narrative strategy in which events are represented in terms of the unforeseen consequences of actions that contradict the intentions of individuals or groups.

Irony is a broad rhetorical concept closely akin to the ideas of false appearance, unexpected opposition, contradiction, and paradox. As a literary device, *irony* "defines by contrast, by juxtaposition of illusion and reality, intention and event" (Struever, 1970: 133). In ancient Greek usage *eironeia* originally meant "dissimulation, ignorance purposely affected" (*OED*) and was particularly associated with the method of the cunning Socrates, who feigned ignorance in debate and praised the intelligence of his less subtle philosophical adversaries. In current popular usage as well as traditional rhetoric, *irony* is most commonly understood in the sense of "verbal" or "rhetorical" irony, that is, a contrived strategy whereby "a writer or speaker signals that he means the opposite of what he appears to say" (Reinitz, 1978: 95; Beckson and Ganz, 1975: 119); since ancient times it has also been more broadly used in the sense of "dramatic irony," a device by which authors, through the entire structure of a work, illustrate a contrast between appearance and reality, truth and illusion (Beckson and Ganz, 1975: 120). In the early nineteenth century, following the work of German critics such as the brothers A. W. and Friedrich Schlegel, *irony* was further broadened to designate an entire attitude or mode of perception that may characterize a writer's poetic vision. In the twentieth century literary theorists have displayed a "preoccupation" with the concept of irony, and it has become a "central idea in literary criticism throughout the world" (Knox, 1973: 632–33).

Since historical narrative often takes the form of a revelation of the unexpected results of past actions, *irony* has been called an "archetypical historical technique" (Struever, 1970: 134). The fact of hindsight makes irony seem especially suited to history—the historian and his readers know (or believe they know) the true consequences of previous events, whereas participants in these events do not: "The most prevalent ironic situation is unanticipated by the protagonists, but expected by the reader" (p. 134). All theories of historiographic irony share a focus on the central role of contradiction and emphasize the reader's need to look beneath the surface to find truth. In ironic historiography the historian poses as a revealer of hidden truth, and through irony the reader is invited to participate in its discovery.

In historical commentary *irony* is usually understood as the representation of human action in terms of its unforeseen consequences, a device favored by ancient authors such as Thucydides, Sallust, and Tacitus. In Sallust and Tacitus, "irony lies in the disparity between conscious purpose and unwilled result, or between facts supplied by the narrative and the protagonist's faithless reporting of the facts" (Struever, 1970: 32; Syme, 1958: 206, 407; 1964: 192, 198). RENAISSANCE historians—for example, Leonardo Bruni—revived many of the literary devices of classical antiquity and made similar use of irony to point up contradictions between words and facts (Struever, 1970: 133). But historical irony can also be understood more broadly in terms of an aloof attitude or cast of mind, for example, in the work of Edward Gibbon and other eighteenth-century scholars who posed as detached exposers of past illusion, ignorance, and folly (White, 1973: 53–54).

Today the word *irony* is often encountered in historical writing in the ill-defined sense of an element of paradox or anomaly that somehow inheres in human affairs—for example, "History is indeed full of ironies" (Howe and Finn, 1974: 4) or "History delights in irony" (Marcus, 1960–61: 128). Traditionally, the word has been used to refer to "a certain complexity which inheres in the data" (Struever, 1970: 133–34), a rhetorical convention that may derive from ancient fatalistic conceits, as in the "irony of fate." Used in this way, the word normally amounts to nothing more than a glib cliché (Howe and Finn, 1974: 5).

Only recently have historians begun to look to poetics, sociology of knowledge, and to some extent speculative philosophy for clues regarding specific ways that the concept of irony may function in historical conceptualization, interpretation, and explanation (e.g., Wise, 1968; 1973: 296–300, 333–43; White, 1973; Reinitz, 1977a; 1977b; 1978). Following trends in literary criticism, *irony* has been analyzed as a broad "ordering principle," an explanatory "paradigm" or "*mental construct*, an analytical tool employed to give order and meaning to the materials of our perceived world" (Wise, 1968: 596, 598, 600,); as a "form for perceiving the past" (Reinitz, 1977a: 283); and as a metaphorical "mode of historical consciousness" (White, 1973: xi).

Some historians of the United States (for instance, Woodward, [1953] 1960: 167–91) have been specifically influenced by the idea of dramatic irony employed by the theologian Reinhold Niebuhr in his *Irony of American History* (1952). Niebuhr understands *irony* as a "dramatic form for structuring the larger units of historical narrative" (Reinitz, 1977a: 276); ironic situations for Niebuhr are those in which the "consequences of an act are diametrically opposed to the original intention, and the fundamental cause of the disparity lies in the actor himself, and his original purposes" (Wise, 1968: 584). What distinguishes "Niebuhrian irony" from other forms of dramatic irony based on the notion of unforeseen consequences is the special stress placed on the historical protagonist's moral responsibility for the consequences of action, even though he may be unaware of them. In this way, Niebuhrian irony to some degree helped to strengthen the trend toward an emphasis on VALUE JUDGMENT in recent American historiography. According to Richard Reinitz (1977b: 118), American historians' use of irony as a framing device in the "Niebuhrian" sense actually antedates Niebuhr's book and has been growing in frequency since the 1930s as the "political and social hopes of American intellectuals . . . have been repeatedly disappointed by the failure of radicalism and the shallow success of reform movements"; Reinitz (1977a: 285, n. 2) detects the strategy—although "usually not directly acknowledged"—in the work of a number of influential recent historians, for example, Perry Miller, Louis Hartz, and Richard Hofstadter.

Reinitz, thus far the chief elucidator of ironic historiography in America, recognizes the possibility of many variations; instead of trying to reduce *irony* to one meaning, he believes that

> students of the literature of history should explore the ways in which irony functions in different historiographic situations. . . . The lack of a rigid agreed upon meaning for the term irony implies that for different purposes historians may use the concept in ways that work best for them, within the broad limits of a range of meanings which necessarily attach to the word. . . . different kinds of irony lie in the eye of the beholder . . . as a form for perceiving the past irony can have contradictory meanings. (1977a: 275–76, 283)

Some of the broadest claims for the place of irony in historiography are made by Hayden White in his complex theory of the historical IMAGINATION. For White (1973: xi), *irony* is more than a verbal contrivance or framing device; it is one of four archetypical "modes of historical consciousness," one of the metaphorical "tropes" that may subliminally "prefigure" a historian's approach to the past as a whole. White believes that *irony* is the cast of mind "in which skepticism in thought and relativism in ethics are conventionally expressed," and he maintains that it is the linguistic mode that typically informs the historiographical REALISM favored by academic historians since the late nineteenth century (1973: 38, 40–41). Although his characterization of irony has been criticized (e.g., Nelson, 1975: 81–82), White's analysis has undoubtedly drawn the attention of some historians to the possible significance of irony as a category for understanding their own work.

References

Beckson, Karl, and Ganz, Arthur. 1975. *Literary Terms: A Dictionary*. New York. This work contains a brief but useful discussion of literary usage, along with two references.

Howe, Daniel Walker, and Finn, Peter Elliot. 1974. "Richard Hofstadter: The Ironies of an American Historian." *Pacific Historical Review* 43: 1–23.

Knox, Norman D. 1973. "Irony." *DHI* 2: 626–34. This is a valuable discussion of the history of the concept in literature and philosophy, with bibliography.

Marcus, John T. 1960–61. "Time and the Sense of History: West and East." *CSSH* 3: 123–39.

Nelson, John S. 1975. Review of Hayden White, *Metahistory: The Historical Imagination in Nineteenth-Century Europe*. In *HT* 14: 74–91.

Reinitz, Richard. 1977a. "The Use of Irony by Historians and Vice-Versa: Toward a Methodology of Liberation." *Clio* 6: 275–88.

———. 1977b. "Vernon Louis Parrington as Historical Ironist." *Pacific Northwest Quarterly* 68: 113–19.

———. 1978. "Niebuhrian Irony and Historical Interpretation: The Relationship between Consensus and New Left History." In Canary and Kozicki: 98–128. This and the above two titles by Reinitz are important contributions toward a theory of irony in the historiography of the United States. All three essays contain valuable bibliographical information in footnote citations.

Struever, Nancy S. 1970. *The Language of History in the Renaissance: Rhetoric and Historical Consciousness in Florentine Humanism*. Princeton, N.J.

Syme, Ronald. 1958. *Tacitus*. Oxford.

————. 1964. *Sallust*. Berkeley, Calif.

White, Hayden. 1973. *Metahistory: The Historical Imagination in Nineteenth-Century Europe*. Baltimore.

Wise, Gene. 1968. "Implicit Irony in Perry Miller's *New England Mind*." *JHI* 29: 579–600. This piece rivals the essays of Reinitz in importance.

————. 1973. *American Historical Explanations*. Homewood, Ill.

Woodward, C. Vann. [1953] 1960. "The Irony of Southern History." In C. Vann Woodward, *The Burden of Southern History*. Baton Rouge, La. This piece displays explicit use of Niebuhr's concept of irony.

Sources of Additional Information

For general bibliography see, in addition to the bibliography in Knox (1973), the titles listed under "Irony" in the *Princeton Encyclopedia of Poetry and Poetics* (Princeton, N.J., 1974): 407–8. Knox has also written the study *The Word "Irony" and Its Context, 1500–1755* (Durham, N.C., 1961). See also the bibliography in D. C. Muecke, *The Compass of Irony* (London, 1969). Important recent studies are Bert O. States, *Irony and Drama: A Poetics* (Ithaca, N.Y., 1971), and Wayne C. Booth, *A Rhetoric of Irony* (Chicago, 1974). For history see Richard Reinitz's study *Irony and Consciousness: American Historiography and Reinhold Niebuhr's Vision* (Lewisburg, Pa., 1980); also Isaac Deutscher, *Ironies of History* (New York, 1966). For comments on historical irony in the thought of Hegel see Sidney Hook, *The Hero in History: A Study in Limitation and Possibility* (New York, 1943), pp. 61, 64. *Beih.* 19 of *HT* (1980) is devoted to comments on White (1973). Also pertinent are various titles in James R. Bennett et al., "History as Art: An Annotated Checklist of Criticism," *Style* 13 (Winter 1979): 5–36.

L

LAWS. 1. In speculative PHILOSOPHY OF HISTORY, invariable rules that govern change in human affairs and provide the basis for social predictions; this meaning is presently discredited in most professional historical circles. 2. Generalizations regarding behavior patterns characteristic of particular societies at given times in the past (rare). 3. In critical PHILOSOPHY OF HISTORY, empirically verifiable hypotheses that provide the basis for deductions about the nature of the past; commonly referred to as COVERING LAWS since the late 1950s.

The notoriously vague and ambiguous idea of social laws is the object of controversy in many disciplines (Walters, 1967: 410). *Webster's New International Dictionary* (2d ed.) defines *law* as "a statement of an order or relation of phenomena that, so far as is known, is invariable under the given conditions." According to Murphey (1973: 74), philosophers generally agree that laws or "law-like statements" (1) cannot be mere summatory generalizations (e.g., the statement "all chairs in this room are made of wood" cannot be construed as a law); (2) must support predictions; and (3) must support "contrary to fact conditionals" (i.e., must support statements about things that might have occurred but did not—see COUNTERFACTUAL ANALYSIS). There is disagreement, however, on the question of whether a law may "contain no ineliminable reference to individual things or to particular times and places." Traditionally, this has been held to be so, but certain philosophers—including some with a strong interest in the philosophy of history—have argued that there can be laws about individual cases (e.g., White, 1965: 48–49). The three definitions given above represent three senses in which the term *law* has been used by historians and philosophers of history: universal, limited, and epistemological. The concept of COVERING LAWS, although related in certain respects to sense two, has been the subject of such intense discussion in recent years that it merits separate consideration in a separate entry and is not discussed here.

Professionally trained historians normally understand *law* in the first sense, aptly characterized by a nineteenth-century scholar as the idea of "principles which govern the character and destiny of nations" (Buckle, [1857] 1959: 109); they typically seek to avoid the term, which they identify with *a priori* generalization and quixotic speculation. This mistrust is partly the consequence of traditions as old as Aristotle, who declared in a famous passage in chapter nine of his *Poetics* that history merely records particular past occurrences, not general truths. Modern reservations, however, are mainly the result of the excesses of nineteenth-century speculative philosophy of history, which, modeled on seventeenth- and eighteenth-century concepts of natural science (Gardiner, 1959: 3–5), proposed to create a SCIENTIFIC HISTORY capable of discovering universal principles of order presumed to exist beneath the chaotic surface of human affairs. This effort failed, eliciting a negative reaction that became the basis for the triumph of a strongly nominalistic and empirical orientation in the modern historical profession.

It is true that nineteenth-century historians and social theorists (e.g. H. T. Buckle, Hegel, Comte, Marx) often believed in the existence of universal historical laws and made the discovery of such rules the principal goal of their work; twentieth-century instances can be cited as well (e.g., Toynbee, 1934–61; Winkler, 1967). In the 1920s, for example, a president of the American Historical Association looked forward to future meetings "when the search for the laws of history and their application will have become the principal part of [the association's] procedure" (Cheyney, [1923] 1927: 28). Moreover, twentieth-century philosophers have occasionally defended the idea of social laws, at least in principle (e.g., Lebergott, 1944; Murphey, 1973: 86). But the historical profession as a whole has become decidedly skeptical concerning the existence of verifiable historical laws. At the end of the nineteenth century influential theorists, reaffirming Aristotle, concluded that history was properly an "idiographic" discipline (one that seeks an "understanding of social situations or individuals in their uniqueness and do[es] not attempt to generalize these descriptions") rather than one of the "nomothetic" sciences (which "search for general laws and are trying to explain nature" [Riegel, 1976: 33; Hughes, 1958: 186–96; Iggers, 1964: 566–67]). This is the position of most professionals today, who generally believe that historians do not seek to discover laws and, at best, occasionally borrow laws from the natural and social sciences for explanatory purposes (Leff, 1971: 66–68; Hughes, 1960: 24). Many philosophers of history also reject the concept of universal historical laws, even though they may not subscribe to the nomothetic-idiographic dichotomy (Mandelbaum, 1939–40; Walsh, 1959: 303–4).

Although the idea of universal historical laws is generally out of favor, there have been occasional arguments in support of more limited concepts of law in history. Frederick J. Teggart (1939) argued, for example, that a statistically verifiable, law-like correlation existed between political events in ancient China and invasions of the Roman empire. Although he did not extend his generalization beyond the period of late antiquity (Zilsel, 1941), his argument was generally greeted with skepticism.

While denying the existence of inexorable laws of social PROCESS, many historians routinely refer to "trends" and subscribe to the more modest view that something called the *logic of situations* must be taken into account in historical work, that is, the idea that "in any given situation not everything is possible and that some things are more likely to happen than others" (Zagorin, 1959: 249). Furthermore, historians attracted to the use of QUANTIFICATION have defended the possibility of formulating limited "generalizations of a middle level" about the past (Aydelotte, 1971: 25–26, 31).

Murray G. Murphey (1973: 74–85) has made what is perhaps the most note-worthy recent contribution toward the idea of a limited concept of law in history. Murphey flatly asserts (pp. 85, 86) that the conventional notion that historians do not discover laws is "not only false, it is pernicious as well. . . . historians are and have been fundamentally concerned with discovering laws." He defends in principle the existence of "laws of social change covering temporally extended intervals of moderately long duration" but adds that "we seem to have very little knowledge as to what they are" (p. 86). Instead of pursuing this aspect of the question, he concentrates on the analysis of law-like, time and space-bound generalizations, for example, descriptions of patterns of thought and behavior in particular societies. Despite their hostility to the idea of laws, he argues, historians typically formulate such generalizations, and he cites various examples to illustrate the point. Murphey believes that such generalizations concerning customary patterns of thought and behavior in specific cultural settings can be properly labeled laws, contending that we may speak of laws in a limited sense with reference to human or cultural individuals.

References

Aydelotte, William O. 1971. *Quantification in History*. Reading, Mass. The author supports the idea that historians may generalize on a "middle" level but avoids calling these generalizations "laws."
Buckle, Henry Thomas. [1857] 1959. *The History of Civilization in England*. In Gardiner: 106–24.
Cheyney, Edward P. [1923] 1927. "Law in History." In Edward P. Cheyney, *Law in History and Other Essays*. New York. Cheyney advances a "tentative formulation" of six general laws that have allegedly governed the course of human history: continuity, impermanence, interdependence, democracy, necessity for free consent, and moral progress. These six are presented as "natural laws, which we must accept whether we want to or not . . . laws to be reckoned with, much as are the laws of gravitation, or chemical affinity, or of organic evolution, or of human psychology" (pp. 24–25). Critics argue that they are not laws but merely expressions of Cheyney's own liberal values.

Gardiner, Patrick. 1959. "Introduction." In Gardiner: 3–8. This concise summary places the idea of historical laws in context.

Hughes, H. Stuart. 1958. *Consciousness and Society: The Reorientation of European Social Thought, 1890–1930*. New York. Chapter six is a good introduction to the development of the distinction between "idiographic" and "nomothetic" sciences in late-nineteenth-century Germany.

————. 1960. "The Historian and the Social Scientist." *AHR* 66: 20–46.

Iggers, Georg G. 1964. "German Historical Thought and the Idea of Natural Law." *Cahiers d'histoire mondiale* 8: 564–75.

Lebergott, Stanley. 1944. "Chance and Circumstance: Are Laws of History Possible?" *JP* 41 (July 20, 1944): 393–411. The author argues that "the laws of natural science are, in general, much more modest, much less impeccably correct, than we are wont to think" and suggests that "the achievement of laws of history no less rigorous than many of the laws of natural science is not an impossible dream" (p. 393).

Leff, Gordon. 1971. *History and Social Theory*. Garden City, N.Y. This is a concise statement of the widespread opinion that "history is a body of knowledge, not a store of axioms or laws which can be applied to events of the same nature" (p. 67).

Mandelbaum, Maurice. 1939–40. "Can There Be a Philosophy of History?" *The American Scholar* 9: 74–84.

Murphey, Murray G. 1973. *Our Knowledge of the Historical Past*. Indianapolis, Ind. This book is original and important.

Riegel, Klaus F. 1976. *Psychology of Development and History*. New York.

Teggart, Frederick J. 1939. *Rome and China: A Study of Correlations in Historical Events*. Berkeley, Calif.

Toynbee, Arnold J. 1934–61. *A Study of History*. 12 vols. Oxford. The section "Law and Freedom in History" in volume nine is devoted to a justification of the author's quest for general historical laws. Toynbee's work was the object of great controversy in the middle decades of the twentieth century, the high-water mark of the historical profession's broad consensus that the search for historical laws is illusory and irrelevant to the main tasks of the discipline.

Walsh, W. H. 1959. " 'Meaning' in History." In Gardiner: 296–307. Walsh expresses the widely shared opinion that "despite everything that has been said on the subject in the last 200 years, no one has yet produced a reputable example of an historical law" (p. 303).

Walters, R. S. 1967. "Laws of Science and Lawlike Statements." *EP* 4: 410–14.

White, Morton. 1965. *Foundations of Historical Knowledge*. New York. Pages 47–53 deal with "laws about individuals."

Winkler, Fred H. 1967. "Some Suggested Laws of Diplomatic History." *The Social Studies* 58: 114–20. The author qualifies his argument by stating that "the effort by the diplomatic historian to develop 'laws' must remain what it essentially is— an exercise in cerebration. . . . he would be foolhardy indeed to declare that they can always be used to predict accurately . . . future behavior" (p. 118).

Zagorin, Perez. 1959. "Historical Knowledge: A Review Article on the Philosophy of History." *JMH* 31: 243–55.

Zilsel, Edgar. 1941. "Physics and the Problem of Historico-sociological Laws." *Philosophy of Science* 8: 567–79.

Sources of Additional Information

See also COVERING LAW. Consult *HT Beih*. For general information and bibliography see Walters (1967), as well as the entry "Gesetz" in *HWP* 3: 480–532. Maurice Mandelbaum, *History, Man, and Reason: A Study in Nineteenth-Century Thought* (Baltimore, 1971), is a major study that touches on the subject of concepts of historical law. Mandelbaum's very important "Societal Laws," *The British Journal for the Philosophy of Science* 8 (1957–58): 211–24, outlines four possible classes of laws—functional, directional, abstractive, and global—and argues that various combinations of these categories are conceivable; only laws of the "functional-abstractive" type are plausible, however. Mandelbaum's "Critique of Philosophies of History," *JP* 45 (July 1, 1948): 365–78, criticizes Toynbee's effort to isolate general laws of history, as does William Dray, "Toynbee's Search for Historical Laws," *HT* 1 (1961–62): 32–54; the latter essay comments on the looseness and confusion with which historians usually invoke or attack the idea of law in history. On the much-disputed question of Marx's understanding of social laws see especially Roy Enfield, "Marx and Historical Laws," *HT* 15 (1976): 267–77, as well as the references listed under HISTORICAL MATERIALISM. Thomas Burger's *Max Weber's Theory of Concept Formation: History, Laws, and Ideal Types* (Durham, N.C., 1976) explores late-nineteenth-century German thought on the subject; see, as well, Wilhelm Windelband's classic address of 1894, "History and Natural Science," *HT* 19 (1980): 165–85. On Murphey's theory of limited historical laws (1973) see particularly the reviews of Louis O. Mink (*AHR* 79 [April 1974]: 482–83) and William Dray (*JP* 72 [Dec. 18, 1975]: 805–9).

LIBERALISM. An intellectual and political orientation that stresses the need for the greatest possible degree of individual freedom from external control—governmental or social.

Liberalism denotes a set of ideas that may vary in detail depending on time and place but that rests on one central conviction: the importance of individual liberty as an ultimate value. Along with its root word *liberal*, *liberalism* has always been employed with extraordinary looseness, as a computer-assisted analysis of German usage demonstrates (Sucharowski, 1975; cf. Geyl, [1956] 1961; Sabine, 1940–41; Kelley, 1969: xvi). Concise definition is difficult because the term may refer to a particular sociopolitical doctrine, bound to a specific period in history (the eighteenth to twentieth century) or to a perennial psychological attitude or sensibility (Cumming, 1969: 2); to complicate matters, the political doctrine of liberalism underwent a partial shift in meaning around 1900.

Bertier de Sauvigny (1970: 154) locates the initial French use of *liberalism* in the 1819 pamphlet *Examen du libéralisme par un libéral*. The *Oxford English Dictionary* cites the first English use of the word in the same year. The word *liberal* is much older but was not traditionally used in a political sense. In early modern usage (for example, in Shakespeare), *liberal* frequently meant "unrestrained" or "licentious." It also had more positive associations: "that which is worthy of a free man" (e.g., *education libéral* or *arts libéraux*) and "that which shows a generous disposition" (e.g., *un maître libéral* or *un don libéral*)

(Bertier de Sauvigny, 1970: 151). Gibbon (1952: 36, 65, 71), for example, referred to "liberal birth and education," "liberal" professions, and a "liberal spirit of public magnificence." An early instance of political usage is a proclamation justifying Napoleon's *coup d'etat* of 1799, which referred to *les idées . . . libérales* in the sense of "generosity applied in the field of politics" (Bertier de Sauvigny, 1970: 151–52).

Political use spread quickly in the early nineteenth century. In 1812 constitutional monarchists in the Spanish Cortes adopted the name *los liberales*—evidently the first group of people to so identify themselves. In France conservatives unintentionally popularized the political meaning of *liberal*—and, after about 1819, *liberalism*—by using the words as derisory labels for their progressive opponents; because *liberal* already suggested "generosity," the terms were readily embraced by those being attacked.

The meaning of *liberalism* quickly expanded: by about 1830 it loosely suggested a general sensibility concerning the relationship between the individual and society (Bertier de Sauvigny, 1970: 154–55). In the United States the term was at first distrusted as an European import and, in the late nineteenth century, was sometimes used in the sense of "visionary crank"; during the 1930s it often served as a substitute for *socialist* and, in the vocabulary of political journalism, signified government-sponsored social and economic reform.

The word's inflation was assisted by associations with unorthodox theology and, especially, with *laissez-faire* economic theory. Although it has long been usual to link liberalism automatically with *laissez-faire* theory (e.g., Laski, 1936)—often to the exclusion or neglect of other meanings—the association with free-market economics was not evident in early usage; the *OED* makes no specific reference to economics in the etymology of either *liberal* or *liberalism*. The connection seems to have come about gradually, primarily as the result of the British Liberal Party's support for free trade and the self-regulating market. From this came the concept of *classical liberalism* (i.e., the ideology of free enterprise), an expression not popularized until the turn of the twentieth century (Walther, 1982: 787, 808–11).

As opposed to the word itself, the concept of liberty as a human value has a long tradition in western history, dating from antiquity (Geyl, [1956] 1961). One broad reading of history—called the "Whig" interpretation after the popular name for the nineteenth-century British Liberal Party (Butterfield, [1931] 1959)—argues that history itself is the story of the progressive achievement of greater human freedom (Acton, 1967; Croce, [1941] 1955; de Ruggiero, 1927). As an articulated doctrine, however—based on "dedication to human reason, science, and education as the best means of building a stable society of free men on earth" (Anchor, 1967: ix)—liberalism dates only from the late seventeenth and eighteenth centuries.

Many tenets customarily associated with liberalism—freedom of conscience, the right to free expression and assembly, the contract theory of government, and so on—first arose in the sixteenth century in defense of new religious ideas or as extensions of medieval corporate and aristocratic "liberties" (by modern standards, actually *privileges*, recognized by custom or granted by royal charter). A key prerequisite (often overlooked in Britain and the United States [e.g., Berlin, 1958], where *liberalism* is typically [though one-sidedly] understood as necessarily opposed to strong public authority [Freeden, 1978: 23]) was the consolidation of the modern state in the seventeenth and eighteenth centuries. With its legal and bureaucratic structure, the state provided a framework of predictability that could minimize caprice and define the limits of authority. By the same token, however, the state represented the centralization of power; it was against this threat to freedom that classic doctrines of liberalism—constitutional government, separation of powers, the theory of "natural rights," *laissez-faire*, and so on—were given final form in Britain and France (de Ruggiero, 1927; Martin, 1929).

In the late nineteenth century a major shift occurred. Long-range goals remained the same—greater individual freedom—but conceptions of the possible means for attaining freedom began to change. From Britain (Freeden, 1978) to Austria (Holleis, 1978), a doctrine of "neo-liberalism," or "new liberalism," crystallized (also called "reform liberalism" or "social liberalism"), based on the idea that liberty for each and all might require increased public regulation. In the United States the same idea was conveyed by the term *progressivism*. Thus, the meaning of *liberalism* was broadened to accommodate government activity to maximize freedom for the greatest possible number of individuals. By the mid-twentieth century this new concept of liberalism had become the working philosophy of most governments in Western Europe and North America.

Historical interest in liberalism peaked at three points in the twentieth century: the turn of the century, when the "Whig" approach flourished (e.g., Acton 1967); the 1930s and early 1940s, when the world economic depression, the popularity of Marxist HISTORICAL MATERIALISM, and the threat of FASCISM challenged the tenets of "classical" liberalism (e.g., Sabine, 1940–41); and the 1950s, when the "cold war" and fear of Soviet TOTALITARIANISM threatened liberal values of both the "classical" and "progressive" variety (e.g., Hartz, 1955; Harris, 1955).

At these times an array of definitions and interpretations of *liberalism* were advanced; they may be grouped into two general categories: psychological and sociopolitical (Cumming, 1969: 2). In the psychological approach, *liberalism* is "a particular tendency of the human mind, manifest in the form of theories and principles regarding the nature of the human mind" (p. 2). The Whig interpretation is a variation on this theme. Qualified extensions of the Whig interpretation still appear (e.g., Hartz, 1955; Coates, Schapiro, and White, 1970), and "liberal" schools of interpretation, which evaluate past behavior in terms of the increase of human liberty, continue to flourish in some quarters (Jarausch, 1983: 282). Although most west European and North American historians are presently committed to the ideals of liberalism (cf. Walsh, [1961] 1966: 67), they are not always convinced that scholarship demonstrates progress toward greater individual freedom (McNeill, 1967: xix).

Despite the fact that most current academic historians hold liberal values, the use of *liberalism* as a frame of reference for historical interpretation has declined dramatically in recent years. More typical of contemporary historiography is the sociopolitical understanding, pronounced in Marxist and non-Marxist usage alike. Here liberalism is treated as a more or less moribund IDEOLOGY, a socially conditioned "belief system" that reflects the special interests of the modern middle class and the values of CAPITALISM (Ashcraft, 1972). This approach assumes that human consciousness is the reflection of transient socioeconomic circumstances and that liberalism is a distorted or limited form of consciousness, now transcended due to changing material conditions (e.g., Lasch, 1978: xiii); " 'the meaning of this limitation . . . is the key to the understanding of the liberal idea' " (Cumming, 1969: 2).

Generally, the past fifty years have been characterized by the efforts of historians to free themselves from the time-bound constraints of the Whig tradition. For several decades it has been fashionable to debunk liberalism and to speak of its "crisis" (Fraser, 1982) or "end" (Lowi, 1979). The pervasiveness of this orientation is reflected in the widespread use of expressions such as *paradox* and *inner contradiction* to refer to liberalism (for instance, Harris, 1955: 508, 515)—conventions that have assumed the status of clichés in the literature. In this respect, historiography reflects a general tendency toward disillusionment with liberalism typical of western literary and academic circles from the 1930s (Becker, 1935) to the 1960s (Wilson, 1967).

References

Acton, Lord [John Emerich Edward]. 1967. *Essays in the Liberal Interpretation of History: Selected Papers*. Chicago. This is a classic example of the nineteenth-century Whig interpretation.

Anchor, Robert. 1967. *The Enlightenment Tradition*. New York.

Ashcraft, Richard. 1972. "Marx and Weber on Liberalism as Bourgeois Ideology." *CSSH* 14: 130–68.

Becker, Carl L. 1935. "Liberalism—A Way Station." In Carl L. Becker, *Everyman His Own Historian: Essays on History and Politics*. New York: 91–100.

Berlin, Isaiah. *Two Concepts of Liberty* (Oxford, 1958). Berlin juxtaposes "negative" and "positive" concepts of freedom and endorses the former. For an opposing view see the review by M. Cohen, "Berlin and the Liberal Tradition," *Philosophical Quarterly* 10 (1960): 216–27.

Bertier de Sauvigny, G. de. 1970. "Liberalism, Nationalism, and Socialism: The Birth of Three Words." *The Review of Politics* 32: 147–66. This is a key essay on early usage, primarily in France.

Butterfield, Herbert. [1931] 1959. *The Whig Interpretation of History*. London. Butterfield defines the *Whig interpretation* in British historiography as "the tendency in many historians to write on the side of Protestants and Whigs, to praise revolutions provided they have been successful, to emphasize certain principles of progress in the past and to produce a story which is the ratification if not the glorification of the present'' (p. v).

Coates, Willson H.; Schapiro, J. Salwyn; and White, Hayden V. 1970. *The Ordeal of Liberal Humanism: An Intellectual History of Western Europe*. New York.

Croce, Benedetto. [1941] 1955. *History as the Story of Liberty*. New York.

Cumming, Robert Denoon. 1969. *Human Nature and History: A Study of the Development of Liberal Political Thought*. Chicago.

Geyl, Pieter. [1956] 1961. ''The Idea of Liberty in History.'' In Pieter Geyl, *Encounters in History*. Cleveland. This is a brief survey of the diverse ways that *liberty* has been understood in the past.

Gibbon, Edward. 1952. *The Portable Gibbon: The Decline and Fall of the Roman Empire*. New York.

Fraser, Peter. 1982. ''British War Policy and the Crisis of Liberalism in May 1915.'' *JMH* 54: 1–26. Fraser analyzes the political demise of the British Liberal Party. He portrays the ''neo-liberal'' party as ''doomed'' because it was ''not adapted to the crudities of mass democracy'' (p. 2).

Freeden, Michael. 1978. *The New Liberalism: An Ideology of Social Reform*. Oxford. This study of turn-of-the-century neo-liberalism in Britain contains an important discussion of essential and non-essential tenets of liberalism, pp. 22–23.

Harris, David. 1955. ''European Liberalism in the Nineteenth Century.'' *AHR* 60: 501–26. This is a summary of conventional mid-century views and clichés, based on the incorrect assumption that ''liberalism after 1848 was living on borrowed time.''

Hartz, Louis. 1955. *The Liberal Tradition in America*. New York. This is an influential study of liberalism in the United States.

Holleis, Eva. 1978. *Die sozialpolitische Partei: Sozialliberale Bestrebungen in Wien um 1900*. Munich.

Jarausch, Konrad H. 1983. ''Illiberalism and Beyond: German History in Search of a Paradigm.'' *JMH* 55: 268–84.

Kelley, Robert. 1969. *The Transatlantic Persuasion: The Liberal-Democratic Mind in the Age of Gladstone*. New York. This comparative study of ''liberal-democratic'' thought in late-nineteenth-century America, Canada, and Britain rejects use of the term *liberalism* on the grounds that too ''many divergent meanings have been stuffed into it and so many scholars have strongly personal commitments to one or another of these meanings'' (p. xvi).

Lasch, Christopher. 1978. *The Culture of Narcissism*. New York.

Laski, H. J. 1936. *The Rise of Liberalism: The Philosophy of a Business Civilization*. New York.

Lowi, Theodore J. 1979. *The End of Liberalism: The Second Republic of the United States*. New York.

Martin, Kingsley. 1929. *French Liberal Thought in the Eighteenth Century*. London.

McNeill, William H. 1967. ''Introduction.'' In Lord Acton, *Essays in the Liberal Interpretation of History: Selected Papers*. Chicago.

Ruggiero, Guido de. 1927. *The History of European Liberalism*. London. This is a famous study of liberalism and its major national variations in Europe, tracing its origins to the middle ages.

Sabine, George H. 1940–41. ''The Historical Position of Liberalism.'' *The American Scholar* 10: 49–58.

Sucharowski, Wolfgang. 1975. *"Liberal" im gengenwärtigen Sprachgebrauch: linguistische, psycholinguistische und semantische Studien zum Jahr 1971*. Munich.
Walsh, W. H. [1961] 1966. "The Limits of Scientific History." In Dray: 54–74.
Walther, Rudolf. 1982. "Exkurs: Wirtschaftlicher Liberalismus." *GG* 3: 787–815.
Wilson, R. J. 1967. "United States: The Reassessment of Liberalism." *Journal of Contemporary History* 2: 93–105. Wilson discusses historians' disillusionment with the values of liberal progressivism in the 1960s. See especially pp. 99–105.

Sources of Additional Information

An excellent starting point is the well-chosen list of titles in Massimo Salvadori, *The Liberal Heresy: Origins and Historical Development* (New York, 1977). For a general bibliography see also William Theodore Bluhm, *Ideologies and Attitudes: Modern Political Culture* (Englewood Cliffs, N.J., 1974), pp. 65–66 and 113–15, and David Sidorsky, ed., *The Liberal Tradition in European Thought* (New York, 1970), pp. 360–62. Several encyclopedias contain articles with helpful bibliographies: for example, Guido de Ruggiero, "Liberalism," *ESS* 9: 435–41; J. H. Hallowell, "Liberalism," *New Catholic Encyclopedia* 8: 701–6; John Plamenatz, "Liberalism," *DHI* 3: 36–61; K. R. Minogue, "Liberalism," *Encyclopedia Americana* 17: 294–97; David G. Smith, "Liberalism," *IESS* 9: 276–82; Harry K. Girvetz, "Liberalism," *Encyclopedia Britannica* 10: 846–51; Maurice Cranston, "Liberalism," *EP* 4: 458–61; Volker Sellin, "Liberalism," *MCWS* 5: 199–212. The latter is especially useful for the literature in German, as is the more comprehensive *Bibliographie zum deutschen Liberalismus* (Göttingen, 1981) compiled by Jürgen C. Hess and E. van Steensel van der Aa; the review essay by Lothar Gall, "Der deutsche Liberalismus zwischen Revolution und Reichsgründung," *Historische Zeitschrift* 228 (Feb. 1979): 98–108; and Rudolf Vierhaus, "Liberalismus," *GG* 3 (1982): 741–85. Lionel Gossman, *Augustin Thierry and Liberal Historiography*, which appeared as *Beih*. 15 of *HT*, is a sensitive reading of the influence of liberal doctrine in early-nineteenth-century historical writing.

M

METAHISTORY. 1. A speculative approach to history, that is, concern with broad, empirically non-verifiable matters such as the general patterns and ultimate meaning of human history; normally (though not always), pejorative when used in this sense. 2. A form of criticism that stands aside from normal historical practice and analyzes history as a mode of inquiry and expression.

The word *metahistory* ("beyond" history, from the Greek *meta*, i.e., "after") has come into limited use among historians and philosophers of history in Britain and North America since 1945. W. H. Dray (1973: 61) states that "it cannot be said that the term has any settled and generally agreed sense," but one may nonetheless trace a tradition of usage in which there are two distinct levels of meaning.

The *OED* suggests that the noun and its variations were employed widely by theologians and philosophers as early as the 1920s. In the early 1950s *metahistory* was employed in Britain primarily as a contrast to "plain" or "ordinary" history—the "pedestrian," non-speculative historiography favored by many modern academic historians (Renier, 1951: 69). The term was described as a "new word and one which is yet unfamiliar to the ordinary reader," one presumed to have been "coined on the analogy of metaphysics" and "concerned with the nature of history, the meaning of history and the cause and significance of historical change" (Dawson, 1951: 9). The word's range of meanings was established in an exchange of views published by the popular British periodical *History Today* in 1951. Alan Bullock (1951: 5), who attributed the term to the philosopher Isaiah Berlin, used it in a depreciatory sense, as something decidedly inappropriate to the historian. He included among its implications the urge toward "historical prophecy" and cited the sweeping social theories of Hegel, Marx, Herbert Spencer, H. G. Wells, Benedetto Croce, and Arnold J. Toynbee as examples. "These interpretations," he wrote (1951: 10), "have this in common: they are all attempts to discover in history patterns, regularities and similarities on whose recurrence is built a philosophical explanation of human existence, or at the very least a panoramic view of the stages of its development." This, he concluded, was tantamount to treating history as a "rag-bag in which every man will find what he wants to find, and what he expects to find."

Bullock's pejorative understanding of the term's meaning was shared in North America as well as Great Britain. As early as 1951 *metahistory* was disparagingly used in a Canadian journal to describe Toynbee's *Study of History* (Underhill, 1951). Although the word was employed as though it needed no definition, the context conveyed a fairly clear meaning, one essentially identical to that of Bullock. Toynbee's method was described as

> that of the poet or seer . . . who sits musing, brooding, letting his imagination play with the suggestive images that crowd into it. A stimulating idea flashes across his mind, and he then looks about for a few historical examples to illustrate it. . . . this sort of thing can hardly be said to constitute scientific proof. It is the method of the intuitive artist rather than the social scientists. (Underhill, 1951: 206)

This is the meaning that most historians are today likely to associate with *metahistory*: non-empirical speculation and system building that moves through the past in seven-league boots (for instance, Fischer, 1970: 66, 194, 254–55). The Austrian-British philosopher Karl Popper (1957) meant to convey something very similar by his idiosyncratic use of the word HISTORICISM about the same time.

Various factors explain the mid-century dissemination of both *metahistory* and *historicism* as pejoratives: a widespread belief that the tyrannies of Nazi Germany and Soviet Russia were sustained by cognitively irresponsible metaphysical views of past and future; the desire of the majority of academic historians to distinguish their activity from "non-scientific" efforts to discover the "meaning" of history, epitomized by Oswald Spengler's *Decline of the West* (1918–22) and Toynbee's *Study of History* (1934–61); and the debate over whether history was properly "philosophical," spurred in part by the publication of idealist interpretations of history such as R. G. Collingwood's *Idea of History* (1946).

But not everyone agreed that metahistory was a threat to "plain history." Christopher Dawson (1951), a Catholic scholar, endorsed the need for a distinction between *metahistory* and *history* proper. For Dawson, however, the two activities had never in fact been clearly separated in the tradition of historiography; he argued that great masterworks of history succeeded "not in spite of [metahistorical] principles but because of them," since concern with the ultimate meaning and pattern of history imparted an element of "profundity" (p. 12). He concluded that "metahistory is not the enemy of true history, but its guide and its friend, provided always that it is good metahistory. . . . the mastery of . . . techniques will not produce great history, any more than a mastery of metrical technique will produce great poetry" (p. 12). To achieve this standard, Dawson continued, "something more is necessary—intuitive understanding, creative imagination, and finally a universal vision transcending the relative limitations of the particular field of historical study" (p. 12). Although he did not explain what he meant by *profundity* and *good* metahistory, the context of Dawson's argument suggests that he meant these ideas to imply an association with Christian doctrine.

Another party to the debate, Max Beloff (1951: 57), alluded to an important second level of meaning in the word—already implicit in Dawson's idea that *metahistory* was concerned with the "nature of history"—when he used the word casually in connection with "those whose concern is to bring some light to bear upon the actual operations of the plain historian, by subjecting his objects and processes to reasoned analysis." Whether Beloff meant to establish the idea that this sort of activity is "metahistorical" is unclear; in any case, a tradition of usage in this second sense has developed (Yolton, 1955: 477; Dray, 1973: 61). In light of what has been said, one may conclude that metahistory can be understood as broadly synonymous with the idea of PHILOSOPHY OF HISTORY, which, according to the widely accepted view of W. H. Walsh ([1951] 1960), may be divided into two subcategories: *speculative* philosophy of history, concerned with the search for pattern and meaning in history (*history* being understood as the course of human development); and *critical* philosophy of history, concerned with inquiry into the nature of history (*history* being understood as a scholarly activity, or "discipline").

References

Beloff, Max. 1951. "Plain History and Meta-History—II." *History Today* 1 (Sept.): 57.

Bullock, Alan. 1951. "The Historian's Purpose: History and Metahistory." *History Today* 1 (Feb.): 5–11.

Dawson, Christopher. 1951. "The Problem of Metahistory." *History Today* 1 (June): 9–12.

Dray, W. H. 1973. "The Politics of Contemporary Philosophy of History: A Reply to Hayden White." *Clio* 3: 55–76.

Fischer, David Hackett. 1970. *Historians' Fallacies: Toward a Logic of Historical Thought*. New York.

Popper, Karl. 1957. *The Poverty of Historicism*. London.

Renier, G. J. 1951. "Plain History and Meta-History." *History Today* 1 (July): 69. Renier concedes, in response to Dawson, that most histories probably contain a metahistorical ingredient but stresses that the motives, goals, and emphasis of the "plain" historian differ fundamentally from those of the metahistorian. The plain historian seeks primarily to tell a story; the metahistorian seeks to elaborate a philosophy. Renier popularized the notion of the plain historian in his *History: Its Purpose and Method* (Boston, 1950).

Underhill, Frank H. 1951. "Arnold Toynbee, Metahistorian." *The Canadian Historical Review* 32: 201–19.

Walsh, W. H. [1951] 1960. *Philosophy of History: An Introduction*. New York.

Yolton, John W. 1955. "History and Metahistory." *Philosophy and Phenomenological Research* 15: 477–92. Yolton uses *metahistory* in the sense of the "theory of meta-disciplines" (e.g., metaethics), which "examine the presuppositions, the methodologies, the concepts of the sciences" (p. 477).

Sources of Additional Information

To date the most noteworthy use of the concept is Hayden White, *Metahistory: The Historical Imagination in Nineteenth-Century Europe* (Baltimore, 1973), an elaborate extension of Dawson's ideas of 1951, informed by mid- and late-twentieth-century poetic and linguistic theory. White uses the term not as a pejorative but as a descriptive category to refer to the tacit, speculative element that he believes inheres in most historical work. The book is at the same time a good example of *metahistory* understood in its second sense, as a supra-disciplinary form of CRITICISM (although it is also an exercise in INTELLECTUAL HISTORY). The study has generated considerable controversy; see especially Adrian Kuzminski, "A New Science?" *CSSH* 18: 129–43; the review by Andrew Esergailis in *Clio* 5: 235–45; and the six essays in *Beih.* 19 of *HT* (1980). White's work may have strengthened a trend to use the term *metahistory* in a purely descriptive, non-pejorative sense; see, for example, the usage of William J. Bouwsma, "From History of Ideas to History of Meaning," *Journal of Interdisciplinary History* 12: 291.

METHOD, METHODOLOGY. 1. A set of research techniques used to authenticate, date, and otherwise evaluate historical EVIDENCE, that is, source CRITICISM. 2. More generally, any research technique or theoretical orientation used to study the past. *Methodology* may also refer to the type of criticism that reflects on the nature and validity of research and interpretive techniques used in historiography.

In historiography, *method* and its derivative *methodology* are commonly used in two senses—one older and more narrow, the other recent and less well defined. The older meaning refers specifically to the rules and systematic procedures of "source CRITICISM"—techniques for the evaluation of historical EVIDENCE—that were codified between the sixteenth and eighteenth centuries and became variously known in the nineteenth century as the "critical method" (Butterfield, 1955: 15; Stern, 1972: 4), the "historical method" (Johnson, 1926: 118; Potter, 1954: xviii), the "historical-critical" or "philological-critical method" (Fueter, [1911] 1936: 461), and the "scientific method" (Holt, 1940: 355). This narrow use of *method* is preserved especially in literature on the history of historical scholarship in the eighteenth and nineteenth centuries. "Philological-critical method" is perhaps the most accurate label (Fueter, [1911] 1936: 453), since many of the techniques in question were refined by philologists and then borrowed by historians—themselves often philologists as well—such as Barthold Georg Niebuhr (1776–1831) and Leopold von Ranke (1795–1886). This "research methodology" (Hughes, 1960: 21) required the historian to examine critically the source materials and systematically to base his narrative upon them (Fueter, [1911] 1936: 461; Momigliano, [1954] 1966: 105). Today this obligation is taken for granted, but before the late eighteenth century this was not generally true:

historians traditionally claimed to base their accounts on original sources, but few readers actually expected them to painstakingly ascertain the authenticity and origin of the existing evidence or to search for new evidence (Fueter, [1911] 1936: 461).

Outside the history of historiography, use of *method* in this sense seems increasingly dated and "redolent of the nineteenth century" (Grew, 1980: 776); the reason, perhaps, is that the rules of source criticism are now (rightly or wrongly [Momigliano, (1954) 1966: 107]) considered self-evident. In the twentieth century the focus of most research has shifted from ancient and medieval to modern history, making problems of dating, ascribing, detecting forgeries, and so on appear less urgent than they formerly seemed. Explicit emphasis on the rules of source criticism in the training of historians has diminished—at least in the United States—and one often encounters the belief that there is no "single method" (Grew, 1980: 776) of history, that the "discipline of history is [simply that of] argument" (Struever, 1980: 67), or that the historian "does not depend on any systematic methodology" (Higham, 1965: 68–69; Barzun, 1972: 55) but may eclectically "pick and choose" his methods from other disciplines or from the conventions of ordinary logic (Hughes, 1960: 33).

The second sense of the word is much more permissive. Here *method* may encompass any operation or mental process of the historian; following the usage of the nineteenth-century German scholar Johann Gustav Droysen ([1858] 1882), it may refer not only to the mechanics of source criticism but to any aspect of the historian's art or craft whatsoever, including analysis of the theoretical and epistemological premises or preconceptions of historiography (Mommsen, 1961: 78–79).

Methodology—overlapping, often synonymous, and equally broad—may refer (1) to any kind of "technical apparatus" (Aydelotte, 1971: 23) used to interpret evidence (particularly if drawn from fields other than history, such as demography, statistics, psychology); (2) to a general philosophical stance, "frame of reference," or theoretical orientation used to interpret the past (Wiener, 1941; Jacobs, 1968; Polišenský, 1980: 22); or (3) to the genre of criticism that deals with the use of special techniques or theories or that seeks "to clarify the basic principles involved in the definition and depiction of history" (Pflug, [1954] 1971: 1; also Sakmann, [1906] 1971; Renier, 1950: 6). In the social sciences generally, the adjective *methodological* has been more specifically defined as "concerning the methods of concept formation" or "concerning the methods of abstracting concepts from empirical reality" (Burger, 1976: 201, n. 22). Types of literature classed as "methodology" include the disciplinary reflections by the profession's elder statesmen, credos, defenses and apologies, and programmatic statements. The word *theory* is also used in this general sense (Gilliam, 1976: 231). In his bibliography of works on "historical theory," for example, Berding (1977: 6) lists titles on "hermeneutics," "explanation and understanding," "comparative methods and typology," "historical objectivity," and "quantification" under the heading "Logic and Methodology." The American journal *History and Theory*, to cite a further instance, publishes articles in all of the areas mentioned above.

Categories (2) and (3) fall into the field that contemporary philosophers call "critical" PHILOSOPHY OF HISTORY. Historians, however, generally prefer *methodology* or *theory* to the term *philosophy*. (In German-speaking countries, *Historik*—"historics," again after Droysen—is sometimes also used [e.g., Bayer, 1974: 222, Rüsen, 1976; Blanke, Fleischer, and Rüsen, 1984]). This preference derives from late-nineteenth-century historiographical manuals, for example, Freeman (1886), Langlois and Seignobos ([1898] 1926), and, most importantly, Bernheim ([1889] 1908). These guides defined the scope, procedures, and characteristic problems of the new science of history; they often dealt not only with source criticism, but with the history of historiography as well as philosophical issues such as DETERMINISM, VALUE JUDGMENT, and CAUSATION. Maurice Mandelbaum ([1938] 1967: 1–2; 1942: 35) worked in this tradition when he called his pioneering studies in critical philosophy of history exercises in "methodology" (Mink, 1978: 212); the usage is still encountered among philosophers (for instance, Nowell-Smith, 1977: 2).

To some extent the words *method* and *methodology* have lately fallen out of favor and are considered "pretentious" in some circles (Aydelotte, 1971: 167). This may simply be the result of loose usage or because the terms have become associated with the self-conscious appropriation of techniques and concepts from other disciplines, especially the quantitative social sciences (Bailyn, 1982: 2)— a practice deplored by some scholars (e.g., Barzun, 1972: 55; Curtis, 1970: 274). It also originates in the terms' close association with "theory" and "philosophy" and the widely held belief that philosophical pursuits merely distract the historian from his proper task, that is, the empirical analysis of concrete events and situations of the past (Malia, 1969: 1019–20). On the other hand, the terms are widely employed by historians attracted to QUANTIFICATION, SOCIAL SCIENTIFIC HISTORY, INTERDISCIPLINARY HISTORY, and PHILOSOPHY OF HISTORY, for whom they have very positive connotations (e.g., Aydelotte, 1971: 23).

References

Aydelotte, William O. 1971. *Quantification in History*. Reading, Mass. The author defends use of the term methodology.
Bailyn, Bernard. 1982. "The Challenge of Modern Historiography." *AHR* 87: 1–24.
Barzun, Jacques. 1972. "History: The Muse and Her Doctors." *AHR* 77: 36–64.
Bayer, Erich., ed. 1974. *Wörterbuch zur Geschichte: Begriffe und Fachausdrucke*. 4th ed. Stuttgart. Bayer defines *Historik* as "in the broadest sense, the answer to the question of how one can and should practice history" (p. 222).
Berding, Helmut. 1977. *Bibliographie zur Geschichtstheorie*. Göttingen. This is a comprehensive guide to the literature, with emphasis on German titles.
Bernheim, Ernst. [1889] 1908. *Lehrbuch der historischen Methode*. 6th ed. Leipzig.
Blanke, Horst; Fleischer, Dirk; and Rüsen, Jörn. 1984. "Theory of History in Historical Lectures: The German Tradition of *Historik*, 1750–1900." *HT* 23: 331–56.

Burger, Thomas. 1976. *Max Weber's Theory of Concept Formation: History, Laws, and Ideal Types*. Durham, N.C.

Butterfield, Herbert. 1955. *Man on His Past: The Study of the History of Historical Scholarship*. Cambridge. This work includes a concise account of early applications of philological criticism to history at the University of Göttingen.

Curtis, L. P., Jr. 1970. "Of Images and Imagination in History." In L. P. Curtis, Jr., *The Historian's Workshop: Original Essays by Sixteen Historians*. New York: 245–76. Curtis believes that "the surest guide to the past is not *Method*, which includes the monastic and monistic faith in model-building," but "imagination"— as if IMAGINATION were not a question of method (p.274).

Droysen, Johann Gustav. [1858] 1882. *Grundriss der Historik*. Leipzig. This work has been published in many subsequent editions.

Freeman, Edward A. 1886. *The Methods of Historical Study*. London.

Fueter, Eduard. [1911] 1936. *Geschichte der neueren Historiographie*. 3rd ed. Munich.

Gilliam, Harriet. 1976. "The Dialectics of Realism and Idealism in Modern Historiographic Theory." *HT* 15: 231–56.

Grew, Raymond. 1980. "The Case for Comparing Histories." *AHR* 85: 763–78.

Higham, John, et al. 1965. *History*. Englewood Cliffs, N.J.

Holt, W. Stull. 1940. "The Idea of Scientific History in America." *JHI* 1: 352–62.

Hughes, H. Stuart. 1960. "The Historian and the Social Scientist." *AHR* 66: 2–46.

Jacobs, Wilbur R. 1968. "Turner's Methodology: Multiple Working Hypotheses or Ruling Theory?" *The Journal of American History* 54: 853–63. Here *methodology* refers to Turner's general approach to historical studies.

Johnson, Allen. 1926. *The Historian and Historical Evidence*. New York.

Langlois, Ch. V., and Seignobos, Ch. [1898] 1926. *Introduction to the Study of History*. New York. This work was originally published in French in 1898 and translated into English in the same year. The authors called their book an "essay on the method of the historical sciences" (p. 3).

Malia, Martin. 1969. "On the Languages of the Humanistic Studies." *Daedalus* 98: 1019–28.

Mandelbaum, Maurice. 1942. "Causal Analysis in History." *JHI* 3: 30–50.

———. [1938] 1967. *The Problem of Historical Knowledge: An Answer to Relativism*. New York. "An examination of the validity of any intellectual discipline," writes Mandelbaum, "properly belongs to that field of philosophy which has often been termed methodology. Methodological investigations are to be distinguished from general epistemology, since they do not concern themselves with problems of perception nor with general formulations of the relation between the knower and the known. They examine the materials and methods of particular sciences with a view to estimating in how far those methods enable the investigator to comprehend the material with which he seeks to deal. Thus it may be said the methodological discussions represent philosophy's attempt to render explicitly the working assumptions of the empirical sciences, and to determine whether these assumptions contain any fundamental contradictions which render them suspect" (pp. 1–2).

Mink, Louis O. 1978. Review of Maurice Mandelbaum, *The Anatomy of Historical Knowledge*. *HT* 17: 211–23.

Momigliano, Arnaldo. [1954] 1966. "A Hundred Years After Ranke." In Arnaldo Momigliano, *Studies in Historiography*. London: 105–11. The author complains that "much of the present historical research is done with little respect for, if not with actual contempt of, the approved rules" (p. 107).

Mommsen, Hans. 1961. "Historische Methode." In Waldemar Besson, ed., *Geschichte: Das Fischer Lexikon*. Frankfurt: 78–91. This is one of the most thorough discussions of the concept in both its narrow and broad senses.

Nowell-Smith, P. H. 1977. "The Constructionist Theory of History." *HT Beih*. 16: 1–28. Here *methodology* refers to "a critical account of history as a discipline, . . . the conceptual and logical articulation of an historian's thought" (p. 2).

Pflug, Günther. [1954] 1971. "The Development of Historical Method in the Eighteenth Century." *HT Beih*. 11: 1–23. Here, as in Sakmann ([1906] 1971), *method* is understood to refer to a general mode of conceptualization.

Polišenský, Josef. 1980. *Aristocrats and the Crowd in the Revolutionary Year 1848: A Contribution to the History of Revolution and Counter-Revolution in Austria*. Albany, N.Y. The author exhibits the typical Marxist understanding of *methodology* as "theoretical orientation." See p. 22.

Potter, David M. 1954. *People of Plenty: Economic Abundance and American Character*. Chicago.

Renier, G. J. 1950. *History: Its Purpose and Method*. Boston.

Rüsen, Jörn. 1976. *Für eine erneuerte Historik. Studien zur Theorie der Geschichtswissenschaft*. Stuttgart/Bad Canstatt.

Sakmann, Paul. [1906] 1971. "The Problems of Historical Method and of Philosophy in Voltaire." *HT Beih*. 11: 24–59.

Stern, Fritz, ed. 1972. *The Varieties of History*. 2d ed. New York.

Struever, Nancy S. 1980. "Topics in History." *HT Beih*. 19: 66–79.

Wiener, Philip P. 1941. "On Methodology in the Philosophy of History." *JP* 38 (June 5): 309–24. Wiener analyzes three general ways of approaching history, which are called "methodologies": "naturalistic empiricism," "classical rationalism," and "organicism." According to Wiener, the analyst of methodology "will seek the more covert forms of reasoning habits which constitute the inner logic, the *logica utens*, of a thinker's view of history. Every thinker's theory of history has a methodological frame of reference and orientation even where there is in his writings no explicit 'philosophy of history' as *logica docens*" (p. 310).

Sources of Additional Information

In general, see the titles cited under CRITICISM and PHILOSOPHY OF HISTORY. Berding (1977) is comprehensive. See also the appropriate sections of the American Historical Association *Guide to Historical Literature* (New York, 1961) and *The Harvard Guide to American History* 1 (Cambridge, Mass., 1974). H. C. Hockett, *The Critical Method in Historical Research and Writing* (New York, 1955), contains a short list of manuals of historical method on pp. 265–66. In addition, Butterfield (1955: 3, n. 1) cites eighteenth-century bibliographies on historical method. For a concise history of the evolution of manuals of historical method see Johnson (1926), chapter five. A new critical edition of Droysen's methodological works, edited by P. Leyh, is now appearing (Stuttgart, 1977-). Of related interest is Peter Caws, "Scientific Method," *EP* 7 (1967): 339–43.

MODEL. See IDEAL TYPE, MODEL.

MODERNIZATION, MODERNITY. In recent social science theory *modern-ization* designates a pattern of social and economic change initiated about 200 years ago in the countries of Western Europe and since extended to many other parts of the world; its characteristics include secularization, rationali-zation in political and economic life, industrialization, accelerated urbaniza-tion, the differentiation of social structures, and an increased level of popular involvement (direct or indirect) in public affairs. *Modernity* is the end result of the modernization process.

The ideas of modernization and modernity, as well as the associated concept of "tradition," have enjoyed wide popularity among social scientists—including many historians—since the 1960s. *Modernization* is an IDEAL TYPE, or conceptual MODEL, created primarily by American sociologists and political scientists—but also by historians (e.g., Black, 1967; Black et al. 1975)—for the purpose of characterizing, comparing, and explaining the broad nature of global change during the past two centuries; the idea first became a focus of attention in the late 1950s, and theoretical interest peaked in the mid- and late 1960s, when modernization theories proliferated in the United States (Wehler, 1975: 8). How-ever, relatively little attention was paid to the rigorous definition of *moderni-zation*, one author frankly asserting, "We are less concerned with [the concept's] definition than its description" (Black et al., 1975: 4). In the 1970s modernization theory was carefully scrutinized, and many defects were identified, leading to a certain disenchantment with the concept (e.g., Tipps, 1973). The idea was nevertheless well established and is now routinely used by historians in various fields of specialization (e.g., Berdahl, 1972: 65–80; Turner, [1972] 1975; Raeff, 1975: 1221–22; Lindenfeld, 1980: 9; Okey, 1982: 9–10). Some historians con-tinue to strongly defend its use in research (Appleby, 1978: 260–61; Brown, 1976: 3–22) and teaching (Alpern, 1982).

The word *modern* in the sense of "of the present" is of sixth-century Latin origin (*OED*); in early modern English it could mean "ordinary" (as is often the case in Shakespeare), but by the seventeenth century it was associated with the RENAISSANCE convention dividing history into "ancient," "medieval," and "modern" periods (Germino, 1970: 298; Gerhard, 1973: 477—see PERIODI-ZATION). The term *modernity* (the "quality or condition of being modern") was in use by the seventeenth century, and *modernize*, *modernizer*, and *modernization* had all been coined by the eighteenth century.

As an explicit concept of social science, "modernization" is a product of post–1945 American social theory; the idea has a lengthy prehistory, however, dating from the eighteenth century and closely related to the ideas of PROGRESS, social evolution, and social development (see PROCESS). The literature of the eighteenth-century European ENLIGHTENMENT often reflects a sense of the pass-ing of old, established ways of life and the emergence of new social patterns, one that foreshadows formal concepts of tradition and modernity (Bendix, 1966–67: 295). According to Richard Koebner (Koebner and Schmidt, 1964: xvi-xvii), from the mid-eighteenth century onward the word *modern* came to "emphasize the conviction that the present age is one of incessant crises leading on to new developments which are not comparable with any of the past" and to imply that "the critical present is at the same time the beginning of an unprecedented new period in human history." "The conviction of being *modern*," Koebner adds, "is assertive. It commits man to a scientific outlook, to social improvement, and economic development."

Sharp contrasts between old and new ways of life were drawn with increasing frequency by European and North American writers in the early nineteenth century, following the French Revolution of 1789 and the onset of INDUSTRIAL-IZATION. At this point, according to Bendix (1966–67: 295, 324), the words *tradition* and *modernity* already implied two distinct social orders, and the contrast between them became the "master theme which underlies a great diversity of topics and influences our understanding of modern society to this day." Particularly important in this regard was interest in the social impact of mechanized industry—reflected in the thought of figures such as Adam Smith and Karl Marx. A by-product of this concern was the famous contrast drawn by the German sociologist Ferdinand Tönnies (1887) between two hypothetical social models: *Gemeinschaft* (the traditional "community," tightly knit, based on common trust and social convention) and *Gesellschaft* (modern "society," based on industry, innovation, the pursuit of individual self-interest). Tönnies' idea is still occasionally used as an organizing concept by historians (e.g., Johnston, 1972: 20–23).

As early as 1933 the *Encyclopedia of the Social Sciences* included an entry on *modernism*, defined in psychological terms as the "attitude of mind which tends to subordinate the traditional to the novel" (Kallen, 1933: 564), but explicit theories of modernization as a process had to await the end of World War II (Tipps, 1973: 200). The tensions of the "cold war," the collapse of Western Europe as a center of world political power, and the emergence of the United States as an arbiter of international relations all stimulated American interest in the general nature and direction of global change, particularly as it effected non-western societies.

Skeptics (e.g., Tipps, 1973: 199, 233; Salamon, 1970: 83) point to the lack of agreement that characterized work on the subject in the 1950s and 1960s. However, critics often exaggerate the degree of confusion that existed. All theories shared certain features; all, for example, sought to explain the broad nature of global change during the past 200 years. All depicted modernization as a process initiated in Europe by the scientific revolution of the sixteenth and seventeenth centuries and the French and INDUSTRIAL REVOLUTIONS of the eighteenth century. The momentum of these events was believed to have acted as a "universal social solvent" (Black et al. 1975: 1; Rostow, [1960] 1971: 174) to undermine established institutions and patterns of life. All theories were based on the contrast between static, ritualistic "tradition," and dynamic, rationalistic "modernity." In sum, *modernization* was broadly used to designate "the process through which a traditional or pretechnological society passes as it is transformed into a society characterized by machine technology, rational and secular attitudes, and highly differentiated social structures'' (O'Connell, 1965: 549).

Beyond this, there is indeed considerable variation, with some theorists emphasizing economic process, others stressing political, psychological, or social factors. Criticisms focus on a wide range of problems, conveniently summarized by Bendix (1966–67), Tipps (1973: 204–23), and Wehler (1975: 18–33). They include (1) lack of precision in defining the concept; (2) lack of consensus among the various theorists; (3) the tendency to overemphasize one factor or even make *modernization* a redundant synonym for some older concept (e.g., for INDUSTRIALIZATION), thus obscuring matters by encouraging the creation of a superfluous new vocabulary; (4) use of the notion of ''tradition'' as an oversimplified model of pre-industrial and ritualistic societies, which inadequately appreciates the persistence of traditional elements in ''modern'' societies and overlooks the mutual influence that old and new ways of life may exert on one another (this argument eventually led some modernization theorists to abandon the concept of ''traditional society'' [e.g., Black et al., 1975: 7]); (5) the tendency to attribute to modernization a ''quasi-automatic,'' self-sustaining quality that verges on a philosophically indefensible DETERMINISM; (6) ethnocentric use of the idea to imply that modernization will necessarily transform the non-European world in the image of contemporary west European and North American society. With respect to the latter point, one of the concept's most severe critics (Tipps, 1973: 210–11) asserts that ''Far from being a universally applicable schema for the study of the historical development of human societies, the nature of modernization theory reflects a particular phase in the development of a single society, that of the United States.''

Despite the weight of such criticisms, many scholars continue to believe that modernization theory is capable of refinement and worthy of retention (e.g., Bendix, 1966–67: 292). Historians in the United States (Appleby, 1978: 260–61) and West Germany (Wehler, 1975: 62–63), while acknowledging flaws in existing theory, have been among the defenders of the concept, and it has become a ''fairly standard reference point'' in many studies in SOCIAL HISTORY (Stearns, 1980: 220). It may be that the extreme position recommending the concept's abandonment (e.g., Tipps, 1973: 223) was itself a momentary product of the disillusionment that gripped many American intellectuals in the aftermath of civil strife in the 1960s and the Vietnam war, a conflict that was often officially justified by appeals to modernization theory.

References

Alpern, Mildred. 1982. ''Modernization and Social History.'' *AHA Newsletter* (March): 12–14.
Appleby, Joyce. 1978. ''Modernization Theory and the Formation of Modern Social Theories in England and America.'' *CSSH* 20: 259–85.

Bendix, Reinhard. 1966–67. "Tradition and Modernity Reconsidered." *CSSH* 9: 292–346. This key source traces the prehistory of the modernization concept and assesses its criticisms.

Berdahl, Robert M. 1972. "New Thoughts on German Nationalism." *AHR* 77: 65–80.

Black, C. E. 1967. *The Dynamics of Modernization: A Study in Comparative History*. New York. This comprehensive and influential theoretical study by a specialist in East European history contains an important bibliographical essay, pp. 186–92.

Black, C. E., et al. 1975. *The Modernization of Japan and Russia: A Comparative Study*. New York, 1975. This collection of essays includes a valuable bibliography.

Brown, Richard D. 1976. *Modernization: The Transformation of American Life*. New York. Pages 3–22 deal specifically with the concept.

Gerhard, Dietrich. 1973. "Periodization in History." *DHI* 3: 476–81.

Germino, Dante. 1970. "Modernity in Western Political Thought." *New Literary History* 1: 293–310.

Johnston, William M. 1972. *The Austrian Mind: An Intellectual and Social History, 1848–1938*. Berkeley, Calif.

Kallen, Horace M. 1933. "Modernism." *ESS* 10: 564–68.

Koebner, Richard, and Schmidt, Helmut Dan. 1964. *Imperialism: The Story and Significance of a Political Word, 1840–1960*. Cambridge.

Lindenfeld, David F. 1980. *The Transformation of Positivism: Alexius Meinong and European Thought, 1880–1920*. Berkeley, Calif. This work exemplifies the way the concept has been assimilated into many traditional exercises in intellectual history.

O'Connell, James. 1965. "The Concept of Modernization." *South Atlantic Quarterly* 64: 549–64. This concise statement was written when theoretical interest was at its height.

Okey, Robin. 1982. *Eastern Europe, 1740–1980: Feudalism to Communism*. Minneapolis. This brief introduction to East European history is based in part on the concept of modernization.

Raeff, Marc. 1975. "The Well-Ordered Police State and the Development of Modernity in Seventeenth- and Eighteenth-Century Europe: An Attempt at a Comparative Approach." *AHR* 80: 1221–43.

Rostow, W. W. [1960] 1971. *The Stages of Economic Growth: A Non-Communist Manifesto*. 2d ed. Cambridge. This is a widely read, influential, and controversial analysis of economic development in the modern world.

Salamon, Lester M. 1970. "Comparative History and the Theory of Modernization." *World Politics* 23: 83–103. This review essay is based on studies of modernization by C. E. Black, Barrington Moore, Jr., and Samuel P. Huntington.

Stearns, Peter N. 1980. "Trends in Social History." In Kammen: 205–30. Stearns discusses modernization as a framework for social history (pp. 218–20) and notes that "references to modernization and some serious use of a model appear in a host of efforts by American social historians"; he cites representative examples.

Tipps, Dean C. 1973. "Modernization Theory and the Comparative Study of Societies: A Critical Perspective." *CSSH* 15: 199–226. This key source surveys the major theories and supplies rich bibliographical information; it situates modernization theory in its historical setting and conveniently summarizes the major objections. The author advocates abandonment of the concept.

Tönnies, Ferdinand. 1887. *Gemeinschaft und Gesellschaft: Abhandlung des Communismus und des Socialismus als empirischer Culturformen.* Leipzig.

Turner, Henry, Jr. [1972] 1975. "Fascism and Modernization." In Henry A. Turner, Jr., ed., *Reappraisals of Fascism.* New York.

Wehler, Hans-Ulrich. 1975. *Modernisierungstheorie und Geschichte.* Göttingen. This is a comprehensive analysis from a specifically historiographical point of view. It includes a convenient roster of characteristics attributed to "tradition" and "modernity" by modernization theorists (pp. 14–15), as well as extensive citations that constitute a valuable source of bibliography. The author persuasively argues that modernization theory is useful in a restricted sense—not for the analysis of present and future change on a global scale but for the comparative study of the past 200 years of European and North American history.

Sources of Additional Information

Key sources regarding the literature are Black (1967), Tipps (1973), and Wehler (1975). See, as well, Daniel Lerner, James S. Coleman, and Ronald P. Dore, "Modernization," *IESS* 10: 386–409; Gino Germani, "Industrialization and Modernization," *The Encyclopedia Britannica*, 15th ed., 9: 520–27; S. N. Eisenstadt, "Studies of Modernization and Sociological Theory," *HT* 13 (1974): 225–52; and Daniel Scott Smith, " 'Modernization' and American Social History," *Social Science History* 2 (1978): 361–67 (a review of Brown [1976]). On "tradition" see the insights of George Boas, "Tradition," *Diogenes*, No. 31 (Fall 1960): 68–79, and, for earlier literature, Max Radin, "Tradition," and Peter Richard Rohden, "Traditionalism," both in *ESS* 15: 62–70. On current Marxist views, which link modernization theory to IMPERIALISM, see W. J. Mommsen, *Theories of Imperialism* (New York, 1980), p. 125. Cesar Graña, *Bohemian versus Bourgeois: French Society and the French Man of Letters in the Nineteenth Century* (New York, 1974), is a study of the psychological repercussions of modernization in the literary life of nineteenth-century France. Robert Anchor, *Germany Confronts Modernization* (Lexington, Mass., 1972), uses the idea to interpret recent German history.

N

NARRATIVE. 1. A true story about the human past. 2. A discursive literary style frequently used by historians to depict sequences of change in the human past. 3. The art by which a historian casts the past, or some segment of it, in a particular story form.

Since the 1950s the issues surrounding the relationship of history and *narrative*—the art of storytelling and story forms—have been closely interwoven with the debate over the nature of historical EXPLANATION. The question has been approached in a wide variety of ways, and no consensus has thus far emerged (Gilliam, 1976: 251).

Narrative—from the Sanskrit *gnâ* via the Latin *gnarus* (the known, the knowable)—means a story told by one who knows the facts (H. White, 1972: 12; 1980: 5, n. 2). *Story*, in the broadest sense, may be defined as "any account, written, oral or in the mind, true or imaginary, of actions in a time sequence" (Holman, 1972: 511). As was formerly true in English (e.g., Fielding's eighteenth-century *History of Tom Jones*), French and German still regularly employ the words for *history*—*histoire*, *Geschichte*—as synonyms for any sort of "tale" or "story." In ancient Latin, *narratio* referred specifically to the part of an oration summarizing facts that made the address necessary. In medieval times this was extended to include attorneys' pleas in courts of law. The term was first linked to accounts of the past in the seventeenth century and was thereafter sometimes used as a synonym for *history* (*OED*; H. White, 1972: 12).

The art of narrative flourished in the eighteenth century, and two related genres were born: the modern novel (Defoe, Fielding, etc.) and the modern narrative history (Hume, Robertson, Gibbon, etc.). Both claimed factual accuracy as a means of distinguishing themselves from fable and romance (Braudy, 1970: 4–5); in its concerted emphasis on telling polished stories about the past, narrative historiography was, further, a departure from the erudite but fragmented curiosity of seventeenth-century ANTIQUARIANISM. Polished narrative thereafter remained prominent in much historiography, especially in the great national histories of the nineteenth century that were typically presented as political epics with clearly defined beginnings, middles, and conclusions. Narrative, being discursive (i.e., *moving* from subject to subject), was considered the expository form most suited to historiograhy, since history was widely believed to replicate a "stream" of events unfolding in time; this view is still frequently encountered today (see PROCESS; also PERIODIZATION). Arnold Toynbee, for example, believed that the historian must

> adapt the mode of his thinking and of his experience to the movement, in the time-stream, of the events that he is trying to convey. . . . human affairs actually present themselves incessantly on the move. They cannot be described or analyzed truly to life in any other [than the narrative] mode. (1975: 299–300)

Occasionally, however, important histories appeared in which movement was not readily apparent; both Jacob Burckhardt's *Civilization of the Renaissance in Italy* (1860) and Johan Huizinga's *Waning of the Middle Ages* (1919), for instance, portray discrete units of the past "synchronically," in cross-section, rather than sequentially. These panoramas of particular points in time appear to be all "middle," without beginning or end. Some analysts, indeed, deny that narrative is characteristic of such "static" works, which do not explicitly treat the past chronologically (e.g., Gruner, 1969: 284). Even if they contain occasional stretches of narrative, some authorities assert (Dray, 1969: 287), they have a "non-narrative overall principle of organization" and therefore cannot on the whole be considered "narrations."

Still, for various reasons many current historians and philosophers continue to consider narrative an important—even indispensable—feature of historiography. An important exception is the French *"Annales* school" (see SOCIAL HISTORY), which, understanding *narrative history* in the narrow sense of the one-dimensional story of past politics, rejects the narrative approach as tendentious and superficial (H. White, 1984: 8–10). Outside France, however, this is not a prevalent attitude. For example, J. H. Hexter (1961: 21), an American historian, believes that "telling a story" (which he juxtaposes to "analysis and argumentation") is the historian's "real business after all." "Ultimately," he writes, "we do our best . . . when we tell the most intelligent story we can about [the human past], or about that part of it which we know." (Hexter's juxtaposition of "analysis" and "narration" stems from a desire—widely evident among historians—to defend a non-theoretical "craft" concept of historiography over against a "social scientific" or "philosophical" understanding of history [cf. H. White, 1984: 2, n. 3; 8].) Morton White (1959: 73), the philosopher largely responsible for inaugurating recent discussion of the relationship between narrative and historiography, calls *narration* the "most typical activity of the historian." Recognizing that historians perform many apparently non-narrative activities—such as reporting individual facts and searching for causal relation-ships—he maintains that they do them all "in the course of developing a narrative."

In England and North America present interest in the role of narrative in history is largely a by-product of controversy surrounding the neo-positivist COVERING LAW theory of historical EXPLANATION, which holds that explanation in history (like explanation in the physical sciences) proceeds by deduction from general LAWS. Although some analysts of narrative accept the covering law model (e.g., M. White, 1965; Munz, 1967), in most cases they argue that historical explanation has less to do with deduction from abstract generalizations than with the unique shape of particular narratives. A. R. Louch (1969: 54), for example, asserts that "the technique of narrative as it is used by historians . . . is not merely an incidental, stylistic feature of the historian's craft, but essential to the business of historical explanation."

In the 1960s a number of British and North American philosophers investigated this problem (for instance, Gallie, 1964; Danto, 1965; M. White, 1965). Each was, in his own way, a "narrativist" (Dray, 1969: 287), concluding that *history* is basically a matter of constructing narratives (Mandelbaum, 1967: 413). Their studies became the basis for a wide variety of claims, for example, that "historical understanding is best discussed by discussing 'what it is to follow a story,' that the logic of historical statements can be sufficiently characterized as a logic of narration or that explanation in history is explicable in terms of story-telling" (Gruner, 1969: 287). It should be noted, however, that these theorists and their critics (see below), all working within the general framework of Anglo-American analytical philosophy of language, used for the most part a simplified model of storytelling, one that would not satisfy current literary criticism. Specifically, they understood *narrative* as only *simple narrative* in the narrow sense of a linear procession of logically connected, declarative statements (e.g., Mandel-baum, 1967: 415, 417–18; cf. H. White, 1984: 24). Plot construction, motific selection, and other themes familiar to the discussion or narrative in modern poetics—that is, the problems of *complex narrative* (cf. Holman, 1972)—were not explored with a view to their possible relationship to history.

In the late 1960s the narrativist model of historical explanation was attacked on grounds that a distinction must be made between *inquiry*—the business of scholarship—and *storytelling*. From this standpoint narrative form, although widely used in historiography, is really incidental to the business of what history is about; narrative is merely one mode of expression, or STYLE (*style* understood here as something detachable from content), which the historian may choose to employ as a "dramatic" means of communicating or ornamenting the results of his research (McCullagh, 1969: 260; Goldstein, 1976: 139–82). This view is shared by many professional historians (e.g., Butterfield, 1968; cf. H. White, 1984: 2, 18). Maurice Mandelbaum—once a supporter of the view that "the historian's whole purpose is to describe, to narrate" (Mandelbaum, [1938] 1967: 5)—now led the way, arguing that "in judging the merits of historiographical works we use standards other than the standards of interest and intelligibility which are, according to recent discussions of historiography, the primary bases on which we evaluate stories'' (1967: 414). Distinguishing sharply between research and the communication of its findings, Mandelbaum maintained that historians are not in the business of telling stories but are engaged in *"inquiry which aims to establish what did in fact occur.''* The form in which the results of inquiry are presented, then, is incidental and similarities between the historian and the storyteller are ''superficial'' (1967: 414).

Many facets of Mandelbaum's argument were endorsed by others. Arguing that ''there are two principally different ways of conceiving and portraying an individual stretch of reality, a static-descriptive or non-narrative and a kinetic-descriptive or narrative way,'' Rolf Gruner (1969: 286–87) supported the idea that narrative is not a necessary condition or ''defining feature'' of written history. W. H. Dray (1969: 292) conceded that historical ''explanations themselves . . . often properly assume narrative form'' but regarded as ''untenable'' the notion that ''all history, or even every important work of history, narrates'' (Dray, 1971: 156). Richard Ely (1969: 275) maintained that Mandelbaum had ''sufficiently established the falsity of the view that historical writing and historical inquiry are essentially matters of constructing stories, narratives, or connected chronicles.'' Ely concurred (p. 283) on the necessity of making a clear distinction between ''the question of how historians *think*, and the question of how historians may, perforce, have to *communicate* what they think.''

Discussion shifted to a new level in Hayden White's work of the early 1970s. Hayden White (1972: 5), who understands *narrative* as a matter of the overall verbal design of a prose work rather than the sequential linkage of sentences (see IMAGINATION; STYLE), reaffirmed Gallie's view that ''historiography is a species of the genus narrative'' and charged that the distinction between *narrative historiography* and *non-narrative historiography* (allegedly exemplified by an author such as Burckhardt) was itself superficial. Even supposedly ''static'' works such as Burckhardt's *Civilization of the Renaissance in Italy*, he suggested, tacitly involve narrative, partly because they *assume* the reader's knowledge of a beginning and end to frame the ''middle'' that they provide. Burckhardt's concept of RENAISSANCE, for example, makes no sense if it is not seen against the background of the Middle Ages and the course of events since the sixteenth century. More importantly, the very assumption that narrative must move chronologically and display clearly manifest beginnings, middles, and ends is much too narrow and reflects the fact that the debates of the 1960s were uninformed by literary theory and its implications for narrative explanation in non-fiction genres. Obviously, many relatively straightforward chronological histories exist—a famous example is Ranke's *History of Germany during the Age of the Reformation* (H. White, 1972: 6). Others, however, such as Tocqueville's *Democracy in America*, tell stories of a different kind—ones with a ''beginning and an extended middle but no ending'' (pp. 6–7). Different subjects, motives, and temperaments may produce different narrative forms; Ranke's symmetrical story is about sequential change, Tocqueville's unfinished tale deals primarily with stability and continuity. The point is that storytelling is complex rather than one-dimensional and may assume different shapes and carry arguments in many different ways. A narrative can "figure a plot," as Ranke's does, or a theme, as Tocqueville's does. Both are stories nonetheless. Burckhardt's *Civilization of the Renaissance in Italy* tells a story that is "all middle"; his book is typical of stories that " 'go nowhere' precisely because they are intended to frustrate expectations that there is anywhere to go in either a significantly moral or a significantly epistemological sense" (H. White, 1972: 10). The effects achieved by such narrative devices may be regarded as explanatory, since they *communicate meaning* to their audiences, but it must be understood that such explanations are based on the "*topoi* of literary 'plots,' rather than the causal laws of science" (H. White, 1984: 21).

References

Braudy, Leo. 1970. *Narrative Form in History and Fiction: Hume, Fielding, and Gibbon.* Princeton, N.J.

Butterfield, Herbert. 1968. "Narrative History and the Spade Work Behind It." *History* 53: 165–80.

Danto, Arthur C. 1965. *Analytical Philosophy of History.* Cambridge.

Dray, William H. 1969. "Mandelbaum on Historical Narrative." *HT* 8: 287–94.

———. 1971. "On the Nature and Role of Narrative in Historiography." *HT* 10: 153–71.

Ely, Richard G. 1969. "Mandelbaum on Historical Narrative." *HT* 8: 275–83.

Gallie, W. B. 1964. *Philosophy and the Historical Understanding.* New York.

Gilliam, Harriet. 1976. "The Dialectics of Realism and Idealism in Modern Historiographic Theory." *HT* 15: 231–56.

Goldstein, Leon J. 1976. *Historical Knowing.* Austin, Tex. Chapter five attempts to "impugn altogether" the claim that narrative is the essential form of history (p. 150).

Gruner, Rolf. 1969. "Mandelbaum on Historical Narrative." *HT* 8: 283–87.

Hexter, J. H. 1961. *Reappraisals in History.* Evanston, Ill.

Holman, C. Hugh. 1972. *A Handbook to Literature.* Indianapolis, Ind.

Louch, A. R. 1969. "History as Narrative." *HT* 8: 54–70.

Mandelbaum, Maurice. 1967. "A Note on History as Narrative." *HT* 6: 413–19. This is a key source for the anti-narrativist position. The author maintains that "what must be established by those who wish to assimilate history to narrative is that the particular connections which historians trace are primarily successive in character, so that the events which enter into an historical account can be regarded as forming a linear chain of episodes" (p. 415); this, he believes, cannot be done. He suggests that the fundamental relationship in history is "a relationship of part to whole, not a relationship of antecedent to consequence" (pp. 417–418).

———. [1938] 1967, *The Problem of Historical Knowledge: An Answer to Relativism.* New York.

McCullagh, C. B. 1969. "Narrative and Explanation in History." *Mind,* N. S., 78: 256–61. McCullagh asserts that the "narrative style is of value simply as a dramatic means of describing historical events, helping the reader to encounter them with the same sort of surprise as the historical characters did themselves" (p. 260).

Munz, Peter. 1967. "The Skeleton and the Mollusc: Reflections on the Nature of Historical Narratives." *New Zealand Journal of History* 1: 107–23.

Toynbee, Arnold J. 1975. "Narrative History: The Narrator's Problems." *Clio* 4: 299–316.

White, Hayden. 1972. "The Structure of Historical Narrative." *Clio* 1: 5–20. White identifies three kinds of historical narrative, typified by works of Ranke, Tocqueville, and Burckhardt: (1) "processionary" (which "takes us from somewhere specific through a well-marked peripety that issues in a specific ending in a known past")—the model of narrativity used by the "narrativists" such as Morton White as well as their philosophical critics such as Mandelbaum; (2) "structuralist" ("more concerned to figure a structure than to describe a process"); and (3) "impressionistic" (one that "neither describes a process nor figures a structure" but "simply positions us before a body of data thematically organized, which is to be savored as by a connoisseur"). This third type is, White argues, "in one sense, the most sophisticated, for it depends for its effects upon the reader's provision of the correct meaning of the events depicted" (p. 11).

————. 1980. "The Value of Narrativity in the Representation of Reality." *Critical Inquiry* 7: 5–27.

————. 1984. "The Question of Narrative in Contemporary Historical Theory." *HT* 23: 1–33.

White, Morton G. 1959. "A Plea for an Analytic Philosophy of History." In Morton G. White, *Religion, Politics and the Higher Learning*. Cambridge, Mass.: 61–74. This is a pioneering call for the study of narrative in historiography: "If we succeed in clarifying the logic of narration, we shall have inaugurated a new era in the philosophy of history with the help of the tools of linguistic philosophy. . . . For narrative history is a unique form of human discourse" (p. 74).

————. 1965. *Foundations of Historical Knowledge*. New York.

Sources of Additional Information

General questions of narrative are debated in special issues of *New Literary History* (6 [Winter 1975] and 11 [Spring 1980]) and *Critical Inquiry* (7 [Autumn 1980]). The most convenient introduction to the literature on narrative and history is the annotated bibliography in Canary and Kozicki: 151–58. Of special interest in this anthology is the essay by Louis O. Mink, "Narrative Form as a Cognitive Instrument," pp. 129–49, which extends Mink's earlier "Autonomy of Historical Understanding" in Dray: 160–92. See also the discussion of Mink's ideas, which have influenced Hayden White, in William H. Dray, "Theories of Historical Understanding," *Transactions of the Royal Society of Canada* 8 (1970): 267–85. Mink has himself written a concise review of the literature entitled "Philosophy and Theory of History" in Iggers and Parker: 17–27, especially 23–26. In the same anthology see Nancy S. Struever, "Historiography and Linguistics," pp. 127–50. Many relevent titles appear in James R. Bennett et al., "History as Art: An Annotated Checklist of Criticism," *Style* 13 (Winter 1979): 5–36. The journal *Clio* is devoted to common problems of literature and history, including narrative. This is to some extent also true of the journal *New Literary History*. Hook: 3–56 includes essays by Morton White, Lee Benson, and Maurice Mandelbaum under the general heading "The Logic of Historical Narration." Along these same lines see Arthur C.

Danto, "Narrative Sentences," *HT* 2 (1962–63): 146–79, and, in the same issue, James William Johnson, "Chronological Writing: Its Concepts and Development," pp. 124–45. For a wide range of relevent continental European as well as English-language titles, see the footnote citations in White (1984). The most complete explication of Hayden White's views is his own *Metahistory: The Historical Imagination in Nineteenth-Century Europe* (Baltimore, 1973). See also his *Tropics of Discourse: Essays in Cultural Criticism* (Baltimore, 1978). For further discussion of White's work see IMAGINATION INTERPRETATION and STYLE. A related work is Paul Veyne, *Writing History: Essay on Epistemology* (Middletown, Conn., 1984). For the views of three well-known historians see G. R. Elton, *The Practice of History* (New York, 1967), pp. 118–41; J. H. Hexter, *The History Primer* (New York, 1971); and Lawrence Stone, "The Revival of Narrative: Reflections on a New Old History," *Past and Present*, No. 85 (Nov. 1979): 3–24. Finally, see Harold Toliver, *Animate Illusions: Explanations of Narrative Structure* (Lincoln, Neb., 1974), and the review of this book by A. R. Louch, *HT* 14 (1975): 335–42.

NATION, NATIONALITY. Related terms of group classification and identity. *Nationality*, usually the narrower and less ambiguous of the two, refers to group consciousness based on a variable range of shared cultural traits—for example, language, historic traditions, social conventions, or values. *Nation* is sometimes synonymous with *nationality* or (especially in French and English usage) may be used in a political sense to designate all citizens of a particular state—regardless of differences in language, traditions, and so on—or to designate states themselves.

Rustow (1968: 7) calls *nation* the "central political concept of recent times," a claim that could arguably be extended to the realm of modern historiography. The early history of professional historical scholarship coincided precisely with the rise of the modern concepts of nation and nationality, and this fact has left a strong imprint on the conventions of historical conceptualization.

> The idea that the people of the world fall naturally into a series of national groups is one of the dominating presuppositions of our time [writes David Potter]. For the historian it takes the form of a basic, almost an indispensable generalization, so that even historians who recognize that exaggerated nationalism is one of the greatest evils of the modern world, still are very prone to conceive of the structure of the world in national terms. (1963: 116; cf. RIIA [1939] 1966: v)

Leopold von Ranke ([n.d.] 1972: 60), the great nineteenth-century exemplar of professional historiography, assumed that historians should focus their attention on "those nations . . . that have played a preeminent, active role in history" and the "influence which these nations have had on one another, with the struggles they have waged with one another, with their development in peace and war." Although many historians have since doubted that history should deal only with the "great" nations, few historians of the modern era have

> questioned the role of *nation* as the basic conceptual unit within which historical problems [are] to be defined. . . . In every country the dominant historiographical

tradition reflects the political forces which define the boundaries of the nation. . . . most modern history is national history. (Sheehan, 1981: 2–3)

Nation is derived from the ancient Latin *natio*, a product in turn of the verb *nascor* ("I am born") (Kemiläinen, 1964: 18). Its earliest meaning seems to have been a "group of people born in the same place," and the Romans used it particularly to refer to alien or distant groups (Rustow, 1968: 8; Kemiläinen, 1964: 18). It already had a broad range of meanings in ancient Latin, however, including a race, a kind, or a class (Kemiläinen, 1964: 13). In the Middle Ages the ancient meanings of *natio* survived, but new senses developed; it could mean common biological ancestry, one's place of birth, or an organization of university students who came from the same region or spoke the same language (Snyder, 1976: 17; Post, 1973: 323). The earliest English use of *nation* cited by the *OED* is from the fourteenth century. Sixteenth-century English usage was extremely loose and, on occasion (as in ancient Latin), the word could be synonymous with *group* or *class*. Edmund Spenser, for example, referred to a "nation" of birds in his *Faerie Queen*, and Ben Jonson called physicians a "subtile nation" (Snyder, 1976: 17). The ancient meaning of nation as "strange people" survived in the nineteenth-century practice of referring to American Indian tribes as "nations." In seventeenth-century Europe continental aristocracies adapted the word to refer to themselves—as the politically active classes in their societies—as opposed to non-noble groups. This understanding was also colored by the belief that the nobility was biologically and morally superior to other groups (Minogue, 1967: 10).

In the seventeenth century, as well, the two chief modern meanings of *nation* began to crystallize: "territorial" and "cultural" (distinguished in German as *Staatsnation* and *Kulturnation*) (Hinsley, 1973: 49; Bertier de Sauvigny, 1970: 156). In the territorial concept, *nation* designates the entire population of a state, and from this developed the custom of using *nation* and *country* interchangeably. In the cultural concept—associated with the word *nation* but, especially after about 1800, also with the word *nationality*—the thing signified is a group (politically organized or not) that shares common cultural ties, especially language, as well perhaps as the idea of common biological ancestry. The two ideas are ambiguous and can easily overlap, and authorities disagree over which concept first predominated. Two things, however, seem clear. First, the practice of referring to states as "nations" was firmly established in early-modern legal and constitutional usage—"To lawyers and diplomats . . . a nation was any sovereign state, whatever its form of government" (Rustow, 1968: 8). This tradition was so well established in the eighteenth century that it was adopted by constitutionalist reformers such as Jean Jacques Rousseau and the Abbé Siéyès; Siéyès, a leader of the French Revolution, called the nation a "body of associates living under one common law and represented by the same legislature" (cited in Hinsley, 1973: 44). This became the basis for the territorial-political concept of nation that predominated in the United States and France during and after the revolutions of 1776 and 1789. In these areas, especially under the impact of the liberal political ideas of the ENLIGHTENMENT, *nation* took on democratic connotations and meant the entire people of a country. "When political orators of the late eighteenth century invoked the nation, they meant the people [i.e., the population as a whole] as supporters of popular government" (Rustow, 1968: 8). This gave rise to the modern concept of "nation-state," a system of government that reflects the public interest of all the inhabitants of a country and in which the entire population ("nation") is considered sovereign.

Second, from about the middle of the eighteenth century there was a major development of the "cultural" idea of the nation—or "nationality" (Kemiläinen, 1964: 42, 47)—especially in Germany and Eastern Europe. This is reflected most clearly in the work of the German philosopher Johann Gottfried von Herder (1744–1803), the "earliest and perhaps the most influential of all the theorists who have insisted that a nation rests on cultural, ethnic and linguistic uniformity and distinctiveness, and can be defined only in cultural, ethnic and linguistic terms" (Hinsley, 1973: 46). Herder's key idea of *Volksgeist* ("national spirit" or NATIONAL CHARACTER) was based on the vague but influential notion that nationality is an innate quality, outwardly manifested in language, culture, and historical development. The world is composed of many distinct nationalities, each characterized and shaped by its own unique essence. This understanding contributed powerfully to the rise of a new appreciation for the cultural diversity of humankind and, in the minds of many central and east European intellectuals, fed the growth of NATIONALISM, the idea that each distinct nation should be self-governing.

In the nineteenth and twentieth centuries the territorial and cultural concepts have existed together—now separately, often in blurred combination; historians (like others) have often used them interchangeably, leading to varying degrees of confusion (Connor, 1975: 3). Use of *nation* to designate the territorial concept and *nationality* for the cultural concept would clarify matters considerably, but this helpful distinction has not been universally adopted (Hayes, 1926: 4–5).

In both forms the idea of nation has been a benchmark for historical research. Before World War I most historians—and many since—were to some degree "nationalistic," that is, patriotic advocates of the interests of their own nation (whether territorially or culturally conceived), and tended to view the past in terms of the triumph of principles identified with their particular country. History has often been depicted as "national pageant," a practice that persists especially in school textbooks. Early critics of the concept of nation such as Marx and Engels, who viewed the idea as an ideological subterfuge, were not generally professional historians, and their views "made little headway against the patriotic school in academic and university circles until well into the twentieth century" (Kennedy, 1974: 343). It is true that the idea of nationalism, an outgrowth of the concepts of nation and nationality, came under critical scrutiny from the 1920s onward; by 1974 one scholar (Kennedy, 1974: 336) could state that "in [professional] circles today the patriotic historian has virtually disappeared from

the universities and research institutes of Western Europe and the United States,''
and today there are many historians whose work could even be called ''anti-
nationalistic.'' But this does not mean that historians now reject the concept of
nation as a framework for their research, only that they are generally more
critical than before of the policies of their governments. Much recent historical
scholarship has been influenced by the idea of ''nation building'' (Rustow, 1968:
13; Sheehan, 1981: 2), a concept developed by political scientists and sociologists
that is to a large degree a new guise for an old approach. Even the Marxist
historical scholarship of central and Eastern Europe, ostensibly based on the
belief that the idea of nation must be subordinated as an analytical concept to
the idea of CLASS, is no exception (e.g., Polišenský, 1980: 61).

References

Bertier de Sauvigny, G. de. 1970. "Liberalism, Nationalism, and Socialism: The Birth
    of Three Words." *The Review of Politics* 32: 147–66. This piece is especially
    good for the history of usage in early-nineteenth-century France.
Connor, W[alker]. 1975. *The Study of Nationalism: A Bibliographic Essay on the Lit-
    erature*. Washington, D.C. Connor stresses the confusion that may arise from
    using the terms *state* and *nation* indiscriminately.
Hayes, Carlton J. H. 1926. *Essays on Nationalism*. New York. In this pioneering work
    on the idea of nationalism the author's remarks on the distinction between *nation*
    and *nationality* are still useful: "In general . . . 'nationality' is far less ambiguous
    than 'nation' and is most commonly and can be most properly used to designate
    a group of people who speak either the same language or closely related dialects,
    who cherish common historical traditions, and who constitute or think they con-
    stitute a distinct cultural society. In this sense, a nationality may exist without
    political unity, and *vice versa*, a political state may embrace several nationalities.
    . . . A nationality, by acquiring political unity and sovereign independence, be-
    comes a 'nation,' or to avoid the use of the troublesome word 'nation,' establishes
    a 'national state.' A national state is always based on nationality, but a nationality
    may exist without a political state. A state is essentially political; a nationality is
    primarily cultural and only incidentally political" (pp. 4–5).
Hinsley, F. H. 1973. *Nationalism and the International System*. London. This is an
    illuminating discussion of the history of the concept of ''nation'' from the four-
    teenth to the twentieth century. Chapter four is entitled ''Concepts of the Nation.''
    The work contains an excellent annotated bibliography.
Kemiläinen, Aira. 1964. *Nationalism: Problems Concerning the Word, the Concept, and
    Classification*. Jyväskyla, Finland.
Kennedy, P. M. 1974. ''The Decline of Nationalistic History in the West, 1900–1970.''
    In Walter Laqueur and George L. Mosse, eds., *Historians in Politics*. London
    and Beverly Hills, Calif.: 329–52.
Minogue, K. R. 1967. *Nationalism*. New York.
Polišenský, Josef. 1980. *Aristocrats and the Crowd in the Revolutionary Year 1848: A
    Contribution to the History of Revolution and Counter-Revolution in Austria*.
    Albany, N.Y. This book is by a prominent Czech Marxist historian.
Post, Gaines. 1973. ''Medieval and Renaissance Ideas of Nation.'' *DHI* 3: 319–24. Post

is occasionally helpful but tends to confuse the ideas of "state" and "nation." Hinsley (1973) is a much better introduction.

Potter, David M. 1963. "The Historian's Use of Nationalism and *Vice Versa*." In Nicholas V. Riasanovsky and Barnes Riznik, eds., *Generalizations in Historical Writing*. Philadelphia: 114–66.

Ranke, Leopold von. [n.d.] 1972. "A Fragment from the 1830s." In Stern: 58–60.

Royal Institute of International Affairs (RIIA). [1939] 1966. *Nationalism*. London. This work was published in the atmosphere of international tension that led to World War II, but it is still useful.

Rustow, Dankwart A. 1968. "Nation." *IESS* 11: 7–13. There is a valuable introduction with a short bibliography.

Sheehan, James J. 1981. "What Is German History? Reflections on the Role of *Nation* in German History and Historiography." *JMH* 53: 1–23. Sheehan deals specifically with German historiography, but the discussion is of general significance. He argues that the category of *nation* is "too narrow to contain certain kinds of relationships . . . too broad a field to capture others. . . . a concentration on national affairs, together with the political orientation such a concentration usually brings with it, has tended to block from our vision large areas of study" (pp. 19–20).

Snyder, Louis L. 1976. *Varieties of Nationalism: A Comparative Study*. Hinsdale, Ill.

Sources of Additional Information

See also NATIONALISM; NATIONAL CHARACTER. Consult the selective bibliography in Hinsley (1973). The bibliography in *MCWS* 6: 20–59 is comprehensive and particularly good on Marxist interpretations of *nation* and *nationality*. Chapter two of Louis L. Snyder's *Meaning of Nationalism* (New Brunswick, N.J., 1954), entitled "The Concept of the Nation," includes the subsection "The Historian's Idea of the Nation." A much-cited source (especially during the 1950s and 1960s) is Karl W. Deutsch, *Nationalism and Social Communication* (Boston and New York, 1953), which presents an influential "functional" definition of *nationality*:

> . . . what counts is not the presence or absence of any single factor, but merely the presence of sufficient communication facilities with enough complementarity to produce the overall result. . . . Membership in a people [i.e., nationality] essentially consists in wide complementarity of social communication. It consists in the ability to communicate more effectively, and over a wider range of subjects, with members of one large group than with outsiders. (p. 71)

See also Hugh Seton-Watson, *Nations and States: An Enquiry into the Origins of Nations and the Politics of Nationalism* (Boulder, Colo., 1977), and Paul R. Brass, "Ethnic Groups and Nationalities: The Formation, Persistence, and Transformation of Ethnic Identities," in Peter F. Sugar, ed., *Ethnic Diversity and Conflict in Eastern Europe* (Santa Barbara, Calif., 1980), chapter seven. Werner Conze, *Die Deutsche Nation* (Göttingen, 1963), analyzes various meanings of the term *Nation* in German. For a critical approach to the idea of nation building see Walker Connor, "Nation-Building or Nation-Destroying?" *World Politics* 24 (April 1972): 319–55.

NATIONAL CHARACTER. The unique quality, or distinctive combination of qualities, that distinguishes a NATIONALITY and its members and sets them apart from all other nationalities.

The concept of national character has recently fallen into disrepute among many historians, despite the fact that since the 1940s a lively interest in the idea has arisen among anthropologists, sociologists, and social psychologists (De Vos, 1968). Historians today are likely to class generalizations about national character (and related ideas such as "national spirit" and "national mind") in the category of myth, prejudice, caricature, or stereotype (Hartshorne, 1968: 1; Stannard, 1971: 202). Nevertheless, the concept has traditionally been widely used in history and is in fact still frequently encountered in historical studies, whether explicitly or (more often) implicitly (Metzger, 1963: 77; Stannard, 1971: 202). According to David Potter (1954: 6, 8), "probably no other class of writers has trafficked in this concept of national character so heavily as have historians. . . . The concept of national character . . . ranks as a major historical assumption and one which has colored the writing of a vast body of historical literature."

The idea of national character evidently predates recorded history and has its origins in a human tendency to generalize regarding the collective characteristics of alien groups: "the practice of attributing group characteristics to bodies of people is apparently as old as the sense of group identity itself—that is, it is an aspect of ethnocentrism" (Potter, 1954: 4). In written history we find generalizations regarding typical group traits of the Asians and the Greeks as early as the *Histories* of Herodotus (c. 484–c. 425 B.C.). More significant for the history of recent historiographical usage, however, is the crystallization of the ambiguous modern concepts of "character" on the one hand (Metzger, 1963: 78–80; McDougall, 1932) and NATION and NATIONALITY on the other. According to the *OED*, *character*—in the sense of the "aggregate of the distinctive features of any thing" or "essential peculiarity"—dates from at least the mid-seventeenth century. The concept of *nation*—in the dual sense of (1) a territorial-political unit and (2) cultural identity or group consciousness (or "nationality")—took form in roughly the same period. Various writers fused the two ideas in the eighteenth century: the Baron de Montesquieu, for example, used the phrase *divers caractères des nations* (Kemiläinen, 1964: 26, n. 64) and sought to link the "spirit of nations" to climate (Boehm, 1933: 233; Potter, 1954: 22); in his *Projet Corse*, Jean Jacques Rousseau maintained that "the first rule that we have to follow is the national character; each people has, or ought to have, its own character" (cited in Hinsley, 1973: 44). Should such a character be lacking, Rousseau believed, it could be manufactured.

Most important was the metaphysical anthropology of the German philosopher Johann Gottfried Herder (1744–1803). Herder thought of nations, or *Völker* ("peoples"), as "corporate personalities" and referred to the "genetic spirit and character of a people" that he believed to be ultimately "inexplicable and indestructable" (cited in Kohn, 1944: 445). His nebulous but influential notion of *Volksgeist* (spirit of the people, national spirit)—a German rendering of the French *esprit des nations* already used by Montesquieu and Voltaire—is often translated into English as "national character" (e.g., Snyder, 1976: 64). *Volksgeist* referred to the unique, ultimately unexplainable essence that Herder believed animated every distinct human culture and was outwardly manifested in language, values, traditions, and so on. His thinking on the subject was often unclear; at times he spoke as if *Volksgeist* was a product of history (i.e., that it changed and evolved); on other occasions he appeared to assume that it is permanent, outside the realm of historical change (Kohn, 1944: 445–46). In these respects his thought foreshadowed the ambiguity of much later usage.

With the immense growth in popularity of the ideas of nation and nationality between the French Revolution and the First World War, the nineteenth century became the heydey of the notion of national character in historical conceptualization. Leopold von Ranke ([n.d.] 1972: 60), for example, believed that a nation's relationship with other nations was shaped by its "peculiar character" and that "no state has ever subsisted without a spiritual base and a spiritual substance." Potter (1954: 21–25) describes three primary ways in which the concept was understood: "supernatural" ("God had designated the given group as a chosen people and had endowed them with the superior qualities that were pleasing in his eyes"); "environmental" (which "stressed the determinitive force of environmental factors"); and "genetic" or "racial" ("If physical traits, such as skin pigment, are transmitted by heredity, then character traits must also be transmitted in this way") (see RACE; RACISM). In the United States Frederick Jackson Turner introduced one of the most influential variations on the "environmental" theme when he published his opinions on the role of the FRONTIER in American history in the 1890s; the Turner thesis still shapes the way some American historians use the concept of national character (for instance, Billington, 1966: 2, 4). Despite widespread use of the idea in the nineteenth century, however, little was done to analyze the concept itself (Potter, 1954: 8, 20). In the opinion of Hartshorne (1968: 6), even today "no one seems to know precisely what the concept means. Or if any author does have an idea, no one else agrees with him. Even the same author is likely to use the term in many different senses"; most importantly, perhaps, "many historians do not recognize that they are dealing with national character at all."

Toward the end of the nineteenth century, during the vogue of biological and racial social doctrines that accompanied the vulgarization of Charles Darwin's theory of evolution (see RACE, RACISM), the conception of national character as a set of hereditarily determined traits was emphasized. These racial doctrines, however, came increasingly into discredit in the 1920s, 1930s, and 1940s, and concurrently the concept of national character that had become so closely associated with them began to fall into disrepute. The work of certain leading historians of NATIONALISM, however (e.g., Hayes, 1926: 11; Kohn, 1944: 10), continued to reflect cautious acceptance of the idea, as long as it was understood as a product of cultural and environmental conditioning rather than heredity. The tradition of cautious acceptance is still represented by the work of some historians (for example, Snyder, 1976: 55–69), but the main tendency since 1945 (theoretically, at least) has been to regard the idea in any form as at best "an exceedingly doubtful and dangerous image to introduce into one's thought" (Fischer, 1970: 190). Research in the field of SOCIAL HISTORY, with its revelation of the wide array of behavior and thought patterns that distinguish different groups *within the nation*, has done much to undermine the idea of a "unified" national character (Stearns, 1980: 216). Explicit interest in national character, now in itself relatively rare, has usually taken the form of inquiry into the idea as a manifestation of the "mythmaking frame of mind" (Taylor, 1961: 22); interest is typically not in "national character itself, but the opinions people had and have about it" (Hartshorne, 1968: ix; Stannard, 1971). Still, Potter (1954: 7) maintains that "Among the more prominent American historical writers, there is hardly one who does not, either occasionally or constantly, explicitly or implicitly, invoke the idea of an American national character"; he cites as examples Henry Steele Commager, Allan Nevins, Arthur M. Schlesinger, Samuel Eliot Morison, and others, some of whom (e.g., Commager, 1950) ironically repudiate literal belief in the concept in the very works in which they use it (Fischer, 1970: 190–91). In the future historians "will undoubtedly continue to toss the term around with the same looseness that they always have" (Stannard, 1971: 219).

There have lately been scattered attempts to refurbish the concept for historiographical use, notably Potter (1954), Metzger (1963), and Murphey (1965), but these efforts have not generally succeeded in vindicating the idea to the satisfaction of critics. Potter bases his approach primarily on ideas borrowed from anthropologists, sociologists, and psychoanalysts—especially Margaret Mead, David Riesman, and Karen Horney—but critics find fatal flaws in the theories of all of these people (Stannard, 1971: 213). Metzger develops two conceptual models of national character—a "Freudian" model and a "dramaturgical" model (suggested by the "role theory" of George Herbert Mead, Jean Piaget, and Erving Goffmann)—but the majority of American-trained historians remain skeptical of psychoanalytic and sociological theory. Murphey, like Potter and Metzger, turns to other disciplines for guidance, specifically to social psychology and the theory of "modal personality" outlined (among others) by Alex Inkeles and Daniel J. Levinson. This approach, which Metzger (1963: 94, n. 36) rejects, requires that the study of national character be based on the "psychological investigation of statistically adequately large and representative samples of persons, studied individually" in order to define "relatively enduring personality characteristics and patterns that are *modal* among the adult members of society" (cited in Stannard, 1971: 203–4). According to Stannard (pp. 213, 217, 219), Murphey's article "was, and still is, by far the most sophisticated handling by an historian of the national character question to date"; however, his ultimate assessment of even this effort conforms to the generally skeptical attitude that post–1945 historians have displayed toward national character, and he concludes that "the skills and resources of the historian are likely to be seen increasingly as inappropriate, or, at best, peripheral, to empirical investigation and analysis of what has generally come to be recognized as a problem in social psychology." Hartshorne (1968: 5) goes further, doubting the possibility of speaking about group character in scientific terms at all: "The task of deducing character or personality from observed behavior belongs to the psychologist and the psychiatrist, and it is difficult enough to do it for individuals without attempting to extend the process to large groups of people."

References

Billington, R. A. 1966. *America's Frontier Heritage*. New York.

Boehm, Max Hildebert. 1933. "Nationalism." *ESS* 11: 231–40.

Commager, Henry Steele. *The American Mind: An Interpretation of American Thought and Character since the 1880s*. New Haven, Conn.

De Vos, George A. 1968. "National Character." *IESS* 11: 14–19. This contains a good bibliography for recent research in disciplines other than history. Significantly, De Vos himself does not refer to the work of any historian, an indication of the lack of serious interest that historians have displayed since 1945.

Fischer, David Hackett. 1970. *Historians' Fallacies: Toward a Logic of Historical Thought*. New York. Fischer warns against even figurative use of the term on the grounds that it is often "impossible for a reader to distinguish a rhetorical device from a conceptual structure" (p. 191).

Hartshorne, Thomas L. 1968. *The Distorted Image: Changing Conceptions of the American Character since Turner*. Cleveland. The introduction contains a convenient summary of the objections that many historians have regarding the concept. Note the author's own opinion (p. x), which is fairly typical of the profession.

Hayes, Carlton, J. H. 1926. *Essays on Nationalism*. New York.

Hinsley, F. H. 1973. *Nationalism and the International System*. London.

Kemiläinen, Aira. 1964. *Nationalism: Problems Concerning the Word, the Concept, and Classification*. Jyväskyla, Finland.

Kohn, Hans. 1944. *The Idea of Nationalism: A Study in Its Origins and Background*. New York. This book contains a convenient discussion of Herder's thought.

McDougall, William. 1932. "Of the Words Character and Personality." *Character and Personality* 1: 3–16. This article, by a social psychologist, compares usage in English and German.

Metzger, Walter P. 1963. "Generalizations about National Character: An Analytical Essay." In Louis Gottschalk, ed., *Generalization in the Writing of History*. Chicago: 77–102.

Murphey, Murray G. 1965. "An Approach to the Historical Study of National Character." In Melford E. Spiro, ed., *Context and Meaning in Cultural Anthropology*. New York: 144–63. Murphey attempts to link group character traits in early-nineteenth-century America to child-rearing practices, as reflected in the lives of twenty-three individuals.

Potter, David M. 1954. *People of Plenty: Economic Abundance and the American Character*. Chicago. Chapter one is perhaps the best concise survey of the history of the concept's role in historiography. Potter attempts to link a theory of American national character to material affluence.

Ranke, Leopold von. [n.d.] 1972. "A Fragment from the 1830's." In Stern: 58–60.

Snyder, Louis L. 1976. *Varieties of Nationalism: A Comparative Study*. Hinsdale, Ill. This book has a brief bibliography and contains a chapter on the idea of national character. The author assumes a commonsense position: "The existence of similar manners—the core of national character—is recognized without minimizing the difficulties involved in interpreting them" (p. 63).

Stannard, David E. 1971. "American Historians and the Idea of National Character: Some Problems and Prospects." *American Quarterly* 23: 202–20. This is a critical survey of recent attempts by historians to vindicate the concept; it also includes a brief survey of work in other disciplines.

Stearns, Peter N. 1980. "Toward a Wider Vision: Trends in Social History." In Kammen: 205–30.

Taylor, William R. 1961. *Cavalier and Yankee: The Old South and American National Character*. New York.

Sources of Additional Information

See also NATION, NATIONALITY; NATIONALISM. The most important studies in English are Potter (1954), Metzger (1963), Murphey (1965), Hartshorne (1968), and Stannard (1971), and the citations in these essays should be consulted for further bibliographical information; Hartshorne's excellent annotated bibliography is a good place to start. Another good source is Michael McGiffert, "Selected Writings on American National Character," *American Quarterly* 15 (1963): 271–88. See also Boyd C. Shafer, "Men Are More Alike," *AHR* 57 (1952): 593–612, and the same author's *Nationalism: Its Nature and Interpreters* (Washington, D.C., 1976), especially p. 14. An older study, in many ways representative of late-nineteenth- and early-twentieth-century views, is Ernest Barker, *National Character and the Factors in Its Formation* (New York, 1927). Hamilton Fyfe, *The Illusion of National Character* (London, 1946), was for some time an influential attack on the concept, linking it to racism. Social science literature is reviewed by Alex Inkeles and Daniel J. Levinson, "National Character: The Study of Modal Personality and Sociocultural Systems," in Gardner Lindzey, ed., *Handbook of Social Psychology* (Cambridge, Mass., 1954): 977–1020, and H.C.J. Duijker and N. H. Frijda, *National Character and National Stereotypes* (Amsterdam, 1960), which cites 988 studies in various languages. The March 1967 issue of *The Annals of the American Academy of Political and Social Science* is devoted to the subject. Peter N. Stearns has written on "National Character and European Labor History," *Journal of Social History* 4 (Winter 1970): 95–124.

NATIONALISM. A political doctrine, emotion, or state of mind based on the assumption that society is best organized in the form of the nation-state and that the nation-state should be the focal point of individual and group loyalty. A nation-state is a system of government that claims to reflect the interests of all of the inhabitants of a country and in which the entire population (or "nation") is considered the repository of sovereignty. See NATION, NATIONALITY.

Between World Wars I and II historians played a central role in developing the concept of nationalism. Historians were recognized as preeminent in the field, and many professional reputations were built primarily or solely on the basis of contributions to the general theory of nationalism or on studies of the role of nationalism in the history of various cultural and political traditions.

Theoretical interest in nationalism has persisted among historians since 1945, although a primary interest in the subject today may be considered slightly archaic, and one may encounter the opinion that the whole question has been overworked and has reached the point of diminishing returns (for example, Minogue, 1967: 22). The value of much theoretical literature is weakened by the fact that attempts to define and analyze *nationalism* are often prolix, elliptical, and undertaken without sufficient attention to the clear definition of NATION and NATIONALITY, the root words upon which the term is built (notable exceptions are Kemiläinen [1964] and Hinsley [1973]). Many studies are further undermined by a tradition of making the subject seem overly complex (for instance, Snyder, 1976: 7, 19; Shafer, 1976: 8). Moreover, use of the concept has become so popular among historians that in some cases it actually hinders understanding: "The very word 'nationalism' has the power of stopping thought. This is true sometimes even of serious historical scholars, who appeal to the idea as a catch-all substitute for explanation" (Minogue, 1967: 16).

The word *nationalism* (*Nationalismus*) was used in medieval Germany to classify university students who came from the same general region or spoke the same language (Kemiläinen, 1964: 48–49, 54). Most scholars, however, cite the Abbé Barruel's *Mémoires pour servir à l'histoire du Jacobinisme* (1797–98) as the earliest case of modern usage. Barruel used the word *nationalisme* to refer to "love for the nation" as opposed to love for mankind: "the instant that men gather together in nations . . . they cease identifying themselves under a common name. *Nationalism*, or love for the nation, takes the place of general love" (cited in Bertier de Sauvigny, 1970: 155). In practice, historians (and others) have often abused the word, employing it anachronistically to refer to remote eras. For this reason, some scholars believe that any use of the term to refer to the period before 1798 is anachronistic; others maintain that the modern concept predates the word and can be legitimately used with reference to earlier dates— at least in the eighteenth century (Shafer, 1976: 18–19, n. 17).

The word itself was not often used before the 1830s and even then was slow to win acceptance; although it was defined in the 1836 *OED* as the belief that "certain nations are objects of divine election," it did not appear in a major French dictionary until the *Larousse* of 1874 (Bertier de Sauvigny, 1970: 159–60). In French and German the terms became closely associated with exaggerated love for the nation and acquired pejorative connotations. References in the current *OED* suggest that the term was established in English by the mid-nineteenth century and could be either pejorative or neutral.

A multitude of famous and obscure nineteenth-century histories were written to serve what would now be called "nationalistic" purposes, that is, promotion of love for the nation and glorification of the nation-state; George Bancroft's *History of the United States from the Discovery of America* (1834–74), František Palacký's *History of Bohemia* (1836–67), Jules Michelet's *History of France* (1833–67), and Heinrich von Treitschke's *History of Germany in the Nineteenth Century* (1879–94) are only a few of the better known works. Although little analytical work was published on the concept of nationalism before World War I—Hayes (1926: 2) asserts that before the mid–1920s there was "no profound systematic treatment of the whole subject . . . in any language"—impressionistic or polemical essays such as Lord Acton's "Nationality" (1862) and Ernest Renan's "Qu'est-ce qu'une Nation?" (1882) provided insights that would be incorporated in later research. In addition, Marx and Engels and their followers such as Rosa Luxemburg, Otto Bauer, and Karl Renner pioneered efforts to relate the idea to social institutions and economic conditions; the Marxist belief that nationalism is a narrow "middle class" IDEOLOGY—a rationalization for *bourgeois* class domination—became influential and is regularly encountered in various explicit or tacit guises in twentieth-century historical writing, much of it by non-Marxists.

A surge of professional historical interest in the general theory of nationalism arose in the aftermath of World War I, a conflict widely attributed to competitive nationalism. The years between 1918 and 1945 were the "heroic" phase of historical thinking on the subject, when the key works of Hayes (1926; 1931) and Kohn (1944) were conceived and published. These studies (which still provide the broad theoretical underpinning for much historical thinking on the subject) depict nationalism as a product of recent European history, dating only from the late seventeenth and eighteenth centuries (although Kohn, especially, traces elements of the nationalist mentality—for example, the idea that a group is a divinely "chosen people"—to Hebrew and classical antiquity). Smith (1971: 27, 29) correctly observes that the theoretical tradition established by Hayes and Kohn is "predominantly diffusionist" and based on the idea that nationalism is fundamentally a psychological condition; it spreads through a "process of imitation and importation" by a "wave-like outward movement of the ideology from its French and English heartlands, using the medium of the tiny educated elites of more backward areas."

Hayes, undoubtedly the most important figure in the history of scholarship on the subject, emphasized language as a key factor in the development of many nationalist movements and compared nationalism to religion in its emotional force. He defined the concept in terms of four overlapping levels of meaning (1926: 5–6): (1) a historical PROCESS, which results in the establishment of modern nation-states; (2) a political doctrine; (3) the activity of a political party, which seeks to put the doctrine into practice; and (4) a "condition of mind" in which loyalty to the nation-state predominates and "of which pride in one's nationality and belief in its intrinsic excellence and in its 'mission' are integral parts." Hayes (1931) also delineated five basic forms in which nationalism has appeared in various parts of the world since the eighteenth century: (1) *humanitarian* nationalism, tolerant, based on the idea that each nation contributes to the welfare of humankind by cultivating its own unique character; (2) *jacobin* nationalism, democratic in impulse but doctrinaire and fanatical toward opposing groups or nations; (3) *traditional* nationalism, which emphasizes the uniqueness of each nation and the necessity of its remaining true to its own particular traditions and history; (4) *liberal* nationalism, based on the idea of representative government and the idea that the world should be organized according to the principle of national "self-determination"; and (5) *integral* nationalism, which emphasizes the priority of national interest over individual freedom and seeks to increase the nation's power at the expense of other nations.

Although it has been criticized and modified in many ways, Hayes' typology still constitutes the basic paradigm for much historical work on nationalism, the central theme of which is the transformation of the original "humanitarian" nationalism of the late eighteenth century into the "integral," illiberal nationalism of the early twentieth century, culminating in the triumph of extreme forms of integral nationalism in the 1920s and 1930s in Fascist Italy and Nazi Germany (e.g., Snyder, 1976: 11).

Kohn, the most prolific and best-known historian of nationalism, formulated a classic definition still used in classrooms, texts, and monographs: "Nationalism is a state of mind, in which the supreme loyalty of the individual is felt to be due the nation-state" (1965: 9). Also influential was his analysis of nationalism in terms of two basic types: (1) West *European* nationalism (characteristic of politically advanced states such as France and Britain; basically tolerant and progressive); and (2) *non-Western* nationalism (typical of areas where advanced states had not yet been formed—Central and Eastern Europe and the non-European world—and which was intolerant and illiberal).

Since 1945 the interests and energies of historians have increasingly moved along new paths and, under the influence of Marxist, Weberian, and other social theories, there has been a growing tendency to concentrate more on social classes than national units.

Interest in nationalism has been kept alive among historians, however, by the rapid decolonization of European possessions overseas and the founding of new national states in Asia and Africa. At the same time, there has been a notable growth in interest in nationalism on the part of political scientists and sociologists, and certain concepts associated with these disciplines have been widely adopted by historians—for example, *nation building* (the growth of ideologies designed to enhance national consciousness and the establishment of national institutions, already anticipated by Hayes [1926: 5]) and MODERNIZATION theory (in which *nationalism* is understood "functionally" as a tool used by elites to enhance mass mobilization, industrialization, urbanization, and so on). Today many historians would probably agree with Smith (1971: 4) that *nationalism* is best understood according to contemporary economic and sociological theory, that is, as "deeply embedded" in the "wider trend" of "economic development and social and cultural modernization"—rather than in terms of the tradition of intellectual history and political theory represented by Hayes, Kohn, and their followers.

References

Bertier de Sauvigny, G. de. 1970. "Liberalism, Nationalism, and Socialism: The Birth of Three Words." *The Review of Politics* 32: 147–66. The author concentrates on French usage.

Hayes, Carlton J. H. 1926. *Essays on Nationalism*. New York. This and the following
study by Hayes are pioneering works that, for their type—that is, studies in the
history of ideas—are unsurpassed, far superior to most subsequent work on the
theory of nationalism. Through his own work and that of his many students at
Columbia University, Hayes was the key figure in popularizing the study of the
concept of nationalism in the United States.

————. 1931. *The Historical Evolution of Modern Nationalism*. New York.

Hinsley, F. H. 1973. *Nationalism and the International System*. London.

Kemiläinen, Aira. 1964. *Nationalism: Problems Concerning the Word, the Concept and
Classification*. Jyväskyla, Finland. This is a key work, though awkwardly written.
Chapter one includes a detailed survey of the history of the words *nation, nationality*, and *people* and their relationships to the word *nationalism*. Footnote
citations are especially rich in subject and bibliographical information.

Kohn, Hans. 1944. *The Idea of Nationalism: A Study in Its Origins and Background*.
New York. This is the most important of Kohn's many studies and perhaps the
single most famous work on the subject.

————. 1965. *Nationalism: Its Meaning and History*. New York. This convenient,
condensed version of Kohn's interpretation includes selections from primary documents, such as Acton's "Nationality" and Renan's "Qu'est-ce qu'une nation?"

Minogue, K. R. 1967. *Nationalism*. New York. This book is interesting for its ironic
stance toward historiographical use of the concept; see especially pp. 19–25 on
the "received view of nationalism."

Shafer, Boyd C. 1976. *Nationalism: Its Nature and Interpreters*. Washington, D.C. This
work is derivative, based essentially on the ideas of Hayes and Kohn; it is useful
as a synopsis of theories of nationalism.

Smith, Anthony D. 1971. *Theories of Nationalism*. London. This work is poorly organized
and often vague and confusing, despite some insights; it should be used with
caution.

Snyder, Louis L. 1976. *Varieties of Nationalism: A Comparative Study*. Hinsdale, Ill.
The comments on Shafer (1976) apply here as well.

Sources of Additional Information

See NATION, NATIONALITY and NATIONAL CHARACTER. Shafer (1976: 15) notes that
"The primary sources and secondary works on nationalism are voluminous, almost more
than any one scholar in a lifetime can hope to encompass." Fortunately, there are a
number of good bibliographies and review essays. Most general and many specialized
encyclopedias contain entries on nationalism that conclude with brief bibliographies—
for example, *The Encyclopedia Britannica, IESS*, and *EP*. Many of these articles were
written by Hans Kohn. For the older literature see Koppel S. Pinson, *Selected Bibliography
on Nationalism* (New York, 1935). More recent are Karl Deutsch and Richard Merritt,
Nationalism and National Development: An Interdisciplinary Bibliography (Cambridge,
Mass., 1970), which lists more than 5,000 items published between 1935 and 1966, and
W[alker] Connor, *The Study of Nationalism: A Bibliographic Essay on the Literature*
(Washington, D.C., 1975), an able discussion of a large selection of titles. Smith (1971),
Snyder (1976), and Shafer (1976) also contain useful bibliographies. *The Canadian Review
of Studies in Nationalism* has, since 1974, periodically issued an updated *Annotated
Bibliography of Works on Nationalism*. Moreover, Shafer prepares current bibliographies
for the *Newsletter* of the recently established Group for the Study of Nationalism. For

Marxist literature see the comprehensive bibliography in the entry "Nationalism, Nationalities Question" in *MCWS* 6: 20–59. Among the studies that deal specifically with historians and the concept of nationalism see especially David M. Potter's "The Historian's Use of Nationalism and *Vice Versa*," in Nicholas V. Riasanovsky and Barnes Riznik, eds., *Generalizations in Historical Writing* (Philadelphia, 1963): 114–66.

NECESSITY. See DETERMINISM.

NEW HISTORY. 1. An early twentieth-century reform movement in American historical studies based on progressive political values, pragmatic and relativistic attitudes toward historical knowledge, a broad conception of the subject matter of history, and the idea of close cooperation between history and the other social sciences; it flourished from World War I through the 1930s. 2. More broadly, any novel or innovative approach to the study of the past.

The label *New History* came into vogue in the United States at the turn of the twentieth century as a designation for efforts to broaden the scope of history beyond its conventional late-nineteenth-century understanding as "past politics." One of the earliest American uses of the term, possibly the first (Bailyn, 1982: 23, n. 47), appeared in E. W. Dow's *American Historical Review* essay "Features of the New History: Apropos of Lamprecht's 'Deutsche Geschichte' " (Dow, 1897–98). As Dow's title suggests, part of the inspiration for the concept of a "new history" came from Europe—especially from Karl Lamprecht's idea of a comprehensive history revolving around the "socio-psychic development" of humankind but also from Henri Berr's notion of "historical synthesis" (Barnes, [1937] 1962: 377—see also INTERDISCIPLINARY HISTORY). It is possible that the phrase itself was originally an European import, for Berr had used it in French as early as 1890 (Siegel, 1970: 323), and Lamprecht habitually employed the adjective *new* to describe his ideas (Weintraub, 1966: 163). However, the underlying idea had strong native roots in America. In 1891, for example, Frederick Jackson Turner called for a broadening of history to embrace social, cultural, and especially economic developments:

> Today the questions that are uppermost, and that will become increasingly important, are not so much political as economic questions. . . . all spheres of man's activity must be considered. Not only is this the only way in which we can get a complete view of the society, but no one department of social life can be understood in isolation from the others. . . . all kinds of history are essential—history as politics, history as art, history as economics, history as religion—all are truly parts of society's endeavor to understand itself by understanding its past. ([1891] 1972: 200–201)

The phrase *new history* was in fairly wide use in the first decade of the century (Higham et al., 1965: 111), even before James Harvey Robinson's collection of essays entitled *The New History: Essays Illustrating the Modern Historical Out-*

look (1912) transformed it into the label for a specific historiographical movement. Robinson, a Columbia historian, made his university a center for the propagation of novel approaches to the study of the past. Others prominently associated with the movement at various times were Charles Beard, James T. Shotwell, Harry Elmer Barnes, Conyers Read, Frederick J. Teggart, and Crane Brinton. For these men, New History became a battle cry that designated a "synthetic," present-oriented approach that was pitted—often belligerently—against the "political fetish" (Barnes, 1925: 11) of late-nineteenth-century historiography. The term remained popular until the 1930s as an identification tag for innovators (e.g., Brinton, [1930] 1961), but by the mid-thirties it began to lose favor due to a growing association with "indiscriminate eclecticism" (Higham et al., 1965: 119).

Higham (pp. 11–15) draws a concise profile of the movement's features: (1) a pragmatic, progressive, present-oriented attitude that emphasized the importance of elements of the past that were relevant to the solution of current problems; (2) a broad conception of history as the study of "all aspects of human affairs"; (3) an "enthusiastic alliance with the social sciences"; and (4) the idea that history is by nature an inexact science due to the fragmentary nature of its evidence, as well as the intrusion of the individual historian's personality into the interpretation of that evidence.

The present-oriented pragmatism of the New History was reflected in the preface of Robinson and Beard's textbook *The Development of Modern Europe* ([1907–8] 1972: 257), which declared that the authors "have consistently subordinated the past to the present. It has been their ever-conscious aim to enable the reader to catch up with his own times; to read intelligently the foreign news in the morning paper . . . permitting the present to dominate the past." Similarly, Barnes (1925: 16) maintained that the "chief way in which history can be an aid to the future is by revealing those elements in our civilization which are unquestionably primitive, anachronistic and obstructive and by making clear those forces and factors in our culture which have been most potent in performing this necessary function of removing these primitive barriers to more rapid progress." Such attitudes later became a source of inspiration to proponents of RADICAL HISTORY in the United States (for instance, Zinn, 1970: 19). Brinton (1939: 151), himself a representative of the movement, somewhat satirically characterized the school's presentism when he declared that the New Historians thought that "if you could somehow get to understand the whole of the past of a society like ours, learn just how all the stupidities, the superstitions, the inequalities and the other defects we see all about us came to be, you could then take sensible measures to improve matters."

The New History's broad approach and its support for alliances with other disciplines testify to its place in the international movement toward an INTERDISCIPLINARY HISTORY. According to Robinson,

> history's chances of getting ahead and of doing good are dependent on its refraining
> from setting itself off as a separate discipline and undertaking to defend itself from

the encroachments of seemingly hostile sciences which now and then appear within its territory. . . . The bounds of all departments of human research and speculation are inherently provisional, indefinite, and fluctuating; moreover, the lines of demarcation are hopelessly interlaced. . . . Each so-called science or discipline is ever and always dependent on other sciences and disciplines. It draws life from them, and to them it owes, consciously or unconsciously, a great part of its chances of progress. (1912: 73)

In this connection, as well, there was sometimes a considerable emphasis on the notion that history—like the new social sciences—was properly concerned not only with the particular and unique (as was traditionally believed) but with the establishment of regularities and the discovery of LAWS of social development. Brinton, for example, believed that

the historian, too, aspires to the discovery of uniformities, or laws, which will enable him to arrange the chaotic past in an order not merely chronological. . . . If we can, for instance, establish the laws under which revolutions run their course, we can possibly prevent revolutions, or make them less destructive, or at least protect ourselves in a measure from them. ([1930] 1961: 1)

Finally, the New History's subjectivist conception of historical knowledge helped lay the foundations for the debate over historical RELATIVISM that flared in the 1930s and 1940s. Turner ([1891] 1972: 200), who had links with the New History, had already posed the essential problem in his essay of 1891 by stating that "Each age tries to form its own conception of the past. Each age writes the history of the past anew with reference to the conditions uppermost in its own time."

Today, the designation New History is sometimes encountered in the loose sense of any novel approach to historical inquiry (for example, Himmelfarb, 1975; Barraclough, 1979). Among professional historians in the United States, however, it is still usually understood to refer to the crusade spearheaded by Robinson, which flourished between about 1900 and 1935. Since the mid–1930s much of the commentary on the movement has been critical and ironic in tone (e.g., Gross, 1974), and it may be true that the New History was often more an affair of manifestoes about what history *ought* to be than empirical scholarship. Still, the New History unquestionably helped to reorient thinking and pave the way for a more ecumenical and methodologically eclectic view of history in the twentieth century.

References

Bailyn, Bernard. 1982. "The Challenge of Modern Historiography." *AHR* 87: 1–24. Page 23, n. 47, contains references to evaluations of the New History and touches on its links to the work of Lamprecht in Germany.
Barnes, Harry Elmer. 1925. *The New History and the Social Studies*. New York. This work typifies the interdisciplinary spirit of the New History.
———. [1937] 1962. *A History of Historical Writing*. Barnes, one of the New History's

most combative proselytizers, assumes in this second edition that the principles
of the New History have triumphed.

Barraclough, Geoffrey. 1979. *Main Trends in History*. New York. The author situates
the New History in the international context. It is a sympathetic treatment.

Brinton, Clarence Crane. [1930] 1961. *The Jacobins: An Essay in the New History*. New
York.

————. 1939. "The 'New History' and 'Past Everything'." *The American Scholar* 8:
144–57. Although Brinton identifies himself with the movement, his tone here
evokes the impression the New History is already dated.

Dow, Earle Wilbur. 1897–98. "Features of the New History: Apropos of Lamprecht's
'Deutsche Geschichte'." *AHR* 3: 431–48.

Gross, David. 1974. "The 'New History': A Note of Reappraisal." *HT* 13: 53–58. This
is a critique informed by Marxist assumptions.

Higham, John, et al. 1965. *History*. Englewood Cliffs, N.J. This concise, predominantly
ironic portrait of the New History stresses elements of continuity between the
older generation and the New Historians, which, the author claims, were obscured
by the bellicose rhetoric of Robinson and Barnes.

Himmelfarb, Gertrude. 1975. "The 'New History'." *Commentary* 59 (Jan. 1975): 72–
78.

Robinson, James Harvey. 1912. *The New History: Essays Illustrating the Modern Historical Outlook*. New York, 1912.

Robinson, James Harvey, and Beard, Charles. [1907–8] 1972. Preface to *The Development of Modern Europe*. In Stern: 257–58.

Siegel, Martin. 1970. "Henri Berr's *Revue de Synthèse Historique*." *HT* 9: 322–34.

Turner, Frederick Jackson. [1891] 1972. "The Significance of History." In Stern: 198–
208.

Weintraub, Karl J. 1966. *Visions of Culture*. Chicago. This book contains an informative
chapter on Lamprecht.

Zinn, Howard. 1970. *The Politics of History*. Boston.

Sources of Additional Information

For literature on some of the leading representatives of the movement in the United States
see *The Harvard Guide to American History* 1 (Cambridge, Mass., 1974): 283–86.
Chapters twelve to fifteen of Barnes ([1937] 1962) contain much subject and bibliographical information. Chapter fifteen is devoted specifically to the "New History." See also
the brief note in Matthew A. Fitzsimmons, Alfred G. Pundt, and Charles E. Nowell,
eds., *The Development of Historiography* (Harrisburg, Pa., 1954), pp. 422–23. For
information on specific aspects of the doctrine and personalities associated with it see
J. R. Pale, "The New History and the Sense of Social Purpose in American Historical
Writing," *Transactions of the Royal Historical Society*, 5th Series, 23 (1973): 221–42;
also, Solomon Gemorah, "Frederick J. Teggart: Scientific Historian of the New History'," *South Atlantic Quarterly* 68 (1969): 478–90.

O
_____

OBJECTIVITY. Impartiality and respect for truth in scholarship; lack of one-sidedness; balance and openness. More generally, conscientious regard for the critical standards of history as a discipline.

Objectivity has been called "the most important and the most baffling topic in critical philosophy of history" (Walsh, [1951] 1960: 94). The word itself is widely used in everyday speech; yet its ordinary meaning is by no means precise. The term always implies respect for truth; yet it is not simply a synonym for *truth* since we can know that a statement or piece of writing is both false and objective at the same time (Dray, 1964: 39–40). The normal and historiographical meaning of the term combines love of truth, fairness, reasonability, absence of the urge to blame or reproach, and lack of ulterior motive. But more specifically, objectivity in history does *not* imply the absence of VALUE JUDGMENT—for example, "A Roman Catholic could quite consistently say that a certain Protestant historian's work was objective, while refusing to stand committed to all the values expressed in it" (pp. 39–40).

Since history's origins in antiquity it has been axiomatic that historians must avoid partisanship while relating true information about the past. Early historians and rhetoricians recognized that these requirements were difficult, but they did not reflect in any penetrating or systematic detail on the conditions that might limit historical knowledge. For ancient writers such as Polybius, Lucian, and Tacitus, this was evidently not an urgent question; for them *historical theory* was a rhetorical matter concerned with the art of pleasing and effective representation (Unger, [1923] 1971: 62–65). *Objectivity* was "equated with the faithful reproduction of the natural and historical world" (p. 62). Indeed, the origins of *objectivity* as a concept and word seem to lie in the supposition—dominant from ancient to early-modern times—that all thought is imitative, that is, that it copies objects external to the mind; thus, "to be objective is to be part of the world of objects, the out-there" (Blake, 1955: 70; cf. Auerbach, 1953). On this assumption, the objective mind is one that "serves as the impersonal mirror of things" (Unger, [1929] 1971: 62), and its only requirement is simply recognition of the need for truth and impartiality. Thus, ancient thought on the subject did not go beyond the superficial level of Cicero's query: "Who does not know that the first law of history is not to dare to tell anything but the truth? further, to dare tell nothing but the truth? that there must be no hint of partiality in his writing? nor of malice?" (cited in Unger, [1923] 1971: 64).

From antiquity forward, however, there were serious and persistent doubts about the reliability of historians' claims to knowledge of the past (see SKEP-TICISM). Herodotus, the "Father of History," was also known in Greek and Roman times as the "Father of Lies" (Finley, 1959: 7). These suspicions were born of important considerations—that the past is by definition gone and can never be the object of direct observation, that evidence regarding the past is fragmentary and often untrustworthy, and so on. This tradition of skepticism was not seriously challenged until the eighteenth and nineteenth centuries, when history evolved into an academic profession with rigorous critical methods, claiming the status of a modern science (see SCIENTIFIC HISTORY). In that era of confidence, expectations about history were often modeled on reigning "positivistic" ideals of natural science: impartiality, unanimous agreement, precision, certainty, the progressive accumulation of knowledge (see POSITIVISM). Even so, many early professionals continued to acknowledge the contingent nature of their claims to truth (Higham, 1965: 101).

Following World War I misgivings resurfaced in the guise of historical REL-ATIVISM, a form of skepticism that stresses the social conditioning of historians as an insurmountable barrier to the reconstruction of the past "as it actually happened." As early as the eighteenth century, the German theologian Johann Martin Chladenius introduced the idea of perspective, or "point of view," as a factor in historiography, but he did not consider it a serious obstacle to historical knowledge (Unger, [1923] 1971: 71–72). Now, in the context of the rise of modern sociological consciousness, perspective—or "subjectivity"—was elevated to the rank of a major epistemological problem. In far-reaching terms *relativism* defined *objectivity* as the "noble" but impossible dream of attaining complete, trans-personal knowledge of the past (e.g., Beard, [1935] 1972). In its more melancholy variations it suggested that historical knowledge rests ultimately on the "acts of faith" of individual scholars (Beard, [1934] 1959), thereby denying the possibility of criteria for assessing the truth-value of historical accounts and reducing historical judgment to the status of taste, opinion, and IDEOLOGY.

Relativism challenged philosophers and historians to devise explicit definitions of objectivity and to mount rigorous arguments in their defense (see below). In the United States, Maurice Mandelbaum ([1938] 1967) and Morton White ([1949] 1959) were early defenders of history—"objectivists" in the terminology of

William Dray (1964: 21). American-trained historians frequently rely on the arguments of these and other philosophers to uphold the cognitive worth of their craft. Since 1945, in consequence, the idea that history has a ''cognitive function to which considerations of evidence and truth are central'' (Goldstein, 1976: 182) has been refurbished, albeit in a weaker, more limited sense than prevailed in the late nineteenth and early twentieth centuries (Passmore, [1958] 1966: 76–78, 91).

Objectivists accept many of the relativists' warnings about the limits of historical inquiry but maintain that these points must not be overemphasized (Mandelbaum, [1938] 1967: 187–89). The relativist definition of *objectivity*, they argue, is simply unreasonable in its demands: no field of learning—physical science included—can legitimately claim finality or even complete agreement among its practitioners. Finality and perfect agreement may be ideals to which sciences sometimes aspire, but they are never attained in practice. In this context, designating a set of conclusions ''objective'' does not imply that they conform to an abstract conception of unalloyed ''truth'' that stands apart from human inquiry, but that ''they are such as to warrant acceptance by all who seriously investigate them'' (Walsh, [1951] 1960: 96).

Objectivists concede that history, as *human* inquiry into past *human* affairs, may indeed be more susceptible to social bias than physical science; the relativists were correct in denying the possibility of perfect value-neutrality in the social sciences. On the other hand, *objectivity* is perhaps best understood not in the extreme sense of absolute disinterest but as ''*a heightened sense of the possibility* of bias, distortion, and error which our points of view as social beings may induce [emphasis added], and the use of all techniques possible to insure an unwavering devotion to the canons of reasonable belief'' (Melden, [1952] 1969: 200). Although it may be humanly impossible to know the ''whole truth'' about the *entirety* of the past as it actually happened, the demand for omniscience would wreak havoc with the truth-claims of any kind of inquiry; it does not follow that logically responsible conclusions about particular aspects of the past cannot be made (p. 196; White, [1949] 1959: 193–96; Nagel, [1952] 1959: 209–10; Hexter, 1961: 189; Fischer, 1970: 43, 65–68). The fact that personal preference and social bias influence the historian's selection and judgment in no way ''precludes the possibility of warranted explanations for the events he studies'' (Nagel, [1952] 1959: 215). Once again, history is not unique in being selective and evaluative: ''No scientist can study everything in his field; he must select some aspect or problem, and in doing so, like the historian, he follows his interests and betrays his values'' (Dray, 1964: 29).

To be sure, the historian labors under the additional handicap that evidence regarding the past is fragmentary. Still, we do have ample evidence about significant portions of the past; this suggests that we may make warranted statements regarding those segments of the past and that ''where materials are lacking statements should not be made, or if statements are made the grounds of judgment should be given'' (Mandelbaum, [1938] 1967: 189).

Interwar relativism was based primarily on sociological and psychological considerations, whereas objectivists build their defense on logical and methodological arguments. "No sociological understanding of the conditions under which the statement was made," writes Mandelbaum (p. 184), "bears the slightest resemblance to an estimate of the truth or falsity of the statement itself" (cf. M. White, [1949] 1959: 199). The adequacy of historical statements depends on their logical relationship to the evidence upon which they purport to be based. At bottom, objectivists suggest, the question to be addressed is: "What can objectivity be in a discipline pursued in the way [history] is?" (Goldstein, 1976: 184; Blake, 1955). Thus, emphasis has shifted from inordinate demands for certainty to the determination of what it is "reasonable to believe," given the time-honored and tested methods employed by historiography; objectivist analysis involves showing that we have generally accepted "standards, or criteria, in terms of which the acceptability of the historical enterprise is really quite reasonable" (Goldstein, 1976: 196, 170; also Mandelbaum, [1938] 1967: 187; Passmore, [1958] 1966: 89). According to a current view—which Walsh ([1951] 1960: 96, 109) labels the "perspective theory"—what makes a mode of inquiry objective is not so much that it faithfully mirrors independent objects (in history's case, can "events" or the "past" really be considered "objects" in any genuine sense? [cf. Blake, 1955: 72–74]) but that it "has evolved a standard way of thinking about its subject matter," that is, that its practitioners are "more or less agreed in the leading assumptions they are to make about their material and the leading principles they are to adopt in dealing with it." What is required is that a discipline depict its subject matter "accurately from its own point of view, but not in any other way" (Walsh, [1951] 1960: 109; Goldstein, 1976: 132).

Disagreement undeniably occurs more frequently in history than in the natural sciences, and it is unlikely that ways will ever be found to eliminate it from historical interpretation; the critical methods of historiography (see CRITICISM) have nonetheless made possible a remarkable degree of agreement regarding the nature of the human past, a consensus shared by members of diverse persuasions within the community of professional historians: Catholics, Protestants, Marxists, and others (Blake, 1955: 63; Goldstein, 1976: xii). "If the test of objectivity is that there are regular ways of settling issues, by the use of which men of whatever party can be brought to see what actually happened," writes Passmore ([1958] 1966: 91), "then I do not see how one can doubt the objectivity of history."

Within this framework some theorists maintain that objectivity in history is best compared to the determination of truth in daily affairs, in journalism, or perhaps in the law, rather than in the physical sciences. In these contexts "All that is . . . said is that to call something objective is to imply that other people—reasonable people, that is—would accept it" (Blake, 1955: 66). "Every controversy which has raged over the justice or injustice of a judicial decision," writes Sidney Hook (1963: 250–51), "has assumed that the concept of historical truth is as meaningful as the concept of scientific truth, and that historical judgment, although often more difficult to establish than a judgment in science and daily life, can be as objective, even if not so firmly warranted." The "reliability of historical judgment," Hook asserts, "is presupposed by all human beings in the business of living."

References

Auerbach, Erich. 1953. *Mimesis: The Representation of Reality in Western Literature.* Princeton, N.J.

Beard, Charles A.[1934] 1959. "Written History as an Act of Faith." In Meyerhoff: 140–51.

———. [1935] 1972. "That Noble Dream." In Stern: 315–28.

Blake, Christopher. 1955. "Can History Be Objective?" *Mind* 72: 61–78. This penetrating analysis stresses that history and natural science have different standards of objectivity. See especially pp. 68–69.

Dray, William H. 1964. *Philosophy of History.* Englewood Cliffs, N.J. Chapter three is entitled "Historical Objectivity."

Finley, M. I. 1959. "Introduction." In M. I. Finley, ed., *The Portable Greek Historians.* New York: 1–21.

Fischer, David Hackett. 1970. *Historians' Fallacies: Toward a Logic of Historical Thought.* New York. Fischer uses the expression *holist fallacy* to designate the belief that historians cannot tell the truth unless they know the "whole truth" (pp. 65–68). Pages 42–43, n. 4, review some of the standard criticisms of historical relativism.

Goldstein, Leon J. 1976. *Historical Knowing.* Austin, Tex. Goldstein uses the "disciplinary," or inquiry-related, approach to defend the possibility of objectivity in history while rejecting the realist assumptions of the correspondence theory of truth (cf. Mandelbaum, [1938] 1967). He argues that "we are confident that we have arrived at a notable degree of historical truth when those members of the historical community engaged in research on the subject in question reach a level of agreement. . . . From a methodological standpoint, this kind of intersubjective agreement is precisely what is meant by objectivity" (pp. 200, 213).

Hexter, J. H. 1961. "The Historian and His Day." In J. H. Hexter, *Reappraisals in History.* Evanston, Ill. This piece is by one of the chief debunkers of relativism among professional historians.

Higham, John, et. al. 1965. *History.* Englewood Cliffs, N.J.

Hook, Sidney. 1963. "Objectivity and Reconstruction in History." In Hook: 250–74. This is a summary of the tenets of historical skepticism and the typical answers of the objectivists.

Mandelbaum, Maurice. [1938] 1967. *The Problem of Historical Knowledge: An Answer to Relativism.* New York. This pioneering study advanced many of the basic objectivist arguments. Mandelbaum's REALISM, based on the correspondence theory of truth (p. 185), is not universally accepted (cf. Blake, 1955: 72–74; Goldstein, 1976). It is shared, however, by many historians (e.g., Fischer, 1970: 87; Passmore, [1958] 1966: 88).

Melden, A. I. [1952] 1969. "Historical Objectivity, A 'Noble Dream'?" In Nash: 193–205.

Nagel, Ernest. [1952] 1959. "The Logic of Historical Analysis." In Meyerhoff: 203–15.

Passmore, J. A. [1958] 1966. "The Objectivity of History." In Dray: 75–94.

Unger, Rudolf. [1923] 1971. "The Problem of Historical Objectivity. A Sketch of its
    Development to the Time of Hegel." *HT Beih.* 11: 60–86.
Walsh, W. H. [1951] 1960. *Philosophy of History: An Introduction.* New York. Chapter
    five is entitled "Can History Be Objective?" See also pp. 19–20 and 36.
White, Morton. [1949] 1959. "Can History Be Objective?" In Meyerhoff: 188–202. An
    excerpt from White's *Social Thought in America,* published in 1949 and revised
    in 1957.

Sources of Additional Information

See also SKEPTICISM; RELATIVISM; SCIENTIFIC HISTORY; VALUE JUDGMENT. The question
of objectivity in history lies at the heart of contemporary Anglo-American "critical"
philosophy of history, and therefore most general studies of this nature touch on it in
some way. See *HT Beih.*; Birkos amd Tambs; Stephens. The footnote citations in Unger
([1923] 1971) are valuable for nineteenth- and early-twentieth-century German literature.
Wilhelm Dilthey's uncompleted "critique of historical reason," designed to vindicate
historical knowledge along lines similar to those that Kant had earlier used to justify
knowledge of the natural world, is discussed in Hajo Holborn, "Wilhelm Dilthey and
the Critique of Historical Reason," in Hajo Holborn, *History and the Humanities* (New
York, 1972): 125–52. See the comments of Sidney Hook in Bull. 54, p. 126; also the
remarks on "objective relativism" on pp. 22–23 of the same volume. Consult, as well,
Charles Frankel, *The Case for Modern Man* (2d ed., Boston, 1959), chapter seven. Nash,
p. 227, includes a short bibliography, "The Problem of Historical Objectivity." The
citations in Higham (1965: 89–144) are an excellent bibliographical source.

P

_____

PAST. In history and critical philosophy of history, *past* may broadly be understood in two opposed ways: (1) according to the understanding of most historians, the *past* is a "real" temporal realm to which their studies more or less accurately refer—a dimension of time once extant but no longer present; (2) according to certain philosophers of history, the *past* to which historical studies refer is a specifically "historical past," a construct (unrelated to any supposed "real" past) that is fabricated by historians for the purpose of accounting for presently existing EVIDENCE.

Speculation about the past dates at least from the late sixth century B.C. and the Greek philosopher Parmenides (Anscombe, 1963: 36). Despite this long history, comparatively little has been written on the subject, and most of what exists is subject to controversy (Weiss, 1952: 507). In both everyday usage and the language of scholarship, *history* is commonly used as a synonym for the *past*; historical studies are usually written in the past tense, they are normally presumed to refer to past EVENTS, and there is general agreement that history as a mode of inquiry in some way involves a concept of "past." The precise nature of that concept and its epistemic status, however, is a subject of disagreement among philosophers and a matter of disinterest to most historians, because they tend to think that the nature of the past per se is a non-empirical question and therefore inappropriate to their own enterprise.

It is difficult to generalize about the conception of past typically held by professional historians, since they seldom reflect on the subject. Even rare instances that specifically address the question tend to lack rigor or be idiosyncratic (for example, Plumb, 1970: 11–17; Tillinghast, 1972: 3–19; Lefebvre, 1975). In their non-theoretical work, however, historians seem routinely to use an understanding close if not identical to the commonsense notion of "the past," one that reflects the everyday sense of irrevocable temporal change, the use of the past tense in language, and the experience of memory (Bond, 1963). Thus, they think of the past in exclusivist terms; the *past* is the one-and-only past, a realm in which "events happened in the way that they happened, and not in any other way" (Fischer, 1970: 66, n. 4). Many historians would concur in the opinion that "history must posit as its ideal . . . knowledge of the concrete actuality" of this past (Oakeley, 1931–32: 248–49). To be sure, most would concede that this "actual" past can never be *completely* or *impartially* known due to sociopsychological factors affecting the historian's perspective, the fragmentary nature of historical evidence, and so on (see REALISM, RELATIVISM).

Moreover, historians and some philosophers often talk about the past in terms of physical existence and sensory perception; they presume that the past with which they deal is "real"—that is, has an independent status apart from their own researches—and exists as a fixed "realm" with a structure and chronological order of its own that can be "discovered" and "reconstructed" (Weiss, 1952: 521–22; Meiland, 1965: 4; Nowell-Smith, 1971: 7, 12, 20–21; Goldstein, 1976b: 67—see REALISM). They think of "the past" as a domain in which events that have occurred are situated; some, perhaps, believe that these no-longer-present events continue to have some kind of direct or indirect existence (Meiland, 1965: 174)—for example, in the form of memory or in the form of items of EVIDENCE, which are widely held to be "traces" or "remains" of the departed past. Most acknowledge that the past, by definition, can never be directly confronted; it is usually held, however, that the correct interpretation of these "traces" will provide the basis for reliable knowledge of past events (p. 190). Historians often believe that historical reconstructions are true insofar as they "correspond" to the structure of the "real" past (pp. 178–79).

It is not difficult to fault the commonsense notion of past that historians widely employ. For example, much confusion results from the habit of thinking of "past" as a single, uniform entity, that is, as *the* past. There are in fact many logically distinct ways to regard the category of pastness—chronological past, remembered past, mythical past, historical past, and so on (Egan, 1973). "Reference to the past is [thus] logically multiform. . . . to speak of the past without indicating that particular form of the past whereof we speak, is to say but little" (Waters, 1955: 253, 264). From this standpoint, one might argue that "certain pasts may be dismissed . . . as alien to history" (Oakeshott, 1933: 102).

Moreover, the entire question is complicated by a persistent, but obviously dubious, tendency to think of ideas like "past," "present," and "future" as things, rather than as names for our sense of temporal relationships (Leahy, 1952–53).

The most significant attacks on the commonsense understanding of past displayed by many historians come from authors working in the related philosophical traditions of historical IDEALISM and CONSTRUCTIONISM (e.g., Oakeshott, 1933; 1962; Collingwood, [1946] 1956; Waters, 1955; Meiland, 1965; Goldstein, 1976a; 1976b). Although the ideas of these critics differ in many respects, their work broadly suggests that we must posit a specifically "historical past" to designate the particular past to which historians refer and sharply distinguish this historical past from the past we know through memory, as well as the commonsense notion of the "real past." The illusion that these pasts are the same is largely due to the fact that statements about them display the same grammatical form—we refer to them in the past tense. In fact, they are logically different. Waters (1955: 261), following Collingwood ([1946] 1956: 252), argues that

> The radical difference between memory and history lies in the fact that history, unlike memory, is not a premise. History is inferred from evidence. History is highly organized, but memory is spontaneous. In memory the past is a spectacle; here alone is "the past recaptured." The historical past is dead. Much of what is now remembered may enter into history, but it is not historical because it is remembered. What historians call sources are no longer restricted to things remembered and recorded. Using unwritten sources . . . the historian reports as factual that which, so far as he knows, was never recorded [or perhaps even never known] by anyone. (Waters, 1955: 261)

The *historical past*, these theorists maintain, is unique to history as a discipline; it is a "constructed," or "constituted," past (Goldstein, 1976b: 208; xx–xxii) based on the interpretation of EVIDENCE according to time-honored rules of history as a METHOD or mode of CRITICISM. As such, it has nothing at all to do with the past as memory (Zagorin, 1956: 8–9; Murphey, 1973: 11–12) or as an objective "reality" that exists apart from the work of historians. To be sure, a "real past" may exist, and the fact that we possess the faculty of memory may inspire us to look for it (Walsh, [1951] 1960: 84–85). Indeed, the great majority of working historians may believe that the object of their inquiry is such a "real past." Each specialized subfield of history, in fact, exhibits at any given time an interpretive consensus, the result of the tradition of scholarship in that area; "the actual starting point of the individual historian is likely to be [this] professional tradition, . . . which is easily mistaken for the real past" (Goldstein, 1962: 179). But these considerations have no bearing on the kind of past to which historical accounts refer. That past is a construct that the historian creates to account for the presence of evidence (Meiland, 1965: 192).

References

Anscombe, G.E.M. 1963. "The Reality of the Past." In Max Black, ed., *Philosophical Analysis: A Collection of Essays.* Englewood Cliffs, N.J.: 36–56.

Bond, Edward J. 1963. "The Concept of the Past." *Mind* 72: 533–44. This is a summary of logical arguments for and against doubt "whether there is such a thing as the past." Bond's own position is an elaboration of Wittgenstein's statement that "Man learns the concept of the past by remembering" (p. 544).

Collingwood, R. G. [1946] 1956. *The Idea of History.* New York. This book is especially noteworthy for its attack on the idea that history is related to the faculty of memory (p. 58).

Egan, Kieran. 1973. "Mythical and Historical References to the Past." *Clio* 2: 291–307. This is a succinct statement of the premise that mythical concepts of past are more than "false accounts" of past events; it argues that the "prime function" of the mythical past is "the establishment of order in man's mental dealings with the world" (p. 294). The author notes that *myth* and *professional historiography* are functionally similar insofar as they both serve to "establish the identity of the group and its individual members" (p. 302) and complementary insofar as historical narratives employ mythic plot forms.

Fischer, David Hackett. 1970. *Historians' Fallacies: Toward a Logic of Historical Thought*. New York.

Goldstein, Leon J. 1962. "Evidence and Events in History." *Philosophical Science* 29: 175–94.

———. 1976a. "Epistemic Attitudes and History." *Philosophy and Phenomenological Research* 37: 181–92.

———. 1976b. *Historical Knowing*. Austin, Tex. This is a controversial attack on the idea that the "real past" has a role to play in history. Interested readers should consult the wide range of critical reviews written in response to the author's arguments. Although he does not repudiate the idea of a "real past," Goldstein argues that "concern about the reality of the past does not fall within the purview of critical philosophy of history" (p. xx).

Leahy, Daniel J. 1952–53. "A Pragmatic Theory of Past, Present, and Future." *The Review of Metaphysics* 6: 369–80. Leahy reflects attitudes common to early-twentieth-century historical RELATIVISM in the United States.

Lefebvre, Henri. 1975. "What Is the Historical Past?" *New Left Review* No. 90: 27–34.

Meiland, Jack W. 1965. *Scepticism and Historical Knowledge*. New York. This book contains a chapter entitled "The Concept of the Past." It is important, despite the fact that its arguments do not specifically refer to historical practice.

Murphey, Murray G. 1973. *Our Knowledge of the Historical Past*. Indianapolis, Ind. Murphey attempts to combine realism and constructionism: "history, like science, arises from man's attempt to understand the environment in which he now lives, and although it is about things or events which have occurred in the [real] past, it is the phenomena of the present which it seeks to explain. . . . the whole of our historical knowledge is a theoretical construction created for the purpose of explaining observational evidence" (pp. 14, 16).

Nowell-Smith, P. H. 1971. *What Actually Happened*. Lawrence, Kans. This is a defense of historical realism that nevertheless points up the fallacy of thinking of the past as a *"territory*, a realm or region in which events are located as objects are in space" (p. 7).

Oakeley, H. D. 1931–32. "The Status of the Past." *Proceedings of the Aristotelian Society*, N. S., 32: 227–50.

Oakeshott, Michael. 1933. *Experience and Its Modes*. Cambridge. Chapter three, an important contribution to the idealist tradition in philosophy of history, argues that historiography must be understood as a kind of present experience.

———. 1962. "The Activity of Being an Historian." In Michael Oakeshott, *Rationalism in Politics and Other Essays*. London: 137–67.

Plumb, J. H. 1970. *The Death of the Past*. Boston. Plumb draws an unusual distinction between the *past* and *history*, based on a narrow and arbitrary definition of the *past* as the authority of uncritically regarded social tradition. What Plumb really appears to mean is some aspect of the mythical past (cf. Egan, 1973).

Tillinghast, Pardon E. 1972. *The Specious Past: Historians and Others*. Reading, Mass. This book contains the rambling, often obscure reflections of an American medievalist. Despite its lack of rigor, the piece does include a lengthy bibliography of titles on historiography and theory of history, some of which touch on the subject of the role of the past in history.

Walsh, W. H. [1951] 1960. *Philosophy of History: An Introduction*. New York. While rejecting the idea that history can be equated with memory, Walsh argues that memory nevertheless provides us with reasons to dismiss the constructionist position that history does not refer to a "real" past (see pp. 89–90).

Waters, Bruce. 1955. "The Past and the Historical Past." *JP* 52 (May, 12, 1955): 253–69. This is a concise statement of the position that the past in historiography should be understood as the product of the particular, "logically distinctive" kind of inquiry performed by historians (p. 253).

Weiss, Paul. 1952. "The Past: Its Nature and Reality." *The Review of Metaphysics* 5: (1952): 507–22. This is an effort to justify philosophically the "reality" of the past, with some consideration to history.

Zagorin, Perez. 1956. "Carl Becker on History. Professor Becker's Two Histories: A Skeptical Fallacy." *AHR* 62: 1–11. Zagorin rejects Becker's definition of *history* as "the memory of things said and done."

Sources of Additional Information

"Comparatively little has been written on the nature and reality of the past—and what little there has been, has satisfied but few" (Weiss, 1952: 507). See also CONSTRUCTIONISM; REALISM. For general information—both substantive and bibliographical—see the following articles in *EP*: Sydney Shoemaker, "Memory," 5: 265–74; J.J.C. Smart, "Time," 8: 126–34; and C.W.K. Mundle, "Time, Consciousness of," 8: 134–39. Consult also J. W. Harvey, "Knowledge of the Past," *Proceedings of the Aristotelian Society*, N. S., 41 (1940–41): 149–66. For realist and constructionist positions with specific regard to history, see the essays by Nowell-Smith, Goldstein, and Walsh in *Beih.* 16 (1977) of *HT*, "The Constitution of the Historical Past."

PERIODIZATION. The division of the past into segments of time—ages, epochs, stages, and so on.

Periodization is a common historical response to the problem of time and "one of the central problems in the writing of history" (Barraclough, 1964: 4); the practice is generally considered "arbitrary" or "artificial" but—for analytical purposes—unavoidable (Gerhard, 1956: 900; 1973: 476; Besson, 1961: 246; Barzun and Graff, 1970: 46).

In daily life we often sense the passing of time as a "stream," or uninterrupted flow (Smart, 1949), and scholars have often stressed the importance of "continuity" as an element in social change (Starr, 1966: 32–33—see PROCESS). In the nineteenth century it was common to objectify time as a "uniform medium in which historical events occur or historical phenomena have their existence,

and which in itself establishes a continuity among these diverse phenomena"
(Gossman, 1978: 25). The Oxford historian E. A. Freeman (1823–92), for example, defended a doctrine of the "unity of history" based on the notion that
there were no radical breaks between ancient, medieval, and modern history
(Gooch, [1913] 1959: 328); in the same spirit another Victorian scholar, F. W.
Maitland (1850–1906), proclaimed history a "seamless web" (Fischer, 1970:
145). More recently, the French historian Fernand Braudel ([1958] 1972) interpreted early-modern European history as a continuous "long term" (*la longue
durée*), and in West Germany, *Kontinuität* became a slogan of revisionist historiography in the 1960s and 1970s (Röhl, 1970).

Yet even casual reflection on the nature of change demands that time be
compartmentalized in units of some kind. Periodization, wrote the Italian philosopher Benedetto Croce ([1919] 1960: 113; 1955: 390), is intrinsic to thought
and periods are essential "support[s] and aid[s] to memory and imagination."
The notion of time as a continuum may easily become a fetish; in fact, we
ordinarily sense time in terms of discontinuity as well as even flow. The assumption that time is a "uniform medium" has in fact increasingly given way
in the twentieth century to the idea that time is "multiform" and is "constituted
differently by the phenomena placed in series" (Gossman, 1978: 25; cf. Kuzminski, 1979: 344). History may indeed have its origins in

> man's awareness of continuity. But this idea is at once modified by that of sepa-
> rateness—of moments, days, years, hours, centuries. Ideas and objects find their
> place in Time, or more exactly in recorded Time (which is History), with the aid
> of Before and After. (Barzun and Graff, 1970: 46)

Furthermore,

> What is important for the study of history is not that its events are related by their
> position in time, which is at best merely a statement to the effect that events
> happened at a particular moment and not at another, but that it is possible to
> delineate time periods within which human events have a *structure* which differs
> in certain respects from their structure at earlier or later periods in the temporal
> process. (Joynt and Rescher, 1961–62: 159–60)

Thus, COLLIGATION—elucidation of events by situating them in the web of special
circumstances in which they occur—implies periodization since it requires scholars to define labels for the temporal contexts they study—for example, RENAIS-
SANCE or ENLIGHTENMENT. Moreover, Freeman's "unity of history" is itself a
form of periodization that packages time in one big unit (cf. Gerschenkron, 1968:
38), and Braudel's "long term" assumes a distinction between "traditional"
and "modern" periods. Even the simplest chronicle displays periodization, if
only by mechanically dividing time into sequential increments of days, weeks,
years, and so on (Besson, 1961: 245).

Dietrich Gerhard (1973: 476), a leading authority, identifies three general
ways in which time has been organized in periodization schemes: (1) simple
chronology, for example, the "enumeration of centuries and years"; (2) stage

theories of social PROCESS, which depict epochs as phases of broader develop-ments such as PROGRESS or DECLINE; and (3) schemes that "summarize the essence of an age."

Periodization is far older than historiography. In mythology and religion we encounter many types of periodization, for example, nostalgic dichotomies that divide time into golden ages and ensuing periods of decadence, cyclical schemes of birth and decay (see RECURRENCE), and fourfold schemes based on the analogy of the four seasons, the stages of human life, and so on (Nisbet, 1969); the Greek poet Hesiod's *Works and Days* (c. 650 B.C.?), for instance, speaks of ages in descending order of gold, silver, bronze, and iron. It was long held that the ancient Greco-Roman conception of time was characteristically cyclical, and that Judeo-Christian doctrine introduced the idea of time as a linear progression of periods toward a definite goal (e.g., Besson, 1961: 245); this contrast has not withstood the scrutiny of recent scholarship, however, and it now appears that cyclical and linear views can be found in "almost any era" (Eisenstein, 1966: 40; also Momigliano, 1966: 5, 8, 10, 13; Starn, 1975: 18; Trompf, 1979; Press, 1982).

Periodization according to generations, political reigns, or dynasties is one of the simplest and oldest ways of establishing intelligible sequences, and modern American textbooks still occasionally arrange U.S. history—however illogi-cally—according to presidential administrations (Fischer, 1970: 146). A favorite device that dates from the seventeenth century (Gerhard, 1973: 477) is the subdivision of time into segments of one hundred years (the "thirteenth century," the "eighteenth century," and so on) on the assumption that such units have self-contained identities (cf. Fischer, 1970: 145). Certain periodization schemes have special social significance because they condition the assumptions of entire cultures regarding time; the current western sense of time, for instance, rests on the threefold sequence "ancient," "medieval," "modern," a tradition born in the fourteenth century and widely accepted by the seventeenth century (Besson, 1961: 245; Spitzlberger and Kernig, 1972: 280).

Although usually agreeing that periodization is unavoidable, historians are typically cautious and often sarcastic when reflecting on the practice. Croce ([1919] 1960: 110) is only one of the better-known theorists to have stressed that *periods* are fabrications that have no existence apart from the minds of historians; *periodization* is at bottom "an affair of imagination, of vocabulary, and of rhetoric, which in no way changes the substance of things." The threat of hypostatization is especially great; convention easily seduces the unwary into taking periodization too literally and naively confusing mental contructs with the EVENTS one wishes to analyze; thus, concepts such as "antiquity," "middle ages," or "Renaissance" are often endowed with a cognitive status they do not deserve. Croce himself illustrated the problem by citing a former teacher who declared "the curtain fell upon the acting of ancient history in 476, to rise again immediately afterward on the beginning of the Middle Ages" (Croce, [1919] 1960: 114).

Other pitfalls are often remarked. R. G. Collingwood ([1946] 1956: 265) warned against the artificial nature of "pigeon-holing schemes" that are often products of "caprice":

> we are constantly presented with a view of history as consisting of good and bad periods, the bad periods being divided into the primitive and the decadent, according as they come before or after the good ones. This . . . is not and never can be historically true. It tells us much about the historians who study the facts, but nothing about the facts they study. (p. 327)

One of the most commonly cited errors is the inflation of one characteristic— an artistic style, perhaps, or a political philosophy—into the distinctive "essence" or defining feature of an entire period. The practice appears on the broadest level in books about "The Age of the Baroque," "The Age of Liberalism," and so on. It is a species of metaphor; the expression "Age of the Baroque," for example, hinges on a term created to characterize the aesthetic imagination at one point in European history (the late seventeenth century); it implies that the whole of life may be *compared* to the way the arts were understood by their leading practitioners at that time. Mandelbaum ([1938] 1967: 280) identifies this as a "phenomenological" approach, one that "holds that the concrete nature of an epoch is an unanalyzable indwelling quality, an essence which pervades the phenomena belonging to it." Put more simply, it is the "old idea that everything has something deep inside it called an essence, some profound inner core of reality" (Fischer, 1970: 68). The temptations of this "fallacy of essences" may be appreciated in light of the psychological gratification it can provide: "it supplies a sense of completeness and encourages a sense of certainty" (Fischer, 1970: 68).

Many critics (for instance, Fischer, 1970: 65–66; Spitzlberger and Kernig, 1972: 286) point to logical difficulties in stage theories of history, which purport to identify phases in the course of human development (such as those of Hegel and Marx). Such schemes suppose that history is a single entity whose total pattern can be comprehended (see METAHISTORY; PHILOSOPHY OF HISTORY; UNIVERSAL HISTORY). This presumed whole is then compared to some mundane whole that we know through direct acquaintance (e.g., the human life cycle, the cycle of seasons, and so on). The problem—aside from simplistic metaphor— is that the "wholeness of the history is . . . not accessible to any proof of its wholeness whatsoever. . . . history, as a unity and a whole, lies beyond our grasp" (Spitzlberger and Kernig, 1972: 286). Such considerations threaten not only grand philosophies of history such as those of Hegel and Marx but may undermine the "cardinal principle" of *all* periodization as well, namely, "the claim to subdivide the 'whole'."

> The wealth of discussions centering on periodization can be formally reduced . . . to one simple problem [write Spitzlberger and Kernig]. If the lapidary formula of the scientist, to the effect that "that which can be measured exists," is stated negatively ("what does not exist cannot be measured") then it follows quite strictly

that the totality of history, which is inaccessable to man and therefore non-existant for him, can admit of no measure and hence of no periodization. (1972: 288)

Such considerations, however, do not render the use of periodization necessarily "false" or even arbitrary.

To object to labels or periods and say that "historians invent them, hence they are false" is a cliché that is itself false to the way things happen, besides amounting to a failure of imagination. Without divisions of time, groupings of men, aggregates of ideas, the historian would be reduced to unreadable, unrememberable chronicling. (Barzun and Graff, 1970: 177; cf. Fischer, 1970: 145)

Maurice Mandelbaum ([1938] 1967: 280) agrees, arguing that "the [responsible] delimitation of epochs rests not upon caprice, but upon something given in the nature of the historical materials."

an epoch [he writes] is defined in terms of some comparatively long-enduring event which takes place within a given locality and concerns a given class of historical phenomena. Thus, the epoch of the Industrial Revolution . . . is an epoch because within one given locality and in one field of historical phenomena, there was a long-enduring event which we may call the rise of the factory system of production. . . . an epoch is characterized by the emergence of a certain comparatively long-enduring event, and the epoch is itself nothing but this event. (p. 282)

What should be recognized is that, necessary as periodization is, the particular forms it takes will depend on the perspectives of historians and the social theories to which they subscribe. In the words of Gerschenkron,

at all times it is the ordering hand of the historian that creates continuities and discontinuities. . . . It is the historian who decides how far back the causal chain should be pursued and who by his fiat creates its "beginning" as he creates endogenous and exogenous events. And it is the historian's own model in terms of which changes in the rate of historical change are defined. (1968: 38)

References

Barraclough, Geoffrey. 1964. *An Introduction to Contemporary History*. New York.
Barzun, Jacques, and Graff, Henry F. 1970. *The Modern Researcher*. New York. This is a revised version of a book that originally appeared in 1957. The authors maintain that "Periods, like centuries, are arbitrary divisions for convenience, nothing more" (p. 46).
Besson, Waldemar, ed. 1961. *Geschichte. Das Fischer Lexikon*. Frankfurt.
Braudel, Fernand. [1958] 1972. "History and the Social Sciences: The Long Term." In Stern: 404–29.
Collingwood, R. G. [1946] 1956, *The Idea of History*. New York. Collingwood treats *periodization* sarcastically in terms of "optical illusions."
Croce, Benedetto. 1955. *History as the Story of Liberty*. New York.
———. [1919] 1960. *History: Its Theory and Practice*. New York.
Eisenstein, Elizabeth L. 1966. "Clio and Chronos: An Essay on the Making and Breaking of History-Book Time." *HT Beih*. 6: 36–64.

Fischer, David Hackett. 1970. *Historians' Fallacies: Toward a Logic of Historical Thought*. New York. Fischer identifies four of the most common "fallacies of false periodization" (pp. 144–46).

Gerhard, Dietrich. 1956. "Periodization in European History." *AHR* 61: 900–13. Gerhard argues that "any division of time into definite periods is artificial. Recent experience has taught [the historian] that even in the midst of upheavals and utter destruction there is no complete break with the past" (p. 908).

———. 1973. "Periodization in History." *DHI* 3: 476–81. This is a basic introduction with an excellent bibliography.

Gerschenkron, Alexander. 1968. "On the Concept of Continuity in History." In Alexander Gerschenkron, *Continuity in History and Other Essays*. Cambridge, Mass.: 11–39. By a well-known economic historian.

Gooch, G. P. [1913] 1959. *History and Historians in the Nineteenth Century*. Boston.

Gossman, Lionel. 1978. "History and Literature: Reproduction or Signification." In Canary and Kozicki: 3–39.

Joynt, Carey B., and Rescher, Nicholas. 1961–62. "The Problem of Uniqueness in History." *HT* 1: 150–62.

Kuzminski, Adrian. 1979. "Defending Historical Realism." *HT* 18: 316–49. "In modern physics," writes the author, "time has become a function of events—just as Braudel suggests—rather than the other way around" (p. 344).

Mandelbaum, Maurice. [1938] 1967, *The Problem of Historical Knowledge: An Answer to Relativism*. New York. Mandelbaum asserts that *periods* are abstractions from the historical process but argues that it is nonetheless an "indisputable . . . fact that historical events may be said to fall into epochs" (p. 281).

Momigliano, Arnaldo. 1966. "Time in Ancient Historiography." *HT Beih.* 6: 1–23.

Nisbet, Robert A. 1969. *Social Change and History: Aspects of the Western Theory of Development*. New York.

Press, Gerald A. 1982. *The Development of the Idea of History in Antiquity*. Kingston and Montreal.

Röhl, J.C.G. 1970. *From Bismarck to Hitler: The Problem of Continuity in German History*. New York. The introduction and conclusion of this anthology provide a thoughtful account of ways the concept of "continuity" has been used in recent German historiography.

Smart, J.J.C. 1949. "The River of Time." *Mind*, N. S., 58: 483–94.

Spitzlberger, Georg, and Kernig, Claus D. 1972. "Periodization." *MCWS* 6: 278–83.

Starn, Randolph. 1975. "Meaning Levels in the Theme of Historical Decline." *HT* 14: 1–31.

Starr, Chester G. 1966. "Historical and Philosophical Time." *HT Beih.* 6: 24–35.

Trompf, G. W. 1979. *The Idea of Historical Recurrence in Western Thought: From Antiquity to the Reformation*. Berkeley, Calif.

Sources of Additional Information

See especially the bibliographies in Spitzlberger and Kernig (1972) and Gerhard (1973); also Malcom M. Willey, "Continuity, Social," *ESS* 4 (1931): 315–18. Paul Egon Hübinger, ed., *Zur Frage der Periodengrenze zwischen Altertum und Mittelalter* (Darmstadt, 1969), is an important collection of articles. J.H.J. van der Pot, *De Periodisering der Geschiedenis: Een overzicht der Theorieën* (The Hague, 1951), is a frequently cited survey of theories of periodization, from antiquity to the present. See also George Boas,

"Historical Periods," *The Journal of Aesthetics and Art Criticism* 11 (1953): 248–54. *HT Beih.* 6 (1966) is devoted to "History and the Concept of Time," and includes the essays by Eisenstein, Momigliano, and Starr cited above. As Starr notes (pp. 24–25), reflection on "time" per se is rare among professional historians and is generally considered an "unwarranted intrusion" into historical analysis, something left "almost entirely to philosophers and theologians." For general bibliography see especially J. T. Fraser, *The Voices of Time: A Cooperative Survey of Man's Views of Time as Expressed by the Sciences and the Humanities* (New York, 1966); the entry on time by J.J.C. Smart in *EP* 8 (1967): 126–34; and Stephen Toulmin and June Goodfield, *The Discovery of Time* (New York, 1965). See also W. von Leyden, "History and the Concept of Relative Time," *HT* 2 (1962–63): 263–85, and J. A. Harrison, who observes that historians come by their ideas of time

> partly through a sort of osmosis from the ethos in which [they are] raised and partly from the kind of training [they get]. Since historians everywhere, or at least the overwhelming majority of them, are trained primarily in their national histories, then their sense of time reflects their national time-patterns, and accordingly their comprehension of history and causality is a reflection of these ideas of time. ("Time and the American Historian," *South Atlantic Quarterly* 64 [Summer, 1965]: 362–66)

Salomon Bochner, "Continuity and Discontinuity," *DHI* 1: 492–504, is suggestive on the relationship of historical continuity to mathematical, philosophical, theological, and scientific usage. Much of the literature on continuity comes from Germany, where scholars have long displayed a special interest in the problems of discriminating between late antiquity and the early Middle Ages: for example, Hermann Aubin, "Zur Frage der historischen Kontinuität im Allgemeinen," *Historische Zeitschrift* 168 (1943): 229–62; G. Adolf Rein, "Zum Problem der historischen Kontinuität," *Ranke-Gesellschaft Jahrbuch* (1955): 9–16; and Paul Egon Hübinger, ed., *Kulturbruch oder Kulturkontinuität im Übergang von der Antike zum Mittelalter* (Darmstadt, 1968), which reprints Aubin (1943). See also S. Körner, "Continuity," *EP* 1 (1967): 205–7, and Joseph Agassi, "Continuity and Discontinuity in the History of Science," *JHI* 34 (Oct.–Dec. 1973): 609–26.

PHILOSOPHY OF HISTORY. Reflection on the nature of history—*history* being understood as either the course of human events or, more narrowly, as the specialized activity of historians. The idea may be subdivided into three categories: *speculative* philosophy of history, concerned with the search for general pattern and meaning in history (understood as the course of human events); *critical* (or *analytical*) philosophy of history, concerned with the analysis of history as a mode of inquiry—its basic assumptions, methods of explanation, and so on; and *pragmatic* philosophy of history, concerned with the practical reasons for studying the past.

The expression *philosophy of history* covers a very broad span of meaning, a fact reflected in Karl Popper's statement (1969: 181) that philosophy of history involves "three big questions": (1) What is the plot of history? (2) What is the use of history? and (3) How are we to write history, or what is the method of history? The term itself, a variation on the expression *philosophical historian* (*philosoph-historicus*), which goes back to Jean Bodin's *Methodus, ad Facilem*

Historiarum Cognitionem of 1566 (Manuel, 1976: 231), was introduced by Voltaire in the essay *La Philosophie de l'histoire* (1765). The idea of reflecting systematically on the nature of history in any or all of the senses cited above is ancient, however, dating at least from the treatise "How to Write History," by Lucian of Samosata (c. A.D. 125–c. 180).

On the other hand, the idea of differentiating clearly between *speculative* and *critical* philosophy of history is recent and is most firmly established among English and American philosophers. Terminologically, these expressions may derive from the general distinction between *critical* and *speculative* philosophy drawn by C. D. Broad in his *Scientific Thought* (1923) (Gruner, 1972: 283). The sharp distinctions between *metaphysics* and *logical analysis* made by continental philosophers such as Rudolf Carnap in the 1920s and 1930s are also important (M. White, 1968: 708). Raymond Aron's *La philosophie critique de l'histoire* (1938) was a very early example of the use of "critical philosophy of history"; but it was not until the early 1950s that the distinction between *speculative* and *critical* philosophies of history was clearly drawn and popularized by the British philosopher W. H. Walsh ([1951] 1960: 13–28).

As yet there is no well-established English expression to refer to the third branch of philosophy of history, which deals with the practical reasons for studying the past, but it has been correctly observed that the terms *speculative* and *critical* do not adequately cover reflection on the "purpose and value of historical study and knowledge" (Gruner, 1972: 284)—a subject that has an ancient tradition and a vast literature. Following German usage (Hahn, 1974: 401–2) and the hint of a precedent in Mandelbaum (1952: 318), one may suggest the label "pragmatics of the discipline of history" or, more simply, "pragmatic philosophy of history."

Until recently, *philosophy of history* was understood by most historians and philosophers to refer only to the first sense noted above, that is, the "attempt to plot the whole past, present, and future of mankind" (Brinton, 1937–38: 245; Mandelbaum, 1948: 365; Gottschalk, 1963: 114). The term is still regularly used in this way by leading historians (e.g., Manuel, 1965: 137; H. White, 1978: 115). This tradition stems primarily from the late eighteenth century and what was then often called *philosophical history*, a term still on occasion used to designate speculative philosophy of history (for instance, Manuel, 1965). If the transcendent meaning in question is borrowed from religious doctrine, the term *theology of history* may also be employed (La Piana, [1943] 1950). In religious and secular forms *philosophical history* was widespread before 1914, when it found expression in the thought of social theorists such as Comte, Hegel, and Marx and in the work of historians such as Guizot in France and Buckle in England, who incorporated speculative social theory into their histories. *Speculative philosophy of history* has continued to grow in popularity in the twentieth century but mainly outside the ranks of professional historiography. Among non-Marxist academic historians, especially those in England and America, *speculative philosophy of history* has come to imply "forcible imposition of a creed upon the facts'' (Barzun, [1943] 1950: 49) and—with isolated exceptions (e.g., Toynbee, 1934–61; Mazlish, 1966: 333–35)—has found few defenders. This is true of many leading philosophers as well (for example, Mandelbaum, 1939–40; M. White, 1968).

Historians recognize that an overlap exists between the concept of "philosophical history" and another eighteenth-century idea, UNIVERSAL HISTORY (world history, the history of humankind). These two concepts are not necessarily synonymous, however. It is possible to conceive of a history of humankind in which there would be no concerted search for underlying pattern, although in fact many universal histories have assumed that one is there to be discovered. The idea of philosophical history is perhaps implicit in most if not all universal histories (and, some would argue, in most histories of any kind—e.g., Gruner, 1972: 287–88, 300; H. White, 1973b: 45–46); nonetheless, it seems best to think of philosophical history as a subcategory of universal history, one that *deliberately* searches for pattern and meaning in the history of humankind.

Today most Anglo-American philosophers who are interested in history are practitioners of "critical" philosophy of history. This approach was foreshadowed in the late nineteenth century by a number of efforts to analyze historical inquiry and its relationship to other kinds of knowledge: in Germany J. G. Droysen's *Grundriss der Historik* (1858) as well as certain writings of Wilhelm Dilthey, Wilhelm Windelband, and Heinrich Rickert; in Italy the work of Benedetto Croce; and in England, F. H. Bradley's *Presuppositions of Critical History* (1874). The real pioneering works of the genre, however, were Maurice Mandelbaum's *Problem of Historical Knowledge* (1938), Carl G. Hempel's essay "The Function of General Laws in History" (1942), and R. G. Collingwood's *Idea of History* (1946)—although none of these men actually used the expression *critical philosophy of history*. This analytical approach to philosophy of history is largely an outgrowth of twentieth-century Anglo-American philosophy's special interest in elucidating the general epistemological foundations of science. Since 1945 critical philosophy of history has been largely concerned with the nature of historical EXPLANATION. Allowing for certain notable exceptions (such as H. White, 1973a), "working" historians have displayed little more substantial interest in this kind of philosophy of history than they have in the older, speculative variety, claiming that it does not sufficiently attend to the actual practice of historians and, in extreme cases, that "philosophic concern with such problems as the reality of historical knowledge or the nature of historical thought only hinders the practice of history" (Elton, 1967: v). The lack of dialogue between historians and critical philosophers of history has been deplored by some philosophers (e.g., Mink, 1964: 538), although it is perhaps an exaggeration to say that philosophical discussion about history has thus far had "no apparent impact on the way historians do their scholarship" (Skotheim, 1974: 444–45).

The third level of philosophy of history—what is here called "pragmatic" philosophy of history—has a long tradition. From Roman times to the eighteenth century there was broad agreement on what has been called the "exemplar theory of history" developed by Greek rhetoricians—particularly Isocrates—on the basis of their reading of Thucydides (Nadel, 1964: 294). According to this tradition history is important and useful because one learns from past examples; history is a form of moral instruction, or "philosophy teaching by example." This idea remained alive in the nineteenth century and is still encountered today (see, for instance, RADICAL HISTORY); the tradition went into decline, however, with the nineteenth-century professionalization of history and the concomitant rise of the idea that the historian should simply "tell what happened" rather than make ethical judgments about the past (see VALUE JUDGMENT). In the twentieth century the tendency among professional historians has been to deny that history is a branch of moral philosophy and a source of direct lessons. There is, nonetheless, a continuing tradition of reflection on the practical value of studying history (although often only in the form of asides or informal essays— e.g., Trevelyan, [1913] 1972), prompted largely by the occasional need of historians to defend the utility of their discipline or justify it to themselves. As a rule, recent historians and philosophers have been decidedly circumspect with regard to this kind of speculation, suggesting that the value of history lies in very general realms such as "social self-knowledge," "intellectual and emotional satisfaction," or the addition of a "temporal dimension to man's awareness of himself" (Dray, 1973: 69).

References

Barzun, Jacques. [1943] 1950. "History, Popular and Unpopular." In Strayer: 29–57.
Brinton, Crane. 1937–38. "Socio-Astrology." *The Southern Review* 3: 243–66.
Dray, W. H. 1973. "The Politics of Contemporary Philosophy of History: A Reply to Hayden White." *Clio* 3: 55–76. Along with White (1973b), this is a good introduction to the basic concerns, assumptions, and various schools of critical philosophy of history.
Elton, G. R. 1967. *The Practice of History*. New York.
Gottschalk, Louis, ed. 1963. *Generalization in the Writing of History*. Chicago. This book contains a useful bibliography that supplements an earlier one published in Bull. 54.
Gruner, Rolf. 1972. "The Concept of Speculative Philosophy of History." *Metaphilosophy* 3: 283–300. This is an effort to refurbish speculative philosophy of history.
Hahn, M. 1974. "Geschichte, pragmatische." *HWP* 3: 401–2. According to Hahn, the expression *pragmatic history* was first used by Polybius and was revived by the eighteenth-century German scholar David Köler in his *De historia pragmatica* (1741).
La Piana, George. [1943] 1950. "Theology of History." In Strayer: 149–86.
Mandelbaum, Maurice. 1939–40. "Can There Be a Philosophy of History?" *The American Scholar* 9: 74–84. This is an attack on speculative philosophy of history, which Mandelbaum identifies with philosophy of history.
———. 1948. "A Critique of Philosophies of History." *JP* 45 (July 1, 1948): 365–78.
———. 1952. "Some Neglected Philosophic Problems Regarding History." *JP* 49 (May 8, 1952): 317–29. Mandelbaum would subsume the "pragmatics of the discipline

of history'' under critical philosophy of history, which he here calls "formal"
philosophy of history.

Manuel, Frank E. 1965. *The Shapes of Philosophical History*. Stanford, Calif. This is
an entertaining introduction to the subject, based on a series of popular lectures.
It should be balanced by Mazlish (1966).

————. 1976. "Edward Gibbon: Historien-Philosophe." *Daedalus* 105: 231–45.

Mazlish, Bruce. 1966. Review of Frank E. Manuel, *The Shapes of Philosophical History*.
HT 5: 325–36. Mazlish argues that *speculative philosophy of history* should be
taken seriously as an alternative to conventional political philosophy, as a contributor to social science theory, and as an aid in enriching our overall historical
awareness.

Mink, Louis O. 1964. Review of Louis Gottschalk, ed., *Generalization in the Writing
of History*. *JP* 61 (Sept. 3): 538–43.

Nadel, George H. 1964. "Philosophy of History before Historicism." *HT* 3: 291–315.

Popper, Karl R. 1969. "A Pluralist Approach to the Philosophy of History." In Erich
Streissler, ed., *Roads to Freedom: Essays in Honor of Friedrich A. von Hayek*.
New York: 181–200.

Skotheim, Robert Allen. 1974. Review of Murray G. Murphey, *Our Knowledge of the
Historical Past. The Journal of American History* 61: 444–46.

Trevelyan, George Macaulay. [1913] 1972. "Clio, a Muse." In Stern: 227–45. This is
a classic example of pragmatic philosophy of history.

Toynbee, Arnold J. 1934–61. *A Study of History*. 12 vols. Oxford.

Walsh, W. H. [1951] 1960. *Philosophy of History: An Introduction*. New York.

White, Hayden. 1973a. *Metahistory: The Historical Imagination in Nineteenth-Century
Europe*. Baltimore.

————. 1973b. "The Politics of Contemporary Philosophy of History." *Clio* 3: 35–53.
Like Gruner (1972), this is a defense of speculative philosophy of history.

————. 1978. "Historicism, History, and the Figurative Imagination." In Hayden White,
Tropics of Discourse: Essays in Cultural Criticism. Baltimore: 101–20.

White, Morton G. 1968. "Toward an Analytic Philosophy of History." In Marvin Farber,
ed., *Philosophic Thought in France and the United States*. Albany, N.Y.: 705–
25.

Sources of Additional Information

See also METAHISTORY; METHODOLOGY; UNIVERSAL HISTORY. Consult *HT Beih.*; Berding. U. Dierse and G. Scholtz, "Geschichtsphilosophie," *HWP* 3: 416–39, is comprehensive and concludes with a lengthy bibliography. In the same volume see the entry on
"theology of history." William H. Dray, *Philosophy of History* (Englewood Cliffs, N.J.,
1964), is a good general introduction. Gardiner, Nash, and Dray are excellent anthologies.
Gardiner has written "Speculative Systems of History" in *EP* 7: 518–23. Three articles
that review recent trends in thought are Perez Zagorin, "Historical Knowledge: A Review
Article on the Philosophy of History," *JMH* 31: 243–55; Rapehael Demos, "The Language of History," in Nash: 279–99; and Louis O. Mink, "Philosophical Analysis and
Historical Understanding," *The Review of Metaphysics* 21 (June 1968): 667–98. For
differing approaches to the subject and an indication of the semantic confusion that to
some extent still exists in this area, see the papers "What Is Philosophy of History?" in
JP 49 (May 1952): 317–62. Hook is a collection of papers that reflects some of the
differences between historians and contemporary philosophers of history. Robert North

has compiled the "Bibliography of Works in Theology and History," *HT* 12 (1973): 55–133.

POPULAR HISTORY. History written for the entertainment and instruction of general audiences rather than for professional specialists, often by non-academic authors motivated primarily by commercial rather than scholarly concerns; frequently pejorative.

There have been few attempts to define *popular history*, but the conception decidedly exists among academic historians and is often displayed in their pro-grammatic statements, book reviews, and methodological asides. Many scholars exhibit a strongly pejorative working notion of "popularization" that encom-passes commercially motivated writing that caters to the uninformed tastes of the mass reading public, as well as the textbook and other non-technical historical writing of professionals themselves (Barzun, [1943] 1950). On the other hand, there have been significant attempts to encourage popularization by specialists, efforts that reflect more positive attitudes.

The idea of popular history is mainly a creation of the early twentieth century, but it incorporates a number of ancient opinions about the nature and purpose of history: for example, historical accounts should be broad in scope and appeal rather than narrowly monographic, they should be entertainingly written, their authors should engage in explicit VALUE JUDGMENT, and they should generally be socially useful and morally edifying. These ideas, characteristic of "prag-matic" PHILOSOPHY OF HISTORY, have a continuous tradition dating from Greek and Roman times (Ševčenko, 1969: 338–39) and are often said to characterize modern popular history. Before the nineteenth century, however, history could reach only an elite audience of the literate and cultivated. The modern sense of *popular history*—historical writing addressed to people in general—had to await the nineteenth-century rise of public education and mass literacy; the awakening of a broad interest in history and consequent demand for history books; refinements in printing technology and the advent of the modern publishing industry; and the specialization of historical studies in universities, which rendered the most advanced research inaccessible to the reading public. Finally, the new concepts of NATION and NATIONALITY encouraged the idea that history should deal with the "people" as a whole; traditional "dynastic his-tory"—the kind that dealt merely with high politics and genteel life—was increas-ingly challenged by history which was national—or "popular"—in scope (Barzun, [1937] 1965: 28). This is graphically reflected in the work of Jules Michelet (1798–1874), whose *The People* was designed to depict the "life of the people, their toils and sufferings" ([1846] 1972: 109). The Michelet tradition is the source of many self-consciously "literary" (i.e., engagingly written) national histories, as well as the genre of high school and university textbook histories of the "American people," the "French people," and so on.

The period immediately following World War I was most important for the appearance of an explicit concept of popular history. By this time there was a large, politically conscious reading public that sought knowledge of the past "not out of a moral imperative but out of the need to integrate and understand its discordant experience" (Higham et al., 1965: 73). Publishers and writers outside the historical profession—editors, journalists, free-lance authors, writers of fiction—recognized the existence of a market for sweeping, strongly interpretive accounts of the past, written in vivid, non-technical terms. Among the best known examples to appear at this time were *Outline of History* (1920) by the British novelist and social critic H. G. Wells, *The Story of Mankind* (1921) by the Dutch-American journalist Hendrik Willem Van Loon, and *The Decline of the West* (1918–22) by the German amateur philosopher Oswald Spengler.

It was essentially the effort of academic historians to grapple with the vogue of non-professional historiography in the 1920s and 1930s that gave birth to an explicit idea of popular history. By the mid–1920s it was common for professional historians—most of whom had "either ignored or positively distrusted the new [reading] public" in the late nineteenth century (Higham et al., 1965: 78)—to unfavorably contrast "popular writing" with "profound systematic treatment" (Hayes, 1926: 2). Prominent among those who contributed to a more precise formulation of the idea of popular history were practitioners of CULTURAL HISTORY (for example, Huizinga, [1929] 1959; Barzun, [1943] 1950), who sought to legitimize their own (relatively new and insecure) branch of history by distinguishing it from non-scholarly popularization. These men roundly denounced writers such as Wells and Van Loon who, they argued, debased history by flattering vulgar tastes that craved present-oriented, simplistic explanation and colorful sensationalism. Such writing was a "hybrid product" of fact and fiction, masquerading as "genuine" history (Huizinga, [1929] 1959: 43). Its chief fault was its failure to honor the uniqueness and integrity of past situations and its effort to force the richness of past experience into "stock patterns." According to Barzun ([1943] 1950: 56), "the great enemy of the historical sense is not error but convention."

At the same time, attacks on popular history often exhibited an uneasiness attributable to the fear that professionals, in their pursuit of uncompromising scholarly integrity, betrayed an obligation to make their findings comprehensible to the general public. According to Huizinga, a

> historical discipline supported only by an esoteric coterie of scholars is insecure: it must be based on the foundation of historical culture which is the possession of every cultivated person. . . . To be full-fledged any field of study must be accepted and supported by the culture nourishing it. . . . the quality of historical knowledge can be considered highest when scholarship succeeds in supplying a critically refined product of so clear a value for life that the general cultured public accepts it, desires it, absorbs it. ([1929] 1959: 33, 40–41, 42)

In America and Britain such concerns led to (usually unsuccessful) efforts to bring professional and popular history closer together. In the United States in the 1930s a group of scholars mounted a campaign to convince the American

Historical Association (AHA) to sponser a popular magazine of history; the idea was rejected after much debate because the majority of members "wanted the AHA to stick to pure scholarship" (Higham et al., 1965: 81). After World War II a popular magazine entitled *History Today* was founded in Britain, and it frequently contained articles by leading historians. In the United States a popular history magazine called *American Heritage* was launched, still without the backing of the AHA. Neither periodical has earned the full respect of members of the profession.

The belief persists in some circles that there is a need for professionally written popularization: "More and more, historians are writing for each other. We are becoming an incestuous profession. . . . We are turning the public off history" (Winkler, 1980: 10, citing Richard B. Morris). But ambivalence persists, even among advocates of professionally written popularization. A recent proposal that the AHA revive the idea of sponsoring a popular magazine of history cautioned that the venture must be a "commercial success" and therefore "must have its share of the bizarre, the mysterious, the heroic, and the monstrous" (Anon., AHA Newsletter, 1981: 4)—terms that illustrate that the profession's attitude toward public tastes and its working concept of popular history are still essentially condescending.

References

Anon. 1981. "AHA Considering Popular History Magazine." *AHA Newsletter* 19 (Sept.): 4.
Barzun, Jacques. [1943] 1950. "History, Popular and Unpopular." In Strayer: 29–57. According to Barzun, *popular history* is a kind of superficial historical consciousness that exists in the minds of most people; its sources are primarily "the textbooks used in the schools and popular literature" (p. 36).
————. [1937] 1965. *Race: A Study in Superstition*. New York.
Hayes, Carlton J. H. 1926. *Essays on Nationalism*. New York.
Higham, John, et al. 1965. *History*. Englewood Cliffs, N.J. Chapter four is relevant to the subject. Higham is optimistic about the possibility of bridging the gap between specialist and public; see pp. 82, 85.
Huizinga, Johan. [1929] 1959. "The Task of Cultural History." In Johan Huizinga, *Men and Ideas*. New York: 17–76. This is one of the most important and representative statements of professional opinion, informed by a genteel fear and disdain of mass culture. It concludes on a pessimistic note, citing the Russian scholar Rostovtzeff: "The ultimate problem remains like a ghost, ever present and unlaid: Is it possible to extend a higher civilization to the lower classes without debasing its standard and diluting its quality to the vanishing point? Is not every civilization bound to decay as soon as it begins to penetrate the masses?" (p. 51)
Michelet, Jules. [1846] 1972. "Introduction: *The People*." In Stern: 109–19.
Ševčenko, Ihor. 1969. "Two Varieties of Historical Writing." *HT* 8: 332–45.
Winkler, Karen J. 1980. "Decline of History Blamed on Tendency of Scholars to Write for Each Other." *The Chronicle of Higher Education*. April 21, 1980: 10–11.

Sources of Additional Information

The modern notion of popular history is in part related to the ancient belief that history is properly a branch of literature and moral philosophy; on this tradition see PHILOSOPHY OF HISTORY. "History as Art: An Annotated Checklist of Criticism," *Style* 13 (Winter 1979): 5–36, includes a number of titles relevant to the subject. H. R. Trevor-Roper's *History: Professional and Lay* (Oxford, 1957) attacks "professionalism for its own sake" and defends "genuine, productive research . . . by men ever conscious of the lay interest"; the essay is reprinted in Hugh Lloyd-Jones et al., *History and Imagination: Essays in Honour of H. R. Trevor-Roper* (London, 1981). Trevor-Roper's position is echoed in P. G. Ingram, "Artistry in History," *British Journal of Aesthetics* 17 (1977): 161–70. Among the many examples of professional writing that exhibit distrust of popular history see especially Gerhard Ritter, "Scientific History, Contemporary History, and Political Science," *HT* 1 (1961–62): 261–79, particularly 268–69. Some of the differences between high-level, non-professional popularization and commercially successful professional historiography may be discerned by comparing two recent books on similar subjects: Frederic Morton, *A Nervous Splendor: Vienna, 1888/1889* (Boston, 1979), and Carl E. Schorske, *Fin-de-Siècle Vienna: Politics and Culture* (New York, 1980). One of the most highly regarded non-academic authors of history in the United States is Barbara Tuchman. Reviews of her many commercially successful books in professional periodicals are often useful in understanding the idea of popular history. Tuchman has published a collection of her own essays entitled *Practicing History* (New York, 1981).

POSITIVISM. The doctrine that the goals and methods of natural science can be transferred to historiography. Within this framework, the term may have several more specific (though sometimes overlapping or partly contradictory) meanings: (1) most commonly, the belief that there are universal, empirically verifiable LAWS of historical development analogous to the laws of natural science and that historians can discover them through the study of the past; (2) an anti-speculative conception of history that stresses empirical research on particular subjects and shuns generalization and the quest for laws; (3) an epistemological position that holds that the methods of reasoning in history are fundamentally similar to those of the natural and social sciences; (4) the belief that historical accounts can be "objective" in the sense that they can reconstruct the past essentially as it happened.

Positivism, one of the major intellectual orientations of the modern world, is based on three interrelated foundations: (1) the repudiation of metaphysics; (2) the idealization of natural science as a model for all human knowledge; and (3) the idea that only experienced phenomena can be explained and belief that experience provides the basis for the discovery of social laws that permit predictions about the future as well as explanations of the past (Mandelbaum, 1971: 11). Today *positivism* is widely used to designate "any thinker or movement which seeks to imitate the rigor of natural science in philosophy, the social sciences, or history" (Lindenfeld, 1980: 2).

The word *positivism* was invented by the French social theorist Auguste Comte

(1798–1857) to designate his own speculative PHILOSOPHY OF HISTORY. Comte maintained that human intelligence historically evolves through three successively higher phases: "theological," "metaphysical," and "positivist." The positivist stage represents the triumph of the experimental and rational spirit of modern natural science, epitomized by Newtonian physics. All knowledge—including the study of society, or "sociology" (also Comte's term)—must undergo this evolution, which is completed when the science in question is capable of discovering its own general laws, understood as "well-authenticated general descriptive statement[s] of uniformities which have been observed to occur in the past" (Mandelbaum, 1971: 11). Ironically, Comte advertised his philosophy as strictly empirical and anti-metaphysical, whereas the very notion of a transhistorical process of human development is itself speculative.

Many nineteenth-century historians were influenced by Comte's views (Higham et al., 1965: 98; Hughes, 1964: 9), especially outside Germany (where IDEALISM was strongly entrenched and—with isolated exceptions such as Karl Lamprecht [1856–1915]—prevented positivistic inroads). Among English-speaking historians, the best-known positivist was the British amateur scholar H. T. Buckle, author of the two-volume *History of Civilization in England* (1857–61). Buckle's work was based squarely on Comte's philosophy; in 1853 he stated that "I have long been convinced that the progress of every people is regulated by principles—or, as they are called, Laws—as regular as those which govern the physical world. To discover these laws is the object of my work" (cited in Semmel, 1976: 373). Higham (1965: 98, n. 9) maintains that Buckle's influence in the United States, "although not yet adequately appraised, is attested in almost all the early manuals on history."

In the late nineteenth century Comte's speculations fell rapidly out of favor and the assumptions of positivists such as Buckle came under increasing attack by historians (e.g., Droysen, [1868] 1972; Acton, 1907; Burger, 1977). While continuing to heed Comte's injunction to be "empirical," and turning increasingly to narrowly defined and painstakingly rigorous documentary research, academic historians generally renounced the quest for grand laws of human development. (It should be noted, however, that this anti-speculative, fact-grubbing approach to historiography is also occasionally called "positivism" [e.g., Collingwood, [1946] 1956: 126–27]). Since the early twentieth century the term *positivism* has served historians primarily as a pejorative code word for an approach that simplistically and naively attempts to transfer the methods of natural science to the study of the human past.

Another distinct though related meaning of *positivism* is associated with "critical" PHILOSOPHY OF HISTORY, where the term refers to the doctrine that the methods of history should be understood in the same logical terms as those of the natural and social sciences (Dray, 1964: 2). Thus, philosophers who subscribe to the COVERING LAW model of historical EXPLANATION—which claims that historical explanation proceeds deductively from general laws or law-like statements, in the same fashion as explanations in natural science—are typically called "positivists" (for example, Nash, 1969: 76). This usage is an outgrowth of the tradition of "logical positivism" in philosophy, which flourished in the 1930s and attempted to transform philosophy from a speculative into an analytical activity whose purpose was to comprehend the process of human inquiry.

Dray (1964: 21) also cites an additional way the term is sometimes used in philosophy of history: to refer to the doctrine that historians can achieve "objective truth" in their accounts (see OBJECTIVITY).

References

Acton, (Lord) John Emerich Edward Dahlberg. 1907. *Historical Essays and Studies*. London: 305–43. Acton criticizes Buckle's "mechanistic sociology."

Burger, Thomas. 1977. "Droysen's Defense of Historiography: A Note." *HT* 16: 168–73. This piece contains a concise summary of the assumptions underlying positivist historiography.

Collingwood, R. G. [1946] 1956, *The Idea of History*. New York. This book contains an influential discussion of "positivistic historiography" in the late nineteenth century, in which *positivism* is identified with "infinite scrupulosity about any and every isolated matter of fact" and only secondarily with "framing laws" (pp. 126–27).

Dray, William H. 1964. *Philosophy of History*. Englewood Cliffs, N.J.

Droysen, Johan Gustav. [1868] 1972, *Outline of the Principles of History*. In Stern: 137–44.

Higham, John, et al. 1965. *History*. Englewood Cliffs, N.J.

Hughes, H. Stuart. 1964. *History as Art and as Science: Twin Vistas on the Past*. New York.

Lindenfeld, David F. 1980. *The Transformation of Positivism: Alexius Meinong and European Thought, 1880–1920*. Berkeley, Calif. This contains a good discussion of the historical roots and nuances of the movement, as well as its contemporary relevance. There is a useful bibliography.

Mandelbaum, Maurice. 1971. *History, Man, and Reason: A Study in Nineteenth-Century Thought*. Baltimore. This is an important study of the major speculative traditions in philosophy of history, including Comtean positivism.

Nash, Ronald H. 1969. *Ideas of History* 2. New York. This book contains a brief bibliography, pp. 157–58.

Semmel, Bernard. 1976. "H. T. Buckle: The Liberal Faith and the Science of History." *The British Journal of Sociology* 27: 370–86. This is an excellent exposition of Buckle's views.

Sources of Additional Information

For entries and bibliographies on positivism see *EP*, *DHI*, *ESS*, and *IESS*. See also the bibliography in Lindenfeld (1980). W. M. Simon's *European Positivism in the Nineteenth Century* (Ithaca, N.Y., 1963) includes a detailed study of Comte's influence. H. Stuart Hughes, *Consciousness and Society: The Reorientation of European Social Thought, 1890–1930* (New York, 1958), is an analysis of the "revolt against positivism" in the late nineteenth and early twentieth centuries. Both Gardiner and Stern contain well-chosen selections from Buckle's *History of Civilization in England*. See also Christopher Parker, "English Historians and the Opposition to Positivism," *HT* 22 (1983): 120–45.

One of the few contemporary apologists for Buckle's vision of positivistic historiography is Lee Benson; see his "Quantification, Scientific History, and Scholarly Innovation," *AHA Newsletter*, 4 (June 1966): 11–16.

PROCESS. Any causally interconnected sequence of social change, deliberate or unintended, that modifies a human situation and leads over time to a particular result.

The ideas of history and process—along with related notions such as "development," "trend," "movement," and (even more loosely) "change" (Beard and Hook, 1946: 117)—have always been associated in western thought; since the early nineteenth century this association has been especially close. The idea of process is inherent in the notion of cause and effect; it is best understood in history in relation to theories of CAUSATION and COLLIGATION, which suggest that historians explain the PAST by identifying the causes and results of human events and arranging them in "internally related" NARRATIVES designed to show "what happened" (Walsh, 1967: 81–83). M. I. Finley ([1954] 1972: 24) states that the "historian's data are individual events and persons; the sum total of their *interrelationships* is the historical process" [emphasis added].

Although historians have devoted less systematic attention to the concept of process than sociologists (e.g., Nisbet, 1969; 1972), a sampling of their remarks on the subject of social change demonstrates that they—along with most philosophers of history—consider the idea of process crucial to the modern understanding of historical scholarship. A special sensitivity to the dynamic and causally interconnected aspects of human affairs is, for instance, normally considered requisite for the historian: the British scholar G. M. Young believes that a sense of "movement and continuity" and a "passionate apprehension of process" are as important for the historian as a sense of form is for the painter (cited in Wedgwood, 1960: 95; cf. Humphreys, 1980: 2). Marxist scholars, following Engels, are convinced that social reality must be understood "not as a collection of things, 'but as a complex of processes' " (quoted in Ashcraft, 1972: 140, n. 51). According to W. H. Walsh (1967: 66), "the identification of continuing processes" is one of the "primary tasks" of the historian, who "makes events intelligible to his readers to the extent to which he succeeds." Finally, R. G. Collingwood argues that history deals essentially with "those processes by which things in the human world have *come to be*"; the "conception of 'turning into,' the conception of becoming," he believed, "is . . . the fundamental idea of all history" (cited in Mink, 1972: 161, 163). For Collingwood, "the historical fact, as it actually exists and as the historian actually knows it, is always a process in which something is changing into something else. This element of process is the life of history" ([1946] 1956: 163).

Even non-theoretical historians would probably agree with this position. The commonsense metaphysic of mainstream historiography, one might suggest, is based on the assumption that meaningful change is the basic feature of social reality—in contrast to the "unhistorical" view that change is meaningless and reality is essentially timeless. It is this profound temporal sensibility that inspires adherents of the French *Annales* school of historiography when they suggest that history's major contribution to twentieth-century social science is *le sens du temps* (Thomson, 1967: 33).

In its principal current sense, *process* means "a continuous and regular action or succession of actions, taking place or carried on in a definite manner, and leading to the accomplishment of some result" *(OED)*. *Historical process*, therefore, does not refer to mere change, but to "an alteration in human affairs which seems to display direction, pattern, or purpose" (Humphreys, 1980: 3). This is evident in ordinary turns of phrase that suggest that social phenomena "come into existence," "turn into" other things, "emerge" or "unfold" as the result of some sort of "logic," and so on (cf. Mink, 1972: 163). In current usage, technical and non-specialized alike, the ideas of history and temporal process are often used interchangeably; that is, the "history" of some thing or person is frequently considered identical with the record of its development in time, its "evolution," its "growth," or its pattern of becoming. To call a thing "historical" is to suggest not only that it is past but also that it has undergone a logically explicable pattern of modification. *Historical mindedness* (or *historical consciousness*) is commonly understood as awareness of "the concept of development within the framework of time" (e.g., Gustavson, 1976: 261). To *historicize* some subject or problem is often considered equivalent to explaining it in terms of "stages in a real process of development" (Mink, 1972: 172). It is this orientation that underlies the historian's emphasis on "chronology," even at the most elementary levels of pedagogy (for example, Ward, 1959: 12–16).

Since historians concentrate on *human* events, *historical process* refers to patterns of change related to the "achievements and failures" of human beings (Beard and Hook, 1946: 117; Walsh, 1967: 71). But this by no means implies that a process must be the product of deliberate human action to be considered historically important (see BIOGRAPHY); although historians may not usually attend to extra-human processes such as climatic or geological change, they may be vitally interested in impersonal, "natural" phenomena whenever they significantly influence or circumscribe human behavior (Walsh, 1967: 68, 71–72). Historians are also conscious of the power of social tradition, which acts to define the limits of possibility in any age; on this score, most would agree with Marx's famous statement in the *Eighteenth Brumaire of Louis Bonaparte* (1852): "Men make their own history, but they do not make it just as they please; they do not make it under circumstances chosen by themselves, but under circumstances directly found, given and transmitted from the past." It is important to recognize the social and non-deliberate (or quasi-deliberate) nature of many historical processes. In many if not most cases—for example, the growth of an institution, the evolution of a political or cultural movement—the scholar must look beyond the conscious will of individuals and think in terms of collective process (Walsh, 1967: 74).

It is true that scholars have occasionally questioned the necessity of *some forms* of process in history. Certain masterworks (for instance, Jacob Burckhardt's *Civilization of the Renaissance in Italy* [1860] or Johan Huizinga's *Waning of the Middle Ages* [1919], both "synchronic," cross-sectional panoramas of societies at particular points in time rather than "diachronic" chronicles of development) demonstrate that history need not depict an *evolutionary* process in simple chronological terms (White, 1973: 230; Colie, 1964: 623). The Dutch scholar Huizinga openly distrusted the "implicit progressivism" of evolutionism, which, he believed, "led to a simplistic linear causality"; he preferred to "examine problems in all their interrelation, by a method that tends to stasis, to a still life rather than a pageant" (Colie, 1964: 623). Again, during the 1950s French social historians such as Braudel and Emmanuel Le Roy Ladurie introduced the notion of *l'histoire immobile* (unmoving history) as appropriate to the social stagnation that evidently characterized much of Europe between the fourteenth and early eighteenth centuries (Darnton, 1984: 24).

One might nevertheless argue that the idea of process is at least tacitly present in all written histories, even those that emphasize stasis, because historical accounts inevitably assume a "before" and "after" that is distinctly different from yet related to the period they discuss. The title of Huizinga's classic (in the original Dutch as well as the English translation) does, after all, suggest slow disappearance, and a sense of "decadence" pervades the work of Burckhardt (who understood his own late-nineteenth-century society in terms of social DECLINE). Indeed, to make complete sense of a cross-sectional work such as Burckhardt's *Renaissance* one must see it as the "middle" of a story that the reader frames by adding a beginning and end. As far as the "unmoving history" of Braudel and Ladurie is concerned, the expression "now seems exaggerated, for it hardly does justice to the religious conflict, grain riots, and rebellions against the extension of state power that disrupted the late medieval pattern of village life"; the phrase served mainly as a rhetorical "corrective to the tendency to see history as a succession of political events" (Darnton, 1984: 24). One might add that even ideas such as stasis, stagnation, and continuity imply some form of process, that is, the *preservation* of elements of the past.

The precise nature of the role of process in classical Greek and Roman historiography has been the subject of recent inquiry. A concept of historical development in the oft-encountered modern sense of the unified social development of humankind is evidently not present in the work of ancient historians. As J. B. Bury suggested ([1930] 1964: 24), "Their records reached back such a short way, their experience was so brief, that they never attained to the conception of continuous process." Most importantly, in antiquity *history* always seems to have been understood as a "human production," never as a "subsistent entity" that could exhibit a pattern of its own (Press, 1977: 293–94).

But this does not mean that ancient historians lacked an idea of historical process. According to Momigliano (1972: 284–92), classical historians were "dominated by the sense of change"; indeed, they were essentially "interpreters of change." Unlike their counterparts in ancient China—"concerned typically not with process but with permanence"—Greek and Latin historians created a "historiography of change." Ancient audiences expected the historian to depict a "process of change" (p. 284), not to uphold tradition or eternal norms. The point of reading history was to learn how to deal with change; it was assumed that "description of changes in the past . . . would help to recognize the causes and foresee the consequences of similar changes in the future" (p. 284).

This does not imply that ancient historians understood *social process* in terms of RECURRENCE, for their "frequent insistence on the exceptional magnitude and importance of the events [they were] going to tell implied that [they] considered that particular change likely to be irreversible" (p. 286). In recent years specialists have debunked the once-popular belief that Greco-Roman historiography was based essentially on the idea of cyclical RECURRENCE—in contrast to the allegedly linear, developmental Judeo-Christian sense of time (see Press, 1977; Trompf, 1979; cf. Plumb, 1970: 70). Theories of cultural recurrence certainly appear in the work of various classical poets and philosophers, but these doctrines seem to have had no profound effect on the work of ancient historians.

Greco-Roman historians studied process especially in the dramatic forms of war and REVOLUTION. What was difficult for them to represent was non-dramatic, gradual change. It is true that Roman historians such as Livy and especially Tacitus stressed social decline. Still "none of the [classical] texts available to us," writes Momigliano (1972: 290), "gives a satisfactory account of long-term slow changes in law and customs." It is thus not true, as Collingwood believed ([1946] 1956: 42–45; Mink, 1972: 162), that ancient historiography lacked a concept of development; it is simply that ancient historians were unable to depict the sort of slow institutional and psychological change that Collingwood considered necessary to the modern science of historiography.

St. Augustine's distinction between sacred and profane history helped lay the basis for the medieval idea of history as a linear process controlled by divine providence (Press, 1977: 286, 288; cf. Plumb, 1970: 76–77), but this was a far cry from the modern idea of secular, self-sustaining social process. Bury ([1930] 1964: 24) maintained that the Christian conception of history as an extension of God's will "bounded and bound men's minds" and made the modern ideas of "progess and development" impossible, since it allowed for "no self-contained causal development, only a dispensation imposed from without." On the other hand, Collingwood believed that the providential idea of history was crucial to the long-term emergence of the notion of secular process, since it encouraged "recognition that what happens in history need not happen through anyone's deliberately wishing it to happen," which he considered "an indispensable precondition of understanding any historical process" (cited in Mink, 1972: 164; cf. Plumb, 1970: 77–78).

Conditions for the transformation of providence into the modern idea of secular process were slowly created after the sixteenth century, partly by advances in natural science. By the late seventeenth century, *nature* had come to be viewed "as a self-organizing system functioning in accordance with inner dynamic forces" (Goudge, 1973: 177). Philosophers of the eighteenth century ENLIGHTENMENT constructed generalized theories of progressive social evolution, built on the analogy of nature as a self-regulating system (p. 178) (see PROGESS). In the nineteenth century the immense prestige of natural science encouraged belief that social change is governed by uniform principles, similar to the LAWS which govern biological or chemical processes.

More specifically, at the end of the eighteenth century—especially in Germany,—painstaking scholars began to interpret historical aspects of human culture in terms of interrelated process. The philologist F. A. Wolf (1759–1824), for example, analyzed the Homeric poems as manifestations of the early development of human imagination (Gooch, [1913] 1959: 25–28). Barthold Georg Niebuhr (1776–1831) stressed that the historian "must discover at least with some probability the general connectedness of events" (Niebuhr, [1811] 1972: 48). Friedrich Karl von Savigny (1779–1861), founder of the "historical school" of law, depicted the western legal traditions in terms of a continuous evolutionary process (Gooch, 1913: 43–49) and so "helped to diffuse the notion that all the institutions of a society or a nation are as closely inter-connected as the parts of a living organism" (Bury, [1930] 1964: 26). Leopold von Ranke (1795–1886), the greatest nineteenth-century exemplar of professional historical scholarship, insisted on a "deep, pervasive connection" between historical phenomena, based on the idea that "What developed in the past constitutes the connection with what is emerging in the present" (Ranke, [n.d.] 1972: 61). While rejecting *a priori* theories of social process fashioned by speculative theorists such as Hegel and Comte, Ranke was nonetheless convinced that empirical scholarship could unearth the thread of an interrelated pattern of human development—a UNIVERSAL HISTORY of humankind (Holborn, [1943] 1950: 78–80). (A residue of providential history persisted in his work, leading him to seek the hand of God behind all social development; this approach was echoed in the United States by romantic historians such as George Bancroft [Higham et al., 1965: 94–95]—see IDEALISM; ROMANTICISM.)

The early nineteenth century is thus vital for the emergence of what Bury aptly called the "genetic" idea of history—the belief that

> the present condition of the human race is simply and strictly the result of a causal series (or set of causal series)—a continuous succession of changes, where each state arises causally out of the preceding; and that the business of historians is to trace this genetic process, to explain each change, and ultimately to grasp the complete development of the life of humanity. ([1930] 1964: 25–26)

This "idea of human development" was, in Bury's words ([1902] 1972: 214), the "great transforming conception" that enabled history to become a respected academic discipline in the nineteenth century (cf. Higham et al., 1965: 94). From Bury's standpoint, the concept of history "as a [single] causal development" meant "the elevation of historical inquiry to the dignity of a science"—

the term *science* implying knowledge "conceived as lying entirely within a sphere in which the law of cause and effect has unreserved and unrestricted dominion" ([1930] 1964: 23, 26—see SCIENTIFIC HISTORY).

The genetic and organic assumptions of Wolf, Niebuhr, Savigny, and Ranke were enhanced in the late nineteenth century, as historians—like sociologists, psychologists, and anthropologists (Burrow, 1966: ix and *passim*)—were influenced by Darwinian evolutionism. It was now widely assumed that historians must "trace in detail a singular causal sequence" (Bury, [1930] 1964: 33) over a considerable length of time, usually some kind of institutional development; the overall framework, in the broadest sense, was the "growth of civilization" (pp. 33, 35). Frederick Jackson Turner ([1891] 1972: 199) aptly cited late-nineteenth-century historians such as Waitz in Germany and Stubbs in England who "expounded the evolution of political institutions, studying their growth as the biologist might study seed, bud, blossom, and fruit." For history, Darwin was especially important because his work "showed that explanation [even in the natural sciences] can be historical without losing its scientific character" (Goudge, 1973: 181).

In the United States Darwinian evolutionism was a "controlling assumption" of the new "scientific" approach aggressively championed by the first cohort of professional historical scholars (Randall and Haines, 1946). "The concept of cumulative, on-going change, operating through an endless chain of tangible causes and effects," writes John Higham (1965: 94), "became for scientific historians the very essence of historical wisdom." The professional avante garde—for example, H. B. Adams and J. W. Burgess—was preoccupied with the now discredited "germ theory" of western institutions, according to which American democracy was the product of a continuous evolutionary process stretching back through medieval England to ancient Germany (Randall and Haines, 1946: 34–35; cf. Hofstadter, 1955: 173–79).

For all its significance, however, it is generally agreed that Darwinism only enhanced the growth of an already well developed concept of historical process (Bury, [1930] 1964: 31–32; Higham et al., 1965: 94–95; Burrow, 1966: 20–21); and, as Bury ([1930] 1964: 26, 28) suggested before the First World War, the vogue of Darwinism created problems because it encouraged the equation of all "genetic process" in history with linear evolutionism. Perhaps Darwinism's major significance lies in the fact that it helped dissipate the residual transcendentalism present in the work of Ranke and others of the earlier generation (p. 33; Higham et al., 1965: 94–95).

As the foregoing survey indicates, the idea of *historical process* may accommodate a broad range of specific positions. It may be understood as something vast and all-encompassing (e.g., "universal history"—as in Ranke's idea of a synthesis of all human experience) or as something quite circumscribed (e.g., the rate of industrialization in a single economic sector). Alternatively, *process* may be a medium-range idea designating patterns of change over periods of a few decades or several centuries (e.g., REVOLUTION; INDUSTRIAL REVOLUTION;

MODERNIZATION). Again, *process* may be understood teleologically (as in Hegel's notion of history as a series of self-transcending stages leading to human freedom) or as something more open-ended and indeterminate. *Patterns of change* may be understood in terms of a single underlying "logic"—for example, DIALECTIC (as in Hegel, Marx, or Collingwood [Mink, 1972])—or in more pluralistic, multi-causal terms; as Humphreys (1980: 3) notes, *process* "may be understood as either linear or rhythmic and cyclical, and . . . its motive force may be thought of as either internal or external to the social system under description."

An understanding of *process* in terms of a unified "logic" of change is typical of many speculative philosophies of history, which characteristically seek to discover unified patterns of "meaning" in the human past. This approach was popular in the eighteenth and nineteenth centuries and produced the great "metahistories" of Hegel, Marx, Comte, and so on (see IDEALISM; HISTORICAL MATERIALISM; POSITIVISM; PHILOSOPHY OF HISTORY; METAHISTORY). Professional historians today are by and large disinterested in abstract theories of history as a single pattern of development and do not normally approach their own work in this spirit. Instead, they tend to view process nominalistically in terms of specific themes, carefully delimited in frameworks of time and place. They stress the importance of discontinuity as well as continuity and view the past not as a unified field but as a spectrum of diverse sequences of change, defined at least in part by the interests and concerns of historians themselves. In depicting such processes, academic historians typically avoid the suggestion of inevitability by allowing for a range of different possible outcomes at points along the way (e.g., Porter, 1975: 305–10 [see DETERMINISM]).

What all concepts of historical process imply—broad or circumscribed—is that pastness may be represented in narrative fashion, either as one unified story (the history of humankind [cf. Mink, 1978]) or as a collection of many unfolding stories. For this reason NARRATIVE, that is, storytelling, is sometimes considered the appropriate mode of EXPLANATION in history—or at least the most characteristic form of western historiography (cf. Plumb, 1970: 77). As an explicit theory, the idea that narrative is the explanatory mode most adequate to history—the "genetic-narrative model" of historical explanation (Porter, 1975: 299–300)—arose in the 1960s in opposition to the COVERING LAW model of historical explanation, which holds that historians explain by deduction from general laws. Narrativists maintain that historians explain by persuading readers to follow a story, a strategy appropriate to the representation of process-related ideas such as genesis, growth, development, evolution, or decline (Fain, 1970: 298; Porter, 1975: 288–300).

But the narrativist position is almost as controversial as the "covering law" theory it was invented to counter; D. H. Fischer (1970: 131), for example, while acknowledging that narration is "one of the more common and most characteristically historical forms," objects that it is "not the only form of explanation [historians] use." Although narrative structure may indeed be well adapted to the representation of process, this obviously does not mean that process *must* be couched in straightforward "story" form, with a clearly defined beginning, middle, and end. One need only remark that the concept of social process is crucial to contemporary sociology, a discipline notorious for its neglect of the "historical nature of social change" (Nisbet, 1972: vi). On the other hand, one might argue that narrative, in a more complex form, is indeed in some sense inseparable from historiography, since the ideas of "before" and "after" are at least implicit in every work of history.

References

Ashcraft, Richard. 1972. "Marx and Weber on Liberalism as Bourgeois Ideology." *CSSH* 14: 13–68.

Beard, Charles A., and Hook, Sydney. 1946. "Problems of Terminology in Historical Writing: The Need for Greater Precision in the Use of Historical Terms." In Bull. 54: 103–30. This piece was actually written by Hook, who warned (pp. 116–17) against confusing use of the terms *change, development, evolution,* and *progress. Change* is "any difference in position, form, quality," and is "always relative to some thing, measure, or standard which in relation to the changing thing either does not change or is changing at a different rate"; *development* is "any change which has a continuous *direction* and which culminates in a phase that is qualitatively *new*"; *evolution* means "gradual" rather than "revolutionary" development; *progress* signifies "a development favorably evaluated from the standpoint of a human interest, end, or ideal."

Burrow, J. W. 1966. *Evolution and Society: A Study in Victorian Social Theory.* Cambridge. Burrow focuses on anthropology and sociology; he seeks to explain why there has been a twentieth-century "repudiation of the evolutionary tradition" in these disciplines (p. xi).

Bury, J. B. [1930] 1964. "Darwinism and History." In Harold Temperly, ed., *Selected Essays of J. B. Bury.* Amsterdam: 23–42. This is a good specimen of late-nineteenth-century attitudes, still valuable for its insights; the essay was orginally published in 1909.

———. [1902] 1972. "The Science of History." In Stern: 210–23.

Colie, R. L. 1964. "Johan Huizinga and the Task of Cultural History." *AHR* 69: 607–30.

Collingwood, R. G. [1946] 1956. *The Idea of History.* New York.

Darnton, Robert. 1984. *The Great Cat Massacre and Other Episodes in French Cultural History.* New York.

Fain, Haskell. 1970. *Between Philosophy and History.* Princeton, N.J.

Finley, M. I. [1954] 1972. "Introduction." In Thucydides, *The Peloponnesian War.* Harmondsworth, Eng.

Fischer, David Hackett. 1970. *Historians' Fallacies: Toward a Logic of Historical Thought.* New York.

Gooch, G. P. [1913] 1959. *History and Historians in the Nineteenth Century.* Boston.

Goudge, Thomas A. 1973. "Evolutionism." *DHI* 2: 174–89. This piece includes a bibliography.

Gustavson, Carl G. 1976. *The Mansion of History.* New York.

Higham, John, et al. 1965. *History.* Englewood Cliffs, N.J. Higham stresses (following

Hofstadter [1955: 6]) the conservative political uses of late-nineteenth-century historical evolutionism; see p. 96.

Hofstadter, Richard. 1955. *Social Darwinism in American Thought*. Boston.

Holborn, Hajo. [1943] 1950. "The Science of History." In Strayer: 61–83. Holborn is perceptive on Ranke; see especially pp. 78–80.

Humphreys, R. Stephen. 1980. "The Historian, His Documents, and the Elementary Modes of Historical Thought." *HT* 19: 1–20.

Mink, Louis O. 1972. "Collingwood's Historicism: A Dialectic of Process." In Michael Krausz, ed., *Critical Essays on the Philosophy of R. G. Collingwood*. Oxford: 154–78. This is a highly original reading of Collingwood's thought.

Momigliano, Arnaldo. 1972. "Tradition and the Classical Historian." *HT* 11: 279–93.

Niebuhr, Barthold Georg. [1811] 1972. Preface to the *History of Rome*. In Stern: 47–53.

Nisbet, Robert A. 1969. *Social Change and History: Aspects of the Western Theory of Development*. New York.

————, ed. 1972. *Social Change*. Oxford. This is an anthology.

Plumb, J. H. 1970. *The Death of the Past*. Boston. Plumb supports the conventional thesis that a strong emphasis on development in history is unique to the west, that it flows from the ancient Hebrew culture through medieval Christianity, that it was secularized in the idea of progress in the age of ENLIGHTENMENT, and that it entered modern historiography in the nineteenth century.

Porter, Dale H. 1975. "History as Process." *HT* 14: 297–313. Porter wants historians to learn from the process philosophy of Alfred North Whitehead.

Press, Gerald A. 1977. "History and the Development of the Idea of History in Antiquity." *HT* 16: 280–96. Press argues that the nature of the idea of history in antiquity has been misunderstood because history has not itself been adequately understood as a historical phenomenon, that is, something that has undergone a *process* of change. He maintains that the modern sense of *history* as "the whole temporal process of the world, or at least of the human world," was "utterly alien" to antiquity (pp. 286–87).

Randall, John Herman, Jr., and Haines, George, IV. 1946. "Controlling Assumptions in the Practice of American Historians." *Bull* 54: 15–52.

Ranke, Leopold von. [n.d.] 1972. "A Fragment from the 1860's." In Stern: 60–62.

Thomson, David. 1967. "The Writing of Contemporary History." *Journal of Contemporary History* 2: 25–34.

Trompf, G. W. 1979. *The Idea of Historical Recurrence in Western Thought: From Antiquity to the Reformation*. Berkeley, Calif.

Turner, Frederick Jackson. [1891] 1972. "The Significance of History." In Stern: 198–208.

Walsh, W. H. 1967. "Colligatory Concepts in History." In W. H. Burston and D. Thompson, eds., *Studies in the Nature and Teaching of History*. London: 65–84. An excellent starting point, this work clarifies the subject in remarkably clear and effective terms. It concludes with an appeal to Hegel's theory of "concrete universals," that is, the treatment of historical phenomena in terms of "unity in diversity" (pp. 81–83).

Ward, Paul L. 1959. *Elements of Historical Thinking*. Washington, D.C.

Wedgwood, C. V. 1960. *Truth and Opinion: Historical Essays*. New York. Wedgwood warns that "like all obsessions, the obsession with process can become dangerous.

For when a highly satisfactory pattern of process has been worked out by the historian he is very unwilling to let it go; yet he may have to let it go if facts come to light which gravely modify it'' (p. 95).

White, Hayden. 1973. *Metahistory: The Historical Imagination in Nineteenth-Century Europe*. Baltimore.

Sources of Additional Information

See also PERIODIZATION, especially references to literature on "time." Nisbet (1969) sets the idea of social process in the general framework of the history of western thought, although his emphasis is on social theory, not historiography per se; his "Notes and References" include many useful citations. Ernst Breisach's *Historiography: Ancient, Medieval, Modern* (Chicago, 1983) includes relevent passages under the label of "development"; see also Maurice Mandelbaum, *History, Man, and Reason: A Study in Nineteenth-Century Thought* (Baltimore, 1971). Goudge (1973) contains a select bibliography on "evolutionism." Chapter two of Gustav Bergmann's *Philosophy of Science* (Madison, Wis., 1957), "Process and History," appeals more to examples drawn from the physical sciences than historiography and is thus of very limited use. Several sections of chapter five of Fischer (1970) may be found pertinent. Press (1977) extends his arguments on the ancient period in *The Development of the Idea of History in Antiquity* (Kingston and Montreal, 1982). Samuel Kinser, "Ideas of Temporal Change and Cultural Process in France, 1470–1535," in Anthony Molho and John A. Tedeschi, eds., *Renaissance Studies in Honor of Hans Baron* (Dekalb, Ill., 1971): 703–55, is primarily useful for the history of the idea of PROGRESS. For an effort to explicate Marx's idea of DIALECTIC in terms of "internal relations," see Bertell Ollman, *Marx's Theory of Alienation* (2d ed., Cambridge, 1976). Suggestive, although not directly related to historiography, is the anthology edited by Douglas Browning entitled *Philosophers of Process* (New York, 1965).

PROGRESS. A doctrine based on the belief that the study of history reveals a pattern of continuous improvement in human society.

In the nineteenth and early twentieth centuries the idea of historical progress was a principal assumption of western thought and a basic framing concept for European and North American historiography (Iggers, 1958: 215). In a classic study ([1920] 1932: 346) the British historian J. B. Bury called the idea of progress a "general article of faith" in western culture. In the mid-twentieth century the idea fell into partial disfavor as a basis for scholarly analysis; in a modified sense it nonetheless remains significant for historical inquiry and explanation.

In everyday usage, *progress* designates "improvement or . . . advance in a desirable direction"; as a doctrine of human history, *progress* denotes "a cumulative advance, throughout all regions of history, toward an all-encompassing encounter with a universal norm and its realization" (Rotenstreich, 1971: 197). There are two schools of thought regarding the origins of the latter idea. The older view, prevalent from the late nineteenth century to the 1930s, held that the idea of historical progress was a uniquely modern by-product of the sev-

enteenth-century "scientific revolution" and the eighteenth-century ENLIGHT-
ENMENT. This idea was popularized, above all, by the French positivist philosopher Auguste Comte (1798–1857) (see POSITIVISM). Comte articulated a "law
of three stages" to account for the cumulative refinement of human thought—
from the theological, through the metaphysical, to the empirical mode of reasoning. Only as the result of the rise of the last—or "positive"—phase of human
history, he maintained, did the idea of progress crystallize. The majority of late-
nineteenth- and early-twentieth-century historians and social theorists—although
not necessarily accepting the law of three stages—subscribed to Comte's view
that the doctrine of progress was uniquely modern. Medieval thought was not
generally believed to reflect an idea of progress, and classical theory was considered "cyclical" rather than "progressive" (see RECURRENCE). A key work
in this tradition is the aforementioned Bury ([1920] 1932), itself based on the
doctrine. Most intellectual histories of the 1920s and 1930s agreed with Bury
"that the idea of progress was quintessentially a modern faith, fathered by modern
science" (Wagar, 1967: 61).

The more recent view (e.g., Edelstein, 1967; Trompf, 1979) holds that the
doctrine of historical progress is not uniquely modern but existed in various
forms in antiquity; moreover, current scholarship stresses continuity between the
traditional Christian idea of providence and the modern, secular idea of progress
(Wagar, 1967: 55; cf. Iggers, 1965: 2–3). The latter theme was first popularized
by the American historian Carl Becker (1932), who depicted the eighteenth-
century idea of progress as a secular version of the Christian idea of redemption.
The "new orthodoxy"—prevalent especially since 1945—holds that the "modern idea of progress cannot be understood . . . without the most searching inquiry
into the mind of antiquity and the Middle Ages. When such an inquiry is made,
it discloses an organic connection between pre-modern and modern conceptions
of history" (Wagar, 1967: 64). This position is reflected in important works
such as Frankel (1948), Sampson (1956), and Manuel (1962).

One cannot say, however, that the older interpretation is completely outdated.
Many scholars still believe that the idea of progress "became *dominant* [my
emphasis] only with the secularization of the Western intellect in the seventeenth
century and the rise of modern science" (Iggers, 1958: 215). Only since the
seventeenth century, they maintain, was

> the perfectibility of man . . . viewed as primarily intellectual in nature and the result of
> conscious intellectual rather than purely immanent social causation. An earthly utopia
> was possible, not as the inevitable outcome of historical forces, but as the conscious
> work of rational individuals who, because of man's increasing enlightenment, were able
> to base society on the foundations of natural law revealed by human reason. (p. 215)

Whatever its origins, in late-eighteenth- and nineteenth-century historiography
the doctrine of progress was virtually "axiomatic" (Fay, 1947: 231–32, 237).
Voltaire's *Age of Louis XIV* (1752), for example, was designed to demonstrate
"the progress of the human mind and of all the arts" (Voltaire, [n.d.] 1972:
37); Edward Gibbon's *Decline and Fall of the Roman Empire* ([1776–88] 1952:

630) came to the "pleasing conclusion that every age of the world has increased and still increases the real wealth, the happiness, the knowledge, and perhaps the virtue of the human race"; and the essayist Thomas Babington Macaulay (1800–1859) understood the history of England as "emphatically the history of progress" (cited by Buckley, 1966: 34). Among the most famous instances is H. T. Buckle's *History of Civilization in England* (1857), which explicitly adopted Comte's law of three stages and became the "first successful popularization of this new way of thinking about history" (Semmel, 1976: 372). Buckle was not an academic historian; that his understanding of the role of "progress" in history was shared by university scholars, however, is plainly illustrated by the Rev. Mandell Creighton's introduction to the *Cambridge Modern History* (1902: 4): "We are bound to assume, as the scientific hypothesis on which history is to be written, a progress in human affairs. This progress must inevitably be towards some end."

In Germany faith in historical progress overlapped with HISTORISM and IDEALISM in the thought of leading scholars such as Johann Gustav Droysen (1808–84), Heinrich von Treitschke (1834–96), and Friedrich Meinecke (1862–1954) (Iggers, 1965: 7). Academic history in the United States was strongly affected as well (Higham et al., 1965: 134, 141, 157, 226), and the American E. P. Cheyney (1927: 22) could still write in the 1920s that "there seems to be a law of moral progress."

Faith in historical progress was not universal among historians, as the case of Jacob Burckhardt demonstrates (Iggers, 1958: 216); another significant exception, F. York Powell ([1898] 1926: vii), referred sarcastically to the "popular newspaper theory of the continuous and necessary progress of humanity" in his introduction to a popular turn-of-the-century historical manual. Nevertheless, the doctrine was very widely held until the 1930s, when disillusionment spread as a result of many factors: the unsuccessful peace settlement that followed World War I, the rise of FASCISM, the deteriorating world economic picture, and so on. Becker's *Heavenly City* was among the first influential works by a historian to debunk the idea. After its publication the trend was increasingly to regard "progress" not as an objective fact of historical development, or immanent force in human affairs, but as a kind of unempirical "faith" that people displayed toward the historical process.

Following World War II the notion lost its status as a grand, controlling idea in historiographical conceptualization and generally became an unfashionable category. The shift was graphically illustrated in Sidney B. Fay's 1946 presidential address to the American Historical Association, which began by asserting that the idea of progress "depends on subjective value-judgments" and declaring that the "concept is logically meaningless. It ought perhaps therefore to be shunned by the historian" (Fay, 1947: 231). Several years later Perez Zagorin expressed a widespread opinion when he wrote:

> There is something not only wrong but immoral in supposing that a principle of automatic progress is at work and that the future must be better than the past. It

is a vulgar conception which makes long-run evolutionary success the test of value, even in the human realm. . . . It is well also to be reminded that no principle of progress can prevent us from destroying the greatest achievements of our predecessors and that lines of development in which many things of the highest value have been created can be reversed and ended unless we take care. (1959: 248)

At mid-century vivid images of total war, Nazi policies of racial extermination, and Soviet tyranny made easy belief in moral progress virtually impossible. In this climate scholars typically concluded that the nineteenth century concept of progress was "a metaphysical assumption of dubious validity" and a "substitute religion" (Buckley, 1966: 41, 42; also Iggers, 1965: 5; Rotenstreich, 1971: 212).

Leonard Krieger's assertion that the idea of progress had "become an anachronism" (1951: 492), however, was something of an exaggeration. Actually, the prevailing orientation since 1945 is based on a qualified idea of progress. That history has—at least since the seventeenth century—reflected a relatively steady advance in material and technological improvement is generally accepted; that the passage of time has witnessed a corresponding ethical or spiritual betterment (a common belief in the nineteenth century) is usually either rejected or regarded unverifiable in principle (Mazlish, 1966: 333). Perez Zagorin's (1959: 248–49) opinion that the idea must be retained in "more modest and chastened form" is perhaps representative. We must speak of progress, writes Zagorin, when we describe ways in which older forms of human endeavor have been superseded by newer ones. There is progress in science, technology, industry, and so on, but we cannot speak of progress (aside from technical refinements) in the arts because "nothing in these orders is superseded." We cannot believe that history in its entirety is progressive, simply because we cannot envision a

> supervening task or problem to which the entire life of humanity is addressed. We cannot possibly say that the men of some particular present are happier than those of the past. But if we believe that better health or longer life or economic security are possible conditions of happiness, then we can say there is progress in these, because they are all problems whose solution accumulating knowledge makes less difficult and in which important successes have been achieved. (p. 249)

References

Becker, Carl. 1932. *The Heavenly City of the Eighteenth-Century Philosophers*. New Haven, Conn.

Buckley, Jerome Hamilton. 1966. *The Triumph of Time: A Study of the Victorian Concepts of Time, History, Progress, and Decadence*. Cambridge, Mass. Chapter three is a brief, readable account that reflects present attitudes.

Bury, J. B. [1920] 1932. *The Idea of Progress*. New York. This book immediately became "the undisputed classic in its field, comparable in influence to Burckhardt's *Civilization of the Renaissance in Italy* in Renaissance studies" (Wagar, 1967: 61).

Cheyney, Edward P. 1927. *Law in History and Other Essays*. New York.

Creighton, Mandell. 1902. "Introductory Note." *The Cambridge Modern History* 1. New York.

Edelstein, Ludwig. 1967. *The Idea of Progress in Classical Antiquity*. Baltimore. This book is radically revisionist in the context of twentieth-century scholarship; Edelstein notes, however, that early-nineteenth-century scholars believed that the idea of progress originated in classical antiquity; the notion that the doctrine was uniquely modern arose in the mid- and late-nineteenth centuries.

Fay, Sidney B. 1947. "The Idea of Progress." *AHR* 52: 231–46. This concise introduction to the subject is based largely on Bury but assumes an ironic position toward the doctrine of historical progress. See especially the conclusion on p. 246.

Frankel, Charles. 1948. *The Faith of Reason: The Idea of Progress in the French Enlightenment*. New York.

Gibbon, Edward. [1776–88] 1952. *The Portable Gibbon: The Decline and Fall of the Roman Empire*. New York.

Higham, John, et al. 1965. *History*. Englewood Cliffs, N.J.

Iggers, Georg G. 1958. "The Idea of Progress in Recent Philosophies of History." *JMH* 30: 215–26.

———. 1965. "The Idea of Progress: A Critical Reassessment." *AHR* 71: 1–17. This is a good summary of the twentieth-century intellectual shift against which decline of the doctrine must be seen. Iggers argues that "While progress seems to be invalidated as a universal idea, there is, nevertheless, a rational basis to the belief that within limited spheres man's actions can create more rational conditions" (p. 16).

Krieger, Leonard. 1951. "The Idea of Progress." *The Review of Metaphysics* 4: 483–94. This piece includes a short bibliography of writings in history, philosophy, and sociology.

Manuel, Frank E. 1962. *The Prophets of Paris*. Cambridge, Mass.

Mazlish, Bruce. 1966. Review of Frank E. Manuel, *The Shapes of Philosophical History*. *HT* 5: 325–36. Mazlish maintains that "While the entity known as 'morality' . . . is still so vague and ill-defined as to preclude any real estimate of 'progress' in the subject, the increasing material complexity of civilization is evident" (pp. 332–33).

Powell, F. York. [1898] 1926. "To the Reader." In Ch. V. Langlois and Ch. Seignobos, *Introduction to the Study of History*. New York.

Rotenstreich, Nathan. 1971. "The Idea of Historical Progress and Its Assumptions." *HT* 10: 197–221.

Sampson, R. V. 1956. *Progress in the Age of Reason*. Cambridge, Mass.

Semmel, Bernard. 1976. "H. T. Buckle: The Liberal Faith and the Science of History." *British Journal of Sociology* 27: 370–86.

Trompf, G. W. 1979. *The Idea of Historical Recurrence in Western Thought: From Antiquity to the Reformation*. Berkeley, Calif.

Voltaire. [n.d.] 1972. "On History: Advice to a Journalist." In Stern: 36–38.

Wagar, W. Warren. 1967. "Modern Views of the Origins of the Idea of Progress." *JHI* 28: 55–70. This is a valuable review of interpretations.

Zagorin, Perez. 1959. "Historical Knowledge: A Review Article on the Philosophy of History." *JMH* 31: 243–55.

Sources of Additional Information

The literature is so extensive that its history has become virtually a field in itself. Carl Becker's article "Progress" in *ESS* 12: 495–99, is a concise statement of his own interpretation, with a useful bibliography of older works. A gloss on Becker's writings is Leo Gershoy, "Carl Becker on Progress and Power," *AHR* 55 (Oct. 1949): 22–35. There are two excellent articles, both including bibliographies, in *DHI* 3: E. R. Dodds, "Progress in Classical Antiquity," pp. 623–33, and Morris Ginsberg, "Progress in the Modern Era," pp. 633–50. The list of sources cited in Ronald Sampson and Casimir N. Koblernicz, "Progress," *MCWS* 7 (1973): 43–50, is especially helpful for Marxist views. W. Warren Wagar, ed., *The Idea of Progress since the Renaissance* (New York, 1969), is a helpful anthology with a "Note on Further Reading." An older anthology is Frederick J. Teggart and George H. Hildebrand, eds., *The Idea of Progress: A Collection of Readings* (Berkeley and Los Angeles, 1949). Recent surveys are Kenneth E. Bock, "Theories of Progress and Evolution," in Werner J. Cahnman and Alan Boskoff, eds., *Sociology and History* (New York, 1964): 21–41, and Robert Nisbet, *History of the Idea of Progress* (New York, 1980). Maurice Mandelbaum's *History, Man, and Reason: A Study in Nineteenth-Century Thought* (Baltimore, 1971) contains many relevant passages. Chapter five of E. H. Carr's *What Is History?* (1961; reprint ed., Harmondsworth, Eng., 1964) is entitled "History as Progress." For the idea among ancient Christians see Theodore E. Mommsen, "St. Augustine and the Christian Idea of Progress: The Background of the City of God," *JHI* 12 (June 1951): 346–74. On the early modern period see Samuel Kinser, "Ideas of Temporal Change and Cultural Process in France, 1470–1535," in Anthony Molho and John A. Tedeschi, eds., *Renaissance Studies in Honor of Hans Baron* (Dekalb, Ill., 1971): 703–55. On the significance of the idea for eighteenth-century historiography see Günther Pflug, "The Development of Historical Method in the Eighteenth Century," [1954], *HT Beih.* 11 (1971): 1–23, especially 21–23; also chapter five of Frank E. Manuel's *Shapes of Philosophical History* (Stanford, Calif., 1965). Bruce Mazlish's views are elaborated in "The Idea of Progress," *Daedalus*, Summer 1963: 447–61. See the remarks of Sidney Hook in Bull. 54: 117. Folke Dovring argues for the "acceleration of progress" understood as "increased leverage on nature" in "The Principle of Acceleration: A Non-Dialectical Theory of Progress," *CSSH* 11 (1969): 413–24. On the idea in America see, in addition to Higham (1965), Arthur A. Ekirch, *The Idea of Progress in America, 1815–1860* (New York, 1944), and David W. Marcell, *Progress and Pragmatism: James, Dewey, Beard, and the American Idea of Progress* (Westport, Conn., 1974); also, Charles A. Beard's "Introduction" to the 1932 edition of Bury's *Idea of Progress.* A classic study of the idea in British historiography is Herbert Butterfield, *The Whig Interpretation of History* (London, 1931).

PSYCHOLOGICAL HISTORY, PSYCHOHISTORY. The application of psychological theory in historical interpretation. *Psychohistory* may refer broadly to the use of any form of psychological theory or more narrowly to the specific use of psychoanalytic theory.

Psychological insight has been linked to historiography since ancient times. Historical writing has always reflected concern for the inner motives, emotions, and sensibilities of past individuals, groups, and societies. Thucydides' late fifth-century B.C. *Peloponnesian War* set a classic example by treating the psychosocial impact of the plague on the population of Athens. In modern times historians have conventionally been expected to be good "judges of character" in the everyday meaning of the phrase. Properly speaking, however, the beginnings of *psychological history* and *psychohistory* (a term widely adopted in the United States since the 1960s) had to await the late-nineteenth-century creation of a body of formal psychological theory; in the strictest sense, these terms refer to work in which

> the author (in text, notes, or appendix) discusses the pertinence of formal psychological theory, uses it knowledgeably, and demonstrates a willingness to follow it wherever it leads—meaning to use it consistently or to acknowledge snags in the attempt to interweave the theory and history. (Brugger, 1981: xii)

The modern idea of psychological history has a long and complex prehistory. Frank Manuel (1972: 212), who defines *psychological history* in very broad terms as history that seeks to transfer the "focus from the deed to the psychic events that transpired in the doer," locates the origins of the modern tradition in the work of two eighteenth-century philosophers, Giambattista Vico (1668–1744) and Johann Gottfried Herder (1744–1803). Working independently, Vico and Herder established the idea that the collective psyche of societies is of central importance to history and that the quality of mental life varies fundamentally according to time and place. Herder, in particular, helped lay the foundations of HISTORISM, the doctrine that every epoch is spiritually unique and that the historian, by steeping himself in the remains of the past, can empathetically "understand" these diverse epochs (see UNDERSTANDING). Herder's famous notion of the *Volksgeist* ("national spirit"—see NATIONAL CHARACTER) was an aspect of what today might be called social psychology. So was the idea of ZEITGEIST ("spirit of the times"), which crystallized in late-eighteenth-century Germany as a designation for the collective mental climate of a given historical period.

This speculative tradition prevailed for most of the nineteenth century, when psychology was still a branch of philosophy. Nineteenth-century histories were normally not explicitly represented as "psychological," but the assumptions and concepts of the intuitive tradition informed many genres, such as nationalistic historiography (for instance, the work of Jules Michelet, who tried to "explore the changing consciousness of Frenchmen in their thousand years of national life" [Manuel, 1972: 213]); the tradition also helped lay the foundations for another genre of historiography, CULTURAL HISTORY, which survives today as a partial heir of the older tradition of psychological history founded by Vico and Herder.

The decisive turning point for the emergence of a more explicit concept of psychological history came in the 1880s and 1890s, with the transformation of psychology from a speculative to an empirical and experimental science. At this time some historians began to call for the systematic application of the various new psychological theories to historical analysis. Wilhelm Dilthey (1833–1911), the German philosopher and historian, is often cited as a pioneer in this regard (Manuel, 1972; Musto, 1977: 249). But although Dilthey was at one point interested in applying the conclusions of experimental psychology to history, and even explicitly called his approach "psychological," his work really belongs primarily to the older philosophical tradition of IDEALISM. More important in the development of a self-consciously psychological approach were Karl Lamprecht (1856–1915) in Germany and Lucien Febvre (1878–1956) in France. Lamprecht (1905: 3, 29) maintained that "History is primarily a socio-psychological science. . . . in itself [it] is nothing but applied psychology. Hence we must look to theoretical psychology to give us the clew to its true interpretation." He tried to fuse the ideas of various nineteenth-century psychologists with the approaches of sociology and cultural history, but his ideas soon fell out of fashion—partly because of the furious opposition of the majority of his German colleagues but also because the psychological theories to which he appealed were soon superseded. Recently his reputation as an innovator has risen somewhat among West German historians who are interested in the application of social psychology to history (for example, Wehler, 1980).

Febvre, working in the context of the new field of social psychology associated with Emile Durkheim, Gustave Le Bon, Charles Blondel, and Henri Wallon, was the French leader in formulating a concept of *histoire psychologique*. In programmatic essays Febvre called upon historians to reconstruct the entire material, mental, and ethical climates of past generations ([1938] 1973) and directed attention to the past "emotional life of man and all its manifestations" ([1941] 1973: 13). It was he, along with his friend Marc Bloch and those who gathered around the journal *Annales* (founded in 1929), who popularized the now fashionable idea of the history of *mentalités* ("collective mentalities") (Hutton, 1981).

In the United States theory first developed along Franco-German lines, that is, in the direction of an adaptation of social or collective psychology à la Lamprecht and Febvre. The NEW HISTORY school of the turn of the century displayed a pronounced interest in Lamprecht (e.g., Barnes, 1925). However, there was also some early interest in Freudian psychoanalysis (for instance, Smith, 1913). As events transpired, interest in Lamprechtian psychological history declined, and the Freudian approach became dominant—not, however, until the 1950s.

Throughout the first half of the twentieth century, American historians generally remained skeptical of the concept of psychoanalytic history. Freud himself supplied models in his psychoanalytic studies of Leonardo da Vinci (1910) and Dostoevsky (1928), but he also made some embarrasssing blunders in his use of evidence (Arzt, 1978: 2). Beyond this, two objections appeared (and continue to seem today) crucial to many historians: (1) Freudian analysis depends largely on the discovery and interpretation of suppressed childhood traumas in the unconscious, and reliable evidence regarding the early years of most historical figures is either scarce or non-existent. (2) Psychoanalysis was a product of late-nineteenth-century European thought; efforts to apply it to earlier periods risk ANACHRONISM, the reading of the assumptions of one period back into other periods. Indeed, this was a problem for all psychological theory, Freudian or otherwise (Febvre, [1938] 1973: 5). For these reasons, most historians remained doubtful or uninterested. As late as 1952 a survey of the influence of psycho-analysis on recent thought failed to mention history at all (Langer, 1958).

A turning point of sorts occurred in the late 1950s. In his presidential address to the American Historical Association in 1957, William L. Langer, a respected diplomatic historian, stressed the "urgently needed deepening of our historical understanding through exploitation of the concepts and findings of modern psychology," and specifically through the use of "psychoanalysis and its later developments and variations as included in the terms 'dynamic' or 'depth psychology' " (Langer, 1958: 284–85). At the same time, the Danish-born psychoanalyst Erik Erikson (1958: 16) published a widely admired study, *Young Man Luther*, in which he used the adjective *psychohistorical* to describe the historical application of his own post-Freudian "ego psychology." Erikson and his admirers subsequently adopted the term *psychohistory* to designate their approach. (The *OED* indicates that the adjective *psychohistorical* appeared in English as early as 1840, but it was certainly not adopted by historians before the late 1950s.) Although Erikson's work and that of his followers was extremely controversial, particularly in its use of EVIDENCE and inference, the way was nonetheless paved for the growth of a psychohistorical "school" in the United States. In the 1960s and 1970s the question of the possibility of a Freudian and post-Freudian "psychohistory" was vigorously debated. There were numerous efforts to define and defend the field (for example, Mazlish, [1971] 1976) and some (occasionally angry) efforts to debunk the approach entirely (Barzun, 1974; Stannard, 1980). A few established historians experimented with the approach (e.g., Pflanze, 1972), and a leading periodical, the *Journal of Modern History*, devoted an entire issue to the subject (June 1975); but it is noteworthy that the editor of the profession's most highly regarded anthology of theoretical writings did not include an essay on psychohistory in the second edition of his book (Stern, 1972)—although he did include new essays on other non-traditional approaches. Currently, the respectability of the concept of psychohistory is "not yet secure" (Arzt, 1978: 1) and psychohistory is "still more a matter of theoretical discussion by social scientists than of scholarly practice by historians" (Bailyn, 1982: 20).

References

Arzt, Donna. 1978. "Psychohistory and Its Discontents." *Biography* 1: 1–36. This excellent review article includes a history of the concept of psychohistory and many valuable bibliographical references.

Bailyn, Bernard. 1982. "The Challenge of Modern Historiography." *AHR* 87: 1–24. This is a critical survey of current trends by a president of the American Historical Association.

Barnes, Harry Elmer. 1925. *The New History and the Social Studies*. Chapter three deals with psychology and history and includes a discussion of Lamprecht's ideas.

Barzun, Jacques. 1974. *Clio and the Doctors: Psycho-History, Quanto-History, and History*. Chicago. This is a bitter attack on the new psychohistory by a representative of the older tradition of psychological and cultural history.

Brugger, Robert J., ed. 1981. *Our Selves/Our Past: Psychological Approaches to American History*. Baltimore. This important anthology of writings by American historians illustrates the application of psychological theory to American history. The introductory essay includes a wealth of bibliographical references in footnote citations, and there is a general bibliography as well.

Erikson, Erik H. 1958. *Young Man Luther: A Study in Psychoanalysis and History*. New York. Erikson refers to the term *psychohistory* as designating one of a number of "hyphenated approaches" that "are a compost heap of today's interdisciplinary efforts" (p. 16).

Febvre, Lucien. [1938] 1973. "History and Psychology." In Peter Burke, ed., *A New Kind of History: From the Writings of Febvre*. New York: 1–11.

———. [1941] 1973. "Sensibility and History: How to Reconstitute the Emotional Life of the Past." In Peter Burke, ed., *A New Kind of History: From the Writings of Febvre*. New York: 12–26.

Hutton, Patrick H. 1981. "The History of Mentalities: The New Map of Cultural History." *HT* 20: 237–59.

Lamprecht, Karl. 1905. *What Is History? Five Lectures on the Modern Science of History*. New York.

Langer, William L. 1958. "The Next Assignment." *AHR* 63: 283–304.

Manuel, Frank E. 1972. "The Use and Abuse of Psychology in History." In Gilbert and Graubard: 211–37. This balanced overview is especially valuable for its concise treatment of pre- and non-Freudian psychological approaches. It seeks to establish a framework of legitimacy for psychological history by linking it to a long tradition of reputable thought and scholarship; Manuel avoids mentioning Lamprecht or using the term *psychohistory*.

Mazlish, Bruce. [1971] 1976. "What Is Psychohistory?" In George M. Kren and Leon H. Rappoport, eds., *Varieties of Psychohistory*. New York.

Musto, David F. 1977. "Psychohistory." *International Encyclopedia of Psychiatry, Psychology, Psychoanalysis, and Neurology* 9. New York: 248–52. Musto includes a brief bibliography.

Pflanze, Otto. 1972. "Toward a Psychoanalytic Interpretation of Bismarck." *AHR* 77: 419–44.

Smith, Preserved. 1913. "Luther's Early Development in the Light of Psychoanalysis." *American Journal of Psychology* 24: 360–77.

Stannard, David E. 1980. *Shrinking History: On Freud and the Failure of Psychohistory*. New York.

Stern, Fritz. 1972. *The Varieties of History: From Voltaire to the Present*. New York.

Wehler, Hans-Ulrich. 1980. "Psychoanalysis and History." *Social Research* 47: 519–36. This piece is by a leading West German historian.

Sources of Additional Information

See also BIOGRAPHY; CULTURAL HISTORY; INTELLECTUAL HISTORY; INTERDISCIPLINARY HISTORY. There is an abundance of theoretical and polemical literature, much less in the way of concrete application. A general guide is Lloyd DeMause, *A Bibliography of Psychohistory* (New York, 1975), well regarded as a reference work despite DeMause's uneven reputation as a practitioner of psychohistory. The importance of the annotated bibliography in Brugger (1981) must be underscored, since it lists not only theoretical titles but "Representative Works in Psychologically Informed" historiography as well.

In addition to Arzt (1978), there are some valuable review essays, for example: Peter Loewenberg, "Psychohistory," in Kammen: 408–32, and Richard L. Schoenwald, "The Psychological Study of History," in Iggers and Parker: 71–84, which concludes with an excellent short bibliography. Among the anthologies are Bruce Mazlish, ed., *Psychoanalysis and History* (Englewood Cliffs, N.J., 1963); Robert J. Lifton, ed., *Explorations in Psychohistory* (New York, 1974) (although only one of the twelve contributors is a professional historian); and George M. Kren and Leon H. Rappoport, eds., *Varieties of Psychohistory* (New York, 1976). See also part three of Richard E. Beringer, *Historical Analysis: Contemporary Approaches to Clio's Craft* (New York, 1978). For balanced critical responses to Barzun's attack on psychohistory (1974), see reviews by Peter Loewenberg (*Clio* 5 [Fall 1975]: 123–27) and Robert D. Schulzinger (*HT* 15 [1976]: 94–103). Philip Pomper has published *The Structure of the Mind in History: Five Major Figures in Psychohistory* (New York, 1985), which discusses the work of Norman O. Brown, Erik Erikson, Freud, Robert J. Lifton, and Herbert Marcuse. Two journals are devoted to the subject: the *Psychohistory Review* (originally the *Group for the Use of Psychology in History Newsletter*) and the (less respected) *Journal of Psychohistory* (originally the *History of Childhood Quarterly*).

Q

QUANTIFICATION, QUANTITATIVE HISTORY. *Quantification* refers to any method of reasoning based on mathematics; *quantitative history* is historical scholarship based to a significant degree on mathematics—from simple arithmetical tabulation to the use of algebraic functions and mathematical modeling.

Systematic use of mathematics in history has grown rapidly in importance since the 1930s, more particularly since 1945 in France and the United States (Furet, 1972: 45). The idea of a special "quantitative" approach to the study of the past—that is, *quantitative history*—crystallized in the 1950s; key dates in this development were, in France, 1949 (the publication year of Fernand Braudel's *Mediterranean and the Mediterranean World in the Age of Phillip II*, based heavily on quantitative data [Price, 1969: 6]) and, in North America, 1957, when pioneering manifestoes were published by Lee Benson and Alfred H. Conrad and John R. Meyer.

Although rigorous use of quantification—even in economic history—was generally neglected in the nineteenth century (Price, 1969: 2) and has been widely advocated in the historical profession only since the 1950s, there were noteworthy precursors of the idea before 1945. Frederick Jackson Turner, a pioneer of the NEW HISTORY in turn-of-the-century America, encouraged his pupils at the University of Wisconsin to tabulate election returns and analyze legislative roll calls. As early as 1896 one of these students, Orin G. Libby, published a call for the quantitative analysis of congressional roll calls in the Annual Report of the American Historical Association. Among economic historians, Eli Heckscher (1929) called for the application of economic theory to economic history, and J. H. Clapham (1931: 328) required that all economic historians possess a "statistical sense," that is, "the habit of asking in relation to any institution, policy, group or movement the questions: how large? how long? how often? how representative?'' There were isolated efforts to quantify social history in the 1930s, for example, Crane Brinton's ([1930] 1965) study of Jacobin Club membership in the French Revolution and Donald Greer's (1935) analysis of victims of the Terror for the same period. The research and teaching of several prominent U.S. historians of the interwar period—for example, James C. Malin, Thomas C. Cochran, Oscar Handlin, Paul Wallace Gates, and Merle Curti—foreshadowed the quantitative approach. It should be emphasized, however, that this was not ''*the* or even *a* dominant aspect of the historiography of the period'' (Price, 1969: 3–4). Moreover, the work of those interested in quantification before 1945 was circumscribed, whether by their limited command of statistical methods, by the deficiency of statistical techniques themselves (Bogue, 1968: 5, 15–16; Aydelotte, 1971: 1–2), or by use of quantification only in the auxilliary, descriptive role of illustrating historical narrative with statistics (Marczewski, 1968: 179).

Since 1945 dramatic changes have occurred. The French government has funded ambitious data-collecting programs through the Sixth Section (social science) of the *École Pratique des Haute Études*. As practiced in France in the 1950s and 1960s, the quantitative approach has involved the use of long-range compilations of national statistics regarding national income, national wealth, and so on, that are used to study long- and medium-term demographic and economic patterns (Marczewski, 1968: 183; Furet, 1972; Le Roy Ladurie and Dumont, 1972; Le Roy Ladurie, 1979: 3–78).

In the United States a major move toward quantitative research began in the mid- and late 1950s in the form of ECONOMETRIC HISTORY (see also ECONOMIC HISTORY) and in political and social history, where it was spearheaded by historians such as Lee Benson (1957; 1961) who were inspired by statistically oriented behavioral theory in political science. (*Behavioral* in this context designates ''a strong interest in the methods, results, and implications of measurement, combined with some desire to produce research that is respectable by social science criteria'' [Bogue, 1968: 6].) In 1964 a history committee of the Mathematics Social Science Board (itself a creation of the Social Science Research Council and the Institute for Advanced Study in the Behavioral Sciences) was established to encourage mathematical competence among professional historians (p. 14); in the same decade the Inter-University Consortium for Political Research was founded at the University of Michigan to serve as a computerized data bank for historical statistics. Some researchers began to extend the methods of statistical analysis beyond economic, political, and social history to intellectual and cultural history through the use of methods such as ''content analysis'' (i.e., mapping the frequency and pattern of key terms and symbols in public and private discourse) (Barraclough, 1979: 88). As a result of such experiments,

> Uniformities have been discovered and quantitative studies have thrown light on a variety of topics: the composition of various social or political groups, business history, agricultural history, roll-call votes in legislatures, patterns of voting in

electorates, the social structure and nature of social mobility, and a number of demographic and ecological questions. (Aydelotte, 1971: 32)

Advocates of quantification argue that use of statistical inference and other "indirect" measurement techniques are crucial "if historians are to succeed in shifting the attention of their discipline from a preoccupation with exceptional individuals to concentration on the life and times of [inarticulate] common people" (Fogel, 1975: 345).

In America (though to a much lesser extent elsewhere [Erickson, 1975: 360]) the historiographical use of mathematics became a storm center of controversy in the 1960s and 1970s, with debate extending at times to the popular press. The acrimony of debate was the result of various factors: champions of the new approach sometimes overstated their case (often, their opponents charged, to secure funding for their costly data-collecting and computer-assisted projects [Vann, 1969: 64; Erickson, 1975: 351–52]); many scholars believed that the subject matter and ultimate "human" questions of history were not susceptible of measurement (for example, Beard, [1934] 1959: 147; Schlesinger, 1962: 770); angry traditionalists maintained that advocates of quantification were purveyors of a pernicious "cult of the new" (e.g., Barzun, 1974: x; cf. Bridenbaugh, 1963: 326); most historians were ignorant (and often frightened) of higher mathematics and disinclined to "retool" in order to meet the challenge of quantification; generational tensions and the long-standing debate over history's relationship to social science became entangled in the controversy (Erickson, 1975: 364—see SOCIAL SCIENTIFIC HISTORY). The use of quantitative methods was perhaps most novel (and to some scholars, disturbing) in ECONOMETRIC HISTORY, where theorists advocated the use of mathematically designed models—some contrary to fact (see COUNTERFACTUAL ANALYSIS)—to assist inquiry and test traditional interpretations (McClelland, 1975: 178; Price, 1969: 11; Fogel, 1975: 337–38). A major concern associated with such innovation—and with quantification generally—was the fear that history, like the physical sciences, might be "transformed into an esoteric subject that is directly accessible only to rigorously trained professionals" and would thus "require a corps of intermediaries or popularizers who could explain to the lay public the findings of professional historians" (Fogel, 1975: 349). By the end of the 1960s one authority (Vann, 1969: 64) could state that "Fear of, and animosity toward, quantitative history is one of the facts of contemporary scholarly life."

During the debate advocates of quantification scored one undeniable point: the issue of whether "counting" should or can be used in history is spurious. When historians employ terms such as *many, most, average, typical, representative, significant, widespread, growing,* and *intense,* as they almost invariably do, they tacitly engage in quantitative reasoning, regardless of whether they support their prose with numbers or equations. Thus, the question is not "*can* there be a quantitative history?" but "*when* should formal quantitative methods be utilized in historical research and explanation?" (Aydelotte, 1971:

40; Fogel, 1975: 329–331). It seems reasonable that such methods should be used whenever they can make historical reasoning more precise.

Although many members of the profession remain skeptical about quantification, an atmosphere of qualified acceptance is growing, based on the realization that quantitative methods "can give to many historical debates a perspective that would otherwise be completely lacking" (McClelland, 1975; cf. Vann, 1969: 74; Fischer, 1970: 90; Ford, 1975: 367; Fogel and Elton, 1983; Himmelfarb, 1984: 20).

References

Aydelotte, William O. 1971. *Quantification in History* (Reading, Mass., 1971). This is a balanced introduction by a "cautious" advocate (p. 3). The author summarizes many of the various claims and criticisms, pp. 18–37, and includes an exchange of letters between himself and a skeptic, J. H. Hexter (chapter 6).

Barraclough, Geoffrey. 1979. *Main Trends in History*. New York. This is a highly sympathetic survey of recent quantitative work in both Europe and North America.

Barzun, Jacques. 1974. *Clio and the Doctors: Psycho-History, Quanto-History, and History*. Chicago. This is an angry attack on quantification; according to Barzun, one "knows as his eye ranges across a chart in all directions that he is not *reading history*" (p. 24).

Beard, Charles A. [1934] 1959. "Written History as an Act of Faith." In Meyerhoff: 140–51. Beard maintains that "occurrences of history—the unfolding of ideas and interests in time-motion—are not identical in nature with the data of physics, and hence in their totality they are beyond the reach of that necessary instrument of natural science—mathematics—which cannot assign meaningful values to the imponderables, immeasurables, and contingencies of history as actuality" (p. 147).

Benson, Lee. 1957. "Research Problems in American Political Historiography." In Mirra Komarovsky, ed., *Common Frontiers of the Social Sciences*. Glencoe, Ill.: 113–83.

———. 1961. *The Concept of Jacksonian Democracy: New York as a Test Case*. Princeton, N.J.

Bogue, Allan G. 1968. "United States: The 'New' Political History." *Journal of Contemporary History* 3: 5–27. This is good for a bibliography through the mid–1960s.

Bridenbaugh, Carl. 1963. "The Great Mutation." *AHR* 68: 315–31. This presidential address to the American Historical Association warns against the seductions of the "Bitch-Goddess Quantification."

Brinton, Crane. [1930] 1965. *The Jacobins: An Essay in the New History*. New York.

Clapham, J. H. 1931. "Economic History as a Discipline," in *Encyclopedia of the Social Sciences* 5: 327–38.

Conrad, Alfred H., and Meyer, John R. 1957. "Economic Theory, Statistical Inference, and Economic History." *The Journal of Economic History* 17: 524–44.

Erickson, Charlotte. 1975. "Quantitative History." *AHR* 80: 351–65. This is a review of five studies published in the early 1970s.

Fischer, David Hackett. 1970. *Historians' Fallacies: Toward a Logic of Historical Thought*. New York. Fischer believes that quantification is "an important tool,

long used by historians and presently in process of a revolutionary refinement''
and that ''every historian should count everything he can, by the best available
statistical method'' (p. 90). His book contains a catalog of logical fallacies often
associated with quantification, pp. 61–2, 90–97, 103–30.

Fogel, Robert William. 1975. ''The Limits of Quantitative Methods in History.'' *AHR*
80: 329–50. This piece is very important for the bibliographical citations in footnotes. It stresses the idea that ''mathematics has long been an intrinsic feature of
historical analysis, but its use has been covert and subliminal'' (p. 330).

Fogel, Robert William, and Elton, G. R. 1983. *Which Road to the Past? Two Views of
History* (New Haven, Conn., 1983). This is an exchange between a champion of
quantification and a well-known traditionalist. Elton (the traditionalist) concedes
that high-quality quantitative economic history is feasible.

Ford, Franklin L. 1975. Review of Emmanuel Le Roy Ladurie, *Le territoire de l'historien*.
AHR 80: 366–67. Ford concludes that ''not everyone will rely as heavily [as Le
Roy Ladurie] on [quantitative] methods, but no one can any longer safely ignore
them'' (p. 367).

Furet, François. 1972. ''Quantitative History.'' In Gilbert and Graubard: 45–61.

Greer, Donald. 1935. *The Incidence of the Terror During the French Revolution: A
Statistical Interpretation*. Cambridge, Mass.

Heckscher, Eli F. 1929. ''A Plea for Theory in Economic History.'' *Economic History*
1: 525–34.

Himmelfarb, Gertrude. 1984. Review of Peter Laslett, *The World We Have Lost Further
Explained*. *The New York Times Book Review*, June 24, 1984: 20–21. The author
asserts that quantitative social science history ''has become so well established
that it is in the mainstream rather than on the cutting edge'' (p. 20).

Le Roy Ladurie, Emmanuel. 1979. *The Territory of the Historian*. Chicago. The author
summarizes French developments, pp. 3–31.

Le Roy Ladurie, Emmanuel, and Dumont, Paul. 1972. ''Quantitative and Cartographical
Exploitation of French Military Archives, 1819–1826.'' In Gilbert and Graubard:
62–106.

McClelland, Peter D. 1975. *Causal Explanation and Model Building in History, Economics, and the New Economic History*. Ithaca, N.Y.

Marczewski, Jean. 1968. ''Quantitative History.'' *Journal of Contemporary History* 3:
179–91.

Price, Jacob M. 1969. ''Recent Quantitative Work in History: A Survey of the Main
Trends.'' *HT Beih*. 9: 1–13. This is one of the best introductory surveys. Price
declares that ''the bulk of historical work now being published is substantially
non-quantitative and that this state of affairs is likely to continue'' (p. 12).

Schlesinger, Arthur, Jr. 1962. ''The Humanist Looks at Empirical Social Research.''
American Sociological Review 27: 768–71. This piece represents the widespread
''humanistic'' view that ''almost all important questions are important precisely
because they are *not* susceptible to quantitative answers'' (p. 770).

Vann, Richard T. 1969. ''History and Demography.'' *HT Beih*. 9: 64–78. Vann cites
use of quantification in the history of the family as ''an extraordinary example of
how the most intimate details in the private lives of quite obscure people, who
produced no literary evidence at all, can nevertheless become the object of our
knowledge'' (p. 74).

Sources of Additional Information

See also COUNTERFACTUAL ANALYSIS; ECONOMETRIC HISTORY; ECONOMIC HISTORY. Because of the intensity of debate over quantification, most writers consciously try to locate themselves within the network of literature on the subject; therefore most works cited above are important for bibliographic information, either in text or footnote citations. See, for example, p. 38, n. 11, in Aydelotte (1971). Aydelotte also wrote "Quantification in History," *AHR* 71 (April 1966): 803–25. Barraclough (1979) cites many of the important contributions in French and German, as well as English. There is a convenient list of titles in all relevant languages in Berding: 183–90. William O. Aydelotte, Allan G. Bogue, and Robert William Fogel, eds., *The Dimensions of Quantitative Research in History* (Princeton, N.J., 1972), is an anthology that reflects a spectrum of the applications of quantification, as is Don Karl Rowney and James Q. Graham, Jr., eds., *Quantitative History: Selected Readings* (Homewood, Ill., 1969). Val R. Lorwin and Jacob M. Price, eds., *The Dimensions of the Past: Materials, Problems, and Opportunities for Quantitative Work in History* (New Haven, Conn., 1972), is another important anthology dealing with developments in various countries. Chapters two, three, and six of Iggers and Parker are very important for bibliography (on demography, econometric history, and the "new political history"). The entire issue of *American Behavioral Scientist* 21 (Dec. 1977) contains several relevant articles. Charles M. Dollar and Richard J. Jensen, *Historian's Guide to Statistics: Quantitative Analysis and Historical Research* (New York, 1971), is a basic manual with an extensive annotated bibliography. Two good reviews of research appear in Kammen: Allan G. Bogue, "The New Political History in the 1970s," pp. 231–51, and J. Morgan Koussner, "Quantitative Social-Scientific History," pp. 433–56. *HT Beih.* 9 (1969) is entitled *Studies in Quantitative History and the Logic of the Social Sciences*. Samuel P. Hays, "Historical Social Research: Concept, Method, Technique," *Journal of Interdisciplinary History* 4 (Winter 1974): 475–82, is a review essay based on four books on quantification. Robert P. Swierenga, "Computers and American History: The Impact of the 'New' Generation," *Journal of American History* 60 (1974): 1045–70, contains a good survey of quantitative work and methodological manuals. See, as well, Eugene J. Watts, "Quantitative Methods in Historical Analysis: A Syllabus," *Historical Methods Newsletter* 5, No. 2 (1972): 59–67, and Theodore K. Rabb, "Guides to Quantitative History: A Review Article," *The Historian* 35 (1973): 271–75. H. Stuart Hughes, "The Historian and the Social Scientist," *AHR* 66 (1960): 20–46, especially 34–36, 38–40, displays an ambivalent but open-minded attitude toward quantification that is probably typical of many historians.

R
_____

RACE, RACISM, RACIALISM. *Race* is a biological concept according to which humankind may be subdivided into distinct categories ("races") based on inherited physical characteristics. *Racism* and *racialism*, synonymous terms, designate the belief that certain human groups are—by virtue of heredity—physically, intellectually, or otherwise collectively superior to other groups and that this innate superiority is a determining factor in social affairs.

The idea of race, formerly an important theoretical template for historical studies, is today almost entirely discredited as an analytical concept in historiography. Mere association of an idea with the notion of race—as in the case of the idea of NATIONAL CHARACTER—is often enough to discredit it in the eyes of historians.

The term *race* has a long tradition in English. In sixteenth-century usage it could mean "a tribe, nation, or people, regarded as of common stock" and, more generally, "a group or class of persons, animals, or things, having some common feature or features" (*OED*). The word has always had a close association with the idea of common physical ancestry.

> It was therefore appropriate in medieval times to any self-conscious group of peoples in Europe, many of whom (like the Roman, French and British aristocracies) chose at times to believe that they were descended from the Trojans. But it could (like "tribe" and "nation" and "people") be extended to cover any set of humans, or animals. (Minogue, 1967: 9)

Systematic racial theories of history date from the eighteenth century, when growing interest in the scientific study of the past was often associated with the notion that social development depends on heredity (for instance, the work of Henri de Boulainvilliers [1658–1722] and the Baron de Montesquieu [1689–

1755]). At this time two distinct ideas of race began to crystallize: (1) the biological conception, or notion, that within the human species "there exist different populations . . . which are distinguished from one another by the possession of certain distinctive hereditary traits" (Montagu, 1964: xi); and (2) the social concept—usually called *racism* or *racialism* (e.g., Hofstadter, [1944] 1955: 172), defined as "the theory that moral and intellectual qualities (and especially inferiorities and superiorities) are genetically determined by racial membership" (Minogue, 1967: 9). The French physician François Bernier (1620–88) was evidently first to classify humankind according to subcategories based on the idea of shared, inherited characteristics (Gossett, 1963: 32–33), a practice that was almost universally accepted in the nineteenth century.

According to one view (Poliakov, 1974), historical interest in race was spurred by biblical criticism and secularization in the eighteenth and nineteenth centuries. Skepticism regarding the Bible and traditional Christian doctrine undermined the Old Testament genealogy of humankind, based on the idea that all people were descended from Adam. This, in turn, stimulated a broad interest in the discovery of secular genealogies, and the social concept of race seemed to provide a scientific category for the purpose.

Various theories of racial origins and classification were devised in the late eighteenth and early nineteenth centuries, although they were usually the work of naturalists, philologists, and physicians rather than historians (Barzun, [1937] 1965; Gossett, 1963; Poliakov, 1974). According to their inclination, historical scholars could pick and choose from this reservoir of ideas; the fact that *race* had no exact definition made it all the more attractive. The most influential of these theories—based on the idea of a link between language and biological ancestry and now regularly debunked as fantasy (Poliakov, 1974)—was the notion of "Aryanism." Aryanism was a by-product of eighteenth-century philologists' discovery of grammatical and lexical similarities between ancient Sanskrit and most modern European languages. On this factual foundation, racial theorists erected the mythical doctrine that Europe had once been settled by a fair-skinned, superior, culture-building "Aryan race" that persisted especially in the northern parts of the continent.

In the early nineteenth century racist assumptions made gradual headway against the traditional Christian doctrine of the brotherhood of man and EN-LIGHTENMENT ideas of natural equality and cosmopolitanism. The social concept of race is present in the work of early-nineteenth-century American historians such as George Bancroft, John Lothrop Motley, and W. H. Prescott, but it is not generally pronounced (Gossett, 1963: 88–94). By the late nineteenth century, however, belief in racial hierarchy and the socially determining role of superior "stock"—"Aryan," "Celtic," and so on—powerfully conditioned historical writing in every western country. The opening chapters of nobel-laureate Theodor Mommsen's famous *History of Rome* ([1854–85] 1898: 9–10), with their references to the "Indo-German stock," the "suppression of races less capable of, or less advanced in, culture by nations of higher standing," and "dark-coloured population[s] less susceptible of culture," are striking illustrations. Likewise, Lord Bryce, eminent British historian of the Holy Roman Empire, argued in his *Race Sentiment as a Factor in History* (1915) that there is "an unquestionable racial strain" in every civilized nation (cited in Snyder, 1954: 15). J. B. Bury, editor of the *Cambridge Ancient History*, considered one of the important tasks of scientific history to be "prosecuting that most difficult of all inquiries, the ethnical problem, the part played by race in the development of peoples and the effects of race blendings" (Bury, [1902] 1972: 222).

At the same time, speculative philosophies of history based on racism were constructed by the Comte de Gobineau ([1853–55] 1915) and H. Stuart Chamberlain ([1899] 1910), men who, although not academic historians, enjoyed wide influence among professional scholars (for instance, Lord Acton [Semmel, 1976:380]) and the lay public. As the quotations from Mommsen and Bryce suggest, the terms *race*, NATION, and NATIONALITY were routinely used loosely and interchangeably (Murphey, 1965: 144–45; Snyder, 1954: 14), a practice legitimized by lexicographers who often defined the word *nation* in terms of "race." In German Europe, the term *Rassenkampf* ("race struggle") was used as early as the 1840s to refer to nationality conflicts and, from the 1870s on, was a vogue word (Ladendorf, [1906] 1968: 258). Although racialist theories have been soundly discredited in the twentieth century on scientific and ethical grounds, the historiographical use of *race* as a synonym for *nationality* is still occasionally encountered (for example, Taylor, [1948] 1976: 24; Okey, 1982: 14)—although from the present viewpoint this usage confuses biological (i.e., inherited) and cultural (i.e., acquired) categories.

The pervasiveness of racialist assumptions in popular writing in turn-of-the-century America was amply reflected in the work of the amateur scholar John Fiske ([1876] 1902: 207–38). Among academic historians, an important racialist school was championed by men such as Herbert Baxter Adams, Albert Bushnell Hart, Andrew D. White, and Moses Coit Tyler, who argued that America's democratic institutions were an "Anglo-Saxon" racial inheritance, ultimately "Teutonic" or "Aryan" in origin. From the 1880s to about 1900, this "germ theory" was the dominant interpretive model of U.S. historians, losing its appeal only as a consequence of the acceptance of Frederick Jackson Turner's FRONTIER thesis and the growth of anti-German feeling during World War I (Saveth, 1939; [1948] 1965; Gossett, 1963). In Europe the social concept of race became a pillar of historiographical orthodoxy in Nazi Germany between 1933 and 1945 (Gilbert, 1947; Werner, 1968).

In the early twentieth century the social concept of race came under critical scrutiny, and some anthropologists—especially Franz Boas (1858–1942)—declared even the biological concept suspect (Lesser, 1968:105). On the eve of World War I James Harvey Robinson (1912: 87–88), leading prophet of the NEW HISTORY in the United States, observed that historians used the word *race* with "great recklessness" and called the "Aryan theory" used by Mommsen "well-nigh as naive and grotesque as the earlier notion of the Tower of Babel."

Robinson maintained that the constant "migrations and fusions" of human history made talk of the persistence of distinct racial strains meaningless; his attitude was particularly influenced by work in the new academic disciplines of anthropology and sociology, which emphasized the role of CULTURE in the determination of behavior, as opposed to physical inheritance. Gradually, historians adopted the view that

> nation is a term used in social science, while race is one used in natural science: the nation designates historical and social characteristics which can be altered by society; race refers to hereditary, biological traits not easily changeable by education and assimilation. . . . in the scientific sense [race] should be applied only to the biological groupings of human types. (Snyder, 1954: 17)

In the 1930s critical retrospectives on the role of the concept in historiography began to appear (such as Barzun, [1937] 1965; Saveth, 1939). The decisive blow against the race concept, however, was ethical rather than scientific; for historians as for the general public, racialist theories of history were ultimately descredited only by Nazi Germany's policies of "racial purification" and extermination in the Second World War.

It should be noted that, despite their present overwhelming rejection of the idea of race as a determinative social factor, historians generally continue to accept the biological concept (e.g., Snyder, 1954: 17; Gossett, 1963: 409).

References

Barzun, Jacques. [1937] 1965. *Race: A Study in Superstition*. New York. This book contains an annotated bibliography that, unfortunately, was not updated for the 1965 edition.

Bury, J. B. [1902] 1972. "The Science of History." In Stern: 210–23.

Chamberlain, H. Stuart. [1899] 1910. *The Foundations of the Nineteenth Century*. London.

Fiske, John. [1876] 1902. "The Races of the Danube." In John Fiske, *Darwinism and Other Essays*. Cambridge, Mass.: 207–38.

Gilbert, Felix. 1947. "German Historiography During the Second World War: A Bibliographical Survey." *AHR* 53: 50–58. Gilbert discusses tensions between racialist and traditionalist historians in Nazi Germany.

Gobineau, Joseph Arthur Comte de. [1853–55] 1915. *The Inequality of Human Races*. London.

Gossett, Thomas F. 1963. *Race: The History of an Idea in America*. Dallas, Tex. This is a concise survey of the main ideas regarding race in Europe as well as America; footnote citations provide a rich bibliography.

Hofstadter, Richard. [1944] 1955. *Social Darwinism in American Thought*. Boston.

Ladendorf, Otto. [1906] 1968. *Historisches Schlagwörterbuch*. Hildesheim.

Lesser, Alexander. 1968. "Franz Boas." *IESS* 2: 99–110.

Minogue, K. R. 1967. *Nationalism*. New York.

Mommsen, Theodore. [1854–85] 1898. *History of Rome*. New York.

Montagu, Ashley, ed. 1964. *The Concept of Race*. New York. This book includes contributions by a number of anthropologists and biologists that are critical not only of the social concept of race but of the biological concept as well.

Murphey, Murray G. 1965. "An Approach to the Historical Study of National Character." In Melford E. Spiro, ed., *Context and Meaning in Cultural Anthropology*. New York: 144–63. Murphey notes that "in an era before modern genetic theory, one often finds race and nationality combined, and historians speak of the English race or the German race, meaning really no more than that Englishmen seem to have certain traits in common and that this community outlasts a generation" (pp. 144–45).

Okey, Robin. 1982. *Eastern Europe, 1740–1980: Feudalism to Communism*. Minneapolis.

Poliakov, Léon. 1974. *The Aryan Myth: A History of Racist and Nationalist Ideas in Europe*. New York. This interesting study of the origins of the idea of an "Aryan" race originally was published in French.

Robinson, James Harvey. 1912. *The New History: Essays Illustrating the Modern Historical Outlook*. New York.

Saveth, Edward N. 1939. "Race and Nationalism in American Historiography: The Late Nineteenth Century." *Political Science Quarterly* 54: 421–41.

———. [1948] 1965. *American Historians and European Immigrants, 1875–1925*. New York. Saveth analyzes the relationship between the "germ theory" in the United States and Social Darwinism.

Semmel, Bernard. 1976. "H. T. Buckle: The Liberal Faith and the Science of History." *The British Journal of Sociology* 27: 370–86.

Snyder, Louis L. 1954. *The Meaning of Nationalism*. New Brunswick, N.J.

Taylor, A. J. P. [1948] 1976. *The Habsburg Monarchy, 1809–1918*. Chicago.

Werner, Karl Ferdinand. 1968. "On Some Examples of the National Socialist View of History." *Journal of Contemporary History* 3: 193–206.

Sources of Additional Information

See NATION, NATIONALITY; NATIONAL CHARACTER. The article on race in *ESS* 13: 25–36 was written by the anthropologist Franz Boas. There are also important entries (with bibliographies) in *IESS* 13: 263–69 and *EP* 7: 58–61. Additional historical studies of race undertaken in the 1930s are Jacques Barzun, *The French Race: Theories of Its Origins and Their Social and Political Implications Prior to the Revolution* (New York, 1932), and Louis L. Snyder, *Race: A History of Modern Ethnic Theories* (New York, 1939). There is a useful bibliography in the volume *Race and Science* (New York, 1961), published under the auspices of UNESCO. Nancy Stepan has published a study of *The Idea of Race in Science: Great Britain, 1800–1960* (Hamden, Conn., 1982). Useful articles include Eric Voegelin, "The Growth of the Race Idea," *Review of Politics* 2 (1940): 283–317, and Geoffrey G. Field, "Nordic Racism," *JHI* 38 (1977): 523–40, which deals with racial attitudes in early-twentieth-century Germany and contains general bibliographical information in footnote citations.

RADICAL HISTORY. Social protest history, that is, history written in conscious opposition to perceived social injustice and dedicated to the furtherance of progressive political and social change.

The word *radical* is derived from the ancient Latin *radix*, meaning "root." Since the late eighteenth century the term has implied thoroughgoing political change in the sense of "going to the root or origin; touching or acting upon what is essential and fundamental" (*OED*). For English, the earliest political use of *radical* cited by the *OED* is 1786. The nouns *radical* and *radicalism* (introduced about 1820 [*OED*]) won wide acceptance in the political vocabulary of the early nineteenth century, a period of rapid change in the wake of the French Revolution. Nineteenth-century historians who consciously used their work to further social change initiated what has become known—especially since the end of World War II—as *radical history*. In broad perspective, the idea of radical historiography is a modern continuation of "pragmatic" PHILOSOPHY OF HISTORY, the ancient tradition that teaches that history should instruct present and future leaders.

Radical historiography's motives are ethical and rhetorical; practitioners assume that the scholar is morally obligated to relate his research to the struggle for positive change and to convert others through his work (Landes and Tilly, 1971: 15). A self-professed representative declares that radical history springs from "the urgent desire for a better world" and condemns politically detached scholarship as "antiquarian" (Zinn, 1970: 29). Radical scholars believe that historians should themselves be "historical protagonists" (Lynd, [1968] 1969: 111) and social "therapists" (Zinn, 1970: 31), oriented to the present and future even more than to the past. From their standpoint, knowledge of the past is not valuable for its own sake but only insofar as it may be used to serve some social purpose.

Radicals regard their activity as progressive or regenerative; their goal is social betterment and human liberation. Zinn (p. 19), for example, is committed to the idea that "the ultimate purpose of social change [is] to enlarge human happiness." This does not mean, however, that radical historiography is necessarily liberal or democratic in spirit (although the concept has normally been so understood in North America and Western Europe since 1945); as Zinn (p. 2) notes, the concept of radical history does not imply a "uniform approach" to writing history. For example, politically committed Nazi and Soviet historians have assumed that their scholarly struggles on the "historical front" serve human improvement and social regeneration (e.g., Pokrovsky, [1931] 1972: 338; Frank, [1935] 1972). Whatever one's political orientation the genre's animating spirit is passionately engaged "social combat" in the service of "ultimate" values and "absolute beliefs" (Zinn, 1970: 3, 20, 51).

Zinn (p. 29) defines *radical history* in terms of a struggle for five goals: (1) intensification of public awareness of present social injustice; (2) exposure of the callousness and hypocrisy of governments; (3) exposure of the hidden IDE-OLOGY—or false value system—that rationalizes injustice; (4) rediscovery of missed opportunities in the past that may serve as progressive models for the future; (5) recognition that well-intentioned reform movements may go wrong.

As a self-conscious stance, *radical history* originated mainly among non-academic social theorists and journalists in nineteenth-century Britain, France, and Germany. (Most professionals of the day upheld the ideal of detachment; Leopold von Ranke [(1824) 1972: 57], a cardinal example, repudiated didacticism, arguing that history should not aspire to "the office of judging the past, of instructing the present for the benefit of future ages.") In France the work of Jules Michelet (e.g., [1846] 1972) exhibits the populist and anti-elitist tone typical of subsequent radial historical writing. Kennedy (1974: 343) cites the liberal politician Richard Cobden along with Karl Marx as "founding fathers" of the radical genre in England. Marx's famous injunction in the *Theses on Feuerbach* (1845)—"philosophers have only *interpreted* the world, in various ways; the point, however, is to *change* it"—continues to sustain radical scholars today (for instance, Lynd, [1968] 1969: 110).

Radical journalistic historiography grew rapidly in Britain on the eve of World War I—J. A. Hobson's *Imperialism: A Study* (1902) and Henry Brailsford's *War of Steel and Gold* (1914) are cases in point (Kennedy, 1974: 343–44). In post–1945 Britain Marxist academic historians such as E. P. Thompson, Eric Hobsbawm, and Christopher Hill carry on this tradition. In North America a liberal school of politically committed scholarship was proclaimed by the academic historian James Harvey Robinson (1912: 24), who declared: "The present has hitherto been the willing victim of the past; the time has now come when it should turn on the past and exploit it in the interests of advance." This "presentist" attitude was an important feature of the NEW HISTORY in the United States until the 1930s, and present-day radicals still draw inspiration from Robinson's "pragmatic" attitude (e.g., Zinn, 1970: 19)—although it has been suggested that Robinson's true goal was the legitimization of America's existing social framework, not its transformation (Gross, 1974: 54). In Germany the overwhelming majority of historical scholars before the 1960s endorsed the existing social order and sought to distance themselves from present concerns; an isolated exception in the 1920s was Eckhart Kehr, the "most brilliant radical historian of Weimar Germany" (Kennedy, 1974: 345; cf. Sheehan, 1968).

Early academic champions of politically engaged history often cited the Italian philosopher Benedetto Croce's view that it is psychologically impossible for historians, social products themselves, to divorce their work entirely from ethical and aesthetic values (Hughes, 1964: 97). The work of post–1945 radicals has also been influenced by the interwar debate over historical RELATIVISM, the doctrine that each account of the past is to some extent dependent upon the individual historian's "frame of reference." Zinn (1970: 40), for example, asserts that there is "no one true picture of any historical situation, no one objective description."

Since 1945 the influence of radical history has spread in academic circles in Western Europe and North America. This is true particularly since the 1960s, when professional scholars occasionally became activists in "new left" causes such as civil rights and opposition to the Vietnam war in America and the reassessment of authoritarian traditions in West Germany. Staughton Lynd

([1968] 1969) and Howard Zinn (1970) exemplify the trend in America, and politically engaged historians such as Fritz Fischer, Immanuel Geiss, Helmut Böhme, and Hans-Ulrich Wehler extend the tradition of socially critical German scholarship initiated by Kehr (Kennedy, 1974: 345). Still, the majority of professional historians are skeptical of protest scholarship, remaining convinced that systematic use of history for present purposes jeopardizes OBJECTIVITY and violates the integrity of the past (Unger, [1967] 1969). Although most would endorse Croce's belief that all history is inevitably political to some degree, the majority would reject "polemic" and discriminate between legitimate historical scholarship and "writing designed to serve a cause"; the former, writes Hughes (1964: 96), can only be the result of "a desperate *and conscious* battle to rise above partisan passion." It is nevertheless true that, especially since the 1960s, belief in the possibility of absolute detachment has given way to the idea that it is appropriate for the historian to profess some kind of personal involvement with his subject matter and to make moral judgments about it (Kammen, 1980: 23). However, the notion that the historian may "ransack" the past "not for its own sake, but as a source of alternative models of what the future might become"—a view seriously advanced by Lynd ([1968] 1969: 117)—is one that few professional historians, even radicals (e.g., Kraditor, 1972: 136)—are willing to endorse. The overwhelming majority of historians continue to believe that the past has an "integrity" (Hofstadter, 1970: 464–65) that must be respected at all costs.

References

Frank, Walter. [1935] 1972. "Guild and Nation." In Stern: 342–44.

Gross, David. 1974. "The 'New History': A Note of Reappraisal." *HT* 13: 53–58.

Hofstadter, Richard. 1970. *The Progressive Historians*. New York. The author asserts that the "activist historian who thinks he is deriving his policy from his history may in fact be deriving his history from his policy, and may be driven to commit the cardinal sin of the historical writer: he may lose his respect for the integrity, the independence, the pastness, of the past" (pp. 464–65).

Hughes, H. Stuart. 1964. *History as Art and As Science: Twin Vistas on the Past*. New York. Hughes, influenced by Croce, argues that the "historian can do no better than write with all honesty in the perspective his own irreducible values set for him. A conservative cannot help writing as a conservative, and a radical as a radical, and they should not feel obliged to apologize for so doing" (p. 99).

Kammen, Michael. 1980. "Introduction." In Kammen: 19–46. Pages 22–25 are relevant; see the footnote citations for a bibliography.

Kennedy, P. M. 1974. "The Decline of Nationalistic History in the West, 1900–1970." In Walter Laqueur and George L. Mosse, eds., *Historians in Politics*. London and Beverly Hills, Calif.: 329–52.

Kraditor, Aileen S. 1972. "American Radical Historians on Their Heritage." *Past and Present*, No. 56: 136–53. This has a good bibliography. Kraditor argues that radicals often lack a proper sense of ANACHRONISM, that is, they "distort our image of the past by depicting it in the image of the present" (pp. 142–43, 145).

Landes, David S., and Tilly, Charles, eds. 1971. *History as Social Science*. Englewood Cliffs, N.J.

Lynd, Staughton. [1968] 1969. "A Profession of History." In Robert Allen Skotheim, ed., *The Historian and the Climate of Opinion*. Reading, Mass.: 107–19. Lynd believes the historian's "first duty is the sensitive chronicling in depth of the important events of his own lifetime" and that historians are most useful "not by deeper but still inconclusive research into the past, but by projecting alternative scenarios for the future. . . . on the basis of the richness of the experience of the past" (pp. 115–16).

Michelet, Jules. [1846] 1972. Introduction to *The People*. In Stern: 109–19.

Pokrovsky, M. N. [1931] 1972. "The Tasks of Marxist Historical Science in the Reconstruction Period." In Stern: 335–41.

Ranke, Leopold von. [1824] 1972. From *Histories of the Latin and Germanic Nations from 1494–1514*. In Stern: 55–58.

Robinson, James Harvey. 1912. *The New History: Essays Illustrating the Modern Historical Outlook*. New York.

Sheehan, James J. 1968. "The Primacy of Domestic Politics: Eckart Kehr's Essays on Modern German History." *Central European History* 1: 166–74.

Unger, Irwin. [1967] 1969. "The 'New Left' and American History: Some Recent Trends in United States Historiography." In Robert Allen Skotheim, ed., *The Historian and the Climate of Opinion*. Reading, Mass.: 135–63. Unger criticizes the radical new left for its "exaggerated present-mindedness," which "suggests a contempt for pure history, history that has not enlisted in the good fight" (p. 155).

Zinn, Howard. 1970. *The Politics of History*. Boston. Zinn reflects the impassioned tone and sense of desperation typical of much radical history of the 1960s and 1970s— see especially the essay entitled "What is Radical History?" (pp. 35–55). He starts from the "premise that there are terrible wrongs all about us" and asserts that the radicals begin with "frank adherence to a small set of ultimate values" (p. 42). Among Zinn's own ultimate values is the belief that "war, poverty, race hatred, prisons, should be abolished; that mankind constitutes a single species; that affection and cooperation should replace violence and hostility"; and that people should enjoy "economic security" (pp. 20, 23).

Sources of Additional Information

See also OBJECTIVITY; VALUE JUDGMENT. On radicalism in general, see the three-volume work edited by Seweryn Bialer and Sophia Sluzar, *Radicalism in the Contemporary Age* (Boulder, Colo., 1977). Robert Blackey, *Modern Revolutions and Revolutionists: A Bibliography* (Santa Barbara, Calif., 1976), pp. 38–39, includes a list of eighteen items on the general idea of radicalism. See also the footnote citations in Kammen: 23–25. Consult, as well, Horace M. Kallen, "Radicalism," *ESS* 13: 51–54, and Egon Bittner, "Radicalism," *IESS* 13: 294–300. See also "Radical" in Raymond Williams, *Keywords: A Vocabulary of Culture and Society* (New York, 1976), pp. 209–11, and the older essay by Alfred Meusel, "Der Radikalismus," *Kölner Vierteljahrshefte für Soziologie* 4 (1924–25): 44–68. Reviews of Zinn (1970) provide a good starting point for understanding mainstream criticisms of radical history. Journals that promote the radical orientation include *Studies on the Left* and *Radical History Review*. J. H. Hexter has written a scathing criticism of Christopher Hill's scholarship in *On Historians* (Cambridge, Mass., 1979), pp. 227–51. For a balanced evaluation of politically committed historiography, especially scholarship on the history of Black Americans, see C. Vann Woodward, "Clio with Soul," (1969) in Stern: 475–90. Consult also Robert James Maddox, *The New Left and the Origins of the Cold War* (Princeton, N.J., 1973); J. M. Siracusa, *New Left Diplomatic History and Historians: The American Revisionists* (Port Washington, N.Y., 1973); Jerold S. Auerbach, "New Deal, Old Deal, or Raw Deal: Some Thoughts on New Left Historiography," *The Journal of Southern History* 35 (Feb. 1969): 18–30; and Paul Buhle et al., "New Left Historians of the 1960s," *Radical America* 4 (1970): 81–106. For a rebuttal of Kraditor (1972) see the remarks of James R. Green in *Past and Present*, No. 69 (Nov. 1975): 122–30; also Kraditor's "Rejoinder," p. 131, in the same issue.

REALISM. The belief that historical inquiry refers to a "real" PAST that was once, but is no longer, present, and that written histories are valid to the extent that they accurately correspond to this real past.

As a theory of knowledge, *realism* may be broadly defined as the position that the "object of knowledge . . . exists independently of an act of a knowing subject" (Moore, 1971: 420). In literature *realism* is the doctrine that art should convey a "truthful impression of actuality as it appears to the normal human consciousness" (Weisstein, 1974: 685). Historical *realism*—also called "representationism" (Mink, 1978b: 215)—is the belief (explicit or, more often, presupposed [Goldstein, 1976a: 181]) that historical accounts *refer* to a "real" PAST that "actually happened"—a realm totally apart from the thought of historians in which "events happened in the way that they happened, and not in any other way" (Fischer, 1970: 66, n. 4, 70; Nowell-Smith, 1971: 3; Goldstein, 1962: 175). The task of the historian, then, is to recover and represent the factual nature of this real past (Fehl, 1971: 19–20; Passmore, [1958] 1966: 85–86; White, [1975] 1978: 105).

Realists assume that historians recapture the real past, or at least some part of it, by analyzing EVIDENCE, understood as presently existing "remains" or "traces" of past EVENTS (for instance, Becker, 1932: 221). Historical accounts are, in turn, deemed reliable insofar as they meet the requirements of a "correspondence" conception of truth, that is, insofar as they *correspond* to a real past (p. 222; MacIver, 1947: 33–34; Walsh, [1951] 1960: 73–85).

It is normally conceded that perfect correspondence may exceed the realm of the humanly possible. According to the qualified or "perspectival" (Gay, 1974: x, 198–217) realism that predominates today, the historian cannot become a completely "impersonal mirror of reality" (Gossman, 1978: 4; Gilliam, 1976: 233); the fragmentary nature of historical evidence, the social conditioning of historians, as well as the impossibility of immediately perceiving a past that is lost forever all prevent the ideal goal of a perfect fit between historical accounts and the real past. Still, according to the realist view, "this does not mean that the real events of a given age change; it [only] means that our comprehension of these facts changes" (Turner, [1891] 1972: 200). The object of historical study is still understood to be these events, and the historian's ultimate goal is to report a "plain, unvarnished tale of real life" (Cheyney, 1927: 166).

Since antiquity realism has been the controlling orientation in historiography, and *history* has often been considered synonymous with *realism*—with the simple reporting of *res gestae* or "what happened" in the past. This was particularly the case in the nineteenth century—the "classic age of European historical thought"—when society as a whole displayed what the German philosopher Dilthey termed an "unsatiable desire for reality" (quoted in Holborn, 1972: 129), and historians and philosophers as temperamentally diverse as Leopold von Ranke, G. W. F. Hegel, and Karl Marx tried in various ways to "constitute history as the ground for a 'realistic' science of man, society, and culture" (White, 1973: 432, 39–40). It was an age that believed that "historical reality is *there*, weaving and reweaving its tangled web, subject like the laws of nature to discovery and perhaps exploitation, but remaining a field of real entities and forces whether discovered or not" (Mink, 1968: 667). In its extreme form, nineteenth-century realism compared history to photography, which (it was widely assumed) "catches everything, however trivial," in a precise replication of actuality (quoted in Higham et al., 1965: 93).

This strong commitment to realism was in part a repudiation of flights of fancy in historical fiction (Bourne, 1901: 249; Higham et al., 1965: 92–93; White, 1973: 163). It was, in addition, a reaction against the "ironic" tone of much eighteenth-century historiography, in which historians (for example, Gibbon) consciously distanced themselves from their narratives (White, 1973: 39–40; 45–48; Gossman, 1978: 22–23). Thus, in nineteenth-century historiography we find "the replacement of the overt eighteenth-century persona of the narrator by a covert [or omniscient] narrator, and the corresponding presentation of the narrative as unproblematic, absolutely binding" (Gossman, 1978: 24).

The classic *dicta* of historiographical realism date from early-nineteenth-century Germany. According to the philosopher Wilhelm von Humboldt, for example,

> The historian's task is to present what actually happened. The more purely and completely he achieves this, the more perfectly has he solved his problem. A simple presentation is at the same time the primary, indispensable condition of his work and the highest achievement he will be able to attain. ([1821] 1967: 57)

Leopold von Ranke's restatement of Humboldt's idea that history should reconstruct the past as it "actually happened" (*wie es eigentlich gewesen*—[1824] 1972: 57) is so famous as to have become "the most hackneyed of all quotations in the philosophy of history" (Nowell-Smith, 1971: 3).

The realism of early-nineteenth-century German theory was not, however, a naive photographic realism, since it was alloyed with philosophical IDEALISM (the dominant current in north German thought at the time). The greater part of Humboldt's discussion of "The Historian's Task," for example, was actually devoted to the problem that an "event . . . is only partially visible in the world of the senses; the rest has to be added by intuition, inference, and guesswork" ([1821] 1967: 57). Ranke, too, for all his emphasis on "strict presentation of the facts,'' shared Humboldt's belief in the need for empathy—a fundamental characteristic of the blend of realism and idealism now known as HISTORISM. The German historists nevertheless believed in a bedrock of God-given historical reality that the properly receptive scholar could at least "divine," if not perfectly perceive (Gossman, 1978: 28, n. 36). This is reflected in Ranke's belief in the possibility of "knowledge of the objectively existing relatedness" of past events ([n.d.] 1972: 59) and his dream of writing a UNIVERSAL HISTORY, one that "comprehends the past life of mankind . . . in its fullness and totality" (pp. 59, 61). Both Humboldt and Ranke assumed that the past has intrinsic form, that it is a kind of "untold story" that can be discovered and represented (Mink, 1978a: 134). Stripped of idealism—as in the historiographical POSITIVISM typical of professional research in the late nineteenth century, or in Marxian HISTORICAL MATERIALISM (Marx and Engels, [1845–46] 1972: 150)—realist sensibility was merely intensified.

Historical RELATIVISM, which preoccupied many historians between World Wars I and II and stressed the inevitable subjectivity of the individual historian, shook the foundations of this orientation, but it did not destroy—or even confront—the ultimate basis of historical realism: the assumption that the past has an inherent structure and that this structure is the object of historical accounts. The basis of most contemporary historiography is a "modified" realism (Gilliam, 1976: 250) reflected in the notion that historians follow a "reality rule," that is, that, like natural scientists, historians are dedicated to

> explanation, understanding, and rendering the best possible account of reality; for the physicist, the reality of the operations of nature; for the historian, the reality of what happened in the past. . . . the historian's goal in his response to the data is to render the best account he can of the past as it really was. (Hexter, 1967: 4, 11)

Despite its pervasiveness, however, systematic defenses of historical realism (e.g., Mandelbaum, [1938] 1967; 1977; Nowell-Smith, 1971; Kuzminski, 1979) are rare and have been mounted only in reaction to ostensible or genuine challenges to realism, such as relativism in the 1930s and CONSTRUCTIONISM in the 1960s and 1970s. Since the nineteenth century the "realistic" nature of historical conceptualization and writing has usually been taken for granted, and some historians simply acknowledge that realism for them is an "article of faith" (for example, Fischer, 1970: 70).

Only a few recent scholars have precisely articulated a concept of historiographical realism and seriously questioned its validity for history as a way of knowing (Meiland, 1965; White, 1973; Goldstein, 1976b; Mink, 1978a; Gossman, 1978: 7). Some of these challenges emphasize similarities between IMAGINATION in history and poetics (White, [1976] 1978); others stress that historians have no way of becoming personally acquainted with a supposed "real" past and must therefore "constitute" or "construct" (not "discover") a "historical" rather than "real" past on the basis of presently existing evidence (Goldstein,

1976b—see CONSTRUCTIONISM). Such arguments have thus far made little headway among historians (Gossman, 1978: 32). As Hexter (1967: 5) notes, "when
[historians] actually get down to writing history they all still commit themselves
to trying to write about the past, as Ranke put it so very long ago, 'wie es
eigentlich gewesen,' as it really happened." This is partly due to historians' fear
that anything less would jeopardize the epistemic legitimacy of their enterprise
and partly attributable to political considerations; for it is widely believed that
historians

> must retain a fundamentally unshakable conviction that the past is real—however
> hard it may be to define its nature and write an unbiased record of it. Fully conceding
> those difficulties, the historian must never concede that the past is alterable to
> conform with present convenience, with the party line, with mass prejudice, or
> with the ambitions of powerful popular leaders. (Woodward, [1955] 1969: 38)

References

Becker, Carl. 1932. "Everyman His Own Historian." *AHR* 37: 221–36. The first two
     pages of this essay demonstrate the correctness of Goldstein (1972) in arguing
     that "realism" underpinned interwar doctrines of "historical relativism" in the
     United States.
Bourne, Edward Gaylord. 1901. "Leopold von Ranke." In Edward Gaylord Bourne,
     Essays in Historical Criticism. New York: 245–61.
Cheyney, Edward P. 1927. *Law in History and Other Essays*. New York.
Fehl, Noah Edward, ed. 1971. *Sir Herbert Butterfield, Cho Yun Hsu, and William H.
     McNeill on Chinese and World History*. Hong Kong.
Fischer, David Hackett. 1970. *Historians' Fallacies: Toward a Logic of Historical
     Thought*. New York.
Gay, Peter. 1974. *Style in History*. New York. Gay's account of his own "perspectival
     realism" is more credo than argument; see especially pp. 198–217.
Gilliam, Harriet. 1976. "The Dialectics of Realism and Idealism in Modern Historio-
     graphic Theory." *HT* 15: 231–56.
Goldstein, Leon J. 1962. "Evidence and Events in History." *Philosophy of Science* 29:
     175–94. This is an early attack on realism by Goldstein, which argues that the
     realist position is "entirely beside the point so far as history as a human enterprise
     is concerned." See especially p. 177.
———. 1972. "Historical Realism: The Ground of Carl Becker's Scepticism." *Philos-
     ophy of the Social Sciences* 2: 121–31.
———. 1976a. "Epistemic Attitudes and History." *Philosophy and Phenomenological
     Research* 37: 181–92. The author suggests that historical realism is based on "the
     [erroneous] tendency to think about historical knowing in perceptual terms"
     (p. 181). Thus, the past is (paradoxically) treated as if it were present. He maintains
     that the "epistemic attitude appropriate to historical evidence is not perceptual
     [i.e., sensory] but hermeneutic" (p. 186).
———. 1976b. *Historical Knowing*. Austin, Tex. This is Goldstein's most comprehensive
     attack on historical realism. He argues that history is not a way of knowing about
     a real past but a way of making sense out of presently existing evidence. He also

maintains, as in his essay on Becker (1972), that historical realism must necessarily (and ironically) culminate in historical SKEPTICISM if carried to its logical extreme.

Gossman, Lionel. 1978. "History and Literature: Reproduction or Signification." In Canary and Kozicki: 3–39. This piece is important for its bibliography in the footnotes, as well as for an analysis of the doctrine of realism.

Hexter, J. H. 1967. "The Rhetoric of History." *HT* 6: 3–13.

Higham, John, et al. 1965. *History*. Englewood Cliffs, N.J.

Holborn, Hajo. 1972. *History and the Humanities*. Garden City, N.Y.

Humboldt, Wilhelm von. [1821] 1967. "On the Historian's Task." *HT* 6: 57–71. This is a classic expression of the blend of realism and idealism typical of nineteenth-century German historical theory.

Kuzminski, Adrian. 1979. "Defending Historical Realism." *HT* 18: 316–49. This is a rare explicit defense of historical realism in the sense of a "literal re-presentation of the facts, . . . a straight-forward description" (p. 348) devoid of subjective interpretation.

MacIver, A. M. 1947. "The Character of a Historical Explanation." *Aristotelian Society Supplementary Volume 21*: 33–50. MacIver argues that the historian's function is to make an "intelligent précis" of some part of the real past (p. 34). See also the response by W. H. Walsh in this same volume.

Mandelbaum, Maurice. [1938] 1967. *The Problem of Historical Knowledge*. New York. This is a classic defense of realism against the challenge of RELATIVISM.

———. 1977. *The Anatomy of Historical Knowledge*. Baltimore. Although he tends to avoid the term *realism* as a label for his position, Mandelbaum is generally considered the foremost philosophical defender of realism in historiography. This study revises some aspects of his earlier (1938) version of realism. See Mink (1978b: 215).

Marx, Karl, and Engels, Friedrich. [1845–46] 1972. "From *The German Ideology*." In Stern: 147–58. This is a graphic illustration of the nineteenth-century preoccupation with the accurate representation of "real life," the realm "where speculation ends . . . [and] real positive science begins" (p. 150). Here the term and concept *real* are used as rhetorical bludgeons.

Meiland, Jack W. 1965. *Scepticism and Historical Knowledge*. New York.

Mink, Louis O. 1968. "Philosophical Analysis and Historical Understanding." *Review of Metaphysics* 21: 667–98.

———. 1978a. "Narrative Form as a Cognitive Instrument." In Canary and Kozicki: 129–49.

———. 1978b. Review of Maurice Mandelbaum, *The Anatomy of Historical Knowledge*. *HT* 17: 211–23. Mink calls Mandelbaum's position a "radical" realism that holds that "societies and their parts and aspects over time are independently real, with structures and characteristics which do not depend on the way we choose to view them" (pp. 214–15).

Moore, Stanley. 1971. "Marx and the Origins of Dialectical Materialism." *Inquiry* 14: 420–29.

Nowell-Smith, P. H. 1971. *What Actually Happened*. Lawrence, Kans. This is a defense of modified realism.

Passmore, J. A. [1958] 1966. "The Objectivity of History." In Dray: 75–94. Passmore maintains that the historian represents the past by building a "scale" or "narrative" model of it (pp. 85–86).

Ranke, Leopold von. [n.d.] 1972. "A Fragment from the 1830's." In Stern: 58–60.

———. [1824] 1972. From *Histories of the Latin and Germanic Nations from 1494–1514*. In Stern: 55–58. Nowell-Smith (1971: 3) correctly notes that Ranke did not actually make his famous statement for epistemological reasons; his intent was to contrast his own impartial approach to history with the traditional idea that the historian should judge the past and use it as an instrument for moral instruction.

Turner, Frederick Jackson. [1891] 1972. "The Significance of History." In Stern: 198–208.

Walsh, W. H. [1951] 1960. *Philosophy of History: An Introduction*. New York. Chapter four contains a convenient discussion of the "correspondence" and "coherence" theories of truth and their relevance for history.

Weisstein, Ulrich. 1974. "Realism." *The Princeton Encyclopedia of Poetry and Poetics*. Princeton, N.J.: 685.

White, Hayden. 1973. *Metahistory: The Historical Imagination in Nineteenth-century Europe*. Baltimore. This is an imaginative and controversial study of the conflicting ways that historians and philosophers of history sought to portray "reality" in the nineteenth century. White denies the possibility of an absolute realism; see p. 433.

———. [1975] 1978. "Historicism, History, and the Figurative Imagination." In Hayden White, *Tropics of Discourse: Essays in Cultural Criticism*. Baltimore: 101–20.

———. [1976] 1978. "The Fictions of Factual Representation." In Hayden White, *Tropics of Discourse: Essays in Cultural Criticism*. Baltimore: 121–34.

Woodward, C. Vann. [1955] 1969. "On Believing What One Reads: The Dangers of Popular Revisionism." In Robin W. Winks, ed., *The Historian as Detective: Essays on Evidence*. New York: 25–38.

Sources of Additional Information

As Kuzminski (1979) notes, there is scant literature that explicitly defends historical realism; his own essay as well as the work of Mandelbaum ([1938] 1967; 1977) and Nowell-Smith (1971) are rare examples. For related literature see CONSTRUCTIONISM; PAST; and IMAGINATION. There is a good general bibliography in Josef de Vries, "Realism," *MCWS* 7: 133–38. See also A. N. Prior, "Correspondence Theory of Truth," *EP* 2: 223–32. For critiques of historical realism see the bibliographical essay in Canary and Kozicki: 151–58 and especially the citations in the article by Gossman (1978). All three essays in *HT Beih*. 16 (1977), "The Constitution of the Historical Past," are relevant. Jack W. Meiland, *Scepticism and Historical Knowledge* (New York, 1965), is centrally concerned with realism (which he calls the "Discovery Theory of History") and the correspondence theory of truth. There is an interesting restatement of the nineteenth-century German blend of realism and idealism in Gerhard Ritter, "Scientific History, Contemporary History, and Political Science," *HT* 1 (1961–62): 261–79, especially 266–67. On Ranke there are relevant passages in Ferdinand Schevill, "Ranke: Rise, Decline, and Persistence of a Reputation," *JMH* 24 (Sept. 1952): 219–34. Also interesting is Hayden V. White, "Romanticism, Historicism, and Realism: Toward a Period Concept for Early Nineteenth Century Intellectual History," in Hayden V. White, *The Uses of History* (Detroit, 1968): 45–58. More generally, John Wild, "What Is Realism?" *JP* 44 (1947): 148–58, discusses several varieties of philosophical realism, as does the less polemical article by R. J. Hirst, "Realism," in *EP* 7: 77–83, which also cites a wide range of titles on the subject. On the theory of realism in literary and aesthetic criticism see René Wellek, "Realism in Literature," *DHI* 4: 51–56, which includes a brief bibliography; also the very influential Eric Auerbach, *Mimesis: The Representation of Reality in Western Literature* (Princeton, N.J., 1953).

RECURRENCE. The idea that human events repeat themselves in some fashion.

The idea of recurrence has occupied an important place in historical thinking from the earliest times to the present. Most concepts of historical repetition assume that lessons can be learned from the study of past events, since they are based on the belief that what has happened before will occur again in some way and can therefore be prepared for.

There are various ways of envisioning the notion of historical recurrence, and they often overlap or interlace in the thought of historians and philosophers of history. Trompf (1979: 2) identifies eight distinct "paradigms" of recurrence: (1) *cyclical* (the view that events display a pattern of at least three fixed stages, returning to the beginning to start over again); (2) *alternation* (the belief that events swing, pendulum-like, between two basic event patterns); (3) *reciprocal* (the idea that recurring types of events elicit recurring types of consequences, so as to display a distinct rhythm—for example, the belief that periods of excess or exaggeration invariably result in returns to a "golden mean"); (4) *reenactment* (the idea that given actions of historical personalities are repeated in the actions of later individuals); (5) *restoration, renovation,* and *renaissance* (the view that a particular set of circumstances represents the revival of an earlier set of circumstances); (6) *typicality* (the belief that social change may be characterized in terms of the repetition of typical patterns); (7) *uniformity of human nature* (the belief that human nature is constant and human behavior will consequently repeat itself in familiar patterns—as in Thucydides' well-known statement [1954: 48] that "human nature being what it is," the events of the past "will, at some time or other and in much the same ways, be repeated in the future"); (8) *parallelism* (the view that striking resemblances between past events or circumstances can be identified and should be emphasized).

The most commonly recognized form of the concept is the notion of historical cycles, which posits the idea that "all events occur in cycles that are more or less alike" (Boas, 1973: 621). Even here, there are many variations: "dichotomies . . . three-phase rhythms . . . four-five-and six-phase rhythms," and so on (Maier, 1964: 42). There are two logically distinct forms of the idea of historical cycles that may or may not be found in combination: the "cosmic" view, or belief that change is universally characterized by cyclical recurrence, and the more limited view that human affairs are cyclical (Boas 1973: 621). The idea of identical recurrence—the belief that historical cycles repeat themselves exactly—has occasionally been held (for instance, by some ancient Stoics and by the German philosopher Nietzsche) but it is rare.

The idea of recurrence probably originated in primordial efforts to explain social phenomena in terms of natural regularities—the solar year, lunar phases, the life cycle, and so on (p. 621). In the western scholarship, concepts of recurrence and cyclical development are traditionally linked closely to ancient Greek and Roman philosophy and historiography (e.g., Manuel, 1965: 3–7; Wagar, 1967: 64). This tradition rests ultimately on ancient sources. Among classical historians Polybius (c. 204–122 B.C.), for example, is regularly cited for his use of the concept of cyclical recurrence with respect to forms of government (for instance, Boas, 1973: 625–26). It is true that Polybius (*History*, Book VI, 3) asserts that there are six kinds of government—monarchy, kingship, tyranny, aristocracy, oligarchy, democracy—and maintains that they recur in a set pattern of progression. Whether he had a cyclical conception of time in general, however, is subject to question.

Recent scholarship challenges the conventional view that Greek historians typically formulated their work in terms of cycles. According to Momigliano (1966: 10), "the first precaution [in dealing with ancient Greek historical thought] is to beware of the cyclical notion of time. Even Greek philosophers were not unanimous about it." Momigliano flatly denies that historians such as Herodotus and Thucydides held cyclical views of time. Aside from a few brief passages on constitutions, even Polybius "operates as if he did not hold any cyclic view of history." Momigliano concludes (pp. 13–14) that "Greek philosophers often thought in terms of cycles, but Greek historians did not. . . . No ancient historian, as far as I can remember, ever wrote the history of a State in terms of births and rebirths" (cf. Nisbet, 1969: 3–61; see also PROCESS).

The position of Trompf (1979: 61, n. 1) is less extreme; although noting the importance of cyclical thought in ancient Greece, he is "unwilling . . . to make pretentious claims about the common assumptions" of the Greeks. In addition, he argues that the concept of linear development played an important role in Greek thought, alongside the concept of recurrence. He also suggests (p. ix) that cyclical themes were important in the Jewish and Christian traditions, especially the gospels of Luke and Acts, as well as some of the earlier Hebrew writings.

Under the impact of Christian dogma, ancient doctrines were largely forgotten during the Middle Ages, although the idea of recurrence by no means died out completely (pp. 2, 116–78). In the Muslim world the medieval Arab historian Ibn Khaldun (1332–1406) wrote a universal history based on the idea that civilizations follow a pattern of growth and decline, modeled on the life cycle of nature (Maier, 1964: 45).

Classical doctrines of recurrence were revived during the sixteenth century, for example, in the *Discorsi* (1531) of Niccolo Machiavelli and the *Ricordi* (1528–30) of Francesco Guicciardini (cf. Burke, 1969: 87–89). An eventual result of this revitalization was the work of the Neopolitan philosopher Giambattista Vico (1668–1744). Vico believed that all societies pass through phases of development and recurrence—*corsi* and *ricorsi*—characterized by three stages: an age of gods, an age of heroes, and an age of men. Each *corso* is followed by a lapse into a new barbarism. Each phase also represents an advance over previous stages, so that an upward, spiral pattern of overall development emerges. Thus, for Vico history "repeats and does not repeat itself. It does not repeat itself in that it comes round to each new phase in a form different from what it had been before, and, as in Hegel's dialectical scheme, it repeats itself, but ever on another level and with ever-changing modifications" (Maier, 1964: 47).

But Vico's work was not widely known until the nineteenth century. In the seventeenth and eighteenth centuries the main trend, under the impact of refinements in natural science, was a growing understanding of time in terms of linear, open-ended PROGRESS, rather than recurrence. This outlook triumphed in the late eighteenth and early nineteenth centuries. At the same time, the growth of the spirit of HISTORISM, especially in Germany but also in other countries, popularized the notion that each historical situation was unique and non-repeatable.

On the other hand, the idea of recurrence never entirely disappeared among academic historians. The nineteenth-century concept of SCIENTIFIC HISTORY often assumed the existence of social regularities, recurring patterns or typologies that could be charted and might become the basis for generalizations about social development. The concept of repetition was central to the work of avante-garde, turn-of-the-century academic historians such as Henri Pirenne, Gustav Schmoller, and Karl Lamprecht, who believed that *history* is "the study of recurrences and the basis of laws of human conduct" (Dhondt, 1971: 34–35) (see LAWS). The dialectical conception of historical development, popularized especially by Hegel and Marx (see DIALECTIC), may also be classified as a variation on the theme of recurrence (Maier, 1964: 48–50).

A revived interest in cycles and recurrence emerged in the late nineteenth century, a by-product of *fin-de-siècle* pessimism and disillusionment with the doctrine of linear progress (Iggers, 1958: 216). This is evident, for example, in a work such as Brooks Adams' *Law of Civilization and Decay* (1895) (Conley, 1972). The early twentieth century witnessed a great revival of the idea of recurrence in the popular historical consciousness, one closely associated with notions of historical DECLINE and DECADENCE. In the climate of cultural pessimism following World War I, there appeared widely read general histories based on ideas of recurrence and decline—most notably Oswald Spengler's *Decline of the West* (1918–22) and Arnold J. Toynbee's *Study of History* (1934–61). In both Spengler and Toynbee what recurs is not particular events and situations but the general pattern of historical development. Spengler's book revived and popularized the ancient biological metaphor of the life cycle— cultures and civilizations are born, mature, decline, and die, only to fertilize the growth of subsequent cultures (Nisbet, 1969: 7–11). But these grand theories of recurrence were decidedly unpopular among academic historians; indeed, debunking the theories of Toynbee and other proponents of recurrence became virtually obligatory for the professional historian of the 1930s, 1940s, and 1950s (e.g., Brinton, 1937–38).

Historians today—especially those trained in Germany and North America—

are generally uninterested in systematically exploring the question of whether human events repeat themselves, regarding the issue as essentially speculative and not susceptible of systematic historical inquiry or empirical demonstration (Iggers, 1965: 7–8). Still, the notion of recurrence appears—often unacknowledged and unrecognized—in much contemporary historical writing. The informal opinion that history oscillates between "periodic recurrences" is sometimes openly espoused (Lovejoy, 1940: 20), and in dealing with public attitudes, historians often loosely evoke the "feeling that all this has happened before" (C. Woodward, 1953: 10). The approach of Llewellyn Woodward (1966: 12) would probably be endorsed by many scholars: "in the variety and flux of human affairs no two situations are exactly similar; the recurrences of history are real, but they are not like those of Halley's comet." One occasionally finds explicit expressions of sympathy with the Thucydidean approach, particularly among those who view history as a social science that can uncover regularities of collective social behavior (e.g., Dhondt, 1971: 30)—but these scholars, except perhaps in France, are presently in a minority within the profession.

References

Boas, George. 1973. "Cycles." *DHI* 1: 621–27. This piece contains a brief bibliography.
Brinton, Crane. 1937–38. "Socio-Astrology." *The Southern Review* 3: 243–66. This is a review of Pitrim A. Sorokin's *Social and Cultural Dynamics*.
Burke, Peter. 1969. *The Renaissance Sense of the Past*. London.
Conley, Patrick T. 1972. "Brooks Adams' Law of Civilization and Decay." *Essex Institute, Historical Collections* 108: 89–98.
Dhondt, Jan. 1971. "Recurrent History." *Diogenes*, No. 75: 24–57. This is a wide-ranging essay on the broad lines of development of modern historical conceptualization. The Belgian Dhondt sees himself as part of a tradition stemming from Pirenne, Schmoller, and Lamprecht in the late nineteenth century, according to which "history [is] the result of massive and anonymous forces. . . . movements and collective behavior patterns," and the study of the past is the "science of the recurrent, of the model, of the study of anonymous forces, and, lastly, of historical laws" (pp. 30, 32).
Iggers, Georg G. 1958. "The Idea of Progress in Recent Philosophies of History." *JMH* 30: 215–26.
———. 1965. "The Idea of Progress: A Critical Reassessment." *AHR* 71: 1–17.
Lovejoy, Arthur O. 1940. "Reflections on the History of Ideas." *JHI* 1: 3–23.
Maier, Joseph. 1964. "Cyclical Theories." In Werner J. Cahnman and Alvin Boskoff, eds., *Sociology and History: Theory and Research*. New York: 41–62. Maier includes discussions of Spengler, Toynbee, Vilfredo Pareto, and Pirtrim Sorokin. The work includes useful bibliographical citations.
Manuel, Frank E. 1965. *Shapes of Philosophical History*. Stanford, Calif. Manuel follows the convention of identifying the idea of cyclical recurrence with Greco-Roman thought and linear development with the Judeo-Christian tradition (pp. 3–7).
Momigliano, Arnaldo. 1966. "Time in Ancient Historiography." *HT Beih.* 6: 1–23. Footnote citations are rich in bibliographical information.

Nisbet, Robert A. 1969. *Social Change and History: Aspects of the Western Theory of Development*. New York.

Thucydides. 1954. *The Peloponnesian War*. Harmondsworth, Eng.

Trompf, G. W. 1979. *The Idea of Historical Recurrence in Western Thought: From Antiquity to the Reformation*. Berkeley, Calif. Trompf challenges conventional ideas and touches on many neglected aspects of ancient, medieval, and early-modern historiography. He predicts that the idea of historical recurrence "is likely to gain in popularity and credibility at the expense of the idea of progress" (p. ix) in the near future. The work is important for its bibliography.

Wager, W. Warren. 1967. "Modern Views of the Origins of the Idea of Progress." *JHI* 28: 55–70.

Woodward, C. Vann. 1953. "The Irony of Southern History." *The Journal of Southern History* 19: 3–19.

Woodward, Llewellyn. 1966. "The Study of Contemporary History." *Journal of Contemporary History* 1: 1–13.

Sources of Additional Information

The extensive bibliography in Trompf (1979) is the best general source of information, although it covers primarily literature on the period up to the Reformation. Bull. 54: 161–62 includes a list of works that appeared in the early twentieth century, at the height of the Spengler and Toynbee controversies. Felix Gilbert, *Machiavelli and Guicciardini: Politics and History in Sixteenth-Century Florence* (Princeton, N.J., 1965), includes bibliographical essays on the two Florentine historians, as well as Renaissance historiography in general. For Vico see Robert Crease, ed., *Vico in English: A Bibliography of Writings by and about Giambattista Vico (1668–1744)* (Atlantic Highlands, N.J., 1978). For further references to the literature of disillusionment with the idea of progress see Johan Huizinga, "The Task of Cultural History" [1929], in Johan Huizinga, *Men and Ideas* (New York, 1959): 73–74, 344, n. 1.

RELATIVISM. A type of historical SKEPTICISM that holds that reliable knowledge of the past is unattainable because every work of history is inevitably limited by the subjective viewpoint of its author—his personal values, preferences, prejudices, socially conditioned perspective, and so on.

From the 1920s through the 1940s the role of subjective judgment in historical scholarship was the central methodological issue in historiography. What was identified in continental Europe as the "crisis of HISTORICISM" (Heussi, 1932) became variously known in the United States as the problem of historical skepticism, historical subjectivism, or, more commonly—following the usage of Mandelbaum ([1938] 1967)—historical *relativism*.

In broad perspective, the relativist debate is one facet of the ancient problem of the reliability of human knowledge, an issue cast in its modern form by eighteenth-century philosophers, especially (as far as history is concerned) by the German idealists led by Immanuel Kant (1724–1804). Kantian IDEALISM, which stressed the tenuousness of human knowledge and the role of IMAGINATION in casting sensory data into comprehensible form, was influential among German theorists who helped to establish the canons of modern historical scholarship; consequently, an appreciation of subjective judgment was prominent in their understanding of historical knowledge. Wilhelm von Humboldt ([1821] 1967: 57–58), for example, held that the historian's work involves

> intuition, inference, and guesswork. The manifestations of an event are scattered, disjointed, isolated. . . . The truth of any event is predicated on the addition . . . of [an] invisible part of every fact, and it is this part, therefore, which the historian has to add. Regarded in this way, [the historian] does become active, even crea-tive—not by bringing forth what does not have existence, but in giving shape by his own powers to that which by mere intuition he could not have perceived as it really was. (pp. 57–58)

That idealist historiography did not succumb to skepticism—or "Pyrrhonism"—was insured by its presumption of the existence of a metaphysical "idea," or "reality," behind appearance; if the historian could not attain perfect knowledge of the past, he could at least elicit a reliable approximation of this hidden reality.

This confidence was gradually eroded as metaphysical orientations were chal-lenged by the advance of empirical science. By the mid-nineteenth century the methods of natural science had become the chief model for human knowledge, and in response, many scholars rushed to translate historical practice into the terminology of science (see SCIENTIFIC HISTORY). Concurrently, Marx and En-gels—with their concept of IDEOLOGY—called attention to the subjective nature of social analysis in the sense of socioeconomically conditioned "false con-sciousness"; at the same time, they somewhat problematically proclaimed the possibility of a "real, positive science" of society (Marx and Engels, [1845–46] 1972: 150), based on the analysis of economic relationships (see HISTORICAL MATERIALISM). Ever since, Marxist historiography has not considered subjec-tivism an insurmountable problem (Kon, 1964).

Other theorists, however—especially the German "neo-idealists" such as Wilhelm Dilthey (1833–1911), Wilhelm Windelband (1848–1915), and Heinrich Rickert (1863–1936)—denied that history's methods were identical to those of natural science. They devised a dualistic theory of knowledge in which the methods of the "humanities," or "cultural" sciences (*Geisteswissenschaften*)—including history—differed fundamentally from those of the "natural" sciences (*Naturwissenschaften*) (Rickman, 1967). According to this distinction, the high level of detachment possible in the natural sciences was not available to the cultural sciences, which dealt with human behavior; here, the values of the individual scholar were an unavoidable ingredient (see VALUE JUDGMENT). More-over, human values had to be understood in terms of their unique historical contexts rather than any set of allegedly timeless standards. The resulting con-troversy (the "crisis of historicism") culminated in the work of Theodor Lessing (1921), who argued that the past has no inherent structure and that historical interpretation is wish fulfillment, and Ernst Troeltsch (1922), who tried unsuc-cessfully to escape the conclusion that all values are historically contingent.

Neo-idealist subjectivism was expounded with special significance for history by the Italian philosopher Benedetto Croce (1866–1952), who advanced a "relativist theory of history" beginning with his *Estètica* (1909). Croce argued that "intuitional knowledge" is the foundation of poetry and history alike, as opposed to "logical knowledge," which underpins natural science (Destler, 1970: 338); history, like art, is the product of "subjective, intuitional thinking." Croce's idea of "living history" referred to

> the intuitive reliving of past experience by the historian. Written history is the narration of particulars and their imaginative reconstruction, the depiction of subjective mental images as reality. Since historical knowledge is the intuitive knowledge of the historian, his viewpoint must necessarily be that of his present, rather than that of the epoch which he describes. (p. 338)

Such reasoning gave rise to Croce's famous dictum ([1919] 1960: 12) that "every true history is contemporary history."

Relativism was nourished in America by the European debates, but there were native roots as well—for example, philosophical pragmatism and the so-called NEW HISTORY, which encouraged historians to "choose their facts according to canons of present relevance" (Higham et al., 1965: 120). Frederick Jackson Turner ([1891] 1972: 200), a pioneer in the "New History," anticipated relativism in his belief that *"Each age writes the history of the past anew with reference to the conditions uppermost in its own time.* . . . There is objective history and subjective history. Objective history applies to the events themselves: subjective history is man's conception of these events."

In the early twentieth century relativism was elaborated systematically by Carl Becker and Charles Beard, both presidents of the American Historical Association. Under Croce's influence (Destler, 1970: 335–42), Becker (1910) pitted relativism against the nineteenth-century ideal of history as a narrative of the past "as it actually happened" (see REALISM, SCIENTIFIC HISTORY, POSITIVISM). *History*, he argued, is an "imaginative reconstruction of vanished events"—a "foreshortened and incomplete representation" based on fragmentary evidence and "colored to suit the convenience of those who make use of it" (1932: 233, 235). Moreover, the very FACTS with which the historian works are products of his own making ([1955] 1959). Therefore, history

> can not be precisely the same for all at any given time, or the same for one generation as for another. . . . It is . . . an imaginative creation, a personal possession which each one of us . . . fashions out of his individual experience, adapts to his practical or emotional needs, and adorns as well as may be to suit his aesthetic tastes. (1932: 227–28)

Charles Beard, usually considered the "foremost spokesman" of historical relativism (Meyerhoff, 1959: 138), developed his position in an atmosphere of general dismay over the "relativity" of values characteristic of the 1920s and 1930s and in reaction to the work of Europeans such as Troeltsch and Heussi; his relativism was the "first serious encounter between the American New History and German neo-idealism'' (Higham et al., 1965: 126). Beard distinguished between the *past* as "actuality," which the historian can never really know, and *written history*, based on incomplete evidence selectively drawn to suit the scholar's personal "frame of reference." The historian's conclusions, he argued—no less than the events and ideas he studies—are time-bound (Beard, [1934] 1959; 1935). In some passages Beard seemed to suggest a "historical solipsism" (Deininger, 1954: 576); in his most extreme statement, Beard maintained that "The historian who writes history . . . consciously or unconsciously performs an act of faith, as to order and movement, for certainty as to order and movement is denied to him by knowledge of the actuality with which he is concerned" (Beard, [1934] 1959: 148). A milder version of the doctrine— "objective relativism"—is found in some parts of Bulletin 54 of the Social Science Research Council (1946: 22–23), which Beard helped to prepare. According to this position, "Every written history . . . is a product of a particular frame of reference; but we can and should become less biased by avoiding all absolutes and recognizing our preconceptions" (Higham et al., 1965: 130).

The writings of Becker and Beard caused confusion and alarm in the American profession, particularly since the "quicksand" (Hughes, 1964: 13) of their subjectivism appeared to follow logically from the assumptions of historiographical REALISM (Goldstein, 1976: 35), that is, the widely shared idea that the object of the historian's study is a "real" past that exists independent of his labors. The position had already been explicitly stated by Turner ([1891] 1972): " 'The whole mode and manner of looking at things alters with every age,' but this does not mean that the real events of a given age change; it means that our comprehension of these facts changes" (p. 200).

Various rebuttals of historical relativism were advanced, beginning in the late 1930s (e.g., Mandelbaum, [1938] 1967; Lovejoy, 1939; M. White, 1949; Danto, 1965). With the onset of the "cold war" in the late 1940s, many western scholars had—in addition to purely philosophical motives—an urgent political reason for rejecting relativism: the desire to refute Soviet charges that western historiography was really an ideological defense of the "bourgeois" social order (e.g., Beck, 1950). The most telling argument against relativism was the simple point that the relativists' demand for "completeness" and "certainty" was epistemologically naive; no form of human knowledge, critics argued, could lay claim to the "whole truth" (Mandelbaum, [1938] 1967: 84; Deininger, 1954: 586; Zagorin, 1956: 5–6, 10–11; Higham et al., 1965: 133). The fallacy of equating *knowledge* with *total knowledge* rendered relativism, in the opinion of some authorities, the "shallowest form" of historical skepticism (Donagan, 1967: 85).

Interest in relativism waned dramatically after mid–1950s, as a sense grew that the debate had reached the point of diminishing returns and that historians should get on with "doing" history. Logical criticism allayed the doubts of many scholars, and some erroneously concluded that the entire question was little more than a passing "fad" that did not affect the actual practice of history (Hexter, 1961: 188; Fischer, 1970: 41). This was a mistake, for the relativist debate was a key event in the history of history itself, one that challenged epistemological complacency, heightened historians' awareness of their "controlling assumptions" (Gershoy, 1956: 17), and stimulated a healthy interest in theory.

Many of relativism's premises were in fact assimilated by the mainstream (e.g., Ferguson, 1948: 386–92), and most scholars "learned to live" with some degree of relativism (Challener and Lee, 1956: 331). For example, the relativists' distinction between the *past* as "actuality" and the *written past*—logically defensible or not (Zagorin, 1956: 5) (see REALISM)—is now part of conventional wisdom. Most historians acknowledged "bias" in interpretation but rejected the debilitating pessimism of a full-blown skepticism; given the existence of rigorous, agreed-upon methods of research and peer criticism as a check, it was generally agreed that research can yield highly probable—if not certain—accounts of the past (Beck, 1950: 462; Gershoy, 1956: 15; Higham et al., 1965: 90, 141). Emphasis was transferred from the fact of disagreement among historians to the "extraordinary amount of agreement . . . that history has managed to achieve under what are clearly epistemologically unpromising conditions" (Goldstein, 1976: xii).

Although relativism is not presently a focus of intense debate, the question continues to surface. The passion with which the idea is occasionally denounced (Fischer, 1970: x, 66) suggests that the issue is still sensitive. Louis Mink (1978: 221), a leading philosopher of history, identifies two recent forms of historical relativism that await adequate assessment: "conceptual relativism" (e.g., Kuhn, [1962] 1970) and "rhetorical relativism" (e.g., H. White, 1973). Conceptual relativism, according to Mink (1978: 221) holds that knowledge is the product of time-bound conceptual frameworks ("paradigms" in Kuhn's terminology) that "cannot be compared with respect to empirical evidence because they differ on what *counts* as evidence." *Rhetorical relativism* refers to the view that the knowledge content of written histories is at least partly tied to the rhetorical form in which that content is cast and that the conclusions of historians are ultimately "cognitively incomparable" since the rhetorical forms historians choose are ultimately matters of aesthetic or ideological taste (p. 222).

References

Beard, Charles A. 1934 [1959]. "Written History as an Act of Faith." In Meyerhoff: 140–51. This was Beard's 1933 presidential address to the American Historical Association.

———. 1935. "That Noble Dream." *AHR*: 74–87. Reprinted in Stern: 315–28.

Beck, Louis W. 1950. "The Limits of Skepticism in History." *The South Atlantic Quarterly* 49: 461–68. Beck deals with only one form of skepticism, "relativism." He brands *relativism* an "invitation to laziness, subjectivity, and pragmatic history at its worst" (p. 468).

Becker, Carl L. 1910. "Detachment and the Writing of History," *The Atlantic Monthly* 106: 524–36.

———. 1932. "Everyman His Own Historian." *AHR* 37: 221–36. Becker's celebrated

1931 presidential address to the American Historical Association, reprinted in Carl L. Becker, *Everyman His Own Historian: Essays on History and Politics* (New York, 1935).

————. [1955] 1959. "What Are Historical Facts?" In Meyerhoff: 120–37. This piece was originally presented as a paper in 1926 but was not published until 1955.

Challener, Richard, and Lee, Maurice, Jr. 1956. "History and the Social Sciences: The Problem of Communications." *AHR* 61: 331–38.

Croce, Benedetto. [1919] 1960. *History: Its Theory and Practice*. New York.

Danto, Arthur C. 1965. *Analytical Philosophy of History*. Cambridge.

Deininger, Whitaker T. 1954. "The Skepticism and Historical Faith of Charles A. Beard." *JHI* 15: 573–88. This defense of Beard suggests that "Beard did not intend to reduce contemporary historiography to an arbitrary subjectivism" (p. 586).

Destler, Chester McArthur. 1970. "The Crocean Origin of Becker's Historical Relativism." *HT* 9: 335–42.

Donagan, Alan. 1967. Review of Jack W. Meiland, *Scepticism and Historical Knowledge*. *Philosophical Quarterly* 17: 85–86.

Ferguson, Wallace K. 1948. *The Renaissance in Historical Thought*. Cambridge, Mass., 1948. This book is a self-styled "object lesson in historical relativism" (p. 386).

Fischer, David Hackett. 1970. *Historians' Fallacies: Toward a Logic of Historical Thought*. New York. Fischer calls *relativism* an "absurd and pernicious doctrine [which] became a popular delusion in the 1930s" (p. 41).

Gershoy, Leo. 1956. "Zagorin's Interpretation of Becker: Some Observations." *AHR* 62: 12–17. This criticism of Zagorin (1956) denies that Becker was a radical skeptic.

Goldstein, Leon J. 1976. *Historical Knowing*. Austin, Tex. This controversial but important criticism of relativism (and historical skepticism of all varieties) is based on a constructionist theory of historiography. Goldstein argues that most current thought about the nature of history rests on a tacit REALISM that "must lead to skepticism on the part of anyone subscribing to it" (pp. 30–31).

Heussi, Karl. 1932. *Die Krisis des Historismus*. Tübingen.

Hexter, J. H. 1961. *Reappraisals in History*. Evanston, Ill.

————. 1970. *The History Primer* (New York, 1970). Hexter was an acrid critic of relativism in the 1950s; ironically, Mink (1978: 25) finds an implicit rhetorical relativism in this work.

Higham, John, et al. 1965. *History*. Englewood Cliffs, N.J. Part II, Chapter 3, is a concise account of historical relativism in the United States.

Hughes, H. Stuart. 1964. *History as Art and as Science: Twin Vistas on the Past*. New York.

Humboldt, Wilhelm von. [1821] 1967. "On the Historian's Task." *HT* 6: 57–71.

Kon, I. S. 1964. *Die Geschichtsphilosophie des 20. Jahrhunderts. Kritischer Abriss*. 2 vols. Berlin. This is a Soviet work. See the review in *HT* 6: 230ff.

Kuhn, Thomas S. [1962] 1970. *The Structure of Scientific Revolutions*. Chicago.

Lessing, Theodor. 1921. *Geschichte als Sinngebung des Sinnlosen*. Munich.

Lovejoy, Arthur O. 1939. "Present Standpoints and Past History." *JP* 36 (Aug. 31, 1939): 477–89. This is a concise summary of relativism's propositions which denies that historiography must be fundamentally present-oriented.

Mandelbaum, Maurice. [1938] 1967. *The Problem of Historical Knowledge: An Answer to Relativism*. New York. This is a pioneering work in the critical philosophy of history.

Marx, Karl, and Engels, Friedrich. [1845–46] 1972. From *The German Ideology*. In Stern: 147–58.

Meyerhoff, Hans, ed. 1959. *The Philosophy of History in Our Time*. Garden City, N.Y.

Mink, Louis O. 1978. Review of Maurice Mandelbaum, *The Anatomy of Historical Knowledge*. *HT* 17: 211–23.

Rickman, H. P. 1967. "Geisteswissenschaften." *EP* 3: 275–79. This entry incudes a brief bibliography.

Social Science Research Council. 1946. *Theory and Practice in Historical Study*. New York. See especially chapter two, "Controlling Assumptions in the Practice of American Historians," by John Herman Randall, Jr., and George Haines, and Sidney Hook's discussion of "frame of reference" (pp. 125–27). Hook notes that "the possession of bias or passion on the part of the historian does not preclude the possibility of his achieving objectivity in testing his hypothesis any more than a physician's passion to relieve men from the ravages of a disease or a chemist's desire to achieve money or fame or destroy his country's enemies precludes the possibility of the discovery of a medical or chemical truth" (p. 126).

Troeltsch, Ernst. 1922. *Der Historismus und seine Probleme*. Tübingen.

Turner, Frederick Jackson. [1891] 1972. "The Significance of History." In Stern: 198–208.

White, Hayden. 1973. *Metahistory: The Historical Imagination in Nineteenth-Century Europe*. Baltimore. See especially pp. xii, 432ff.

White, Morton. 1949. *Social Thought in America*. New York.

Zagorin, Perez. 1956. "Carl Becker on History. Professor Becker's Two Histories: A Skeptical Fallacy." *AHR* 62: 1–11. Zagorin summarizes the present mainstream position: "Though the statements of fact in which the historian deals cannot be certain [in the mathematical] sense, they are none the less knowledge for that. We need not have certainty in order to know; for if we agree that knowledge consists of ideas for which we can show evidence, then we have knowledge so far as our evidence extends and in proportion as it is good. . . . Whether acquired by the historian or the natural scientist, knowledge is, in principle, always open to doubt, since the evidence yet to be established may require the revision of our conclusions" (pp. 10–11).

Sources of Additional Information

See also OBJECTIVITY; VALUE JUDGMENT; SKEPTICISM. Consult *HT Beih.*; Stephens; Birkos and Tambs; and sections 10 and 21 of Berding. Of general interest is D. H. Monro, "Relativism in Ethics," *DHI* 4: 70–74, including the bibliography. Thomas Robischon, "What Is Objective Relativism?" *JP* 55 (1958): 1117–32, discusses the origins and meaning range of the expression *objective relativism*, although not with specific reference to historiography. See also the citations in two interesting articles in *JMH* 21 (March 1949): Bert James Loewenberg, "Some Problems Raised by Historical Relativism," pp. 17–23, and Willson H. Coates, "Relativism and the Use of Hypothesis in History," pp. 23–27. Jack W. Meiland, *Scepticism and Historical Knowledge* (New York, 1965), discusses various types of relativism and denies that Croce was a relativist. Review articles include Chester McArthur Destler's rambling "Some Observations on Contemporary Historical Theory," *AHR* 55 (April 1950): 503–29, and Maurice Mandelbaum's, "Concerning Recent Trends in the Theory of Historiography," *JHI* 16 (Oct. 1955): 506–17. Volume one of A. S. Eisenstadt, ed., *The Craft of American History: Selected Essays* (New York, 1966), includes relevant bibliography in the section "Objectivity and Truth in History." On Becker and Beard consult John C. Rule and Barbara Stevens Crosby, "Bibliography of Works on Carl Lotus Becker and Charles Austin Beard, 1945–1963," *HT* 5 (1966): 302–14. William Appleman Williams, "A Note on Charles Austin Beard's Search for a General Theory of Causation," *AHR* 62 (Oct. 1956): 59–80, contains a partial defense of Beard's position, especially 75–76. Jack W. Meiland, "The Historical Relativism of Charles A. Beard," *HT* 12 (1973): 405–13, defends Beard against the charge of self-contradiction. On Hayden White, see *HT Beih.* 19 (1980).

RENAISSANCE. "Rebirth" (Fr.). 1. A period in European (and especially Italian) history roughly comprising the late fourteenth, the fifteenth, and the early sixteenth century and characterized by renewed interest in classical antiquity and a general cultural revival. 2. Broadly, any period in which there is renewed interest in the cultural achievements of classical Rome or, more generally still, any period of intellectual and aesthetic vigor that follows a period of cultural quiescence or decline.

The idea of a historical period known as the Renaissance is the product of six centuries of development. The term is important not only as a label for a particular era in western culture but because its history illuminates the genesis of the entire modern scheme of historical PERIODIZATION. The idea has also attracted the interest of philosophers who seek to understand the use of COLLIGATION in historical interpretation (Stalnaker, 1967; McCullagh, 1978).

The idea's history is exceptionally well documented. Its origins lie in fourteenth-century Italy, which experienced a growth of interest in the Latin rhetoric of pre-Christian authors. The germ of the idea is usually traced to the Italian poet Petrarch (1304–74), whose works display a nostalgic "admiration for pagan Roman literature, the city of Rome, and the ideal of republican virtue" (Ferguson, 1948: 8). Petrarch used the word *antiqua* (ancient) to refer to pre-Christian times and *nova* (modern) to designate the Christian era, including his own times. The former he represented as a glorious age of achievement, the latter as a period of decline and "darkness." He longed for a cultural renewal modeled on the presumed intellectual and moral perfection of ancient Rome (p. 8; Hay, 1973: 121).

Petrarch neither used the term *renaissance* nor glorified his own day; his age, he believed, was simply another chapter in the history of "modern" decline. His interest in pagan antiquity spread, however, and his intellectual successors— for example, Giovanni Boccaccio, Giovanni Villani—came to believe that they were reviving the stylistic excellence of "ancient" Latin and Greek letters. Indeed, the ideas of the "Middle Ages" and "Antiquity" were by-products of the development of the idea of the "Renaissance." "This contrast, and the traditional three-fold periodization, ancient, medieval and modern, which goes with it, are the most essential and lasting components of the concept" (Stalnaker,

1967: 167). As it emerged in fifteenth-century Italy, the Renaissance concept consisted of the "sense of belonging to a new age, the antecedent period of darkness, and behind that the ancient world of light; [also] the assumption that Latin letters are the basis for all cultural activity, in the fine arts as well as in literature" (Hay, 1973: 122).

The term *rebirth* (It. *rinascita*) was itself not popularized until the mid-sixteenth century, when Giorgio Vasari used it to characterize the history of Italian art from the thirteenth century onward in his famous *Lives of the Great Painters, Sculptors, and Architects* (1550) (B. Ullman, 1955: 23). Vasari "created for the first time a conception of Renaissance art as an organic whole, developing by clearly marked stages, each of which was admirable in relation to its place in the steady progression toward the perfect style of his own day" (Ferguson, 1948: 61). Metaphorically, Vasari appealed to the cycle of nature; the arts, he argued, are comparable in their development to the human body, with its pattern of birth, growth, decline, and death. By using this comparison he hoped that his readers would "recognize the progress of the renaissance (*renascita*) of the fine arts and the perfection to which they have attained in their own time" (quoted in Hay, 1973: 123).

Vasari's book was widely read throughout Europe, and the notion of a rebirth of the visual arts in Italy became conventional wisdom. The Dutch humanist Erasmus was first to adapt the term *rebirth* to literature (p. 124). In French, *renaissance* in the sense of a "rebirth of the fine arts" appears as early as the sixteenth century but did not completely establish itself until the late seventeenth century, as reflected in Pierre Bayle's *Historical and Critical Dictionary* (1697) and in the *Dictionary* (1701) of Furetière (B. Ullman, 1955: 23–24; Ferguson, 1948: 69–70). Eighteenth-century French ENLIGHTENMENT authors commonly contrasted the Renaissance of arts and letters with the "barbarism" of the Middle Ages—for example, Voltaire (Ferguson, 1948: 90).

This usage was firmly established by the early nineteenth century, as illustrated in the work of writers such as Stendhal and the historian Guizot; in Sismondi's *Histoire de la renaissance de la liberté en Italie* (1832), the term was extended to politics (Febvre, [1950] 1973: 259; Huizinga, [1920] 1959: 253). Thus, it gradually acquired a broad range of associations, reaching beyond the realm of the arts. In *Le bal de Sceaux* (1829) the novelist Balzac already used the word to mean an entire epoch—one of his characters "could argue fluently on Italian or Flemish painting, on the Middle Ages or the Renaissance' " (cited in Huizinga, [1920] 1959: 253). The expression "the period of the Renaissance" appeared in English in 1845, and "the Renaissance period" was used by Ruskin in his *Stones of Venice* in 1851 (Panofsky, 1960: 5, n. 2).

In light of this evidence, Lucien Febvre's suggestion ([1950] 1973: 259; cf. Panofsky, 1960: 6, n. 1) that the French historian Jules Michelet "invented" the period concept of the "Renaissance" in the 1850s—that is, the idea of a distinct epoch characterized by a cultural unity all its own—is clearly wrong. The period concept was already well established before Michelet published the seventh volume of his *Histoire de France*, entitled *La Renaissance*, in 1855. Indeed, Febvre himself states that Michelet used the term in the period sense in a course of lectures delivered in 1840 (Febvre, [1950] 1973: 260, 262–64, 267, n. 8). Moreover, although Michelet broadened the term's range to mean not only a revival of literature and the arts but a rebirth in all facets of life—the "discovery of the world and of man"—he used it somewhat narrowly to refer only to sixteenth-century France (Ferguson, 1948: 178). (It must be stressed that the notion of an early-modern transformation of consciousness was a well-established part of literary tradition; without using the term *Renaissance*, for example, Voltaire [(n.d.) 1972: 39] referred to the fifteenth century as "the time when there occurred in the human mind as in the world itself, a revolution which changed everything.") However it is true that Michelet was important in introducing the idea to formal historical scholarship (Ferguson, 1948: 173) and that the French writer's usage directly influenced the key figure in the recent history of the concept, the Swiss historian Jacob Burckhardt.

More than any single work, Burckhardt's *Civilization of the Renaissance in Italy* (1860) established the Renaissance in the modern imagination. Although he wrote in German, Burckhardt borrowed Michelet's French term, and his example has since been followed by historians of all languages (Ferguson, 1940: 1, n. 1). Moreover, Burckhardt adopted Michelet's idea that the Renaissance was a general awakening of human consciousness, of "the discovery of the world and the discovery of man." It was thus the "prototype of the modern world" (Ferguson, 1948: 194), a decisive stage in the secularization of western consciousness and the birth of modernity. Every aspect of life was related to this general theme.

Nurtured in the tradition of central European LIBERALISM—an amalgam of IDEALISM and neo-humanism—Burckhardt portrayed the essence of the Renaissance as the discovery of modern individualism; "his picture of the Renaissance leaves a vivid impression of rampant individualism, creative energy and moral chaos, with the supernatural sanctions and Christian traditions of the middle ages giving way to something more like the ancient pre-Christian ways of thought" (Ferguson, 1940: 4). In fifteenth- and sixteenth-century Italy he discovered the roots of those values he treasured most (and feared would be lost) in his own age.

It was a romantic picture, at once subtle and susceptible to easy vulgarization, one that has provided enduring inspiration for serious scholarship and much historical fiction as well. "The story of the historiography of the Renaissance after Burckhardt is the story of extension and articulation of his thesis followed by attack on the theory, principally by medieval historians, followed by modification and revision" (Stalnaker, 1967: 169). In light of the fact that his interpretation would later be criticized as one-sided, it is important to note that Burckhardt began his "essay" with a caveat:

> In the wide ocean upon which we venture, the possible ways and directions are many; and the same studies which have served for this work might easily, in other

hands, not only receive a wholly different treatment and application, but lead also to essentially different conclusions. Such indeed is the importance of the subject that it still calls for fresh investigation, and may be studied with advantage from the most varied points of view. ([1860] 1954: 3)

With few exceptions, Burckhardt's interpretation was accepted by scholars for more than fifty years. The British scholar John Addington Symonds (1840–93), for example, considered the Italian Renaissance "the first transcendent springtide of the modern world" (cited by Ferguson, 1948: 201). The period since World War I, however, has witnessed a sharp counter-reaction on many fronts, especially among medievalists. This gave rise to the "problem of the Renaissance," that is, the relationship of the Renaissance to the Middle Ages, to modern times, and, indeed, the question of whether there ever was a "Renaissance." By 1940 Wallace Ferguson wrote:

For more than a generation . . . scholarly critics have been attacking Burckhardt's conception of the Renaissance from the most varied points of view, so that, though it remains a commonly recognized historical period, there is no longer any general agreement as to its character, its causes, or even its geographical and chronological limits. (1940: 1–2)

The general result of this revisionism has been a rejection of the notion of medieval times as the "dark ages" and increased emphasis on elements of continuity between the "Middle Ages" and the "Renaissance" (for instance, Nisbet, 1973: 482).

Moreover, historians of science (for example, Sarton, 1929; Thorndike, 1943) maintain that the fourteenth, fifteenth, and sixteenth centuries do not constitute a "prototype of the modern world" from the standpoint of the growth of the natural sciences. With regard to the advancement of science, they argue, the Renaissance was not a genuine "rebirth" but a period of decline.

On the other hand, medievalists have themselves been partly responsible for broadening *renaissance* into a general historical concept by discovering cultural "rebirths" in earlier periods. We have, for instance, books on "renaissances" in the twelfth and even eighth centuries (see Haskins, 1927; W. Ullmann, 1969). Thus, opponents of Burckhardt's thesis have ironically helped to preserve his period concept; as Stalnaker (1967: 164) notes, the expression *a renaissance*, so employed, "means partly just 'rebirth' or 'revival' and partly 'something like *the Renaissance.*'"

On the whole, the defenders of the Renaissance period concept have sucessfully defended themselves, although many concessions to the critics have been made. Their defense has succeeded not because they reject the factual arguments of their critics but because they deny the "relevance of these facts to the general thesis that the identity of the Renaissance cannot be maintained" (p. 172). Admitting that individualism, classical revivals, and so on may be found in earlier periods, they argue that what is important is not that these developments occurred but *the specific way in which they occurred*. In this regard, they maintain, there were crucial differences between the Middle Ages and the Renaissance. Thus, the idea persists that the Renaissance was an "age" with its own unique character and identity (Ferguson, 1940: 6–8; 1948: 393–94; Hay, 1973: 127; Stalnaker, 1967: 164).

References

Burckhardt, Jacob. [1860] 1954. *The Civilization of the Renaissance in Italy*. New York. This is the Modern Library edition, based on the S. G. C. Middlemore translation of 1878.

Febvre, Lucien. [1950] 1973. "How Jules Michelet Invented the Renaissance." In Peter Burke, ed., *A New Kind of History: From the Writings of Febvre*. New York: 258–267.

Ferguson, Wallace K. 1940. *The Renaissance*. New York.

————. 1948. *The Renaissance in Historical Thought: Five Centuries of Interpretation*. Cambridge, Mass. This key source traces the history of interpretation from the fourteenth century to the present. It includes a comprehensive bibliography of the literature to 1948 and Ferguson summarizes flaws in Burckhardt's interpretation, yet believes that "for all its faults of exaggeration, it contained much brilliantly penetrating analysis, and a great deal of evident truth. And it was no more one-sided than many later revisions" (p. 194).

Haskins, C. H. 1927. *The Renaissance of the Twelfth Century*. Cambridge, Mass.

Hay, Denys. 1973. "Idea of Renaissance." *DHI* 4: 121–29. Hay believes that "Burckhardt's interpretation has, on the whole, stood the test of time" (p. 126). He includes a convenient bibliography.

Huizinga, Johan. [1920] 1959. "The Problem of the Renaissance." In Johan Huizinga, *Men and Ideas: Essays by Johan Huizinga*. New York: 243–87. This is an important early study.

McCullagh, C. Behan. 1978. "Colligation and Classification in History." *HT* 17: 267–84.

Nisbet, Robert. 1973. "The Myth of the Renaissance." *CSSH* 15: 473–92.

Panofsky, Erwin. 1960. *Renaissance and Renascences in Western Art*. Stockholm. The footnotes are rich in bibliography.

Sarton, G. 1929. "Science in the Renaissance." In J. W. Thompson et al., *The Civilization of the Renaissance*. Chicago.

Stalnaker, Robert C. 1967. "Events, Periods, and Institutions in Historians' Language." *HT* 6: 160–79.

Thorndike, Lynn. 1943. "Renaissance or Prenaissance?" *JHI* 4: 65–74. This is a strong attack on the concept of the Renaissance. Thorndike denied that the thought of the Italian humanists was genuinely "modern" and refers to the term *renaissance* as a "catch-word" that should be abandoned (p. 74).

Ullman, B. L. 1955. *Studies in the Italian Renaissance*. Rome. Chapter one is informative on early uses of terms for "reawakening" and "rebirth" in Latin, Italian, and French.

Ullmann, Walter. 1969. *The Carolingian Renaissance and the Idea of Kingship*. London.

Voltaire. [n.d.] 1972. "On History: Advice to a Journalist." In Stern: 36–38.

Sources of Additional Information

Bibliographical resources are excellent. See Ferguson (1948) and Hay (1973). Besides Hay's essay, volume four of *DHI* contains the articles "Renaissance Humanism," "Renaissance Idea of the Dignity of Man," and "Renaissance Literature and Historiography," all with bibliographies. André Chastel et al., *The Renaissance: Essays in Interpretation* (London, 1982), includes Hay's essay "Historians and the Renaissance During the Last Twenty-Five Years," pp. 1–32. Consult also the annotated bibliography in Karl H. Dannenfeldt, ed., *The Renaissance: Medieval or Modern?* (Boston, 1959); the *Bibliothèque d'Humanisme et Renaissance* (Geneva, 1941–   ) and the *Bibliographie internationale d'Humanisme et de Renaissance* (Geneva, 1966–   ); Federico Chabod, "The Concept of the Renaissance," in Federico Chabod, *Machiavelli and the Renaissance* (London, 1958), a bibliographical essay that surveys the literature to 1957; the annotated bibliography in volume one of Peter Gay, *The Enlightenment: An Interpretation* (New York, 1966), pp. 506–15, 517–20; the annotated bibliography in Charles R. Young, ed., *The Twelfth-Century Renaissance* (New York, 1969); and G. W. Trompf, "The Concept of the Carolingian Renaissance," *JHI* 34 (1973): 3–26. Ilan Rachum has published *The Renaissance: An Illustrated Encyclopedia* (New York, 1979), which contains both bibliographical and substantive information. On Burckhardt, Werner Kaegi's four-volume *Jacob Burckhardt: Eine Biographie* (Basel, 1947–1976) is widely cited; see also the chapter on Burckhardt in Hayden White's *Metahistory: The Historical Imagination in Nineteenth-Century Europe* (Baltimore, 1973). J. H. Hexter expresses second thoughts about his earlier attacks on the Renaissance concept in *On Historians* (Cambridge, Mass., 1979), pp. 4–5.

REVOLUTION. Any sudden, fundamental, and permanent break with past social tradition. With regard to politics, the idea is closely—though not necessarily—associated with violent change.

Revolution has been a key concept of historical analysis since the rise of history as a specialized discipline two centuries ago; academic historiography and the modern idea of revolution arose side by side. Under the impact of early-nineteenth-century political upheaval and INDUSTRIALIZATION, many authors perceived that society was undergoing rapid and irreversible change; *revolution* was the term (or catch-word) most commonly identified with the more dramatic forms of social change. By the late nineteenth century the notion of revolution was a major intellectual tool used by historians (whether radical, conservative, or moderate) to conceptualize the story of past, present, and future: "Historians found revolutions everywhere in history," notes Felix Gilbert (1973: 162). "What had been the defection of the Netherlands became the Dutch Revolution. The revolt of the Protestants in Prague was named the Bohemian Revolution." Indeed, nineteenth-century historiography was largely an exercise in the conceptualization and explanation of revolution, which was broadly perceived as the central problem of modern society. To some extent this is still true; the great modern historians have traditionally been much more attracted to revolutionary themes than to the study of stability (Plumb, 1967: xvii).

The idea of sudden social change is very old, and the term *revolution* (from Latin *revolutio*) dates from late antiquity; the concept of social revolution is only two centuries old, however, and the meaning of the term *revolution* has itself changed dramatically in the recent past. Contemporary understanding of the history of the modern term and concept is based on pioneering works by Rosenstock-Hüessy (1938) and Griewank ([1955] 1971). These scholars established the idea that *revolution*, in its social meaning, is a product of the modern era and that its crystallization was only possible in the context of a specifically modern outlook on the world.

The ancient Greeks had no single equivalent for the modern term *revolution*, but philosophers such as Plato and Aristotle reflected on the nature of social change, and Greek historians played a crucial role in establishing traditional western attitudes on the subject. For example, Thucydides' *Peloponnesian War*, written in the late fifth century B.C., dramatically describes the psychology of social upheaval and civil war in the Greek city-states (cf. Zagorin, 1973: 23). Moreover, the *Histories* (VI, 9, x) of Polybius (c. 203–c. 120 B.C.) contain an explicit theory of change, at least insofar as systems of government are concerned: political constitutions, Polybius asserts, change in the circular manner of a revolving wheel—in recurring cycles that always return to the same place (Hatto, 1949: 499). This idea of change as RECURRENCE was influential among the Romans; however, the Latin term *revolutio*—introduced only in late antiquity (p. 509)—was never commonly used by Roman authors and was employed only in the non-political sense of "movement" or "migration." Indeed, the entire cast of ancient political thought made it difficult for a modern idea of revolution—with its implications of an open future—to exist, since ancient philosophers tended to envision political change in terms of a limited number of forms that alternated according to set principles of nature—monarchy, tyranny, aristocracy, oligarchy, democracy, anarchy (Koselleck, 1969: 827).

The link between *revolutio* and political change was forged during the Italian RENAISSANCE. Sixteenth-century Florentine historians such as Jacapo Nardi and Francesco Guicciardini used *revoluzione* in a specifically political sense to describe recent changes in their city's government, still wedding the word, however, to the ancient, transhistorical idea that change represents a cyclical return to the order of the past (Hatto, 1949: 503, 511). From Italy this usage spread to northern and Western Europe, where its popularity was enhanced by Copernicus' usage in his *De revolutionibus orbium caelestium* (*On the Revolutions of the Heavenly Bodies*, 1543), and especially by the early-modern fascination with astrology, which encouraged people to associate human affairs with the "revolutions" of the stars and planets (Griewank, [1955] 1971: 16). This reinforced the idea that change was circular or cyclical, a return to the order of the past. *Revolution* in the sense of "restoration" came into wide use as a political term in the seventeenth century, especially in politically volatile England. Thus, Clarendon and Thomas Hobbes used the word in connection with the Stuart Restoration in 1660 (pp. 15, 17). The first rebellion to be widely labeled a revolution was England's "Glorious Revolution" of 1688, but even here the term implied a return to a previous legal order upset by King James II (Zagorin, 1973: 26).

Only in the eighteenth century, as it became linked to the idea of historical change as PROGRESS toward an open future, did the term gradually assume its modern meaning of profound change that inaugurates a new order. Eighteenth-century writers continued to use the term in its traditional, circular sense but also employed it in ways that foreshadowed the new meaning; moreover, they began to broaden its associations beyond politics. In his *Discourse on the Origins of Inequality* (1755), for example, Jean-Jacques Rousseau referred to the revolutionary impact of technological innovation (Hatto, 1949: 506). Diderot's famous *Encyclopédie* (1751–65) contained an entry discussing *révolution* in terms of "important change in government" (Gilbert, 1973: 154). The old meaning persisted, however. In their rebellion against England, for instance, American colonists rarely used *revolution* in the modern sense, assuming that they were working to restore a just order that had been undermined by British misrule (pp. 155–56).

Most authorities agree that the decisive turning point in the term's history was the French Revolution of 1789–99—a series of political and social upheavals accepted to this day (sometimes uncritically [Zagorin, 1973: 31]) as the chief standard for measuring modern revolution. Now two previously separate ideas were fused: *revolution* as a change of government and *revolution* as "ushering in a new social order and a new stage in world history" (Gilbert, 1973: 156). The French experience also brought the idea of violence into close association with *revolution* and linked the word to the prospect of inevitable and "progressive" change, that is, change that results in greater freedom for the majority of people (p. 157). The assumption of the inevitability of revolutionary change was subsequently enshrined in a whole body of historical and social literature, for example, Alexis de Tocqueville's melancholy LIBERALISM, Whig historiography in England, and the populist historiography of Jules Michelet in France (Kramnick, 1972: 52). It became a central preoccupation, as well, in imaginative literature, philosophy, economics, and natural science.

Marx's theory of HISTORICAL MATERIALISM represents an especially important landmark in the history of modern usage. Building on ENLIGHTENMENT and Hegelian foundations (see IDEALISM), Marx and Engels built an entire social philosophy around the idea of revolutionary "transcendence" (see DIALECTIC), as well as a concrete program for political, social, and economic change. Their work strengthened the new tendency to view *revolution* in terms of human emancipation and as a comprehensive phenomenon—social, economic, cultural, and psychological as well as political (Gilbert, 1973: 161). This fostered increasingly broad use of the term, for example, introduction of the expression INDUSTRIAL REVOLUTION in the early and mid-nineteenth century. It also led to the idea, still popular, that revolutionary change implies profound "structural" transformation; a mere change of government, no matter how dramatic or violent, is not enough (cf. Zagorin, 1973: 27–28; Gilbert, 1973: 164).

The Soviet Revolution of 1917 reinforced historians' preoccupation with the term and encouraged efforts to understand *revolution* as a generic phenomenon. There is little agreement on this matter, however.

> Terminology remains a basic problem. No consensus exists as to just how to define revolution. Most definitions have been tautologies, characteristics selected because they are found in specific movements and specific movements chosen to support the definition because they manifest those characteristics. (Lipsky, 1976: 508)

Zagorin (1973: 28) expresses a widespread sentiment: "Perhaps it is impossible to establish a completely satisfactory definition of the term, so complex are the phenomena and variables to be included."

The most influential American study is still the "brilliantly suggestive" *Anatomy of Revolution* ([1938] 1965) by the Harvard historian Crane Brinton (Zagorin, 1973: 30–31; Kramnick, 1972: 27; Lipsky, 1976: 499). Brinton built his general theory of revolution on a comparison of four events: the Puritan Revolution of mid-seventeenth-century England, the American and French Revolutions of the eighteenth century, and the Soviet Revolution of the twentieth century. It is worth noting that attempts to construct general theories of revolution often betray a residue of the Greek cyclical idea. It is thus not entirely accurate to say that ancient connotations of "perpetual return" have been "buried" (e.g., Kramnick, 1972: 31) in modern thinking about revolution. Most Marxist and much liberal historiography rests on the idea of revolution as an irreversible break with the past. On the other hand, an influential tradition represents *revolution* in terms of a "paradoxical" combination of the new and the repetitive; indeed, this may be the dominant twentieth-century view not only among historians but among many political scientists and sociologists (for example, Johnson, 1964) who interpret change in terms of "dysfunction" or "deviation" from "normal" states of social stability and returns to these states of "equilibrium" (Kramnick, 1972: 46–49; Stone, 1966).

The idea dates from at least Edmund Burke's *Reflections on the Revolution in France* (1790) and Burke's famous prediction—inspired by ancient models—that France's break with authority would culminate in another form of authoritarianism. It reappears in Alexis de Tocqueville's *Old Regime and the French Revolution* (1856), in which Tocqueville suggests that Napoleon's regime echoed the centralizing policies of the Bourbon monarchs; it is basic, as well, to Brinton's comparative theory, which stresses the tendency for revolutionary extremism to generate authoritarian counterrevolution. Much additional literature identifies a pattern that culminates in the reglorification of authority (Kramnick, 1972: 59; Laqueur, 1968: 505). The view is not rigidly cyclical because restoration is not presented as an exact copy of the old order; rather, it melds ideas of old and new into an ironic spiral in which revolution yields fundamental change in specific institutions, economic relations, and so on, yet results in social forms that are reminiscent of traditional structures.

References

Brinton, Crane. [1938] 1965. *The Anatomy of Revolution*. New York. This book is still a "touchstone for current scholarly inquiry" (Kramnick, 1972: 27); it "established the area of study, the methodology for investigation and the basic working premises" (Lipsky, 1976: 499).

Gilbert, Felix. 1973. "Revolution." *DHI* 4: 152–67.

Griewank, Karl. [1955] 1971. "Emergence of the Concept of Revolution." In Bruce Mazlish, Arthur D. Kaledin, and David B. Ralston, eds., *Revolution: A Reader.* New York: 13–18. This piece is an excerpt from Griewank's *Der neuzeitliche Revolutionsbegriff* (Weimar, 1955).

Hatto, Arthur T. 1949. "Revolution: An Enquiry into the Usefulness of an Historical Term." *Mind* 58: 495–517. This piece is a good, short introduction to the subject.

Johnson, Chalmers. 1964. *Revolution and the Social System.* Stanford, Calif. This is an influential theoretical work by a political scientist.

Koselleck, R. 1969. "Der neuzeitliche Revolutionsbegriff als geschichtliche Kategorie." *Studium Generale* 22: 825–38. Koselleck discusses the changing historical relationships between the ideas of "revolution" and "civil war."

Kramnick, Isaac. 1972. "Reflections on Revolution: Definition and Explanation in Recent Scholarship." *HT* 11: 26–63. The footnotes provide bibliography on the taxonomy, classification, origins, periodization, and dynamics of revolution.

Laqueur, Walter. 1968. "Revolution." *IESS* 13: 501–07. Laqueur expesses the common view that "Since force begets force . . . violent revolution, though intended to overthrow despotism, very often culminates in a new tyranny" (p. 505).

Lipsky, W. E. 1976. "Comparative Approaches to Study of Revolution: A Historiographic Essay." *Revolutionary Politics* 38: 494–509.

Plumb, J. H. 1967. *The Origins of Political Stability: England, 1675–1725.* Boston.

Rosenstock-Hüessy, E. 1938. *Out of Revolution: Autobiography of Western Man.* New York.

Stone, Lawrence. 1966. "Theories of Revolution." *World Politics* 18: 159–76.

Zagorin, Perez. 1973. "Theories of Revolution in Contemporary Historiography." *Political Science Quarterly* 88: 23–52. This is a useful survey of recent trends in theory and research, especially recent work in sociology and political science. It contains a concise list of objections to the Marxist theory of revolution (pp. 31–34). In contrast to most authorities, Zagorin rejects the idea that revolution must be a comprehensive social transformation and would include "most peasant revolts, urban insurrections, and provincial or national separatist rebellions" (pp. 28–29).

Sources of Additional Information

Robert Blackey, ed., *Modern Revolutions and Revolutionists: A Comprehensive Guide to the Literature* (Santa Barbara, Calif., 1982), cites more than 5,000 titles. Berding: 263–77 lists many of the important works. See especially the footnote references in Zagorin (1973) and Lipsky (1976). Zagorin also has an extensive discussion of the concept's history in chapter one of his *Court and the Country* (New York, 1969), which cites more titles. Consult, as well, Jean Baechler, *Revolution* (New York, 1975). There is a concise list of works in n. 30 (pp. 513–14) of James H. Billington, *Fire in the Minds of Men: Origins of the Revolutionary Faith* (New York, 1980). The revised and expanded edition of Brinton ([1938] 1965) contains a very good bibliography. Brinton's theory of revolution resembles the idea of historical "crisis" set forth by the nineteenth-century Swiss historian Jacob Burckhardt—see Burckhardt's "Crises of History" in his *Force and Freedom: Reflections on History* (New York, 1943). A number of anthologies on the subject have appeared that contain helpful bibliographies: for example: Carl J. Friedrich, ed., *Nomos VIII: Revolution* (New York, 1966); Bruce Mazlish, Arthur D. Kaledin, and David B. Ralston, eds., *Revolution: A Reader* (New York, 1971); James Chowning Davies, ed., *When Men Revolt and Why: A Reader in Political Violence and Revolution* (New York, 1971). See also Krishan Kumar, *Revolution: The Theory and Practice of A European Idea* (London, 1971). Various sections of George Rudé's long historiographical essay *Debate on Europe: 1815–1850* (New York, 1972) are pertinent. A recent German work is Karl-Heinz Bender, *Revolutionen: Die Entstehung des politischen Revolutionsbegriffes in Frankreich zwischen Mittelalter und Aufklärung* (Munich, 1977). Of related interest is I. Bernard Cohen, "The Eighteenth-Century Origins of the Concept of Scientific Revolution," *JHI* 37 (1976): 257–88. A thoughtful analysis of Brinton's general theory of revolution is George H. Nadel, "The Logic of the *Anatomy of Revolution*, with Reference to the Netherlands Revolt," *CSSH* 2 (1959–60): 474–84.

ROMANTICISM. Cultural movement characteristic of early-nineteenth-century literature (including historical writing), aesthetic and social thought, and general taste and sensibility. Among the range of ideas associated with the word, the following are especially important: anti-formalism, in contrast to prevailing eighteenth-century neo-classical styles and attitudes; emphasis on intuition, sympathetic feeling, and emotional expression; fascination with the individual, the unique, and the exotic; interest in social tradition and organic PROCESS.

The word *romanticism* (Ger. *Romantik*) was evidently coined by the German poet Novalis in the late 1790s. The term was an outgrowth of *romantic*, which, in seventeenth- and eighteenth-century French, English, and German usage, acquired a wide span of associations ranging from "fanciful" to "marvelous" and "picturesque" (Wellek, 1973: 187–88). Around 1800, German scholars and critics began to use the word to serve their rebellion against the conventions of prevailing neo-classicism. *Romanticism* gradually came to designate an emotional mode of expression (allegedly discovered in the work of early-modern dramatists such as Shakespeare and Calderón), which contrasted favorably with aesthetic approaches based on adherence to formal rules. Most influential in formulating and popularizing this understanding was the critic August Wilhelm Schlegel. In a series of lectures delivered in Jena, Berlin, and Vienna between 1798 and 1809, Schlegel established a contrast between *classical* and *romantic* styles based on the distinction between *formalist* and *anti-formalist* impulses. In the first two decades of the nineteenth century Schlegel's ideas spread to France, Italy, and England, particularly through the influence of the French writer Madame de Staël. In Italy the word was first used in 1818 during quarrels between defenders of old and new literary styles. Thus, the idea of a "romantic school" was introduced (Wellek, 1973: 190–91). The idea was slow to take hold in English. Its development can be traced in the work of many early-nineteenth-century writers, including historians such as Thomas Carlyle and Thomas Babbington Macaulay—even though they may not always have used the word itself (p. 194). By the late nineteenth century it was firmly established in the language of international scholarship (e.g., Rudolf Haym, *Die Romantische Schule* [1870]; Ricarda Huch, *Blütezeit der Romantik* [1899]).

The meaning and usefulness of the idea have been widely debated since about 1900. In an influential essay, Arthur O. Lovejoy ([1924] 1948: 232) asserted that "The word 'romantic' has come to mean so many things that, by itself, it means nothing. It has ceased to perform the function of a verbal sign." The terms *romantic* and *romanticism* have not been without defenders among cultural and literary historians, however (for example, Barzun, 1940; 1961; Wellek, [1949] 1963). A widespread opinion holds that although "some scholars have, in despair, suggested that it be abandoned . . . the phenomenon would not become less complex with the abandonment of the term, and there is no reason to suppose that its successor would be any clearer" (Beckson and Ganz, 1975: 215). Lovejoy himself ([1936] 1960) later identified one feature that, he maintained, characterized the various forms of romanticism: "diversitarianism," by which he meant the "idealization of diversity" in contrast to the "uniformitarianism" of eighteenth-century neo-classicism.

Historians have used the idea widely for various purposes, for example, as a concept of COLLIGATION to explain events in the early nineteenth century (Barzun, 1950; Evans, 1952) and as a label to collectively designate anti-rational traditions in modern culture and politics (Talmon, 1960). Of particular interest is the degree of acceptance that the concept enjoys in explanations of the early-nineteenth-century history of historical conceptualization and writing itself. Since the late nineteenth century historians have widely held that the early-nineteenth-century "romantic" sensibility for the unique, the particular, and the "individual"—what Lovejoy called "diversitarianism"—was of key importance among historians (especially in Germany) in stimulating a heightened sense of ANACHRONISM, a new appreciation of the need for imaginative insight and sympathetic UNDERSTANDING (*Einfühlung, Verstehen*) into the past, and that romanticism fed the rise of HISTORISM, that is, the doctrine that past personalities, events, and situations must be understood in terms of their own unique contexts and not judged by present standards and values. This position is explicit, for example, in the unpublished notes of the British historian Lord Acton (Butterfield, 1955: 70–74), as well as in the published studies of various German scholars, culminating in the works of Friedrich Meinecke ([1936] 1972; 1939). Through Meinecke's work, especially, the idea of romanticism's centrality for the development of modern historiography has been transmitted to the general literature on historiography (for example, Butterfield, 1955: 17–18, 34). Recent research on the development of historiography in the seventeenth and eighteenth centuries suggests that the special emphasis traditionally placed on romanticism for the development of modern historical thinking may in some respects be "antiquated" (Kelly, 1982: 320). Nevertheless, the dominant attitude today holds that romanticism, if not as decisive as previously believed, was still a "great stimulus to historians" (Butterfield, 1955: 74).

References

Barzun, Jacques. 1940. "To the Rescue of Romanticism." *The American Scholar* 9 (1940): 147–58.

———. 1950. *Berlioz and the Romantic Century*. Boston, 1950. This book is by a strong defender of the concept.

———. 1961. *Classic, Romantic and Modern*. Boston. This is a revised version of *Romanticism and the Modern Ego*, originally published in 1943.

Beckson, Karl, and Ganz, Arthur. 1975. *Literary Terms: A Dictionary*. New York.

Butterfield, Herbert. 1955. *Man on His Past: The Study of the History of Historical Scholarship*. Cambridge. This book is a good introduction. See particularly the footnote citations on pp. 17 and 34–35.

Evans, D. O. 1952. *Social Romanticism in France, 1830–1848*. New York.

Kelly, Donald R. 1982. Review Essay. *JMH* 54: 320–26.

Lovejoy, Arthur O. [1924] 1948. "On the Discrimination of Romanticisms." In Arthur O. Lovejoy, *Essays in the History of Ideas*: 228–37. Baltimore. Lovejoy argues that scholars should think in terms of many romantic movements rather than one unified movement.

———. [1936] 1960. *The Great Chain of Being*. New York.

Meinecke, Friedrich. 1939. *Vom geschichtlichen Sinn und vom Sinn der Geschichte*. Leipzig. This book contains the essay "Klassizismus, Romantizismus und historisches Denken im 18. Jahrhundert."

———. [1936] 1972. *Historism: The Rise of a New Historical Outlook*. London.

Talmon, J. L. 1960. *Political Messianism: The Romantic Phase*. New York.

Wellek, René. [1949] 1963. "The Concept of Romanticism in Literary History." In René Wellek, *Concepts of Criticism*. New Haven, Conn. Wellek argues against Lovejoy ([1924] 1948) in favor of the idea of a unified romantic movement.

———. 1973. "Romanticism in Literature." *DHI* 4: 187–98. This piece has a convenient history of the term, with bibliography.

Sources of Additional Information

The literature is vast. A journal called *Studies in Romanticism* is devoted to the subject. Among the important general bibliographies are A. C. Elkins, Jr., and L. J. Forstner, eds., *The Romantic Movement Bibliography, 1936–1970*, 7 vols. (Ann Arbor, Mich., 1973), and David V. Erdman, ed., *The Romantic Movement: A Selective and Critical Bibliography* (New York, 1979–). John B. Halsted, ed., *Romanticism: Problems of Definition, Explanation, and Evaluation* (Boston, 1965), is one of many anthologies of critical writings on the topic; it contains a useful annotated bibliography. Volume 4 of *DHI* contains not only the excellent essay by Wellek (1973) but the entries "Romanticism (ca. 1780-ca. 1830)," "Romanticism in Political Thought," and "Romanticism in Post-Kantian Philosophy"; all conclude with bibliographies. *JHI* 2 (June 1941) includes articles by Lovejoy on "The Meaning of Romanticism for the Historian of Ideas," and Barzun on "Romantic Historiography as a Political Force in France." Harry Elmer Barnes, *A History of Historical Writing* (1937; reprint ed., New York, 1962), includes a discussion of the relationship of romanticism to historiography, as does Matthew A. Fitzsimmons et al., *The Development of Historiography* (Harrisburg, Pa., 1954). The histories of Augustin Thierry, Thomas Carlyle, and especially Jules Michelet have received attention as expressions of romanticism; on Thierry and Carlyle see, for example, Emery Neff, *The Poetry of History: The Contribution of Literature and Literary Scholarship to the Writing of History since Voltaire* (New York, 1947). On Michelet see especially Edward K. Kaplan, *Michelet's Poetic Vision: A Romantic Philosophy of Nature, Man, and Woman* (Amherst, Mass., 1977), although it is based primarily on Michelet's non-historical works. Among studies of early American historiography see especially David Levin, *History as Romantic Art: Bancroft, Prescott, Motley, and Parkman* (Stanford, Calif., 1959); also George H. Callcott, *History in the United States, 1800–1860: Its Practice and Purpose* (Baltimore, 1970), especially chapter one, "The Intellectual Origins of Romantic History."

S

SCIENTIFIC HISTORY. 1. Scholarship that honors the generally agreed-upon methods and standards of history as a discipline: that is, the techniques of source CRITICISM, the spirit of OBJECTIVITY (fairness and impartiality—readiness to subordinate personal feeling to established FACT), an awareness of ANACHRONISM (feeling for the fundamental difference between past and present), and a sense of secular CAUSATION. 2. A research orientation, modeled on the natural sciences, that seeks through the study of the past to isolate general LAWS of social development. In some cases—especially in current SOCIAL SCIENTIFIC HISTORY—these laws are understood in a limited sense, as applying only to individual societies at a particular point in time. In the nineteenth and early twentieth centuries, however, the search for general principles was most often understood as a quest for universal laws of human behavior and social process.

The word *science* has been linked to historiography in a number of senses during the past two centuries. Many scholars prefer to avoid the term because its meanings are easily conflated, and because some of these meanings are widely considered unacceptable in relation to history (for instance, Aydelotte, 1971: 35). This is true especially of historians trained in English-speaking countries. Continental European scholars experience far fewer doubts about the possibility of scientific history, since German and French writers still frequently employ *science* in the loose sense of the ancient Latin *scientia*: any organized body of knowledge (e.g., Ritter, 1961–62; Holborn, [1943] 1950: 63). This is roughly equivalent to the meaning now suggested by the term *discipline* in England and America (Iggers, 1975: 4). The older sense was once common in English usage and is still occasionally encountered (for example, Wedgwood, 1960: 71; Collingwood, [1946] 1956: 249). To employ the word in this older sense in contemporary Britain or America, however, is to risk serious misunderstanding (Mink, 1969: 184; Iggers, 1975: 4), for English has come to associate *science* narrowly with experimental and quantitative *natural science* during the past 200 years (Leith, 1971: 158). In the contemporary Anglo-American historical profession there is consequently wide feeling that *history* is best considered a "craft" rather than a full-fledged science (Brinton, 1963: 81). Many professional philosophers agree (e.g., Blake, 1955: 68–70; Passmore, [1958] 1966: 93)—although not always for the reasons historians typically cite. On the other hand, those British and American scholars who defend the idea of SOCIAL SCIENTIFIC HISTORY—thus far a minority—strongly endorse the notion of linking history and science (for instance, Benson, 1972). Their idea of science differs, however, from the traditional sense still popular on the European continent.

The concept of scientific history arose in the eighteenth century as a by-product of the desire to render all branches of inquiry more systematic, rigorous, and precise. Historians of the day such as Voltaire in France, Gibbon and Robertson in Britain, and Niebuhr in Germany sought to

> go beyond antiquarian interest in the noteworthy details of the past to the broader reconstruction of aspects of past reality on the basis of convincing evidence . . . [and to] grasp meaningful connections among events and structures. . . . [This marked the] transition from erudition to a discipline which considered itself a science (*Wissenschaft*). (Iggers, 1975: 9)

Like the natural sciences, history became a search for interrelationships between phenomena, an organized effort to discover order in apparent disorder. Once connections were established, they could be represented in coherent narratives displaying each development as the logical outgrowth of earlier events (Holborn, [1943] 1950: 74). This shift was in turn closely linked to a new association between history and universities—especially in Germany, which assumed the lead in refining historical scholarship as a "science" (Iggers, 1975: 12–14).

While these changes were under way, certain theorists (such as the Baron de Montesquieu [1689–1755]) advanced the notion that historical inquiry might lead to the discovery of social LAWS that would lay the foundations for a predictive "science of man" (see also POSITIVISM). To some degree this was a revival of the ancient idea that the grounds of human action are universal, that historical inquiry can reveal their operation, and that knowledge of these principles may serve as a guide to conduct (as in Thucydides). Initially, however, this revival was mainly an affair of speculative philosophers. The earliest professional historians, while touting the idea of "historical science," doubted that historical inquiry would lead to the discovery of universal truths; historians at the University of Göttingen, for example, believed their task to be the reconstruction of unique experiences and situations of the past, rather than the discovery of general rules of conduct (Iggers, 1975: 15). Historians and philosophers alike, however, appealed to science as an ideal and to an understanding of science as a style of inquiry whose "methods and rules do not in the last analysis rest on personal hunches . . . but are governed by intersubjectively acceptable rules'' (p. 5; 1962–63: 20). The generation of Leopold von Ranke (1795–1886)—the most important early role model of ''scientific history''—understood the term primarily in the latter sense (Iggers, 1975; 1962–63: 20).

In the mid- and late nineteenth century, amidst growing admiration for the achievements and applications of experimental science, the expectation spread that history might be transformed into a predictive ''science of man.'' POSITIVISM and HISTORICAL MATERIALISM were merely two of the many expressions of this dream. In this setting the very word *science* became a ''fetish'' (Holt, 1940: 352), even for some historians (particularly outside of Germany). The adjective *scientific* was brandished for scholarly and non-scholarly purposes alike: as a form of disciplinary self-flattery, as a means to distinguish *history* from *literature* and *speculative philosophy*, and so on.

Curiously, late-nineteenth-century historians spent little time reflecting on the meaning of *science*. Often the word meant nothing more than the methodical and conscientious effort to reconstitute the past ''as it actually happened'' (pp. 354–55). Painstaking archival research was certainly a key ingredient, as was the kind of detachment in which the scholar's personality disappeared behind his work. From this standpoint the problem was simply to ''get the facts'' and get them straight, not to speculate or generalize (Aydelotte, 1971: 22). Once established the facts would presumably ''speak for themselves'' (Holt, 1940: 358; Aydelotte, 1971: 15). Beyond this, *scientific history* often implied the attainment of a high if not complete degree of certainty, and the idea that research is cumulative, that is, that collective knowledge of the past advances steadily through the publication of ever more precise monographic studies (Higham et al., 1965: 101, 103).

At the same time, it was widely assumed that the defining feature of a science was the capacity to establish laws, and this ''nomothetic'' orientation (Iggers, 1975: 33) sometimes overlaid the more modest understanding of science as rigorous scholarship. Darwin's theories had made an enormous impact on public opinion, and some late-nineteenth-century historians hoped that scientific historiography might isolate a social law similar in scope to the principle of ''natural selection,'' one that would revolutionize and unify social inquiry (Saveth, 1960: 2). This expectation was shared by (among others) the British historian H. T. Buckle (1821–62), the French scholar Paul Lacombe (1848–1921), and the maverick of German scholarship Karl Lamprecht (1856–1915). In the United States Henry Adams asserted that to become a true science history must ''establish its laws'' (cited in Holt, 1940: 356). This orientation persisted well into the twentieth century, as illustrated in Charles Cochrane's opinion ([1929] 1965: 167) that history is scientific ''in so far as it yields useful generalizations about human action.'' Even today it enjoys a residual existence in many discussions on the ''scientific'' or ''non-scientific'' nature of history. In modifed form it also persists in the COVERING LAW model of historical EXPLANATION advanced by the philosopher C. G. Hempel ([1942] 1959).

The confident nineteenth-century models of scientific history began to break down around the turn of the twentieth century, as philosophers began to doubt the possibility of absolute certainty and precision in any branch of human inquiry. Neo-idealist thinkers such as Wilhelm Dilthey, Wilhelm Windelband, and Heinrich Rickert in Germany and Benedetto Croce in Italy underscored differences between the "cultural" or "human" sciences (*Geisteswissenschaften*)—including history—and the "natural" sciences (*Naturwissenschaften*) (Rickman, 1967). Following Windelband's celebrated address on the subject in 1894, many historians began to separate *Geschichte* from *Naturwissenschaft* on the grounds that history is *idiographic* (i.e., concerned with understanding unique events), whereas natural science is *nomothetic*, or concerned with the establishment of general laws. There was a heightened appreciation of the individual historian's personality in framing historical problems, selecting evidence, and devising interpretations, an awareness that helped spawn historical RELATIVISM—a doctrine that (especially in North America) denied that history was a "science" at all. It was, at best, an "art," or some autonomous mode of inquiry in itself. *Craft* now became a favored substitute for *science*, for this word connoted rigor and intellectual honesty but carried the less scientistic suggestion of acquired skill and personal finesse (for instance, Fogel and Elton, 1983: 101, 106).

Simultaneously, however, a chastened version of the nomological concept of historial science gradually emerged in connection with the idea of social science (see SOCIAL SCIENTIFIC HISTORY). Frederick Jackson Turner's presidential address to the American Historical Association in 1910 maintained, for example, that "if history could not be made into a [exact, natural] science, it might at least be infiltrated by the social sciences to the end that true understanding might be achieved" (Saveth, 1960: 10). As it has developed in the twentieth century, the social scientific orientation differs from the earlier nomethetic approach insofar as it usually does not seek to discover *universal* laws of social reality but attempts to utilize explicit sociological and economic MODELS to uncover social regularities in relatively delimited historical settings (p. 14; Fogel and Elton, 1983: 25, 29). From this viewpoint, although it may not be possible to posit laws that govern human behavior in widely separated periods (e.g., ancient Greece and modern Western Europe), it may indeed be possible to generalize regarding the social constants and regularities in a particular spatio-temporal context—for example, Puritan New England (Murphey, 1973: 84–85). In this limited sense, then, advocates of historical social science such as the American Lee Benson maintain that the "primary goal of scientific history or history as social science 'is to help develop general laws of human behavior' " (Aydelotte, 1973: 263; also Benson, 1972; Fogel and Elton, 1983).

For most historians today, however, the term *science* (when it is employed at all) still implies "little more than a conscientious search for facts and an attempt at their interpretation so as to discover what went on in the past" (Saveth, 1960: 17; cf. Walsh, 1973: 204–5). The philosopher John Passmore agrees:

If we mean by "science" the attempt to find out what really happens, then history is a science. It demands the same kind of dedication, the same ruthlessness, the same passion for exactness, as physics. . . . If, however, we mean by science the search for general theories, then history is not a science; indeed, in so far as it tries to show us something through a particularized pattern of action, it stands closer to the novel and the drama than it does to physics. ([1958] 1966: 93)

References

Aydelotte, William O. 1971. *Quantification in History*. Reading, Mass.
————. 1973. "Lee Benson's Scientific History: For and Against." *Journal of Interdisciplinary History* 4: 263–72.
Benson, Lee. 1972. *Toward the Scientific Study of History: Selected Essays*. Philadelphia.
Blake, Christopher. 1955. "Can History Be Objective?" *Mind*, N.S., 64: 61–78. Blake considers the older, continental European usage "obsolescent" (p. 69).
Brinton, Crane. 1963. Review of Louis Gottschalk, ed., *Generalization in the Writing of History*. AHR 69: 80–82. According to Brinton, "writing history is a craft, perhaps an art, and a science only in the sense that the historian must observe complete respect for facts, data, concrete 'reality,' and that he must seek for complete detachment, scientific objectivity" (p. 81).
Cochrane, Charles Norris. [1929] 1965. *Thucydides and the Science of History*. New York.
Collingwood, R. G. [1946] 1956. *The Idea of History*. New York. The author considers the identification of *science* and *natural science* to be an instance of "slang usage" (p. 249).
Fogel, Robert William, and Elton, G. R. 1983. *Which Road to the Past? Two Views of History* (New Haven, Conn., 1983). Fogel equates *scientific history* with *cliometrics*. By this he means the use of explicit social science models to study "repetitive occurrences" (p. 29). See ECONOMETRIC HISTORY.
Hempel, Carl G. [1942] 1959. "The Function of General Laws in History." In Gardiner: 344–56.
Higham, John, et al. 1965. *History*. Englewood Cliffs, N.J.
Holborn, Hajo. [1943] 1950. "The Science of History." In Strayer: 61–83. This piece is a good illustration of the conflation of the broad and narrow meanings of *historical science* (see pp. 63, 70).
Holt, W. Stull. 1940. "The Idea of Scientific History in America." *JHI* 1: 352–62. This essay was written at the height of the relativism's influence in America.
Iggers, Georg G. 1962–63. "The Image of Ranke in American and German Historical Thought." *HT* 2: 17–40.
————. 1975. *New Directions in European Historiography*. Middletown, Conn.
Leith, James A. 1971. "Peter Gay's Enlightenment." *Eighteenth-Century Studies* 5: 157–71.
Mink, Louis O. 1969. *Mind, History, and Dialectic: The Philosophy of R. G. Collingwood*. Bloomington, Ind.
Murphey, Murray G. 1973. *Our Knowledge of the Historical Past*. Indianapolis, Ind.
Passmore, J. A. [1958] 1966. "The Objectivity of History." In Dray: 75–94.
Rickman, H. P. 1967. "Geisteswissenschaften." *EP* 3: 275–79.

Ritter, Gerhard. 1961–62. "Scientific History, Contemporary History, and Political Science." *HT* 1: 261–79.

Saveth, Edward N. 1960. "Scientific History in America: Eclipse of an Idea." In Donald Sheehan and Harold C. Syrett, eds., *Essays in American Historiography: Papers Presented in Honor of Allan Nevins*. New York: 1–19.

Walsh, W. H. 1973. "History as Science and History as More Than Science." *The Virginia Quarterly Review* 49: 196–212. Walsh understands *historical science* as "history using the full resources of modern scholarship to carry out its primary task of finding out what happened in the past" (pp. 204–5).

Wedgwood, C. V. 1960. *Truth and Opinion: Historical Essays*. New York.

Sources of Additional Information

See also COVERING LAW; LAW; OBJECTIVITY; POSITIVISM; SOCIAL SCIENTIFIC HISTORY. Consult *HT Beih.*; Stephens; Birkos and Tambs. There is a vast literature on the question of whether *history* is an "art," a "science," a combination of both, or something entirely different; see, for example, H. Stuart Hughes, *History as Art and as Science: Twin Vistas on the Past* (New York, 1964). Fritz Stern's widely used anthology *The Varieties of History* (New York, 1972) provides a good sampling of nineteenth- and twentieth-century views; see especially the famous exchange between J. B. Bury and G. M. Trevelyan in Stern: 209–45. Also relevant is Jacques Barzun, *Clio and the Doctors* (Chicago, 1974); many of the essays of J. H. Hexter (for instance, those collected in *Doing History* [Bloomington, Ind., 1971]); Isaiah Berlin, "History and Theory: The Concept of Scientific History," *HT* 1 (1961–62): 1–31; Helen P. Liebel, "History and the Limitations of Scientific Method," *University of Toronto Quarterly* 34 (Oct. 1964): 15–30; and Haskell Fain, "History as Science," *HT* 9 (1970): 154–73. In all of this work it is, as Maurice Mandelbaum remarked, a "commonplace" that "historians are concerned with particular events that occurred at specific times and places, and not with them only in so far as they represent events of a given type" (*The Anatomy of Historical Knowledge* [Baltimore, 1977], p. 4). The role of Ranke is discussed in Iggers (1962–63). Ranke's own essay "On the Character of Historical Science" is included in Leopold von Ranke, *The Theory and Practice of History*, ed. Georg G. Iggers and Konrad von Moltke (Indianapolis, Ind., 1973): 33–46. As Higham (1965: 99) notes, "Ranke himself . . . was a romantic idealist, who always sought an intuitive apprehension of the universal within the particular." On Lamprecht see Karl Lamprecht, *What Is History? Five Lectures on the Modern Science of History* (New York, 1905). On two other individual historians see Solomon Gemorah, "Frederick J. Teggart: Scientific Historian of the 'New History'," *South Atlantic Quarterly* 68 (1969): 478–90, and Donald E. Emerson, "Hildreth, Draper, and Scientific History," in E. F. Goldman, ed., *Historiography and Urbanization: Essays in American History in Honor of W. Stull Holt* (Baltimore, 1941): 139–70.

SKEPTICISM. 1. Doubt concerning the reliability of historical scholarship, based on a variety of possible reasons: for example, the fact that EVIDENCE regarding the past is fragmentary and subject to INTERPRETATION, that the past is not an object of immediate perception, that individual historians view the past from different, socially conditioned perspectives, and so on. 2. Less commonly, a critical attitude toward evidence of the past. 3. Also less commonly, the position that disclaims the ethical worth of studying history or denies the existence of laws or discoverable patterns in the record of the past.

The words *skeptic* and *history* are semantically related—in ancient Greece both terms meant "inquiry" (Stough, 1969: 3). Philosophy recognizes differing degrees of skepticism. The most radical form holds that no knowledge at all is possible; milder varieties hold that our capacity to know is limited in various ways. *Skepticism* is sometimes referred to as "Pyrrhonism," after the ancient philosopher Pyrrho (c. 360–270 B.C.), who taught that reality is unknowable since all statements about it are equally plausible.

In history *skepticism* usually refers to the position that "denies the possibility . . . of having knowledge of the past on the basis of evidence about the past" (Meiland, 1965: 4). However, the word may also designate positions that deny the ethical value of history—that is, disclaim the idea that there is any discoverable pattern or "meaning" in history (Phillips, 1947: 449; White, 1973: 433)— or affirm the historian's need to adopt a questioning attitude toward his sources (Johnson, 1926: 50, 98). *Skepticism* and RELATIVISM are sometimes used interchangeably (e.g., Beck, 1950); properly speaking, however, *historical relativism* refers to a species of skepticism—the sort that denies the possibility of uncontested historical knowledge due to the subjective limitations of individual scholars. Because of the large body of literature on the subject, relativism is discussed in a separate entry in this dictionary.

Among the Greeks, some form of historical skepticism was virtually unavoidable, since their accounts were based primarily on memory of the immediate past (which they themselves recognized as highly fallible), rather than critical use of evidence about the remote past (Goldstein, 1970: 9, n. 14); the methods of source CRITICISM would not be codified until the sixteenth and seventeenth centuries (see below). Herodotus, the "father of history," was regularly called a "liar" in ancient times (Momigliano, [1958] 1966: 127–28). Perhaps the great emphasis that ancient historians placed on chance, destiny, and the supernatural reflects an implicit skepticism about their own work (Grant, 1970: xvii).

In the Middle Ages skepticism was not articulated since it was identified with pagan philosophers, but tacit doubt about human knowledge in general—and the past in particular—was a natural consequence of the Christian doctrine of human fallibility. This attitude continued into the early-modern period (Hay, 1977: 128), when it merged with revived interest in ancient skepticism during the RENAISSANCE. Early-modern skepticism is vital to the history of subsequent historical scholarship, since it stimulated a defense of historiography based on the development of new, rigorously systematic methods of source criticism.

Historians disagree on the extent to which explicit skepticism intensified in the sixteenth century. The usual view (for instance, Hay, 1977: 127–29; Haddock, 1980: 46–48) holds that skepticism was strengthened by various factors: for example, the sectarian conflicts of the Reformation (when competing confessions advanced contradictory versions of the ecclesiastical past) and humanistic scholarship (which classified history as a branch of rhetoric, designed to persuade rather than to inform). Many authorities underscore on the significance of Heinrich Cornelius Agrippa (1486–1535), who denied history's cognitive validity on the basis of a combination of Christian arguments concerning the frailty of reason and references to the contradictory nature of many historical accounts (Haddock, 1980: 48). Cochrane (1981: 481), however, doubts the importance of sixteenth-century historical skepticism, arguing that Agrippa—whose arguments were in any case not profound—was the only important philosopher of the period to question history's reliability. Those who subscribe to the traditional view typically cite the florid remarks of the poet Sir Philip Sidney, who doubted both the cognitive and moral worth of history and described the historian as

> laden with old mouse-eaten records, authorizing himself (for the most part) upon other histories, whose greatest authorities are built upon the notable foundation of hearsay. . . . being captivated to the truth of a foolish world, [the historian] is many times a terror from well doing, and an encouragement to unbridled wickedness. . . . affirming many things, [he] can, in the cloudy knowledge of mankind, hardly escape from many lies. ([1595] 1970: 88, 91, 97)

Cochrane (1981: 481), however, maintains that Sidney's indictment "was quickly forgotten."

All specialists agree that historical Pyrrhonism reached a peak in the seventeenth-century thought of figures such as René Descartes, La Mothe Le Vayer, and Pierre Bayle (p. 482; Hay, 1977: 130–31; Haddock, 1980: 45; Momigliano, 1950: 295–307). Descartes, perhaps the most important, required knowledge to be mathematically precise and reduced history to the status of rumor, gossip, or "romantic fiction" because it did not satisfy his demand for comprehensiveness and certainty (Lévy-Bruhl, [1936] 1963: 191; Haddock, 1980: 49–51); his Pyrrhonism was a logical consequence of his general attack on tradition as a foundation for knowledge, since most history of the day was based on the uncritical acceptance of traditional authorities. To this point in time, the "good historian had been distinguished on the ground that his tale was both pleasing and instructive; but it was not thought essential that he should concern himself unduly with the evidence which warranted his account" (Haddock, 1980: 57). Descartes had many influential followers—for example, Malebranche and Bayle—who popularized his contempt for the study of the past. The epigrams attributed to Fontenelle ("history is nothing but a fable men have agreed upon") and Voltaire (history is a "pack of tricks the living play on the dead") reflect this tradition.

Against skepticism, the defense of historiography was taken up by ecclesiastical and legal scholars from the mid-sixteenth century onward—François Baudoin, Jean Bodin, John Bolland, Jean Mabillon, and others (Hay, 1977: 130; Kelley, 1970: 116–48). These writers attacked skepticism by devising methods for verifying the authenticity of EVIDENCE, which they divided into "primary" and "secondary" categories (see METHOD, CRITICISM, ANTIQUARIANISM). Mabillon's *De Re Diplomatica* (1681) was especially important. The critical techniques codified by these opponents of Pyrrhonism prepared the way for history's emergence as a systematic discipline in the late eighteenth and early nineteenth centuries.

Historical skepticism diminished radically in the nineteenth century—a period of unprecedented confidence in the reliability and value of knowledge of the past, when history was widely understood as a rigorous science (see SCIENTIFIC HISTORY). Doubters such as the German philosopher Friedrich Nietzsche were isolated exceptions. Even Nietzsche, while questioning the worth of history as practiced in his lifetime, believed that knowledge of the past was necessary for "life and action" (Nietzsche, [1874] 1949: 3).

In some respects, however, Nietzsche's thought foreshadowed a twentieth-century resurgence of skepticism, and the growth of outright hostility toward historical consciousness (White, [1966] 1978). In particular, Nietzsche touched on the roles of partisanship and social conditioning in historiography:

> How difficult it is to find a real historical talent, if we exclude all the disguised egoists and the partisans who pretend to take up an impartial attitude for the sake of their own unholy game! And we also exclude the thoughtless folk who write history in the naive faith that justice resides in the popular view of their time, and that to write in the spirit of the time is to be just. . . . The measurement of the opinions and deeds of the past by the universal opinions of the present is called "objectivity" by these simple people. ([1874] 1949: 37)

Such doubts—based on the idea of the "truly subjective nature" of historiography (p. 38)—became the basis for historical RELATIVISM, which eventually affected the thought of many historians themselves. For relativists, the problem was that

> every historian regards the documents or evidence from his own point of view; his values, standards, and interests greatly influence what he says about the past. As a result of the difference, different historians will give different interpretations of the past. Their "bias" will determine or influence their interpretation of the past. How, then, is it to be determined which, if any, of these different interpretations is correct? (Meiland, 1965: 35)

But although such considerations troubled many scholars from the 1920s through the 1940s (Deininger, 1954; Zagorin, 1956), they did nothing to stem the publication of scholarly works about the past. By the 1950s concern about relativism had largely subsided. A measure of "bias" in historical accounts was now accepted as inevitable, and it was conceded that scholarship could not produce "certain" knowledge; in this sense, a mild form of skepticism is integral to the present orthodoxy: "Whether acquired by the historian or the natural scientist, knowledge is, in principle, always open to doubt, since the evidence may have been misunderstood or because new evidence yet to be established may require the revision of our conclusions" (Zagorin, 1956: 10–11). Nevertheless, given the existence of rigorous methods of source criticism, it is generally agreed that professional research can indeed result in highly reliable accounts of the past (pp. 10–11).

At present, only a small number of historians hold explicit positions that might suggest a more radical form of historical skepticism. A noteworthy case is Hayden White (1973), whose "rhetorical relativism" (Mink, 1979: 25–26) is based on the belief that the western cultural tradition has produced four distinct ways in which historical narratives can be conceived, argued, and "emplotted."

> When it is a matter of choosing among alternative visions of history [White concludes], the only grounds for preferring one over another are *moral* or *aesthetic* ones. . . . without any apodictically provided theoretical grounds for preferring one over another, we are driven back to moral and aesthetic reasons for the choice of one vision over another as the more "realistic." . . . we are free to conceive "history" as we please, just as we are free to make of it what we will. (1973: 433)

In White's controversial schema, however, the number of possible visions of the past is not infinite but is restricted to variations on the four rhetorical "tropes" (metonymy, synechdoche, metaphor, irony) that he identifies as fundamental to the art of narrative in the western tradition.

It should be noted that the position of those contemporary philosophers of history known loosely as "positivists" implies a strong form of historical skepticism, since it denies history the status of a full-fledged science, that is, one that can yield reliable knowledge on par with the natural sciences (see COVERING LAW; POSITIVISM).

Different, but also significant, is the relationship between *skepticism* and the philosophical position known as CONSTRUCTIONISM (Goldstein, 1970, 1972, 1976; Meiland, 1965). The small number of theorists who hold this view, while rejecting historical skepticism, ironically maintain that *skepticism* is the inevitable result of historical REALISM—that is, the view that the historian's task is the recovery of a "real" past that exists independently of historical research. The constructionist position is based on the argument that the existence of a "real" past, independent of the historian's operations, cannot be demonstrated; more importantly, even if it could be proven to exist, such a past could not possibly be the object of anyone's direct acquaintance and thus could not be known in a commonsense way. We can indeed lay claim to reliable knowledge of the past, constructionists maintain, but only if we recognize that this is not knowledge of a commonsense "real" past, "as it actually happened" but of a technical "historical past" that the community of historical scholars constructs on the basis of EVIDENCE (Nowell-Smith, 1971: 16; Goldstein, 1970: 16, 20; 1972: 126). It is not clear if this position is held by any professional historians.

References

Beck, Lewis White. 1950. "The Limits of Skepticism in History," *The South Atlantic Quarterly* 49: 461–68. This article is an attack on historical relativism.
Cochrane, Eric. 1981. *Historians and Historiography in the Italian Renaissance*. Chicago.
Deininger, Whitaker T. 1954. "The Skepticism and Historical Faith of Charles A. Beard." *JHI* 15: 573–88.
Goldstein, Leon J. 1970. "Collingwood's Theory of Historical Knowing." *HT* 9: 2–26.

The author maintains that Collingwood held a constructionist position with regard to historical skepticism.

————. 1972. "Historial Realism: The Ground of Carl Becker's Scepticism." *Philosophy of the Social Sciences* 2: 121–31. Goldstein makes somewhat unorthodox use of the terms *skepticism* and *relativism*, based on the idea that "systems of knowledge are *relative* to the disciplined techniques or methodologies of knowing in terms of which knowledge is established. Thus, historical knowledge is relative to those methods of inquiry which constitute the discipline of history. Presumably anyone who took historical knowledge and the ways in which it is acquired seriously would not expect to be called a *sceptic* with respect to the possibility of such knowledge, and thus it would seem that one could be a relativist without being a sceptic."

————. 1976. *Historical Knowing*. Austin, Tex.

Grant, Michael. 1970. *The Ancient Historians*. New York.

Haddock, B. A. 1980. *An Introduction to Historical Thought*. London.

Hay, Denys. 1977. *Annalists and Historians: Western Historiography from the Eighth to the Eighteenth Centuries*. London.

Johnson, Allen. 1926. *The Historian and Historical Evidence*. New York.

Kelley, Donald R. 1970. *Foundations of Modern Historical Scholarship*. New York.

Lévy-Bruhl, Lucien. [1936] 1963. "The Cartesian Spirit and History." In Raymond Klibansky and H. J. Paton, eds., *Philosophy and History: Essays Presented to Ernst Cassirer*. New York: 191–96.

Meiland, Jack W. 1965. *Scepticism and Historical Knowledge*. New York. 1965. In the most extensive recent examination of the question Meiland argues that Benedetto Croce and Michael Oakeshott held constructionist positions with regard to historical skepticism. Critics (e.g., Maurice Mandelbaum [*AHR* 71 (April 1966): 894]) note that Meiland's arguments are of a general philosophical nature, not oriented toward the specific practice of historians.

Mink, Louis O. 1979. "Philosophy and Theory of History." In Iggers and Parker: 17–27.

Momigliano, Arnaldo. 1950. "Ancient History and the Antiquarian." *Journal of the Warburg and Courtauld Institutes* 13: 285–315. The author discusses seventeenth-century historical skepticism in some detail and includes a wealth of bibliography.

————. [1958] 1966. "The Place of Herodotus in the History of Historiography." In Arnaldo Momigliano, *Studies in Historiography*. London: 127–42.

Nietzsche, Friedrich. [1874] 1949. *The Use and Abuse of History*. New York.

Nowell-Smith, P. H. 1971. *What Actually Happened*. Lawrence, Kans. This book is a vigorous defense of historical REALISM and a repudiation of all forms of historical skepticism.

Phillips, Herbert J. 1947. "Historical Skepticism." *JP* 44 (Aug. 14, 1947): 449–59.

Sidney, Sir Philip. [1595] 1970. "An Apologie for Poetrie." In Walter Jackson Bate, ed., *Criticism: The Major Texts*. New York: 82–106.

Stough, Charlotte, L. 1969. *Greek Skepticism: A Study in Epistemology*. Berkeley, Calif.

White, Hayden. 1973. *Metahistory: The Historical Imagination in Nineteenth-Century Europe*. Baltimore.

————. [1966] 1978. "The Burden of History." In Hayden White, *Tropics of Discourse: Essays in Cultural Criticism*. Baltimore: 27–50.

Zagorin, Perez. 1956. "Carl Becker on History. Professor Becker's Two Histories: A Skeptical Fallacy." *AHR* 62: 1–11.

Sources of Additional Information

See OBJECTIVITY; RELATIVISM. For general background and bibliography (without specific reference to historiography) see two essays by Richard H. Popkin: "Skepticism," *EP* 7 (1967): 449–61, and "Skepticism in Modern Thought," *DHI* 4 (1973): 240–51; also Phillip de Lacy, "Skepticism in Antiquity," *DHI* 4 (1973): 234–40. For the early-modern period see especially Kelley (1970) and Julian H. Franklin, *Jean Bodin and the Sixteenth-Century Revolution in the Methodology of Law and History* (New York, 1963). For the late seventeenth and eighteenth centuries there is useful substantive and bibliographical information in the three essays in *HT Beih*. 11 (1971), especially Rudolf Unger's "Problem of Historical Objectivity: A Sketch of Its Development to the Time of Hegel." For literature on all aspects of twentieth-century historical skepticism see the entry RELATIVISM. The views of Meiland and Goldstein are controversial; see the titles cited under CONSTRUCTIONISM, especially *HT Beih*. 16 (1977). On Hayden White's position see the collection of essays in *HT Beih*. 19 (1980).

SOCIAL HISTORY. Historical writing that concentrates on the study of social groups, their interrelationships, and their roles in economic and cultural structures and processes; often characterized by the use of social science theory and quantitative methods.

Since the 1950s (Hobsbawm, 1972: 3) the idea of social history has been the pivot of many important and novel developments in European and American historiography. In the United States "so many lines of inquiry opened up that social history seemed to dominate research on all fronts" (Darnton, 1980: 329). The notion itself is admittedly vague; it is not necessarily linked to any particular methodology, and even practitioners concede that it is "difficult to define social history sharply" (Conze, 1967: 9; Stearns, 1980: 211). Nevertheless, proponents maintain that a "certain degree of consensus exists, however fuzzy and inarticulate . . . and this is satisfactory for most purposes" (Stearns, 1967: 3). More broadly, late-twentieth-century historians (whether or not they label themselves "social historians") have generally become highly sensitive to the "social dimension" of human action; it is now widely agreed that

> the activities of human beings owe many of their special characteristics to the fact that they are social activities, undertaken not by individuals acting in isolation but by beings who are members of organizations of every degree of complexity, the nature of which they have for the most part to take for granted . . . and the operation of which often seems to proceed by a logic of its own. Modern historians . . . have grasped the all-important fact that men appear on the stage of history in a variety of roles, and that what they do . . . is determined, often to a very significant extent, partly by ways of proceeding which are commonly accepted, partly by what others concerned in the activity do or are expected to do. (Walsh, [1962–63] 1969: 248–49)

Although social history has only recently become a major specialization within the field of history, the term itself has been used since the nineteenth century, and the core of the idea is even older. A prerequisite for the concept's crystallization was the emergence of a distinct idea of "society," and this only occurred in the late eighteenth and early nineteenth centuries. Before that time a sharp distinction was not customarily made between *political* and *social* phenomena, and assumptions about "state" and "society" were intertwined in the ancient ideas of *societas civilis* ("civil society") and *res publica*, or "commonwealth." In contrast to the modern idea that social groups may have fundamentally opposing interests, it was assumed that all members of a community dwelt together in a unified, though stratified and hierarchical, "body politic." In this framework

> state and society could not yet be conceived separate from one another. . . . It was a patriarchal system, in which order was achieved through the responsible cooperation of citizens or social classes in communal activities from the provincial diets to the village councils. Consequently, there could be no social history distinct from political history. (Conze, 1967: 9–10)

The breakdown of this outlook began in the mid-eighteenth century, with the rise of the modern, impersonal idea of the state as something that even the ruler himself served. Then during the French Revolution various groups claiming to represent the "general will" (or public interest) of "the nation" rose up against the state, conceived as an instrument of oppression (see NATIONALISM). This was often explained by the progressive intelligentsia as the triumph of "society"—a new idea that had democratic and egalitarian implications. *Societas civilis* no longer functioned as the ideal for human relationships. The meaning of *human history* could now be conceived in terms of the "social question," an expression coined around 1840 (pp. 10–12).

During the nineteenth century *social history* was understood in three sometimes overlapping senses (Hobsbawm, 1972: 2). First, it might designate the history of the impoverished or "lower classes," as well as their efforts to improve their condition; within this context it might refer more specifically to the history of SOCIALISM or the labor movement. Second (especially in English), it might designate histories of popular mores, mundane life, customs, fashions, and so on. Thus understood, *social history* was often loosely conceived and superficial and usually implied light entertainment about subjects that—compared to the history of politics—were considered marginally significant (Zeldin, 1976: 238). The approach culminated in G. M. Trevelyan's *English Social History* (London, 1944), which defined *social history* simply as "history with the politics left out." In German this form of popularization was called *Kulturgeschichte*, or *Sittengeschichte* (the "history of mores," after Voltaire's *Essai sur les moeurs* [1756]—see also CULTURAL HISTORY; POPULAR HISTORY). In the early-twentieth-century United States it was frequently teamed with INTELLECTUAL HISTORY to become "social and intellectual history," an outgrowth of the NEW HISTORY of James Harvey Robinson, Frederick Jackson Turner, Charles A. Beard, and others (cf. Brinton, [1930] 1961: 2–3); this was in some ways a forerunner of the notion of the "social history of ideas" that emerged in the 1960s.

Third, *social history* was used in tandem with ECONOMIC HISTORY to mean "social and economic history," with an emphasis on the evolution of systems of production and distribution (e.g., Pirenne, 1936; Dopsch, [1918] 1937). This idea arose in the late nineteenth century, partially due to the slowly spreading influence of Marxian HISTORICAL MATERIALISM but, more generally, simply as the result of a growing appreciation of industrialization (see INDUSTRIAL REVOLUTION) and its social impact—especially for the division of labor and the dynamics of social stratification. In this context, social "classes" were defined in terms of the economic function of their members in the productive system (see CLASS). A turn-of-the-century scholar summarized the essence of this approach in the following terms:

> the conception of history has been broadened until it is now well recognized that political history is only one phase of that wider activity which includes all the phenomena of social life. . . . it is now conceded that the history of mankind is the history of man in society, and therefore social history in its broadest sense. (Seligman, 1907: 2)

This "socioeconomic" tradition is more important than any other for understanding concepts of social history that have developed since the 1950s (Hobsbawm, 1972: 2; Zeldin, 1976: 238).

Particularly important for the emergence of present views is the work of the French "*Annales* school," which evolved after the founding of the journal *Annales d'histoire économique et sociale* in 1929 by Lucien Febvre and Marc Bloch (Stoianovich, 1976; Ricoeur, 1980; also INTERDISCIPLINARY HISTORY). Febvre, Bloch, and their disciples sought to create a comprehensive, "total" history, one that delved beneath traditional "event history"—*histoire événementielle*, that is, the history of discrete political events—and identified allegedly more profound, "structural" layers of reality (Ricoeur, 1980: 10–11; also PROCESS). Febvre and Bloch favored *social* as an adjective for their brand of history just because it was so imprecise: "They wanted to show that the object of their study was the whole of life" (Zeldin, 1976: 240). As demonstrated particularly in the work of Fernand Braudel ([1949] 1975), the *Annales* goal was ecological history: "All aspects of life—from climate to topography to architecture, from popular culture to capitalist values to high art—were sketched in to create a comprehensive multidimensional cubist portrait of the society" (Henretta, 1979: 1297). Here, social history was vastly more than "history with the politics left out." Politics, while not ignored, was treated as a social phenomenon, like other aspects of life, and regarded as one among many levels of historical reality, often the most superficial. This ideal of "holistically" studying past life in the entirety of its relationships is a key feature of contemporary understandings of social history (Hexter, 1972: 523, 537–38; Henretta, 1979: 1297; Stearns, 1967: 4).

In France historians continue to refine the comprehensive *Annales* approach, with particular emphasis on historical demography and the use of QUANTIFI-CATION. In Britain social history since the 1950s has been strongly conditioned by Marxian HISTORICAL MATERIALISM and has focused more on specific social groups and institutions (the family, the revolutionary "crowd," laboring classes, religious sects, and so on) than on the broad studies of space and time that the French have favored (Henretta, 1979: 1296). In West Germany the prime focus has been the sociological analysis of politics (*politische Sozialgeschichte*), based on a combination of Marx's ideas and those of the pioneer sociologist Max Weber (see IDEAL TYPE) (Kocka, 1977: 9–47; 1980: 434).

In the United States the lack of a strong tradition of SOCIALISM works against the growth of an explicitly Marxist historiography (Henretta, 1979: 1306). We-ber's influence is strong, but the range of American approaches to social history is much wider and more diffuse than in France, Britain, or West Germany; there is no clearly identifiable Braudelian, Marxian, or Weberian theoretical consensus. To some extent the popularity of social history has been attributable to fashion, generational tension within the profession, and political engagement; in many cases, the word *social* is used as a mere slogan by the self-consciously anti-traditional (Zeldin, 1976: 237). It is impossible to generalize about any one dominant approach or focus. *Social history* is an umbrella label that covers many varieties of method, perspective, time frame, and subject. What ties everything together is a prime concern with human *groups* and *group behavior* in the past and, more generally, the explicit use of social theory. The main American contribution has been a taste for novelty and the extension of sociological inquiry into a very wide range of diverse topics (Stearns, 1980: 220–221). Within this context one notes the development of subfields such as the history of the family, crime, sexuality, leisure, women, ethnic minorities, urbanization, and so on. A key theme—though by no means universal—has been the effort to construct history "from the bottom up" by accounts of the daily lives, viewpoints, and experiences of "ordinary" people, rather than through the eyes of social elites (pp. 205, 212; Henretta, 1979: 1309; Kocka, 1980: 445).

Wherever it is practiced today, social history typically breaks with the convention that historians should avoid generalizations and the self-conscious use of theory (Kocka, 1980: 456). Contemporary social history puts less stress than traditional history on the study of unique events and personalities and more emphasis on general social relationships and problems. To this extent it is strongly influenced by the idea of SOCIAL SCIENTIFIC HISTORY and borrows freely from disciplines such as sociology and anthropology.

References

Braudel, Fernand. [1949] 1975. *The Mediterranean and the Mediterranean World in the Age of Phillip II*. New York. This book is the classic expression of the *Annales* idea of "total" history.
Brinton, Crane. [1930] 1961. *The Jacobins: An Essay in the New History*. New York.

Brinton asserts that "Our new social history must . . . never lose sight of its ultimate goal, the discovery of generalizations which will have as much as possible the force of scientific laws. . . . To save social history from mere rambling among details some specific problem must be set" (pp. 2–3).

Conze, Werner. 1967. "Social History." *Journal of Social History* 1 (Fall 1967): 7–16.

Darnton, Robert. 1980. "Intellectual and Cultural History." In Kammen: 327–54. See especially the analysis of the growth of social history in American research and teaching from the late 1940s to the late 1970s.

Dopsch, Alfons. [1918] 1937. *The Economic and Social Foundations of Medieval Civilization.* London.

Henretta, James A. 1979. "Social History as Lived and Written." *AHR* 84: 1293–1322. This is a concise review of the *Annales* school and British social history and their effect on work in the United States.

Hexter, J. H. 1972. "Fernand Braudel and the *Monde Braudellien . . .*" *JMH* 44: 480–539.

Hobsbawm, E. J. 1972. "From Social History to the History of Society." In Gilbert and Graubard: 1–26. A British Marxist, Hobsbawm expresses a view that is especially unsettling to traditionalists: the "artisan technique of older historians is plainly inadequate" for many topics in social history that "require cooperative teamwork and the utilization of modern technical equipment" (p. 16).

Kocka, Jürgen. 1977. *Sozialgeschichte: Begriff—Entwicklung—Probleme.* Göttingen. This book is particularly important for its bibliography in the footnote citations. It reflects the self-conscious sense of West German historians about their own "backwardness" in the field of social history (e.g., p. 50).

———. 1980. "Theory and Social History: Recent Developments in West Germany." *Social Research* 47: 426–57. This is a good survey of West German understandings of the term—essentially a shortened English version of the author's *Sozialgeschichte*, cited above. It discriminates between three kinds of West German social history: *political social history*, in which politics are explained in terms of social and economic factors; *social-scientific history*, which focuses on "social classes and social groups, work, urbanization," and so on; and *history of society* (*Gesellschaftsgeschichte*), which "refers to attempts to write the history of a complex system like a whole society during a specific period" (p. 448).

Pirenne, Henri. 1936. *Economic and Social History of Medieval Europe.* London.

Ricoeur, Paul. 1980. *The Contribution of French Historiography to the Theory of History.* Oxford.

Seligman, Edwin R. A. 1907. *The Economic Interpretation of History.* New York.

Stearns, Peter N. 1967. "Some Comments on Social History." *Journal of Social History* 1: 3–6.

———. 1980. "Toward a Wider Vision: Trends in Social History." In Kammen: 205–30. This piece includes much bibliography on the United States. Stearns notes that the "field's charm is its enthusiasm for novelty and . . . its rawness" (p. 208).

Stoianovich, Traian. 1976. *French Historical Method: The Annales Paradigm.* Ithaca, N.Y.

Walsh, W. H. [1962–63] 1969. "Historical Causation." In Nash: 234–52.

Zeldin, Theodore. 1976. "Social History and Total History." *Journal of Social History* 10: 237–45. This article contains many fresh insights.

Sources of Additional Information

Since social historians tend to be self-consciously reflective about their work, there is already a large body of literature. For bibliography see especially the footnote citations in Henretta (1979), Kocka (1977; 1980), and Stearns (1980); also "Social History," *IESS* 6: 455–62. Several sections of Berding are pertinent. For an excellent, concise bibliography see Geoff Eley, "Some Recent Tendencies in Social History," in Iggers and Parker: 55–70. Review articles on developments in Italy, West Germany, Eastern Europe, Britain, France, and elsewhere are contained in a special issue of *Social Research* 47 (Autumn 1980), "Theory and Social History." The *Journal of Social History* 10 (Winter 1976) is also devoted to social history; see especially Richard T. Vann's "Rhetoric of Social History," pp. 221–36. Along similar lines see Alfred Cobban's seminal "Vocabulary of Social History," *Political Science Quarterly* 71 (1956): 1–17. Georg G. Iggers, *New Directions in European Historiography* (Middletown, Conn., 1975), is very useful, as is Gordon Leff, *History and Social Theory* (Garden City, N.Y., 1971). Since the late 1950s a number of specialized journals have been founded; in the United States the most important are *CSSH*, the *Journal of Social History*, and the *Journal of Interdisciplinary History*. In France the name of Bloch and Febvre's journal has been changed to *Annales: Économies, Sociétés, Civilisations*. The most important journal in England is *Past and Present*; in West Germany the major vehicle is *Geschichte und Gesellschaft*. In opposition to the long-standing aversion to sociology in the historical profession, Peter Burke's *Sociology and History* (London, 1980) discusses ways the two disciplines can contribute to one another. For additional reading on the late-eighteenth- and early-nineteenth-century separation of the concepts of "state" and "society," see Kocka (1977: 51–59); also two articles by Manfred Riedl: "Gesellschaft, bürgerliche," *GG* 2 (1975): 719–800, and "Gesellschaft, Gemeinschaft," *GG* 2 (1975): 801–62. On the *Annales* school see the entire issue of *JMH* 44 (1972). There is a critique of the *Annales* approach in Alan Bullock, *Is History Becoming a Social Science? The Case of Contemporary History* (Cambridge, 1976). For women's history see Lois W. Banner, "On Writing Women's History," *Journal of Interdisciplinary History* 2 (1972): 347–58, and Frederickson in Kammen (1980): 470–71. Urban history is discussed in John B. Sharpless and Sam Bass Warner, Jr., "Urban History," *American Behavioral Scientist* 21 (1977): 221–44, and William H. Hubbard, "Politics and Society in the Central European City: Graz, Austria, 1861–1918," *Canadian Journal of History* 5 (1970): 25–45; also in the same issue, Gordon A. Craig, "The City and the Historian," pp. 47–55. On historical demography see Richard T. Vann, "History and Demography," *HT Beih.* 9 (1969): 64–78; Monte D. Wright, "Demography for Historians," *Rocky Mountain Social Science Journal* 7 (1970): 1–10; T. H. Hollingsworth, *Historical Demography* (Ithaca, N.Y., 1969); and Allan N. Sharlin, "Historical Demography as History and Demography," *American Behavioral Scientist* 21 (1977): 245–62. Examples of the idea of "history from the bottom up" include Jesse Lemisch, "The American Revolution Seen from the Bottom Up," in Barton Bernstein, ed., *Towards a New Past: Dissenting Essays in American History* (New York, 1968): 3–45; Herbert G. Gutman, *Work, Culture, and Society in Industrializing America: Essays in American Working Class and Social History* (New York, 1976); and Gutman's *Black Family in Slavery and Freedom, 1750–1925* (New York, 1976).

SOCIAL SCIENTIFIC HISTORY. Historical scholarship based on the explicit use of general social theory (drawn especially from sociology, psychology, economics, political science, and anthropology), which seeks to identify regularities of social development and emphasizes systematic comparison of past events and situations. It may also involve the belief that the aims and methods of historical inquiry are (or should be) essentially similar to those of natural science.

The idea of social scientific history was born in the early nineteenth century and has had an uneven development in both Europe and America; since 1945 it has grown in popularity. The opinion that "History and the social sciences in the United States mutually divorced each other in the period after World War II" (Gustavson, 1976: 338) is certainly incorrect; the growing number of historical monographs informed by social science theory and the appearance of new journals dedicated to interdisciplinary social research testifies to the fact that social scientific history is a "trend, not a fad" (Briggs, 1973: 556—see INTER-DISCIPLINARY HISTORY). Even scholars who are temperamentally opposed to the methods of social science occasionally speak of the "disputed, perhaps vanishing frontier between history and the social and behavioral sciences" (Curtis, 1970: 265). It should be recognized, however, that traditions linking history to social science frequently blur the nature of that relationship, and those who advocate a social scientific approach often seem "basically confused as to whether they [merely] wish to use social science, or be social scientists" (Danto, 1955: 501). It is widely held that social science, strictly speaking, is "interested in the establishment or testing of social, cultural, or psychological generalizations of universal validity" or in supplying "material for such establishment or testing in the form of a 'case study' " (Gruner, 1969: 285). Only a minority of current historians in the United States, England, or Germany would describe their aims in these terms. The differences between champions of social scientific history, in the purest sense, and those who advocate or accept a social scientifically oriented history, lies chiefly in the readiness of the latter to use social science theory as a guide to research but their unwillingness to accept the idea that history can become a "nomothetic" science—that is, one that seeks to discover general LAWS or norms (e.g., Hughes, 1960: 37; Bullock, 1976: 21).

The general concept of social science originated in the eighteenth century. It is based on a "monistic" or "unified" understanding of science that presumes that the empirical and quantitative methods of natural science provide a model for all human inquiry, including the study of social and ethical problems. The term *social physics* appeared as early as 1713 in George Berkeley's *De Motu* (Trompf, 1977: 117, n. 14); other terms such as *moral science* and *social art* were used in late-eighteenth-century France and England to convey the idea that social laws analogous to the laws of nature could be discovered and utilized to increase human happiness (Baker, 1964). The actual term *social science* (*science sociale*) originated in France during the French Revolution. Baker (pp. 215–18) suggests that it may first have been employed in a pamphlet of 1791 by Dominique-Joseph Garat and that it was an outgrowth of *art social*, an expression that meant the "art of maximizing the happiness of a nation" by extending the methods of natural science to the study and reform of society. Popularized in France by intellectual lights such as Condorcet (1743–94) and Destutt de Tracy (1754–1836) (see IDEOLOGY), it was introduced to America by an 1817 translation of Destutt de Tracy's works and to Britain in the 1820s—apparently via Spanish translations of the French term (pp. 223–26).

In the early and mid-nineteenth century various social philosophers—for example, Hegel, Comte, Marx, Spencer—constructed influential variations on the theme of a unified science of society; history was usually assumed to be one facet of this comprehensive science, a view reflected in the social criticism of Marx and Engels, as well as the historical research of H. T. Buckle (1821–62). This work was closely associated with the philosophical orientation known as POSITIVISM (see also HISTORICAL MATERIALISM). Simultaneously, however, history was being professionalized. Most of the new breed of academic historians, eager to assert the independence of their discipline vis-à-vis speculative and moral philosophy, rejected the idea that history was properly concerned with the discovery of general social laws. They identified their fledgling discipline with the study of particular events, with a strong emphasis on politics.

At the turn of the twentieth century the positivistic idea of a unified social science gave way to the more modest idea of a number of separate "social sciences" that differed widely in theory and parctice, and the modern academic disciplines of sociology, psychology, economics, anthropology, and political science took shape (Hughes, 1958). This gave rise to a revised conception of history and social science, based on the idea that history should be more comprehensive than the study of "past politics" and the belief that historians should make systematic use of the findings and concepts of the new disciplines. This attitude was exemplified in Germany by the work of Max Weber (known primarily as a sociologist, although he was vitally concerned with historical problems) and Karl Lamprecht (whose ideas were repudiated by the mainstream of the German historical profession); in France by Henri Berr, Lucien Febvre, and Marc Bloch (who laid the foundations of the "Annales School"); and in the United States by James Harvey Robinson and other advocates of the NEW HISTORY. As a result of these turn-of-the-century efforts, history is still often categorized in university curricula as a "social science." The new generation of scholars sacrificed some of the older confidence in the possibility of discovering general laws of social development, although this dream was by no means entirely rejected. They strongly retained a faith in the utilitarian value of research as a means to social reform and in the use of theory as a guide to inquiry. In the United States traditions established by the "new" social scientific orientation eventually led to controversial pleas for greater cooperation between history and social science, underwritten by the Social Science Research Council: *Theory and Practice in Historical Study* (1946); *The Social Sciences in Historical Study* (1954); and *Generalization in the Writing of History* (1963). Aside from programmatic statements and manifestoes, there were notable attempts to translate the idea of social science history into practice (e.g., Brinton, [1930] 1961; [1938] 1965). Following World War II some historians continued this tradition, emphasizing the importance of methodological self-consciousness and the need to delve beneath particular events in quest of general patterns which might be helpful for comparative, or even predictive, purposes (Landes and Tilly, 1971: 9–10; Cochran, [1954] 1972). With the refinement of statistical methods and the adaptation of computer technology to social analysis, there was a trend toward QUANTIFICATION, although this was not always regarded as an essential condition of social science history (Landes and Tilly, 1971: 10, 73). A few partisans in the 1960s, a period of significant revival for the concept, even displayed attitudes reminiscent of mid-nineteenth-century positivism, such as the idea that the modes of explanation in history and the natural sciences are identical (for instance, Fogel, 1966: 656) or the belief that social scientific inquiry might legitimately postulate laws of social development (Benson, 1966).

It should be noted, however, that social scientific history, even in the form of scholarship merely oriented toward social science, has often met with passionate opposition. In Germany the idea never gained a foothold until after 1945, when Marxism was established as the philosophical orthodoxy of the East German Democratic Republic and there was a strong West German revival of interest in Max Weber, as well as Marx. In France, birthplace of the social science concept, opposition has been much less strong; indeed, the social or "human sciences" approach (*sciences humaines*) has become the reigning orthodoxy, exemplified in the *Annales* approach of Bloch, Febvre, and their disciples Fernand Braudel and Emmanuel Le Roy La Durie (see INTERDISCIPLINARY HISTORY; SOCIAL HISTORY). In Britain and the United States there has been strong, often emotional opposition by champions of history as an autonomous "humanistic" discipline, properly concerned with unique, non-quantifiable phenomena as opposed to theory, generalization, and collective behavior (e.g., Barzun, 1974). Most typical, however, is a middle position that "history is *with* the social sciences but not really *of* them. History stands between the social sciences and the humanities" (Eisenstadt, 1966: 124–25; Shafer, 1960). In practice, this amounts to a cautious, eclectic pragmatism based on the use of methods and concepts associated with sociology, psychology, and so on, wherever they seem to be useful in handling specific historical problems.

References

Baker, K. M. 1964. "The Early History of the Term 'Social Science'." *Annals of Science* 20: 211–26. This article contains references to earlier studies of the history of the term.

Barzun, Jacques. 1974. *Clio and the Doctors: Psycho-History, Quanto-History, and History.* Chicago.

Benson, Lee. 1966. "Quantification, Scientific History, and Scholarly Innovation." *AHA Newsletter* 4 (June 1966): 11–16.

Briggs, Asa. 1973. "Doing the New History," *Journal of Interdisciplinary History* 3: 555–58.

Brinton, Crane. [1930] 1961. *The Jacobins: An Essay in the New History*. New York. This work is based on the belief that the "new social history must . . . never lose sight of its ultimate goal, the discovery of generalizations which will have as much as possible of the force of scientific laws" (p. 2).

————. [1938] 1965. *The Anatomy of Revolution*. New York.

Bullock, Alan. 1976. *Is History Becoming a Social Science? The Case of Contemporary History*. Cambridge. This is a sober and judicious assessment.

Cochran, Thomas C. [1954] 1972. "The Social Sciences and the Problem of Historical Synthesis." In Stern: 348–59. This piece is by a leading proponent of social scientific history.

Curtis, L. P., Jr. 1970. "Of Images and Imagination in History." In L. P. Curtis, Jr., *The Historian's Workshop: Original Essays by Sixteen Historians*. New York: 245–76.

Danto, Arthur C. 1955. Review of Social Science Research Council, *The Social Sciences in Historical Study, JP* 52 (Sept. 1): 500–502.

Eisenstadt, A. S., ed. 1966. *The Craft of American History: Selected Essays* 2. New York.

Fogel, R. W. 1966. "The New Economic History." *The Economic History Review*, 2d Series, 19: 642–56.

Gruner, Rolf. 1969. "Mandelbaum on Historical Narrative." *HT* 8: 283–87.

Gustavson, Carl G. 1976. *The Mansion of History*. New York.

Hughes, H. Stuart. 1958. *Consciousness and Society: The Reorientation of European Social Thought, 1890–1930*. New York.

————. 1960. "The Historian and the Social Scientist." *AHR* 66: 20–46. Sympathetic to social scientific history, this article is one of the most balanced introductions to the topic. Hughes maintains that historians widely use social science concepts without acknowledging them—even to themselves: "In many cases . . . [the historian] does not really 'apply' them at all. He lets them remain in the back of his mind, without bringing them explicitly into the foreground of his historical writing. He does not parade his knowledge of social science theory: he simply permits his thought to be informed by it. . . . A process of this kind subtly alters the character of a historian's work in ways that even the writer himself may be unaware of" (pp. 33–34).

Landes, David S., and Tilly, Charles, eds. 1971. *History as Social Science*. New York. This book is essential reading by two leading advocates. It contains results of an opinion survey of U.S. historians on the question of social scientific history.

Shafer, Boyd C. 1960. "History, Not Art, Not Science, But History: Meanings and Uses of History." *Pacific Historical Review* 29: 159–70.

Trompf, G. W. 1977. "Social Science in Historical Perspective." *Philosophy of the Social Sciences* 7: 113–38. This article is important, particularly for the history of the idea of social science in the nineteenth century.

Sources of Additional Information

See especially SCIENTIFIC HISTORY; also COMPARATIVE HISTORY; HISTORICAL MATERI-ALISM; INTERDISCIPLINARY HISTORY; LAWS; POSITIVISM; SOCIAL HISTORY. The literature, much of it polemical, is vast. See *HT Beih.*; Stephens; Birkos and Tambs. For general bibliography several sections of Berding are directly relevant. The bibliographies in Bull. 54 and Louis Gottschalk, ed., *Generalization in the Writing of History* (Chicago, 1963), are very important. Ronald P. Formisano, "History and the Social Sciences: A Review Essay," *Historical Methods Newsletter* 4 (1971): 84–87, is a critical survey. An important anthology, containing samples of social scientific history as well as theoretical articles, is Edward N. Saveth, ed., *American History and the Social Sciences* (New York, 1964). On the debate in the United States see especially John Higham et al., *History* (Englewood Cliffs, N.J., 1965), particularly pp. 106–44. See also Charles Tilly, "In Defense of Jargon," *Canadian Historical Association, Annual Report* (1966): 178–86, and Robert William Fogel and G. R. Elton, *Which Road to the Past? Two Views of History* (New Haven, Conn., 1983). The entire issue of the periodical *American Behavioral Scientist* 21 (Nov.-Dec. 1977) is devoted to the theme of history and the social sciences. On France see Traian Stoianovich, *French Historical Method: The Annales Paradigm* (Ithaca, N.Y., 1976); Charles Morazé, "The Application of the Social Sciences to History," *Journal of Contemporary History* 3 (1968): 207–15; and chapter two of Georg G. Iggers, *New Directions in European Historiography* (Middletown, Conn., 1975). Among the journals that encourage a social scientific approach are *Social Science History, CSSH,* and the *Journal of Interdisciplinary History.*

SOCIALISM. A doctrine of social reform that stresses cooperation and the rationalized, public management of economic life and generally seeks to further the interests of the working class. The general term embraces a broad variety of more specific programs—for example, democratic socialism, communism, anarchism.

Like other major social creeds of the past two centuries (e.g., LIBERALISM, FASCISM, NATIONALISM), socialism has exercised an important influence on the writing of history. Cole (1967: 468) notes that the term has carried various meanings throughout the years but identifies three basic features that most forms share: (1) the belief that any society founded on large-scale private ownership is unjust; (2) the conviction that a more equitable form of society can be established, one that will contribute to the moral and material improvement of humankind; and (3) the idea that social revolution is imperative (although the specific means for achieving the transformation are widely disputed; *revolution* may imply either violence or gradual [but thoroughgoing] reform). The extent to which the new society will be democratic and egalitarian is a matter of debate, but—theoretically, at least—socialists have usually been on the side of democracy and legal equality (cf. Lichtheim, 1969: 5–6); radical economic egalitarianism, in which each person would have exactly as much as everyone else, is not a necessary requirement.

The word's etymology has been extensively researched (Bestor, 1948; Bertier de Sauvigny, 1970). It first appeared in Italy, where Ferdinando Facchinei used *socialist* in his 1765 commentary on Beccaria's *On Crime and Punishment* to designate admirers of Rousseau's social contract theory. In 1785 Appiano Buonafede employed *socialismo* to specify the notion that sociability is a natural human condition (Bertier de Sauvigny, 1970: 161).

This early Italian usage—although remotely related to current meaning—bears slight resemblance to our primary understanding of the term today, that is, an inclusive label for doctrines of progressive economic and social reform. The crucial period in the term's evolution occurred in England and France between 1825 and 1840 (Bestor, 1948: 290; Lichtheim, 1969: 6). As labels for reformism, *socialist* and *socialism* were first introduced by British followers of Robert Owen in the 1820s and for some time were employed narrowly to refer specifically to Owen's ideas. The earliest-known written use of *socialist* in this spirit appears in an 1822 letter from Edward Cooper to Owen, although it is clear from the context that the term was already in spoken use among the Owenites (Bertier de Sauvigny, 1970: 163). Thereafter, the word occasionally reappears in Owenite discourse—for example, in the *Co-operative Magazine* in 1827 (which Bestor [1948: 277] cites as the first Owenite use of the term in print). By 1833 the Owenites may be said to have adopted both "socialist" and "socialism," even though Owen himself continued to use other terms to designate his ideas until 1837 (Bertier de Sauvigny, 1970: 163–64).

Socialisme did not appear in French—at least not in print—until 1831, when the Protestant journal *Le Semeur* used it in a positive sense to stand for the overcoming of "individualism" (p. 162). Here, as in other French usage of the early 1830s, the meaning is very ill defined. The term was gradually rendered more precise, especially after contacts were established between the Owenites and disciples of the French social theorist Fourier (1772–1837) (p. 163). According to Bestor (1948: 278) *Sozialist* and *sozialistisch* appeared in German in 1840 and *Sozialismus* in 1842.

By about 1840, in France as elsewhere, *socialism* was commonly understood to refer to a variety of doctrines that criticized existing property relations and advocated a transformation of economic life along egalitarian lines (Lakoff, 1973: 289). It was typically used in juxtaposition to another neologism—*individualism*—which appeared in France in 1827 and in England in 1840 as a label for the cult of self-interest associated with the ideas of Adam Smith, Malthus, Ricardo, and Bentham and immediately became the "standard antonym" to *socialism* (Bestor, 1948: 282; Lakoff, 1973: 289). Writing in 1847 Pierre Leroux, a sometime follower of Henri de Saint-Simon, asserted: "For the past several years it has been normal to refer as 'socialists' to all those thinkers who are interested in social reform, all those who criticize and disapprove of individualism" (cited in Bertier de Sauvigny, 1970: 163).

Still, the close association with Owenism persisted to the end of the 1840s. This is suggested by Friedrich Engels' testimony that he and Marx called their famous tract of 1848 the "communist" rather than the "socialist" manifesto because socialism was too closely linked to the ideas of Owen, Fourier, and middle-class reformism (Bestor, 1948: 291).

As for *communism* and *communist*, these terms derived from the French *commun* (the common, the generality). *Communiste* appeared among the Parisian secret societies that opposed the July Monarchy (1830–48) and began to attract working-class membership in the late 1830s; it first occurred in print in 1840 in

Étienne Cabet's article "Le démocrate devenu communiste, malgré lui." In the same year the word was introduced to English readers by the Owenite John Goodwyn Barmby in Owen's *New Moral World*, where Barmby used both *communist* and *communism*. As early as 1841 the London *Times* used both words; in America Emerson employed them in 1844. The terms appeared in German in 1842 (Bestor, 1948: 279–81).

Due to its Owenite associations, *socialism* increasingly acquired connotations of moderation and gradualism after 1840, whereas the newer term *communism*— at least on the continent—assumed more militant overtones of revolutionary, working-class opposition to the established order (p. 291; Lichtheim, 1969: 7). This did not always apply in Britain and America, however, where *communism* was embraced in the mid-nineteenth century by a number of non-violent religious groups (Bestor, 1948: 292).

From about 1850 forward *socialism* gradually lost its specific ties to Owenism and evolved into the inclusive term for progressive social reform, embracing communism. Already in the late 1840s, Fourierists and others in France (e.g., the anarchist Proudhon) were using the word to denote their doctrines; the expression *Christian socialist* appeared in English at least as early as 1850 (p. 293). After the mid–1860s *socialism* was adopted by groups as diverse as followers of the American religious reformer John Humphrey Noyes and the Marxists— who, under Engels' lead, began to style themselves "scientific socialists" rather than communists in the 1870s. As Bestor (p. 294) notes, "By 1888 Engels was actually finding it necessary to explain why he and Marx had called their 1848 document a Communist, rather than a Socialist, Manifesto." By now *communism* was restricted to the idea of community property and had largely lost its earlier connotations of revolutionary militancy (pp. 294–95).

These revolutionary connotations were revived in March 1918 when, following the Soviet Revolution, Lenin's Bolshevik faction changed its name from the Russian Social-Democratic Labor Party to the Russian Communist Party. The Soviets' purpose was to evoke the militant associations of the 1848 *Communist Manifesto*, in opposition to the idea of gradualism. As a result of the Soviet Party's leading role in furthering twentieth-century revolution, *communism* has regained the revolutionary connotations it lost in the late nineteenth century (p. 300). Soviet discourse nevertheless agrees with western usage in recognizing *socialism* as the more inclusive term; the Soviet Union is officially the "Union of Soviet *Socialist* Republics," and Soviet communism is considered one of many possible varieties of socialism, albeit the most "scientific" form (pp. 300–301).

Literature on the origins of *socialism* as a concept, as opposed to the history of the word itself, falls into two broad categories. One school, approaching the problem from the standpoint of the history of great ideas (see INTELLECTUAL HISTORY), pushes the doctrine's beginnings back to antiquity and defines *socialism* in its simplest form as of the timeless "belief that all producers ought to share equally in the fruits of combined labor" (Lakoff, 1973: 284; Gray,

1946). This scholarship stresses the heritage of Hellenic philosophy and myth, Judaic tradition, Christian charity and monasticism, Reformation millenarianism, and so on in the belief that socialism is a modern variant of the age-old western egalitarian tradition.

In contrast, the more important authors (e.g., Lichtheim, 1969: vii, 5; 1970: 3–4; Cole, 1967), while acknowledging some justification for this sweeping approach, deemphasize pre-modern egalitarian traditions and stress developments since the late eighteenth century. They view socialism as a very modern idea, one comprehensible only in the specific historical context of eighteenth-century ENLIGHTENMENT social theory, the sociopolitical legacy of the French Revolution, and the unprecedented conditions created by the early INDUSTRIAL REVOLUTION.

From this standpoint the advent of industrialization represents a particularly crucial watershed, since it introduced entirely new possibilities of wealth creation that made material well-being for all people a distinct possibility, rather than the fantasy that it had always necessarily been in the past. Once the enormous productive powers unleashed by industrialization were recognized, it was only natural that some moralists would argue that the new affluence should be made available to all (Lichtheim, 1969: 10); it was equally natural that economic egalitarianism would attract, for the first time, a mass following.

It should be stressed that the growth of socialist theory cannot be separated from the history of *laissez-faire* doctrine, since the economic individualism of Smith, Malthus, and others, which became the reigning social philosophy in the early nineteenth century, served as a foil for socialist thought; socialism crystallized as a repudiation of free enterprise LIBERALISM.

In the second approach, the story typically begins with a discussion of reformist thought on the eve of the French revolution (e.g., Rousseau, Mably, Morelly), and the key founders of socialism are identified as Henri de Saint-Simon, Robert Owen, Charles Fourier, and the German team of Marx and Engels. The central figures are those who—following Saint-Simon—grasped the significance of industrialization and concluded that modern industry might become the basis of equity and material well-being for all. Although variations on the socialist theme proliferated in the years immediately before 1848, two broad orientations may be identified (Cole, 1967: 469; Lichtheim, 1969: 5; Lakoff, 1973: 285). The first approach, associated with Owen in England and Fourier in France, made the small, cooperative community the focus of efforts to reform society. This assumed that socialism would be built by rational persuasion and example; the world would be converted to socialism through the proselytizing efforts of people of goodwill. The second view—identified with Saint-Simon and later Marx and Engels—regarded socialism as the outgrowth of a logic of historical development, apart from the efforts of well-meaning individuals and groups. Lakoff (1973: 285) calls this the "distinction between socialism as a theory of the planned community and socialism as the outcome of an historically determined revolution." In Marxism the logic of development was understood to be inseparably

tied to the evolution of systems of economic production (see HISTORICAL MA-
TERIALISM). In a famous tract of 1883, Engels labeled the first of these approaches
"utopian" and the second "scientific." For the Marxists, the term *scientific*
implied

> the proving, by logical argument and study of history, of two quite simple prop-
> ositions: first, that under the existing capitalist system, the proletariat, the laboring
> class, is systematically and continuously robbed of its just share of the fruits of
> production; second, that "changes in the modes of production and exchange," and
> not any other factor, such as "man's insight into eternal truth and justice" are
> leading inevitably to a reversal of the system that will remove the bourgeois
> capitalist class from the seats of power and replace it by the organs of the proletariat.
> (Cole, 1967: 470)

Non-Marxists, however, are apt to regard Marxism as decidedly "utopian" in
its own way, usually on the grounds that it is founded on a non-empirical theory
of social development (for example, Lakoff, 1973: 290).

Marxism is nevertheless recognized as the "classical formulation" of socialism
(Lichtheim, 1969: 10), a fusion of earlier French and English ideas achieved
through the synthesizing power of German philosophy. From the 1870s onward
the popularizing efforts of Engels made Marxism a touchstone of sorts for socialist
movements in all countries, one that provided a philosophical rallying point for
the Second Socialist International founded in 1889. One must say a touchstone
"of sorts" because heated disputes over the meaning of Marx's legacy divided
Marxists themselves, giving rise to the doctrines of "revisionism," "social
democracy," and "bolshevism" (Nettl, 1973).

As far as historiography is concerned, from the 1890s onward, but especially
after World War I (Barraclough, 1979: 20), Marxian socialism began to exert a
significant influence on serious scholarship. This was reflected in works that
were either avowedly Marxist or in non-Marxist studies informed by the categories of Marxist analysis. Studies of the former type might be couched in
reserved terms of a socialist perspective on some past event—a classic example
is Jean Jaurès' famous *Socialist History of the French Revolution* (Jaurès, [1901–
9] 1972: 158), written from the angle of one among several possible "general
conception[s] of life and society"—or from the militant standpoint that Marxism
constitutes the only scientific framework for historical analysis, one that transforms history into a weapon of political combat (for example, Pokrovsky, [1931]
1972). Today, Marx's and Engels' doctrine of HISTORICAL MATERIALISM underpins the entire historical cast of mind in the Soviet Union and other communist
countries (Iggers and Parker, 1979: 277–79) and also among western Marxists.

Equally important is Marxism's impact on non-Marxist scholarship. Marxist
or Marxian-influenced ideas of IDEOLOGY and ALIENATION, as well as many of
the general premises of historical materialism, are pervasive in west European
and North American scholarship today, usually as implicit assumptions rather
than explicit concepts. The current orthodoxy in scholarship on modern Germany,

for example (both in Europe and the United States), is based on a combination of the ideas of Marx and the non-Marxist sociologist Max Weber (Iggers, 1975: 80–122). Generally speaking, the genres of RADICAL HISTORY and SOCIAL HISTORY have been strongly influenced by the Marxist idea of social liberation (cf. Iggers, 1975: especially 123–74).

References

Barraclough, Geoffrey. 1979. *Main Trends in History*. New York. This book includes a section on "Marxism and Marxist history," pp. 17–28.
Bertier de Sauvigny, G. de. 1970. "Liberalism, Nationalism, and Socialism: The Birth of Three Words." *The Review of Politics* 32: 147–66. This brief review of French and Italian scholarship updates Bestor (1948) in some respects.
Bestor, Arthur E., Jr. 1948. "The Evolution of the Socialist Vocabulary." *JHI* 9: 259–302. This basic work is expecially important for its bibliographical information in footnote citations.
Cole, Margaret. 1967. "Socialism." *EP* 7: 467–70. This piece is brief but useful and has a short bibliography.
Gray, Alexander. 1946. *The Socialist Tradition—Moses to Lenin*. London.
Iggers, Georg G. 1975. *New Directions in European Historiography*. Middletown, Conn.
Iggers, Georg G., and Parker, Harold T. eds. 1979. *International Handbook of Historical Studies: Contemporary Research and Theory*. Westport, Conn.
Jaurès, Jean. [1901–09] 1972. "Critical Introduction to *The Socialist History of the French Revolution*." In Stern: 158–64.
Lakoff, Sanford A. 1973. "Socialism from Antiquity to Marx." *DHI* 4: 284–94. This piece has a good bibliography. It stresses the "quasi-religious character of Marxian socialism" as an extension of Hegel's "radical Christian theology" (p. 290).
Lichtheim George. 1969. *The Origins of Socialism*. New York. There is a rich bibliography in the endnotes.
———. 1970. *A Short History of Socialism*. New York. This book has a helpful reading list. In English, Lichtheim has written most perceptively on the subject. His work is often strongly opinionated and sympathetic to socialism.
Nettl, J. P. 1973. "Social Democracy in Germany and Revisionism." *DHI* 4: 263–76. This entry includes an excellent bibliography.
Pokrovsky, M. N. [1931] 1972. "The Tasks of Marxist Historical Science in the Reconstruction Period." In Stern: 335–41.

Sources of Additional Information

See ALIENATION; HISTORICAL MATERIALISM; DIALECTIC; RADICAL HISTORY. For further information on the history of the term *socialism* consult the German titles cited in Bestor (1948), n. 95. A comprehensive bibliographical source is G. D. H. Cole, *History of Socialist Thought*, 7 vols. (London, 1953–1960). On Marxism see the "Note on Sources" in George Lichtheim, *Marxism: An Historical and Critical Study* (2d ed., New York, 1965), pp. ix-xi. An invaluable source of substantive and bibliographical information on a wide range of subjects, including historiography, is *MCWS*. For current Soviet positions consult *The Great Soviet Encyclopedia*. On Marxist historiography in the Soviet Union and other socialist nations—including the People's Republic of China—see the section "The Socialist Countries" in Iggers and Parker: 277–363.

SOURCE. See EVIDENCE.

STYLE. A historian's characteristic mode of expression; the way he makes use of language and poetic conventions.

The word *style* is widely used but seldom well defined by historians; "it would seem that style is something historians try hard to have," writes Richard Vann (1976: 226), "but would rather not talk about." The word's meaning-range has been extended in recent years, paralleling developments in literary criticism, linguistics, and poetics (Struever, 1979: 139). There appears to be no firm consensus regarding when, precisely, the term should be used: *style*, *rhetoric*, and *form* are often used in vague, synonymous, or overlapping ways.

The term is often invoked in exhortations or asides, as though its meaning were self-evident. Most commonly, it is used in the narrow sense of the "well-turned phrase or striking illustration" (Bogue, 1968: 23) or "lucidity and grace of writing" (Woodward, 1968: 24)—the understanding informally conveyed by the casual notion of "good style." One tradition assumes that style is the consciously contrived manipulation of words, desirable perhaps, but peripheral to history and separable from its underlying cognitive purpose. This assumption underpins the belief that a "book which claims to be a work of science rather than a work of art can plead for a gentle judgment of its diction and presentation" (Niebuhr, [1811–12] 1972: 49), as well as the notion that "the historians' tradition of casting their conclusions in the form of narratives is a stumbling block to the achievement of their goals" (Goldstein, 1967: 40). This ancient distinction between *style* and *argument*—"*how* an historian says something" as opposed to "*what* he says"—is reflected in the traditional rhetorical terms *elocutio* and *disputatio* (Struever, 1980: 66–67). In his essay "The Way to Write History," Lucian of Samosata (c. 125–c. 180) discussed style in terms of lucidity, elevated diction, color, phrasing, and rhythm, representing it as "adornment" or "ornament" added consciously, after the historian has collected and organized his facts (1905: 130–31). G. M. Trevelyan ([1913] 1972) reaffirmed this view when he exalted a "limpid style . . . the easy flowing connection of sentence with sentence and paragraph with paragraph" and maintained that "in the case of history, all this artistic work is superimposed on the labours of scholarship" (p. 240). This "neo-classical," ornamental concept of style is still widely shared (for example, Elton, 1967: 109, 115–16; Schoenwald, 1979: 77), although Lionel Gossman (1978: 39) notes that it is "remote from the modern [imaginative] writer's conception of his art."

There is an old tradition that style—even if ornamental—is important to history, stemming from the classical idea that history is a branch of rhetoric and the historian is a "man of letters." Lucian (1905: 126) expected his "perfect historian" to display two basic qualities: "political insight" and the "faculty of expression,'' the first innate, the latter "acquired by long practice, unremitting toil, and loving study of the classics." This attitude—reinforced during the RENAISSANCE (Struever, 1970)—persists in an informal way among working historians today, particularly in English-speaking countries, where historical studies were professionalized late in comparison to Germany and France. It should be noted that there were occasional attempts in the nineteenth and early twentieth centuries to deal in a more formal analytical way with the aesthetic and poetic dimensions of historiography (Droysen, [1858] 1882; Croce, [1919] 1960). Such efforts, however, held little interest for the great majority of historians. The informal but self-conscious "gentleman's" approach to style is reflected in the work of famous British historians such as Gibbon—still regularly praised for his literary prowess—Thomas Carlyle, George Babbington Macaulay, and Trevelyan, and, in twentieth-century America, Allan Nevins and Samuel Eliot Morison. However, the literary approach to history was strongly challenged at the end of the nineteenth century in the name of SCIENTIFIC HISTORY (e.g., Turner, [1891] 1972: 198–99; Bury, [1902] 1972: 210–11) and partially discredited on the grounds that the quest for "good style" might lure the scholar away from the quest for truth (Wedgwood, 1960: 71). Even Trevelyan, who fought mightily to defend style in history, believed that "there is an undoubted temptation to the [historian-]artist to neglect . . . small, inconvenient pieces of truth" ([1913] 1972: 241).

Since the 1930s a few historians, inspired in part by movements in literary criticism and philosophy, have developed an analytical interest in historiography as a kind of NARRATIVE discourse, and some have attempted to go beyond the neo-classical concept of style. The "dated" idea of style as "decoration" (Gay, 1974: 189) was renounced as early as the 1930s by Carl Becker (1932: 233–34) in favor of the belief that the ways historians use language cannot be separated from what they say. The idea has been expressesd and extended more recently in various ways, for example, John Higham's assertion (1965: 141) that

> Whereas academic historians traditionally considered "style" as an icing on the cake of scholarship . . . many now realize that style as an external application is inevitably artificial; for any authentic craft blends manner and matter, form and substance, in a single creative process. (cf. Hexter, 1967: 11; Gay, 1974: 189)

Hayden White (1973) and Peter Gay (1974) have made the most noteworthy attempts to extend the idea of style in history. Gay (1974: 3), inspired by Buffon's eighteenth-century remark that *le style est l'homme meme*, maintains that style is both "form and content" and that "manner is indissolubly linked to matter." Gay's position is really a partial revision of neo-classical tradition rather than a radical departure. While rejecting the idea that style and content are easily separable categories, he continues to view style primarily as the deliberate art of adroitly manipulating words, that is, "the management of sentences, the use of rhetorical devices, the rhythm of narration" (p. 7). Style for Gay is still basically "literary style," something exercised primarily on the conscious level—although he does mention "emotional" and "professional" style in passing and suggests the possibility of a much broader and complex concept when he says that *style* ultimately refers to "style of thinking," that is, "nothing less than the historian's total perception of the past, the constraints within which he works and the truths he is uniquely capable of grasping. . . . a historian's most fundamental and therefore least examined assumptions about the nature of the world, its ontological makeup" (p. 10).

White (1973), drawing on linguistic and poetic theory, seeks to define this broader, more diffuse notion of style. His *Metahistory* is the most challenging assertion to date of the centrality of style to the practice of history; indeed, he understands *style* as *prior* to content, since it is the historian's "style of language" that "constitutes the facts themselves" (Nelson, 1975: 90). For White, *style* designates the historian's total mode of conceptualization rather than his conscious manner of expression. He approaches the historical work as a "verbal structure in the form of a narrative prose discourse" (White, 1973: ix) and believes that historical writing must be subjected to "rhetorical analysis, so as to disclose the poetical understructure of what is meant to pass for a modest prose representation of reality" ([1975] 1978: 105). Here *style* operates on the conscious and, particularly, the unconscious level. It is the complex sum of a number of possible culturally and politically conditioned conceptual "strategies" (formal argument, emplotment, ideological implication, metaphorical "prefiguration") and expository "modes of articulation" (e.g., contextual, tragic, conservative) by virtue of which the historian gains "explanatory effect": "a specific combination of modes comprises . . . the historiographical 'style' of a particular historian or philosopher of history" (1973: x). The entire theory is founded on the assumption that there is a subliminal, "deep level of consciousness on which a historical thinker chooses conceptual strategies by which to explain or represent his data" (p. x).

References

Becker, Carl. 1932. "Everyman His Own Historian." *AHR* 37: 221–36.
Bogue, Allan G. 1968. "United States: The 'New' Political History." *Journal of Contemporary History* 3: 5–27.
Bury, J. B. [1902] 1972. "The Science of History." In Stern: 210–23.
Croce, Benedetto. [1919] 1960. *History: Its Theory and Practice*. New York.
Droysen, Johann Gustav. [1858] 1882. *Grundriss der Historik*. Leipzig.
Elton, G. R. 1967. *The Practice of History*. New York.
Gay, Peter. 1974. *Style in History*. New York.
Goldstein, Leon J. 1967. "Theory in History." *Philosophy of Science* 34: 23–40.
Gossman, Lionel. 1978. "History and Literature: Reproduction or Signification." In Canary and Kozicki: 3–39.
Hexter, J. H. 1967. "The Rhetoric of History." *HT* 6: 3–13. Hexter asserts that "the relation of writing history, of its rhetoric, to history itself is quite other than it has traditionally been conceived. That rhetoric is ordinarily deemed icing on the cake of history; but our recent investigation indicates that it is mixed right into

the batter. It affects not merely the outward appearance of history, its delight and seemliness, but its inward character, its essential function—its capacity to convey knowledge of the past as it actually was'' (p. 11).

Higham, John, et al. 1965. *History*. Englewood Cliffs, N.J.

Lucian of Samosata. 1905. ''The Way to Write History.'' In *The Works of Lucian of Samosata* 2. Oxford.

Nelson, John S. 1975. Review of Hayden White, *Metahistory: The Historical Imagination in Nineteenth-Century Europe. HT* 14: 74–91.

Niebuhr, Barthold Georg. [1811–12] 1972. Preface to *History of Rome*. In Stern: 47–50.

Schoenwald, Richard L. 1979. ''The Psychological Study of History.'' In Iggers and Parker: 71–85.

Struever, Nancy S. 1970. *The Language of History in the Renaissance*. Princeton, N.J.

———. 1979. ''Historiography and Linguistics.'' In Iggers and Parker: 127–50. Struever includes a general bibliography on stylistics and rhetoric, as well as rich bibliographical notes.

———. 1980. ''Topics in History.'' *HT Beih*. 19: 66–79. This is an important essay; the author defends the traditional rhetorical distinction between *disputatio* and *elocutio* against Hayden White's alleged conflation of the two.

Trevelyan, George Macaulay. [1913] 1972. ''Clio, A Muse.'' In Stern: 227–45. This is a classic disscussion of the ''literary'' function of history.

Turner, Frederick Jackson. [1891] 1972. ''The Significance of History.'' In Stern: 198–208. This is a nice expression of the late-nineteenth-century's desire to emancipate history from the realm of ''literature'' and assert its autonomy as a discipline. Turner's idea of literature is narrowly based on nineteenth-century romantic fiction—still true of many historians today.

Vann, Richard T. 1976. ''The Rhetoric of Social History.'' *Journal of Social History* 10: 221–35. Vann notes that the ''frontier between logic and rhetoric is a disputed and fluctuating one. At times rhetoric has been confined almost to a consideration of the annoying intractabilities of language which escape careful logical tidying-up; at others, under the category of 'invention,' rhetoric almost captures the citadel of epistemology itself'' (p. 221).

Wedgwood, C. V. 1960. ''Literature and the Historian.'' In C. V. Wedgwood, *Truth and Opinion: Historical Essays*. New York. The volume contains other relevant essays.

White, Hayden. 1973. *Metahistory: The Historical Imagination in Nineteenth-Century Europe*. Baltimore.

———. [1975] 1978. ''Historicism, History, and the Figurative Imagination.'' In Hayden White, *Tropics of Discourse: Essays in Cultural Criticism*. Baltimore. The entire volume is pertinent, especially the essay ''The Fictions of Factual Representation,'' pp. 121–34.

Woodward, C. Vann. 1968. ''History and the Third Culture.'' *Journal of Contemporary History* 3: 23–35.

Sources of Additional Information

See also IMAGINATION, INTERPRETATION. For the concept of ''style'' in general see the essays ''Style'' and ''Stylistics'' in the *Princeton Encyclopedia of Poetry and Poetics* (Princeton, N.J., 1974), pp. 814–18. James R. Bennett et al., ''History as Art: An

Annotated Checklist of Criticism," *Style* 13 (Winter 1979): 5–36, includes many relevant titles. Also invaluable are the essays and annotated bibliography in Canary and Kozicki. Gay (1974) also contains an annotated bibliography. On Droysen's nineteenth-century approach to historical "representation" (*Darstellung*) see H. W. Hedinger, "Historik, ars historica," *HWP* 3: 1132–37; also the article "Darstellungsformen" in Waldemar Besson, ed., *Das Fischer Lexikon: Geschichte* (Frankfurt, 1961): 61–65, and the entry "Historik" in Erich Bayer, ed., *Wörterbuch zur Geschichte: Begriffe und Fachausdrücke*, 4th ed. (Stuttgart, 1974): 222. Emery Neff, *The Poetry of History* (New York, 1947), and P. G. Ingram, "Artistry in History," *British Journal of Aesthetics* 17 (1977): 161–70, approach *style* in a spirit similar to Gay's. Robert D. Schulzinger's review in *HT* 15 (1976): 94–103 is a perceptive critique of Gay's views on style. *HT Beih.* 19 (1980) is devoted to reaction to Hayden White's *Metahistory*. White has written "The Problem of Style in Realistic Representation: Marx and Flaubert," in Berel Lang, ed., *The Concept of Style* (Philadelphia, 1979): 213–29.

T

TIME. See PERIODIZATION; PROCESS.

TOTALITARIANISM. Theoretical concept used by many social scientists since the 1930s to describe the most advanced forms of twentieth-century dictatorship, especially the regimes of Nazi Germany, Fascist Italy, and Soviet Russia. It designates those political systems that, utilizing advanced methods of mass communication, education, administration, and technology, endeavor to monopolize and control every aspect of the life of a society, private (thought control through propaganda, indoctrination, ritual) as well as public. This aim of "total" control is said to distinguish the most extreme forms of twentieth-century authoritarianism from older forms of despotism, since earlier forms were satisfied if the individual merely acquiesced and were not concerned with, or capable of, actively mobilizing the entire population.

The term *totalitarianism* has had an up-and-down career in the language of twentieth-century politics. Introduced in the 1920s, it became a vogue word in the 1950s and was often used as a rhetorical bludgeon in the ideological debates of the "cold war." By the 1970s the idea had fallen out of fashion in many scholarly circles.

The idea of totalitarianism originated in Italy in the 1920s. Theorists of Italian FASCISM, for example, the philosopher Giovanni Gentile and the Italian dictator Mussolini himself, were among early users of the word; it is not entirely clear if the word originated as an ideal among Mussolini's more radical supporters or as a term of derision among his opponents (Nolte, 1975: 330–31; Schapiro, 1972: 13). Mussolini first used the word on June 22, 1925, when he referred to the "fierce totalitarian will" of his political movement. About the same time, Mussolini's liberal opponents adopted the word as a pejorative to designate Fascist authoritarianism. The term appeared in English at least as early as 1926 with the publication of Luigi Sturzo's *Italy and Fascismo* (Schapiro, 1972: 13–14). In a famous essay on Fascism in the *Encyclopedia Italiana* ([1932] 1977: 331), Mussolini defined the idea as an extreme form of state control: "Fascism reaffirms the State as the true reality of the individual. . . . for the Fascist, everything is in the State, and nothing human or spiritual exists, much less has value, outside the State. In this sense Fascism is totalitarian."

Opponents of Fascism in Italy and abroad turned the word into a general term of opprobrium, and, already in the late 1920s it was extended to refer to the communist system of Soviet Russia. When Hitler came to power in Germany in 1933, the term was extended to the Nazi regime. Many scholars came to consider Germany under Nazi rule the most extreme manifestation of totalitarianism—a uniquely modern form of despotism that seeks to mobilize the population emotionally to create a total consensus in support of the regime (Bracher, 1981: 15).

In the United States in the mid–1930s totalitarianism became a concept for the comparative analysis of authoritarian regimes (for instance, Kohn, [1935] 1939: 83), and this usage was rapidly adopted by west European and North American historians, sociologists, and political scientists (Mommsen, 1981: 148). Marxist scholars rejected the use of *totalitarianism* to refer to the Soviet regime and worked to transform the word FASCISM—which originally designated only Mussolini's political movement in Italy—into a generic concept to describe non-socialist dictatorships. By the late 1930s, however, the term *totalitarianism* was in broad scholarly use in Europe and the United States to refer to the specific regimes of Fascist Italy, Nazi Germany, and the Soviet Union, as well as to designate generally a new, more effective form of tyranny made possible by modern technology and bureaucratic rationalization. Events such as the Soviet purges of the late 1930s and the Nazi-Soviet Non-Aggression Pact of August, 1939, reinforced the notion that, despite rhetorical differences, the Soviet dictatorship and the self-styled central European totalitarian regimes were essentially similar in the way they functioned and in their significance for modern history.

During World War II the concept declined in popularity owing to the fact that after June 1941 the western democracies and Soviet Russia were allied against Nazi Germany and Fascist Italy. The term was revived to enjoy its greatest vogue, however, after 1945. In the tense atmosphere of the "cold war" during the late 1940s and 1950s, *totalitarianism* became a means of classifying the despotic features shared by authoritarian regimes opposed by the liberal west. The Soviet Union was now the main object of interest, Nazi Gemany having been defeated. Interest in Fascist Italy as a totalitarian state waned because—despite the term's Italian origin—Mussolini never achieved a degree of total control comparable to that enjoyed by Hitler and Stalin. During the 1950s the term often degenerated to the level of polemical cliché, but the most important scholarly studies of the concept were also published: Arendt (1951); Talmon (1952); Friedrich (1954); and Friedrich and Brzezinski (1956). The idea was widely accepted by professional historians (for example, Iggers, 1958), who usually located its earliest origins in the revolutionary thought of late-eighteenth- and early-nineteenth century France and Germany.

In the 1960s a shift in scholarly opinion resulted in a sharp decline in the concept's popularity, although the opinion that the concept "had nearly gone out of use even in scholarly literature" by the early 1970s (Nolte, 1981: 172) is an overstatement. On the theoretical level it still found defenders (such as Bracher, 1973), it remained alive on the level of popular polemic (e.g., Revel, 1977), and certain academic historians continued to find it useful (for instance, Hunt, 1974). Nevertheless, a dramatic change had occurred, which was the result of several factors: the relaxation of extreme centralization in the Soviet Union following the death of Stalin in 1953 (leading some observers to think that Stalin's regime had been an aberration, not the reflection of an inherently totalitarian nature of Soviet communism); detailed research in the administrative history of German National Socialism, which revealed a degree of inefficiency, caprice, and improvisation seemingly incompatible with the abstract concept of total social control; and a renaissance of Marxist theory in the 1960s—influential far beyond the orbit of Marxist scholarship itself—that debunked the theory of totalitarianism as an ideological weapon of the cold war, emphasized philosophical differences between Soviet communism and the dictatorships of Hitler and Mussolini, and advocated the revival of the concept of Fascism as the proper category for understanding the central European tyrannies (Mommsen, 1981: 164). By the late 1960s the trend was clearly established; the theory of totalitarianism had fallen out of favor among historians as a conceptual framework for the explanation of twentieth-century tyranny (for instance, Sauer, [1967] 1975: 94–97). This remains broadly true (e.g., Allen, 1981; Mommsen, 1981); a notable exception is the West German scholar Karl Dietrich Bracher (1973; 1981: 12–33), who continues to defend the idea's usefulness as an IDEAL TYPE for understanding twentieth-century dictatorships of the past and extremist politics of the present.

References

Allen, William S. 1981. "Totalitarianism: The Concept and the Reality." In Ernest A. Menze, ed., *Totalitarianism Reconsidered*. Port Washington, N.Y.: 98–106.

Arendt, Hannah. 1951. *The Origins of Totalitarianism*. New York. This is one of the most widely read and influential studies.

Bracher, Karl Dietrich. 1973. "Totalitarianism." *DHI* 4: 406–11. This piece has a useful bibliography.

———. 1981. "The Disputed Concept of Totalitarianism: Experience and Actuality." In Ernest A. Menze, ed., *Totalitarianism Reconsidered*. Port Washington, N.Y.: 12–33. The author rejects the idea that the concept of totalitarianism was a mere by-product of the cold war. See especially pp. 16–18.

Friedrich, Carl J., ed. 1954. *Totalitarianism*. Cambridge, Mass. Proceedings of a conference of the American Academy of Arts and Sciences. The conference participants included a number of historians.

Friedrich, Carl J., and Brzezinski, Zbigniew K. 1956. *Totalitarian Dictatorship and Autocracy.* Cambridge, Mass. This book includes one of the best annotated bibliographies of the 1950s. A second, revised edition published by Friedrich in 1965 contains additional bibliography.

Hunt, Richard N. 1974. *The Political Ideas of Marx and Engels: Marxism and Totalitarian Democracy, 1818–1850.* Pittsburgh, Pa. Chapter one includes a convenient discussion of J. L. Talmon's theory of the origins of *totalitarianism.*

Iggers, Georg G. 1958. *The Cult of Authority: The Political Philosophy of the Saint-Simonians. A Chapter in the Intellectual History of Totalitarianism.* The Hague.

Kohn, Hans. [1935] 1939. "Between Democracy and Fascism." In Guy Stanton Ford, ed., *Dictatorship in the Modern World.* Minneapolis: 79–92.

Mommsen, Hans. 1981. "The Concept of Totalitarian Dictatorship vs. the Comparative Theory of Fascism: The Case of National Socialism." In Ernest A. Menze, ed., *Totalitarianism Reconsidered.* Port Washington, N.Y.: 146–66.

Mussolini, Benito. [1932] 1977. "The Doctrine of Fascism." In John Louis Beatty and Oliver A. Johnson, eds., *Heritage of Western Civilization* 2. 4th ed. Englewood Cliffs, N.J.: 321–41.

Nolte, Ernst. 1975. "Fascismus." *GG* 2: 329–36.

———. 1981. "Despotism—Totalitarianism—Freedom-Oriented Society." In Ernest A. Menze, ed., *Totalitarianism Reconsidered.* Port Washington, N.Y.: 167–78.

Revel, Jean-François. 1977. *The Totalitarian Temptation.* Garden City, N.Y.

Sauer, Wolfgang. [1967] 1975. "National Socialism: Totalitarianism or Fascism?" In Henry A. Turner, Jr., ed., *Reappraisals of Fascism.* New York: 93–116. This is an important review essay.

Schapiro, Leonard. 1972. *Totalitarianism.* New York. This work is good on the origins of the term.

Talmon, J. L. 1952. *The Origins of Totalitarian Democracy.* Boston. This book is a controversial attempt to locate the roots of *totalitarianism* in the intellectual history of late-eighteenth-century France, especially in the thought of Jean-Jacques Rousseau.

Sources of Additional Information

See also FASCISM. Consult Berding: 317–28 for a substantial list of titles on "Faschismus und Totalitarismus." A good introduction to the history of scholarly opinion is Ernest A. Menze, ed., *Totalitarianism Reconsidered* (Port Washington, N.Y., 1981), an anthology that reflects the ideas of historians who have been mainly concerned with the history of Nazi Germany rather than Fascist Italy or the Soviet Union. Robert Allen Skotheim, *Totalitarianism and American Social Thought* (New York, 1971), deals with the development of the concept among American intellectuals. For the state of opinion at the beginning of World War II see *Proceedings of the American Philosophical Society* 82, No. 1 (Philadelphia, 1940)—the published results of a symposium on the "totalitarian state." The annotated bibliographies in Friedrich and Brzezinski (1956; 2d ed., 1965) are among the best. Paul T. Mason, ed., *Totalitarianism: Temporary Madness or Permanent Danger?* (Boston, 1967), is an anthology that includes an annotated bibliography. See also the entry "Totalitarianism," *IESS* 16: 106–13. Especially valuable is Leonard B. Schapiro, "Totalitarianism," *MCWS* 8: 188–201, which includes a lengthy bibliography. Robert Burrowes, ''Totalitarianism: The Revised Standard Version,'' *World Politics* 21 (Jan. 1969): 272–94, a review essay based on later editions of Arendt (1951) and Friedrich and Brzezinski (1956), includes many bibliographical references in footnote citations.

U

UNDERSTANDING. (Ger. *Verstehen*). The German term *Verstehen* denotes a relationship of empathy with past situations that enables the historian to "relive" or "reenact" past events (see also IMAGINATION). The English word *understanding* may (1) share the German meaning; (2) be used as a synonym for EXPLANATION, that is, the logical method by which historians make the past intelligible; or (3) designate a mental state achieved *as a result of* the procedures of historical explanation and INTERPRETATION.

As a technical term, *understanding* was introduced to historiography in the late nineteenth century, largely through the work of two German scholars: the historian Johann Gustav Droysen (1808–84) (Burger, 1977; 1978) and the philosopher Wilhelm Dilthey (1833–1911). Since 1945 their concept of *Verstehen* (understanding) has fallen increasingly out of favor, at least in the English-speaking world. The notion of historical "understanding" is still widely employed in English, although usually in a loose, quasi-technical sense—often in ambiguous association with the word *explanation*.

The concept of *Verstehen* ("empathetic understanding" [Gruner, 1967: 157]) was the outgrowth of several causes: the eighteenth-century philosophies of Johann Gottfried von Herder (Barnard, 1963: 198) and Immanuel Kant, historiographical ROMANTICISM, the doctrine of HISTORISM, and the nineteenth-century conflict between the philosophical orientations of POSITIVISM and IDEALISM. Positivism, popularized by the French theorist Auguste Comte (1798–1857), was based on the idea of the "unity of science," that is, the belief that all valid inquiry is logically uniform and is ideally represented by the method of deduction from universal generalizations (or LAWS) often employed by natural science. Positivists sought to model the methods of historical inquiry on those of natural science in the belief that history might thereby attain a degree of precision on par with the natural sciences (see also SCIENTIFIC HISTORY).

In sharp contrast, the German idealists were epistemological dualists who distinguished two realms of reality—"nature" and "spirit." Denying that knowing is always logically uniform, they differentiated knowledge of physical nature (which roughly conformed to the positivist model) from knowledge of human affairs (which referred to matters of "spirit," incapable of being grasped in terms of physical laws). According to this distinction, the natural sciences (*Naturwissenschaften*)

> approach their subject matter from "the outside"; they describe regularities in nature through the observation of natural phenomena. In the human sciences [*Geisteswissenschaften*], however, the subject matter is accessible to the social scientist in a way not possible for the natural scientists. For example, because the historian is a man studying the actions of other men, he can know their actions from "the inside," as it were. (Nash 1969: 5–6; also Rickman, 1967; Windelband [1894] 1980)

In contrast to the natural sciences, the human sciences comprehend human events in terms of the *unique, non-repeatable contexts* in which they occur, not in terms of generalizations and regularities. Consciously or not, the idealists refined an idea advanced by the eighteenth-century Italian philosopher Giambattista Vico— that "human beings can possess a type of knowledge concerning things they themselves produce [i.e., cultural phenomena] which is not obtainable about the phenomena of nature" (Abel, 1948–49: 211).

Dilthey, the key figure in this regard, made a clear distinction between *explanation* and *understanding*; for him these were "concepts on the same level although opposed to each other—natural sciences explain, social sciences understand" (Gruner, 1967: 153). Like *explanation*, *understanding* (*Verstehen*) is a method and not merely a condition; it is a cognitive procedure based on the human capacity for "intellectual empathy" (Nash 1969: 6). Unlike *explanation*, *understanding* is not a *logical* process but a largely emotional and intuitive experience through which the practitioner of the human sciences establishes a "psychological rapport" with the object of his study (Antoni, [1940] 1959: 170). Through this process he "internalizes" the past by "imagining what emotions may have been aroused by the impact of a given situation or event" (Abel, 1948–49: 215). By steeping himself in the records of the past, the historian may intuitively enter into a sympathetic relationship with the past and can to some degree reexperience the past and "rethink" the thoughts of historical personalities.

In the early twentieth century the concept of *Verstehen* was widely employed in Germany and beyond. In the United States the idea was often associated with historical RELATIVISM (Beard and Hook, 1946: 128). Max Weber, a pioneer of historical sociology, made the notion a pillar of his method (Hughes, 1958: 310–14; Burger, 1976: 102–15; Oakes, 1977); and the idea was refined in various ways by idealist philosophers such as Benedetto Croce and R. G. Collingwood (Goldstein, 1970).

Collingwood's *Idea of History* (1946) became perhaps the single most widely admired philosophical work among English-language historians, although it is doubtful that all would completely accept the British thinker's special approach to historical understanding as "rethinking" (Higham et al., 1965: 142–44), a position that many philosophers consider "untenable" (e.g., Cebik, 1970: 77). On the other hand, according to Allen Johnson—the author of a popular historical manual of the 1920s (1926: 150)—the "tacit postulate that an historian may enter into the thoughts and feelings of men of other times" underpins "all histories and manuals of historical method." Citing the German historian Sybel on the possibility of penetrating to the "inmost being of another person, to note the genesis of his perceptions, and to take the measure of his very concepts and feelings," Johnson expressed "qualified" approval on the grounds that all historians accept the principle of the "identity of human nature in all times and places."

Today, although the doctrine of *Verstehen* remains popular in continental Europe (for instance, Besson, 1961: 84–85; Nolte, [1963] 1965: x), it has lost much of its appeal among English-speaking philosophers and historians (Cohen, 1973: 299). To be sure, the idea of "intellectual empathy" still exerts a fascination; for instance, John Higham (1965: 143)—a well-known student of United States historiography—writes that "No amount of scientific analysis or synthesis can take the place of that crucial act of human empathy by which the historian identifies himself with another time and place, re-enacting the thoughts and reliving the experience of people remote from himself." A good part of the idea's continuing attraction lies in its usefulness for asserting the "autonomy" of history from the natural and social sciences—something many historians are eager to defend.

But like so much in the German idealist tradition, *Verstehen* has come to be regarded since 1945 as a dangerous appeal to "romanticism," intuition, and the irrational. H. Stuart Hughes (1958: 187), for instance, refers to "the method of inner understanding, or *Verstehen*" as "the most difficult intellectual problem that I have confronted . . . the murkiest of the many dark corners in the labyrinth of German social science method." According to some philosophers (for instance, Gruner, 1967: 161) the very idea that understanding is a cognitive method "rests on a confusion of explanation and understanding." Among social theorists, apart from scattered defenders (such as Rickman, 1967), *Verstehen* is regarded as at best only a "heuristic idea" (Gruner, 1967: 161) that may be the basis for intuitive "hunches"—hypotheses that must be rigorously tested with reference to evidence (Abel, 1948–49: 217–18).

In recent English-language literature *understanding* has been used in a variety of senses—usually in close association with the related questions of historical EXPLANATION and NARRATIVE—and the line between *explanation* and *understanding* is not often clearly drawn. Many studies that use the word *understanding* seem to assume that the meaning of the word is self-evident (for example, Mink, 1965; Skinner, 1969). In much of the literature there is a tendency to "label any intellectual achievement above the level of fact-stating an instance of explanation" (Levich, 1964–65: 338). A few authors discriminate clearly between the two concepts: Gruner (1969: 351), for example, maintains that, unlike explanation,

> the logical grammar of "to understand" is such that it cannot denote an activity. Hence it is of a type which is different from that of "to identify" and "to explain" both of which do denote activities. Understanding x is an achievement, a product; identifying x and explaining x are activities, processes. Consequently, saying that understanding *is* identifying or *is* explaining is to commit a logical error. And the same holds true for any statement to the effect that understanding is an operation of identifying of explaining. (p. 351)

Again:

> To have understood something only means that it has become comprehensible or intelligible or even familiar, i.e., we no longer regard it as strange, bewildering and unaccountable. . . . [The condition of understanding is achieved] by connecting, in some way or other, the phenomenon to be understood with other phenomena which we have understood already, that is by establishing "a linkage of what we do not understand to what we do understand." (1967: 151–52)

Levich (1964–65: 338–41), on the other hand, treats *understanding* as the broadest category of comprehension, a heading under which other logically distinct categories, such as "explanation" and "interpretation," are subsumed. Like Gruner, he apparently believes that *explanation* is an activity or method, while *understanding* is a *condition* or *state* arrived at as the *result* of some such activity.

But others ignore the problem of the relationship between *explanation* and *understanding* or treat the two concepts as practically synonymous (Beard and Hook, 1946: 127–28; Martin, 1977: 14, 43, 90, 240). In fact, "no firm terminology has been established, and 'understanding,' 'explanation,' 'empathy,' etc. have been used in similar or different ways, as the case may be, sometimes even by one and the same writer" (Gruner, 1967: 151).

References

Abel, Theodore. 1948–49. "The Operation Called *Verstehen*," *The American Journal of Sociology* 54: 211–18. This is a widely cited critique of the idea.

Antoni, Carlo. [1940] 1959. *From History to Sociology: The Transition in German Historical Thinking*. Detroit. Antoni calls Dilthey's doctrine of "understanding through reliving" (*nacherlebendes Verstehen*) an "unhealthy" doctrine that "fruitlessly occupied German thought at the beginning of the twentieth century" (p. 170).

Barnard, F. M. 1963. "Herder's Treatment of Causation and Continuity in History." *JHI* 24: 197–212. This piece contains references to numerous passages in Herder's work that anticipate the doctrine of *Verstehen* (p. 198).

Beard, Charles A., and Hook, Sydney. 1946. "Problems of Terminology in Historical Writing." Bull. 54: 103–30.

Besson, Waldemar. 1961. *Geschichte: Das Fischer Lexikon*. Frankfurt.

Burger, Thomas. 1976. *Max Weber's Theory of Concept Formation*. Durham, N.C.

———. 1977. "Droysen's Defense of Historiography: A Note." *HT* 16: 168–73.

———. 1978. "Droysen and the Idea of *the Verstehen*." *Journal of the History of the Behavioral Sciences* 14: 6–19. This article is a concise exposition of Droysen's theory of history.

Cebik, L. B. 1970. "Collingwood: Action, Re-enactment, and Evidence." *The Philosophical Forum* 2: 68–90. Cebik states flatly that the "doctrine of re-enactment makes little sense" (p. 68).

Cohen, Howard. 1973. "*Das Verstehen* and Historical Knowledge," *American Philosophical Quarterly* 10: 299–306. Cohen asserts that the idea of *Verstehen* "has been out of vogue for some 30 years now" (p. 299). This article contains an interesting analysis of Michael Scriven's recent effort to revive *Verstehen* in modified form.

Goldstein, Leon J. 1970. "Collingwood's Theory of Historical Knowing." *HT* 9: 3–36. This is a rare defense of Collingwood's idea of history as "rethinking" the past; n. 48 contains references to the work of Collingwood's many critics.

Gruner, Rolf. 1967. "Understanding in the Social Sciences and History." *Inquiry* 10: 151–63. Gruner complains that careless use of the term *understanding* by philosophers is "no less than a scandal" (p. 151).

———. 1969. "The Notion of Understanding: Replies to Cunningham and Van Evra." *Inquiry* 12: 349–56. This article is by one of the few recent philosophers to reflect systematically on the use of *understanding* as a term in contemporary philosophy of history.

Higham, John, et al. 1965. *History*. Englewood Cliffs, N.J.

Hughes, H. Stuart. 1958. *Consciousness and Society: The Reorientation of European Social Thought, 1890–1930*. New York.

Johnson, Allen. 1926. *The Historian and Historical Evidence*. New York.

Levich, Marvin. 1964–65. Review of Sidney Hook, ed., *Philosophy and History: A Symposium*. *HT* 4: 328–49.

Martin, Rex. 1977. *Historical Explanation: Re-enactment and Practical Inference*. Ithaca, N.Y. Martin states that Collingwood treated the terms *explanation* and *understanding* "as virtual synonyms" (p. 43).

Mink, Louis O. 1965. "The Autonomy of Historical Understanding." *HT* 5: 24–47. Reprinted in Dray: 160–92.

Nash, Ronald H. 1969. *Ideas of History* 2. New York. This book contains a selection of writings titled "Positivism and Idealism: The Problem of Historical Understanding" (pp. 3–74).

Nolte, Ernst. [1963] 1965. *Three Faces of Fascism: Action Française, Italian Fascism, National Socialism*. New York. This book is by a leading West German scholar who believes that "Historical understanding . . . is a very different matter from abstract speculation. To understand means to grasp the differentiated within its context" (p. x).

Oakes, Guy. 1977. "The Verstehen Thesis and the Foundation of Max Weber's Methodology." *HT* 16: 11–29.

Rickman, H. P. 1967. "Geisteswissenschaften." *EP* 3: 275–79. In this defense of *Ver-*

stehen, Rickman notes that "The term *Geisteswissenschaften* was coined . . . to translate John Stuart Mill's phrase 'the moral sciences' " (p. 275). The entry includes a bibliography.

Skinner, Quentin. 1969. "Meaning and Understanding in the History of Ideas." *HT* 8: 3–53. Skinner contrasts *explanation* and *understanding*; the former is expository, the latter is interpretive, or hermeneutic (p. 46).

Windelband, Wilhelm. [1894] 1980. "Rectorial Address, Strasbourg, 1894." *HT* 19: 169–85. See also Guy Oakes' introduction to this famous lecture, pp. 165–68.

Sources of Additional Information

See also EXPLANATION; INTERPRETATION. The literature on *Verstehen* is extensive. Consult Abel (1948–49), n. 6, for a list of some of the older German works. See especially Joachim Wach, *Das Verstehen: Grundzüge einer Geschichte der hermeneutischen Theorie im 19. Jahrhundert*, 3 vols. (Tübingen, 1926–33), for a survey of the origins of the idea. On "empathy" consult Charles Edward Gauss, "Empathy," *DHI* 2: 85–89 (with bibliography), and Jørgen B. Hunsdahl, "Concerning Einfühlung (Empathy): A Concept Analysis of Its Origin and Early Development," *Journal of the History of the Behavioral Sciences* 3 (1967): 180–91. In English there are a number of books on Dilthey that contain helpful bibliographies; among the more recent are H. Michael Ermarth, *Wilhelm Dilthey: The Critique of Historical Reason* (Chicago, 1978), and Theodore Plantinga, *Historical Understanding in the Thought of Wilhelm Dilthey* (Toronto, 1980); both stress the degree to which Dilthey's thought has been misinterpreted. See also Michael J. Maclean, "Johann Gustav Droysen and the Development of Historical Hermeneutics," *HT* 21 (1982): 347–65. The introduction to Wilhelm Dilthey, *Der Aufbau der geschichtlichen Welt in den Geisteswissenschaften* (Frankfurt, 1970), an anthology of Dilthey's writings, concludes with a bibliography, as does Section II of Nash (1969), "Positivism and Idealism: The Problem of Historical Understanding." For the literature on Collingwood see the bibliography in Michael Krausz, ed., *Critical Essays on the Philosophy of R. G. Collingwood* (Oxford, 1972), pp. 327–48, as well as Louis O. Mink's essay in the same volume, "Collingwood's Historicism: A Dialectic of Process," pp. 154–78; Mink argues that most commentary on Collingwood's doctrine of "rethinking" is superficial. See also the footnote citations in Margit Hurup Nielsen, "Re-enactment and Reconstruction in Collingwood's Philosophy of History," *HT* 20 (1981): 1–31. *JP* 63 (Oct. 13, 1966): 566–82 includes a Symposium on "Historical Understanding. The Problem of Other Periods," with contributions by Arthur C. Danto, Alan Donagan, and J. W. Meiland.

UNIVERSAL HISTORY. Historical writing that attempts to depict the history of the human race as a whole, understood as a unified process of development.

Universal history means "the history of mankind" or "world history"—in the words of Thomas Carlyle ([1840] 1972: 101), "the history of what man has accomplished in this world." The idea of a comprehensive history of the human race from the earliest times originated in antiquity (Momigliano, 1978). The history of the Greco-Persian war by Herodotus (c. 484–c. 425 B.C.), the "father of history," might be considered a precursor of the genre, since it incorporated in eclectic fashion many of the legends and traditions of peoples of the then-known world. More important for the early notion of a unified human history was Ephorus (c. 405–330 B.C.), who attempted to survey the entire political and military history of the Greeks—an effort that necessarily involved some attention to nations with whom the Greeks came into contact. Ephorus' attention, however, always focused on the Greeks; for him, "universality existed only in the form of excursuses subordinated to Greek history" (p. 11).

The most important non-Christian pioneer of universal history was the Greek Polybius (c. 203–c. 120 B.C.). Writing after the campaigns of Alexander the Great (which briefly unified much of the near east) and at the beginning of Rome's ascendency, Polybius—inspired in part by Ephorus—attempted to write a comprehensive history of his contemporary world. His task was facilitated by the system of universal chronology associated particularly with Eratosthenes (c. 275–c. 195 B.C.) (p. 17).

The growth of the Roman empire and the advent of Christianity, both ecumenical in thrust, spurred the concept of universal history. Many scholars regard the idea as primarily a creation of Christian thought, attributable especially to the notion of providence, which viewed history as a single event originating in God's will (for instance, Leyden, 1970: 219; Mommsen, 1961: 323–24); divine will was the thread that ultimately unified everything. Providence was used by the Church father Eusebius of Caesarea (c. A.D. 263-c. 339) to create a new genre in his *Ecclesiastical History*. "Ecclesiastical history," a popular form of historiography from the early Middle Ages to the Counter-Reformation, surveyed God's creation from the beginning of time, with an emphasis on the triumph of Christianity over paganism and heresy. As conceived by Eusebius, it supplied a framework for the narration of human affairs, based on a six-stage scheme of PERIODIZATION drawn from Jewish tradition (Hay, 1977: 27–28): (1) from creation to the great flood; (2) from the flood to the birth of Abraham; (3) from Abraham to David; (4) from David to the Babylonian captivity; (5) from captivity to Christ's birth; (6) from Christ's birth to his second coming. The second coming would be followed by the seventh and last age of God's eternity.

These stylistic conventions gradually broke down in the early-modern period. In the sixteenth century, for example, Jean Bodin ([1555] 1945) proposed a secular universal history based on the interaction of geography, climate, and human culture. The last great traditional Christian universal history was Bishop Bossuet's *Discours sur l'histoire universelle* (1681).

In the eighteenth century the idea of ecumenical history was transformed into secular "philosophical history" (see PHILOSOPHY OF HISTORY), a genre that represented the past in terms of the growth of human reason. Providence was replaced as the unifying thread by the abstract idea of PROGRESS, a process believed to occur in accordance with the dictates of natural LAW. A single story line of development was assumed to exist, a "hidden plan" that the "philosophical historian" discovered and revealed to his audience (Walsh, 1967: 69). "The *cultural development* of humanity . . . became the underlying theme of a new universal history" (Mommsen, 1961: 325). ENLIGHTENMENT figures such as Immanuel Kant, Friedrich Schiller, and the Marquis de Condorcet made the idea of secular progress the foundation of their views about history. Voltaire (1694–1778), more than anyone else, popularized the modern concept of universal history in the third volume of his *Essai sur les moeurs et l'esprit des nations* (1754), which he entitled *Essai sur l'histoire universelle* (p. 325).

But the idea of providence was not entirely forgotten by historians; after being temporarily submerged during the Enlightenment, it resurfaced in the early nineteenth century in combination with the spirit of cosmopolitanism. This is strikingly reflected in the idealist scholarship of the German historian Leopold von Ranke (1795–1886) and his followers (Liebel, 1963–64: 317; Holborn, [1943] 1950: 79–80). Ranke, a devout Lutheran, envisioned *universal history* as the end product of all national histories, an ideal made possible by "a thoroughgoing study of the relationships of nations, languages, civil institutions, religions, origins and effects of wars—in short, of God's 'plan' " (Liebel, 1973: 145, 153). His project for a universal history best reflects the early-nineteenth-century dream of combining painstaking scholarship on particular national traditions with the general idea of a history of the human race.

Various factors worked to gradually undermine this idea of universal history among academic historians. The outlook of HISTORISM, for example, encouraged the study of unique contexts rather than general patterns and rejected the idea of a single, uniform human nature. *Historism* and *universal history* coexisted in delicate equilibrium in Ranke, but Ranke's successors were unable to sustain that balance, and a nominalistic emphasis on the unique gradually triumphed over cosmopolitanism (Mommsen, 1961: 327, 331). Indeed, Ranke's own effort to write a universal history late in life "was severely criticized . . . , as universal history was considered outmoded by the Bismarckian generation of historians" (Liebel, 1973: 159, n. 48). The trend toward specialization and the orientation toward increasingly narrow, monographic research that accompanied the professionalization of historiography, as well as the growing tendency to conceptualize the past in terms of NATIONALISM and the individual NATION, all acted to weaken the idea of universal history—at least among academics—in the late nineteenth and twentieth centuries.

In their most serious work, current professional scholars have in practice generally shelved universal history. They tend to think that the idea's scope is simply far too vast for the resources of careful scholarship and assume, as well, that any world history will soon be rapidly outdated because its organizing principle—time- and place-bound of necessity—is likely to be rejected by future generations (Ritter, 1961–62: 276–77). According to Louis Mink,

> the view of historical knowledge most widely shared in our time is precisely the denial of the claims of universal history. Instead of the belief that there is a single story embracing the ensemble of human events, we believe that there are many stories, not only different stories about different events, but even different stories about the same events. (1978: 139–40)

Only among Marxists, in this regard heirs of the eighteenth-century doctrine of progress, does the concept now enjoy wide professional support.

The notion nevertheless survives in various forms, for example, school textbooks, speculative philosophies of history (such as Spengler, 1918–22; Toynbee, 1934–61), popularizations (Van Loon, 1921; Durant, 1935–75), occasional programmatic calls for a "new" universal history to counteract narrow specialization and ethnocentrism (e.g., Mommsen, 1961: 322, 331–32; Steensgaard, 1973), and the odd, professionally written world history designed to satisfy such pleas (for example, McNeill, 1963).

More importantly, Mink (1978) suggests that universal history less obviously persists among both laypersons *and professionals* as the commonsense presupposition that the past has an inherent narrative structure—the assumption (seldom if ever consciously articulated) that history is a hidden "untold story" that historians discover, or attempt to discover, for their readers. It is this assumption that lies behind the conviction—shared by many historians and some philosophers of history—that "all historical works must ultimately be regarded as contributing to history-in-the-large" (Dray, 1971: 155–56; Kracauer, 1966: 66–67). Accordingly, Mink argues (1978: 140–41), "the concept of universal *history* has not been abandoned at all, only the concept of universal *historiography*."

The idea that the past is an untold story is nicely illustrated in the thought of Ranke, who presumed that historical events have an inner connection of their own and that this connection "is not something arbitrarily assumed: it existed in a particular way and could be no other" (Ranke, [n.d.] 1972: 60–62). This position, which would be endorsed by many academic historians today, has significant implications:

> we assume that everything that has happened belongs to a single and determinite realm of unchanging actuality. . . . [We have] the concept of a totality of "what really happened." We reject the possibility of a historiographical representation of this totality, but the very rejection presupposes the concept of the totality itself. (Mink, 1978: 140–41)

But, Mink objects (p. 147), there "can in fact be no untold stories at all, just as there can be no unknown knowledge. There can be only past facts not yet described in a context of narrative form." He therefore suggests that we recognize the fallacious nature of this presupposition and abandon it entirely.

References

Bodin, Jean. [1555] 1945. *Method for the Easy Comprehension of History*. New York.

Carlyle, Thomas. [1840] 1972. From *On Heroes, Hero Worship, and the Heroic in History*. In Stern: 101–07.

Dray, W. H. 1971. "On the Nature and Role of Narrative in Historiography." *HT* 10: 153–71. Dray cites R. G. Collingwood as a philosopher who believed that "the unity of the historical world, the existence of 'one history,' is a [necessary] *presupposition* of historical inquiry." Dray maintains, however, that this is not the same as believing that history "might yield one super-story. . . . It is not a presupposition of every historical work that there exists a final narrative account of history-in-the-large to be discovered. What is required is only that every account, narrative or otherwise, be consistent with the rest" (pp. 155–56).

Durant, Will. 1935–75. *The Story of Civilization*. 11 vols. New York.

Hay, Denys. 1977. *Annalists and Historians: Western Historiography from the Eighth to the Eighteenth Centuries*. London.

Holborn, Hajo. [1943] 1950. "The Science of History." In Strayer: 61–83. This piece contains a concise sketch of Ranke's idea of universal history.

Kracauer, Siegfried. 1966. "Time and History." *HT Beih*. 6: 65–78. The author cites celebrated historians such as Ranke, Henri Pirenne, and Marc Bloch as scholars who regarded the "chimera" of universal history "the goal of all historical pursuits" (pp. 66–67).

Leyden, W. von. 1970. Review of Jacqueline de Romilly, *Time in Greek Tragedy*. *HT* 9: 209–29.

Liebel, Helen P. 1963–64. "Philosophical Idealism in the *Historische Zeitschrift*, 1859–1914." *HT* 3: 316–30. Liebel briefly discusses the views of the German historian Friedrich Wilhelm Giesebrecht on the complementary relationship between *national* and *universal* history.

————. 1973. "Ranke's Fragments of Universal History." *Clio* 2: 145–59. This article highlights the tension between Ranke's emphasis on the particular and his aspiration to the general. It includes translations of a few of Ranke's fragmentary writings on universal history.

McNeill, William H. 1963. *The Rise of the West: A History of the Human Community*. Chicago.

Mink, Louis O. 1978. "Narrative Form as a Cognitive Instrument." In Canary and Kozicki: 129–49. Mink maintains that rejecting the idea that the past is an untold story "does not imply that there is nothing determinate about the past, since individual statements of fact . . . remain unaffected. But it does mean that the significance of the past is determinate only by virtue of our own disciplined imagination" (p. 148).

Momigliano, Arnaldo. 1978. "Greek Historiography." *HT* 17: 1–28.

Mommsen, Wolfgang. 1961. "Universalgeschichte." In Waldemar Besson, ed., *Geschichte: Das Fischer Lexikon*. Frankfurt: 322–32. This piece includes one of the best concise discussions of the concept.

Ranke, Leopold von. [n.d.] 1972. "A Fragment from the 1860s." In Stern: 60–62.

Ritter, Gerhard. 1961–62. "Scientific History, Contemporary History, and Political Science." *HT* 1: 259–79.

Spengler, Oswald. 1918–22. *Der Untergang des Abendlandes*. Munich.

Steensgaard, Niels. 1973. "Universal History for Our Times." *JMH* 45: 72–82. This plea for a new universal history is nonetheless critical of recent UNESCO efforts in this direction.

Toynbee, Arnold J. 1934–61. *A Study of History*. Oxford.

Van Loon, Hendrik Willem. 1921. *The Story of Mankind*. New York.

Walsh, W. H. 1967. "Colligatory Concepts in History." In W. H. Burston and D. Thompson, eds., *Studies in the Nature and Teaching of History*. London: 65–84.

Sources of Additional Information

Berding includes a convenient list of titles on universal history, pp. 61–65. There is a compact survey of the modern history of the idea, with emphasis on Bodin, Bossuet,

Voltaire, and Condorcet, in R. V. Sampson, *Progress in the Age of Reason: The Seventeenth Century to the Present Day* (Cambridge, Mass., 1956), pp. 95–123. Friedrich Schiller's classic "Nature and Value of Universal History: An Inaugural Lecture [1789]" has been translated in *HT* 11 (1972): 321–34. On Ranke see Leonard Krieger, *Ranke: The Meaning of History* (Chicago, 1977), as well as collections of Ranke's writings edited by Georg G. Iggers and Konrad von Moltke (Indianapolis, Ind., 1973) and Roger Wines (New York, 1981). Chapter four of Herbert Butterfield, *Man on His Past: The Study of the History of Historical Scholarship* (Cambridge, 1955), is titled "Ranke and the Conception of 'General History' "; see also pp. 44–50 of the same book. On Eusebius see J. H. Wallace-Hadrill, *Eusebius of Caesarea* (London, 1960).

V

VALUE JUDGMENT. The (tacit or explicit) assessment of past individuals, events, or circumstances from the standpoint of some set of ethical norms.

The question of value judgment arises in at least two related contexts in history: first, in connection with the problem of ethical relativism; second, with respect to the rendering of moral judgments by historians. The former problem involves the question of whether there are universally valid norms by which the morality of human actions may be judged. Strictly speaking, this is more properly a philosophical or religious question than a historical one. Nevertheless, when historians survey the vast array of conflicting value systems that have existed in time they may be led to wonder, with the nineteenth-century philosopher Wilhelm Dilthey, if "historical consciousness" does not demonstrate "the relativity of every metaphysical or religious doctrine" (cited in Meyerhoff, 1959: 226). E. H. Carr ([1961] 1964: 83), for example, believes that an effort to judge the past relative to an absolute standard of morality is "unhistorical and contradicts the very essence of history." For a more complete discussion of the implications of this problem for historiography, see entries HISTORISM and RELATIVISM. With respect to the second question—which is addressed here—the problem is not only whether moral judgments are appropriate in historiography but whether, given the nature of history as a discipline, they are avoidable at all.

One of the oldest ideas associated with historical study is the assumption that written history should erect guideposts to right conduct; by displaying instances of exemplary behavior, and by revealing the failures and character flaws of historical individuals, history—according to this tradition—is an edifying and sobering form of "philosophy teaching by example," and the historian is an agent of moral judgment and instruction (Nadel, 1964).

This orientation—one facet of the ancient tradition of "pragmatic" PHILOS-

OPHY OF HISTORY—gained renewed popularity in the eighteenth century, precisely on the eve of the rise of modern academic historiography. The ENLIGHTENMENT idea of historical PROGRESS (the notion that history is the story of the material and moral improvement of the human race) injected new life into the ancient doctrine; written history was a bar of judgment before which the moral worth of past ideas and actions might be reviewed. According to Friedrich Schiller's inaugural lecture as professor of history at Jena ([1789] 1972: 322), history "embraces the whole moral world" and "must render the account of everything [man] has given and received." Voltaire, to cite a second instance, was eager in his historical works to pass judgment on the past—especially the Middle Ages, when "nobles knew nothing but war and idleness; the clergy lived in disorder and ignorance; and the people, devoid of industry, stagnated in poverty" (Voltaire, [1752] 1972: 43).

> The great errors of the past [Voltaire wrote] are . . . very useful in many ways. . . . One cannot remind oneself too often of crimes and disasters. . . . It is necessary to bring to mind repeatedly the usurpations of the Popes, the scandalous strife of their schisms, the madness of theological quarrels, the wars engendered by these quarrels, and the horrors that resulted. If this knowledge were not made familiar . . . the public could be as stupidly blind as in the time of Gregory VII. ([n.d.] 1972: 45)

The eighteenth-century's readiness to render moral verdicts in history is understandable in light of its assumption that the historian's goal is not knowledge of the past for its own sake, but rather study of those events that have a direct bearing on present issues. In Schiller's words, the historian must select for scrutiny only those events

> which have had on the contemporary state of the world and on the condition of the generation now alive an influence which is essential, undeniable, and easy to discern. It is thus the relevance of an historical fact to the contemporary state of the world to which attention must be paid in assembling materials for world-history. ([1789] 1972: 331)

The early nineteenth century, however, witnessed a sharp reaction against this notion, at least among the new academic historians. The idea now emerged that the past should be understood for its own sake and in terms of its own context, not in light of present values or partisan viewpoints (see ANACHRONISM; HISTORISM). The *locus classicus* for this position is the famous Preface to Leopold von Ranke's *Histories of the Latin and Germanic Nations from 1494–1514* (1824). Ranke's book dealt, among other things, with the Reformation, a subject whose history was beset by partisan controversy. In this context Ranke declared: "To history has been assigned the office of judging the past, of instructing the present for the benefit of future ages. To such high offices this work does not aspire: It wants only to show what actually happened (*wie es eigentlich gewesen*)" (Ranke, [1824] 1972: 57). This statement subsequently became the inspiration for the tradition of value-neutral historical scholarship, a conception that triumphed in mid- and late-nineteenth-century professional historiography. Now, in the eyes of the majority of its academic practitioners, history would become an objective science, characterized by the same impersonal detachment that typified the natural sciences (see also OBJECTIVITY).

To be sure, nineteenth-century academic historiography did produce outspoken opponents of value-neutral scholarship. Lord Acton ([1887] 1955: 336), for instance, believed that history's very status as a "science" required it to be "an arbiter of controversy, a guide of the wanderer, the upholder of that moral standard which the powers of earth, and religion itself, tend constantly to depress." Andrew D. White (1885: 7), first president of the American Historical Association, maintained that the great, synthetic works of history had to spring from the "ethical ground" and show "what developments have been good, aiding in the evolution of that which is best in man and society" as well as "what developments have been evil, tending to the retrogression of man and society." The well-known German scholar J. G. Droysen maintained, in opposition to Ranke, that history is important because "it makes man not only more intelligent but also should and will make him better" (cited in Maclean, 1982: 352). Droysen's own studies on Prussian history were conscious efforts to demonstrate the worth of his liberal and nationalist values. " 'Objectivity,' " he declared, "is not the historian's greatest glory," (p. 363); instead, that honor resides in the scholar's function as an instrument of moral and political education, or *Bildung*. But Droysen—although he enjoyed considerable prestige—was nonetheless considered distinctly "idiosyncratic" by the majority of his German colleagues. The main trend in academic circles—both within Germany and abroad—followed Ranke's own judgment of Droysen: any effort to consciously blend critical scholarship with ethical or political values would degenerate to *Tendenzgeschichte* ("partisan history") (p. 357).

Today, however, belief in the possibility of clinical detachment in the study of the past is no longer the rule. Conventional wisdom holds that the historian must strive for the greatest possible impartiality but nonetheless necessarily imposes his own socially conditioned ethical categories on the past to a greater or (preferably) lesser degree. Granted, gratuitous value judgment sometimes does enter into historical inquiry, but this can and must be avoided; the idea that history should serve an overt ethical purpose, that it should "kindle the anger and awaken the indignation of men" (Butterfield, [1931] 1959: 243; cf. Zinn, 1970), is decidedly not a mainstream view (see RADICAL HISTORY). Nevertheless, it is now normal to think that an important source of any historian's approach is a (conscious or unconscious) "moral or ideological decision," and historians typically speak in terms of "schools" of interpretation: liberal, conservative, Marxist, and so on (H. White, [1972–73] 1978: 67).

This shift is the result of many factors: for example, late-nineteenth-century neo-idealist epistemology, which drew a sharp distinction between the value-neutral methods and aims of the "natural" sciences and the unavoidably normative categories of the "human" sciences (see IDEALISM; UNDERSTANDING);

the rise of sociological consciousness, which viewed the historian as a social product whose work was inevitably conditioned by the prevailing values of his society and social CLASS (see RELATIVISM); the growing influence of Marxian HISTORICAL MATERIALISM, which, in its concept of IDEOLOGY, complemented the sociological view that knowledge is a socially conditioned human construct; and the desire—emerging especially at the turn of the twentieth century and typified by the NEW HISTORY in the United States—to make history "relevant" to present social problems. Present liberal orthodoxy is reflected, for example, in Breisach (1983: 409–10), who speaks of the "inevitability" of INTERPRE-TATION and asserts:

> To acknowledge interpretation as an integral part of historiography is to recognize the link between a historical account and the person of the historian, making it doubtful that historians can avoid affirming values altogether. Indeed, even those scholars who demand freedom from values most ardently affirm at least one value: the freedom to explore the past and formulate interpretations without restrictions, a freedom given only in at least minimally democratic states. . . . A relatively value-free historiography can only exist as long as individuals are free to inquire and draw their own conclusions. Thus paradoxically the aim of a neutrality on values can only be preserved if contemporary historians support a democratic society, itself a historical and value-laden phenomenon.

It is true, nevertheless, that the nineteenth-century ideal of value-free scholarship is still occasionally encountered in the work of well-known historians; in his *Origins of the Second World War* (1961), for instance, the British historian A. J. P. Taylor echoes Ranke's dictum in declaring that "it is no part of the historian's duty to say what ought to have been done. His sole duty is to find out what was done and why" (cited in Dray, 1978: 168). Among current English-language historians, Herbert Butterfield ([1931] 1959) has even advanced a sustained argument against the use of value judgment in history. Butterfield's opinions, although not representative of the profession as a whole, merit closer review.

Ironically, Butterfield's position is frankly presented as the product of his own moral code, a liberal-Christian ethic based on the axiom "judge not, lest ye be judged"; his argument also draws on the nineteenth-century tradition of HIS-TORISM, the doctrine that we are obligated to understand past events in light of their own unique circumstances and values (see also ANACHRONISM; COLLIGA-TION; UNDERSTANDING). As sinners before God, Butterfield maintains, our knowledge is always incomplete; in our frailty we can never ultimately know the motives that prompt human action or perfectly understand the factors that give rise to those motives. As historians, we must strive to understand previous epochs completely in their own terms and so avoid the presumption of imposing our own time-bound cultural and political values on the past. We must, in other words, undertake an "act of self-emptying" to truly understand our subject (p. 229). A sharp distinction must be drawn between the categories of day-today life, where—for practical reasons—moral judgments are unavoidable, and the realm of "technical history," where the imperatives of dispassionate description and explanation must reign supreme. In the latter sphere the best we can make are "quasi-aesthetic" judgments, never verdicts of moral responsibility. In Butterfield's view, the historian is barred even from passing moral judgment on figures such as Hitler or Stalin—men who, by everyday conventions, would surely be considered monsters.

In sum, history must be a "high and austere academic discipline," not a stage for conflict between "right" and "wrong" where the historian melodramatically parades his own biases and partisanship. Indeed, Butterfield argues that by conscientiously avoiding value judgments we actually serve a "higher" morality; for by acknowledging the limits of our ability to evaluate the past, historians and their audiences experience a chastening sense of contrition that assists in "drawing together again the torn fabric of historic life, and healing the wounds of mankind and deepening our insight into human destiny" (p. 248). History, in Butterfield's view, should be a moral exercise for *us*, not an instrument for the vindication or condemnation of others. He concedes that history conceived in this way "may never exist in its absolute purity"; we are all "sinners," and the historian can never become an ethical tabula rasa. Nevertheless, when history is approached in this spirit, "its assertions have a higher authenticity in so far as the ideal is attained" (p. 229). At bottom, Butterfield wants to establish an ideal standard of humility and impartiality to which the "technical" historian should unwaveringly aspire.

Much of Butterfield's argument will not be objectionable to most historians, especially what he has to say about the scholar's need to study the past in terms of "imaginative sympathy"; still, many current historians are apt to find his central message muddled, perhaps pernicious, or, at best, epistemologically and ethically naive—especially in the aftermath of World War II and its horrors. He states, for example, that in historiography "it is impossible to think one man essentially more wicked than another save as one might say: 'All men are sinners and I the chief of them' " (p. 234). He thinks it is possible to divide experience into two discrete realms: that of the everyday world and that of technical history. But others (for example, Berlin, [1954] 1959: 265–71) deny this on grounds of their belief that the categories of historical analysis are identical to those of everyday reality. Technical history, they argue, does indeed have its own standards, but they are neither separable from nor superior to the historian's ethical responsibility as part of the human community. Historians deal with human beings, not molecules and atoms, and human actions have an inner, ethical side (Berlin, 1961–62: 24). It would be unnatural, unrealistic, and impossible for the historian to think of his subject matter in the same dispassionate terms as, say, a physicist, whose concern is mere physical objects and their relationships. History, in other words, is a "humanistic" discipline that deals with purposeful agents. Its subject matter is value-laden from the beginning. To "understand" in the technical historiographical sense does not necessarily imply the need to withhold judgment, justify, or forgive; in any case, the road to hell is often paved with good intentions.

On the other hand, one might argue that the value-charged nature of history's subject matter does not present a serious problem; Meyerhoff (1959: 226), for example, concedes that "moral issues and conflicts of values permeate history as they do ordinary life." He maintains, however, that "No special problem arises over the interests and values which the historian finds in his material; presumably, he treats them . . . like any other 'fact,' " that is, in a spirit of ethical detachment.

A more serious question is whether evaluative categories are inherent in the *method* of history, as opposed to its subject matter. Butterfield speaks as if value judgment is something the historian can largely (if not entirely) control—as though, by an act of will, the historian could purge his work of normative concepts. Although some theorists would concur—notably those who wish to defend history's status as an objective science against doctrines such as idealism and relativism (for example, Mandelbaum, [1938] 1967)—many historians and philosophers would disagree, arguing that ethical distinctions are, to some degree, intrinsic to the structure of historical inquiry itself and that the categories of historical "description," "explanation," and "value judgment" intertwine and overlap (e.g., Walsh, [1961] 1966). Even supposing the historian were able to eliminate all evaluative *terminology* from his discourse, the necessity of *selecting* material to include in his narrative, so as to create an impression of the relative significance of that which is "memorable" in the past, would defeat any effort to purge moral judgment from history as a form if inquiry (Dray, 1967: 27–30). As Walsh ([1961] 1966: 63) points out, this is not a question of "mere selection" but of "selection in accordance with criteria of [intrinsic] importance"; history, writes Walsh (p. 69), "is always written from a particular point of view, a phrase which includes the acceptance of a certain moral outlook." Certainly, most current historians would agree that even the "mere description" of an event such as the extermination of millions of people in Nazi death camps invariably involves some form of INTERPRETATION, that is, some process of *selection* and *emphasis* that presupposes at least implicit ethical judgment and discrimination (cf. Carr, [1961] 1964: 79). This is true even in cases where historians attempt to establish causal relationships between past events; for in the assessment of historical causation, where the category of human "responsibility" is involved, it is often impossible to avoid "reference to [a conception of] appropriate standards of conduct. The historian's concept of cause, in other words, is a humanistic, not a physical one" (Dray, 1967: 30).

References

Acton, John Emerich Edward Dalberg (Lord). [1887] 1955. *Essays on Freedom and Power*. Cleveland and New York.
Berlin, Isaiah. [1954] 1959. *Historical Inevitability*. In Meyerhoff: 249–71.

———. 1961–62. "History and Theory: The Concept of Scientific History." *HT* 1: 1–31.

Butterfield, Herbert. [1931] 1959. *History and Human Relations.* In Meyerhoff: 228–49. Butterfield believes that "we need no help from the historian to bring us to the recognition of the criminality of religious persecution or wholesale massacre or the modern concentration camp or the repression of dissident opinions. And those who do not recognise that the killing and torturing of human beings is barbarity will hardly be brought to that realisation by any labels and nicknames that historians may attach to these things" (p. 244). Butterfield's overall position should be seen in light of his previous study of the liberal bias in British historiography, *The Whig Interpretation of History* (London, 1931).

Breisach, Ernst. 1983. *Historiography: Ancient, Medieval and Modern.* Chicago.

Carr, E. H. [1961] 1964. *What Is History?* Harmondsworth, Eng. Chapter three contains a lively discussion of some aspects of the issue, especially pp. 75–84. See also p. 107.

Dray, W. H. 1967. "History and Value Judgments." *EP* 4: 26–30. Dray argues that value judgment is part of the disciplinary logic of history. His piece includes a bibliography.

———. 1978. "Concepts of Causation in A. J. P. Taylor's Account of the Origin of the Second World War." *HT* 17: 149–74. This excellent analysis shows that we cannot always believe what historians say about their own practice. Taylor professes to make no moral judgments; yet his controversial work (which attempts to portray Hitler as a conventional European statesman) is replete with ethical assumptions—as are the attacks of his critics.

Maclean, Michael J. 1982. "Johann Gustav Droysen and the Development of Historical Hermeneutics." *HT* 21: 347–65.

Mandelbaum, Maurice. [1938] 1967. *The Problem of Historical Knowledge.* New York.

Meyerhoff, Hans, ed. 1959. *The Philosophy of History in Our Time.* Garden City, N.Y.

Nadel, George H. 1964. "Philosophy of History before Historicism." *HT* 3: 291–315.

Ranke, Leopold von. [1824] 1972. Preface to *Histories of the Latin and Germanic Nations from 1494–1514.* In Stern: 55–58.

Schiller, Friedrich von. [1789] 1972. "The Nature and Value of Universal History." *HT* 11: 321–34.

Voltaire. [1752] 1972. Introduction to *The Age of Louis XIV.* In Stern: 40–44.

———. [n.d.] 1972. "On the Usefulness of History." In Stern: 44–45.

Walsh, W. H. [1961] 1966. "The Limits of Scientific History." In Dray: 54–74.

White, Andrew D. 1885. "On Studies in General History and the History of Civilization." *Papers of the American Historical Association* 1: 1–28.

White, Hayden. [1972–73] 1978. "Interpretation in History." In Hayden White, *Tropics of Discourse.* Baltimore: 51–80.

Zinn, Howard. 1970. *The Politics of History.* Boston.

Sources of Additional Information

See OBJECTIVITY; INTERPRETATION; RADICAL HISTORY; also *HT Beih.*; Stephens; Birkos and Tambs. For a short list of general philosophical studies see William K. Frankena, "Value and Valuation," *EP* 8: 32. Bert James Loewenberg, "Some Problems Raised by Historical Relativism," *JMH* 21 (Mar. 1949): 22, n. 19, cites a number of titles to support the author's belief that the historian must "cope with values, not . . . strive to circumvent them." Dray (1967) concludes with a short bibliography, and there is a brief list of relevant titles in Nash, p. 227. In the same volume see Dray's "Historian's Problem of Selection," pp. 216–27; chapter three of Dray's *Philosophy of History* (Englewood Cliffs, N.J., 1964) also contains a clear summary of the issues. For additional information on Schiller's views see the "Editors Note," in Schiller ([1789] 1972: 321), as well as Louis O. Mink, "Narrative Form as a Cognitive Instrument," in Canary and Kozicki: 135–36. C. Vann Woodward's, "Clio With Soul" [1969], in Stern: 475–90, addresses the question of at what point "the historian's moral engagement [may] compromise the integrity of his craft" (p. 475). In this connection see also John Higham, "Beyond Consensus: The Historian as Moral Critic," *AHR* 67 (April 1962): 609–25; Bruce Mazlish, "History and Morality," *JP* 55 (March 13, 1958): 230–40; and Ann Low-Beer, "Moral Judgments in History and History Teaching," in W. H. Burston and D. Thompson, *Studies in the Nature and Teaching of History* (London, 1967): 137–58. Also relevant is Hayden White's discussion of the ethical-ideological dimension of historical analysis in *Metahistory: The Historical Imagination in Nineteenth-Century Europe* (Baltimore, 1973).

VERSTEHEN. See UNDERSTANDING.

W

WORLD HISTORY. See UNIVERSAL HISTORY.

Z

ZEITGEIST, CLIMATE OF OPINION. Both terms designate the idea that thought in a given historical period may be understood in terms of an underlying identity, a "genius" or animating principle that pervades and conditions mental behavior, conscious and unconscious alike. *Zeitgeist* (Ger., "spirit of the time") means the psychic reality characteristic of a historical epoch. *Climate of opinion*, less comprehensive in implication, designates a unique constellation of ideas and assumptions that typifies the thought of a particular historical period or social group.

Zeitgeist and *climate of opinion* are related expressions closely associated with the procedures of PERIODIZATION and COLLIGATION. Once fashionable (cf. Brinton, 1963: 43), both terms (but especially *Zeitgeist*) are now slightly passé (Schorske, 1980: xxii; Colton, 1981: 295–96); their explicit use today is encountered mainly in the work of journalists and popularizers and only occasionally—usually with caveats—in the writing of academic historians (e.g., Hughes, 1958: 8; 1960: 43; Skotheim, 1969: 1–3; Gombrich, 1969: 31, 42). H. Stuart Hughes (1960: 43), for example, calls *Zeitgeist* a "cultural Lorelei that has seduced generation after generation of speculative historians." Nevertheless, the assumptions these words evoke are still basic to much serious historical writing, particularly in the subfields of INTELLECTUAL HISTORY and CULTURAL HISTORY (Schoeps, 1959: 9–29; Gilbert, 1972: 155; Beringer, 1978: 57). The ideas are clearly manifest in the common practice of classifying periods according to a particular "style," or mode of thinking—for example, "Baroque age," "age of Enlightenment," or "era of Liberalism" (Stromberg, 1975: 567–68)—and they may appear in a variety of guises (e.g., "intellectual climate" [Skinner, 1969: 38] or "historical temper of the time" [Snyder, 1976: 27]).

Both terms predate the early-nineteenth-century rise of academic historiography. *Zeitgeist* is an outgrowth of the notion *Geist der Zeit*, current among German intellectuals in the late eighteenth century and inspired by the French expressions *esprit du siècle* and *esprit du temps* (employed by Voltaire and Montesquieu in the mid-eighteenth century) (Sakmann, [1906] 1971: 39; Pflug, [1954] 1971: 9, 12–13, 16, 22; Schoeps, 1959: 13). Grimms' *Deutsches Wörterbuch* cites 1789 as the earliest date of use. In its origins, the German expression is closely related to the notion of *Volksgeist* ("spirit of the people," or NATIONAL CHARACTER), which crystallized about the same time:

> Just as the term *Volksgeist* was conceived as a definition of the spirit of a nation taken in its totality across generations, so Zeitgeist came to define the characteristic spirit of a historical era taken in its totality and bearing the mark of a preponderant feature which dominated its intellectual, political, and social trends. (Rotenstreich, 1973: 535)

The idea is found in various implicit or explicit guises in the thought of figures such as Herder, Kant, Schiller, Fichte, Goethe, Hegel, and Marx and later in the work of the philosopher-historian Wilhelm Dilthey, a pioneer of intellectual history. (Dilthey also popularized the related notion of *Weltanschauung* ["world view"]—the idea of the characteristic metaphysical outlook of an age.) It was particularly suited to German idealist historiography and philosophy of history, which posited the movement of "reason" or "spirit" (*Geist*) behind the course of human events (cf. Lichtheim, 1967: 189—see IDEALISM).

As far as English usage is concerned, the earliest case cited by the *OED* is an 1893 edition of Matthew Arnold's *Literature and Dogma*, although this is far too late. It seems likely that the idea was introduced in England in the early nineteenth century, during the vogue of German philosophy and letters among British intellectuals. Thomas Carlyle ([1830] 1972: 97) employed *spirit of the age* as early as 1830, and in 1831 John Stuart Mill referred to the phrase as a "novel expression" that had been in use for perhaps fifty years (Mill, [1831] 1942: 1). Mill understood the term to mean the "character" or "dominant idea of any age" and to imply the idea of "comparing one's own age with former ages, or with our notion of those which are yet to come." It was, he believed, an idea "essentially belonging to an age of change" (pp. 1–2). Mill's view may also have been inspired by his reading of French as well as German writers, for example, Henri de Saint-Simon and Auguste Comte. In early-nineteenth-century American historiography the idea of Zeitgeist was implicit in the conventional belief that the scholar must be capable of intuitively "feeling" himself into the spiritual "essence" of a period or situation (Callcott, 1970: 149).

The American historian Crane Brinton (1963: 43–44), alluding to the idea of a "whole of many parts," sought to illustrate the notion of Zeitgeist by referring to

> late eighteenth-century culture in the Western world, what most Americans mean when they speak of "colonial" styles. The costumes of both ladies and gentlemen, the architecture, as restored in Williamsburg, the furniture, the music of Mozart

and Haydn, the paintings of Gainsborough and Copley, all this and a lot more could be nothing else in space-time but eighteenth-century Western culture. (p. 43)

The origins of the expression *climate of opinion* are less well documented; it was employed in the late nineteenth century by the Irish historian W. E. H. Lecky (Semmel, 1976: 382), although it was apparently introduced to North America by the philosopher Alfred North Whitehead in the 1920s (1925: 3). Whitehead claimed to have discovered it in the work of an unnamed seventeenth-century author. (The synonymous expression *mental climate* was at any rate already current in English, having been used by John Stuart Mill in the nineteenth century [Rotenstreich, 1973: 536]; in 1920 J. B. Bury used the term *intellectual climates* in his widely read *Idea of Progress* [(1920) 1932: 7].) For Whitehead, *climate of opinion* designated a collective "state of mind," a notion that suggests a loose relationship to the origins of social psychology in the early twentieth century. The expression was popularized among historians by Carl Becker's widely read study of ENLIGHTENMENT thought, *The Heavenly City of the Eighteenth-Century Philosophers* (1932: 5).

Becker (p. 5) understood *climate of opinion* to mean "those instinctively held preconceptions in the broad sense, that *Weltanschauung* or world pattern" that characterizes a particular time and place. In French the idea is conveyed by the term *mentalité*—the focus of much recent interest in continental European historiography (see INTELLECTUAL HISTORY; CULTURAL HISTORY). Becker also hinted at another aspect of *climate of opinion* (and *Zeitgeist* as well): in asserting that those nurtured in the "modern" intellectual climate can "describe [the medieval] climate of opinion [but] cannot live in it" (p. 6), he suggested that these terms imply that mental phenomena are time-bound. Just as a tropical plant cannot survive in arctic conditions, so ideas bred in one age cannot truly "live" in another. This assumption links the concepts to certain features of nineteenth-century HISTORISM, specifically the idea that social phenomena are comprehensible only in terms of their own unique contexts. Both *climate of opinion* and *Zeitgeist* are used to "denote the boundaries of an age that limit and channel the development of thought and culture" (Beringer, 1978: 55).

Referring to *Zeitgeist*, Brinton (1963: 43) insisted that "There *is* such a thing, a total impression made by a huge number of details that somehow fit together." Many historians would have to agree that their work is indeed based on such a premise. Still, the logical problems associated with the use *Zeitgeist* and *climate of opinion* are not difficult to identify, and they help to explain why explicit use of these terms has become rare. In *Faust*, Goethe already pointed to a key problem: "My friend, the ages of the past are to us a book with seven seals. What you call the spirit of the past (Geist der Zeiten) is at bottom only the spirit of the historians, in which the past is reflected" (Bayard Quincy Morgan translation, 1954).

A major pitfall is glib oversimplification, that is, the danger that an author— ignoring the complexity, variety, and contradiction almost always present in any human situation (Geyl, 1955: 80)—may select only a few criteria to characterize the "essence" of a given culture, period, or social stratum (Gilbert, 1972: 155). This practice

> may become little more than an excuse to take any phenomenon and exaggerate its importance until it contains the spirit of the age, or at least a major component thereof. The result is distortion by gross generalization. Seeking the great synthesis, the scholar is altogether too likely to find common elements that may not really exist. (Beringer, 1978: 56)

This error might be classified under the category that D. H. Fischer labels the "fallacy of essences," which springs from the unverifiable premise that

> everything has something deep inside it called an essence, some profound inner core of reality. According to this view, facts about a man, a nation, an age, a generation, a culture, an ideology, or an institution are significant in the degree to which they display the essence of the entity in question. (1970: 68)

This idea may be "psychologically gratifying," since it "supplies a sense of completeness and . . . certainty," but it is "not susceptible to reasoned refutation." In Fischer's view, the "essentialists' significant facts are not windows through which an observer may peek at the inner reality of things but mirrors in which he sees his own a priori assumptions reflected" (p. 68).

Although recognizing such dangers, many historians would defend the concepts of "Zeitgeist" and "climate of opinion," as useful (perhaps even unavoidable in some cases), provided their unverifiability is frankly recognized (cf. Hughes, 1958: 8). Most would concur in the opinion that, at their worst, they constitute the kind of glib thinking that seeks to apply the mentality of popular fashion to historical interpretation (Beringer, 1978: 57–58).

References

Becker, Carl L. 1932. *The Heavenly City of the Eighteenth-Century Philosophers*. New Haven, Conn.

Beringer, Richard E. 1978. *Historical Analysis: Contemporary Approaches to Clio's Craft*. New York. Beringer devotes an entire section to the use of *Zeitgeist* in intellectual history.

Brinton, Crane. 1963. *Ideas and Men: The Story of Western Thought*. Englewood Cliffs, N.J. Originally published in 1950, this book was a standard text in the 1950s and 1960s.

Bury, J. B. [1920] 1932. *The Idea of Progress*. New York.

Callcott, George H. 1970. *History in the United States, 1800–1860*. Baltimore.

Carlyle, Thomas. [1830] 1972. "On History." In Stern: 91–101. Even at this early date Carlyle mocked the expression *spirit of the age* as an "algebraical symbol" employed by "cause-and-effect speculators" (p. 97).

Colton, Joel. 1981. "Intellectual History in the 1980s." *Journal of Interdisciplinary History* 12: 293–98.

Fischer, David Hackett. 1970. *Historians' Fallacies: Toward a Logic of Historical Thought*. New York.

Geyl, Pieter. 1955. *Use and Abuse of History*. New Haven, Conn. Geyl argues that historians must be constantly sensitive to the "abundant fullness and to the infinite complexity" of life (p. 80).

Gilbert, Felix. 1972. "Intellectual History: Its Aims and Methods." In Gilbert and Graubard: 141–58. See especially Gilbert's acute observations on p. 155.

Gombrich, E. H. 1969. *In Search of Cultural History*. Oxford. Gombrich refers to *Zeitgeist* as a "mental shortcut" that often leads to "second-hand stereotypes" (pp. 31, 42).

Hughes, H. Stuart. 1958. *Consciousness and Society: The Reorientation of European Social Thought, 1890–1930*. New York. On "spirit of the times," Hughes, a leading intellectual historian, writes: "Most of us think that such a spirit exists. . . . But who is bold enough to say exactly what this spirit is? Who is confident that he knows how to locate it or to define it? The paradoxical truth is that the discovery of the spirit of the times is at once a technical near-impossibility and the intellectual historian's highest achievement" (p. 8).

————. 1960. "The Historian and the Social Scientist." *AHR* 66: 20–46. Hughes defends the use of central grouping symbols in history.

Lichtheim, George. 1967. "Forward to Utopia." In George Lichtheim, *The Concept of Ideology and Other Essays*. New York: 177–89.

Mill, John Stuart. [1831] 1942. *The Spirit of the Age*. Chicago.

Pflug, Günther. [1954] 1971. "The Development of Historical Method in the Eighteenth Century." *HT Beih*. 11: 1–23.

Rotenstreich, Nathan. 1973. "Zeitgeist." *DHI* 4: 535–37. This piece has a brief bibliography.

Sakmann, Paul. [1906] 1971. "The Problems of Historical Method and of Philosophy in Voltaire." *HT Beih*. 11: 24–59.

Schoeps, Hans-Joachim. 1959. *Was ist und Was Will die Geistesgeschichte? Über Theorie und Praxis der Zeitgeistforschung*. Göttingen. This work is a classic statement of the position that the proper object of intellectual history is "the Zeitgeist and its transformations" (p. 9), written in the tradition of German idealist historiography and historical theory.

Schorske, Carl E. 1980. *Fin-de-Siècle Vienna: Politics and Culture*. New York. Schorske abjures the "positing in advance of an abstract categorical common denominator— what Hegel called the *Zeitgeist*, and Mill 'the characteristic of the age' " (p. xxii). A major part of Schorske's purpose, however, is the discovery of "unitary patterns" in the form of "shared concerns" and "shared ways of confronting experience."

Semmel, Bernard. 1976. "H. T. Buckle: The Liberal Faith and the Science of History." *The British Journal of Sociology* 27: 370–86.

Skinner, Quentin. 1969. "Meaning and Understanding in the History of Ideas." *HT* 8: 3–53.

Skotheim, Robert Allen, ed. 1969. *The Historian and the Climate of Opinion*. Reading, Mass. Skotheim defines *climate of opinion* as "the fundamental assumptions and attitudes shared by significant elements of a population at a given time . . . the basic intellectual viewpoint of the group in question . . . an intellectual temper." He is careful to note that in any given period or group, there are often "competing basic outlooks" (pp. 1–2).

Snyder, Louis L. 1976. *Varieties of Nationalism: A Comparative Study*. Hinsdale, Ill.

Stromberg, R. N. 1975. "Some Models Used by Intellectual Historians." *AHR* 80: 563–73. Stromberg argues that "Concepts of periodization . . . are nearly the same thing as Zeitgeist. 'Renaissance,' 'Enlightenment,' 'Romantic Era,' and so on . . . stand for the view that in each period a leading idea or theme dominated the culture and gave a special tone to everything" (p. 568).

Whitehead, Alfred North. 1925. *Science and the Modern World*. New York.

Sources of Additional Information

See the brief bibliography in Rotenstreich (1973). Dorothy Ross, "The 'Zeitgeist' and American Psychology," *Journal of the History of the Behavioral Sciences* 5 (1969): 256–62, contains some interesting bibliographical citations. For the idea in Herder see F. M. Barnard, "Herder's Treatment of Causation and Continuity in History," *JHI* 24 (1963): 197–212, especially, 198, 209–10. For more on the concept of Zeitgeist in the thought of Wilhelm Dilthey, as well as the related idea of *Weltanschauung* ("world view"), see Michael Ermarth, *Wilhelm Dilthey: The Critique of Historical Reason* (Chicago, 1978), and Theodore Plantinga, *Historical Understanding in the Thought of Wilhelm Dilthey* (Toronto, 1980). *Zeitgeist* is analyzed as a form of methodological "monism" in Maurice Mandelbaum, "The History of Ideas, Intellectual History, and the History of Philosophy," *HT Beih.* 5 (1965): 33–66, especially 48ff. See also William Appleman Williams, "A Note on Charles Austin Beard's Search for a General Theory of Causation," *AHR* 62 (1956): 59–60, especially 70; Wallace K. Ferguson, *The Renaissance in Historical Thought* (Cambridge, Mass.), pp. 82, 177, and *passim*; Charlotte W. Smith, *Carl Becker: On History and the Climate of Opinion* (Ithaca, N.Y., 1956); Pieter Geyl, "Jan Romein, or Bowing to the Spirit of the Age," in Pieter Geyl, *Encounters in History* (Cleveland, 1961), pp. 321–27; and P. H. Nowell-Smith, "History as Patterns of Thought and Action," in L. Pompa and W. H. Dray, eds., *Substance and Form in History* (Edinburgh, 1981): 145–55, especially 151–55.

Index

About the Author

HARRY RITTER is Professor of History at Western Washington University, Bellingham, Washington. He has contributed to the essay collection *The Quest for the New Science* and has written articles in *Central European History*, *East European Quarterly*, and *Austrian History Yearbook*.